CCH
a Wolters Kluwer business

# The Executor's Handbook

*4th Edition*

CCH Canadian Limited
300-90 Sheppard Avenue East
Toronto Ontario
M2N 6X1
1 800 268 4522
www.cch.ca

Leanne D. Kaufman, LL.B., LL.M.

RBC Wealth Management

Published by CCH Canadian Limited

**Important Disclaimer:** This publication is sold with the understanding that (1) the authors and editors are not responsible for the results of any actions taken on the basis of information in this work, nor for any errors or omissions; and (2) the publisher is not engaged in rendering legal, accounting or other professional services. The publisher, and the authors and editors, expressly disclaim all and any liability to any person, whether a purchaser of this publication or not, in respect of anything and of the consequences of anything done or omitted to be done by any such person in reliance, whether whole or partial, upon the whole or any part of the contents of this publication. If legal advice or other expert assistance is required, the services of a competent professional person should be sought.

*Edited by:*
Brenna Wong

**Library and Archives Canada Cataloguing in Publication**

Kaufman, Leanne D.
The executor's handbook / Leanne D. Kaufman. — 4th ed.

Includes index.
Previous eds. by: Jennifer A. Greenan.
ISBN 978-1-55496-433-8

1. Executors and administrators — Canada — Popular works.
I. Greenan, Jennifer. Executor's handbook. II. Title.

KE831.K39 2011 346.7105'6 C2011-907245-9
KF778.Z9K39 2011

ISBN 978-1-55496-433-8



Typeset by CCH Canadian Limited.
Printed in Canada.

# Dedication

Dedicated to the memory of Isabel K. Smith (1909–2011), an inspirational woman who devoted most of her life to helping others in this area.

# Table of Contents

# Preface

While we are responsible for the contents within this publication, and although all efforts have been made to ensure the accuracy contained within, laws do frequently change and the reader is urged to seek competent legal and accounting advice. This handbook is a tool to assist the personal representative and is not intended to replace specific professional advice.

# Acknowledgments

I am pleased to have had the opportunity to collaborate on *The Executor's Handbook, 4th Edition*, with my esteemed colleagues and contributors, Anne Chaurette, K. Thomas Grozinger, and Shamim Panchbhaya; it was, as usual, a pleasure. In addition, many thanks go to Brenna Wong, CCH Canadian Limited, for her editorial assistance. Finally, my acknowledgment and thanks to John M. Hamilton, President, Royal Trust Corporation of Canada for his support in this, and all, endeavours.

Leanne D. Kaufman, B.A., LL.B., LL.M.
October 2011

# Contributors

### Anne Chaurette

Anne Chaurette is Senior Trust Specialist for The Royal Trust Company (Quebec). She was admitted to the Quebec Bar in 1989. She graduated from the University of Montreal in 1980 with an LL.L., and became a member of La Chambre des Notaires du Québec in 1981. She is a member of the Society of Trust and Estate Practitioners (STEP). Ms. Chaurette works mainly in the areas of wills, estates, trusts, mandates, and protective supervision regimes. She has contributed to in-house publications and continuing education programs.

### K. Thomas Grozinger

K. Thomas Grozinger is Principal Trust Specialist for Royal Trust Corporation of Canada in the Professional Practice Group, Estate and Trust Services, RBC Wealth Management. He is a member of the Law Society of Upper Canada and is certified as a Specialist in Estates and Trusts Law. He holds the TEP designation from the Society of Trust and Estate Practitioners (STEP). Mr. Grozinger has contributed articles for continuing legal education programs, in-house publications, and the *Estates, Trusts and Pensions Journal*, receiving a Widdifield Award for one of his articles that appeared in that journal.

### Shamim Panchbhaya

Shamim Panchbhaya, CA, CFP, TEP, is a Senior Tax Manager with RBC. She provides Canadian and United States tax technical support to all RBC business units including Estate and Trust Services. She is a member of the CICA, the Canadian Tax Foundation, the Society of Trust and Estate Practitioners, and CSI Global Education Inc.

1

# Overview of Estate Administration

## Introduction

A personal representative acting in the administration of an estate has a challenging road ahead. Often, this is a difficult task, not only in an administrative sense, but also in an emotional sense. This handbook is designed to assist you, the personal representative, in the performance of your duties. It is also designed to enhance your understanding of the liabilities you may incur as a result of this position.

Along with the advice and guidance of your legal counsel and other professionals, this handbook acts as a guide. Depending on your situation, you may choose to seek assistance from a professional such as a trust company, legal counsel, accountant, or other individual with expertise in the administration of estates. If this is the case, you should clarify from the outset exactly what each party's responsibilities will be, but be mindful of the general duty on executors (subject to some exceptions) not to delegate their decision-making authority.

When an individual dies, the assets he or she owned must be located and protected; these assets form what is called the deceased's estate. At the same time, the debts (including taxes) of the deceased must also be determined and then paid out of the estate assets. After the debts have been paid, what remains in the estate is either distributed to the beneficiaries named in the deceased's will, held in trust as directed in the will, or distributed according to the provincial[1] laws of intestacy. When an individual dies without a will, the person is said to have died "intestate". Other provincial laws, such as those governing matrimonial property and dependants' relief, may also impact how the estate is distributed.

The following terms must be clarified before proceeding:

- **Executor/Estate Trustee with a Will/Liquidator:** In most provinces, the individual appointed under a will to administer an estate is referred to as the "executor". In Ontario, an executor is referred to as an "estate trustee with a will". In Quebec, the role is referred to as a "liquidator". The meaning of these terms is the same. For simplicity, most references in this book to this position will be to an "executor".
- **Administrator/Estate Trustee without a Will/Liquidator:** In situations where there is no will or where there is a will but no executor is appointed or available to act, the court appoints an "administrator" to look after the estate. In Ontario, an administrator is referred to as an

[1] Throughout this book, reference will be made to "provinces". Any reference to provinces will include the territories, unless expressly stated otherwise.

"estate trustee without a will". In Quebec, the role is referred to as a "liquidator"; if a liquidator is not appointed in the will, the heirs of the estate may act as the liquidator or may appoint a liquidator. For simplicity, all references in this book to this position will be to an "administrator".

- **Personal Representative:** The general term for a person who administers an estate is "personal representative". The term includes both an executor and an administrator. Because many duties for executors and administrators are similar, the term "personal representative" will be used predominantly throughout the remainder of this book.

An executor is given the power to administer the estate from the will, but an administrator must make an application to the court to be granted such power. Each province has legislation that sets out who may apply to become an administrator and who has priority over whom to succeed in such an application.

## A Word About the Law

Throughout this book, you will see references to various pieces of legislation and governing laws. The laws of succession (governing the administration of estates) and trusts are provincial in nature, meaning that each province has its own laws, both statutory and judge-made. Many of the concepts and principles are common from province to province, but there are some significant differences. We have tried to make this text applicable regardless of the province governing the estate; however, competent legal advice should always be sought.

Legislation is amended as required by changing times and priorities of the various governments, meaning the legislative references we give at the time of writing may no longer be in effect by the time you read this. For example, both British Columbia and Alberta have introduced significant changes to the statutes governing wills, estates, and succession in those provinces. Because the new legislation has not been brought into force as of the date of writing, the legislative references in this book do not reflect the amendments. However, both provinces are expected to proclaim their new legislation in force in 2012. Given the nature of these changes, if you are administering an estate in British Columbia or Alberta in or after 2012, legal advice is highly recommended.

## Renouncing Appointment as Executor

No one is obligated to act as an executor. If you have been appointed as an executor under a will, you can renounce this position at the outset by signing a "form of renunciation". If you are undecided as to whether you wish to act as executor, you should not interfere in the affairs of the estate until you have made a decision to proceed. If you do intermeddle with the affairs of the estate, the right to renounce may be lost (and a court order may be required to discharge you) and you risk liability arising from any improper administration of the estate. In Quebec, no one is obligated to act as an executor unless the person is the sole heir.

If more than one executor is named in the will and one of them renounces the appointment, the remaining executor or executors may apply for probate (where applicable), provided the will does not expressly require a certain number of executors. In the event that the will does not designate an alternate executor and the only named executor does not wish to proceed, an application must be made to the court to appoint someone else as an administrator. If the deceased died intestate or did not appoint an executor under her will, or if the appointed executor is prevented from acting, an application must be made to the court to appoint an administrator.

In Quebec, if the deceased died intestate or if the appointment of an executor is without effect, the heirs may designate an executor. Failing agreement among the heirs, or if it is impossible to appoint or replace the executor, the court may appoint or replace an executor.

If an executor or administrator obtains letters probate or letters of administration and later wishes to resign, she cannot do so unless the resignation is permitted by the will or a court order is obtained. However, in Quebec, an executor may resign at any time; no form is required for the submission of such resignation, but a notice of resignation is to be given to beneficiaries, co-executor(s), and any person empowered to appoint a replacement.

## Receiving Professional Assistance

Your duties as the personal representative are generally administrative in nature. If you are confused as to these duties, your legal counsel can advise you and provide information regarding the various options available.

If you decide to accept the role of executor or administrator but feel that you do not have the time or skills necessary to carry out all the administrative functions, a variety of alternative arrangements are possible. Your legal counsel, accountant, or a professional trust company may be prepared to take over various functions for a fee generally payable from the estate. If these third parties take over such functions, your compensation as the personal representative may need to be reduced accordingly. The estate will not compensate you for duties not performed. Additionally, remember that although many duties can be delegated, the ultimate responsibility for decision-making rests with the personal representative. In the Ontario case of *Wagner v. Van Cleef*,[2] the administrator of the estate delegated all of his duties to a legal counsel. This was an unfortunate decision, as the legal counsel eventually absconded after having misappropriated approximately $216,000 from the estate. In the end, the administrator was held *personally liable* for the loss to the estate.

The professional estate administrator's duties can be as wide or narrow as the executor wishes, provided that the executor retains the discretionary decision-making power (unless the will or the law in your jurisdiction permits certain powers to be delegated). In fact, depending on the level of involvement you desire, the professional can take over most of your estate administration tasks.

☞ It is important to remember that the professional does not act on behalf of the beneficiaries or the deceased, but acts on behalf of you, the personal representative of the estate.

You may also be appointed jointly with another individual or professional as co-executors. In that case, you share the duties and responsibilities, but it may be more administratively feasible to assign certain tasks to just one or the other.

## Organizing the Paperwork

As the personal representative, you will be dealing with a variety of people and a number of documents. It is essential to ensure that you keep records of important documents and transactions. You should also maintain records of the time spent on any estate-related duties, particularly if you intend to seek compensation. Although the beneficiaries may never ask you to account for the compensation you seek, they have the right to do so; therefore, it is nonetheless wise to record the time spent on such duties in the event that you are required to account for it.

Acting as a personal representative is somewhat akin to running a small business, so treat it as such. Set aside an area in your filing cabinet, desk, etc., and

[2] (1991), 5 O.R. (3d) 477 (Div. Ct.).

organize it in a manner appropriate for you. For example, you could have a folder for each of the following:

- **Correspondence:** Have a folder for correspondence from your legal counsel and any other correspondence related to the estate.
- **Assets:** If there are numerous assets, you may choose to set up subfolders for different types of assets such as:
  - — real estate (deed and mortgage documents);
  - — records of cash on hand and the particulars of bank accounts;
  - — investment account information;
  - — life insurance policies;
  - — automobiles; and
  - — other personal assets, including art, jewellery, furniture, collectibles, digital assets, etc.
- **Debts:** If there are numerous debts, you may choose to organize them into subfolders such as:
  - — funeral expenses;
  - — hospital or physicians' bills;
  - — hydro, water, telephone, cable, fuel, and property tax bills;
  - — bank loans and mortgages;
  - — credit cards and other credit accounts; and
  - — business loans.
- **Application for probate/administration (where required):** For this task, you will need certain documents such as the original will (or a notarial copy) and notarial copies of the letters probate (called "certificate of appointment of estate trustee" in Ontario) or letters of administration, once issued. You should also keep notarial copies of the death certificate.
- **Time sheets:** Keep an accurate record of the time spent administering the estate.
- **Income tax:** Keep a separate folder for income tax returns, etc.
- **Accounting records:** Keep a detailed accounting of the money and assets that are in your possession, all income or other funds received during the course of the administration, and any funds paid out for whatever reason.

# Simplified Overview of Estate Administration Where a Will Exists

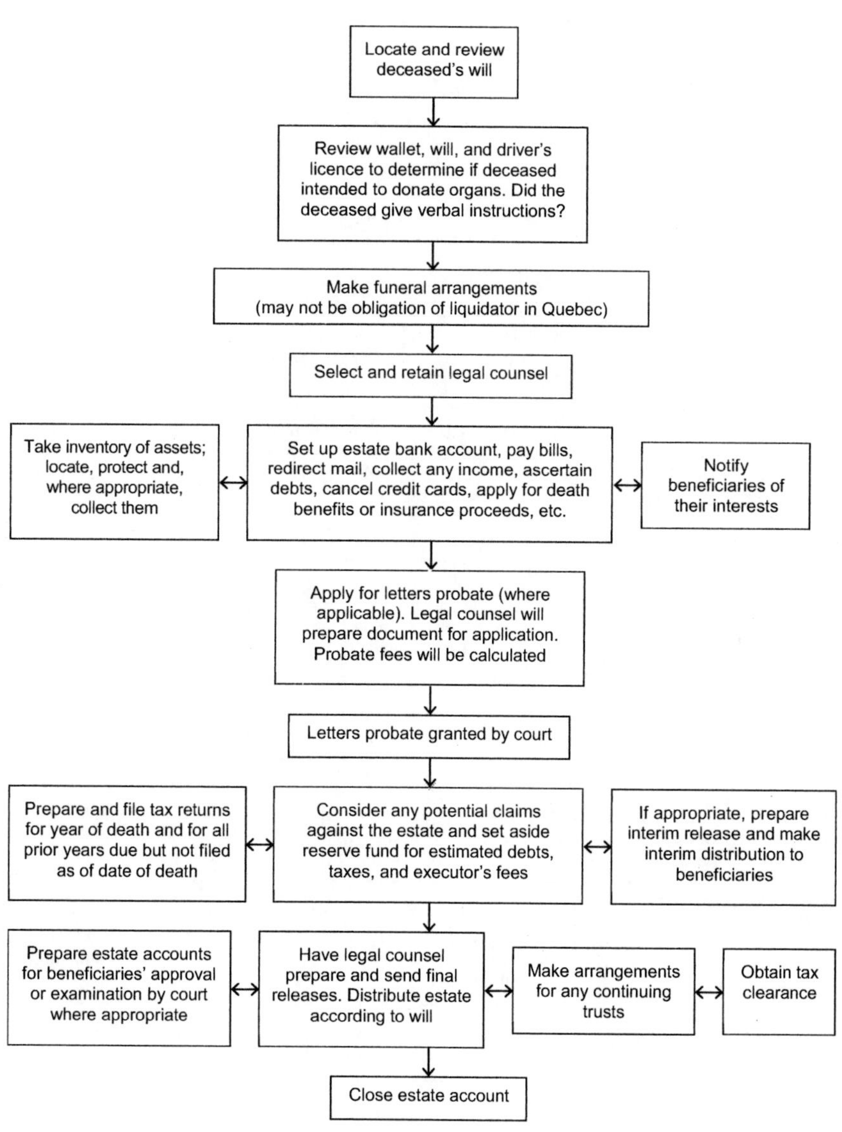

## Simplified Overview of Estate Administration Where No Will Exists

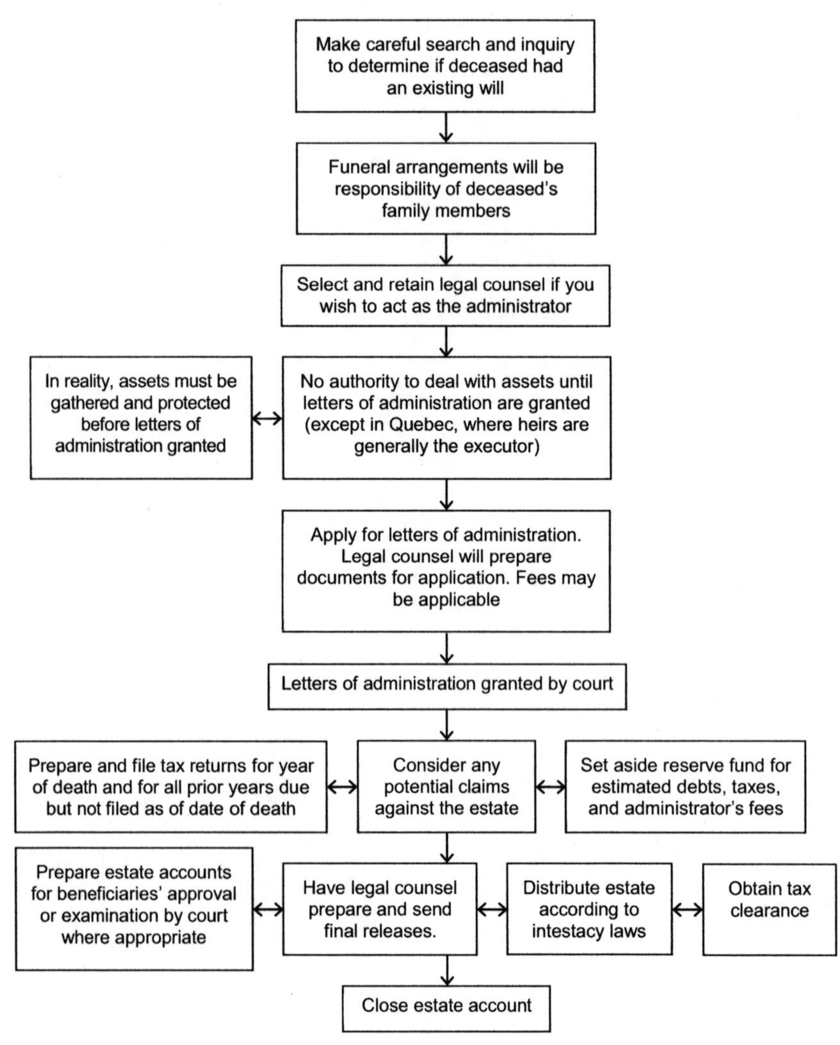

# Estate Administration Checklists

## Initial Matters

### Immediate

- ❏ Locate and review the last will of the deceased to determine who the deceased appointed as executor(s) of the estate and to determine:
  - if there are any directions regarding organ donation; or
  - if there are instructions with respect to funeral arrangements.
- ❏ Make appropriate funeral arrangements and pay for this expense (see "Funds to Pay for the Funeral Checklist" in chapter 2 for further information).
- ❏ Obtain statement/proof of death from the funeral home and, if needed, apply for a provincial death certificate.
- ❏ Arrange for the care of any pets.
- ❏ In respect of farm property, arrange for the care and management of livestock and crops.
- ❏ Dispose of all perishable assets (e.g., if the deceased owned a business that sold perishable produce) so that the value of the estate is not diminished.

### Subsequent

- ❏ Retain legal counsel.
- ❏ Review the will with your legal counsel.
- ❏ Determine, with the assistance of your legal counsel, whether the will is valid (i.e., whether the will was properly executed).
- ❏ Understand how the assets of the estate are to be distributed.
- ❏ Review what duties the legal counsel will be performing and what duties you, the executor, will be performing.
- ❏ Obtain notarial copies[3] of the will.

---

[3] A notarial copy is a photocopy of the original document that is certified as being a true or genuine copy of the original. Your legal counsel can certify the copy.

- ❑ Search for assets and safeguard such assets until they are distributed or sold (assets should be protected as soon as possible, as things such as jewellery and cash can often "disappear" if left unsecured):
  - search for cash, securities, jewellery, and other valuables, and arrange for safekeeping;
  - where appropriate, lock up the residence and notify the police that the home is vacant; in winter, ensure that the house remains heated or drain the pipes to prevent freezing;
  - examine insurance coverage and insure estate assets (motor vehicle, house, furniture, jewellery, art, etc.) against perils and fire; and
  - for motor vehicles, check the insurance policy for adequate coverage and permitted uses; if someone is using the vehicle and there is inadequate coverage, the estate may be liable or the personal representative may be personally liable.
- ❑ Determine whether immediate family members have any urgent financial needs. If so, and if those persons cannot wait for the estate to distribute assets, look to the following sources of funds:
  - life insurance policies — only viable if the designated beneficiary(ies) is immediate family;
  - employment pay — if the deceased was an employee at the time of death, there may be some type of termination pay available (only viable if payable to a family member rather than to the estate);
  - death benefit — there may be a death benefit through the employee's pension plan (only viable where directly payable to the family);
  - Canada Pension Plan — if the deceased contributed to the CPP, you may be able to obtain a lump-sum death benefit, while the surviving spouse and children may be entitled to monthly payments; and
  - Régie des rentes du Québec — if the deceased contributed to the Régie des rentes du Québec, you may be able to obtain a lump-sum death benefit, while the surviving spouse and children may be entitled to monthly payments.
- ❑ Contact the Canada Revenue Agency (1-800-959-8281) and inform them of the deceased's death if any of the following situations apply:
  - the deceased was receiving the GST/HST credit;

- the deceased was receiving (or the deceased's spouse/common-law partner was receiving) the Canada Child Tax Credit ("CCTB") or the Universal Child Care Benefit ("UCCB"); or
- the deceased was a child for whom GST credit, CCTB, and/or UCCB payments were being paid.

❑ Contact Service Canada (1-800-O-Canada; 1-800-622-6232) if the deceased was receiving Old Age Security (i.e., OAS pension, allowance, or allowance for the survivor benefits) or Canada Pension Plan benefits (i.e., retirement, disability, or survivor benefits), as these benefits must be cancelled. Benefits are payable for the month in which the death occurs, but any benefits paid after that month must be returned.

❑ Contact the Régie des rentes du Québec if the deceased was receiving Quebec Pension Plan benefits; in Quebec City, call 418-643-5185; in Montreal, call 514-873-2433; elsewhere, call 1-800-463-5185. As with CPP benefits, QPP benefits are payable for the month of death, but any benefits received after that month must be returned.

❑ Search for contact information for the deceased's advisers.

❑ Establish who the beneficiaries are and obtain their full names and addresses.

❑ Open an estate bank account as soon as the bank will permit it (depending on what documents, such as probate, the bank requires to open the estate account).

❑ Organize the interim management of the deceased's business, where applicable. If you, as the personal representative, decide to run the business, you must consider matters of personal liability. Professional advice should be sought.

❑ Collect income generated by the estate assets or payable to the deceased.

❑ Apply for any benefits payable on death, including the CPP or QPP death benefit, life insurance proceeds, and death benefits from pension plans or annuities. Deposit these benefits to the estate account.

❑ Locate any original investment certificates, bonds, deeds, etc.

❑ Determine if any registered plans or insurance policies have designated beneficiaries or if the proceeds belong to the estate.

- ❑ Check leases and tenancy agreements, arrange for the payment or collection of rent, and give notice, if appropriate.
- ❑ Note that banks and other financial institutions may refuse to honour cheques that were written by the deceased but not cleared prior to death.
- ❑ Redirect or cancel subscriptions to newspapers and magazines.
- ❑ Redirect mail.
- ❑ Cancel the deceased's social insurance number, passport, permanent resident card, provincial health insurance coverage, provincial driver's licence, cable, telephone, club memberships, subscriptions, and credit cards.
- ❑ Review the deceased's investments, if any, to determine suitability and whether any are particularly risky or volatile and whether any need to be sold immediately.

## Interim Matters

- ❑ Prepare an inventory of original assets, including a safety deposit box listing, real estate, monies on deposit at financial institutions, personalty, life insurance, any interest in an estate or trust, and any other investments.
- ❑ Arrange for valuation of assets where necessary.
- ❑ Advertise for creditors and prepare an inventory of debts.
- ❑ Ascertain any debts by or to family members and locate evidence regarding loan balances.
- ❑ Notify the beneficiaries of their interests.
- ❑ Assess whether it is necessary to apply for a grant of probate.
- ❑ If probate is determined necessary, instruct your legal counsel to apply for the appropriate grant or certificate from the court.
- ❑ Supply your legal counsel with the information required to make the application for probate.
- ❑ Obtain letters probate or certificate of appointment and have notarial copies made.

- ❑ Pay bills, mortgage payments, property taxes, insurance premiums, and credit cards.
- ❑ Prepare and file income tax returns for the deceased's year of death and for all prior years due but not filed at the date of death.
- ❑ Make reasonable inquiries for next of kin if required.
- ❑ Consider any claims or potential claims against the estate and obtain legal advice if necessary:
  - assess the rights of the surviving spouse under provincial family law; depending on the province, the personal representative may be required to advise the surviving spouse that she might have a claim and should seek independent legal advice; and
  - assess the rights of any dependants who were financially dependent on the deceased.
- ❑ Set aside reserve funds for estimated debts, taxes (including potential taxable capital gains on property such as a cottage), and the personal representative's compensation.
- ❑ Organize the sale of assets, if necessary, such as to pay debts and legacies.
- ❑ Prepare an interim release and make an interim distribution to beneficiaries, if appropriate.

## Final Matters

- ❑ Depending on the circumstances, you may have to convert investments and other assets to cash and deposit funds into the estate account, or invest the estate balance in interest-earning investments, pending final distribution to beneficiaries.
- ❑ Re-register assets in the estate's name, if applicable.
- ❑ File a T3 income tax return.
- ❑ Obtain a clearance certificate from the Canada Revenue Agency ("CRA") and from Revenu Québec, if applicable.
- ❑ Settle and pay all legitimate claims against the estate.

- ❑ Prepare a transfer/deed for conveyance of real property, if required by the will or the law. As real estate transactions can be quite complex, your legal counsel will most likely prepare the legal documents.
- ❑ Arrange rollover of RRSPs or RRIFs to the spouse or dependent child, if required.
- ❑ Arrange rollover of TFSA to spouse, if required.
- ❑ Prepare and maintain estate accounts for approval by the beneficiaries or examination by the court, where appropriate.
- ❑ Calculate compensation for performance of your duties. (See chapter 10 for more information on the personal representative's compensation.)
- ❑ Prepare final accounting of assets, income, and payments out.
- ❑ Have your legal counsel prepare and send the final releases.
- ❑ Remember to ensure that any matrimonial property or dependants' relief limitation periods have expired before distributing the estate (unless consents or a court order have permitted distribution).
- ❑ If there is no will, distribute assets according to rules for intestate succession.
- ❑ Dispose of or distribute personalty according to instructions in the will.
- ❑ Prepare cheques, pay legacies, and transfer bequests as provided in the will.
- ❑ Invest assets for establishment of trusts, if the will so directs.
- ❑ Prepare cheques and pay balances to residuary beneficiaries.
- ❑ Advise beneficiaries regarding inclusion of income from the estate in their income tax, if appropriate.
- ❑ Close the estate account.

## Important Limitation Periods and Deadlines

It should be noted that many provinces have limitation periods (the period within which any claims against the estate must be made) that are tied to the date that probate is applied for or obtained. If probate is not obtained for any reason, it may leave the time period open indefinitely for a matrimonial property claim or dependants' relief claim to be made.

## Matrimonial Property Claims

In most provinces, a surviving spouse may have the right to make an application to claim a share of the deceased's property — known as a matrimonial property claim — and has a time limit within which to do so. Although only some provinces specifically state that the personal representative cannot distribute the estate until this limitation period has expired, it would normally be prudent to wait until the end of the limitation period to do so, unless consent of the spouse or a court order provides otherwise. The limitation periods are as follows:

- **Alberta,[4] Manitoba, Nova Scotia, and Saskatchewan:** The surviving spouse must bring a claim within six months of the grant of letters probate or letters of administration.[5]
- **New Brunswick:** The surviving spouse must bring a claim within four months after the death of the deceased spouse.
- **Newfoundland and Labrador:** The surviving spouse must bring a claim within one year after the death of the deceased spouse.
- **Northwest Territories and Nunavut:** The surviving spouse must bring a claim within six months after the day on which probate or letters of administration were granted.
- **Ontario:** The surviving spouse must bring a claim within six months after the deceased spouse's death.
- **Quebec:** Marriage entails the establishment of a family patrimony consisting of certain property of the spouses, regardless of which of them holds a right of ownership in that property. One spouse may, from the death of the other spouse, renounce such rights in whole or in part by notarial act. The renunciation must be entered in the register of personal and movable real rights. If the spouse does not enter a renunciation

[4] Alberta only permits an application if a matrimonial property application could have been commenced before the spouse's death; in other words, the spouses suffered a marriage breakdown during their joint lives. For example, if the spouses had been living separate and apart for one year prior to the deceased spouse's death, the surviving spouse could make an application.

[5] For Alberta and Saskatchewan, the legislation states that a claim must be brought within six months of the date of *issue* of the grant of letters probate or administration.

within a period of one year from the date of death of the deceased, the spouse is deemed to have accepted the family patrimony.

- **Yukon:** There are no similar provisions, although a claim that began before the death of the deceased spouse can continue.

See the "Matrimonial Property Claims Table" on page 82 in chapter 5 for more information.

## Dependants' Relief Claims

In all provinces, a dependant of the deceased may have the right to make an application to claim a share of the deceased's property — known as a dependants' relief claim — and has a time limit within which to do so. Although only some provinces specifically state that the personal representative cannot distribute the estate until this limitation period has expired, it would be prudent in all cases to wait until the end of the limitation period to do so, unless consent of the dependants or a court order provides otherwise. The limitation periods are as follows:

- **Alberta, British Columbia, Manitoba, Newfoundland and Labrador, Northwest Territories, Nova Scotia, Nunavut, Ontario, Prince Edward Island, Saskatchewan, and the Yukon:**[6] The dependant must bring a claim within six months after the grant of probate or administration.

- **New Brunswick:** The dependant must bring a claim within four months after the death of the deceased.

- **Quebec:**[7] Every creditor of support (i.e., married or civil union spouses and relatives in the direct line in the first degree) may, within six months from the date of death of the deceased, claim a financial contribution from the succession as support.

See the "Dependants' Relief Claims Table" on page 85 in chapter 5 for more information.

---

[6] B.C. legislation states that the claim must be brought within six months from the date of issue of probate of the will. In B.C. and Nova Scotia, dependants' relief applications can only be brought where there is a will, so the reference to grant of administration should be ignored for these provinces.

[7] In Quebec, dependants' relief is referred to as "survival of the obligation to provide support".

## Income Tax Returns

### Returns for the Deceased

Following are the deadlines for the tax returns that you may have to file on behalf of the deceased:

- **Prior-year return:**
  - — where the taxpayer died before May in the terminal year, the return for the immediately prior year is due within six months of death; or
  - — where the taxpayer died in May or after, the return was actually due on April 30th of the year of death and as a result no extension is permitted.
- **Final return for taxpayer or spouse/common-law partner not operating a business:**[8]
  - — where the taxpayer died before November in a year, the return must be filed by April 30 of the next calendar year; or
  - — where the taxpayer died in November or December, the return must be filed within six months of the date of death.
- **Final return for taxpayer or spouse/common-law partner operating a business:**
  - — where the taxpayer died between January 1 and December 15, the return must be filed by June 15 of the next calendar year; or
  - — where the taxpayer died between December 16 and December 31, the return must be filed within six months of the date of death.
- **Balance owing from the final return:**[9]
  - — where the taxpayer died before November in a year, the balance owing must be paid by April 30 of the next calendar year; or
  - — where the taxpayer died in November or December, the balance owing must be paid within six months of the date of death.

---

[8] Where the deceased's will creates a testamentary trust that would qualify as a spouse/common-law partner trust except that it provides for the payment of testamentary debts, the *Income Tax Act* extends the time for filing the tax return of the deceased to 18 months after death. However, the balance due date is the same as noted in the "Balance owing from the final return" list. If the payment is not made by the balance due date, interest will be charged at the prescribed rate.

[9] This due date also applies to a taxpayer who operated a business.

- **Partnership or sole proprietorship stub period return:** Subject to the same filing deadlines as for the T1 final return (above).
- **Testamentary trust stub period return:** Subject to the same filing deadlines as for the T1 final return (above).
- **Rights or things separate return:** The return must be filed by the later of: (a) 90 days after the mailing of a notice of assessment for the final return; or (b) one year after the date of death.
- **Election to opt out of the regular spousal rollover under subsection 70(6.2):** This election is to be made in the final return.
- **Election under subsection 164(6) to carry back a loss from the estate's first taxation year to the terminal year:** This election must be made in writing by the later of: (a) the filing deadline for the final return; or (b) the filing deadline for the estate's first taxation year.
- **Election to pay deceased's tax in yearly instalments under subsection 159(5):** The election Form T2075 must be filed by the filing deadline for the final return.

### Estate Returns

Following are the deadlines for the tax returns that you may have to file on behalf of the estate:

- **T3 return:** The first tax period of the estate begins on the day after the person dies and ends at any time the personal representative chooses within the next 12 months. The T3 return must be filed no later than 90 days after the estate's tax year end (the balance owing is due at this time as well).
- **T3 returns for subsequent years:** If the administration of the estate is not completed within 12 months, then a T3 return must be filed for each of the estate's taxation years. The T3 return for these subsequent years must be filed no later than 90 days after the estate's tax year end (the balance owing is due at this time as well).

## Guardianship of Children

The role of guardian of a child is usually filled by the child's parents. If a child's parents are no longer living, someone will need to look after the child and her property; for such situations, it is common for parents to appoint guardians for their children in their wills. Some parents choose to name one person (or persons) to look after the child and another person to look after the child's property. Most provinces have legislation that provides that parents can appoint persons to act as guardians in their place and that such appointment can be made by deed or will.

It should be noted, however, that while a parent is an automatic guardian of the person, a parent may not automatically be the guardian of the child's property. A court order is generally required.

Although a parent's choice of guardian is a very important factor to be considered in the question of guardianship of children, it is not always conclusive. There are several cases in which the parent's choice of guardian was not followed.[10] The courts will always consider what is in the best interests of the child.

In Quebec, in addition to having the rights and duties connected with parental authority, the father and mother are tutors to their minor child for the purposes of representing the child in the exercise of the child's civil rights and administering the child's patrimony.

[10] For example, in *Kiehlbauch v. Franklin* (1980), 20 A.R. 31 (T.D.), the Court awarded custody of the children to the grandparents with whom the children had been living for the four years after their mother's death and not to the persons appointed by the father in his will.

2

# Organ Donations and Funeral Arrangements

## Organ or Body Donations

As the executor of the estate, it is unlikely that you will be involved in any organ donation consent issues that might arise after a person's death unless you are also a family member. However, you may have access to information that might assist the family in making an organ donation decision.

Each province has a different method for signing up as an organ donor: consent may be given on a person's health card or driver's licence, or in a registry. The deceased's legal counsel may have notes from the time the will was drafted, and other documents may also provide valuable insight into the deceased's wishes regarding organ donation. Therefore, if you, as the executor, come into possession of any pertinent documentation, it is important to pass this information along. If family members are aware of the deceased's wish to donate organs, they are more likely to consent to a donation than if they are unaware of such a desire.[1]

## Consent

### Donor's Consent While Alive

The donation of human organs is governed by provincial legislation. According to the law in each province, an individual may consent to an organ donation, and that consent is supposed to remain valid after the individual's death. However, the reality is that in many jurisdictions, family members have the power to override a person's consent to donate organs after that person's death.

In Quebec, the Commission de l'éthique de la science et de la technologie's April 2004 consultation paper "Ethical Issues Surrounding the Donation and Transplantation of Organs" referred to a study[2] that revealed that 70% of Quebec physicians believe the family's consent needs to be obtained in order for an organ donation to proceed after an individual's death. However, according to the *Civil Code of Quebec*, an adult or a minor 14 years or older can consent to an after-death organ donation.

British Columbia and Ontario have organ donor registries. In British Columbia, donors can register online[3] or complete a form and return it by mail.

[1] Trillium Gift of Life Network, "Backgrounder: Trillium Gift of Life Network — Attitudinal Research", April 15, 2004. In 2004, research conducted by Navigator Ltd. demonstrated that 94% of family members were either very likely (85%) or somewhat likely (8%) to donate a family member's organs when they were aware of the donor's desire to donate, as opposed to only 66% who stated they would be likely to donate organs if they were unsure of the family member's donation wishes.

[2] The study was carried out by the Committee promoting organ and tissue donation at the University Hospital Centre in Quebec.

[3] www.transplant.bc.ca.

If a person is declared brain dead, the medical staff will enter the individual's personal health number into the organ donor registry system; if the individual has registered, a copy of the registration form will be validated and shown to the family. According to the British Columbia Transplant website, the organ donor registry form is a legal document, and the medical staff will always follow the deceased person's wishes according to the donor's registry form. They will inform the person's family of the person's desire to permit an organ donation; however, the medical staff is not required to obtain the family's consent.

In Ontario, donors can also register online[4] or complete a consent form and return it by mail. The decision to consent is maintained in a government database and is disclosed at a time "only for the purpose of ensuring that [the] decision to donate is known and respected".[5] Unlike in British Columbia, however, the final decision regarding donation rests with family members.

### Consent of Family Members After Person's Death

According to provincial legislation, if the deceased did not express any intentions regarding organ donation before death, family members may consent to the donation of organs after the person dies. (This applies, as well, in the case of a child who could not give consent while alive because of his age.) Provincial legislation sets out the order of priority of different family members for this purpose. If a higher-priority family member refuses to give consent, a lower-priority family member's consent is irrelevant. For example, if the deceased's spouse declines to consent to an organ donation, the deceased's child's consent cannot override the spouse's decision.

The order of priority is generally as follows; refer to the table on the next page for greater detail:

1. the deceased's spouse;[6]
2. the deceased's adult children;
3. either of the deceased's parents;
4. any one of the deceased's adult brothers or sisters;
5. any other of the deceased's adult next of kin.

The consent cannot be acted upon if it is known that the deceased would have objected to the consent.

---

[4] www.beadonor.ca.

[5] See www.beadonor.ca/faqs.

[6] In many provinces, this also applies to the deceased's common-law partner.

## Organ Donation Consent Table

| Province | Age | Form of Consent by Donor | Priority of Consent (after Donor's Death) | Form of Consent by Other Person |
|---|---|---|---|---|
| Alberta | 18 | In writing, dated and signed by:<br>● Donor and witness; or<br>● If donor cannot sign, 2 witnesses | ● Spouse or adult interdependent partner (if not estranged)<br>● Adult child<br>● Parent or guardian<br>● Adult sibling<br>● Adult next of kin | In writing, dated and signed by:<br>● Consenter and witness; or<br>● If consenter cannot sign, 2 witnesses |
| British Columbia | 19 | ● In writing, signed; or<br>● Orally in presence of 2 witnesses during last illness | ● Spouse<br>● Adult child<br>● Parent<br>● Adult sibling<br>● Adult next of kin<br>● Person lawfully in possession of body | ● In writing, signed;<br>● Orally in presence of 2 witnesses; or<br>● By telegraphic, recorded telephonic, or other recorded message |
| Manitoba | 18[1] | ● In writing;<br>● Any type of recorded message;<br>● Orally in presence of 2 witnesses; or<br>● By telephone to 2 witnesses | ● Proxy[2] if deceased was 18 or over at time of death<br>● Spouse or common-law partner<br>● Adult child<br>● Parent or legal guardian<br>● Adult sibling<br>● Person lawfully in possession of body | ● In writing;<br>● Any type of recorded message;<br>● Orally in presence of 2 witnesses; or<br>● By telephone to 2 witnesses |
| New Brunswick | 19 | ● In writing; or<br>● Orally in presence of 2 witnesses during last illness | ● Spouse or common-law partner<br>● Adult child<br>● Parent<br>● Sibling<br>● Adult next of kin<br>● Person lawfully in possession of body | ● In writing; or<br>● Orally in presence of 2 witnesses |
| Newfoundland and Labrador | 19 | ● In writing; or<br>● Orally in presence of 2 witnesses during last illness | ● Spouse<br>● Adult child<br>● Parent<br>● Adult sibling<br>● Adult next of kin<br>● Person lawfully in possession of body<br>● Where person died in hospital, administrative head of hospital | ● In writing, signed;<br>● Orally in presence of 2 witnesses; or<br>● By telegraphic, recorded telephonic, or other recorded message |

| Province | Age | Form of Consent by Donor | Priority of Consent (after Donor's Death) | Form of Consent by Other Person |
|---|---|---|---|---|
| Northwest Territories | 19 | ● In writing; or<br>● Orally in presence of 2 witnesses during last illness | ● Spouse<br>● Adult child<br>● Parent<br>● Adult sibling<br>● Person lawfully in possession of body | Not specified |
| Nova Scotia[3] | 19 | ● In writing; or<br>● Orally in presence of 2 witnesses during last illness | ● Spouse<br>● Adult child<br>● Parent<br>● Adult sibling<br>● Adult next of kin<br>● Person lawfully in possession of body | ● In writing, signed;<br>● Orally in presence of 2 witnesses; or<br>● By telegraphic, recorded telephonic, or other recorded message |
| Nunavut | 19 | ● In writing; or<br>● Orally in presence of 2 witnesses during last illness | ● Spouse<br>● Adult child<br>● Parent<br>● Adult sibling<br>● Person lawfully in possession of body | Not specified |
| Ontario | 16 | ● In writing; or<br>● Orally in presence of 2 witnesses during last illness | ● Spouse[4]<br>● Child<br>● Parent<br>● Sibling<br>● Next of kin<br>● Person lawfully in possession of body | ● In writing, signed;<br>● Orally in presence of 2 witnesses; or<br>● By telegraphic, recorded telephonic, or other recorded message |
| Prince Edward Island | 16 | Not specified | ● Guardian<br>● Spouse<br>● Child<br>● Parent<br>● Sibling<br>● Next of kin<br>● Person who shared a residence with the deceased immediately before the death and has knowledge of deceased's wishes | Not specified |
| Quebec | 14[5] | ● In writing; or<br>● Orally in presence of 2 witnesses | ● Mandatary, tutor, or curator<br>● Spouse (married, civil union, or *de facto*)<br>● Close relative<br>● Person who shows special interest | Not specified |

| Province | Age | Form of Consent by Donor | Priority of Consent (after Donor's Death) | Form of Consent by Other Person |
|---|---|---|---|---|
| Saskatchewan | 18 | ● In writing; or<br>● Orally in presence of 2 witnesses during last illness | ● Spouse (unless separated)<br>● Adult child<br>● Parent<br>● Adult sibling<br>● Adult next of kin<br>● Person lawfully in possession of body | ● In writing, signed;<br>● Orally in presence of 2 witnesses;<br>● By telegraphic, recorded telephonic, or other recorded message; or<br>● By telephonic message received by 2 people who recorded in writing the consent |
| Yukon | 19 | ● In writing; or<br>● Orally in presence of 2 witnesses during last illness | ● Spouse<br>● Adult child<br>● Parent<br>● Adult sibling<br>● Adult next of kin<br>● Person lawfully in possession of body | ● In writing, signed;<br>● Orally in presence of 2 witnesses; or<br>● By telegraphic, recorded telephonic, or other recorded message |

Footnotes:

[1] A direction may be given by a person who is under 18 but not under 16 years of age where: (a) a parent or legal guardian of the person consents to the direction; or (b) without the consent required under clause (a) if the parent(s) or legal guardian(s) of the person is unavailable.

[2] "Proxy" means the proxy appointed in a health care directive made in accordance with *The Health Care Directives Act*. However a proxy will not have priority if the proxy was restricted from making organ donation decisions in the directive.

[3] Rules according to the *Human Tissue Gift Act*. This Act is to be replaced by Nova Scotia's *Human Organ and Tissue Donation Act*. At the date of this writing, the *Human Organ and Tissue Donation Act* had not yet been proclaimed into force.

[4] "Spouse" means a person (a) to whom the person is married; or (b) with whom the person is living or, immediately before the person's death, was living in a conjugal relationship outside marriage, if the two persons (i) have cohabited for at least one year, (ii) are together the parents of a child, or (iii) have together entered into a cohabitation agreement under section 53 of the *Family Law Act*.

[5] A minor under the age of 14 can also donate organs with the consent of his parental authority or tutor.

## Funeral Arrangements

### Executor's Responsibility

As a general rule, the executor of the estate, rather than the spouse or other family members of the deceased, is responsible for making the funeral arrangements. (However, in Quebec, the responsibility for the funeral and disposal of the remains lies with the deceased's heirs and successors.) Regardless of the deceased's intentions, whether previously stated in a letter or specified in the will, the executor has the final decision in determining the type of ceremony and burial (however, please see the following discussion entitled "Legislation Impacting Funeral Arrangement Authority"). Common sense should prevail in such matters. Excluding input from the deceased's family with respect to the funeral arrangements (unless you have a valid reason for doing so) and ignoring any reasonable requests or suggestions they might have is laying the foundation for a challenging estate administration process ahead.

If there is no executor, then a family member has the right to make the funeral arrangements, and indeed may be obliged to do so. In determining the order of priority with respect to control over the funeral arrangements when no executor exists, the spouse would normally have first priority, followed by the next closest relative.

Irrespective of who is making the arrangements, it is preferable to follow the wishes of the deceased. The estate is required to pay only for a funeral arrangement that is fitting to the deceased's position in life. If family members desire a more elaborate ceremony and burial, the executor should obtain a written direction from the family members, and the direction should also specify that the family members are personally liable for the extra expense.

In the Alberta case of *Kosic v. Kosic*,[7] the deceased named his two sons from a previous marriage as his executors. They spent approximately $12,600 on the funeral arrangements. The deceased's wife argued that the funeral expenses were inappropriately luxurious and inappropriately religious, given the modest, non-religious lifestyle he lived. The Court disagreed with her and accepted the executor's evidence that it was a middle-of-the-road funeral, similar in status to the funerals of the deceased's friends in the community.

If an executor or any other person who undertakes to dispose of the deceased's remains fails to do so, he is guilty of an indictable offence under section 182 of the *Criminal Code*.

## Legislation Impacting Funeral Arrangement Authority

Much of the provincial legislation regarding funerals and funeral homes deals primary with issues related to consumer protection, but some provinces set out an order of priority for dealing with human remains following death. British Columbia's law is set out below; Alberta's regulation under the *Cemeteries Act* has a similar list of priority.

### British Columbia — *Cremation, Interment and Funeral Services Act*

In British Columbia, as a result of the *Cremation, Interment and Funeral Services Act*, the deceased's written preference (subject to the *Human Tissue Gift Act*), as stated in a will or a pre-need cemetery or funeral services plan, is binding on the person who has the right to control the disposition. However, if

[7] 2002 ABQB 325.

compliance with such preference or plan would be unreasonable, impracticable, or would create hardship, the plan does not have to be followed.

The *Cremation, Interment and Funeral Services Act* also sets up a priority structure with respect to the disposition of the deceased's remains. The right to control the disposition of human remains occurs in the following order of priority:

1. the personal representative named in the will of the deceased;
2. the spouse[8] of the deceased;
3. an adult child of the deceased;
4. an adult grandchild of the deceased;
5. if the deceased was a minor, a person who was a legal guardian of the deceased at the date of death;
6. a parent of the deceased;
7. an adult sibling of the deceased;
8. an adult nephew or niece of the deceased;
9. an adult next of kin of the deceased;
10. the Minister under the *Employment and Assistance Act* or, if the official administrator under the *Estate Administration Act* is administering the estate of the deceased under that Act, the official administrator;
11. an adult person having a personal or kinship relationship with the deceased.

If the person who has the right to control the disposition is not available or is unwilling to act, the right passes to the next person on the priority list. If the right to control passes to persons of equal rank, the order of priority is determined by agreement among them; if an agreement cannot be reached, priority begins with the eldest person and descends in order of age.

In a British Columbia case,[9] a husband had his wife's remains cremated and placed in a cemetery plot alongside his mother's remains. He told the

[8] "Spouse" under the *Cremation, Interment and Funeral Services Act* means a person who (a) is married to another person, (b) is united to another person by a marriage that, although not a legal marriage, is valid at common law, or (c) has lived and cohabited with another person in a marriage-like relationship, including a marriage-like relationship between persons of the same gender, for a period of at least 2 years immediately before the other person's death.

[9] *Re Popp Estate*, 2001 BCSC 183.

Court that when his father died, he would remove his wife's remains and bury his father beside his mother, but that he was uncertain as to what he was going to do with his wife's remains at that point. The wife's son stated that he wanted his mother's remains to be placed in its own site where he could visit and that would be identified with its own plaque. The Court ordered the wife's remains to be disinterred and inurned in a columbarium.[10] According to legislation, the person who has the right to control the disposition of the deceased's remains (the husband, in this case) is only entitled to control the disposition of such remains so long as he or she does not act capriciously. By failing to declare his intentions regarding his wife's remains, the husband was, in the opinion of the Court, acting capriciously.

### Quebec — *Civil Code of Quebec*

In Quebec, according to article 42 of the *Civil Code of Quebec*, a person who has reached the age of majority may direct the nature of his funeral and the disposal of his body. A minor may also do so with the written consent of the person having parental authority or of his tutor. If no such wishes were made by the deceased, the funeral and disposal of the remains lie with the deceased's heirs and successors.

## Costs Involved in Funeral Arrangements

Funerals can be quite expensive: the cost for a funeral in Canada can range anywhere from $1,500 (no service, basic casket) to $15,000. The average cost of a funeral is typically between $6,000 and $10,000, depending on the type of service and the choices made regarding items such as coffins, graves, and markers. Funeral homes offer a wide array of services, such as providing death certificates; assisting with obituary notices; embalming; dressing; casketing; cremating; providing space for the visitation; directing the funeral service; and providing the funeral coach or hearse, the family limousine, prayer cards, acknowledgment cards, and flowers. Some costs, such as those paid to the graveyard for the plot and marker, may be payable in addition to the funeral home expenses.

## Funds To Pay for the Funeral Checklist

Funeral fees and expenses are a first charge on the estate, provided that they are reasonable given the size of the estate and the deceased's position in life. The following are possible sources of funds from which the bills may be paid:

[10] A columbarium is a form of vault that has spaces where urns containing the cremated remains of deceased individuals can be placed.

- ❑ **Prepaid funeral arrangement:** Find out whether the deceased had a prepaid funeral arrangement. Details may have been left with the will or related documents.

- ❑ **Bank:** Banks may be willing to provide funds from the deceased's bank account to cover the cost of the funeral, particularly if the funds are paid directly to the funeral home.

- ❑ **Life insurance policy:** The executor or legal counsel may also be able to obtain funds from the life insurance company through which the deceased owned a policy. The executor should look through the deceased's belongings to determine whether such a policy exists.

- ❑ **Employee benefits:** The deceased's employer may have a benefits package that includes funds for such purposes.

- ❑ **Social assistance:** If there are no other financial means to pay for a funeral, the government may provide funding for a simple burial. For example, in Nova Scotia, according to the *Employment Support and Income Assistance Policy*:

> In the event of a death of a resident of the Province, where no provision for burial has been made, either by the deceased or his/her family, the Department may pay for funeral expenses and the cost of the burial subject to the approved funeral rate schedule. . . .
>
> The family or representative of the deceased must make application and demonstrate financial eligibility on behalf of the deceased for all or part of the allowable funeral costs.

According to the Nova Scotia Funeral Rates Schedule, up to a maximum of $2,700 plus taxes may be paid for professional services and merchandise; up to a maximum of $1,100 plus taxes may be paid for cash disbursements for certain things such as cemetery charges, grave liners, newspaper and radio notices, clothing for the deceased, honorariums (clergy, music), and a grave lot.

British Columbia's Ministry of Human Resources may also provide funeral and burial services if the deceased's funds are insufficient and no one else can assist. Indian and Northern Affairs' Income Assistance Program may also be available to assist with funeral and burial costs for eligible individuals.

The relevant government or agency should be contacted to determine what benefits, if any, are available.

- ❑ **Funeral home arrangements:** If you are having difficulty finding the funds immediately, you should inquire as to whether the funeral home has any special payment plan, such as an instalment plan.

- ❑ **Canada Pension Plan:** The CPP pays out survivor and dependants' benefits and, in eligible cases, a death benefit, which is a lump-sum payment that amounts to six times the amount of the deceased contributor's monthly retirement pension, to a maximum of $2,500. Death benefits are payable upon approval of an application for payment of a death benefit. An application form can be downloaded from the Service Canada website at **www.servicecanada.gc.ca**. Additionally, many funeral homes carry the form. The application form and instructions are reproduced at page 172 in Appendix A.

- ❑ **Quebec Pension Plan:** The QPP pays out survivor and dependants' benefits and, in eligible cases, a death benefit, which is a lump-sum payment of $2,500 in respect of an eligible contributor. An application form can be downloaded from the Régie des rentes du Québec website at **www.rrq.gouv.qc.ca**. Additionally, the Régie also allows individuals to submit applications online. The application form is reproduced at page 197 in Appendix A.

- ❑ **Workers' compensation:** In the event the deceased died as a result of an injury or industrial disease incurred in the course of employment, the surviving spouse and children will receive an income-replacement benefit from the workers' compensation board. The workers' compensation board in every jurisdiction pays an additional lump-sum benefit for burial expenses and a certain amount for transportation of the body. The executor should contact the local workers' compensation board for details. More information is available in chapter 4.

- ❑ **Last Post Fund:** The Last Post Fund is a non-profit organization whose purpose is to ensure, insofar as possible, that no war veterans, military disability pensioners, or civilians who meet wartime service eligibility criteria are denied a dignified funeral and burial because of a lack of sufficient funds. Applications can be made online at **www.lastpostfund.ca**. The Last Post Fund is financially supported by Veterans Affairs Canada and by private donations.

- ❑ **Motor vehicle insurance:** If the cause of death was in relation to a motor vehicle accident, you should contact the insurance agent or the provincial insurance corporation for any available benefits. For example, in British Columbia, the Insurance Corporation of British Columbia will reimburse burial and funeral expenses of up to $2,500 if an insured person is killed in a motor vehicle crash.

- ❑ **Department of National Defence military funeral benefits:** The Department of National Defence ("DND") will pay funeral and burial expenses for currently serving members up to the limits outlined in the regulations.[11] Section 210.20(5) of the DND's Compensation and Benefit Instructions sets the rate at $12,700, with an annual increase based on the Consumer Price Index.

## Airline Discounts for Family Members

If family members need to fly to attend the funeral, they may be able to obtain discounted fares. The family member should inform the airline agent or travel agent of the situation and inquire as to whether a bereavement fare is available with that airline and, if so, what information and documentation are required to obtain the reduced fare. Keep in mind that there may be sale fares that are cheaper than any bereavement fare offered.

According to Air Canada's website,[12] bereavement fares are fixed discounts off specific full fares; lower priced fares may be available through regular booking channels. Bereavement fares can be booked by calling Air Canada Reservations and providing certain information. To receive the bereavement fare at the airport counter, the family member must present a copy of the death certificate; otherwise he will have to apply for a Bereavement Travel Refund after the travel is complete. Refund applications must be made within 90 days of bereavement and may only apply to select international flights.

WestJet offers bereavement fares on every flight for those with a death in the immediate family. As noted on the website,[13] although the bereavement fares are lower than their regular fares, WestJet sometimes has last-minute sales that can be cheaper than the bereavement fare. Bereavement fares can only be booked through WestJet's Sales Super Center at 1-888-WESTJET or 1-800-538-5696.

---

[11] www.cmp-cpm.forces.gc.ca.

[12] www.aircanada.com/en/travelinfo/before/bereavement.html.

[13] www.westjet.com.

# 3

# Letters Probate and Letters of Administration

## What Is Probate?

Probate is the judicial process whereby the authority of an executor is confirmed by the court.[1] However, the executor's authority actually stems from the will and not from the formal document[2] issued by the court. Accordingly, an executor has full legal authority to deal with the assets of the deceased from the moment of the testator's death. Probate is generally required to demonstrate to third parties, such as financial institutions and others holding assets or income of the deceased, that the executor named in the will has the authority to act.

If the deceased died intestate or the executor named in a will is unable or unwilling to act, someone must be appointed to administer the estate of the deceased. In these circumstances, the authority of the person named in the grant stems from the grant itself.

Whether there is a will or not, probate entails paying a tax that is determined by the estate's value.[3] Because there is no maximum for the tax chargeable (except in Alberta, the Northwest Territories, Nunavut, and the Yukon), probate tax for large estates can be substantial.

## Letters Probate

Letters probate (called a "certificate of appointment of estate trustee with a will" in Ontario) is a formal court document that provides evidence to third parties that the will has been proved and registered in court and that the executor is authorized to deal with the estate.

Letters probate will generally be required (outside of Quebec) in situations such as the following:

- if the estate is involved in litigation;
- if there is real property to be transferred (required in most provinces);
- if there are assets over a certain value held by a bank or trust company (most financial institutions will not transfer such assets without letters probate);

---

[1] In Quebec, probate is not required for wills executed before a notary. Where required in Quebec, it is a process whereby the court confirms that the will is the will of the deceased and that it meets the requirements of the law. If the deceased was a member of a First Nation, the provisions of the federal *Indian Act* may govern the process, not the provincial legislation set out in this chapter.

[2] Traditionally, this document is referred to as "letters probate"; in Ontario, the document is called a "certificate of appointment of estate trustee with a will", as noted in chapter 1.

[3] Among Canadian provinces, only Quebec does not impose a probate tax. A nominal, flat filing fee applies for the probate of holograph wills and wills made in the presence of witnesses.

- if shares (particularly publicly traded shares) are to be transferred (corporations usually insist on letters probate before they will transfer shares); and
- if Canada Savings Bonds over a certain value are to be transferred.

In Quebec, letters probate must be obtained for all holograph wills and wills made in the presence of witnesses.

## Is Probate Necessary?

Most executors want to know whether or not probate is actually necessary. Because the executor's authority comes from the will itself and not from the court, if the estate is relatively small and uncomplicated or holds only certain types of assets, probate may not be necessary. More particularly, probate may not be necessary to deal with:

- CPP survivor benefits;
- jointly held property with right of survivorship;
- personal effects;
- automobiles;
- life insurance, RRSPs, RRIFs, TFSAs, and other proceeds payable to a named beneficiary;
- certain securities;
- certain bank deposits;
- shares of a private corporation; and
- certain real property.

### Concerns of Third Parties

Aside from any statutory requirements, such as those regarding real property, probate becomes necessary when third parties who must transfer properties to executors require assurance that they will not become liable for doing so. The grant of probate by a court gives third parties such as transfer agents and financial institutions confirmation that the will was validly executed, that the testator possessed the required mental capacity and did not make the will under some undue influence that might render the will invalid, and that a subsequent will will not turn up and name someone else as the executor. If a probated will is later proved invalid, a third party who delivered property to that will's executor is protected from liability.

### Executor's Liability

Probate also serves to protect the executor. Generally, an executor who acts with the care and diligence that a reasonable and prudent person would be expected to display in conducting her own affairs would not be personally liable for losses suffered by the estate. However, the result may be different if the executor did not have the authority to act. If the person named in a will proceeds to administer the deceased's estate without probate and that will is later successfully challenged, that person may be personally liable for any losses suffered by the estate as a result of her actions.

Similarly, in some provinces, probate is important in determining the rights of the deceased's dependants. Ontario's *Succession Law Reform Act*, for instance, provides a six-month limitation period during which dependants can lodge an application for support against a deceased's estate. This limitation period runs *not* from the date of death, but *from the date probate is granted*. (In some provinces, the legislation does not refer to the date of grant of probate; refer to chapter 1.) Any distribution of assets made before the expiry of this period could result in the executor having to make a payment out of her own personal funds, if a dependant successfully brings an application for support and sufficient assets do not remain in the estate. The executor would be personally liable for the amount of the dependant's support won, to the extent of the distributed assets.

Therefore, unless the executor is also the only residuary beneficiary and is sure that there is no later will, the executor may be well advised to seek the protection afforded by probate.

As discussed in chapter 1, in some provinces, matrimonial property claims are also tied to the date of grant of probate.

## Probate Taxes

Probate fees were supposed to be "administrative charges" for the courts' work in issuing letters probate and letters of administration. However, in 1998, the Supreme Court of Canada in *Re Eurig Estate* ruled that probate fees were not fees, but were, in fact, a direct tax. The Supreme Court stated that there was no relationship between the probate fees charged and the costs involved in the administration. So what difference has the ruling made? Not much, except that now probate fees are recognized as a tax.

Probate taxes are calculated on the value of the estate (note that not all assets are necessarily included in this valuation; in some provinces, it is based only on the property located in that province). The greater the value of the estate, the higher the probate tax. Alberta, the Northwest Territories, Nunavut, and the Yukon set a maximum amount that can be charged as probate tax, but the other provinces have no such restriction.

In most provinces, the deceased's personal debts (other than mortgages on real property) cannot be deducted from the value of the estate. For example, if the estate assets are worth $500,000 and the deceased had a $300,000 bank loan, the probate tax would be calculated on $500,000. However, the law in each province must be reviewed. In Alberta, for example, probate tax is based on an estate's net value, not gross value; therefore, all debts, such as credit card and cable bills, can be deducted before the probate tax is calculated.

## Probate Taxes Table[4]

| Province | Probate tax |
|---|---|
| Alberta | Value of Estate<br>$10,000 or under ........ $25<br>Between $10,001–$25,000 ........ $100<br>Between $25,001–$125,000 ........ $200<br>Between $125,001–$250,000 ........ $300<br>Over $250,000 ........ $400 |
| British Columbia | • For estates less than $25,000, there are no taxes.<br>• For estates greater than $25,000, a $200 flat fee plus<br>– $6 for each $1,000 (or part thereof) in excess of $25,000, up to $50,000, plus<br>– $14 for each $1,000 (or part thereof) in excess of $50,000. |
| Manitoba | • For estates $10,000 or under, $70.<br>• For estates over $10,000, $70 plus $7 for every $1,000 (or part thereof) over $10,000. |
| New Brunswick | Value of Estate<br>$5,000 or under ........ $25<br>Between $5,001–$10,000 ........ $50<br>Between $10,001–$15,000 ........ $75<br>Between $15,001–$20,000 ........ $100<br>Over $20,001 ........ $5 per $1,000 (or part thereof) value |

[4] Court filing fees may apply in addition to the fees set out in the table.

| | |
|---|---|
| Newfoundland and Labrador | • \$60 for the first \$1,000 plus<br>• \$0.50 for each additional \$100 over \$1,000 (or part thereof) value |
| Northwest Territories | Value of Estate<br>\$10,000 or under .......... \$25<br>Between \$10,001–\$25,000 .......... \$100<br>Between \$25,001–\$125,000 .......... \$200<br>Between \$125,001–\$250,000 .......... \$300<br>Over \$250,000 .......... \$400 |
| Nova Scotia[5] | Value of Estate<br>\$10,000 or under .......... \$78.54<br>Between \$10,001–\$25,000 .......... \$197.48<br>Between \$25,001–\$50,000 .......... \$328.65<br>Between \$50,001–\$100,000 .......... \$920.07<br>Over \$100,000 .......... \$920.07 plus<br>\$15.53 for every \$1,000 (or part thereof) over \$100,000 |
| Nunavut | Value of Estate<br>\$10,000 or under .......... \$25<br>Between \$10,001–\$25,000 .......... \$100<br>Between \$25,001–\$125,000 .......... \$200<br>Between \$125,001–\$250,000 .......... \$300<br>Over \$250,000 .......... \$400 |
| Ontario | • \$5 per \$1,000 (or part thereof) on the first \$50,000 value plus<br>• \$15 per \$1,000 (or part thereof) over \$50,000<br>No tax if the estate's value is \$1,000 or less. |
| Prince Edward Island | Value of Estate<br>\$10,000 or under .......... \$50<br>Between \$10,001–\$25,000 .......... \$100<br>Between \$25,001–\$50,000 .......... \$200<br>Between \$50,001–\$100,000 .......... \$300<br>Over \$100,000 .......... \$400 plus<br>\$4 for each \$1,000 (or part thereof) over \$100,000 |
| Quebec | • \$99 for individual applicants.<br>• \$111 for corporations or other non-individual applicants.<br>Notarial wills do not require probate. |
| Saskatchewan | • \$7 on each \$1,000 (or part thereof). |
| Yukon | • For estates under \$25,000, there is no tax.<br>• For estates \$25,000 or over, \$140. |

## Examples

The following simple examples illustrate the probate tax or fee calculation. Professional advice in the relevant jurisdiction should be sought to assist with actual calculations in complex situations.

[5] Rates may vary depending on the date of grant of probate.

### Example 3.1 — Alberta Probate Tax

Mary had an estate with a net value of $650,000 in Alberta when she died:

| | |
|---|---|
| Tax on value over $250,000 | $400 |
| Total probate tax | $400 |

### Example 3.2 — Prince Edward Island Probate Tax

Tom had an estate with a gross value of $650,000 in Prince Edward Island when he died:

| | |
|---|---|
| Tax on first $100,000 value | $ 400 |
| Tax on remaining $550,000 value | $2,200 |
| Total probate tax | $2,600 |

### Example 3.3 — Ontario Probate Tax

Bob owned the following when he died:

- a home worth $200,000 (the home had a $77,000 mortgage)
- paintings worth $85,000
- a car worth $15,000
- a line of credit of $10,000

The value of Bob's estate is $223,000 for Ontario probate purposes; the $77,000 mortgage is deducted from the value of the estate, but the $10,000 line of credit is not.

| | |
|---|---|
| Tax on first $50,000 value ($5 × 50) | $ 250 |
| Tax on remaining $173,000 value ($15 × 173) | $2,595 |
| Total probate tax | $2,845 |

## Renouncing

Renunciation is the act of a person giving up the right to be the executor of the deceased's estate. An executor may renounce at any time after the deceased's death, provided that she has not intermeddled in the estate and the letters probate have not yet been issued. (See "Renouncing Appointment as Executor" in chapter 1 for more information.)

In Quebec, the liquidator of the deceased's estate may resign at any time by giving notice to the beneficiaries of the estate and any co-liquidators and by providing them with a final account of her administration.

## Applying for Letters Probate

Each province has legislation regarding the application for letters probate; the procedure varies somewhat from province to province. After you have filed the application with the appropriate court office, the letters probate will be issued at a later date. After you receive the letters probate, you should have notarial copies made. Notarial copies are simply copies certified by a lawyer or notary public as being exact copies of the original letters probate.

Normally, your legal counsel will prepare the documentation required for the application.[6] The following documents may be required to obtain letters probate (although the required documents vary from province to province):

- application form;
- original will and codicils (if any);
- affidavit of execution of will (states that the will was properly signed or, if the will is a holograph will, states that the handwriting is that of the deceased);
- death certificate;
- affidavit stating that notice of the application has been served on all persons entitled to share in the estate;
- valuation of assets;
- probate tax;
- renunciation from every executor alive who is not applying to be appointed as an executor (if applicable);
- security, if the executor is a foreign executor; and
- in British Columbia, a certificate of Wills Notice Search.

### Application Form

An application form is required, although it may be called something else, such as a petition or a *praecipe*.

[6] In Quebec, probate can be obtained either by filing a motion for probate before the Superior Court where the deceased resided or by a notary on the application of any interested person.

### Will and Codicil

Ideally, the will and any codicils are easily located or, better yet, the testator informed you of the will's location beforehand. If not, you will have to do some investigating. You should contact the deceased's lawyer, check the deceased's personal papers at home or at the office, and check any safety deposit boxes. If the will is in a safety deposit box, you may encounter some problems. Financial institutions generally only allow those individuals who have letters probate to access safety deposit boxes (but you need the will in the safety deposit box to obtain letters probate!). Nonetheless, you will hopefully be able to reach an agreement with the financial institution where you present them with a death certificate and an employee of the institution accompanies you while you review the contents of the safety deposit box.

In British Columbia, the Vital Statistics Agency operates a wills registry. You can search for a Wills Notice, which the testator may have filed; it identifies the person who made the will, where the will is located, and the date of the will. A certificate of Wills Notice Search is required in the British Columbia probate process. In Quebec, a wills search can be done at the Registres des dispositions testamentaires et des mandates held by the Chambre des Notaires.

### Affidavit of Execution of the Will or Codicil

The affidavit of execution is simply an affidavit sworn by one of the witnesses to the will, stating that the will or codicil was properly signed and witnessed. Lawyers usually have the witnesses swear such an affidavit when the will or codicil is signed and keep copies of the affidavits with the will. If the affidavits are not with the will you have located, you should contact the lawyer who drafted the will to determine if she has the affidavits. Where it is impossible to obtain an affidavit of execution of the will or codicil, the signature of the deceased may be proved by other means, such as an affidavit from a third party verifying the testator's handwriting.

Individuals may also make holograph wills. A holograph will is a will written by the testator entirely in her own handwriting. Witnesses are not required for a holograph will. As a result, an affidavit attesting that the handwriting is the testator's is generally required.

In Quebec, a will executed before a notary under her minute does not require an affidavit of execution of the will.

### Service of the Notice of Application and Affidavit of Service

The personal representative of the estate may be required to provide an affidavit stating that a notice of the application has been served on all persons entitled to share in the estate. The notice requirements vary among the provinces. Below are some examples.

#### Example 3.4 — Service of Notice in British Columbia

Notice must be mailed or delivered to the following persons:

- beneficiaries under the will;
- a person entitled to apply under the *Wills Variation Act* with respect to the will;
- a common-law spouse[7] or a surviving spouse who was separated from the deceased for not less than one year prior to the death of the deceased;
- if the probate relates to a Nisga'a citizen, notice must be given to the Nisga'a Lisims Government;
- if the beneficiary is a minor, notice must be given to the minor's parent or guardian (if there is one), unless the parent or guardian is the applicant, and to the Public Guardian and Trustee; and
- if the beneficiary is mentally challenged or has a representative or a committee, notice must be given to such representative or committee (if there is one), unless that person is the applicant, and to the Public Guardian and Trustee.

#### Example 3.5 — Service of Notice in Ontario

Notice of the application for a certificate of appointment of estate trustee with a will must be served on the following persons by regular letter mail to the person's last known address:

- all persons (except minors), including charities, entitled to share in the distribution of the estate;
- if a person who is entitled to a share in the distribution of the estate is less than 18 years of age, notice must be served not on the minor, but on the minor's parent or guardian and on the Children's Lawyer;
- if there are unborn or unascertained beneficiaries, notice must be served on the Children's Lawyer; and
- if a person who is entitled to a share of the estate is mentally incompetent or incapable of managing his or her affairs, notice must be served

[7] A common-law spouse is defined in the British Columbia *Estate Administration Act* as a person who (i) is united to another person by a marriage that, although not a legal marriage, is valid by common law, or (ii) has lived and cohabited with another person in a marriage-like relationship, including a marriage-like relationship between persons of the same gender, for a period of at least two years immediately before the other person's death.

on the person and the person's guardian with authority to act in the proceeding, or if there is no such guardian, on an attorney under a power of attorney with authority to act in the proceeding, or if there is no such attorney, on the Public Guardian and Trustee.

## Valuing the Assets

As the executor, you may be required to compile a list of the deceased's assets and debts and their values. Normally, an executor is required to list and/or record the values of only those assets that form part of the estate. Therefore, you would not have to list jointly owned real estate or bank accounts subject to the right of survivorship;[8] insurance, registered plans, and pension plans payable to a named beneficiary; or Canada Pension Plan survivor's benefits: this property passes directly to the beneficiary and does not form part of the estate.

Some provinces may require a particular form of inventory. In Ontario, the application for certificate of appointment includes a section entitled "value of assets of estate". The total value of the assets of the estate must be provided, including separate values for personal property and real estate. Legislation was introduced in Ontario in 2011 that allows the government to reassess the estate administration tax payable if it is believed that all of the required information was not provided, or if the information was incorrect due to neglect, carelessness, or wilfully misleading behaviour. The government has four years to perform this reassessment. Penalties (fines and possibly prison) may result if an executor is found guilty of failing to comply with the law. As of the date of writing, regulations under this new legislation were not yet available.

## Paying the Probate Taxes

Probate taxes are payable at the time of filing the application. (See the "Probate Taxes Table" at page 37.)

## Letters of Administration[9]

An individual who dies without a will is said to have died intestate. Because the deceased did not make a will naming an executor, an administrator must be appointed by the court to administer the estate. Letters of administration (called "certificate of appointment of estate trustee without a will" in Ontario) are proof of an administrator's authority to administer the estate. Unlike an executor, who administers the estate by following the wishes set out in the deceased's

[8] Right of survivorship does not apply in Quebec. When an asset is held jointly, each of the joint owners is presumed to be the owner of an equal share unless there is proof to the contrary.

[9] This section does not apply in Quebec.

will, an administrator has no such document to follow. Instead, each province has legislation that specifies how an intestate's estate is to be distributed. Most of the provinces have fairly similar legislation in this regard.

It is recommended that the administrator's lawyer prepare the application for letters of administration, as this can be a time-consuming and difficult process.

## Appointing the Administrator

Generally, the court alone has the right to appoint an individual to administer an estate. In Quebec, the heirs of the intestate deceased are the liquidators, and they must act jointly unless they designate someone else to act. There are certain obvious restrictions as to who cannot act as administrator, such as a minor, a mentally incompetent person, or a prisoner. In most provinces, the legislation sets out who may apply to the court to be an administrator.

Normally, the court would appoint the spouse or the closest living relative of the deceased to act as the administrator, provided that that person wishes to act. However, the persons entitled to apply to be the administrator, such as the spouse and other relatives, may not wish to do so. In such case, they may request that someone else be appointed as administrator.

In some provinces, common-law partners may stand on similar footing to married spouses when it comes to the right to be appointed as administrator of the deceased's estate. For example, the Ontario *Estates Act* states that the court may appoint the person to whom the deceased was married immediately before death or the person with whom the deceased was living in a conjugal relationship outside marriage immediately before death. In the British Columbia *Estate Administration Act*, which sets out the priority of appointment to be the administrator, a spouse includes a person who lived with the deceased in a marriage-like relationship for at least two years immediately prior to the deceased's death, regardless of whether the person is of the same or opposite sex. In Nova Scotia, if same-sex or opposite-sex partners register a domestic partner declaration under the *Vital Statistics Act*, they have the same rights as a spouse under the Nova Scotia *Probate Act*, which sets out the priority of appointment.

A number of other persons or institutions may be appointed to administer the estate; for example, a trust company, a creditor, or a provincial public trustee. In a financially complex situation, the relatives may prefer to have a trust company appointed as the administrator of the estate. It is also possible to have joint administrators; for example, the deceased's wife and adult child could act as joint administrators.

Although the courts have broad discretion in determining who can or cannot become an administrator, in practice, most provinces observe the following order of priority of the deceased's relatives:

1. spouse (including common-law spouse in some provinces);
2. adult child or children;
3. adult grandchild or grandchildren;
4. adult great-grandchildren or other descendants;
5. parent;
6. brother(s) or sister(s).

As a general rule, the spouse has the right to administer the intestate's estate in priority to other applicants. However, if the marriage was dissolved prior to the deceased's death, the surviving spouse has no right to make an application.

In Quebec, the position of liquidator falls automatically to the heirs, and the heirs, by majority vote, may designate the liquidator.

### Does an Individual Have To Act?

As the application to be appointed the administrator of an estate is voluntary, generally no person can be compelled to act as an administrator. A person entitled to a prior right of administration may need to renounce her right before administration would be given to someone lower in priority. For example, if the deceased's husband is alive, he may have to renounce his right to administer the estate before the deceased's daughter could become the administrator.

In some jurisdictions, such as Manitoba, a person interested in the estate may compel someone with higher priority to agree to either act or renounce, and if no one agrees to act, the interested person may apply for the grant.

In Quebec, the law states that no person "is bound to accept the office of liquidator unless he is the sole heir".

## Applying for Letters of Administration[10]

Certain documents must be filed before letters of administration are granted. These documents are normally prepared by a lawyer. The following documents are normally filed to obtain letters of administration (although the requirements vary slightly from province to province):

- application form;
- affidavit;
- renunciations and consents (or in some jurisdictions, confirmation of renunciation and consent in the applicant's affidavit);
- inventory (in some jurisdictions, this is not required until after the grant is issued);
- security;
- probate tax;
- affidavit stating that notice of the application has been served on all persons entitled to share in the estate; and
- in British Columbia, a certificate of Wills Notice Search.

### Application Form

The application form varies from province to province. In Ontario, the form requires information such as the deceased's residential address, date of death, and next of kin who are entitled to a share in the estate.

### Affidavit

The person applying to become the administrator of the estate must swear an affidavit; the information may include a statement saying that a will could not be located and specifying the person's relationship to the deceased.

### Renunciation and Consent

Before the court can appoint a person as the administrator, any other individuals who have a prior right to be the administrator of the estate must renounce this right. Additionally, written consent may be required from those persons who have an equal right to be an administrator and from all other persons who are entitled to share in the distribution of the estate.

---

[10] This section does not apply in Quebec.

### Bond/Security

The administrator may be required to provide the court with a bond as security for the collection, administration, and accounting of the property of the deceased. Review the requirements of the applicable province; in some cases, the bond may be decreased or dispensed with altogether. In British Columbia, for example, the court may dispense with the bond where:

- there are no debts for which the estate is or may be liable;
- the estate is of small value;
- the administrator is the beneficiary; or
- all parties who may be beneficially interested in the estate consent in writing.

### Notice

The applicant must give notice of the application to any person who is entitled to a share of the estate. Notice may also need to be served on appropriate government agencies or another person, if the entitled person is below the age of majority or is mentally incapable.

## Paying the Probate Taxes

Probate taxes are payable at the time of filing the application. (See the "Probate Taxes Table" at page 37.)

# Inventory of Assets

## Introduction

As the personal representative, you are responsible for the administration of the estate's assets. However, if you have little experience in estate administration, a professional, including legal counsel or a trust company, can assist you with this responsibility or at least advise you as to what must be done. Remember that if you do seek assistance, fees will be payable, and if the fees are paid by the estate, this may reduce the compensation payable to the executor.

You (or your representative) should gather, as soon as possible, all information relating to the deceased's liabilities and assets. Once you have located the assets of the deceased and taken them into possession, you will have to take an inventory and have the assets valued.

Assets should be recorded and should undergo a valuation for the following reasons:

- to calculate the value of probate taxes, where applicable;
- to determine capital gains and capital losses for income tax purposes;
- to calculate foreign taxes, if any;
- to keep records if you intend to seek compensation;
- for miscellaneous purposes such as buy–sell agreements, sale or distribution of assets, insurance on assets, etc.;
- to calculate the value of property for family/matrimonial property issues;
- to preserve assets;
- to provide an accurate accounting to the beneficiaries; and
- to attend to immediate issues.

To locate the estate assets, you should speak to the deceased's family and employer, search the deceased's home and place of business, and review the deceased's personal records (including electronic records found on a personal computer) and income tax return from the previous year. You should also make inquiries at financial institutions and insurance companies located near the deceased's home.

☞ See the "Sample Inventory — Assets of the Deceased" at page 207 in Appendix A.

### Quebec

With respect to the settlement of an estate in Quebec, the liquidator is required to prepare a complete and detailed inventory of all the assets and liabilities left by the deceased. Once the inventory is completed, a notice advising of the location where the inventory can be consulted must also be published in a newspaper circulated in the locality of the deceased's last known address.

The law permits the heirs and successors of an estate to unanimously exempt the liquidator from making and publishing an inventory where the estate is solvent, but this may have serious consequences. Failure to make an inventory or publish it is considered a deemed acceptance of the estate and renders the heirs liable for any and all debts of the estate, even if the debts are greater than the heirs' net entitlement from the estate.

Before agreeing to forgo an inventory (and consequently giving up the protection that the law provides through the publishing of the notice of closure of the inventory), you should remember that the solvency of an estate can be threatened during the course of its liquidation if a debt only becomes known during the administration of the estate. If hesitation over publishing an inventory is based on privacy or confidentiality concerns, it should be noted that the only information appearing in the notice is the name of the deceased and where the inventory may be consulted. The notice does not provide any information regarding the assets and liabilities of the estate or any information regarding the heirs.

## Assets That Pass Outside the Estate

Certain assets of the deceased may not be included in the valuation of the estate, either for probate purposes (where required) or for distribution to the beneficiaries under the will.

In provinces other than Quebec, jointly owned assets, such as real estate held in joint tenancy and joint bank accounts with right of survivorship, do not form part of the deceased's estate, and therefore do not pass through the hands of the personal representative; rather, they go directly to the surviving joint tenant(s). Note that if an asset is held jointly but with no right of survivorship, the deceased's share may form part of the estate. You may require legal advice to determine if the assets are held jointly with or without the right of survivorship.

It should also be noted that the question of ownership of jointly held property between a parent and a child after the parent's death has been the subject of some litigation. For example, a mother might open a joint account with her son (as a matter of convenience for the mother) although the funds in the account are solely those of the mother; after the mother's death, the other children or beneficiaries of the estate might claim that the mother did not intend for the bank funds to belong only to the son after her death. Two Supreme Court of Canada cases, *Pecore v. Pecore*[1] and *Madsen Estate v. Saylor*,[2] involved an aging father who opened a joint account with his daughter; upon the father's death, litigation ensued. In *Pecore*, the Court determined that the evidence clearly demonstrated that the father intended his daughter to receive whatever was in the joint account at the time of his death. In *Madsen*, however, the Court found that the father did not intend to make a gift of the joint account to the daughter; thus, the proceeds of the joint account became part of the estate.

In addition, assets such as insurance proceeds, RRSPs, RRIFs, and pension benefits that have validly designated beneficiaries (other than the estate) go directly to the beneficiary and do not pass through the hands of the personal representative. Care must be taken to ensure that the beneficiary designations on these policies or plans remain valid and were not revoked by a will or other instrument made after the designation. These assets are not included in the estate inventory and are excluded for the purposes of calculating probate fees, but the personal representative must be aware of these assets.

### Example 4.1 — Assets That Pass Outside the Estate

Eddie Executor reviews the assets of the estate of Bob Brown. Bob Brown named his sister, Sue Brown, as the beneficiary of his RRSPs. Eddie assumes that he does not need to be informed about the RRSPs. However, Eddie is wrong. Eddie is responsible for filing Bob Brown's final tax return, and the value of the RRSPs must be included in the final return.

## Real Estate

Normally, a lawyer will handle any transactions relating to the transfer of real estate, as this process can be quite complicated. You may assist the lawyer in determining what real estate exists and whether there are any mortgages. Title to any real estate believed to be owned by the deceased should be searched to confirm ownership and find out whether any charges or liens are registered against it.

---

[1] 2007 SCC 17.

[2] 2007 SCC 18.

The deceased's interest in real estate may not be immediately obvious. The deceased may own a home, but may sometimes have an additional property such as a cottage. You will need to determine whether the property was owned by the deceased alone or whether someone else has an interest in the property. If someone else does have an interest in the property, you will need to determine whether the property was held as joint tenants or as tenants-in-common. If the deceased owned the property as a joint tenant, the property normally passes directly to the surviving joint tenant by right of survivorship.[3] Any property that the deceased owned as a tenant-in-common will have to be dealt with as part of the estate, as such property does not pass by right of survivorship outside of the estate.

As soon as the deceased's interest in the property is determined, if no one is occupying the home, certain precautions should be taken to ensure that the home is not damaged or vandalized. It would be advisable to notify the police that the home is vacant. Other preventative measures, such as turning off the water in the winter to prevent the pipes from freezing, may also be advisable.

You will have to ensure that the taxes and mortgage payments are made, and you must also determine whether the utilities, phone, etc., should be disconnected. If not, these bills will have to be paid. Additionally, you must check the homeowner's insurance policy to ensure that the insurance is still valid, particularly if the home is vacant; there may be action required, such as periodic visits to a vacant home, to preserve coverage. You should also make certain that the home has adequate insurance coverage and that the loss payee is changed to the name of the executor(s). If a beneficiary is living in the home, you may need to make arrangements with the beneficiary regarding expenses and rent.

The deceased may also have owned rental or commercial property, which would have to be dealt with by you or your solicitor. You should inform the tenants of the deceased's death and request that all rent cheques be made payable to the estate.

As a requirement of the *Income Tax Act*, capital gains or losses resulting from the deemed disposition of property must be recorded.[4] You will be responsible for attesting to the fair market value of the real estate, and as a matter of prudence, you may want to obtain an appraisal of the property's fair market value from a real estate appraiser or a real estate agent. Real estate agents

[3] There may, however, be some family-law implications to consider. According to section 26 of the Ontario *Family Law Act*, if a spouse dies owning an interest in a matrimonial home as a joint tenant with a third party and not the other spouse, the joint tenancy shall be deemed to have been severed immediately before death. The joint tenancy would therefore become a tenancy in common.

[4] See chapter 6 for more information on capital gains/losses and income tax in general.

may provide an opinion as to value or an appraisal for free, as they would ultimately like to be involved in the sale of the property, whereas real estate appraisers will charge a fee. If the value of the property is unlikely to be a point of contention, a real estate agent's appraisal might suffice. However, more weight would be given to a value determined by a qualified real estate appraiser.

## Mortgages

The deceased may have died holding a vendor take-back mortgage or an investment mortgage. If so, you will have to determine the balance of the outstanding mortgage and whether the payments are up to date or in arrears. You will have to contact the mortgagor (borrower) and request that all future mortgage payments be made payable to the estate.

## Bank Accounts and Safety Deposit Boxes

### Bank Accounts

Normally, you will be able to determine the value and location of the deceased's accounts by reviewing the deceased's personal records (both paper and electronic files). These accounts may be located in banks, credit unions, and/or trust companies. As discussed earlier in this chapter, joint bank accounts usually pass to the survivor rather than to the estate (however, there are circumstances where this would not be the case).

You should call the financial institutions that the deceased had accounts with and inform them of the deceased's death. This prevents unauthorized individuals from dealing with the deceased's assets. You should also write a letter to the financial institutions to notify them of the deceased's death and request the following:

- the deceased's account numbers and balances;
- information regarding joint accounts;
- information regarding the existence of other property held by the bank, such as that held in safety deposit boxes; and
- information regarding any loans, mortgages, or any other liabilities of the deceased.

☞ See the "Sample Letter to Bank Concerning Accounts and/or Assets" at page 212 in Appendix A.

Open an estate bank account as soon as possible. The financial institution will advise you of its requirements, which may include a notarial copy of the will and the death certificate. Deposits can generally be made to the estate account before letters probate or letters of administration are issued; however, withdrawals are normally not permitted until such documents have been issued. A financial institution may release nominal amounts to you on an exception basis or may agree to pay directly from the account certain estate expenses that cannot wait until probate has been obtained; however, they generally are not obligated to do so.

If you engage a professional trust company to assist you with the administration of the estate, it may be able to open a single account where you can consolidate all of the deceased's bank and investment accounts, pay the estate debts and expenses, and eventually distribute the balance to the beneficiaries. The accounting system used by the trust company should also generate statements for you that you can use in your accounting to the beneficiaries.

It is important to keep detailed and accurate records of all receipts and disbursements, as this will make accounting to the beneficiaries a much easier task (see chapter 9 for information regarding estate accounts).

## Safety Deposit Boxes

Contact the bank or trust company manager at the location where the safety deposit box exists and make arrangements for the listing of the contents of the box. The listing is done in the presence of a bank employee and the personal representative (or an individual authorized to stand in for the personal representative) and is necessary in order to obtain details of the assets in the box. As with bank accounts, to gain access to a safety deposit box, you may need to provide a notarial copy of the will and an undertaking to provide a notarial copy of letters probate or letters of administration, if the financial institution so requires. Additionally, if you are not going to be present at the bank, an authorization must be provided for the person who will be attending the bank in your place.

☞ See the "Sample Authorization To View Safety Deposit Box" at page 213 in Appendix A.

## Joint Accounts and Joint Safety Deposit Boxes

Joint accounts and joint safety deposit boxes held with right of survivorship[5] are normally conveyed to the survivor by presenting the financial institution with a notarial copy of the death certificate. If there are any questions regarding the deceased's capacity or intention to have the account held jointly, it may be possible to have the account frozen until the issues are resolved.

## Life Insurance

To determine whether any life insurance policies exist, search the deceased's personal effects. Further information may be available through the deceased's employer. In some circumstances, the OmbudService for Life & Health Insurance may be able to assist with a search for a policy of a deceased throughout its member companies. In order to do so, there must be both (a) some reasonable basis for the search (i.e., a solid reason for believing that a policy does exist); and (b) specific data available about the deceased. For more information, visit the OmbudService website.[6]

If a life insurance policy is found, contact the insurance company to determine what information it requires and whether the deceased has any other insurance policies with that company. You should also request written confirmation of the benefits payable, the name of the beneficiary, and what the insurance company needs in order to transfer the life insurance policy proceeds to the named beneficiary or, if there is none, to the estate. If there are any pressing financial concerns, you may need to act immediately to ensure that the proceeds of the policy are paid out as quickly as possible.

Note that if the insurance policy is payable to a named beneficiary as opposed to the estate, it is the beneficiary's responsibility to apply for the proceeds and not the personal representative's responsibility.

☞ See the "Sample Letter Regarding Life Insurance Policy" located at page 214 in Appendix A.

[5] The right of survivorship does not apply in Quebec.

[6] www.olhi.ca/policy_search.html.

## Automobiles

Automobiles will need to be valued for the purposes of the inventory of the estate and, where necessary, sale. Prices may be determined by comparisons to similar models based on local advertisements, or by a dealer or auctioneer.

Contact your local provincial motor vehicles department to determine what steps are required to transfer ownership of the deceased's motor vehicle(s). You should also record the model, year, serial number, and licence number of each of the deceased's vehicles.

## Canada Savings Bonds

Rules and forms relating to the transfer and redemption of Canada Savings Bonds can be found on the Canada Savings Bonds website.[7] The relevant forms and information include:

- Estate Transfer Form and Guidelines (2351);
- Quebec Estate Transfer Form and Guidelines (534); and
- Bank of Canada Business Rules.

Letters probate are not necessary to transfer Canada Savings Bonds in the following situations:

- the deceased made a specific bequest of the bonds;
- the bonds do not exceed $75,000 and the surviving spouse is the sole beneficiary under the will;
- the bonds do not exceed $50,000 and the children are the sole beneficiaries under the will;
- the bonds do not exceed $50,000 and the spouse and children are the sole beneficiaries under the will;
- the bonds do not exceed $20,000 and the parents, siblings, or other family members are the sole beneficiaries under the will (i.e., no spouse and no children); and
- the bonds do not exceed $20,000 and the common-law spouse, same-sex partner, or friend is the sole beneficiary under the will.

However, other documentation, as specified in the Bank of Canada Business Rules, will be required.

---

[7] www.csb.gc.ca.

Somewhat similar rules are applicable in intestate situations. Letters of administration are not required to transfer Canada Savings Bonds in the following situations:

- the bonds do not exceed $75,000 and the spouse is claiming the bonds (i.e., no children);
- the bonds do not exceed $50,000 and the spouse and children are claiming the bonds;
- the bonds do not exceed $50,000 and the children are claiming the bonds; and
- the bonds do not exceed $20,000 and the parents or siblings (if parents are deceased) are claiming the bonds (i.e., no spouse and no children).

☞ See "Transfer or Redemption of Canada Saving Bonds from a Deceased Owner" at page 215 in Appendix A.

Bonds that have a surviving joint tenant can be transferred without limitation. The bonds must be registered in two or more names with the words "and survivor". When one of the registered owners dies, the registration can be transferred to the survivor(s) upon presentation of proof of death.

Canada Savings Bonds, legal documents, and correspondence should be mailed to:

Canada Savings Bonds
Transfer & Exchange Unit
P.O. Box 2770, Station D
Ottawa ON K1P 1J7

☞ See "Canada Savings Bonds — Estate Transfer Form and Guidelines (Form 2351)" at page 221 and "Canada Savings Bonds — Quebec Estate Transfer Form and Guidelines (Form 534)" at page 227 in Appendix A.

## Other Marketable Securities Including Shares, Bonds, and Mutual Funds

To determine whether the deceased held any shares or bonds, you should search his personal effects and safety deposit box for evidence of securities in physical form (i.e., original share certificates or bonds). It is now more common, however, for shares, bonds, and units of mutual or pooled funds to be held in an account with an investment professional. You should therefore contact the deceased's investment adviser or financial planner to determine if the adviser holds any accounts in the name of the deceased. Units in mutual funds may also be held directly with a mutual fund company or a mutual fund dealer. Review the deceased's files (including electronic files), banking statements, and prior years' tax slips/returns for clues as to the types of assets held by the deceased, and where held.

If you discover any securities, find out what information or documentation the investment professional or firm requires to release the securities to you or to grant you authority over the deceased's account. These requirements may be similar to those of the banks.

If there is no broker involved and the deceased held securities in certificate form, you will have to determine the identity of the transfer agent. The share certificates or bonds will have the name of the transfer agent for the company whose stocks or bonds are held in the deceased's name (however, note that the transfer agent may have changed). Once you determine the identity of the transfer agent, you should contact the transfer agent by telephone or letter and inform him of the death of the deceased.

The following documents may be required in order to have share certificates transferred:

- a notarial copy of letters probate or letters of administration, where applicable;
- a certified true copy of the will, if letters probate or letters of administration are not applicable;
- the share certificate;
- a declaration of transmission; and
- a power of attorney.

☞ See the "Sample Letter To Transfer Shares" at page 234 and "Sample Power of Attorney for Stocks" at page 235 in Appendix A.

The following documents are often required to transfer bonds of a corporation:

- a notarial copy of letters probate or letters of administration, where applicable;
- a certified true copy of the will, if letters probate or letters of administration are not applicable;
- the original bond;
- a declaration of transmission; and
- a power of attorney.

When you complete the power of attorney and the declaration of transmission, it is generally not necessary to obtain printed forms. The form of the document is not crucial. As long as the wording is essentially the same as the form shown at page 236, the document should be acceptable.

☞ See the "Sample Power of Attorney for Bonds" at page 236 in Appendix A.

For income tax purposes, the securities must be valued in order to determine any capital gains. For shares traded on a stock exchange, use the stock's closing value on the date of the deceased's death. This value can be provided by the broker or obtained by checking the stock listings for the date of death. You may require assistance with this.

Bonds, on the other hand, should specify the interest rate and when the interest is to be paid. As a general rule, the value of the bond is the face value as of the date of death, plus the interest owing from the last interest payment before the deceased's death to the date of death. Special assistance may also be required with these valuations, as bonds may also have a capital gain or loss if they are sold or transferred prior to their maturity.

## Employee Benefits

Contact the deceased's employer to determine if there are any benefits owing or available in connection with the deceased's employment. Employee benefits could include such things as death benefits, salaries or commissions owing, benefits payable under a group pension plan maintained by the employer, deferred profit-sharing plans, or retiring allowances. If the employer is a large company, the human resources department should be able to provide you with the necessary information.

☞ See the "Sample Letter to Deceased's Employer" at page 237 in Appendix A.

## Business Interests

The deceased may have had business interests in a sole proprietorship, a partnership, or a corporation. After determining the deceased's business interests, you must have these interests valued and determine who will perform such a valuation. Additionally, in some circumstances (e.g., in a small, privately owned corporation that was run by the deceased), arrangements will have to be made to ensure that the business is operated properly.

If there is a business that was owned and operated by the deceased, the administration of the estate will necessarily be more complex. You should review the will (if there is one) to determine if the deceased specified how the business is to be operated or whether the business is to be sold. The most pressing matter will be to arrange competent interim management, to wind up the company immediately, or to sell it.

☞ Warning! A personal representative who is interested in operating the business must consider his own potential personal liability.

If the deceased acted as director or officer for any board, business, or organization (including charitable or not-for-profit organizations or those in which the deceased was invested), those organizations must be notified. If the deceased was the sole shareholder and director of a company or business, it will be necessary to find a replacement director as quickly as possible. It may be necessary for you, as executor, to take over as director in order to facilitate the administration of the company and protect it as an asset of the estate; professional assistance, including legal and tax advice, should be sought.

## Registered Plans and Pension Plans

The deceased may have designated either an individual or the estate as the beneficiary[8] of his registered plans (including registered retirement savings plans ("RRSPs"), registered retirement income funds ("RRIFs"), tax-free savings accounts, registered education savings plans, and registered disability savings plans ("RDSPs")) or pension plan proceeds. Both the will and the plan contract should be reviewed to determine the most recent designated beneficiary. Contact the plan administrator to determine what documents are required to obtain the proceeds.

Special rules regarding the entitlement to the proceeds of an RRSP or RRIF may also apply based on provincial pension laws if the plan is a registered pension or a locked-in RRSP or RRIF. In addition, if the deceased was the beneficiary of a RDSP, special rules may apply (including the possible requirement to pay back certain government grants) if death occurs within 10 years of the receipt of the grant. Each type of registered plan has its own specific rules regarding what happens on death; advice should be sought either from the financial institution administering the plan or from your professional adviser.

Please note that you should review chapter 6, "Income Taxation", before dealing with registered plans.

## Personal Property

Naturally, the deceased will have owned personal property such as furniture, clothing, jewellery, and antiques. You are responsible for locating and valuing this property, ensuring that the property is stored in a safe place, and arranging for or maintaining adequate insurance. If the deceased collected antiques or other collectibles, or had jewellery that may be of value, it is advisable to hire a qualified appraiser.

## Digital Assets

If the deceased had a personal computer, it is possible that the deceased conducted online banking, investing, shopping, gaming, or gambling. All of these activities may have created assets or liabilities for the estate, and the contents of computers, along with online activities, should be reviewed.

[8] Beneficiary designations on Quebec registered plans are only valid under certain conditions. If there is any doubt as to the validity of the designated beneficiary, you should seek legal advice.

If you are unable to obtain information (such as user or login information or passwords), there are service providers who can assist you. These individuals or firms may be able to find information on a hard drive or track the deceased's online activity to lead you to other assets or liabilities. They may also be able to assist with the sale or transfer of virtual assets owned by the deceased, including online businesses and domain names.

It is important to secure all digital assets and online accounts, as they may be targets for identify theft.

## Canada and Quebec Pension Plan Benefits

### Canada Pension Plan

Under the Canada Pension Plan ("CPP"), monthly pensions are paid to a deceased contributor's surviving spouse or common-law partner[9] and dependent children under the age of 18 (or between ages 18 to 25 if attending school full time at a recognized institution). In addition, the CPP provides for a death benefit, which is a lump-sum payment.

The amount of survivor's pension that a spouse or common-law partner will receive depends on a variety of factors, such as the age of the survivor, whether the survivor is receiving his own retirement pension, the amount of the deceased's retirement pension, and whether the survivor is disabled or has children. The personal representative should advise the surviving spouse/common-law partner to apply for his benefits as well as any benefits for dependants. The survivor will need to provide the following:

- the death certificate of the deceased;
- the deceased's social insurance number (if the social insurance number is not provided, a certified true copy of the deceased's original birth certificate must be submitted);[10]
- the surviving spouse or common-law partner's social insurance number (if the social insurance number is not provided, a certified true copy of his or her original birth certificate must be submitted);[10]

[9] A "common-law partner" is defined in the *Canada Pension Plan* as a person (regardless of sex) who is cohabiting in a conjugal relationship with the CPP contributor at the relevant time, having so cohabited with the contributor for a continuous period of at least one year.

[10] Although a birth certificate is normally not necessary, the Canada Pension Plan has the right to request proof of birth at any time, when deemed necessary.

- the social insurance numbers of the children of the deceased (if the social insurance numbers are not provided, certified true copies of their original birth certificates must be submitted);[10]
- a certified true copy of the marriage certificate, if the applicant was married to the deceased; and
- a statutory declaration, if the applicant was living in a common-law relationship with the deceased.

☞ See "How To Apply for the CPP Survivor's Pension and Child(ren)'s Benefit(s)" and the "Application for CPP Survivor's Pension and Child(ren)'s Benefits" at page 182 in Appendix A.

The CPP death benefit is a lump-sum payment that amounts to six times the amount of the deceased's monthly retirement pension (the retirement pension is earnings-related) to a maximum of $2,500. If there is a will, the executor named in the will must apply for the death benefit within 60 days of the date of death. If there is no will, or if the executor does not apply within 60 days of the date of death, the death benefit will be paid, after application, to a party in the following order of priority:

1. the person or institution who paid or who was responsible for paying the deceased's funeral expenses;
2. the surviving spouse or common-law partner of the deceased;
3. the next of kin of the deceased.

☞ See "How To Apply for the CPP Death Benefit" and the "Application for CPP Death Benefit" at page 172 in Appendix A.

Four times a year, the federal government produces an Income Security Programs Information Card ("ISP card") that sets out the maximum payment that can be made for each type of Canada Pension Plan and Old Age Security benefit. The ISP cards can be viewed online at **www.servicecanada.gc.ca/eng/isp/statistics/rates/infocard.shtml**.

## Quebec Pension Plan

The Quebec Pension Plan ("QPP") operates in much the same manner as the CPP. Monthly pensions are paid to surviving spouses and orphans of the deceased. A surviving spouse is a person who, on the day of the death of the contributor: (i) is married to the contributor; (ii) is in a civil union with the contributor; or (iii) provided the contributor is either legally separated or neither married nor in a civil union on the day of death, has been living with the contributor in a *de facto* union (opposite or same-sex) for at least three years or for at least one year if a child was born from their union, they adopted a child, or one of them adopted a child of the other.

The amount of surviving spouse's pension varies as a result of several factors, such as the age of the spouse, the contributions made by the deceased to the QPP, and whether the surviving spouse is disabled or supports dependent children of the deceased.

The death benefit is a lump-sum payment of $2,500. The death benefit is paid to the person or charity who paid the funeral expenses (but only up to the amount paid if less than $2,500). An application must be made, with accompanying receipts, within 60 days of the contributor's death. Otherwise, the death benefit will be paid to the first of the following applicants:

- the heirs of the contributor;
- the surviving spouse of the contributor (if no surviving heirs);
- the descendants of the contributor (if no surviving heirs or surviving spouse);
- the ascendants of the contributor (if no surviving heirs, spouse, or descendants).

If the deceased made sufficient contributions to the QPP, children of the deceased under the age of 18 may be eligible for an orphan's pension. The amount is fixed by the government and ends when the child turns 18.

More information about QPP benefits can be found on the Régie des rentes du Québec's website at **www.rrq.gouv.qc.ca**. An application for survivor benefits may also be made online on the Régie's website.

☞ See the "Application for QPP Survivors' Benefits" at page 197 in Appendix A.

## Workers' Compensation Survivor Benefits[11]

In the event that an employee dies as a result of an injury or industrial disease incurred in the course of employment, the surviving spouse[12] and children will receive an income-replacement benefit from the Workers' Compensation Board ("WCB").[13] Most jurisdictions reduce the benefit amount if a CPP or QPP survivor's pension is also being paid out. All jurisdictions pay an additional lump-sum benefit for burial expenses and a certain amount for transportation of the employee's body.

Other than the lump-sum amounts that may be paid, spousal benefits are usually based on a fixed percentage of the deceased's pre-injury net earnings. The amounts may also be dependent on the spouse's age, the number and ages of the dependent children, and whether or not the spouse is an invalid. Special rules may also apply if spouses are separated.

Previously, spousal benefits generally ceased upon remarriage, and the spouse was paid a lump sum upon such remarriage; however, this is no longer the case.

The benefits for dependent children generally terminate at age 18 or 19 (depending on the province), but may be extended if the child is disabled or attending school.

In most provinces, survivors are required to file their WCB compensation claims as soon as possible after the date of death. Failure to give notice to the WCB in a timely manner may result in a denial of compensation benefits. The time period varies among the provinces, but is usually between six months and one year from the date of death. For example, in New Brunswick, Newfoundland and Labrador, Ontario, P.E.I., Quebec, and Saskatchewan, the time limit is six months from the date of death. In British Columbia, Manitoba, the Northwest Territories, and Nunavut, the time limit is one year; and in Alberta, it is two years from the date of death.

If the deceased was already receiving WCB benefits, there may be outstanding amounts owing to the estate.

---

[11] More information may be obtained from the website for the Canadian Centre for Occupational Health and Safety, including links to each provincial board. See www.ccohs.ca.

[12] A surviving spouse in all jurisdictions means a married spouse or a common-law partner, for the purposes of workers' compensation benefits.

[13] In most jurisdictions, the corporate body that manages the workers' compensation insurance business is known as the Workers' Compensation Board. In New Brunswick, it is called WorkSafeNB. In Newfoundland and Labrador, it is called the Workplace Health, Safety and Compensation Commission. In Ontario, it is called the Workplace Safety and Insurance Board. In Quebec, it is called the Commission de la santé et de la sécurité du travail (Occupational Health and Safety Commission). In British Columbia, it is called WorksafeBC. In the Yukon, it is called the Workers' Compensation, Health and Safety Board.

## Travel Reward Programs and Other Bonus Points

The deceased may have accumulated points of substantial value under a reward system established by an airline or credit card company. Sometimes these points may be transferred upon the deceased's death, and it may be necessary to assign or use the points within a given time. As a result, the company administering the reward points should be contacted fairly early in the administration of the estate to determine the status of such points and whether they can be transferred.

## Firearms

In general, the executor would have the same rights to possess firearms, during the administration of the estate, as the deceased had to possess such firearms during his lifetime. As a result, even if you are not personally licensed to possess firearms, you may keep them in your possession for a reasonable period of time until the estate is settled.[14] If the deceased did not have a valid licence and registration certificate for the firearm, then he was in illegal possession. According to the RCMP's fact sheet "Inherited Firearms", this puts you "at risk of penalties for possessing the firearm unless you act quickly to comply with the law — for example by transferring it to a properly licensed individual in some cases, or by turning it in to a police or firearms officer for disposal". If you are uncertain as to whether or not the deceased had a registration certificate, call 1-800-731-4000. The firearms can be transferred by phone (1-800-731-4000) or by paper application. As executor, you will be required to complete the RCMP's Declaration of Authority to Act on Behalf of an Estate.

☞ See the RCMP's "Fact Sheet on Inherited Firearms" at page 238 in Appendix A.

[14] This is not the case if a court has prohibited you from possessing firearms, although you are still permitted to transfer the firearms to someone who can legally possess them.

# 5

# Debts of the Estate

## Introduction

The deceased will most likely have a collection of unpaid bills that will need to be dealt with before the personal representative can distribute the estate. It is your duty, as the personal representative, to determine what debts exist and whether the debts are legitimate. The debts and liabilities of the estate could include such things as funeral expenses, medical expenses, income tax liabilities, utility bills, personal guarantees, apartment leases, and obligations to provide maintenance under a separation agreement or court order. The debts and liabilities that arose prior to death as well as those that arose as a consequence of death must be paid. You may also have to deal with obligations under a buy–sell agreement, if the deceased was an owner of a private corporation.

☞ Warning! Proceed with caution. If you distribute the assets of the estate without paying the debts of the estate first, you may be held personally liable for the unpaid debts.

## Ascertaining the Debts

The more familiar the personal representative is with the affairs of the deceased, the less arduous the task of determining the estate's debts is likely to be. As the personal representative, you must complete a thorough inquiry into what debts are owed by the estate. To do this, you should search the deceased's personal papers and electronic files at home (and at work, if you are permitted access). You should also speak to any professionals with whom the deceased had dealings in the past, such as financial advisers, lawyers, and accountants, to determine if there are any outstanding debts.

### Debt Checklist

The following are debts to look for and people or organizations to contact:

- ❑ **Funeral or burial expenses:** Contact the funeral home.
- ❑ **Medical expenses:** If the deceased had personal care assistance or other outstanding medical expenses, contact the organization that provided these services to determine if any money is owing.
- ❑ **Mortgage liabilities:** If the deceased had mortgage payments, contact the institution that acts as the mortgagee (e.g., the bank).

- ❑ **Apartment or other residential lease:** If the deceased rented an apartment or home, ensure that the rent owing is paid. Also remember to give notice to terminate the lease.
- ❑ **Nursing home:** If the deceased lived in a nursing home prior to death, contact the administrators of the home to ensure that no money is owing.
- ❑ **Telephone company:** Contact the telephone company (land line and/or mobile) to determine whether any outstanding balance is owing and ensure that the telephone has been disconnected.
- ❑ **Cable company:** Contact the cable company to determine if there are any outstanding balances owing and ensure that the cable has been disconnected.
- ❑ **Utility bills:** Ensure that no amounts are owing to the utility companies. Remember to discontinue such services, if necessary.
- ❑ **Internet service providers:** Contact the company to determine if any amounts are outstanding and to discontinue the service.
- ❑ **Credit cards and lines of credit:** Contact credit card companies and banks where the deceased was a client to determine if the deceased owed any debt on credit cards or other debts such as lines of credit.
- ❑ **Electronic accounts:** Review the online activity of the deceased as well as credit card and bank statements to determine if the deceased had any accounts that existed only online (for example, a PayPal account) and to validate whether there are any amounts owing to creditors.
- ❑ **Property taxes:** Contact the local government to determine if any taxes are outstanding.
- ❑ **Income tax liabilities:** Ensure that all income tax owing will be paid.
- ❑ **Business debts:** If the deceased was operating a business as a partnership or sole proprietorship, the debts of the business may also have to be paid.
- ❑ **Maintenance:** Review any separation agreement or court order(s) to determine whether maintenance must continue to be paid after the individual's death. You may have to set up a reserve fund to pay such obligations. You may also wish to negotiate with the recipient to see

whether a lump sum would be accepted rather than ongoing payments. This would prevent the estate from being tied up with future payments.

- **Personal guarantees:** Personal guarantees are often given in a business context to support the financial obligations of a business. They may also be given in a non-business context, such as to provide a guarantee for a family member. Most guarantees given to a bank are continuing guarantees, and they will become the responsibility of the estate. You may need to set up a reserve fund in the event that the guarantee is called sometime in the future.

## Advertising for Creditors

The requirement to advertise for creditors varies among the provinces. For example, in Nova Scotia, the personal representative is required to advertise for creditors in Nova Scotia's *Royal Gazette* for six months. In Prince Edward Island, the Registrar of the Estates Section is responsible for advertising for creditors in that province's *Royal Gazette*. In Saskatchewan, there are other specific legislative requirements regarding advertising for creditors.

In other provinces, such as Ontario, Alberta, and British Columbia, the law does not specifically require such an advertisement. However, if the personal representative distributes the estate without advertising and a creditor later makes a claim against the estate, the personal representative may be held liable to pay the debt herself. If an advertisement is made, however, the executor may distribute the assets once the time period has expired[1] without being personally liable for subsequent claims made by creditors.

Regardless, in those provinces where advertising is optional, the personal representative may decide that advertising for creditors is a needless expense, particularly in certain circumstances, such as where the personal representative is the sole beneficiary. Nonetheless, if you, as the personal representative, feel uncertain as to whether all the debts have been located, you may wish to advertise. If not, you may wish to obtain an indemnity from the beneficiaries receiving the estate, promising to repay any amounts they receive that are later found to be owing to creditors (along with any penalties and interest accruing).

[1] This assumes that all other debts of the estate have been paid and the time limitations for potentials claims have expired.

### Quebec

In Quebec, heirs are not held liable for the debts of the estate beyond the value of the property they take, subject to the following requirements on the part of the liquidator:

- making an inventory including the assets and liabilities of the estate;
- publishing the closure of the inventory in the register of personal and movable real rights by registration of a notice identifying the deceased and indicating the place where the inventory may be consulted by interested persons; and
- publishing the notice in a newspaper circulated in the locality of the deceased's last known address.

However, the heirs can still be held personally liable for the debts of the estate if:

- all the heirs unanimously exempt the liquidator from making an inventory; or
- before the inventory, the heirs mingle the property of the estate with their personal property (unless the property was already mingled before the death, such as in the case of cohabitation).

The liquidator must inform those who have an interest in the estate and any known creditors of the registration of the notice of closure and of the place where the inventory may be consulted; the liquidator must provide a copy of the inventory to them if that can easily be done.

Known creditors and legatees by particular title who have been neglected in the payments made by the liquidator may be able to make a claim against the liquidator as well as an action against any heirs who have received advances and any legatees by particular title who have been paid to their detriment.

### Contents of the Notice

Some provinces set out the contents and nature of the notice in their legislation, some do not. Nonetheless, there is normally some standard for giving notice, and the personal representative should make inquiries as to the appropriate manner of notice for the province in which the estate is being handled.

In Ontario, although there is no obligation on the personal representative to advertise for creditors and there is no prescribed form of notice, the following practice has developed: an advertisement is inserted once a week for three successive weeks in the local newspaper in the region where the person lived or carried on a business prior to death; it allows at least 30 days from the time the notice was first published to the end date for the filing of all claims. Although in reality many creditors will never even see such an advertisement, this procedure is a method by which you, the personal representative, can protect yourself. However, if a creditor gives notice of a debt and you proceed to distribute the assets anyway, advertising cannot be used as a mechanism to protect yourself, as you are obviously not acting in good faith.

☞ See the "Sample Advertisement for Creditors (Provinces Other Than Quebec)" and the "Sample Advertisement for Creditors (Quebec)"at pages 242 and 243 in Appendix A.

In Quebec, the law provides that the notice for the closure of the inventory should identify the deceased and indicate the place where the inventory may be consulted by interested persons.

## Paying the Debts of the Estate

The personal representative has a responsibility to ensure that all debts of the estate are paid before any distribution is made to the beneficiaries. Note that if the estate is insolvent, the entire estate will be consumed by the creditors, and the beneficiaries will receive nothing.

In general, you can exercise a great deal of discretion in determining whether a debt or claim against the deceased's estate is legitimate. This does not mean, however, that you can pay just anyone who claims that she was owed money by the deceased. You must act in a reasonable and cautious manner and be satisfied that the debt or claim is actually enforceable against the estate.

In provinces other than Quebec, if the deceased died intestate, you have the power to sell estate assets to pay the debts of the deceased. On the other hand, if a will exists, your work may become somewhat more complicated, as the deceased may have specified in the will that some individuals are to receive specific assets from the estate. Thus, the funds or assets that you can use to pay the debts may depend on what the will says.

The personal representative must review the will to determine if the testator specified how the debts are to be paid. Unless otherwise stated in the will, the debts are generally paid out of the residuary estate. The residuary estate is that portion of the estate that has not otherwise been particularly bequeathed or devised. If the will contains a residuary clause that disposes of both real estate and personal property, the residuary real estate and personal property is treated as a single fund.

The deceased may have specified in the will that certain beneficiaries will be responsible for carrying the debt associated with certain assets. For example, if a father left his car to his son, he may have specified in his will that the son is to pay for the car loan. If the father did not leave specific instructions in his will, the car loan would have to be paid out of the residue of the estate.

If a debt is owed to someone who is also left a specific gift in the will of the deceased, advice may be required in order to determine if the gift is considered to pay off the debt owing. In Quebec, the law specifically provides that a legacy to a creditor is not presumed to have been made as compensation for a claim.

In some circumstances, there are sufficient assets available to pay all the debts and liabilities but not enough left to make all the gifts specified in the will. It will be necessary to determine how the debts and liabilities will be paid, and which assets will be used to pay such debts. The order in which the assets are used to pay debts may mean that some beneficiaries will receive the benefits to which they were entitled under the will while other beneficiaries will not. If it comes to this, you should definitely consult your legal counsel regarding the payment of debts, as this could be a very troublesome area. As you can imagine, it can be quite difficult to explain to one beneficiary why she did not receive a gift under the will while another beneficiary did.

To determine which assets should be used to pay off debts, the assets are divided into different categories. If the first class of assets does not have sufficient funds to pay the debts, then you must access funds from the next class, and so on. The rules regarding the order of assets from which debts are to be paid can be complex. They are generally paid out of the residue first. If there are insufficient funds in the residue, competent advice should be sought, but in general, the order of assets from which debts are to be paid is as follows:[2]

1. **Residuary estate:** Debts are to be paid out of the residuary estate first.
2. **Real estate:** Any real estate that the testator specified should be put into trust to pay debts.
3. **Real estate or personal property:** Any real estate or personal property charged with the payment of debts.
4. **General legacies:** Gifts of money that do not come from a particular fund. For example, "I give my friend Rita $10,000".

[2] The new legislation in British Columbia, not yet in force as of the date of writing, may slightly modify these rules.

5. **Demonstrative legacies:** Gifts of money that are to be paid out of a particular fund. For example, "I give to David the sum of $500, if David survives me, and I direct my Trustees to sell my golf clubs to produce the amount of this legacy".

6. **Specific legacies:** Gifts of particular things, specified and distinguished from all other things. For example, "I give my diamond necklace to my niece Ellen Christina". The necklace would have to be converted into cash to pay the debts.

7. **Real estate (specific devises):** Gifts of specific real property to beneficiaries. For example, "I give lot 1 of my property, known as the river lot, to my mother, Noreen". The property would have to be sold and converted into cash to pay the debts.

### Example 5.1 — Paying Debts from Legacies

John makes the following bequests in his will:

- To Sonya: my 2008 wine-coloured sedan
- To Lora: the shares in JAG Co. owned by me at my death
- To Chris: $100,000 out of the proceeds of my life insurance
- To Demetri: $40,000
- To Thane: $20,000
- To Pam: the residue

At death, John's estate is as follows:

| | |
|---|---|
| Assets | |
| 2008 car | $ 10,000 |
| Shares in JAG Co. | $ 40,000 |
| Life insurance proceeds | $100,000 |
| Other assets | $ 50,000 |
| Total assets | $200,000 |
| Debts | |
| Debts, taxes, etc. | $ 10,000 |
| Net Value of Estate | $190,000 |

Ordinarily, debts are paid out of the residue of the estate. In this example, in order to pay the $10,000 debt and all the non-residuary beneficiaries (i.e., everyone other than Pam) in full, the gross value of the estate has to equal $220,000. Since the gross value of the estate is only $200,000, there is a shortfall of $20,000. Therefore, there is no residue, and it will be necessary to use other assets to pay the debt.

Sonya's and Lora's legacies are specific (gifts of specific personal property such as jewellery), Chris's legacy is demonstrative (gift of money paid out of a particular fund), and Demetri's and Thane's legacies are general (gifts of money that do not come from a particular fund). There are sufficient assets to pay the legacies to Sonya, Lora, and Chris. Therefore, the debt must be paid from the general legacies made to Thane and Demetri. Instead of receiving their full amounts of $40,000 and $20,000, respectively, Thane will receive $26,667 and Demetri will receive $13,333.

## Quebec

In Quebec, if the property of the succession is sufficient to pay all the creditors and all the legatees by particular title, the liquidator pays the known creditors and known legatees by particular title as and when they present themselves.

If there may be insufficient funds in the estate, the liquidator may not pay the debts of the succession or the legacies by particular title until the expiry of 60 days from registration of the notice of closure of inventory or from the exemption from making an inventory. However, if circumstances require it, before the expiry of that time the liquidator may pay the ordinary public utility bills and the debts in urgent need of payment.

If the property of the estate is insufficient, the liquidator may not pay any debt or any legacy by particular title before drawing up a full statement of the property, giving notice to the interested persons, and obtaining homologation by the court of a payment proposal that contains a provision for a reserve for the payment of any future judgment.

The liquidator, in accordance with her payment proposal, first pays the preferred or hypothecary creditors according to their rank and then pays the other creditors (except with regard to claims for support); if she is unable to repay them fully, she pays them *pro rata* to their claims. If property remains after the creditors have been paid, the liquidator pays the creditors of support, *pro rata* to their claims if she is unable to pay them fully, and then pays the legatees by particular title.

The liquidator may sell property bequeathed as legacies by particular title or reduce the legacies by particular title if the other property of the estate is insufficient to pay all the debts. The sale and/or reduction is done in the order and in the proportions agreed to by the legatees. Where the property is still insufficient, the liquidator sells the objects of legacies of determined things, then the objects of legacies having preference, or reduces such legacies *pro rata* to their values.

However, the legatees may always agree to another mode of settlement or be relieved by giving back their legacies or equivalent value.

If the property of the succession is insufficient to pay all the legatees by particular title, the liquidator, in accordance with her payment proposal, first pays those having preference under the will and then pays the legatees of an individual property. The other legatees then incur the reduction of their legacies *pro rata*, and the remainder is partitioned among them *pro rata* to the value of each legacy.

## Debts and Liabilities Attached to Specific Property

As previously mentioned, the general rule is that the debts of the deceased are paid out of the residue of the estate. Specific legacies, such as a car or jewellery, may be used to pay debts only when the residue is insufficient to pay all the debts. This rule applies even if a specific legacy has a liability attached to it. Referring to example 5.1 above, if the car bequeathed to Sonya had an outstanding car loan attached to it, the personal representative would have to pay the car loan with funds from the residue of the estate. Sonya would receive the car free of the loan. Similarly, if RRSP or RRIF proceeds are being transferred to a beneficiary who is neither the spouse nor a dependent child of the deceased, the estate rather than the beneficiary would incur the tax liability.

However, there are some exceptions to the general rule. In Ontario, for example, the legislation provides that where the deceased leaves real estate to a beneficiary, the beneficiary is responsible for the mortgage. But this would not occur if the deceased clearly stated in the will that the property is to be transferred and the mortgage is not to be the responsibility of the beneficiary.

## Insolvent Estates

An insolvent estate is one that does not have sufficient assets to cover the debts owing. If the estate is insolvent, the road ahead will be difficult. As the personal representative, you cannot simply choose who you wish to pay. Any money left over is divided among the estate's creditors in the manner specified by law.

When it becomes evident that the estate is insolvent, the personal representative may decide to declare bankruptcy. It may also be possible to reach an agreement among the creditors without resorting to the formal procedures under the *Bankruptcy and Insolvency Act*. However, an agreement is a viable option only if there is reason to believe that a consensus can be reached among the creditors, and where the personal representative has concluded that it is not necessary to obtain the protection of a judgment or order.

## Claims of Spouses and Dependants

### Spousal Rights

The term "spousal rights" refers to the surviving spouse's[3] right to claim a share of the deceased's property if the spouse is not satisfied with the provisions made under the will or under the provincial intestacy law. In provinces that permit such rights, the spouse is given a limited period of time to commence a court action. If a spousal claim is made against the estate, you should consult your lawyer, as the surviving spouse's claim may have an impact on the distribution of the estate.

In Manitoba, Nova Scotia, and Saskatchewan, the surviving spouse must bring a claim within six months of the grant of letters probate or letters of administration. In New Brunswick, the surviving spouse must commence an action within four months of the death of the deceased. In Newfoundland and Labrador, the spouse must commence an action within one year of the death of the deceased, and in Ontario, the surviving spouse must file an election with the Estate Registrar of Ontario within six months of the death of the deceased.

Alberta's current legislation only permits an application if a matrimonial property application could have been made prior to the spouse's death; in other words, only a surviving spouse who suffered a marriage breakdown during the joint lives of the spouses can make a claim for distribution of property under the Alberta *Matrimonial Property Act*. Changes to the *Matrimonial Property Act* have been passed (but as of the date of writing are not yet in force) that would allow a spouse to claim his or her share of matrimonial property from the estate of a spouse on the death of the first spouse. If eligible to make an application, a surviving spouse in Alberta must bring an application for a matrimonial property order within six months from the date of issue of the grant of probate or letters of administration.

In Quebec, a surviving spouse has a personal right under the Family Patrimony Rules, aside from rights under intestacy law or under the will. This right is exercisable upon separation, divorce, nullity of marriage, or death.

---

[3] It is important to bear in mind that the definition of spouse varies from province to province and, in some cases, varies in the same province from one piece of legislation to the next. For example, "spouse" may or may not include common-law partners, adult interdependent partners, and same-sex partners, depending on the province and the law in question.

In Prince Edward Island and the Yukon, the matrimonial property legislation does not permit a surviving spouse to apply for a division of assets upon the death of one of the spouses. However, if an action was started before a spouse's death, it may be continued by or against the deceased spouse's estate. Otherwise, a surviving spouse may be entitled to a remedy under the provincial dependants' relief legislation, which is discussed below.

In provinces where spousal rights exist, the personal representative may be required to advise the surviving spouse that she may have such rights and that she should seek the advice of her legal counsel. It would be wise to discuss this matter with your own legal counsel before proceeding with written notice to the spouse. An election by a spouse to claim under the family/matrimonial property legislation is frequently not in the best interests of other beneficiaries, so your duty to all those involved makes this a complicated matter.

### Example 5.2 — Spousal Rights in Ontario

This example discusses the provisions of the Ontario *Family Law Act*, simply to provide an example of how one province deals with spousal rights.

In Ontario, if a will exists, the surviving spouse may elect to take under:

- the will of the deceased spouse; or
- the *Family Law Act*.

If the spouse does not make an election within six months after the deceased's death, the spouse is deemed to have elected to receive the amount under the will.

If a will does not exist, the surviving spouse may elect to take under:

- the provincial intestacy law (for more information regarding intestacy laws, see chapter 8); or
- the *Family Law Act*.

If the spouse does not make an election within six months after the date of the deceased's death, the spouse is deemed to have elected to take under the intestacy law of Ontario.

If the deceased had a will dealing with some property but not other property, the surviving spouse may elect to take under:

- the will, and receive the entitlement under the provincial intestacy law; or
- the *Family Law Act*.

The *Family Law Act* provides for the equalization of the spouses' net family property in certain circumstances including separation, divorce, or death. The "net family property" of a spouse is the value of the increase in her net worth during the marital relationship. To calculate net family property, it is necessary to calculate each spouse's net worth as of the date of the marriage and as of the date of the deceased's death.

If the net family property of the deceased spouse exceeds that of the surviving spouse (with some exceptions), the surviving spouse is entitled to one-half the difference of the two figures. For example, if the deceased husband had net family property totalling $800,000 and the surviving wife's net family property is $400,000, the difference between the net family properties is $400,000, and the wife is entitled to $200,000.

In calculating a spouse's net family property as of the date of the deceased's death, the following are not included:

(a) property, other than a matrimonial home, that was acquired by gift or inheritance from a third person after the date of the marriage;

(b) income from property referred to in (a) above, if the donor or testator expressly stated that it is to be excluded from the spouse's net family property;

(c) damages, or a right to damages, for personal injuries, nervous shock, mental distress, or loss of guidance, care, and companionship, or the part of a settlement that represents those damages;

(d) proceeds, or a right to proceeds, of a policy of life insurance that are payable on the death of the life insured;

(e) property, other than a matrimonial home, into which property referred to in (a) to (d) above can be traced;

(f) property that the spouses have agreed by a domestic contract is not to be included in the spouse's net family property;

and the following are subtracted:

- the spouse's debts and other liabilities, and
- the value of property, other than a matrimonial home,[4] that the spouse owned on the date of the marriage, after deducting the spouse's debts and other liabilities, calculated as of the date of the marriage.

Only the surviving spouse has the right to file the election, except in a case where the surviving spouse is incapacitated. In that case, the spouse's attorney under a power of attorney may make the election. The personal representative cannot file the election on behalf of the spouse.

[4] Note that the value of the deceased's interest in the matrimonial home is included in her net family property even if the home was owned at the date of the marriage.

## Matrimonial Property Claims Table[1]

| Province | Definition of Spouse | Limitation Period | Restriction on Distribution of Estate | Priority of Spousal Claim |
|---|---|---|---|---|
| Alberta[2] | Married spouse only | Within 6 months of issue of grant of probate or administration | During limitation period, no distribution without written consent of spouse or court order | Has priority over a dependants' relief order |
| Manitoba | ● Married spouse ● Common-law partner where partners (a) had registered under *Vital Statistics Act*; or (b) had cohabited in conjugal relationship for at least 3 years | Within 6 months of grant of probate or administration; court may extend period | During limitation period, no distribution unless spouse's written permission obtained or matrimonial property claim has been settled | Has priority over a dependants' relief order |
| New Brunswick | Married spouse only | Within 4 months of death of deceased; court may extend period | Not specified but prudent to wait for expiry of limitation period | Has priority over a dependants' relief order |
| Newfoundland and Labrador | Married spouse only | Within 1 year of death of deceased; court may extend period | Not specified | Not specified |
| Northwest Territories/ Nunavut | ● Married spouse; ● Person who lived in conjugal relationship for at least 2 years, or in relationship of some permanence and is natural/ adoptive parent of child with deceased | Within 6 months of grant of probate or administration | During limitation period, or if personal rep. receives notice of an application, no distribution of estate without written consent of spouse or court order | Has priority over a dependants' relief order |
| Nova Scotia | ● Married spouse ● Domestic partner registered with Vital Statistics | Within 6 months of grant of probate or administration; court may extend period | Not specified but prudent to wait for expiry of limitation period | Not specified |

| Province | Definition of Spouse | Limitation Period | Restriction on Distribution of Estate | Priority of Spousal Claim |
|---|---|---|---|---|
| Ontario | Married spouse only | Within 6 months of death of deceased | During limitation period, or if personal rep. receives notice of an application, no distribution of estate without written consent of spouse or court order; however, reasonable advances to dependants of deceased for their support allowed | Has priority over dependants' relief order, but does not have priority over a dependants' relief order in favour of a child of the deceased |
| Quebec[3] | Married spouse or civil union spouse of same or opposite sex | Renunciation to partition of family patrimony to be entered in the register of personal and movable real rights within 1 year of death, failing which spouse is deemed to have accepted the partition | Before dividing the succession, the family patrimony must be partitioned | |
| Saskatchewan | • Married spouse<br>• Common-law partner of 2 years | Within 6 months of grant of probate or administration | During limitation period, no distribution of estate without written consent of spouse or court order, otherwise personal rep. may be personally liable | Has priority over a dependants' relief application |

Footnotes:

[1] British Columbia does not allow matrimonial property claims. Prince Edward Island and the Yukon do not permit a surviving spouse to make an application for a division of assets; however, if an action was commenced before a spouse's death, it may be continued by or against the deceased spouse's estate.

[2] Alberta's current legislation permits a matrimonial property application only if it could have been commenced immediately before the spouse's death; in other words, only a surviving spouse who suffered a marriage breakdown during the joint lives of the spouses can make a claim for distribution of property. However, new legislation (not yet in force as at the date of writing) provides that a spouse will be entitled to claim his or her share of matrimonial property from the estate of a spouse on the death of the first spouse. The upcoming changes to the law will also permit a deceased's spouse or adult interdependent partner to automatically be entitled to stay in the home shared with the deceased for three months following the death of the deceased.

[3] In Quebec, spousal rights are under the Family Patrimony Rules. If the deceased was married or in a civil union, the family patrimony must be partitioned before dividing the succession. Family patrimony includes the family residences or the rights that confer use of them, the movable property with which they are furnished and that serves for the use of the household, the motor vehicles used for family travel, the benefits accrued during the marriage under a retirement plan, and the registered earnings earned during the marriage pursuant to the QPP or similar plans. Property devolved to a spouse by succession or gift before or during the marriage is excluded from the family patrimony.

## Dependants' Relief

Every province in Canada has legislation to ensure that the dependants of the deceased are provided for by the estate. The definition of "dependant" varies from province to province; however, it generally includes certain family members who are financially dependent on the deceased, such as the deceased's spouse and children. Most provinces have extended the application of their dependants' relief legislation to encompass common-law same-sex and opposite-sex relationships. In Manitoba and Ontario, a brother or sister of the deceased can also be classified as a dependant, so long as he or she was financially dependent on the deceased. It is necessary to review the legislation of the relevant province to determine who can or cannot qualify as a dependant. Furthermore, simply because an individual may potentially be a dependant does not mean that the individual would succeed in an application. Each province's legislation sets out the grounds for reviewing any application for support.

Dependants must make a claim within a fixed period of time, which varies among the provinces. The personal representative should not distribute the assets of the estate until this time limit has expired. If the personal representative does make a distribution of the estate before the expiry of the limitation period, she may be held personally liable to the extent that there are insufficient assets left in the estate to satisfy an amount awarded to a dependant.

In Quebec, dependants' relief is called the "survival of the obligation to provide support". A dependant is called a "creditor of support" and generally includes a spouse, child, and parent. The share granted to a surviving spouse or child cannot exceed one-half of what she would have been entitled to receive on intestacy, less what she actually received. This results in a maximum of 1/6 of the estate (called the "succession") for the surviving spouse and 1/3 of the succession for all the surviving children. The maximum claim of an ex-spouse cannot exceed the lesser of 12 months' support or 10% of the succession's value. The maximum share to the deceased's parents cannot exceed the lesser of six months' support or 10% of the succession's value.

A dependant can make an application for dependants' relief regardless of whether the deceased died testate (with a will) or intestate (without a will), except in British Columbia and Nova Scotia where a dependant can only make an application if the deceased died with a will.

All the provinces specify that an award can be made out of the "estate" or the "whole estate", but only Saskatchewan defines what estate means: all of the deceased's property less "the amount of the deceased's funeral, testamentary and administration expenses and debts and liabilities payable out of the estate". The Newfoundland Court of Appeal stated in *Downton v. The Royal Trust Company* (1980), 34 Nfld. & P.E.I.R. 303, that the "whole estate of the deceased" (as stated in legislation) from which a dependants' relief award is to be made can only mean the estate's value after deducting its liabilities, including expenses from its winding up; as a result, the logical conclusion for all jurisdictions is that estate means "net estate".

Property gifted in a will, in accordance with the provisions of a contract entered into by the deceased in her lifetime in good faith and for valuable consideration, is generally exempted from dependants' relief orders (except to the extent the property's value, in the court's opinion, exceeds the consideration paid).

In some provinces, certain assets and transactions are to be taken into consideration in valuing the estate and are to be available to satisfy a dependants' relief award (e.g., joint accounts).

## Dependants' Relief Claims Table

| Province | Definition of Dependant | Limitation Period and Other Restrictions |
|---|---|---|
| Alberta[1] | ● Spouse<br>● Adult interdependent partner<br>● Child under age 18<br>● Child 18 or over unable by mental or physical disability to earn a livelihood | Within 6 months of grant of probate or administration[3, 4, 6, 7] |
| Alberta[2] | ● Spouse<br>● Adult interdependent partner<br>● Child, grandchild, or great-grandchild under age 18<br>● Child 18 or over unable by mental or physical disability to earn a livelihood<br>● Child 18 to 22 who is a full-time student | Within 6 months of grant of probate or administration[3, 4, 6, 7] |
| British Columbia[8] | ● Spouse (married, or person of same or opposite sex living in a marriage-like relationship and cohabiting for at least 2 years)<br>● Child (based on case law, includes birth/adopted child, adult independent child in some cases, but not step-child not adopted by deceased or birth child adopted by third party) | Within 6 months of issue of probate[3, 4] |
| Manitoba | ● Spouse<br>● Divorced spouse who has a maintenance/support agreement<br>● Common-law partner<br>● Minor child<br>● Child unable by reason of disability, etc., to support self<br>● Grandchild, parent, grandparent, adult child, or sibling who was substantially dependent on deceased at time of deceased's death | Within 6 months of grant of probate or administration[3, 5, 6, 7] |

| Province | Definition of Dependant | Limitation Period and Other Restrictions |
|---|---|---|
| New Brunswick | ● Spouse<br>● Common-law partner<br>● Child<br>● Parent in need who has cared for and provided support to deceased | Within 4 months of death of deceased[3, 5, 6] |
| Newfoundland and Labrador | ● Spouse<br>● Child | Within 6 months of grant of probate or administration[3, 5, 6] |
| Northwest Territories/ Nunavut | ● Spouse<br>● Child under age 19<br>● Child 19 or over unable by mental or physical disability to earn a livelihood<br>● Person cohabiting with deceased for 1 year before death of deceased and was dependent on deceased for support<br>● Person cohabiting with deceased at time of deceased's death and between whom one or more children were born<br>● Person who at time of death of deceased was acting as foster parent of children of deceased in same household and who was dependent on deceased for support | Within 6 months of grant of probate or administration[3, 5, 6, 7] |
| Nova Scotia[8] | ● Spouse<br>● Domestic partner registered with Vital Statistics<br>● Child (based on case law, can be adult) | Within 6 months of grant of probate[3, 4, 6, 7] |
| Ontario | ● Spouse<br>● Ex-spouse<br>● Common-law partner who cohabited continuously for 3 years, or in a relationship of some permanence if they are the natural or adoptive parents of a child<br>● Parent, grandparent, sibling, child, or grandchild<br>● All of above must be someone to whom the deceased was providing support or was under a legal obligation to provide support immediately before death | Within 6 months of grant of probate or administration[3, 5, 6, 7] |
| Prince Edward Island | ● Spouse<br>● Person divorced from deceased who, for at least 3 years immediately prior to death of deceased, was dependent on deceased for support<br>● Child under age 18<br>● Child 18 or over unable by mental or physical disability to earn a livelihood<br>● Grandparent, parent, or descendant who, for at least 3 years immediately before deceased's death, was dependent on deceased for support | Within 6 months of grant of probate or administration[3, 5, 6, 7] |
| Quebec | ● Spouse<br>● Former spouse<br>● Child<br>● Parent<br>(In Quebec, a dependant is called a "creditor of support") | Within 6 months of death of deceased |

| Province | Definition of Dependant | Limitation Period and Other Restrictions |
| --- | --- | --- |
| Saskatchewan | ● Spouse<br>● Common-law partner who cohabited with deceased as a spouse continuously for at least 2 years, or in a relationship of some permanence if they were parents of a child<br>● Child under age 18<br>● Child 18 or over (a) unable by mental or physical disability to earn a livelihood; or (b) by reason of need or other circumstances, who ought to receive a greater share of estate | Within 6 months of grant of probate or administration[3, 4, 6, 7] |
| Yukon | ● Spouse or common-law spouse (relationship valid at common law, or person cohabited with deceased for at least 12 months before deceased's death)<br>● Child under age 16<br>● Child 16 or over unable by mental or physical disability to earn a livelihood<br>● Grandparent, parent, descendant, or divorced spouse who, for at least 3 years immediately before death of deceased, was dependent on deceased for support | Within 6 months of grant of probate or administration[3, 5, 6, 7] |

Footnotes:

[1] Rules according to the *Dependants Relief Act*. This Act will be replaced by the *Wills and Succession Act*. At the date of this writing, the *Wills and Succession Act* had not been proclaimed into force, so both sets of rules are included in this table.

[2] Rules according to the *Wills and Succession Act*. See note above.

[3] A late application may be possible if a judge considers it just; the order would only apply to estate assets that remain undistributed at date of application. B.C. legislation does not specifically provide for late applications, but there have been cases where the courts have allowed it. In Manitoba, a court will allow an application if the court is satisfied that (a) the dependant was unaware of the death until after the expiry of the limitation period; (b) the dependant's need for maintenance and support did not arise until after the expiry of the limitation period; or (c) circumstances beyond the control of the dependant prevented her from making an application within the limitation period.

[4] No distribution of estate property during limitation period unless all of deceased's dependants consent or a court permits. If the personal representative distributes the estate (or part of it) before the limitation period ends and a court subsequently makes a dependants' relief award to a dependant, the personal representative is held personally liable to the extent that there are insufficient assets left in the estate to satisfy the amount awarded (B.C. does not set out this liability in its legislation). However, the personal representative can continue with other estate-related duties (i.e., taxes and funeral expenses must be paid regardless of a dependants' relief application).

[5] Although not specifically stated in legislation that the personal representative cannot distribute the estate during the limitation period, it would be prudent to wait until the period expires before distributing the estate. As acknowledged in some court decisions, it is possible that the personal representative could be held personally liable if such distribution occurred. Newfoundland and Labrador's legislation states that a personal representative may proceed with the distribution until notice of an application is served on her.

[6] If a dependants' relief application is made and notice of the application is served on the personal representative, she cannot distribute the estate until the judge disposes of the application (or, in Manitoba, Nova Scotia, Ontario, PEI, and Yukon, if all dependants consent or a court orders otherwise). If the personal representative contravenes this provision, she is held personally liable to the extent that there are insufficient assets left in the estate to satisfy the amount awarded to the dependant (New Brunswick does not set out this liability in its legislation). In Alberta and Saskatchewan, the personal representative is also guilty of an offence and liable to a fine or, in Alberta, if the fine is not paid, imprisonment up to 60 days. However, the personal representative can continue with other estate-related duties (i.e., taxes and funeral expenses must be paid regardless of a dependants' relief application).

[7] Reasonable advances are allowed for the support of dependants who are beneficiaries.

[8] A dependant can only bring an application where the deceased died testate (with a will).

# 6

# Income Taxation

## Introduction

There are no estate or succession taxes in Canada. Nonetheless, to a certain extent the income taxes imposed at death amount to the same thing under a different name. Income tax laws are very complex, and depending on the deceased's circumstances, you, the personal representative, may have a very challenging road ahead. If the estate is complex (e.g., if the deceased owned a business) or if you have little or no experience in filing income tax returns, you will probably require the assistance of a lawyer and/or an accountant experienced in estate income tax matters. The Canada Revenue Agency ("CRA") provides useful tools for preparing and filing the deceased's tax returns, such as "What To Do Following a Death" (information sheet RC4111) and "Preparing Returns for Deceased Persons" (guide T4011). The CRA also has a useful web page for executors and administrators that provides links to relevant estate-related tax documents: **www.cra-arc.gc.ca/formspubs/clntgrp/ndvdls/xctrs-eng.html**.

☞ See "What To Do Following a Death (Information Sheet RC4111)" at page 246 and "Preparing Returns for Deceased Persons (Guide T4011)" at page 250 in Appendix B.

Formerly, the definition of "spouse" in the *Income Tax Act* included opposite-sex common-law partners but not same-sex partners.[1] However, as a result of the Supreme Court of Canada decision in *M. v. H.*, in which the Court struck down a same-sex limitation denying support payments to same-sex common-law couples under the Ontario *Family Law Act*, the federal government amended its legislation, extending coverage to same-sex couples. The *Income Tax Act* no longer defines the term spouse and now includes a definition of "common-law partner": a common-law partner of a taxpayer at any time means a person who cohabits in a conjugal relationship with the taxpayer, provided that: (a) they have so cohabited throughout a continuous one-year period before that time; or (b) the person is a parent of the taxpayer's child (natural or adopted); or (c) the person has custody and control of the taxpayer's child and the child is wholly dependent on that person for support. As it currently stands, if you previously lived in a common-law relationship with a taxpayer for at least 12 continuous months and then resumed living together again, you and the taxpayer would immediately become common-law partners again. Under *proposed changes* at the time of this writing, a person will be a taxpayer's common-law partner only if the current relationship has lasted

[1] Same-sex marriage was legalized in July 2005.

12 continuous months. This does not apply to persons defined as common-law partners as a result of (b) or (c) above.[2]

## Liability of the Personal Representative

Before any distribution is made to those entitled to share in the estate, the personal representative must obtain a clearance certificate from the CRA, which indicates that outstanding taxes, interest, and penalties have been paid. Otherwise, the personal representative will be liable for the payment of any outstanding taxes, up to the value of the assets distributed.

The personal representative's liability is limited to the amount of assets available in the estate to pay the taxes.[3] For example, estate X owes the CRA $40,000 and the estate assets are worth $30,000. If the personal representative of estate X distributes the assets of the estate to the beneficiaries under the will without obtaining a clearance certificate from the CRA, the personal representative would be held personally liable for $30,000, as the estate was never worth $40,000.

In situations where the personal representative is also the sole beneficiary of the estate (e.g., the spouse of the deceased), a clearance certificate is often not obtained prior to the winding up of the estate, as the personal representative will be liable one way or another for any unpaid taxes.

## Income Tax Returns Checklist

You must file the following returns for the deceased taxpayer:

- ❑ **Overdue returns:** Any income tax returns for previous years in which the deceased failed to file a return. Such a return should be filed as soon as possible, as penalties and interest are charged on taxes owing from the date that the deceased was supposed to file the return.
- ❑ **Prior-year return:** A return for the immediately preceding taxation year, if the taxpayer had not filed it before death. (For example, Sue died on February 1, 2011 and had not filed her 2010 tax return; the personal representative must file a T1 tax return for 2010.)

---

[2] According to July 16, 2010 draft legislative proposals to implement outstanding income tax technical measures previously included in Bill C-10.

[3] According to July 16, 2010 draft legislative proposals to implement outstanding income tax technical measures previously included in Bill C-10, for assessments completed after December 20, 2002, the personal representative would also be responsible for any and all interest that is charged as a result of these assessments.

- ❑ **Final return:** A T1 return referred to as the "final return" (or "terminal return") must be filed. The final return is for the period of January 1 of the year of death to the date of death. The final return is the return that the deceased would have made if he were still living. (For example, in Sue's situation above, the final return would be for the period of January 1, 2011 to February 1, 2011.)

You must file the following returns for the estate:

- ❑ **T3 return:** If the administration of the deceased's estate is completed within 12 months of the date of death, only one (first and final) T3 return for the estate must be filed.
- ❑ **T3 return for subsequent years:** If the administration of the estate is not completed within 12 months, then a T3 return must be filed for each of the estate's taxation years until the administration is completed.

## Returns for the Deceased

### Overdue Returns

Any T1 tax returns that the deceased failed to file for previous years (other than the prior-year return and the final return) should be filed as soon as possible. Remember that the CRA charges interest and penalties on taxes owed from the date that the deceased should have filed the tax returns.

### Prior-Year Return

If the deceased taxpayer died before he filed the tax return for the year before he died, a T1 return should be filed. This T1 return must be filed and the taxes paid by the later of these two dates:

- the deceased taxpayer's normal filing deadline (usually April 30 or June 15); or
- six months after the date of death.

#### Example 6.1 — Prior-Year Return

Heather Brown died on March 10, 2011. At that time, she had not filed her 2010 tax return, which was not due until April 30, 2011. The personal representative would have until September 10, 2011 to file Heather's 2010 income tax return.

## Final Return

The taxpayer's final taxation year is referred to as the "terminal year". The terminal year begins on January 1 of the year of death and ends on the day of death. Taxes must be paid on all income in the terminal year (e.g., employment income, RRSP payments, etc.). This is also the return in which all accrued capital gains as of the date of death must be accounted for and reported.

Although it is referred to as the "final return", there is no special form; simply use the T1 General Income Tax and Benefit Return.

If the deceased:

- died between January 1 and October 31, the final return must be filed by April 30 of the following year; or
- died between November 1 and December 31, the final return must be filed within six months after the date of death.

If the deceased taxpayer or his spouse/common-law partner carried on a business in the year of death and the deceased:

- died between January 1 and December 15, the return must be filed by June 15 of the following year; or
- died between December 16 and December 31, the return must be filed within six months after the date of death.

According to the CRA, the personal representative can file the final return any time after the date of death and the return will be processed at that time. If you file the final return on the previous year's tax form, in the next year you may request the CRA to reassess the return and apply any tax changes that were introduced in the year of death. However, unless the estate is very simple, it may be easier to wait until the new year's forms are available.

Besides the deadline for filing the tax return, there is also a deadline for paying the balance due on the final tax return. If the deceased:

- died between January 1 and October 31, the balance due date is April 30 in the following year; or
- died between November 1 and December 31, the balance due date is six months after the date of death.

If you are late filing the final return and an amount is owing, a late-filing penalty will be charged. The CRA also charges interest on both the balance owing and the penalty. The penalty is 5% of the balance owing plus 1% of the balance owing for each full month that the return is late, to a maximum of 12 months. If the return was filed late for reasons beyond your control, the CRA *may* cancel this penalty and the interest owing. For more information, see the CRA's Information Circular IC07-1, "Taxpayer Relief Provisions".

☞ See "Taxpayer Relief Provisions (Information Circular IC07-1)" at page 283 in Appendix B.

## Separate Returns

In addition to the final return, you have the option of filing separate T1 returns for certain sources of income. If filing separate returns would result in an overall lower tax liability, you will likely have a duty to file such returns. Each separate return includes only the individual source of income in question. Additionally, for each separate return, most of the personal tax credits, such as the basic personal credit and the married status tax credit, can be fully claimed. Other tax credits, such as the medical expense credit, the charitable donation credit, and the education credits, must be divided up among the different returns.

### Rights or Things Return

"Rights or things" are amounts that were not paid at death but, had that person not died, would have been included in his income. See the discussion regarding "Other Income in the Terminal Year" on page 103 of this chapter for examples of rights or things. If the rights or things are not being transferred to a beneficiary, the personal representative has the option of filing a separate T1 return for the rights or things income. The separate return assumes that the taxpayer is another person, and it includes only the value of the rights or things. This is beneficial because the marginal tax rate that applies to the rights or things will normally be lower than the tax rate applicable to the other income in the regular final return.

In order to file the separate return, you must elect to do so by the later of two dates: one year after the date of death or 90 days after the mailing of the notice of assessment for the final return. The income tax payable for the rights or things income may be paid in instalments over 10 years, if the deceased's personal representative elects to do so.

### Partnership/Sole Proprietorship Stub Period Return

If the deceased person was a partner in a business or a sole proprietor of a business, you may also have the option of filing a separate T1 return for the partnership/sole proprietorship "stub period". The stub period is from the end of the business's last fiscal period to the date of death. The filing of such a return is only permitted if the person died after the business's fiscal period but before the end of the calendar year in which the fiscal period ends. For example, Mr. Brown was the sole proprietor of a shoe company with a fiscal year end on March 31. Mr. Brown died on June 25, 2011. As the personal representative, you would be able to file a separate stub period return for the business income from April 1, 2011 to June 25, 2011, instead of including this income in the final return.

### Testamentary Trust Stub Period Return

If the deceased was receiving income from a testamentary trust (a trust established by someone else's will), you may be able to file a separate T1 return for such income. If the deceased died after the trust's year end but before the end of the calendar year in which the fiscal period ends, you can file a stub period return. For example, Mr. Thomas was receiving income from a trust that had been set up for him in his mother's will. The fiscal year of the trust was from May 1 to April 30. Mr. Thomas died on July 15, 2011. As the personal representative, you can file a separate stub period return for the trust income from May 1, 2011 to July 15, 2011.

## Income and Capital Gains

In Canada, individuals pay income tax on income, which includes capital gains. Calculating the income tax owing is a three-step process:

1. The taxpayer's income for the year is first determined.
2. From the taxpayer's income, the taxable income is calculated.
3. From the taxpayer's taxable income, the tax payable is calculated.

In addition to the common sources of income from employment and business, income includes such things as commissions, tips, salary, rental payments received, and interest payments received. Capital gains, on the other hand, are income (profits) from selling property. A capital gain usually occurs when property is sold (but not sold in the ordinary course of business, such as inventory) for a profit. It is important to distinguish between a capital gain and income, because a taxpayer pays less tax on a capital gain than on normal income. Capital gains usually arise from the sale of property, such as real estate or shares in a corporation.

## Deemed Disposition of Property at Death

The *Income Tax Act* deems a taxpayer to have disposed of his assets immediately before death at fair market value. As a result, if an asset has increased in value since it was acquired, this increase may be subject to tax in the terminal year. However, if the asset is left to the deceased's spouse/common-law partner or to a qualifying spousal/common-law partner trust, the asset will be rolled over to the spouse, common-law partner, or trust. A spousal or common-law partner rollover means that the asset is transferred to the spouse/common-law partner and no tax on the asset is payable until the surviving spouse or common-law partner dies or disposes of the property.

## Calculation of Capital Gain

The capital gain is calculated by subtracting the "adjusted cost base" from the "proceeds of disposition". The adjusted cost base is basically the original cost of the property plus any expenses to acquire it (e.g., real estate commissions and legal fees); you may also be able to add the cost of additions or improvements to the property. As discussed above under "Deemed Disposition of Property at Death", the CRA deems that the deceased disposed of all of his assets immediately before death. In reality, there is no actual disposition or sale of property. As the personal representative, you will most likely have to get the assistance of a qualified appraiser to determine what the proceeds of disposition should be. Fifty per cent of a capital gain is taxable.

Capital Gain = Proceeds of Disposition "P" - (Adjusted Cost Base "ACB" + Outlays and Expenses "OE")
= P - (ACB + OE)

Taxable Capital Gain = 50% × Capital Gain

### Example 6.2 — Capital Gain

In 1990, Doris purchased a cottage for $200,000. It was not her principal residence. Doris died in 2011 and the fair market value of the cottage was $300,000. The personal representative calculated the capital gain as follows:

Capital Gain = P - (ACB + OE)
= $300,000 - $200,000
= $100,000

Taxable Capital Gain = 50% × $100,000
= $50,000

## Capital Property

Capital property can be non-depreciable, such as land, or depreciable, such as a vehicle.

### Non-Depreciable Capital Property

Non-depreciable capital property, as the name implies, is property that does not depreciate. The deceased is deemed to have disposed of non-depreciable capital property for its fair market value immediately prior to death. If the non-depreciable property has increased in value from the amount paid originally, there is a capital gain. On the other hand, if the deemed fair market value is less than the original purchase price, there is a capital loss.

### Depreciable Capital Property

Depreciable capital property is generally any property for which the taxpayer is allowed a deduction for capital cost allowance. For an asset to be depreciable, it must have been acquired for the purpose of gaining and producing income. For example, an asset such as a truck used for business purposes depreciates in value over time and is considered to be depreciable property. Over time, as these assets lose their value, the *Income Tax Act* allows the taxpayer to deduct an allowance for depreciation from his revenue. This deduction is called the capital cost allowance ("CCA"). The balance remaining after deducting the capital cost allowance from the original cost of the property is called the undepreciated capital cost ("UCC").

The *Income Tax Regulations* specify the amount that a taxpayer is allowed to deduct as CCA. This amount is determined by the class of property within which the asset falls. For example, a trailer used to earn income from business or property is eligible for a CCA of 30%. If CCA is deducted in the year that the asset was purchased, the taxpayer is usually only allowed to deduct one-half the amount that he would otherwise be allowed to deduct. CCA cannot be claimed in the terminal year.

The deceased is deemed to have disposed of depreciable capital property for its fair market value immediately prior to death. If the fair market value is precisely equal to the UCC, there are no tax issues to resolve. If the fair market value is less than the UCC, there is a **terminal loss**; the terminal loss can be deducted from ordinary income and capital gains. If, on the other hand, the fair market value is more than the UCC, the situation is more complicated. In general, where the fair market value is greater than the UCC, the amount by which the fair market value exceeds the UCC but is less than the original cost is **recaptured** and treated as ordinary income. Therefore, recapture = (lesser of

(i) proceeds of disposition or (ii) original cost) - UCC. The amount by which the sale price exceeds the original cost of the asset is a capital gain.

### Example 6.3 — Recapture, Capital Gain, and Terminal Loss

Joe purchased a trailer for $20,000 for his business in 2009. He had claimed CCA on the trailer, so at his death in 2011, the UCC was $11,900.

- If the fair market value of the trailer is $11,900, there will be no tax consequences.
- If the fair market value of the trailer is $15,000, there will be a recapture of $3,100 (lesser of ($20,000 or $15,000) - $11,900).
- If the fair market value of the trailer is $21,000, there will be both a recapture and a capital gain:

| | |
|---|---|
| Recapture | = (lesser of P or Original Cost) - UCC |
| | = (lesser of $20,000 or $21,000) - $11,900 |
| | = $8,100 |
| Capital Gain | = P - (ACB + OE) |
| | = $21,000 - $20,000 |
| | = $1,000 |
| Taxable Capital Gain | = 50% × Capital Gain |
| | = $500 |

- If the fair market value of the trailer is $10,000, there will be a terminal loss of $1,900.

## Personal-Use Property and Listed Personal Property

Personal-use property is defined as any property that is used primarily for the personal use or enjoyment of a taxpayer or any person related to the taxpayer. Personal-use property includes such things as furniture, cars, and boats. If the taxpayer disposes of personal-use property and there is a gain, it is treated as a capital gain; however, losses on such property usually cannot be deducted.

For personal-use property, if the proceeds of disposition are less than $1,000, there is no gain for income tax purposes. However, if the proceeds of sale exceed $1,000, there may be a capital gain. If the adjusted cost base is less than $1,000, it is deemed to be $1,000; otherwise, the adjusted cost base remains the same.

Losses on personal-use property are allowed only for listed personal property, which is a subclass of personal-use property. So if the taxpayer suffers a loss on personal-use property other than listed personal property, such loss cannot be used to offset capital gains. Listed personal property is defined in the *Income Tax Act* as personal-use property that is:

- a print, etching, drawing, painting, sculpture, or other similar work of art;
- jewellery;
- a rare folio, manuscript, or book;
- stamps; or
- coins.

A gain from listed personal property is included in the taxpayer's return and may be offset by a loss on any listed personal property. It is important to note that a listed personal property loss can offset a gain only on listed personal property; it cannot be used to offset any other type of gain.

### Example 6.4 — Listed Personal Property

Bob purchased a painting in 2004 for $10,000 and a diamond necklace in 2009 for $15,000. Bob died in 2011. In 2011, the fair market value of the painting was $5,000 and the fair market value of the necklace was $25,000.

Listed Personal Property Gain (necklace) = P - ACB
= $25,000 - $15,000
= $10,000

Listed Personal Property Loss (painting) = P - ACB
= $5,000 - $10,000
= ($5,000)

Net Gain = Listed Personal Prop. Gains - Listed Personal Prop. Losses
= $10,000 - $5,000
= $5,000

Taxable Net Gain = 50% × $5,000
= $2,500

### Principal Residence

A principal residence is a housing unit that the taxpayer, his spouse or common-law partner, or his child ordinarily inhabits. After 1981, only one residence of the family unit (taxpayer, spouse or common-law partner, and unmarried children under the age of 18) can qualify as a principal residence. A housing unit includes a house; apartment or unit in a duplex, apartment building, or condominium; cottage; mobile home; trailer; and houseboat.

The land on which the housing unit is built may also qualify as part of the principal residence, so long as it can reasonably be regarded as contributing to the use and enjoyment of the housing unit. If the property is greater than one-half hectare (1.24 acres), the taxpayer must be able to establish that the excess property is necessary for the use and enjoyment of the home in order for that part of the property to be eligible for the principal-residence exemption.[4]

The deceased's principal residence is subject to the deemed disposition rules. However, the principal-residence exemption will, in most circumstances, exempt the deceased from any tax. An individual can designate only one property as his principal residence for one particular taxation year.

The expression "ordinarily inhabited" is not defined in the *Income Tax Act*. However, the housing unit must only be ordinarily inhabited *in* the year, not throughout the year. This means, for example, that if a taxpayer sells one house and buys another in the same year, he may be considered to ordinarily inhabit both in the year, so that either may be his principal residence. Living in the home on a periodic basis (such as in the case of a vacation property) may constitute ordinary inhabitation, even where the total time spent on the property makes up only a small portion of the year.

The tax-exempt portion of the gain equals one plus the number of years that the home was the taxpayer's principal residence, divided by the number of years the taxpayer owned the home, multiplied by the total gain. Therefore, if the home is the taxpayer's principal residence for every year but one, the entire gain is still exempt.

$$\text{Gain Exemption} = \frac{1 + \text{No. of Years as Principal Residence after 1971}}{\text{No. of Years Taxpayer Owned Property after 1971}} \times \text{Gain}$$

Principal Residence Capital Gain = Gain - Gain Exemption

**Example 6.5 — Principal Residence Gain Exemption**

Sarah bought a home for $100,000 in 1990. She died in 2011, and the fair market value of the home was $200,000. The home was designated as her principal residence for every year but one.

Capital Gain = $200,000 - $100,000
= $100,000

[4] According to paragraph 15 of the CRA's Interpretation Bulletin IT-120R6, "Principal Residence", the excess land must clearly be necessary for the housing unit to properly fulfill its function as a residence and not simply be desirable. Generally the use of land in excess of 1.24 acres in connection with a particular lifestyle (such as keeping pets or for country living) does not mean that the excess land is necessary for the use and enjoyment of the housing unit as a residence.

| | |
|---|---|
| Gain Exemption | = [(1 + 21)/22] × $100,000 |
| | = 1 × $100,000 |
| | = $100,000 |
| Principal Residence Capital Gain | = Gain - Gain Exemption |
| | = $100,000 - $100,000 |
| | = $0 |

☞ See "Principal Residence (Interpretation Bulletin IT-120R6)" at page 298 in Appendix B.

### Family Farms

Normally, when an individual dies, the *Income Tax Act* deems that the individual's property has been disposed of at fair market value, and a capital gain or loss must be calculated. However, the *Income Tax Act* makes an exception in the case of family farms. The deceased's family farm property can be rolled over when such property is left to the deceased's children. A rollover means that no tax repercussions occur immediately. Rather, the capital gain is calculated when the person to whom the property is transferred disposes of the property. Basically, a rollover defers the payment of tax.

The *Income Tax Act* allows a rollover of farmland or of depreciable property that was used principally in the business of farming before the taxpayer's death.

For the purpose of the farm rollover, "child" includes:

- the taxpayer's natural or adopted child;
- the taxpayer's grandchild or great-grandchild; and
- a person who, before reaching the age of 19, was dependent on the taxpayer and was in the taxpayer's custody and control.

More information on intergenerational transfers of farm property can be found in the CRA's Interpretation Bulletin IT-349R3, "Intergenerational Transfers of Farm Property on Death", which can be viewed on the CRA website at **www.cra-arc.gc.ca**.

### Fishing Property

As a result of the 2006 Federal Budget, the ability to roll over property to children, grandchildren, and great-grandchildren has been extended to fishing property disposed of after May 1, 2006.

## Buy–Sell Agreements

Shares of a corporation and interests in a partnership are normally considered capital property and, as such, are subject to the deemed disposition rules. Frequently in the case of a private, closely held corporation or partnership, there will be a shareholders' (partnership) agreement in place with a buy–sell clause that applies on the death of one of the shareholders (partners). Under a typical buy–sell agreement, the deceased's shares are sold to the remaining shareholder(s) or purchased for cancellation by the corporation at the buy–sell price under the agreement. If the buy–sell price is not considered the fair market value of the subject shares, there are numerous potential income tax concerns, especially where the shares are left to a non-arm's length person. If the estate is involved in such an agreement, you should seek the advice of your lawyer or accountant.

## Spousal Rollover of Capital Property

A spousal rollover occurs when property is left to the deceased's spouse, common-law partner, or a spousal/common-law partner trust; any tax payable on any accrued gains of the property are deferred until either the death of the surviving spouse or common-law partner or the sale or gifting of the property by the spouse, common-law partner, or spousal/common-law partner trust. Certain requirements must be met in order for the rollover to apply. For example, the deceased must have been resident in Canada immediately before his death, and the property must be transferred to the deceased's resident Canadian spouse, common-law partner, spousal/common-law partner trust (also resident in Canada), or both the spouse/common-law partner and trust as a consequence of the deceased's death. The property must vest indefeasibly[5] in the spouse or common-law partner no later than 36 months after the date of death. The vesting period can be extended where the legal representative applies in writing to the Minister within the 36-month period and the Minister considers that a longer period is reasonable in the circumstances.

## Paying Tax in Instalments

If any tax liability occurs as a result of the deemed disposition rules for capital property, the tax owing can be paid in instalments over a 10-year period.[6] So long as sufficient security is provided to the CRA, the tax can be paid by equal annual instalments. It is important to note that if the personal representative

[5] In other words, the spouse or common-law partner who receives the property has a right to absolute ownership of it.

[6] Certain other types of income may qualify for instalment payments, such as rights or things income.

elects to pay the tax by instalments, interest is charged to the estate on the balance of tax remaining unpaid.

See "Election To Defer Payment of Income Tax (Form T2075)" at page 319 in Appendix B.

## Other Income in the Terminal Year

The deceased's final return, as filed by the personal representative, is basically the return the deceased would have filed if still living. For example, any salary or wages, commissions, tips, or rental payments earned in the year are normally included. However, certain provisions of the *Income Tax Act* relate solely to the terminal year and the computation of income in that year. These provisions deal with such things as periodic payments and rights or things.

### Periodic Payments

Periodic payments are payments that are payable to a person on a regular basis. The periodic payments that were not received by the deceased but which had accumulated to the date of death are taxable in the final return. (The amounts accruing after the date of death and received by the estate are included in the estate's return; the amounts accruing after the date of death and received by a beneficiary are included in the beneficiary's income.) Periodic payments include such things as:

- interest;
- rent;
- royalties;
- annuities;
- salaries and wages; and
- other amounts paid periodically.

The final return includes periodic payments that were not received by the deceased prior to death. Periodic payments are deemed to accrue on a daily basis up to the date of death.

### Example 6.6 — Periodic Payments

On January 1, 2011, Josie loaned $10,000 to Bob at an interest rate of 10% per annum. The interest to be earned for 2011 would be $1,000. Bob paid $500 interest on July 1 and was to pay $500 on December 31. Josie died on July 31. The period from July 1 to July 31 was 30 days. Accrued interest to the date of death is:

$$\text{Accrued Interest} = \frac{30}{183} \times \$500$$
$$= \$81.97$$

## Rights or Things

Where the deceased at the time of death has rights or things (other than capital property) that, if they had been disposed of during the taxpayer's lifetime, would have been included in an income tax return, the value of such rights or things must be included in the final return. Rights or things include:

- uncashed matured bonds;
- dividends that are declared but unpaid as of the date of death;
- Old Age Security benefits due and payable before the date of death;
- farm crops that have been harvested; and
- work in progress of a professional (e.g., doctor, lawyer, dentist) who was a sole proprietor and who had elected to exclude work in progress when calculating his income.

It will most likely be preferable to have the income classified as a right or thing because such income can be reported on a separate return (as discussed under "Separate Returns" on page 94) or can be taxable to the deceased's beneficiaries in certain circumstances.

If the personal representative transfers the right or thing to a beneficiary of the estate within one year of the date of the death or within 90 days from the date of the notice of assessment for the final return (whichever is later), the value does not have to be included in the final return. Rather, the beneficiary will pay the tax owing at the time those rights or things are realized. This can be advantageous for two reasons: first, the income can be spread over several beneficiaries, which will likely result in a lower rate of tax; second, the tax owing will be deferred until realized by the beneficiary. What does "realize" mean? A dividend is realized when it is received by the beneficiary. For example, unpaid salary, vacation pay, commission, etc., are normally realized when the beneficiary receives the cheque from the employer.

## Special Rules for RRSPs, RRIFs, RPPs, and TFSAs

### Registered Retirement Savings Plans

Where the deceased had a Registered Retirement Savings Plan ("RRSP"), at his death he is deemed to have disposed of the RRSP, and the full amount of the RRSP is to be added to the deceased's final return. Generally, the full value of the RRSP will be included in the deceased's final return, even if it is paid out to a designated beneficiary. However, in certain circumstances, if the deceased designated his spouse, common-law partner, or a dependent child or grandchild as the beneficiary, the RRSP will not be taxed in the hands of the estate.

#### Financially Dependent Child or Grandchild

The *Income Tax Act* makes special provision for dependent children or grandchildren who are minors and dependent children or grandchildren who, regardless of age, are financially dependent by reason of mental or physical infirmity. A dependent child is one who, at the date of the deceased's death, was financially dependent on the deceased for support. Unless the contrary is established, it is assumed that a child is not financially dependent if the child's income for the preceding tax year is more than the basic personal amount for the preceding year. For deaths occurring after 2002, the income threshold used for determining the financial dependency of a mentally or physically infirm child or grandchild is equal to the basic personal amount plus the disability amount for the preceding year.

#### Matured RRSP

If the plan has matured — for example, if the deceased was receiving annuity payments from the RRSP prior to death — and the surviving spouse or common-law partner is designated as the beneficiary to receive the remaining annuity payments, these payments will be included in the surviving spouse's or common-law partner's income. The RRSP will not be included in the deceased's income. If a financially dependent child or grandchild is designated as the beneficiary and the amounts qualify as a refund of premiums (explained below), the value of the RRSP payments will not be included in the income of the deceased in the year of death.

#### Unmatured RRSP

If the deceased died before the plan matured — that is, the plan did not pay retirement income — usually the RRSP is paid out in a lump sum to his estate or to the beneficiary named in the plan. Again, the deceased taxpayer will have to pay tax on this amount, unless the amount passes directly to his spouse, common-law partner, or financially dependent child or grandchild. The spouse, common-law partner, child, or grandchild can defer paying the tax on the amount if the amount qualifies as a "refund of premiums", as described below. If, under the RRSP, the estate is designated as the beneficiary, the amount will be included in the income of the deceased taxpayer, unless one of the elections noted below applies.

### Refund of Premiums

A refund of premiums is essentially any amount paid out of a deceased's RRSP to a:

- spouse or common-law partner, where the RRSP has not matured; or
- financially dependent child or grandchild, regardless of whether the plan has matured or not.

A refund of premiums must be paid in a lump sum and included in the beneficiary's income unless the amount is rolled over into another specified tax deferral plan. If the spouse or common-law partner is the beneficiary, he can roll over the amount into an RRSP, RRIF, or annuity, thereby deferring taxes. If the refund of premiums is transferred to a child or grandchild, the RRSP can be rolled over to an annuity that is payable until the child reaches 18 years of age. A child or grandchild who, regardless of age, was dependent on the deceased parent or grandparent by reason of physical or mental infirmity can make a tax-deferred transfer of a refund of premiums to an RRSP, RRIF, or eligible annuity.[7]

If the deceased died prior to 1999, amounts paid to financially dependent children or grandchildren would only qualify as a refund of premiums if there was no surviving spouse. From 1999 onwards, amounts paid to a financially dependent child or grandchild qualify as a refund of premiums even if there is a surviving spouse.[8]

#### *Joint Election for Unmatured RRSP*

The personal representative and the spouse, common-law partner, child, or grandchild may file a joint election so that all or a portion of the RRSP is deemed to be received by the spouse, common-law partner, child, or grandchild

[7] In Bill C-10, *Income Tax Amendments Act, 2006*, a proposed new section will allow a trust to be named as the annuitant under a life annuity if certain conditions are met. The *Income Tax Act* already permits this in the case of a minor term annuity (annuity to age 18). Finance has advised that this proposal is still under consideration.

[8] Amounts qualify as a refund of premiums for deaths occurring in 1996, 1997, and 1998 where there was a surviving spouse and if the spouse and the personal representative filed a joint election before May 2000.

as a refund of premiums. This can only occur where you, as the personal representative, are entitled to receive the RRSP amounts for the benefit of the spouse or child. The spouse, common-law partner, child, or grandchild beneficiary can roll over the refund of premiums so that the tax will be deferred.

### *Joint Election for Matured RRSP*

Where the plan has matured and the estate is the recipient of the remaining amounts owing under the plan, the personal representative and the spouse or common-law partner may file a joint election so that the amounts to be paid to the estate will be deemed to have been received by the spouse or common-law partner. It is not necessary that the amounts received by the estate actually be paid to the spouse or common-law partner. It is important to note that, in order to make this election, the RRSP amounts are held by the personal representative for the *benefit* of the spouse or common-law partner.

☞ See "Death of an RRSP Annuitant (Information Sheet RC4177)" at page 320 in Appendix B.

## Home Buyers' Plan

The Home Buyers' Plan ("HBP") allows an individual to withdraw up to $25,000 in a calendar year from his RRSP to buy or build a qualifying home. In essence, the withdrawal must be repaid in equal instalments over 15 years. If the amount due in a year is not repaid, it will have to be included in the individual's income for that year.

Generally, if an individual participating in the HBP dies, his personal representative has to include the HBP balance in the deceased's income for the year of death. Therefore, the amount to be included in the income for the year is equal to the individual's HBP balance before death, less any RRSP contributions made before death and designated as an HBP repayment for the year of death.

### Example 6.7 — HBP Taxation

Belle participated in an HBP, and at the time of her death in 2011 the balance in the plan was $10,000. She had made a $1,000 RRSP contribution before her death and she had planned to designate that contribution as an HBP repayment. In the final return, the personal representative will have to include $9,000 ($10,000 - $1,000) as RRSP income.

If a deceased person who participated in an HBP is survived by a spouse or common-law partner who was resident in Canada immediately before the deceased's death, the spouse or common-law partner and the deceased's personal representative can jointly elect to have the deceased's repayment liability transferred to the surviving spouse or common-law partner.

☞ See "Home Buyers' Plan (Guide RC4135)" at page 326 in Appendix B.

### Lifelong Learning Plan

The Lifelong Learning Plan ("LLP") allows an individual to withdraw funds from his RRSP to pay for his (or his spouse's or common-law partner's) education or training. The amount withdrawn has to be repaid over a period of no more than 10 years. Any amount that is due in a year and not repaid is included in the individual's income for that year.

Normally, if an individual who is participating in the LLP dies, the LLP balance will have to be included in the individual's income for the year of death in the final return. If the deceased person contributed to an RRSP in the year of death, the personal representative can designate it as a repayment under the LLP.

If the deceased individual had a Canadian resident spouse or common-law partner at the time of death, the spouse or common-law partner and the deceased's personal representative can elect to have the surviving spouse or common-law partner assume the repayment obligations under the LLP of the deceased.

☞ See "Lifelong Learning Plan (Guide RC4112)" at page 344 in Appendix B.

### Additional RRSP Contributions After Death

If the deceased had unused RRSP contribution room and is survived by a spouse or common-law partner, as the personal representative, you may choose to contribute to a spousal or common-law partner RRSP and make an additional deduction on the deceased's income. The contributions to the surviving spouse's or common-law partner's RRSPs can be made in the year of death or during the first 60 days after the end of the year.

## Registered Retirement Income Funds

Where the deceased had a Registered Retirement Income Fund ("RRIF"), he is deemed to have received the fair market value of the RRIF immediately before death. The exceptions to this fair market value disposition are very similar to the exceptions applicable to RRSPs, such as where the RRIF is transferred to the spouse, common-law partner, or financially dependent children or grandchildren.

☞ See "Death of a RRIF Annuitant (Information Sheet RC4178)" at page 361 in Appendix B.

## Registered Pension Plans

The deceased is not taxed on the amount of a Registered Pension Plan ("RPP") at death. Rather, if the deceased was a member of an RPP, the beneficiary who receives the benefits of the RPP is taxed on the amount received. If the beneficiary is the spouse of the deceased and receives a lump-sum benefit, the spouse can roll over the lump-sum amount into his RRSP, RRIF, or another RPP of which he is a member. The rollover is not available for periodic payments made out of an RPP.

For deaths occurring after 2002, if a lump-sum payment is made to the deceased's child or grandchild who was financially dependent on the deceased due to a physical or mental disability, the payment may be rolled over to the child or grandchild's RRSP or RRIF or may be used to acquire a qualifying annuity.

## Tax-Free Savings Accounts

The Tax-Free Savings Account ("TFSA") is a tax-exempt account registered with the CRA that allows Canadian residents to permanently shelter their savings from taxes on income and capital gains. TFSAs became available on January 1, 2009.

Where the deceased had a TFSA, neither he nor any beneficiaries are taxable on the date-of-death value.

There are two possible designations that can be made by a TFSA holder. The holder can designate a beneficiary on the account, much like an RRSP or RRIF. Or, similar to a RRIF, the holder can designate a successor holder on the TFSA. Note that these options are not available to Quebec residents.

### Designated Beneficiary

A holder can designate any person as a beneficiary of the TFSA: a spouse or common-law partner (referred to as a "survivor"), child, sibling, relative, friend, or charity.

### Beneficiary Other Than Survivor

If a beneficiary other than the survivor is designated in the TFSA contract or the will, at the time of the original holder's death, the named beneficiary becomes entitled (subject to provincial law) to the assets of the TFSA, and the plan will terminate. Any payments made out of the TFSA to the beneficiary in excess of the fair market value of the deceased holder's TFSA at the time of death will be taxable in the hands of the beneficiary.

### Survivor Named as Beneficiary

If the beneficiary is a survivor of the deceased holder, a survivor payment can be paid directly to the survivor as a beneficiary under the plan, or indirectly as a payment to the estate that the survivor is entitled to receive under the will. A survivor payment is a payment from the TFSA of the deceased holder to the survivor that is paid during the rollover period.

A survivor has the option to contribute and designate all or a portion of the survivor payment as an exempt contribution to his own TFSA without affecting his own unused TFSA contribution room. The exempt contribution cannot exceed the fair market value of the deceased holder's TFSA at the time of death. Furthermore, the survivor must notify the CRA that he is making an exempt contribution within 30 days of making the contribution. This can be done using Form RC240, "Designation of an Exempt Contribution Tax-Free Savings Account (TFSA)".

☞ See "Designation of an Exempt Contribution Tax-Free Savings Account (Form RC240)" at page 367 in Appendix B.

### Successor Holder

In provinces that recognize TFSA beneficiary designations, the survivor can be designated as a successor holder in the TFSA contract or in the will. A survivor can be named in the deceased holder's will as successor holder to a TFSA if the provisions of the will state that the successor holder acquires all of the holder's rights, including the unconditional right to revoke any beneficiary designation. Upon the death of the original holder, the survivor becomes the new account holder of the TFSA. The TFSA continues to exist under the name of the survivor, and both its value at the date of the original holder's death and any income earned after that date continue to be sheltered from tax under the new successor holder.

#### No Named Beneficiary or Successor Holder

Where no successor holder or beneficiary has been designated in the TFSA contract or in the will, the TFSA property will become part of the deceased holder's estate and distributed in accordance with the terms of the will.

☞ See "Tax-Free Savings Account Guide for Individuals (RC4466)" at page 369 in Appendix B.

## Tax Credits

### Personal Tax Credits

The personal representative can claim the full personal tax credits. If separate returns for rights or things, a trust, or a business are being filed, the personal tax credits can also be claimed on those returns. These personal tax credits include:

- basic personal amount;
- age amount;
- spousal/common-law partner amount;
- caregiver amount;
- eligible dependant amount; and
- infirm dependant amount.

### Medical Expenses Credit

The personal representative may claim a tax credit for medical expenses paid (that are more than a specified amount)[9] within any 24-month period that includes the date of death. In other words, you can claim expenses that were charged and paid after death. A living individual may claim medical expenses only for a 12-month period ending in the calendar year.

[9] For example, in the 2011 tax year, you can claim medical expenses that are more than the lower of (a) $2,052 or (b) 3% of the deceased's total net income.

### Charitable Donations Credit

The personal representative can claim charitable donations made by the deceased both in the year of death and through his will. If the donations exceed the amount allowable in the year of death, you can deduct as much as is allowable in the year prior to the year of death.

## The Estate as Taxpayer

The death of a taxpayer creates a new taxpayer: the deceased's estate. The estate comes into existence on the date of the individual taxpayer's death. You must remember that this tax return is separate from that of the person who died. The CRA requires this return in order to tax any income earned by the estate and to tax the beneficiaries on any income distributed to them. You are required to file a return annually on behalf of the estate from the date of death until all the assets are distributed to the beneficiaries.

For income tax purposes, the estate is generally treated as an individual. Within 90 days after the end of the taxation year, the estate's tax return for each taxation year must be filed and the tax paid. The appropriate return is the trust income tax return, which is the T3 Trust Income Tax and Information Return. The CRA also provides a guide called T3 Trust Guide. The return must be filed if income from the estate's property is subject to tax, and the estate:

- has tax payable;
- has a taxable capital gain or has disposed of capital property;
- has provided a benefit of more than $100 to a beneficiary for upkeep, maintenance, and taxes for property maintained for the beneficiary's use; or
- receives from the trust property any income, gain, or profit that is designated, paid, or payable to one or more beneficiaries, and the trust has:
  - — total income from all sources of more than $500,
  - — income of more than $100 designated, paid, or payable to any single beneficiary,
  - — made a distribution of capital to one or more beneficiaries, or
  - — allocated any portion of the income to a non-resident beneficiary.

The CRA does not require you to file a T3 where all of the estate's property is distributed immediately after the deceased's death, or if the estate did not earn any income before the distribution.

## Returns for the Estate

You must file the following returns for the estate:

- **T3 return:** If the administration of the deceased's estate is completed within 12 months of the date of death, a T3 return (first and final) must be filed for the estate.
- **T3 return for subsequent years:** If the administration of the estate is not completed within 12 months, a T3 return must be filed for each of the estate's taxation years until it is completed.

As a testamentary trust is considered an individual for income tax purposes, the estate is subject to the graduated tax rates that apply to individuals. As the personal representative, you may choose a taxation year ending on the calendar year, the anniversary of the date of death, or any other date within 12 months of the date of death; there may be certain tax advantages to selecting one of these taxation years, depending on the circumstances. Unlike individuals, an estate cannot claim personal tax credits. In computing the estate's income for the year, you can deduct all amounts that became payable in that year to a beneficiary. You should also deduct any money the estate paid to maintain property, such as a cottage or home, held for the use of the beneficiary who is the life tenant of the property.

## The Estate's Capital Gains

Just as the individual taxpayer is deemed to have disposed of property for its fair market value, the estate is deemed to have acquired the property for its fair market value. If you then sell the property for a value greater than its new adjusted cost base (its fair market value), the estate will have a capital gain, and one-half of the capital gain is taxable. If, on the other hand, you sell the property for less than its fair market value, the estate will have a capital loss, which can be used to offset any capital gains. Where the estate incurs a capital loss in its first taxation year, that loss can be carried back to the deceased's terminal year; in such a case, you will have to file an amended final return.

### Deemed Disposition — 21-Year Rule

In general, trusts are required to report a deemed disposition every 21 years on most capital property. Therefore, the trust will have to report capital gains, capital losses, income, and recapture. The 21-year rule exists to prevent the perpetual deferral of capital gains; otherwise, a trust could remain in existence and avoid capital gains indefinitely. The 21-year rule can be avoided by transferring the trust property to the beneficiaries before the end of the 21-year period.[10] No tax will be owing as a result of the transfer; however, once the beneficiaries dispose of the property or it is deemed disposed of upon the beneficiaries' death, the tax will be payable.

## Death Benefits

A death benefit includes amounts received on the death of an employee, in recognition of the employee's service in an office or employment. The CPP death benefit is not included in the definition of death benefit (the tax treatment of the CPP death benefit is discussed below). A death benefit payable is not reported on the deceased's final return, but is income of the estate or the beneficiary to whom it is paid. An amount up to $10,000 may be received tax free.

## CPP Death Benefit

The personal representative is required to include the amount of the CPP death benefit in the T3 tax return for the year in which the amount was received by the estate. However, if the estate pays the death benefit to a beneficiary, the estate is entitled to a deduction, and the amount will be included in the beneficiary's income. An election is available whereby the personal representative can choose not to include the deduction so that the estate will have to pay the tax as opposed to the beneficiary.

## Beneficiaries

### Income Transferred to Beneficiaries

For income transferred to beneficiaries, you must complete and provide the beneficiaries with a T3 slip, which can be obtained from the CRA. These forms indicate the amount of income that the beneficiaries must report on their personal income tax returns. You must send a copy of the T3 slip to the CRA.

[10] There might, however, be other issues affecting the trustee's ability to distribute the property, such as the terms of the will itself.

When income is paid from the estate to a non-resident beneficiary, in general such income is subject to a 25% withholding tax. However, you must check to see if there is a tax treaty with the country where the beneficiary resides. You can pay only part of the amount to the non-resident beneficiary; the remainder goes to the CRA. The tax must be received by the CRA or a Canadian financial institution on or before the 15th day of the month after the month during which the tax was withheld.

Income of the estate that is paid or payable to a beneficiary in the estate's taxation year must be included in the beneficiary's income. As well, the value of all benefits received by the beneficiary from the estate is included in the beneficiary's return. However, it is important to remember that this does not apply to distributions of capital property, such as a house, car, or boat, in satisfaction of the beneficiary's capital interest. On the other hand, any amount paid by the estate for the upkeep of or taxes on property maintained for the beneficiary's use is included in the beneficiary's income.

### Property Transferred to Beneficiaries

The distribution to the beneficiary of capital property in the estate as consideration for all or part of the beneficiary's capital interest takes place on a tax-deferred rollover basis. A capital interest is defined as a right to receive all or any part of the capital property of the estate. The estate is deemed to have disposed of the property at its cost amount, and the beneficiaries are deemed to have acquired it at the same amount.

## Clearance Certificate

A clearance certificate certifies that all tax, Canada Pension Plan contributions, Employment Insurance premiums, interest, and penalties payable by the taxpayer have been paid, or that the CRA has accepted security for payment. The *Income Tax Act* requires you to obtain a clearance certificate prior to any distribution of property of the estate. If you distribute the estate assets before receiving the clearance certificate, you will be personally liable for any unpaid amounts (i.e., taxes, interest, penalties, etc.). Under *proposed legislation,* for assessments completed after December 20, 2002, the personal representative will also be responsible for any and all interest that is charged as a result of these assessments.[11]

[11] According to July 16, 2010 draft legislative proposals to implement outstanding income tax technical measures previously included in Bill C-10, *Income Tax Amendments Act, 2006*, Part 2 (as passed in House of Commons).

According to paragraph 2 of the CRA Information Circular 82-6R8, "Clearance Certificate", you do not need a clearance certificate before each distribution, as long as you keep enough property to pay any liability to the CRA. Basically, the clearance certificate requirement and the personal liability imposed on the personal representative are mechanisms for the CRA to ensure that tax returns are filed. Often, personal representatives make interim distributions either with or without the knowledge of their personal liability in this regard. The key factor to keep in mind is that if you are going to make an interim distribution before obtaining a clearance certificate, it is absolutely essential that you set up a fund that will cover the amounts owing to the CRA; otherwise, it could be a very costly mistake.

You may apply for a clearance certificate by sending CRA form TX19, "Asking for a Clearance Certificate" to the Assistant Director, Audit at your tax services office.

In Information Circular 82-6R8, "Clearance Certificate", the CRA states that a clearance certificate will not be issued until all income tax returns have been filed and assessed and all applicable amounts paid. Therefore, the request for the certificate should not be made until after the assessment notice for the final return of the estate has been received.

It is important to remember that the issuance of a clearance certificate relieves only you, the personal representative, from liability for any unpaid amount. It does not cancel the taxpayer's liability. In other words, it does not prevent the CRA from going after the remaining assets in the estate or from going after the beneficiaries of the estate, to the extent of the estate assets distributed to them.

☞ See "Asking for a Clearance Certificate (Form TX19)" at page 388 and "Clearance Certificate (Information Circular 82-6R8)" at page 389 in Appendix B.

## United States Estate Taxes

If you are acting as the personal representative in an estate where the deceased owned property in the United States, you should speak to your lawyer or accountant.

The estate could be subject to federal estate tax on all of the deceased's assets located in the U.S. Although non-resident aliens (non-resident alien basically means, in this context, a Canadian who owns property in the U.S.) are only taxed on assets located in the U.S., the taxpayer's worldwide gross estate is relevant for calculating certain deductions. Additionally, it should be noted that individual U.S. states may also impose separate estate, death, or inheritance taxes.

The personal representative should note that a U.S. estate tax return (Form 706-NA) is required to be filed for every non-resident alien, if the deceased owned more than $60,000 of property in the U.S.

If there is no executor or administrator appointed, qualified, and acting in the U.S., every person in actual or constructive possession of any of the deceased's property situated in the U.S. is considered an "executor" for estate tax purposes and is required to make and file a return. Where two or more persons are liable for filing the return, it is preferable for all to join in the filing of one complete return.

Form 706-NA, "United States Estate (and Generation-Skipping Transfer) Tax Return", is used for the estates of non-resident decedents who were not citizens. This return must be filed and the estate tax paid within nine months after a decedent's death (unless an extension was granted).

These estates are entitled to the same filing and payment extensions that are available to U.S. citizens and residents. An extension may be requested by using Form 4768, "Application for Extension to File a Return and/or Pay U.S. Estate (and Generation-Skipping Transfer) Taxes". Extensions are not granted for more than six months, unless the executor is abroad. The estate tax return cannot be amended after the expiration of the extension period granted for filing.

☞ See IRS Form 706-NA "United States Estate (and Generation-Skipping Transfer) Tax Return" at page 392 and "Instructions for Form 706-NA" at page 394 in Appendix B.

On December 17, 2010, President Obama signed into law the *Tax Relief, Unemployment Insurance Reauthorization, and Job Creation Action of 2010* (the "2010 Tax Act"). This legislation made significant, but temporary, changes to the federal estate tax.

The 2010 Tax Act reinstates estate tax for 2010 through 2012. These changes affect U.S. citizens, individuals domiciled in the U.S., and Canadian citizens and residents who are subject to U.S. estate tax on account of owning U.S. assets.

The legislation retroactively reinstates estate tax with a top rate of 35 per cent and increases the U.S. estate tax exemption to $5 million for 2010, 2011, and 2012.

Furthermore, for estates of individuals who died in 2010, the estate's executor may elect to treat the estate as if the 2010 Tax Act had not been enacted, in which case the estate would not be subject to estate tax and the modified carryover basis rules would apply. IRS Notice 2011-66 states that the election must be made on Form 8939, "Allocation of Increase in Basis for Property Acquired from a Decedent", on or before November 15, 2011.

If no election is filed by the executor, the estate will be subject to the new estate tax regime, which provides for a stepped-up basis in property passing from the decedent.

The 2010 Tax Act also allows the executor of a deceased spouse's estate to transfer any unused portion of the exemption to the surviving U.S. citizen or U.S. resident spouse.

The changes introduced by the 2010 Tax Act are scheduled to be in effect only through December 31, 2012. Absent further legislation, the 2010 Tax Act will sunset at that time, and the federal estate tax laws in effect in 2001 will return, along with higher tax rates and lower exemptions. Therefore, unless legislation is passed before the end of 2012, 2013 will see the reinstatement of an exemption of only $1 million (indexed for inflation) and a maximum tax rate of 55 per cent.

The *Third Protocol to the Canada–U.S. Income Tax Convention* was ratified on November 9, 1995. The intention behind the Protocol was to grant some relief from double taxation that might occur on death of an individual as a result of the different taxation methods used in the U.S. and in Canada. Under the Protocol, Canadians are entitled to the unified tax credit, which is available to U.S. citizens. However, the means by which it is calculated in the case of non-resident Canadians is different from how it is calculated for U.S. citizens. As a result of the unified credit, for deaths occurring during the years 2010 to 2012, if the value of a Canadian resident's worldwide assets is less than $5 million, a Canadian resident will not be subject to U.S. federal estate tax. Other credits or deductions from the estate may also be available, such as charitable deductions, deductions for estate expenses, and marital deductions.

# Testamentary Trusts

## Introduction

A trust is an arrangement by which the assets of one person (the "settlor") are transferred to an individual or institution (the "trustee") for the benefit of another person or persons (the "beneficiary(ies)"). The trustee follows the directions set out in the trust agreement and manages the trust property for the benefit of the beneficiary. In Quebec, a trust results from an act where a settlor transfers property from her patrimony to another patrimony constituted by her, which she appropriates to a particular purpose and which a trustee undertakes, by acceptance, to hold and administer. For the purposes of the *Income Tax Act*, a trust is either a testamentary trust or an *inter vivos* trust.

A testamentary trust, which is the subject of our discussion in this chapter, is defined in the *Income Tax Act* as a trust that arises on and as a consequence of the death of an individual. In effect, a testamentary trust allows the testator to extend control over her property after her death. The provisions for a testamentary trust (the trust agreement) are outlined in the Last Will and Testament of the deceased settlor. Often the trustee named in a testamentary trust is also the executor of the estate. If the trust is a discretionary trust, the trustee may also be given the power to allocate the trust property to the beneficiaries of the trust. Therefore the trustee may be given the authority to distribute the income and/or capital to the beneficiaries as she sees fit.

An *inter vivos* trust is one that is created by the settlor while alive, and is basically any trust that is not a testamentary trust. The actual trust agreement containing the provisions for an *inter vivos* trust is a separate legal document.

Beneficiaries may be income beneficiaries, capital beneficiaries, or both. An income beneficiary receives income earned from the property held in trust. For example, the beneficiary may receive interest payments from GICs (the property/capital) held in trust. A capital beneficiary, on the other hand, is entitled to the capital of the trust, such as the GIC, other investments, or real estate.

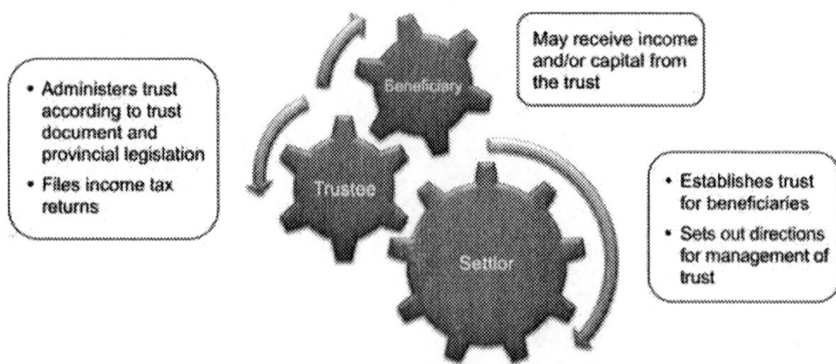

• Administers trust according to trust document and provincial legislation
• Files income tax returns
Beneficiary
Trustee
Settlor
May receive income and/or capital from the trust
• Establishes trust for beneficiaries
• Sets out directions for management of trust

## Trustee's Duties

A trustee, as the name implies, is in a "trust" relationship. As a trustee, you owe a number of duties to the beneficiaries of the trust. If you fail to fulfil these duties, you may be held personally liable.

- **Duty of loyalty to beneficiaries:** As a trustee, you should never place yourself in a position where a conflict of interest might occur. Your duty to the beneficiaries must outweigh any personal interests. For example, unless the trust specifically permits the trustee to purchase trust property, in general, such a purchase should not occur. (However, an exception has evolved that allows a purchase where it would be advantageous for the trust, and hence the beneficiaries; an example may be where the property must be sold in any event, and the trustee is willing to pay more than any other bidder for the property.)
- **Duty of reasonable care:** You must act with the care and diligence that a reasonable and prudent person would use in conducting her own affairs. As far as investments are concerned, the types of investments in which a trustee can invest may be set out in the trust document (i.e., the will) itself. If they are not, then the relevant provincial legislation would apply. Not so long ago, some jurisdictions used a "legal list" approach (a list of permissible investments set out in legislation) to trustee investments. This approach was considered too restrictive, and many provinces have now adopted some form of the "prudent investor" standard or rule. The prudent investor standard of care generally permits a trustee to make any investment that a prudent investor would make.[1]
- **Duty to act personally:** Unless the trust document or legislation provides otherwise, you must act personally in your duties, and, except as noted below, you cannot delegate such duties. You should review the trust document, as the authority to delegate duties may very well be granted by the document. You are allowed to seek advice to assist you in making decisions, to the extent that it is normal practice to employ such persons in the circumstances. Notwithstanding this advice, it is you, the

[1] Where the will or trust instrument does not provide guidance on trustee investments so that the trustee is governed by the relevant provincial legislation, it is important that the trustee becomes thoroughly familiar with the terms and requirements of that legislation, as there are some differences between the provinces. For example, the trustee legislation of Ontario refers to the "prudent investor" standard of care, while the Manitoba trustee legislation uses a "person of prudence" (or "prudent person") standard. Where a trustee is unsure of the rules regarding trustee investments, the trustee should seek legal advice. Note: a trustee may also obtain advice about investments from an investment professional and, depending on the terms of the will or trust instrument and the governing law, a trustee may also, subject to certain requirements, be able to delegate trustee investment responsibility to an investment manager that was prudently selected.

trustee, who must ultimately make the final decision. The case of *Wagner v. van Cleef*[2] is an example of the personal liability that can occur when a trustee fails to properly supervise the activities of those to whom she delegated her power. In *Wagner*, the administrator delegated all of his duties to the estate solicitor, who subsequently absconded with all the estate assets. The administrator was held personally liable. The Court held that, although the administrator did not act dishonestly, he acted unreasonably in totally delegating his responsibilities.

- **Duty to act with an "even hand":** Unless the will or trust investment provides otherwise, you must treat the beneficiaries fairly and equally. You cannot give preferential treatment to one beneficiary to the exclusion of others. This is particularly applicable to a situation where there is both an income beneficiary and a capital beneficiary. For example, if Joe dies and names his sister Lucy as the income beneficiary of his estate and his nephew Bob as the capital beneficiary, the trustee cannot favour Bob by making an investment that has significant growth potential but yields little income to Lucy.

  It is important to note that the trust instrument can override any of the above-mentioned duties. For example, a trust instrument might allow the trustee to purchase assets from the trust, which might otherwise be considered to be a violation of the trustee's duty of loyalty. If a trust instrument does alter the above-noted duties, the trustee should only do what is expressly permitted by the instrument. If there is any doubt as to what is permissible, you should seek the advice of a lawyer.

- **Duty to account:** It should also be noted that one of the fundamental duties of a trustee is to always have the trustee's accounts for the trust ready for inspection and examination, and, as required, to provide certain information concerning the trust. The duty to keep adequate and complete accounts is described in more detail in chapter 9.

## Spousal/Common-Law Partner Trusts and Trusts for Children

Testamentary trusts are commonly family trusts, meaning that they are created by an individual for the benefit of family members. Such trusts include spousal or common-law partner trusts and trusts for minors or children with special needs. (See chapter 6 for a discussion of the tax implications of a spousal/common-law partner trust.) Spousal or common-law partner trusts usu-

[2] (1991), 5 O.R. (3d) 477 (Div. Ct.).

ally provide that the spouse or common-law partner of the settlor is the only person entitled to income and capital from the trust during the spouse's or common-law partner's lifetime.[3] As for minor children, because they are not legally capable of owning property until they reach the age of majority, a trust for minors enables a parent to specify when and how much money can be distributed to her child. Additionally, the deceased might have a child who is physically or mentally challenged and, in order to look after that child's interest, has established a trust to benefit that child.

### Example 7.1 — Spousal Trust Clause in a Will

My Trustees shall hold the residue of my estate in trust and shall pay to my wife, Lisa Low, during her lifetime, the income derived from the residue, with power to my Trustees during that period to pay to my wife any amount out of the capital of the residue remaining that my Trustees in their absolute discretion consider appropriate from time to time.

## Trusts and Taxation

For tax purposes, a testamentary trust is considered to be an individual taxpayer: it is subject to the same graduated tax rates as individuals. When a settlor transfers property to a spousal or common-law partner trust, a rollover occurs, and the capital gains tax that might otherwise be payable is deferred until the spouse or common-law partner disposes of the property or dies. If the property is not transferred to a spousal or common-law partner trust, a deemed disposition of the settlor's property occurs, which might result in either a capital gain or a capital loss.

The trustee, executor, or other legal representative is required to file a T3 trust return for each taxation year of the trust, within 90 days from the year end. The CRA requires that a T3 be filed for any taxation year of a trust where the trust's income is subject to tax, and the trust:

- has tax payable;
- has a taxable capital gain or has disposed of capital property;
- has provided a benefit of more than $100 to a beneficiary for upkeep, maintenance, and taxes for property maintained for the beneficiary's use; or

[3] For the trust to qualify as a spousal trust under the *Income Tax Act*, no one other than the spouse or common-law partner can be entitled to receive the income or capital of the trust property during the spouse's or common-law partner's lifetime.

- receives from the trust property any income, gain, or profit that is designated, paid, or payable to one or more beneficiaries, and the trust has:
  - — total income from all sources of more than $500,
  - — income of more than $100 allocated to any single beneficiary,
  - — made a distribution of capital to one or more beneficiaries, or
  - — allocated any portion of the income to a non-resident beneficiary.

The CRA's T3 Trust Guide can be viewed online at **www.cra-arc.gc.ca/E/pub/tg/t4013**.

It is important to note that a trust would be disqualified as a testamentary trust if anyone transfers property to the trust other than the deceased individual on or after and as a consequence of the death. Therefore, if a person other than the deceased transfers property to the deceased's estate, the estate becomes an *inter vivos* trust for the purposes of the *Income Tax Act* and is subject to a flat tax at the highest marginal tax rate.

## Deemed Disposition — 21-Year Rule

In general, every 21 years trusts are required to report a deemed disposition on most capital property. Therefore, the trust will have to report capital gains, capital losses, income, and recapture. This 21-year rule exists to prevent the perpetual deferral of capital gains; otherwise, a trust could remain in existence and avoid capital gains indefinitely.

Note that this 21-year rule will not generally apply to qualifying spouse or common-law partner trusts.

# Distribution of the Estate

## Introduction

It is time to distribute the remaining assets of the estate to the beneficiaries when you answer yes to all of the following questions:

- Have letters probate/administration[1] been obtained?
- Have all the assets been gathered?
- Have all the debts and claims in relation to the estate been settled?
- Have the limitation periods for spousal elections and dependants' support passed?
- Have the necessary income tax returns been filed and has the clearance certificate from the CRA been received?

Barring provisions in the will that state otherwise, in provinces other than Quebec, the personal representative generally has one year to gather the assets and settle the affairs of the estate. Commonly known as the "executor's year", this one-year period starts on the date of death. The executor is not required to pay a legacy before the end of the executor's year. At the end of the one-year period, the beneficiaries are entitled to demand payment of their legacies; interest on such legacies begins to run at that point.

If the will provides for trusts, then assets must be set aside for these trusts and registered in the trustees' names. On the other hand, assets to be distributed to beneficiaries should be registered in the beneficiaries' names. Whenever property is distributed to a beneficiary, the personal representative must ensure that the beneficiary gives written acknowledgment of receipt of the property, together with a release from any claims arising from the estate, to the personal representative.

Unless the will provides otherwise, money or property should not be paid directly to a minor. The will would most likely have a provision stating that the money or property must be held in trust until the minor reaches at least the age of majority. The executor is usually named as the trustee responsible for a minor child's trust, but provision may be made in the will to pay funds to a child's parent or guardian. (See chapter 7 for more information on the trustee's duties and responsibilities in managing a trust.)

---

[1] Known as "certificate of appointment of estate trustee" in Ontario.

## Distribution Where There Is a Will

As long as there have been no spousal elections under matrimonial property legislation or dependants' relief claims (see chapter 5), the personal representative may begin to implement the testator's instructions in the will. This can be a much more complex task than one would ever think. For example, see the discussion in chapter 5 regarding insufficient funds in the residue to pay the debts of the estate.

## Special Rules Affecting Distribution of Gifts

Three special rules can affect distribution: ademption, lapse, and abatement. These are set out below.

### Ademption — Gift Not in Existence Upon Death

If the gift specified in the will does not exist at the date of death, the gift fails and the beneficiary receives nothing, unless the will provides that the beneficiary may claim the proceeds from the disposition of property in substitution of the original gift. The gift is said to have "adeemed".

For example, a testator provides in his will, "I leave my cherry wood dining room table and china cabinet to my nephew Jacob". If the testator sold the dining room table and china cabinet before his death, Jacob would receive nothing. However, if the provision stated, "I leave my cherry wood dining room table and china cabinet to my nephew, Jacob. If such dining room table and china cabinet do not exist as of the date of my death, I leave whatever other furniture that I own at the date of my death", and the dining room table and cabinet are not in existence, Jacob would be entitled to any other furniture that does exist.

### Lapse — Beneficiary Dies Before Testator

If the beneficiary under the will predeceases the testator, the gift fails or "lapses". The gift would not go to the beneficiary's estate, but would instead fall into the residue of the testator's estate. If, however, the lapsed gift is the residue of the estate, the lapsed gift would become an intestacy and would pass to the testator's next of kin. Read the provisions of the will carefully. The testator may have provided for a "gift-over" to another person in case the intended beneficiary predeceased the testator. For example, "I leave my violin to George. If George is not living at that time, I leave the violin to my sister Susy".

However, you must take note of the anti-lapse provisions in the provincial legislation that governs the distribution of a lapsed gift when a beneficiary who predeceases the testator is a close relative. For example, in Ontario, the *Succession Law Reform Act* specifies that where a testator makes a bequest to his child, grandchild, brother, or sister, and such person predeceases the testator but is survived by a spouse or issue, the gift would not lapse but would go to the family member's spouse or issue.

### Abatement — When Insufficient Funds Exist

As discussed in chapter 5, in a situation where, after the debts have been paid, not enough assets remain to satisfy all the designated gifts in full, the gifts are said to "abate". In paying the deceased's debts, the residue of the estate is used first. If more funds are needed, then the personal representative must access funds from the next class of assets.

## Legacies/Bequests and Devises

The terminology describing the various types of gifts under a will can be confusing. It is important to understand the differences between these gifts, particularly when difficulties in the distribution of the estate assets arise. A legacy, also known as a bequest, is a testamentary gift of personal property (meaning anything other than real estate); legacies are characterized as specific, general, demonstrative, or residuary. A devise is a testamentary gift of real property (real estate).

In Quebec, a legacy is a direct disposition by the testator of the whole or part of his property, even of a specific item, for the benefit of someone. There are three kinds of legacies: universal, by general title, and by particular title.

### General Legacy (Provinces Other Than Quebec)

A general legacy is a gift of money that does not come from a particular fund. It is a gift that must be raised from the general estate. For example, "I give my friend Rita $10,000". General legacies are paid out only after specific devises, specific legacies, and demonstrative legacies have been paid out. If nothing is left after the distribution of these gifts, the general legacy beneficiary will not receive his gift.

What if the total amount of the legacy is not available? In the example above, if there were only $5,000 left after the rest of the estate was distributed, Rita would then receive $5,000 and no more.

If the phrase in the will were changed to "I give to my friends Rita and Don $5,000 each", and if there were only $5,000 remaining in the estate, Rita and Don would each receive $2,500. The gifts are said to "abate ratably"; in other words, they are to be distributed proportionately to the amount gifted. If, under the terms of the will, Rita was to receive $8,000 and Don was to receive $2,000, but only $5,000 was left to distribute, Rita would receive $4,000 and Don would receive $1,000.

### Demonstrative Legacy (Provinces Other Than Quebec)

A demonstrative legacy is a gift of money or stock that is to be paid primarily (although not exclusively) out of a particular fund. Demonstrative legacies are paid first out of the specific fund earmarked for their payment. If that fund is inadequate, the unpaid portion of the gift becomes a general legacy. For example, "I give to David the sum of $1,000, if David survives me, and I direct my Trustees to sell my computer to produce the amount of this legacy". If the computer sells for only $500, the remaining $500 owing to David becomes a general legacy.

### Specific Legacy and Specific Devise

A specific legacy is a gift of a particular thing, specified and distinguished from all other things. For example, "I give my diamond necklace to my niece Ellen Christina".

A specific devise is a gift of a specific parcel of real property. For example, "I give to my mother, Noreen, my cottage located on lot 6 and known as the river lot".

If a specific legacy or specific devise is disposed of in order to pay the debts of the estate, the beneficiary will receive something only if there are funds left after the debts and liabilities are paid. If cash remains after the debts and liabilities are paid, it must be divided proportionately among the beneficiaries who were entitled to receive the property.

### Legacy by Particular Title (in Quebec)

A legacy by particular title is a gift of a particular thing, specified and distinguished from all other things. For example, "I give my diamond necklace to my niece Ellen Christina". Any legacy that is neither a universal legacy nor a legacy by general title is a legacy by particular title. A legacy by particular title lapses if the bequeathed property perished totally during the lifetime of the testator or if the legatee predeceased the testator, unless the will provides otherwise.

It is important to note that a legatee by particular title who accepts the legacy is not an heir of the estate. He is not liable for the debts of the deceased on the property of the legacy unless the other property of the succession is insufficient to pay the debts, in which case he is liable only up to the value of the property he takes.

### Legacy by General Title (Quebec Only)

A legacy by general title entitles a person to take (1) the ownership of an aliquot (fractional) share of the succession; (2) a dismemberment of the right of ownership of the whole or of an aliquot share of the succession; or (3) the ownership or a dismemberment of the right of ownership[2] of the whole or of an aliquot share of all the immovable or movable property of the deceased. For example:

- a legacy of a universality of property: "I bequeath to David all my immovable [and/or, as the case may be, movable, private, common, acquest, corporeal, incorporeal] property";
- a legacy of a share of property: "I bequeath to David a quarter (1/4) share of all my property, movable and immovable";
- a legacy of a share in a universality: "I bequeath to David a quarter (1/4) share of all my immovable [and/or, as the case may be, movable, private, common, acquest, corporeal, incorporeal] property";
- a legacy to several legatees with assignment of shares: "I bequeath all my property, movable and immovable, as follows: (a) to my niece Shirley, a half (1/2) share; to my niece Rose, a quarter (1/4) share; to my niece Monica, a quarter (1/4) share".

### Universal Legacy (Quebec Only)

A universal legacy is a bequest of the entirety of a person's property. For example:

- a legacy in absolute ownership: "I bequeath all my property, movable and immovable, to David, hereby constituting him my universal legatee";
- a legacy of the residue of property: "I bequeath the residue of all my property, movable and immovable, to David, hereby constituting him my residuary universal legatee".

---

[2] There is a dismemberment of the right of ownership when there is a division of the attributes of a thing split between two holders. The dismemberments of ownership impose a restraint on the owner's enjoyment or use of the property but not on his title as owner. Usufruct, use, servitude, and emphyteusis are dismemberments of the right of ownership and are real rights. As an example, usufruct is the right of use and enjoyment, for a certain time, of property owned by another as one's own, subject to the obligation of preserving its substance.

## Residue

The residue of the estate is simply the surplus of a testator's estate remaining after all the debts, legacies, and devises have been dealt with. The residue is often left to one or more beneficiaries, such as the testator's spouse and children.

The will may specify that the residue of the estate be distributed *per stirpes* or *per capita*. If the residue is divided among the beneficiaries *per capita* and one of the beneficiaries dies, that beneficiary's share goes back into the residue to be divided among the surviving beneficiaries. On the other hand, the will may specify that the residue be divided among, for example, the testator's issue "in equal shares *per stirpes*". If a member of the group among which the assets are being divided is not alive at the time of distribution, the children of that deceased member would divide among them the share their parent would have received had the parent been alive. If one of those children is deceased, then the child's children would take such share, and so on.

### Example 8.1 — Distribution in Equal Shares *Per Stirpes*

In Ian's will, he stated that the residue was to be divided among his issue in equal shares *per stirpes*. In this example, Ian's wife predeceased him, and his children Charles and Calista and his granddaughter Geraldine also predeceased him. As his son Chris is alive, Chris will take his 1/3 share of Ian's estate. If Charles and Calista were alive, they would have each taken a 1/3 share of the estate. However, as Charles is not alive, his 1/3 share is distributed to his children, George and Gina. George and Gina are each entitled to 1/2 of Charles's 1/3 share; that is, they are entitled to 1/6 of the estate. As Calista and Geraldine both predeceased Ian, Eve is entitled to 1/3 of the residue of her great-grandfather's estate.

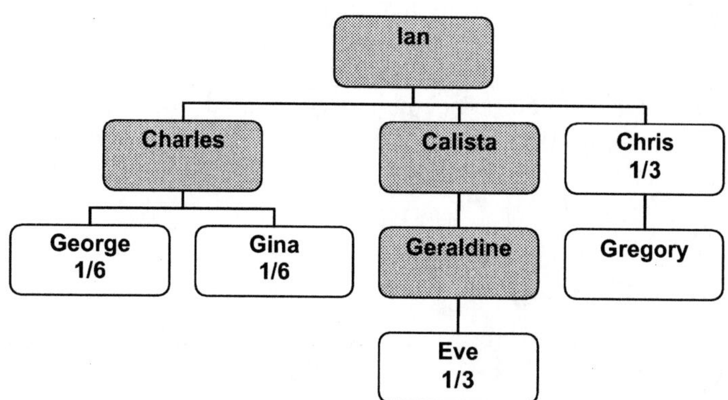


In Quebec, if the residue is divided among several beneficiaries, and one of the beneficiaries dies prior to the testator, the children of that deceased legatee would divide among them the share their parent would have received had the parent been alive (subject to certain conditions applicable to the concept of "representation", unless representation is excluded by the testator expressly or by the effect of the disposition of the will). It is important to note that there is no representation in the matter of legacies by particular title, unless the testator has so provided. If representation does not take place, it may give rise to "accretion", where the co-legatees of the residue would divide among them the share of the legatee who predeceased the testator. Accretion does not apply to legacy by general title unless the testator has so provided. Regarding legatees by particular title, accretion would only apply where property is bequeathed to them jointly and a lapse occurs with regard to one of them.

## Distribution Where There Is No Will (Intestacy)

### Order of Priority

Unlike the situation where there is a will, when a person dies intestate, the distribution of the estate is governed by provincial legislation. The following is a general order of priority for the distribution of an intestate estate. In reality, this is quite complex and your legal advisers would handle most of this. However, it is helpful to know the basic order of priority:

1. spouse[3] and children;
2. father and mother;
3. brothers and sisters;
4. nephews and nieces;
5. grandfather and grandmother;
6. uncles and aunts.

An intestate's children, grandchildren, great-grandchildren, and so forth are called the deceased's descendants, and they have priority over the deceased's ascendants (parents of the intestate) and collaterals (brothers, sisters, nephews, and nieces of the intestate).

### Preferential Share

In most Canadian provinces, an intestate's spouse is entitled to a "preferential share". A preferential share is simply an amount that the spouse is entitled to, in preference to others, after the estate's debts and liabilities have been paid. When

[3] This may include a common-law partner, depending on the jurisdiction. See the "Intestate Distribution Table" on page 139 for specific provincial information.

the net value of the estate is less than the preferential share, the surviving spouse is entitled to receive the entire net estate. When the value of the estate is greater than the preferential share, the surviving spouse is entitled to the preferential share plus a certain percentage of the value of the estate above the amount of the preferential share, known as the distributive share. See the "Intestate Distribution Table" at page 139 for the preferential share values.

### Example 8.2 — Preferential Share

Sue and Bob live in Ontario and have one child. Bob dies without leaving a will. The value of his estate is $400,000. If Sue decides to take her share pursuant to the *Succession Law Reform Act* (rather than pursuant to the *Family Law Act*), she would be entitled to the first $200,000 (after the payment of debts and liabilities) as her preferential share.

| | |
|---|---|
| Value of Bob's estate | $400,000 |
| Sue's preferential share | - 200,000 |
| Residue | $200,000 |
| Sue's distributive share (1/2 of residue) | $100,000 |
| Child's distributive share (1/2 of residue) | $100,000 |
| Total amount for Sue | $300,000 |
| Total amount for child | $100,000 |

## Quebec Family Patrimony

In Quebec, if the intestate was married or in a civil union, the family patrimony must first be partitioned and the matrimonial or civil union regime liquidated before continuing with the distribution of the intestate's estate.[4]

## Special Provisions Regarding the Home

Some jurisdictions set out special provisions regarding the matrimonial home. In British Columbia, if the matrimonial home is to go to someone other than the spouse, the home must be held in trust for the spouse during his lifetime.[5]

In Nova Scotia, the Northwest Territories, and Nunavut, a spouse may elect to take the home in place of the preferential share if the home's value is greater than $50,000. However, if the home's value is less than $50,000, the spouse may elect to receive the home as part of the preferential share.

In Quebec, the surviving married or civil union spouse may, in preference to any other heir, require that the family residence or the rights conferring use

[4] For additional information, see the Quebec Justice Department's web page entitled "Successions" at www.justice.gouv.qc.ca/english/publications/generale/success-a.htm#nowill.

[5] In Alberta and British Columbia, new legislation not in force at the time of writing may affect the treatment of the matrimonial home in those provinces.

of it, together with the movable property used in the household, be placed in his share. If the value of the property exceeds the share due to the spouse, he keeps the property, subject to a payment as compensation.

## Distributive Share

The distributive share is the portion of the estate to which the heirs are entitled on intestacy. In provinces that provide for the preferential share, the distributive share is calculated after the preferential share is determined.

## Descendants of the Deceased

In general, although there are exceptions, the children of the intestate share in the estate with the surviving spouse, as long as the surviving spouse's preferential share does not consume the entire estate.

In most provinces, an intestate's estate is distributed *per stirpes* among the issue. Under the *per stirpes* method, it is always possible that someone from a more remote generation will receive a larger inheritance than someone from a closer generation. For example, a great-grandchild could receive more than a grandchild.

Unlike most of the other provinces, Manitoba has adopted a *per capita* at each generation method. The estate is divided at the closest generation to the intestate that has a surviving member, and all surviving members of a generation who are entitled to share will share in equal portions.

Ontario's rules are based on a *per stirpes* distribution but are not identical to those of the other provinces that use the *per stirpes* method. In Ontario, the estate is divided at the generation closest to the intestate that has a surviving member. Therefore, if there are no surviving children of the intestate but there are surviving grandchildren, all of the grandchildren would take a share not based on their deceased parent's share, but as a member of the closest generation with a surviving member (basically a *per capita* division). However, if there are surviving children and deceased children, the children of the deceased children would take their parent's share (basically a *per stirpes* division). Depending on the situation, the Ontario method can have both *per stirpes* and *per capita* elements.

In Quebec, the persons called to the estate are those who belong to the order of persons closest to the deceased by relationship. In all cases where representation is permitted, partition is affected by roots (*per stirpes*). If one root has several branches, the subdivision is also made by roots in each branch, and the members of the same branch share among themselves on a *per capita* basis.

### Example 8.3 — *Per Stirpes* Distribution

Ian died intestate, and he was predeceased by his wife and his two children, Charles and Calista. Charles had three children and Calista had one child, all of whom survived Ian. Under the *per stirpes* method, Charles's three children will share his 1/2 share of the estate, and thus each will receive only 1/6 of the entire estate, while Calista's child will receive 1/2 of the estate.

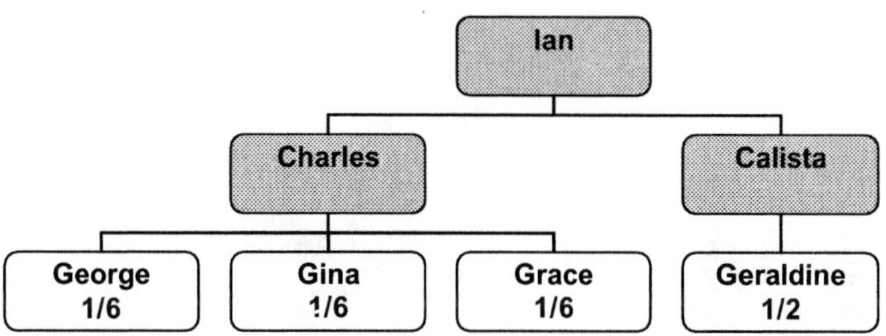


### Example 8.4 — *Per Capita* at Each Generation Distribution

Using the same scenario as example 8.3 above, under the *per capita* at each generation method in Manitoba, since the grandchildren are the closest generation of the intestate having surviving members, the division of the estate will occur at this generation, and all of the grandchildren will share equally, with each entitled to 1/4 of the estate.[6]

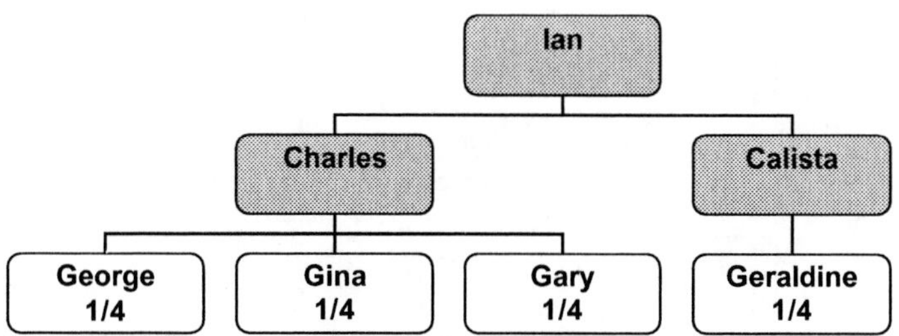


[6] If this scenario were to occur in Ontario, the distribution would also look like this.

### Example 8.5 — *Per Stirpes* Distribution

Ian died intestate, and he was predeceased by his wife and two of his three children. As his son Chris is alive, Chris will take his 1/3 share of the estate. If Charles and Calista were alive, they would each take 1/3 of the estate. But as Charles is not alive, his 1/3 share is distributed to his children, George and Gina. Thus, George and Gina are each entitled to 1/2 of Charles's 1/3 share, or 1/6 of the estate. As Calista is not alive, her 1/3 share of the estate goes to Geraldine.[7]

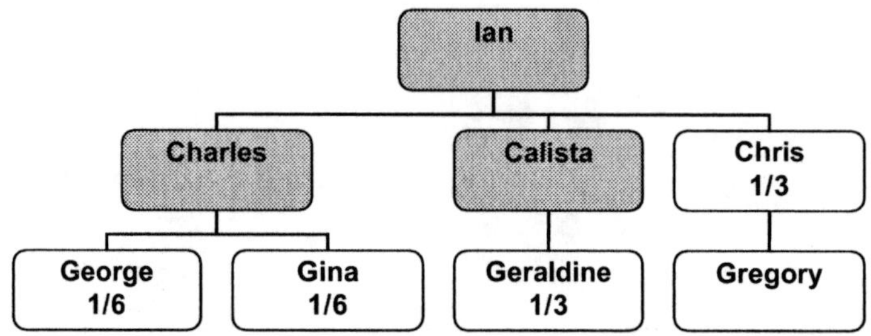


### Example 8.6 — *Per Capita* at Each Generation Distribution

Using the same scenario as example 8.5 above, under the *per capita* at each generation method in Manitoba, Chris will receive his 1/3 share of Ian's estate, while Charles's and Calista's shares are combined into a single share that amounts to 2/3 of the estate and is distributed as if Chris and Gregory had predeceased Ian. Therefore, Charles's and Calista's children will each receive a 2/9 share of the estate.

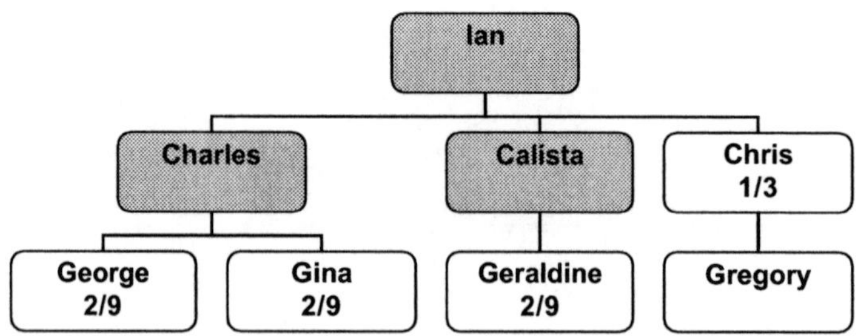


[7] If this scenario were to occur in Ontario, the distribution would also look like this.

## Ascendants and Collaterals of the Deceased

### Parents (Ascendants)

In Alberta, British Columbia, Manitoba, New Brunswick, Newfoundland and Labrador, the Northwest Territories, Nova Scotia, Nunavut, Ontario, Prince Edward Island, Saskatchewan, and Yukon, if an intestate dies leaving no surviving spouse or issue, the estate goes to his father and mother in equal shares, if both are living. If either is deceased, the estate goes to the surviving parent.

In Quebec, parents are privileged ascendants. If the intestate's spouse survives and there are no surviving children, the parents are entitled to 1/3 of the estate and the surviving spouse is entitled to 2/3 of the estate.

### Brothers and Sisters (Collaterals)

In Alberta, British Columbia, New Brunswick, Newfoundland and Labrador, the Northwest Territories, Nova Scotia, Nunavut, Ontario, Prince Edward Island, Saskatchewan, and Yukon, if an intestate dies leaving no surviving spouse, issue, father, or mother, the estate goes to his brothers and sisters in equal shares. If any brother or sister is deceased, the children of the deceased brother or sister take, in equal proportions, the share that their parent would have taken, if living.

This is where the law in Manitoba diverges once again from the legislation of the majority of the other provinces. In Manitoba, if an intestate dies without a surviving spouse, issue, father, or mother, the estate goes to issue of either or both the intestate's parents to be distributed *per capita* at each generation (see the discussion above for a better understanding of *per capita* at each generation). If there are also no surviving issue of parents but there are one or more surviving grandparents:

- half of the estate goes to the paternal grandparents or to the survivor of them; if both of the paternal grandparents predeceased the intestate, the estate is distributed among the issue of the paternal grandparents or either of them on a *per capita* at each generation basis; and
- half of the estate goes to the maternal grandparents or their issue in a like manner.

If there is only a surviving grandparent or issue of a grandparent on either the paternal or maternal side, the entire estate goes to the kindred on that side. If there are then no surviving grandparents or issue of a grandparent, the intestate's estate is divided into four shares and 1/4 goes to each set of great-grandparents or their issue. The specifics of this division can be found in the Manitoba *Intestate Succession Act*.

In Quebec, if an intestate's spouse and descendants are not living, the intestate's siblings and the intestate's parents share in the estate equally.

### Nephews and Nieces

In Alberta,[8] British Columbia,[8] New Brunswick, Newfoundland and Labrador, the Northwest Territories, Nova Scotia, Nunavut, Ontario, Prince Edward Island, Saskatchewan, and Yukon, if an intestate dies leaving no surviving spouse, issue, father, mother, brother, or sister, the estate goes to the nephews and nieces in equal shares, and in no case is representation admitted.[9]

In Quebec, however, nephews and nieces of the intestate in the first degree are privileged collaterals. If an intestate dies leaving only a surviving spouse and a niece and nephew, then the surviving spouse is entitled to 2/3 of the estate, and the niece and nephew are entitled to the remaining 1/3 of the estate.

### Remote Next of Kin

In general, if the nephews and nieces class is non-existent, the estate is divided equally among all members of the closest class of next of kin. The law simply keeps calculating various groups of relatives until it reaches the last living relative. In Quebec, relatives beyond the eighth degree do not inherit.

## Escheat

Although it does not happen very often, if an intestate leaves no spouse or other relatives, the estate would pass to the provincial government. Most provinces have legislation regarding this matter.

---

[8] In Alberta and British Columbia, new legislation not in force at the time of this writing makes a different distribution than indicated here in the sections labelled "Nephews and Nieces" and "Remote Next of Kin".

[9] The phrase "in no case is representation admitted" means that if any of the intestate's nieces or nephews have predeceased the intestate and had issue of their own, the deceased niece's or nephew's issue are *not* entitled to take the share of the deceased niece or nephew. For example, X's closest relatives were his two nieces, Y and Z. Y had two children, A and B. Y predeceased X, and X died intestate. Z would be entitled to all of the estate; A and B would not be entitled to a share.

## Intestate Distribution Table

The following table summarizes how a deceased's estate must be distributed according to each province's law of intestate distribution.

| Province | Spouse Only | Children Only | Spouse and One Child | Spouse and Children | No Spouse or Children |
|---|---|---|---|---|---|
| Alberta[1, 3] | All to spouse | All to children[4] | 1st $40,000 to spouse; rest split equally[4] | 1st $40,000 to spouse; 1/3 rest to spouse; 2/3 rest to children[4] | 20 |
| Alberta[2, 3] | All to spouse | All to children[4] | If all children are also spouse's, all to spouse; if any children not spouse's, 1/2 to spouse, 1/2 to children[4] | | 21 |
| British Columbia[5, 7] | All to spouse | All to children[4] | 1st $65,000 to spouse;[8] rest split equally | 1st $65,000 to spouse;[8] 1/3 rest to spouse; 2/3 rest to children[4] | 20 |
| British Columbia[6, 7] | All to spouse | All to children[4] | If all children are also spouse's, 1st $300,000 to spouse; if any children not spouse's, 1st $150,000 to spouse | | 21 |
| Manitoba[10] | All to spouse | All to children[11] | If all children are also spouse's, all to spouse; if any children not spouse's, greater of $50,000 or half of estate to spouse,[12] plus 1/2 rest to spouse and 1/2 rest to children[11] | | 20 |
| New Brunswick | All to spouse | All to children[4] | Marital property to spouse; rest split equally[4] | Marital property to spouse; 1/3 rest to spouse; 2/3 to children[4] | 20 |
| Newfoundland and Labrador | All to spouse | All to children[4] | Split equally[4] | 1/3 to spouse; 2/3 to children[4] | 20 |
| Nova Scotia[13] | All to spouse | All to children[4] | 1st $50,000 to spouse;[14] rest split equally[4] | 1st $50,000 to spouse;[14] 1/3 rest to spouse; 2/3 to children[4] | 20 |
| Ontario | All to spouse | All to children[4] | 1st $200,000 to spouse; rest split equally[4, 15] | 1st $200,000 to spouse; 1/3 rest to spouse; 2/3 to children[4, 15] | 20 |
| Prince Edward Island | All to spouse | All to children[4] | Split equally[4] | 1/3 to spouse; 2/3 to children[4] | 20 |
| Quebec[16] | All to spouse[17] | All to children[4] | 1/3 to spouse; 2/3 to child[4] | 1/3 to spouse; 2/3 to children[4] | 20 |
| Saskatchewan[7] | All to spouse | All to children[4] | 1st $100,000 to spouse; rest split equally[4] | 1st $100,000 to spouse; 1/3 rest to spouse; 2/3 rest to children[4] | 20 |
| Northwest Territories/ Nunavut[18] | All to spouse | All to children[4] | 1st $50,000 to spouse;[14] rest split equally[4] | 1st $50,000 to spouse;[14] 1/3 rest to spouse; 2/3 rest to children[4] | 20 |
| Yukon[19] | All to spouse | All to children[4] | 1st $75,000 to spouse; rest split equally[4] | 1st $75,000 to spouse; 1/3 rest to spouse; 2/3 rest to children[4] | 20 |

Note: In some cases, provincial Family Law Acts can override these distribution formulas.

Footnotes:

[1] Rules according to the Alberta *Intestate Succession Act*. This Act is to be replaced by the *Wills and Succession Act*. At the date of this writing, the *Wills and Succession Act* has not been proclaimed into force, so both sets of rules are included in this table.

[2] Rules according to the Alberta *Wills and Succession Act*. See note above.

[3] In the Alberta *Intestate Succession Act* and *Wills and Succession Act*, in addition to "spouse", equal rights are given to an "adult interdependent partner". An adult interdependent partner is a person who: (a) has lived with the other person in a relationship of interdependence (share one another's lives, are emotionally committed to one another, and function as an economic and domestic unit) for a continuous period of not less than 3 years, or has lived in a relationship of some permanence if there was a child of the relationship by birth or adoption; or (b) entered into an adult interdependent partner agreement with the other person.

[4] If a child (of the intestate) is deceased, the child's issue (i.e., grandchildren, great-grandchildren of the intestate) takes the child's share.

[5] Rules according to the B.C. *Estate Administration Act*. This Act is to be replaced by the *Wills, Estates and Succession Act*. At the date of this writing, the *Wills, Estates and Succession Act* has not been proclaimed into force, so both sets of rules are included in this table.

[6] Rules according to the B.C. *Wills, Estates and Succession Act*. See note above.

[7] In British Columbia and Saskatchewan, "spouse" includes common-law partners.

[8] Plus household furniture and life interest in family home.

[9] Plus household furnishings.

[10] In Manitoba, the *Intestate Succession Act* provides that common-law partners are entitled to the same rights as married couples. A common-law partner is a person who: (a) registered a common-law relationship with the intestate; or (b) cohabited with the intestate in a conjugal relationship (i) for a period of at least 3 years, or (ii) for a period of at least one year and they are together the parents of a child.

[11] If a child is deceased, the child's children (i.e., the intestate's grandchildren) share in the estate.

[12] Plus life interest in family home plus a possible equalization payment under the *Family Property Act*.

[13] In Nova Scotia, individuals in common-law relationships who register as domestic partners with Vital Statistics have the same rights and obligations as spouses under the *Intestate Succession Act*.

[14] Spouse may elect to receive house and contents in lieu of $50,000.

[15] Subject to possible equalization claim under *Family Law Act*.

[16] In Quebec, intestate successions devolve to the surviving married or civil union spouse. Civil union couples, whether of the same or opposite sex, have similar legal rights and obligations as married spouses.

[17] In Quebec, if relatives survive in addition to the spouse (but no children), then 2/3 to surviving spouse, 1/3 to the privileged ascendants or privileged collaterals. Privileged ascendants are the deceased's mother and father; privileged collaterals are the deceased's brothers and sisters and their descendants in the first degree.

[18] In the NWT and Nunavut, "spouse" includes a common-law partner if the couple has cohabited: (a) for a period of at least 2 years; or (b) in a relationship of some permanence and are the natural or adoptive parents of a child.

[19] In the Yukon, if an intestate dies leaving a common-law spouse, under the *Estate Administration Act*, the court may order that whatever portion of the intestate's property that it deems appropriate be retained and allotted to the common-law spouse for support and maintenance.

[20] When there is no surviving spouse or children, estate generally goes in this order: parents; if neither survive, brothers/sisters; if none survive, nephews/nieces; if none survive, next of kin; if no traceable next of kin, all goes to provincial government. Review the commentary on descendants, ascendants, and collaterals (especially for Manitoba and Quebec) for specific details of distribution when there is no surviving spouse or child.

[21] When there is no surviving spouse or children, estate generally goes in this order: parents; if neither survive, brothers/sisters; if none survive, half to grandparents and their descendants on one side, half to grandparents and their descendants on other side; if none survive, half to great-grandparents and their descendants on one side, half to great-grandparents and their descendants on other side, but only to 4th degree of relationship (but persons of 5th or greater degree of relationship may make claim); if no next of kin, all goes to provincial government. See provincial legislation for more detail.

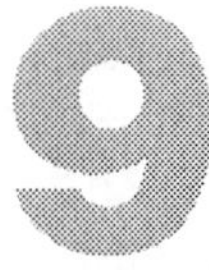

# Estate Accounting

## Introduction

The duty to keep adequate and complete accounts is an important responsibility of the personal representative and should never be overlooked. As the personal representative, you must maintain a complete record of your activities, and you would be well advised to keep all necessary documentation to support your accounts (e.g., receipts for money paid); such documents are often referred to as "vouchers". Additionally, you cannot mix the estate accounts with your own personal accounts, and you must at all times be able to show the beneficiaries any relevant information regarding the estate property. If the beneficiaries request to inspect the accounts, you must permit their inspection of them as well as any supporting documentation.

Unless the accounts are passed in court (discussed below), no particular form of accounts is necessary. However, whichever method is chosen, the work carried out by the personal representative must be clearly documented. If the accounts are passed in the court, they must be in the form acceptable in that province.

Your accounts must generally include:

- a statement of assets that came to the estate from the deceased;
- an account of all money received;
- an account of all money disbursed;
- an account of all property remaining on hand;
- a statement of all investments purchased and disposed of;
- a statement of all contingent or other liabilities of the estate at the closing date of the accounts; and
- a statement of compensation claimed by the personal representative (see chapter 10 for more information).

## The Passing of Accounts

A passing of accounts is the submission of the estate accounts by the personal representative for scrutiny by a court. Basically, through the passing of accounts, the court approves the way in which the personal representative administered the estate.

In most situations, a formal passing of accounts is not required. The personal representative would simply send her accounts along with a "release" to the beneficiaries. A release is a form in which the beneficiary acknowledges receiving money or assets and releases the personal representative from any claims the beneficiary may have against her. The release is signed by the beneficiary in the presence of a witness. As mentioned above, the estate accounts include the records of money and property received and distributed as well a record of any compensation claimed by the personal representative.

☞ See the "Sample Release of Executor/Liquidator" at page 244 in Appendix A.

Review the legislation in the appropriate province to ensure that you follow the proper procedure. For example:

- In Quebec, if the liquidation of the estate takes more than one year, the liquidator must, at the end of the first year and at least once a year thereafter, render an account of management to the heirs, creditors, and legatees who have not been paid. The liquidator, at any time and with the agreement of all the heirs, may render an amicable account without judicial formalities. It is only if an amicable account cannot be rendered that the account is rendered in court.
- In Nova Scotia, a personal representative must pass her accounts within 18 months from the date of the grant; however, a passing of accounts is not required if: (i) the deceased died testate; (ii) all the unpaid beneficiaries are adult and competent; and (iii) all the unpaid beneficiaries and any surety agree, in writing and in the manner prescribed, that an accounting is not required.
- In Saskatchewan, a personal representative must render an account within two years of the grant of letters probate/letters of administration. With the consent of or release from each beneficiary of the estate (or from the public guardian and trustee if the beneficiary is a minor) and proof that all debts of the estate have been paid, the personal representative may apply to court for an order discharging her without passing accounts.

Note that obtaining the consent of beneficiaries (in lieu of passing accounts) might not always be possible; one or more of the beneficiaries may refuse to give consent. In such situations, passing accounts before a court will be necessary in order to ensure that no claims for personal liability can later be brought against the executor.

The personal representative may choose to pass the accounts on her own accord. It may be particularly wise to do this if there are insufficient assets in the estate to cover all the gifts under the will or to cover the potential claims from third parties.

☞ Always respond promptly to legitimate questions asked by beneficiaries, and provide access to information and documents in a timely manner. Suspicion is often bred by delays and lack of information. If you want to avoid a passing of accounts, be prepared, be organized, and respond to questions promptly! You can provide information to the beneficiaries as you proceed, so long as you advise them that this information is subject to change as the administration of the estate progresses.

If a passing of accounts is necessary, notice of the passing of accounts must be given to anyone who has an interest in the estate, such as the beneficiaries and creditors. There are special rules regarding the service of notice to minors, mentally incompetent persons, and charities.

In the passing of accounts process, a formal hearing would occur if the judge is not satisfied that an unopposed judgment should be granted or where an interested party has filed a notice of objection to the passing of accounts. In the formal hearing, the judge has the power to inquire into any complaint or claim of misconduct. If the judge is satisfied with the claim, the judge may order the personal representative to pay whatever the court deems appropriate.

If the court approves the accounts, this confirms that the personal representative acted appropriately in handling the affairs of the estate. It is always best to settle any differences outside of court, as court proceedings can become a costly endeavour. Often the legal costs for the passing of accounts are paid out of the residue of the estate, which in the end are coming out of the residuary beneficiaries' pockets.

## Sample Estate Accounts

In the following example accounts, Hillary Winston died on September 20, 2010. Her estate is quite simple and consists only of a home in Athenaville, Ontario, valued at approximately $200,000, the house contents, a LeDevine oil painting, a cottage in Prince Edward Island valued at $50,000, and a bank account at ABC Bank in Athenaville that has a balance of $10,000. The following is a simplified version of what the estate accounts might look like.

ESTATE OF HILLARY WINSTON

STATEMENT OF ACCOUNTS

SEPTEMBER 20, 2010 (Date of Death) to APRIL 1, 2011

**ESTATE OF HILLARY WINSTON**

**STATEMENT OF ACCOUNTS**

**SEPTEMBER 20, 2010 (Date of Death) to APRIL 1, 2011**

**TABLE OF CONTENTS**

1

# ESTATE OF HILLARY WINSTON
## STATEMENT OF ACCOUNTS
## SEPTEMBER 20, 2010 (Date of Death) to APRIL 1, 2011

### SUMMARY

| | |
|---|---|
| **CAPITAL ACCOUNT** | |
| Capital Receipts | $270,000.00 |
| Capital Disbursements | 29,050.00 |
| Balance | $240,950.00 |
| **INVESTMENT ACCOUNT** | NIL |
| **REVENUE ACCOUNT** | |
| Revenue Receipts | $ 325.00 |
| Revenue Disbursements | $ 195.00 |
| Balance | $ 130.00 |
| Total | $241,080.00 |

| | |
|---|---|
| **SUMMARY OF ASSETS REMAINING** | |
| Bank Account (as at April 1, 2011) | $241,080.00 |
| Less: | |
| Proposed Claim for Compensation | $ 7,489.26 |
| **BALANCE** | $233,590.74 |

2

ESTATE OF HILLARY WINSTON

STATEMENT OF ACCOUNTS

SEPTEMBER 20, 2010 (Date of Death) to APRIL 1, 2011

STATEMENT OF ORIGINAL ASSETS

| **Particulars** | | **How Realized** Page | Item |
|---|---|---|---|
| **Money on Deposit** | | | |
| ABC Bank, Account 55555-77 | $ 10,000.00 | 3 | 1 |
| **Real Property** | | | |
| 210 Retriever Lane, Athenaville, Ontario | $200,000.00 | 3 | 2 |
| 11 Oceanfront Lane, Prince Edward Island | $ 50,000.00 | 3 | 3 |
| **Personal Property** | | | |
| LeDevine Oil Painting | $ 5,000.00 | 3 | 4 |
| Contents of 210 Retriever Lane, Athenaville, Ontario | $ 5,000.00 | 3 | 5 |
| | $270,000.00 | | |

3

## ESTATE OF HILLARY WINSTON
## STATEMENT OF ACCOUNTS
## SEPTEMBER 20, 2010 (Date of Death) to APRIL 1, 2011

### CAPITAL RECEIPTS

| No. | Date | Particulars | Amount |
|---|---|---|---|
| 1. | September 20, 2010 | ABC Bank, Account No. 55555-77 | $ 10,000.00 |
| 2. | December 1, 2010 | Sale of 210 Retriever Lane, Athenaville, Ontario | $200,000.00 |
| 3. | February 10, 2011 | Sale of 11 Oceanfront Lane, Prince Edward Island | $ 50,000.00 |
| 4. | February 20, 2011 | Sale of LeDevine Oil Painting | $ 5,000.00 |
| 5. | March 15, 2011 | Proceeds from sale of contents of 210 Retriever Lane, Athenaville, Ontario | $ 5,000.00 |
| | | | $270,000.00 |

4

**ESTATE OF HILLARY WINSTON**

**STATEMENT OF ACCOUNTS**

**SEPTEMBER 20, 2010 (Date of Death) to APRIL 1, 2011**

**CAPITAL DISBURSEMENTS**

| No. | Date | Particulars | Amount |
|---|---|---|---|
| 1. | September 30, 2010 | Forest Valley Funeral Home: funeral expenses | $ 5,000.00 |
| 2. | October 28, 2010 | Minister of Finance: probate taxes | $ 3,550.00 |
| 3. | December 1, 2010 | Athenaville Real Estate Co. Payment of real estate commission on sale of 210 Retriever Lane, Athenaville, Ontario | $10,000.00 |
| 4. | February 10, 2011 | Island Real Estate Co. Payment of real estate commission on sale of 11 Oceanfront Lane, Prince Edward Island | $ 2,500.00 |
| 5. | March 15, 2011 | Payment to Receiver General: 2010 income tax | $ 5,000.00 |
| 6. | April 1, 2011 | Payment of legal fees and disbursements | $ 3,000.00 |
| | | | $29,050.00 |

5

**ESTATE OF HILLARY WINSTON**

**STATEMENT OF ACCOUNTS**

**SEPTEMBER 20, 2010 (Date of Death) to APRIL 1, 2011**

**REVENUE RECEIPTS**

| No. | Date | Particulars | Amount |
|---|---|---|---|
| 1. | October 1, 2010 | ABC Bank<br>Interest for Sept./10 at 3% | $ 25.00 |
| 2. | November 1, 2010 | ABC Bank<br>Interest for Oct./10 at 3% | $ 50.00 |
| 3. | December 1, 2010 | ABC Bank<br>Interest for Nov./10 at 3% | $ 50.00 |
| 4. | January 1, 2011 | ABC Bank<br>Interest for Dec./10 at 3% | $ 50.00 |
| 5. | February 1, 2011 | ABC Bank<br>Interest for Jan./11 at 3% | $ 50.00 |
| 6. | March 1, 2011 | ABC Bank<br>Interest for Feb./11 at 3% | $ 50.00 |
| 7. | April 1, 2011 | ABC Bank<br>Interest for Mar./11 at 3% | $ 50.00 |
| | | | $325.00 |

6

**ESTATE OF HILLARY WINSTON**

**STATEMENT OF ACCOUNTS**

**SEPTEMBER 20, 2010 (Date of Death) to APRIL 1, 2011**

**REVENUE DISBURSEMENTS**

| No. | Date | Particulars | Amount |
|---|---|---|---|
| 1. | October 1, 2010 | Payment to Ontario Hydro: hydro for home at 210 Retriever Lane, Athenaville, Ontario | $ 50.00 |
| 2. | October 15, 2010 | Payment to Bell Canada: phone | $ 15.00 |
| 3. | November 1, 2010 | Payment to Ontario Hydro: hydro for home at 210 Retriever Lane, Athenaville, Ontario | $ 50.00 |
| 4. | November 15, 2010 | Payment to Bell Canada: phone | $ 15.00 |
| 5. | December 1, 2010 | Payment to Ontario Hydro: hydro for home at 210 Retriever Lane, Athenaville, Ontario | $ 50.00 |
| 6. | December 15, 2010 | Payment to Bell Canada: Phone | $ 15.00 |
| | | | $195.00 |

7

ESTATE OF HILLARY WINSTON

STATEMENT OF ACCOUNTS

SEPTEMBER 20, 2010 (Date of Death) to APRIL 1, 2011

STATEMENT OF UNREALIZED ORIGINAL ASSETS

NIL

8

ESTATE OF HILLARY WINSTON
STATEMENT OF ACCOUNTS
SEPTEMBER 20, 2010 (Date of Death) to APRIL 1, 2011

STATEMENT OF OUTSTANDING LIABILITIES

NIL

9

ESTATE OF HILLARY WINSTON

STATEMENT OF ACCOUNTS

SEPTEMBER 20, 2010 (Date of Death) to APRIL 1, 2011

STATEMENT OF INVESTMENTS

NIL

10

**ESTATE OF HILLARY WINSTON**

**STATEMENT OF ACCOUNTS**

**SEPTEMBER 20, 2010 (Date of Death) to APRIL 1, 2011**

**STATEMENT OF COMPENSATION**

| | |
|---|---|
| **Capital Receipts** | |
| $270,000.00 × 2.5% | $6,750.00 |
| **Capital Disbursements** | |
| $29,050.00 × 2.5% | $ 726.25 |
| **Revenue Receipts** | |
| $325.00 × 2.5% | $ 8.13 |
| **Revenue Disbursements** | |
| $195.00 × 2.5% | $ 4.88 |
| | $7,489.26 |

# 10

# Personal Representative's Compensation

## Introduction

As personal representatives are usually beneficiaries and family members of the deceased, compensation may not always be claimed. Nonetheless, as the personal representative, you are entitled to compensation unless the will or the law specifically states otherwise. In Quebec, according to the *Act respecting trust companies and savings companies*, a trust company is entitled to collect or receive for its services rendered or to be rendered (including services that are gratuitous according to law) any agreed remuneration over and above ordinary legal expenses.

The authority for claiming compensation may come from provincial legislation, from provisions set out in the will, or from a contract (an agreement either between the testator and the personal representative or between the personal representative and the beneficiaries after the testator's death).[1] So if you are acting pursuant to a will, before reviewing the guidelines below, ensure that there are no provisions set out in the will regarding compensation. If there are compensation provisions in the will, you will most likely be bound to that amount of compensation. If there is any doubt, you should seek legal advice.

In certain provinces, if a bequest (apart from the residue) is made to you in the will and you are acting as the executor, there is a presumption that the bequest is the compensation to be awarded to you. Notwithstanding this presumption, if there is any evidence that the testator intended to give you the bequest in addition to a separate amount for compensation, a court would generally allow it.

In Quebec, there is no such presumption. The liquidator is entitled to remuneration if he is not an heir; if he is an heir, he may be remunerated if the will so provides or the heirs so agree. A legacy made to the liquidator as remuneration lapses if he does not accept the office. If the liquidator ceases to hold the office, he has a right to remuneration proportionate to the value of the legacy and the time for which he held office.

---

[1] Generally, where an agreement for executor's compensation was made between the testator and the appointed executor, the terms will not be valid unless the agreement has been incorporated by reference into the will (this is the case at least in Ontario, pursuant to the rationale in *Re Taylor*, [1967] 2 O.R. 557 (Surr. Ct.). Note, however, that Manitoba's *The Trustee Act* provides that in order to be valid, the agreement must first be approved by a judge (s. 90(5)).

## Approaches To Determining Compensation

Generally, provincial legislation simply states that personal representatives are entitled to "fair and reasonable" compensation for their efforts. However, some provinces (British Columbia, Newfoundland and Labrador, Nova Scotia, and Prince Edward Island) have set a limit on the amount of compensation that a personal representative may claim. In British Columbia, for example, the *Trustee Act* limits the personal representative's remuneration to:

- 5% of the gross aggregate value, including capital and income, of all the assets of the estate; and
- a care and management fee of 0.4% of the average market value of the assets.

In Prince Edward Island and Nova Scotia, a personal representative may be permitted a commission not exceeding 5% of the amount received, over and above all necessary expenses incurred. In New Brunswick, prior to 1984, there was a 5% limit imposed by legislation; although this limit has been removed, it is unlikely that the courts would permit an award in excess of 5% absent any exceptional circumstances.

In Quebec, a liquidator is entitled to reimbursement of the expenses incurred while executing his duties. If the liquidator is an heir, the will may specify his remuneration. If remuneration is not mentioned in the will, it is to be set by the heirs. If the heirs disagree as to the remuneration, it is to be fixed by the court. If testamentary trusts are created, trustees are entitled to the remuneration fixed in the act, by usage, or by law, or to the remuneration established according to the value of the services rendered. A trustee is also entitled to the reimbursement of the expenses incurred in fulfilling his office.

It is important that you recognize that your claim for compensation may be challenged.[2] Therefore, it is essential to keep organized records of the amount of time spent in the administration of the estate, in order to justify your claim for compensation.

In most provinces, the personal representative is usually entitled to a certain percentage of the value of the estate; however, simply applying the percentage standard regardless of the amount of work involved in the administration may not suffice if the fees are questioned. These percentages are often

[2] See *Langevin (Succession de)*, 2003-41041 (REJB) (Qc. Sup. Ct.). This Quebec case suggests that a court (1) has the ability to modify administrator fees that are unreasonable in given circumstances; (2) may evaluate reasonability in light of the proportion of fees to the amount of assets administered by relying on the principle of proportionality; and (3) may even look to norms outside the province for a comparative standard in determining appropriate fees.

seen by the courts as only a rough guide; the fees you request must be fair and reasonable, taking into account all of the circumstances.

In Quebec, the *Civil Code of Quebec* authorizes the compensation of a personal representative subject to certain conditions but does not provide specific guidance as to how to calculate the compensation.

In Ontario, the *Trustee Act* authorizes the compensation of a personal representative, but does not provide specific guidance as to how to calculate the compensation. However, a court-recognized tariff has evolved, and the following formula has developed.

**Example 10.1 — Percentages Method Formula (Ontario)**

| Fees Charged Against Capital of Estate | Fees Charged Against Revenue of Estate | Management Fees |
|---|---|---|
| • 2.5% on capital receipts (i.e., original assets that are sold)<br>• 2.5% on capital disbursements (i.e., total value of all capital disbursements made, such as legacies made under the will and debts) | • 2.5% on revenue receipts (i.e., all revenue received by estate or trust)<br>• 2.5% on revenue disbursements (i.e., all revenue disbursed from estate assets) | • $^{2}/_{5}$ of 1% per year of average annual value of estate or trust for ongoing estates and trusts (i.e., where there is no immediate distribution) |

For an example of how the percentages formula is calculated, please refer to the sample estate accounts at the end of chapter 9.

As mentioned above, the use of percentages is not solely conclusive in determining the amount of compensation. Courts frequently look to the following five factors (the "five-factor approach") in determining the personal representative's remuneration:

- the size of the trust;
- the care and responsibility involved;
- the time occupied in performing the duties;
- the skill and ability shown; and
- the success resulting from the work performed by the personal representative.

In a Prince Edward Island judgment,[3] the personal representative sought the maximum fee of 5%, but the Court awarded her a fee of 3.5%. The Court stated that it rarely awarded the full fee of 5%, and referred to the five-factor approach when determining the appropriate fee.

In an Ontario Court of Appeal decision,[4] the Court held that the appropriate manner to test the compensation claimed was to first look at the results of the percentage approach, and then cross-check this mathematical approach with the more general and subjective five-factor approach.

## Care and Management Fees

Where the distribution of the estate is delayed, the personal representative may be entitled to a care and management fee. In such situations, the personal representative is required to supervise the assets until they are distributed; as a result, he should be duly compensated for such efforts. In an estate administration where there are no instructions for the establishment of ongoing trusts (as opposed to a continuing trust administration), this fee compensates personal representatives for the added burden and responsibilities in maintaining the estate where the estate assets could not, for legitimate reasons, be distributed outright within a reasonable time.[5] Such a fee allows for a court to take into account activities performed by personal representatives that are not compensated under any other category of compensation.

## Special Fees

There may be situations where the personal representative feels that the compensation awarded under the regular methods outlined above is insufficient, and requests a special fee from the court. Such fees are rarely awarded. In order to obtain such an amount, the personal representative must illustrate that he performed some work beyond the normal effort exerted in a typical estate administration. A special fee might be awarded where the estate is very complicated or where the personal representative is involved in complex litigation.

---

3 *Re Cahill Estate*, 2002 PESCTD 83.

4 *Laing Estate v. Hines*, (1998) 41 O.R. (3d) 571.

5 See *Krentz Estate v. Krentz*, [2011] O.J. No. 1124 (Q.L.) (Sup. Ct.), especially at para. 128.

## Pre-Taking Compensation

It is generally considered a breach of trust for the personal representative to pay himself without the consent of the beneficiaries or a court order. Nonetheless, there have been a variety of cases in which the personal representative was allowed to pre-take compensation. If you, as the personal representative, wish to pre-take compensation, you should consult your legal counsel first. Otherwise, some problematic legal issues may arise.

In Quebec, it is important to recall that the beneficiaries have no real rights in the trust property. Moreover, the *Civil Code of Quebec* specifies that the trustee has the control and exclusive administration of the trust property. The law does not require a trustee who is in a potential conflict of interest to obtain the beneficiaries' consent; notification suffices. Thus, obtaining consent of the beneficiaries appears unnecessary at law for matters related to the administration of the trust. However, because the beneficiary of a trust is entitled to be informed about matters affecting the trust and its administration, it may be advisable to notify such beneficiaries of the pre-taking of compensation, when appropriate.

## Taxation of Personal Representative's Fees

A personal representative's fees for the administration of an estate are included in his income tax return as either income from business or employment income. For example, a personal representative such as a trust company would include the fees as income from business, since the trust company acts as a personal representative in the course of business. On the other hand, an individual who is not a "professional" personal representative would include the fees as employment income.

## Deductions from Compensation To Pay Third Parties

If the personal representative hires a third party to perform certain duties in his place, the personal representative's compensation may be reduced. The estate cannot be expected to pay both the personal representative and the third party for work that is completed by the third party alone and would otherwise be considered the responsibility of the personal representative to complete.

However, there are exceptions to this rule. If the estate is fairly complex and you hired an accountant to prepare T1 income tax returns and T3 trust and information returns, the accountant would most likely be paid out of the estate rather than out of your compensation. On the other hand, if the estate is small and simple and you hired an accountant to prepare the returns, your compensation may be reduced. If you are required to manage a variety of investments and the will has given you broad investment powers or is silent in this regard but the governing law permits delegation of trustee investment responsibility, the fees for investment advice or investment management, as the case may be, may be paid out of the estate, especially if you lack expertise in this area.

If your legal counsel performs duties that are actually the duties of the personal representative, then once again, your compensation may be reduced. Additionally, if your legal counsel provides services for your own personal benefit, you cannot charge the resulting costs to the estate. For example, if you seek legal advice or assistance in determining your compensation for acting as the personal representative of the estate, jurisprudence indicates that the lawyer's fees generated should be paid by you personally and not by the estate.[6]

## Division of Compensation

As a general rule, compensation is awarded on the basis that there is one personal representative, unless otherwise provided in the will. If there is more than one, once the compensation is awarded, the personal representatives are responsible for dividing the compensation among themselves as they deem appropriate. Usually compensation is divided equally among the personal representatives, assuming that the workload was equal.

## Costs and Expenses

Jurisprudence supports the proposition that, as a general principle, executors are entitled to be indemnified for all properly incurred costs and expenses incurred by them in the due administration of the estate.[7]

[6] However, the British Columbia Court of Appeal decision in *Goldman v. Kanee Estate*, [1991] B.C.J. No. 2857, suggests otherwise.

[7] See *Thompson v. Lamport*, [1945] S.C.R. 343. In Ontario, see also section 23.1 of the *Trustee Act*.

# 11

# Estates under the *Indian Act*

## Introduction

The federal *Indian Act* and its associated regulations govern testamentary matters for First Nations people who are registered or entitled to be registered as Indians under the *Indian Act* and who ordinarily reside on reserve lands.

The portions of the *Indian Act* that deal with estate matters do not apply to a First Nations person who does not ordinarily reside on a reserve or on Crown land.[1] However, as noted by the Law Reform Commission of Nova Scotia,[2] "People may be considered to ordinarily reside on reserve lands even if they are away, as long as they are only away temporarily, such as to attend school, to work or to stay in a health care facility." In *Canada (A.G.) v. Canard*,[3] the Supreme Court held that a member of a reserve who was working on a farm not located on the reserve at the time of his death was still ordinarily resident on the reserve.

As a result of the *Indian Act*, the Minister of Aboriginal Affairs and Northern Development Canada (the "Minister") is granted the authority to make decisions regarding a deceased First Nations person's estate and can act as an administrator when necessary. According to the Aboriginal Affairs and Northern Development Canada website:[4]

> **Program Description**
>
> The Decedent Estates Program provides for the administration of the estates of deceased First Nation individuals who were ordinarily residents on a reserve before their death.
>
> The program carries out the following activities:
>
> - appointing estate administrators/executors;
> - approving/voiding wills;
> - transferring reserve lands;
> - distributing estate assets according to the will or the intestacy provisions of the *Indian Act* (section 48);
> - determining heirs;
> - performing a quasi-judicial role in weighing evidence and allegations raised relating to the conduct of the administration of an estate, the validity of a will, etc.;

---

[1] The *Indian Act* could apply to those residing outside a reserve. Normally this would only occur in specified circumstances, such as where none of the heirs wish to act in the administration of the estate.

[2] *Final Report: Reform of the Nova Scotia Wills Act*, November 2003, page 12.

[3] [1976] 1 S.C.R. 170.

[4] www.aadnc-aandc.gc.ca.

- developing and conducting estate planning and awareness workshops;
- tracking information relating to the administration of all estates reported to the department.

**Client Group**

First Nation individuals who ordinarily reside on reserve.

**Summary**

As estate administration is a private family matter, the Decedent Estates Program's goal is to empower First Nation members to administer the estates of deceased First Nation individuals who were ordinarily residents on a reserve before their death. The department's role is that of "Administrator of last resort." A departmental employee will only be appointed if no eligible non-departmental individual is willing and able to administer the estate.

Before the administration of an estate can proceed, you must determine whether the *Indian Act* applies or not. If the *Indian Act* does apply, it is possible to make a request to the Minister to transfer the proceeding to a provincial court. It is best to speak to a lawyer who has experience in these matters.

## Wills

The will-making requirements under the *Indian Act* and the *Indian Estate Regulations* are far less stringent than the general will-making requirements set out in provincial legislation. According to the *Indian Act*, a will can be any written instrument signed by the testator in which she indicates her intention with respect to the disposition of her property on death, whether or not the written instrument conforms with the laws of general application in any province at the time of her death.

In *Bernard Estate v. Bernard*,[5] the testator lived on a reserve in New Brunswick. He left all of his estate to his son; his son's wife was one of the witnesses at the signing of the will. According to New Brunswick law, a witness to the signing of a will cannot be a beneficiary or a spouse of a beneficiary; if so, the gift to the beneficiary will fail. In *Bernard*, the Court was asked whether the gift to the son was void by reason of his wife's witnessing of the will. The judge stated:

> It is clear that the provisions of s. 45 of the *Indian Act* and particularly those of s. 15 of the Indian Estates Regulations conflict with the requirements as to formalities in the *Wills Act*. Section 15 specifically provides that any written instrument signed by an Indian may be accepted by the Minister as a will whether or not it conforms with the requirements of the laws of general application. This, in my view, has

[5] (1986), 23 E.T.R. 15 9 (N.B.Q.B.).

> the effect of overriding any provincial legislation which stipulates the need for formalities in the making of a will.

As a result, the judge concluded that pursuant to section 45 of the *Indian Act*, a will does not need to be witnessed. Since there is no witness requirement, the witnessing of the will by the son's wife was unnecessary. It therefore followed that since the witnessing was unnecessary, the son's wife's witnessing of the will did not invalidate the son's gift.

The Minister has the deciding authority over whether a document is considered a will or not. According to section 45(3) of the *Indian Act*:

> No will executed by an Indian is of any legal force or effect as a disposition of property until the Minister has approved the will or a court has granted probate thereof pursuant to this Act.

The Minister may also declare the will of a First Nations person as void either in its entirety or in part, if the Minister is satisfied that:

- the will was executed under duress or undue influence;
- the testator lacked testamentary capacity at the time of execution of the will;
- the terms of the will would impose hardship on persons for whom the testator had a responsibility to provide;
- the will purports to dispose of land in a reserve in a manner contrary to the interest of the band or contrary to the *Indian Act*;
- the terms of the will are so vague, uncertain, or capricious that proper administration and equitable distribution of the estate would be difficult or impossible to carry out in accordance with the *Indian Act*; or
- the terms of the will are against public interest.

## Intestacy

The *Indian Act* also specifies how a deceased's property is to be distributed if the person dies intestate.

### Distribution to Survivor

A survivor is defined as the surviving spouse or common-law partner of the deceased. The Minister has the power to direct that the survivor has the right to occupy any reserve lands that the deceased occupied at the time of death. This provision may not apply if the survivor is not a member of the reserve. Special rules may apply if there is more than one survivor.

If the net value of the estate does not exceed $75,000, the entire estate goes to the survivor.

If the net value of the estate exceeds $75,000, $75,000 goes to the survivor, and the remainder is divided as follows:

- if the intestate had no issue,[6] the remainder goes to the survivor;
- if the intestate left one child, 1/2 of the remainder goes to the survivor; or
- if the intestate left more than one child, 1/3 of the remainder goes to the survivor.

The above distribution of the estate occurs so long as there are any children or issue of the children alive.

### Where Children Not Adequately Provided For

Notwithstanding the provisions above, if the Minister is satisfied that any children of the deceased are not adequately provided for, the Minister may direct that all or any part of the estate that would otherwise go to the survivor go to the children instead.

## Distribution to Issue

If an intestate dies leaving issue, her estate is distributed (subject to the rights of any survivor) *per stirpes* among such issue.[7]

## Distribution to Parents

If an intestate dies leaving no survivor or issue, the estate goes to the intestate's parents in equal shares if both of them are living. If either of them is dead, the estate goes to the surviving parent.

---

[6] "Issue" are the descendants, i.e., children, grandchildren, great-grandchildren, etc.

[7] *Per stirpes* denotes a method of dividing an estate. For example, if the assets are being divided among a group, and a member of the group is not alive at the time of distribution but all of her children are alive, the share of assets that the deceased member would have received is divided equally among her children. See chapter 8 for more information regarding *per stirpes* distribution.

## Distribution to Brothers, Sisters, and Their Issue

If an intestate dies leaving no survivor, issue, or father or mother, the estate is distributed among her brothers and sisters in equal shares. If any brother or sister is not alive, his or her children would take the share to which their parent would have been entitled, if living. If the only persons entitled are children of deceased brothers and sisters, they would take on a *per capita* basis.[8]

## Reserve Land

A person who is not eligible to reside on a reserve cannot receive that reserve land through a gift in a will or through intestacy. Such a person is only entitled to the proceeds from the sale.

## Additional Information

For more information and assistance regarding the administration of an estate, contact the Department of Aboriginal Affairs and Northern Development Canada at 1-800-567-9604.

[8] *Per capita* denotes a method of dividing an estate where an equal share is given to each of a number of persons, all of whom stand in equal degree to the deceased. Under a *per capita* distribution, if a beneficiary predeceases, her share is divided among the surviving beneficiaries. The children or descendants of the deceased beneficiary get nothing. See chapter 8 for more information regarding *per capita* distribution.

# Estate Assets and Debts

# How To Apply for the CPP Death Benefit

Service Canada

Disponible en français

Information Sheet

## How to Apply for the Canada Pension Plan (CPP) Death Benefit

### Getting started

Please read this information sheet before you complete your application. The explanations match the box numbers on the application form.

Please use a **pen** to complete your application and be sure to **print** as clearly as possible.

Fill out as much of the application form as you can. If you need help, have a list of your questions ready and call us at the telephone numbers we have listed in the section called **"How to contact us"**. Please have the deceased's Social Insurance Number ready.

**HOW TO CONTACT US**

To learn more about Canada Pension Plan, Old Age Security Program and Service Canada on-line services, please visit our Internet site at:
**servicecanada.gc.ca**
OR
You can call:
**In Canada or the United States**:
**1-800-277-9914** (English)
**1-800-277-9915** (French)
**1-800-255-4786** TTY
**From all other countries:** 613-990-2244
(we accept collect calls)

| CHECK LIST | |
|---|---|
| **Information/Documents You Need to Provide** | |
| Death certificate | * |
| Indicate the deceased's Social Insurance Number on all documents before sending them to us (except originals) | * |
| **If you have already provided these documents to the Canada Pension Plan or Old Age Security Program, you do not have to provide them again.** | |

If you need to send us documents, try to send us certified photocopies instead of the original documents. This way there is no risk that your original documents will be lost in the mail. See the section titled **"Send certified photocopies instead of originals"** for more information.

### Basic eligibility factors for the Canada Pension Plan Death benefit

To qualify for a Death benefit:

- the deceased must have made enough contributions to the Canada Pension Plan; **and**
- you must apply in writing and submit the necessary documents.

*This Information Sheet contains general information concerning the Canada Pension Plan Death benefit. The information reflects the Canada Pension Plan legislation. If there are any differences between what is in the Information Sheet and the Canada Pension Plan legislation, the legislation is always right.*

SC ISP-1200-A (2010-08-01) E

Page 1 / 5

Canadä

### Who should apply for the Canada Pension Plan Death benefit?

The CPP Death benefit is a one-time, lump-sum payment made to the estate of the deceased contributor.

**If there is a will**, the executor named in the will to administer the estate must apply for the Death Benefit within 60 days of the date of death.

**If there is no will**, or if the executor did not apply for the death benefit within 60 days of the date of death, one of the following persons should apply. Payment of the death benefit will be made in the following order of priority, upon application, to:

- the Administrator appointed by the Court; **or**
- the person or institution who has paid, **or** who is responsible for the payment of, the deceased's funeral expenses; **or**
- the surviving spouse or common-law partner of the deceased; **or**
- the next-of-kin of the deceased.

### Did the deceased contribute to the Quebec Pension Plan (Régime de rentes du Québec)?

A person may contribute to both the Canada Pension Plan and Quebec Pension Plan. The contributions made under both plans are combined when a benefit entitlement is calculated. If the deceased spouse or common-law partner only contributed to the Quebec Pension Plan, or if he/she contributed to both plans and resided in Quebec, or the last province of residence in Canada was Quebec at the time of death, you should contact:

La Régie des rentes du Québec
P.O. Box 5200
Quebec, Quebec
G1K 7S9

### Send certified photocopies instead of original documents

With your application, you usually have to send us certain documents. If you have to send us documents, try to send us certified photocopies instead of the original documents. If you do decide to send your original documents, you may want to send them by registered mail. We will return all the original documents you send us. Keep in mind, however, that **we can only accept a photocopy if it is readable and if you have someone certify it as a true copy of the original.**

If you can bring your original documents into any Service Canada office, our staff will photocopy the documents and certify them for free. If you cannot visit a Service Canada office, you can ask one of the following people to certify your photocopy:

- Accountant
- Chief of First Nations Band
- Employee of a Service Canada Centre acting in an official capacity
- Funeral Director
- Justice of the Peace
- Lawyer, Notary, Magistrate
- Manager of Financial Institution
- Medical and Health Practitioners: Chiropractor, Dentist, Doctor, Ophthalmologist, Optometrist, Pharmacist, Psychologist, Nurse Practitioner, Registered Nurse
- Member of Parliament or their staff
- Member of Provincial Legislature or their staff
- Minister of Religion
- Municipal Clerk
- Official of a federal or provincial government department, or one of its agencies
- Official of an Embassy, Consulate or High Commission
- Official of a country with which Canada has a reciprocal social security agreement
- Police Officer
- Postmaster
- Professional Engineer
- Social Worker
- Teacher

People who certify photocopies must compare the original document to the photocopy, state their official position or title, sign and print their name, give their telephone number and indicate the date they certified the document.

They must also write the following statement on the photocopy: **This photocopy is a true copy of the original document which has not been altered in any way.**

If a document has information on both sides, both sides must be photocopied and certified. You cannot certify photocopies of your own documents and you cannot ask a relative to do it for you.

Please write the deceased's Social Insurance Number on any photocopies that you send us.

SC ISP-1200-A (2010-08-01) E

Page 2 / 5

### Filling out your application

The following information explains how to complete the application form. Where needed, explanations have been provided. These explanations match the box numbers on the application form.

If you have any questions, please call us at the telephone numbers listed in the section called **"How to contact us"**.

## Section A: Information about the deceased

### Box 1A
### Social Insurance Number

Enter the deceased contributor's Social Insurance Number in this box.

The Death Benefit is based on how much, and for how long, the deceased contributed to the Canada Pension Plan. The deceased's earnings and contributions to the plan are kept in a "Record of Earnings" file under his/her Social Insurance Number. To make sure that we use the deceased's record of earnings, you must indicate the deceased's Social Insurance Number in question 1A.

If the deceased had more than one Social Insurance Number, please attach a note to your application, listing all numbers assigned to the deceased.

### Box 1B
### Date of birth

You do not need to provide proof of birth for the deceased if you provided their Social Insurance Number in the application. However, the Canada Pension Plan has the right to request proof of birth at any time, when deemed necessary.

If you did not provide the Social Insurance Number of the deceased, then you must submit a certified true copy of the deceased's original birth certificate.

If you do not have one of these documents and the deceased was born in Canada, you can obtain a copy of the deceased's birth certificate by contacting the provincial or territorial birth, marriage or death registration office in the province or territory where the deceased was born.

For people born in Canada, acceptable birth certificates are ones issued by a Provincial birth, marriage or death registration office. You can find the telephone numbers in the provincial or territorial government listings of the telephone book (usually listed as a Provincial Vital Statistics office). If you cannot get one of these documents, please call us. One of our service delivery agents will let you know what other kind of documents you can use to confirm the deceased's date of birth.

### Box 2B
### Date of death

You must submit proof of the deceased contributor's date of death with your application. To be accepted as proof, the document must give the name, date and place of death. The document must also be on official letterhead or contain a seal, and provide the name and/or signature of the person or authority issuing the document. The following documents may be accepted as proof of date of death.

**ACCEPTABLE DOCUMENTS FOR PROOF OF DEATH:**

- Burial or Death Certificate
- Certification of Death from another country, if an agreement on social security exists with that country
- Life or Group Insurance Claim along with a statement signed by a medical doctor
- Medical Certification of Death
- Memorandum of Notification of Death issued by the Chief of National Defence Staff
- Notarial copy of Letters of Probate
- Official Death Certificate
- Official Notification from the Public Trustee for a Province
- Registration of Death
- Statement of a medical doctor, coroner or funeral director
- Statement of Verification of Death from the Department of Veterans Affairs

SC ISP-1200-A (2010-08-01) E

Page 3 / 5

### Box 3
### Marital status at the time of death

Under the Canada Pension Plan, a Survivor's pension can be paid to the person who, **at the time of death**, was the legal spouse or common-law partner of the deceased contributor. Benefits can also be paid to the surviving children of the contributor.

If you feel this applies to you, please contact us to obtain an application for **"Canada Pension Plan Survivors pension"**.

### Box 7
### Did the deceased ever live or work in another country?

Canada has international agreements on social security with many countries. If your answer to question 7 is **yes**, you should provide us with the name of the country and the insurance number issued to the deceased by that country.

The deceased may have accumulated credits that could help qualify the estate or survivors for Canadian benefits under an international social security agreement. The deceased's Canada Pension Plan credits can also help qualify the estate or the survivors for a foreign pension. You will be advised in writing if either of the above conditions apply to the deceased.

### Box 9
### Child Rearing Provision

This provision may help the estate qualify for the Canada Pension Plan Death benefit or increase the amount of the Death benefit. If the deceased received Family Allowances or was eligible to receive the Child Tax Benefit on behalf of any children born after December 31, 1958, obtain and complete the form titled **"Canada Pension Plan Child Rearing Provision"** and return it with your application.

### Non-Resident Tax

If you are a non-resident of Canada for income tax purposes, we may deduct a Non-Resident Tax from the Canada Pension Plan Death benefit. The tax rate is 25% unless the country you live in has a tax treaty with Canada that reduces the rate or exempts you from paying the tax.

## Section D: Applicant's declaration

To complete the application, you have to sign and date it in this section.

**NOTE:** If you make a false or misleading statement, you may be subject to an administrative monetary penalty and interest, if any, under the *Canada Pension Plan,* or may be charged with an offence. Any benefits you received or obtained to which there was no entitlement would have to be repaid.

## Section E: Witness's declaration

If you signed your application with a mark, a witness has to sign and date the application in that section and provide their name, address, relationship to you, and telephone number in case we need to contact that person.

## Other information you should read before mailing your application

### Before you mail your application

Before you send this application form to us, please make sure that you have:

- **completed, signed** and **dated** your application; **and**
- *enclosed certified photocopies or any original documents we need.*

Please refer to the **"Check List"** at the beginning of this information sheet for the documents we need.

### When we receive your application

Once we receive your application and any supporting documents, we will contact you if we need more information. We will send you a letter once we have completed our review to let you know if you are eligible.

If you have not heard from us by the time you expect your Death benefit, please contact us at the telephone numbers listed in the section called **"How to contact us"** at the beginning of this information sheet.

SC ISP-1200-A (2010-08-01) E

Page 4 / 5

### What you must do after you receive the Death benefit

#### If you move

You *must* tell us if you move. This way, we will be able to send you the tax slip you will need for income tax purposes.

## Other pensions / benefits

### Retirement pension

If the deceased made contributions to the Canada Pension Plan, was over the age of 70 at the time of his/her death, and had not applied for or received a Canada Pension Plan retirement pension, you should contact us and request an application. The application must be made within one year of the date of death.

### Old Age Security pension

If you are between the ages of 60 and 64, you may be eligible for an Allowance for the Survivor. For more information on this subject, please contact us.

### Protection of personal information

The information requested is required under the Canada Pension Plan (CPP). We may not be able to give you a benefit if you do not give us all the information we need. We will keep this information in the Personal Information Bank HRSDC PPU 146. Your personal information is governed by the *Privacy Act* and we may disclose it where we are authorized to do so under the CPP.

Under the *Canada Pension Plan* and the *Privacy Act* you have the right to look at the personal information about you in your file. You can ask to see your file by contacting a Service Canada office. To find out how to get your personal information through the Access to Information Coordinator's office, see the Info Source, a directory that lists all the information banks and the information they contain. Copies of the Info Source are available in all Service Canada offices.

Print to PDF

SC ISP-1200-A (2010-08-01) E

Page 5 / 5

# Application for CPP Death Benefit

Service Canada

Protected when completed - B
Personal Information Bank HRSDC PPU 146

Disponible en français

## Application for a Canada Pension Plan Death Benefit

**It is very important that you:**
- send in this form with supporting documents (see the information sheet for the documents we need); **and**
- use a **pen** and **print** as clearly as possible.

### SECTION A - INFORMATION ABOUT THE DECEASED

**FOR OFFICE USE ONLY**

AGE ESTABLISHED — AA
ESTABLISHED DATE OF DEATH — PROV. CODE — AA
SURNAME - VALIDATOR — AR

**1A.** Social Insurance Number

**1B.** Date of Birth — Year / Month / Day

**1C.** Country of Birth (If born in Canada, indicate province or territory)

**2A.** Sex ☐ Male ☐ Female

**2B.** Date of Death *(See the information sheet for a list of acceptable proof of date of death documents)* Year / Month / Day

**3.** Marital status at the time of death *(See the information sheet for important information about marital status)*
☐ Single ☐ Married ☐ Separated ☐ Common-law ☐ Surviving spouse or common-law partner ☐ Divorced

**4A.** ☐ Mr. ☐ Mrs. ☐ Ms. ☐ Miss — Usual First Name and Initial — Last Name

**4B.** Name at birth, if different from 4A. (e.g. maiden name, legal name change, etc.) — First Name and Initial — Last Name

**4C.** Name on social insurance card, if different from 4A. — First Name and Initial — Last Name

**5.** Home Address at the time of death (No., Street, Apt., R.R.) — City

Province or Territory — Country other than Canada — Postal Code

**6A.** If the address shown in number 5 is outside of Canada, indicate the province or territory in which the deceased last resided.

**6B.** In which year did the deceased leave Canada?

**7.** Did the deceased ever live or work in another country? ☐ No ☐ Yes

**If yes**, indicate the names of the countries and insurance numbers. (If you need more space, use the space provided on page 4 of this application). Also, indicate whether a benefit has been requested.

| | Country | Insurance Number | Has a benefit been requested? |
|---|---|---|---|
| a) | | | ☐ Yes ☐ No |
| b) | | | ☐ Yes ☐ No |
| c) | | | ☐ Yes ☐ No |

Service Canada delivers Human Resources and Skills Development Canada programs and services for the Government of Canada.

SC ISP-1200 (2010-08-01) E

Page 1 / 4

Canada

Social Insurance Number

| | | | |
|---|---|---|---|
| **8A.** Did the deceased ever receive or apply for a benefit under the: | Canada Pension Plan? ☐ Yes ☐ No | Old Age Security? ☐ Yes ☐ No | Régime de rentes du Québec? (Quebec Pension Plan?) ☐ Yes ☐ No |
| **8B. If yes** to any of the above, provide the Social Insurance Number or account number. | | | |

**9.** Was the deceased or the deceased's spouse eligible to receive Family Allowances or was the deceased, the deceased's spouse or the common-law partner eligible to receive the Child Tax Benefit for any children born **after December 31, 1958**?

Deceased contributor ☐ Yes ☐ No Deceased's spouse or common-law partner ☐ Yes ☐ No

## SECTION B - INFORMATION ABOUT THE SETTLEMENT OF THE ESTATE

(See "Who should apply for the Death benefit" on the information sheet)

**10.** Is there a will?

☐ Yes Please provide the name and address of the executor in number 11 and go to section C.

☐ No Go to number 12.

| | | | |
|---|---|---|---|
| FOR OFFICE USE ONLY | The Estate of | | A |
| **11.** ☐ Mr. ☐ Mrs. ☐ Ms. ☐ Miss | First Name and Initial | Last Name | B |
| Mailing Address (No., Street, Apt., P.O. Box, R.R.) | City | TYPE NM ADR / FOREIGN CODE / LANG. | C |
| Province or Territory | Country other than Canada / Postal Code | CONS. CODE / NO. LNS / A.L. | D |

**12.** There is no will and I am applying for the Death benefit as:

☐ an administrator appointed by the court **(Please give your name and address in number 11)**

☐ the person responsible for the funeral expenses **(You must submit the funeral contract or funeral receipts with your application.)**

☐ the spouse or common-law partner of the deceased

☐ the next-of-kin (Please specify your relationship) __________

☐ other (Please specify) __________

## SECTION C - INFORMATION ABOUT THE APPLICANT

| | | | |
|---|---|---|---|
| **13.** ☐ Mr. ☐ Mrs. ☐ Ms. ☐ Miss | First Name and Initial | Last Name | A |
| **14.** Relationship of applicant to the deceased | | | |
| FOR OFFICE USE ONLY | For the Estate of | | |
| Mailing Address (No., Street, Apt., P.O. Box, R.R.) | City | TYPE NM ADR / FOREIGN CODE / LANG. | B |
| Province or Territory | Country other than Canada / Postal Code | CONS. CODE / NO. LNS / A.L. 20 | C |

SC ISP-1200 (2010-08-01) E Page 2 / 4

Social Insurance Number

## SECTION D - APPLICANT'S DECLARATION

I hereby apply on behalf of the estate of the deceased contributor for a Death benefit. I declare that, to the best of my knowledge, the information given in this application is true and complete.

**NOTE:** If you make a false or misleading statement, you may be subject to an administrative monetary penalty and interest, if any, under the *Canada Pension Plan*, or may be charged with an offence. Any benefits you received or obtained to which there was no entitlement would have to be repaid.

**APPLICANT'S SIGNATURE** ______________________ **APPLICATION DATE** Year Month Day

**TELEPHONE NUMBER** ______________________

**NOTE: We can only accept a signature with a mark (e.g. X) if a responsible person witnesses it. That person must also complete the declaration below.**

## SECTION E - WITNESS'S DECLARATION

**If the applicant signs with a mark, a witness (friend, member of the family, etc.) must complete this section.**

I have read the contents of this application to the applicant, who appeared to fully understand and who made his or her mark in my presence.

| Name | Relationship to applicant | Telephone number |
|---|---|---|
| Address | Signature | Date (Year Month Day) |

## FOR OFFICE USE ONLY

**BENEFIT INFORMATION**

NUMBER OF LINES

| ACTION | BNFT | AL | B/C | D | E | F | G | S | CPP NUMBER | APP. REC'D Y M D | DT. EFF. M Y | |
|---|---|---|---|---|---|---|---|---|---|---|---|---|
| | DTH | 20 | | 00 | | | | 00 | | | | EA |

**MONETARY INFO**

| CODE | CHILD SQNC | RECOVERY BNFT | RECOVERY CHILD | SIGN | UNDER/OVPMNT | ACCRUED RECOVERY CPP | ACCRUED RECOVERY QPP | DT EFF. M Y | CPP WITHHOLD ARREARS | CPP WITHHOLD RATE | QPP WITHHOLD ARREARS | QPP WITHHOLD RATE | |
|---|---|---|---|---|---|---|---|---|---|---|---|---|---|
| | | | | | | | | | | | | | FA |
| | | | | | | | | | | | | | FA |
| TOTAL | | | | | | | | | | | | | FB |

FA - CTB PERIODS

| | START Y M D | END Y M D | | | START Y M D | END Y M D | |
|---|---|---|---|---|---|---|---|
| (1) | | | GB | (3) | | | GB |
| (2) | | | GB | (4) | | | GB |

Application taken by: (Please print name and phone number)

| Application approved pursuant to the Canada Pension Plan. | Date |
|---|---|
| | Authorized Signature |

| | DATE | TYPE OF REJECT | BATCH NO. | CYCLE | DATE | SIGNATURE |
|---|---|---|---|---|---|---|
| 1 | | | | | | |
| 2 | | | | | | |
| 3 | | | | | | |
| 4 | | | | | | |

SC ISP-1200 (2010-08-01) E

Page 3 / 4

Social Insurance Number

**Use this space, if needed, to provide us with more information. Please indicate the question number concerned for each answer given. If you need more space, use a separate sheet of paper and attach it to this application**

SC ISP-1200 (2010-08-01) E

Page 4 / 4

Print to PDF

# Service Canada Offices

**Mail your forms to:**
The nearest Service Canada office listed below.
From outside of Canada: The Service Canada office in the **province where you last resided**.

**Need help completing the forms?**
Canada or the United States: **1-800-277-9914**
All other countries: **613-990-2244** (we accept collect calls)
TTY: **1-800-255-4786**
**Important**: Please have your social insurance number ready when you call.

**NEWFOUNDLAND AND LABRADOR**
Service Canada
PO Box 9430 Station A
St. John's NL A1A 2Y5
CANADA

**PRINCE EDWARD ISLAND**
Service Canada
PO Box 8000 Station Central
Charlottetown PE C1A 8K1
CANADA

**NOVA SCOTIA**
Service Canada
PO Box 1687 Station Central
Halifax NS B3J 3J4
CANADA

**NEW BRUNSWICK AND QUEBEC**
Service Canada
PO Box 250 Station A
Fredericton NB E3B 4Z6
CANADA

**ONTARIO**
**For postal codes beginning with "L, M or N"**
Service Canada
PO Box 5100 Station D
Scarborough ON M1R 5C8
CANADA

**ONTARIO**
**For postal codes beginning with "K or P"**
Service Canada
PO Box 2013 Station Main
Timmins ON P4N 8C8
CANADA

**MANITOBA AND SASKATCHEWAN**
Service Canada
PO Box 818 Station Main
Winnipeg MB R3C 2N4
CANADA

**ALBERTA / NORTHWEST TERRITORIES AND NUNAVUT**
Service Canada
PO Box 2710 Station Main
Edmonton AB T5J 2G4
CANADA

**BRITISH COLUMBIA AND YUKON**
Service Canada
PO Box 1177 Station CSC
Victoria BC V8W 2V2
CANADA

Disponible en français

ISP-3501-CPP-04-10E

Canada

# How To Apply for the CPP Survivor's Pension and Child(ren)'s Benefit(s)

Service
Canada

Information Sheet

## How to Apply for the Canada Pension Plan Survivor's Pension and Child(ren)'s Benefit(s)

**Getting started**

Please read this information sheet before you complete your application. The explanations match the box numbers on the application form.

Please use a **pen** to complete your application and be sure to **print** as clearly as possible.

Fill out as much of the application form as you can. If you need help, have a list of your questions ready and call us at the telephone numbers we have listed in the section called "**How to contact us**". Please have the deceased's Social Insurance Number ready.

**HOW TO CONTACT US**

To learn more about Canada Pension Plan, Old Age Security Program and Service Canada on-line services, please visit our Internet site at:
**servicecanada.gc.ca**
OR
You can call:
**In Canada or the United States,**
**1-800-277-9914** (English)
**1-800-277-9915** (French)
**1-800-255-4786** TTY
**From all other countries:** 613-990-2244
(we accept collect calls)

**CHECK LIST**

| Information/Documents You Need to Provide | Survivor's Pension | Child(ren)'s Benefits |
|---|---|---|
| Death certificate of the deceased | * | * |
| Marriage certificate if you were married to the deceased | * | |
| A Statutory Declaration if you were living in a common-law relationship with the deceased. | * | |
| Indicate your Social Insurance Number on all documents before sending them to us (except originals) | * | * |

**If you have already provided these documents to the Canada Pension Plan or Old Age Security Program, you do not have to provide them again.**

If you need to send us documents, try to send us certified photocopies instead of the original documents. This way there is no risk that your original documents will be lost in the mail. See the section titled "**Send certified photocopies instead of originals**" for more information.

*This Information Sheet contains general information concerning the Canada Pension Plan Survivor's Pension and Child(ren)'s Benefit(s). The information reflects the Canada Pension Plan legislation. If there are any differences between what is in the Information Sheet and the Canada Pension Plan legislation, the legislation is always right.*

Disponible en français

SC ISP-1300-A (2010-08-01) E



Canada

**Basic eligibility factors for the Canada Pension Plan Survivor's pension**

To qualify for a Survivor's pension:

- you must have been legally married or in a common-law union with your deceased spouse or common-law partner at the time of his/her death; **and**
- your deceased spouse or common-law partner must have made enough contributions to the Canada Pension Plan; **and**
- you must apply in writing and submit the necessary documents.

If you were legally separated from your deceased spouse at the time of his/her death, you may still qualify for a Survivor's pension.

**NOTE**: If you were under 35 years of age at the time of your spouse's or common-law partner's death, you do not qualify for a Survivor's pension unless:

- you are disabled; **or**
- had a dependent child of the deceased at the time of your deceased spouse's or common-law partner's death.

**Definition of spouse and common-law partner**

Under the *Canada Pension Plan:*

- a **spouse** is a person to whom you are legally married;
- a **common-law partner** is a person of the opposite sex or same sex who has been living in a conjugal relationship for at least one year.

**Did your deceased spouse or common-law partner contribute to the Régime de rentes du Québec (Quebec Pension Plan)?**

A person may contribute to both the Canada Pension Plan and Quebec Pension Plan. The contributions made under both plans are combined when a benefit entitlement is calculated. If your deceased spouse or common-law partner only contributed to the Quebec Pension Plan, or if he/she contributed to both plans and resided in Quebec, or the last province of residence in Canada was Quebec at the time of death, you should contact:

La Régie des rentes du Québec
P.O. Box 5200
Quebec, Quebec
G1K 7S9

**Send certified photocopies instead of original documents**

With your application, you usually have to send us certain documents. If you have to send us documents, try to send us certified photocopies instead of the original documents. If you do decide to send your original documents, you may want to send them by registered mail. We will return all the original documents you send us.

We can only accept a photocopy of an original document if it is legible and if it is a certified true copy of the original. Our staff at any Service Canada Centre will photocopy your documents and certify them free of charge. If you cannot visit a Service Canada Centre, you can ask one of the following people to certify your photocopy:

- Accountant
- Chief of First Nations Band
- Employee of a Service Canada Centre acting in an official capacity
- Funeral Director
- Justice of the Peace
- Lawyer
- Magistrate
- Manager of Financial Institution
- Medical and Health Practitioners: Chiropractor, Dentist, Doctor, Ophthalmologist, Optometrist, Pharmacist, Psychologist, Nurse Practitioner, Registered Nurse
- Member of Parliament or their staff
- Member of Provincial Legislature or their staff
- Minister of Religion
- Municipal Clerk
- Notary
- Official of a federal or provincial government department, or one of its agencies
- Official of an Embassy, Consulate or High Commission
- Official of a country with which Canada has a reciprocal social security agreement
- Police Officer
- Postmaster
- Professional Engineer
- Social Worker
- Teacher

**Send certified photocopies instead of original documents (continued)**

People who certify photocopies must compare the original document to the photocopy, state their official position or title, sign and print their name, give their telephone number and indicate the date they certified the document.

They must also write the following statement on the photocopy: **This photocopy is a true copy of the original document which has not been altered in any way.**

If a document has information on both sides, both sides must be photocopied and certified. You cannot certify photocopies of your own documents and you cannot ask a relative to do it for you.

Please write your Social Insurance Number on any photocopies that you send us.

**Filling out your application**

The following information explains how to complete the application form. Where needed, explanations have been provided. These explanations match the box numbers on the application form. If you have any questions, please call us at the telephone numbers listed in the section called **"How to contact us"**.

## Section A: Information about your deceased spouse or common-law partner

**Box 1A**
**Social Insurance Number**

Enter your deceased spouse's or common-law partner's Social Insurance Number in this box.

The Survivor's pension is based on how much, and for how long, the deceased contributed to the Canada Pension Plan. We keep a record of the contributions made to the Canada Pension Plan by individuals under their Social Insurance Number. To make sure that we use your deceased spouse's or common-law partner's record, you must indicate his/her Social Insurance Number in question 1A.

If the deceased had more than one Social Insurance Number, please attach a note to your application, listing all numbers assigned to the deceased.

**Box 1B**
**Date of birth**

You do not need to provide proof of birth for the deceased if you provided their Social Insurance Number in the application. However, the Canada Pension Plan has the right to request proof of birth at any time, when deemed necessary.

If you did not provide the Social Insurance Number of the deceased, then you must submit a certified true copy of the deceased's original birth certificate.

If you do not have this document and the deceased was born in Canada, you can obtain a copy of the deceased's birth certificate by contacting the provincial or territorial birth, marriage or death registration office in the province or territory where the deceased was born.

For people born in Canada, acceptable birth certificates are ones issued by a Provincial birth, marriage or death registration office. You can find the telephone numbers in the provincial or territorial government listings of the telephone book (usually listed as a Provincial Vital Statistics office). If you cannot get one of these documents, please call us. One of our service delivery agents will let you know what other kind of documents you can use to confirm the deceased's date of birth.

**Box 2B**
**Date of death**

You must submit proof of your deceased spouse's or common-law partner's date of death with your application. To be accepted as proof, the document must give the name, date and place of death of your deceased spouse or common-law partner. The document must be on official letterhead or contain a seal, and provide the name and/or signature of the person or authority issuing the document. The following documents may be accepted as proof of date of death.

SC ISP-1300-A (2010-08-01) E    Page 3 / 8

| ACCEPTABLE DOCUMENTS FOR PROOF OF DEATH |
|---|
| - Burial or Death Certificate<br>- Certification of Death from another country, if an agreement on social security exists with that country<br>- Life or Group Insurance Claim along with a statement signed by a medical doctor<br>- Medical Certification of Death<br>- Memorandum of Notification of Death issued by the Chief of National Defence Staff<br>- Notarial copy of Letters of Probate<br>- Official Death Certificate<br>- Official Notification from the Public Trustee for a Province<br>- Registration of Death<br>- Statement of a medical doctor, coroner or funeral director<br>- Statement of Verification of Death from the Department of Veterans Affairs |

**Box 3**
**Marital status at the time of death**

If you were married to the deceased **at the time of death**, we need documents to confirm the date of your marriage. When possible, **a certified true copy of your original marriage certificate should be submitted**.

If you are unable to obtain this document, please contact us to obtain the form titled **"Statutory Declaration of Legal Marriage"**, along with any additional documentation and return it with your application.

If you and the deceased were living in a common-law relationship, the form titled **"Statutory Declaration of Common-law Union"** and additional documentation must be submitted to confirm the start date of your common-law union. Please contact us to obtain this form.

**Box 6**
**Did your deceased spouse or common-law partner ever live or work in another country?**

Canada has international agreements on social security with many countries. If your answer to question 6 is **yes**, you should provide us with the name of the country and the insurance number issued to the deceased by that country.

The deceased may have accumulated credits that could help qualify the estate or survivors for Canadian benefits under an international social security agreement. The deceased's Canada Pension Plan credits can also help qualify the estate or the survivors for a foreign pension. You will be advised in writing if either of the above conditions apply to the deceased.

## Section B: Information about you (the surviving spouse or common-law partner)

**Box 7A**
**Your Social Insurance Number**

Enter your Social Insurance Number in question 7A. If you have more than one Social Insurance Number, please attach a note to your application, listing all your Social Insurance Numbers.

**Box 7B**
**Your date of birth**

Please enter your date of birth in this box.

You do not need to provide proof of birth with your application. However, the Canada Pension Plan has the right to request proof of birth at any time, when deemed necessary.

**Box 8A**
**Written communication**

In this box, please tell us in which language you would like to get letters from us. Check only one box.

**Box 8B**
**Verbal communication**

Please check the language — English or French — you would like to use when you talk to us.

You can choose a different language for written communication than the one you choose for verbal communication. For example, you can ask to receive your letters in English, and you can ask to use French when talking to one of our agents.

**Box 14**
**Are you disabled?**

If you were under the age of 35 at the time of your spouse's or common-law partner's death, you may be entitled to receive a Canada Pension Plan survivor's pension only if you have a dependent child or if you are disabled. Your disabling condition can be physical or mental.

According to the Canada Pension Plan legislation, your disability must be **"severe and prolonged"**. **"Severe"** means your condition prevents you from working regularly at any job, and **"prolonged"** means your condition is long term or may result in your death. The **"severe"** and **"prolonged"** criteria must both be met at the time of application.

If you feel this applies to you and you have not already applied for the disability pension, please contact us.

**Box 18**
**Direct Deposit**

You can sign up for Direct Deposit by completing Question 18.

Here is an example of a cheque which identifies the information we need.

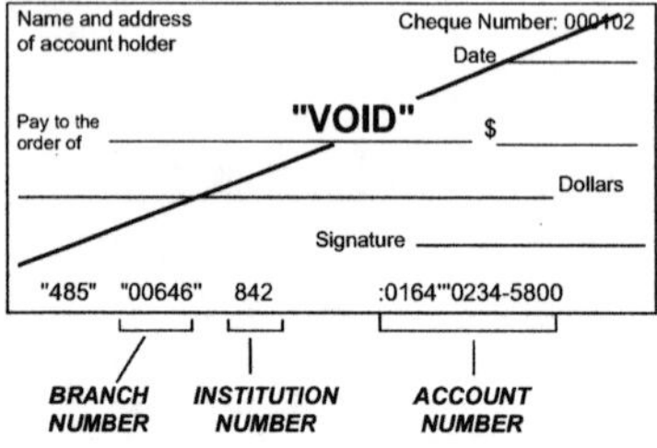


**Box 19**
**Voluntary income tax deduction**

Your Canada Pension Plan benefit is taxable. Fill out Box 19 if you would like to have us take off monthly voluntary income tax deductions from your Canada Pension Plan benefit. You should consider your personal tax situation before choosing an amount. If you decide to have us withhold voluntary income tax deductions, you may request an amount now, and have it changed at a later date. This service is available to Canadian residents only.

## Section C: Information about the child(ren) of the deceased

The child(ren) of the deceased could be eligible for a surviving child's benefit. To be eligible, the child(ren) must be the deceased's:

- natural child;
- legally adopted child;
- child adopted in fact; **or**
- a child who was legally or in fact in the care and custody of the deceased.

The child must also be a dependent child of the deceased. A dependent child is a child who, at the time of death of the deceased, was:

- under the age of 18; **or**
- between the ages of 18 and 25 and was attending school or university full-time.

A child may receive up to two benefits under the Canada Pension Plan if both parents were Canada Pension Plan contributors and are either deceased or are disabled, and if all conditions of eligibility are met for both benefits.

If a child is 18 years old, he/she must complete and submit the forms **"Application for Canada Pension Plan Child's Benefit (for children between ages 18 and 25)"** and the **"Declaration of Attendance at School or University"**. The child must be attending school or university full-time to receive or continue to receive the benefit.

SC ISP-1300-A (2010-08-01) E

Page 5 / 8

**Box 20**
**Do you have any children under the age of 18?**

If you have children under the age of 18 in your care and custody, please complete question 20.

**NOTE**: If a child was in the care and custody of the deceased but is now in the care and custody of someone other than you, that person must apply on the child's behalf for that child to receive the benefit.

You do not need to provide proof of birth for the children if you provided their Social Insurance Number in the application. However, the Canada Pension Plan has the right to request proof of birth at any time, when deemed necessary. If you did not provide the Social Insurance Number of the children, then you must submit a **certified true copy of the children's original birth certificate.**

If you do not have this document and the children were born in Canada, please refer to the previous section **1B "Date of Birth"**, on how to obtain birth evidence.

**Box 21**
**Do you have any children between the ages of 18 and 25 attending school, college or university full-time?**

If you have children between the ages of 18 and 25, please complete question 21 and we will send an application to each child that is listed. The child must be attending school or university full-time to receive the benefit.

**When will my survivor's pension and child(ren) benefit(s) start?**

If your application is approved, your survivor's pension will normally begin the later of:

- the month after the death of the contributor;
- the $11^{th}$ month prior to the month your application is received.

The child(ren) benefit(s) will begin the later of:

- the month after the death of the contributor;
- the month after the birth of the child;
- the $11^{th}$ month prior to the month your application is received.

You can receive a retroactive payment for up to 11 months from when we receive your application but this retroactive period cannot cover any months prior to the month after the month of death of the contributor or the month after the month of birth of the child. If you are covered under the Incapacity provision (see the following section), retroactive payments could be made for more than 11 months.

**Incapacity**

Protection is available for persons who did not apply for a Canada Pension Plan pension benefit since they were unable to apply or to ask someone to apply on their behalf because of their medical condition. If you feel this applies to you, please contact us to obtain a **"Declaration of Incapacity"** form.

**Non-Resident Tax**

If you are a non-resident of Canada for income tax purposes, we may deduct a Non-Resident Tax from your monthly benefit. The tax rate is 25% of your monthly benefit unless the country you live in has a tax treaty with Canada that reduces the rate or exempts you from paying the tax.

Sometimes you can benefit from paying tax at the same rate as residents of Canada by filing a yearly Canadian income tax return. The Canada Revenue Agency will determine if you are due for a refund of any Non-Resident Tax you may have paid. You can also reduce the amount of tax we withhold from your survivor's benefit by completing a yearly **"Application by a Non-Resident of Canada for a Reduction in the Amount of Non-Resident Tax Required to be Withheld"** (Form NR5).

This form can be obtained by writing to the:
International Tax Services Office
Canada Revenue Agency
2204 Walkley Road
Ottawa, Ontario
K1A 1A8

or by calling:
**Outside North America:** English 613-952-3741
French 613-954-1368

SC ISP-1300-A (2010-08-01) E

Page 6 / 8

## Applicant's declaration

To complete the application, you have to sign and date it in this section.

**NOTE:** If you make a false or misleading statement, you may be subject to an administrative monetary penalty and interest, if any, under the *Canada Pension Plan,* or may be charged with an offence. Any benefits you received or obtained to which there was no entitlement would have to be repaid.

## Witness's declaration

If you signed your application with a mark, a witness has to sign and date the application in that section and provide their name, address, relationship to you, and telephone number in case we need to contact that person.

## Other information you should read before mailing your application

**Before you mail your application**

Before you send this application form to us, please make sure that you have:

- **completed**, **signed** and **dated** your application; **and**
- enclosed certified photocopies or any original documents we need.

Please refer to the **"Check List"** at the beginning of this information sheet for the documents we need.

**When we receive your application**

Once we receive your application and any supporting documents, we will review your application and contact you if we need more information. We will send you a letter once we have completed our review to let you know if you are eligible.

If you have not heard from us by the time you expect your first payment, please contact us at the telephone numbers listed in the section called **"How to contact us"** at the beginning of this information sheet.

**What you must do after your pension starts**

**If you move**

You must tell us if you move, even if your pension is being sent to another address or is being deposited directly into your financial institution account. This way, we will be able to send you important information and the tax slips you need for income tax purposes. Also, if you move outside of Canada or from one country to another, your tax status may change. **If you do not inform us of an address change and you should have paid a higher tax rate, you will have to repay any overpayments.**

**If you change financial institutions or account numbers**

If your payment is directly deposited, please let us know if you change financial institutions or accounts. Do not close your old account until you are sure that your pension is being deposited into your new account.

**If the Canada Pension Plan recipient dies**

The estate representative must inform Service Canada as soon as possible of the death of the recipient. Your estate can receive benefits for the month of your death. If we do not get the information quickly enough, any benefits paid after the month of death will have to be paid back.

**If you become disabled or cease to be disabled**

Please notify us if you become disabled or cease to be disabled.

SC ISP-1300-A (2010-08-01) E

Page 7 / 8

## Other pensions / benefits

### Child Rearing Provision

This provision may help you increase the monthly amount of your pension. If you received Family Allowances (FA) or were eligible to receive the Child Tax Benefit on behalf of any children born after December 31, 1958, this provision may apply to you. In this case, complete the form titled **"Canada Pension Plan Child Rearing Provision"** and return it with your application.

If you were a spouse as defined under the Canada Pension Plan prior to the repeal of the Family Allowances Program in 1993 and you received the Family Allowances but your deceased spouse was the person who remained at home and was the primary caregiver for these children, you can waive your rights in favour of the deceased. If you wish to waive your rights, complete the **"Canada Pension Plan Child Rearing Provision"** form and return it with your application.

### Retirement Pension

If the deceased made contributions to the Canada Pension Plan, was at least 70 years of age at the time of his/her death, and had not applied for or received a Canada Pension Plan retirement pension, you should contact us and request an application. The application must be made within one year of the date of death.

### Old Age Security Pension

If you are between the ages of 60 and 64, you may be eligible for the Allowance for the Survivor. For more information on this subject, please contact us.

**Protection of personal information**

The information requested is required under the Canada Pension Plan (CPP). We may not be able to give you a benefit if you do not give us all the information we need. We will keep this information in the Personal Information Bank HRSDC PPU 146. Your personal information is governed by the *Privacy Act* and we may disclose it where we are authorized to do so under the CPP.

Under the *Canada Pension Plan* and the *Privacy Act* you have the right to look at the personal information about you in your file. You can ask to see your file by contacting a Service Canada office. To find out how to get your personal information through the Access to Information Coordinator's office, see the Info Source, a directory that lists all the information banks and the information they contain. Copies of the Info Source are available in all Service Canada offices.

# Application for CPP Survivor's Pension and Child(ren)'s Benefits

Service Canada

Protected when completed - B
Personal Information Bank HRSDC PPU 146

Disponible en français

## Application for a Canada Pension Plan Survivor's Pension and Child(ren)'s Benefits

***It is very important that you:***

send in this form with supporting documents (see the information sheet for the documents we need); **and**

use a **pen** and **print** as clearly as possible.

### SECTION A - INFORMATION ABOUT YOUR DECEASED SPOUSE OR COMMON-LAW PARTNER (The deceased contributor)

| **1A.** Social Insurance Number | **1B.** Date of Birth<br>Year Month Day | **1C.** Country of Birth (If born in Canada, indicate province or territory) | FOR OFFICE USE ONLY<br>AGE ESTABLISHED — AA |
|---|---|---|---|
| **2A.** Sex<br>☐ Male ☐ Female | **2B.** Date of Death<br>*(See the information sheet for a list of acceptable proof of date of death documents)* | Year Month Day | DATE OF DEATH ESTABL. — PROV. CODE — AA |
| **3.** Marital status at the time of death<br>*(See the information sheet for important information about marital status)* | ☐ Single ☐ Married ☐ Separated<br>☐ Common-law ☐ Surviving spouse or common-law partner ☐ Divorced | | SURNAME - VALIDATOR — AR |

**4A.** ☐ Mr. ☐ Mrs. ☐ Ms. ☐ Miss — Usual First Name and Initial — Last Name

**4B.** Name at birth, if different from 4A. (e.g. maiden name, legal name change, etc.) — First Name and Initial — Last Name

**4C.** Name on social insurance card, if different from 4A. — First Name and Initial — Last Name

**5.** Home Address at the time of death (No., Street, Apt., R.R.) — City

Province or Territory — Country other than Canada — Postal Code

If the address shown above is outside of Canada, indicate the province or territory in which the deceased last resided. ▶

**6.** Did your deceased spouse or common-law partner ever live or work in another country? ☐ No ☐ Yes ▶ **If yes**, indicate the names of the countries and the insurance numbers. (If you need more space, use the space provided on page 6 of this application.) Also, indicate whether a benefit has been requested.

| | Country | Insurance Number | Has a benefit been requested? |
|---|---|---|---|
| a) | | | ☐ Yes ☐ No |
| b) | | | ☐ Yes ☐ No |
| c) | | | ☐ Yes ☐ No |

Service Canada delivers Human Resources and Skills Development Canada programs and services for the Government of Canada.

SC ISP-1300 (2010-08-01) E — Page 1 / 6 — Canada

Next Page Last Page

SIN

## SECTION B - INFORMATION ABOUT YOU (The surviving spouse or common-law partner)

| 7A. Social Insurance Number | 7B. Date of Birth Year Month Day | 7C. Country of Birth (If born in Canada, indicate province or territory) | FOR OFFICE USE ONLY |
|---|---|---|---|

AGE ESTABLISHED | AS

DSB START M Y | DSB END M Y | AS

Your Language Preference — 8A. Written Communications *(Check one)* ☐ English ☐ French — 8B. Verbal Communications *(Check one)* ☐ English ☐ French

**9A.** ☐ Mr. ☐ Miss ☐ Ms. ☐ Mrs. — Usual First Name and Initial — Last Name

TYPE NM ADR | FOREIGN CODE | LANG | B

**9B.** Name at birth, if different from 9A. (e.g. maiden name, legal name change, etc.) — First Name and Initial — Last Name

CONS. CODE | NO. LNS | A.I. 2 1 | C

TYPE NM ADR | FOREIGN CODE | LANG | CB

**9C.** Name on social insurance card, if different from 9A. — First Name and Initial — Last Name

CONS. CODE | NO. LNS | A.I. 2 1 | CC

**10.** Mailing Address (No., Street, Apt., P.O. Box, R.R.) — City

Province or Territory — Country other than Canada — Postal Code

Telephone Number(s) — **11A.** Area code and telephone number at home — **11B.** Area code and telephone number at work (if applicable)

**12.** Home Address, if different from mailing address (No., Street, Apt., R.R.) — City

Province or Territory — Country other than Canada — Postal Code

**13A.** Are you receiving or have you ever applied for a benefit under the:

Canada Pension Plan? ☐ Yes ☐ No — Old Age Security? ☐ Yes ☐ No — Régime de rentes du Québec? (Quebec Pension Plan) ☐ Yes ☐ No

**13B. If you answered yes** to any of the above, provide the Social Insurance Number or account number under which you applied. ▸

**14.** Are you disabled? ☐ No ☐ Yes

**15A.** Were you married to the deceased?

☐ Yes ▸ Date of marriage *(Please submit your marriage certificate)* ▸ Year Month Day

☐ No ▸ When did you start living together? ▸ Year Month Day

**15B.** Were you still married at the time of your spouse's death? ☐ Yes ☐ No

**16.** Were you still living together at the time of your spouse's or common-law partner's death? ☐ No ☐ Yes ▸ **If yes** and you are the common-law partner of the deceased, please obtain and complete the form titled "Statutory Declaration of Common-law Union" and return it with this application.

**17.** If you were under 45 years of age at the time of your spouse's or common-law partner's death, were you responsible for the care of:

**a)** a child of your deceased spouse or common-law partner **under 18 years of age** who was not in your care and custody? ☐ Yes ☐ No

**b)** a disabled child of your deceased spouse or common-law partner **over 18 years of age**? ☐ Yes ☐ No

**c)** a child of your deceased spouse or common-law partner **between the ages of 18 to 25** in full-time attendance at school or university? ☐ Yes ☐ No

**IF YOU ANSWERED "YES" TO ANY OF THE ABOVE, PLEASE EXPLAIN THE CIRCUMSTANCES IN THE SPACE PROVIDED ON PAGE 6 OF THIS APPLICATION AND INDICATE WHETHER OR NOT YOU ARE STILL CARING FOR THE CHILD.**

SC ISP-1300 (2010-08-01) E — Page 2 / 6

First Page — Next Page — Previous Page — Last Page

SIN

**18.** Direct Deposit *(For Canada only)*

For Direct Deposit outside Canada, please contact us at 1-800-277-9914 (from the United States) and at 613-990-2244 from all other countries (we accept collect calls).

If your application is approved, do you want your monthly payments deposited into your account at your financial institution?

☐ No (Go to question 19)

☐ Yes - Complete the boxes below (you may want to contact your financial institution to get this information).

Branch Number (5 digits) ____ Institution Number (3 digits) ____ Account Number (maximum of 12 digits) ____

Name(s) on the account ____ Telephone number of your financial institution ____

You can attach an unsigned personalized cheque with the word "VOID" on the front of the cheque and your social insurance number on the back.

**19.** Voluntary Income Tax Deduction **This service is available if you live in Canada.**

Your Canada Pension Plan benefit is taxable income. If we approve your application, would you like us to deduct **federal income tax** from your monthly payment? *(See the information sheet for more information)*

☐ No ☐ Yes ▸ **If yes**, indicate the dollar amount you want us to deduct each month. **Federal Income Tax** ____

## SECTION C - INFORMATION ABOUT THE CHILD(REN) OF THE DECEASED

**20.** Do you have any children **under the ages of 18**? ☐ No ☐ Yes ▸ **If yes**, please provide the following information.

**a)** Child's Usual First Name and Initial ____ Last Name ____

Sex ☐ Male ☐ Female | Date of Birth Year Month Day ▸ | Social Insurance Number

Is the child in your care and custody since birth? ☐ Yes ☐ No ▸ **If no**, please indicate since when: Year Month Day

Is the child **still** in your care and custody? ☐ Yes ☐ No ▸ **If no**, please provide a letter of explanation.

Is the child a:

☐ child of your deceased spouse or common-law partner

☐ legally adopted child of your deceased spouse or common-law partner

☐ other (Explain circumstances in the space provided on page 6 of this application)

| FOR OFFICE USE ONLY ▸ | AGE ESTABLISHED | CANCELLATION | DPND END M Y | DSB. START M Y | DSB. END M Y | A.L. | DA |
|---|---|---|---|---|---|---|---|

**b)** Child's Usual First Name and Initial ____ Last Name ____

Sex ☐ Male ☐ Female | Date of Birth Year Month Day ▸ | Social Insurance Number

Is the child in your care and custody since birth? ☐ Yes ☐ No ▸ **If no**, please indicate since when: Year Month Day

Is the child **still** in your care and custody? ☐ Yes ☐ No ▸ **If no**, please provide a letter of explanation.

Is the child a:

☐ child of your deceased spouse or common-law partner

☐ legally adopted child of your deceased spouse or common-law partner

☐ other (Explain circumstances in the space provided on page 6 of this application)

| FOR OFFICE USE ONLY ▸ | AGE ESTABLISHED | CANCELLATION | DPND END M Y | DSB. START M Y | DSB. END M Y | A.L. | DB |
|---|---|---|---|---|---|---|---|

SC ISP-1300 (2010-08-01) E Page 3 / 6

First Page Next Page Previous Page Last Page

SIN

**21.** Do you have any children **between the ages of 18 and 25** attending school, college or university full-time? ☐ No ☐ Yes ▶ **If yes**, please provide the following information

**a)** Child's Usual First Name and Initial | Last Name | Date of Birth (Year Month Day)

Mailing Address (No., Street, Apt., P.O. Box, R.R.) | City

Province or Territory | Country other than Canada | Postal Code

**b)** Child's Usual First Name and Initial | Last Name | Date of Birth (Year Month Day)

Mailing Address (No., Street, Apt., P.O. Box, R.R.) | City

Province or Territory | Country other than Canada | Postal Code

**22.** Are any of the children named in questions 20 and 21 receiving or have they applied for a benefit under:

**a)** the Canada Pension Plan? ☐ No ☐ Yes

**b)** Régime de rentes du Québec? (Quebec Pension Plan) ☐ No ☐ Yes

▶ **If yes**, to either or both, indicate the name of the child(ren) and the Social Insurance Number under which benefits are being received or have been applied for.

| Child's Usual First Name and Initial | Social Insurance Number |
|---|---|
| | |
| | |
| | |
| | |

**23.** Have you been wholly or substantially maintaining all of the children listed in question 20 and 21, since the death of your spouse or common-law partner? ☐ Yes ☐ No ▶ **If no**, please explain on page 6 of this application.

## SECTION D - INFORMATION ABOUT THE APPLICANT

(If not the surviving spouse or common-law partner named in Section B)

**24.** Social Insurance Number | Your Language Preference | **25A.** Written Communications *(Check one)* ☐ English ☐ French | **25B.** Verbal Communications *(Check one)* ☐ English ☐ French

**26.** ☐ Mr. ☐ Mrs. ☐ Ms. ☐ Miss | Usual First Name and Initial | Last Name

A

**27.** Mailing Address (No., Street, Apt., P.O. Box, R.R.) | City | TYPE NM ADR | FOREIGN CODE | LANG.

B

Province or Territory | Country other than Canada | Postal Code | CONS CODE | NO. LNS | A.L.

C

Telephone Number(s) | **28A.** Area code and telephone number at home | **28B.** Area code and telephone number at work (if applicable)

**Please explain on a separate sheet of paper why you are making this application**

SC ISP-1300 (2010-08-01) E Page 4 / 6

First Page Next Page Previous Page Last Page

SIN

## APPLICANT'S DECLARATION

I hereby apply for a Survivor's Pension and/or child(ren)'s benefits under the provisions of the Canada Pension Plan. I declare that, to the best of my knowledge, the information on this application is true and complete. I realize that my personal information is governed by the *Privacy Act* and it can be disclosed where authorized under the Canada Pension Plan.

**NOTE:** If you make a false or misleading statement, you may be subject to an administrative monetary penalty and interest, if any, under the *Canada Pension Plan*, or may be charged with an offence. Any benefits you received or obtained to which there was no entitlement would have to be repaid.

**APPLICANT'S SIGNATURE X** ____________________ **APPLICATION DATE** Year Month Day ____________

***NOTE:*** **We can only accept a signature with a mark (e.g. X) if a responsible person witnesses it. That person must also complete the declaration below.**

## WITNESS'S DECLARATION

**If the applicant signs with a mark, a witness (friend, member of the family, etc.) must complete this section.**

I have read the contents of this application to the applicant, who appeared to fully understand and who made his or her mark in my presence.

| Name | Relationship to applicant | Telephone number |
|---|---|---|
| Address | Signature | Date Year Month Day |

## FOR OFFICE USE ONLY

BENEFIT INFORMATION: ACTION | BNFT | AL | B/C | D | NUMBER OF LINES E | F | G | S (00) | CPP NUMBER | APP. REC'D D M Y | DT. EFF. M Y | CHILD SQNC — EA

ACCESS CODE | ACTION | BNFT | DT EFF. M Y | CHILD SQNC | MISCELLANEOUS 1 (OLD) (NEW) | MISCELLANEOUS 2 (NEW) | B/C | D | E | NUMBER OF LINES F | G (00) | S (00) — EC

MONETARY INFO: CODE | CHILD SQNC | RECOVERY BNFT CHILD | SIGN | UNDER/OVPMNT | ACCRUED RECOVERY CPP | QPP | DT EFF. M Y | CPP WITHHOLD ARREARS | RATE | QPP WITHHOLD ARREARS | RATE — FA, FA, FB

TOTAL

FA - CTB PERIODS

START M Y | END M Y

(1) GB (3) GB

(2) GB (4) GB

Application taken by: (Please print name and phone number)

Application approved pursuant to the Canada Pension Plan. | Date

Effective Date (month) (year) | Authorized Signature

| | DATE | TYPE OF REJECT | BATCH NO. | CYCLE | DATE | SIGNATURE |
|---|---|---|---|---|---|---|
| 1 | | | | | | |
| 2 | | | | | | |
| 3 | | | | | | |
| 4 | | | | | | |

SC ISP-1300 (2010-08-01) E Page 5 / 6

First Page Next Page Previous Page Last Page

SIN

**Use this space, if needed, to provide us with more information. Please indicate the question number concerned for each answer given. If you need more space, use a separate sheet of paper and attach it to this application.**

SC ISP-1300 (2010-08-01) E

Page 6 / 6

First Page Next Page Previous Page Last Page

# Service Canada Offices

**Mail your forms to:**
The nearest Service Canada office listed below.
From outside of Canada: The Service Canada office in the **province where you last resided**.

**Need help completing the forms?**
Canada or the United States: **1-800-277-9914**
All other countries: **613-990-2244** (we accept collect calls)
TTY: **1-800-255-4786**
**Important**: Please have your social insurance number ready when you call.

**NEWFOUNDLAND AND LABRADOR**
Service Canada
PO Box 9430 Station A
St. John's NL A1A 2Y5
CANADA

**PRINCE EDWARD ISLAND**
Service Canada
PO Box 8000 Station Central
Charlottetown PE C1A 8K1
CANADA

**NOVA SCOTIA**
Service Canada
PO Box 1687 Station Central
Halifax NS B3J 3J4
CANADA

**NEW BRUNSWICK AND QUEBEC**
Service Canada
PO Box 250 Station A
Fredericton NB E3B 4Z6
CANADA

**ONTARIO**
**For postal codes beginning with "L, M or N"**
Service Canada
PO Box 5100 Station D
Scarborough ON M1R 5C8
CANADA

**ONTARIO**
**For postal codes beginning with "K or P"**
Service Canada
PO Box 2013 Station Main
Timmins ON P4N 8C8
CANADA

**MANITOBA AND SASKATCHEWAN**
Service Canada
PO Box 818 Station Main
Winnipeg MB R3C 2N4
CANADA

**ALBERTA / NORTHWEST TERRITORIES AND NUNAVUT**
Service Canada
PO Box 2710 Station Main
Edmonton AB T5J 2G4
CANADA

**BRITISH COLUMBIA AND YUKON**
Service Canada
PO Box 1177 Station CSC
Victoria BC V8W 2V2
CANADA

Disponible en français

ISP-3501-CPP-04-10E

Canadä

First Page Previous Page Print to PDF

# Application for QPP Survivors' Benefits

## Application for Survivors' Benefits

### Information

You can file your application for survivors' benefits on our Web site at **www.rrq.gouv.qc.ca/deces.** It's quicker. Postal delays are eliminated and you will obtain immediate confirmation that we have received your application.

There are **three types of survivors' benefits** that can be paid following the death of a person who contributed sufficiently to the Québec Pension Plan:

- Death benefit;
- Surviving spouse's pension;
- Orphan's pension.

#### Death benefit

The maximum death benefit is 2 500 $. It is **taxable** and must be declared in the estate's income tax return in most cases.

The death benefit is paid to the person or charitable organization that paid the funeral expenses or to the heirs.*

If an application and a photocopy of proof of payment are filed with the Régie **within 60 days** of the death, **priority is given to the person or charitable organization that paid the funeral expenses.**

* If there are no heirs or if they have renounced the estate, the death benefit can be paid to other persons.

#### Surviving spouse's pension

The surviving spouse's pension is paid monthly. The amount of the pension depends on the contributions that the deceased person made to the Québec Pension Plan. It can be paid to the deceased's spouse by marriage or by civil union. If the deceased was not married or in a civil union, the pension is paid to the person recognized as the de facto spouse. In some circumstances, it can also be paid to the deceased's legally separated spouse.

Even if you are already receiving a surviving spouse's pension under the Québec Pension Plan or the Canada Pension Plan, you can file another application following the death of your last spouse. However, you cannot receive more than one surviving spouse's pension. The Régie will begin payment of the new pension only if the amount of that pension is greater than the pension already in payment.

#### Orphan's pension

The orphan's pension is a monthly pension of a set amount. It is paid to the person providing for the needs of a child of the deceased. That child must be **under the age of 18 at the time of the deceased's death.** The following children are eligible:

- A child of the deceased, whether or not they lived together;
- A step-child of the deceased who lived with the deceased;
- Any other child who lived with the deceased or whom the deceased supported.

Payment of the orphan's pension ends when the child turns 18.

#### Additional information

Please note that the surviving spouse's pension and the orphan's pension are:

- payable as of the month following the death and can be paid retroactively, up to a maximum of 12 months from the date the application is received, except in rare cases;
- adjusted in January of each year, based on the increase in the cost of living;
- **taxable.**

#### If the deceased worked outside Canada

If the deceased did not make sufficient contributions to the Québec Pension Plan or the Canada Pension Plan, his or her contributions to a social security plan in another country with which Québec has an agreement could give you entitlement to survivors' benefits.

The spouse or children of the deceased could also be entitled to benefits from that country. For more information, visit www.rrq.gouv.qc.ca/programmes/regime_rentes/ententes_internationales.

**Continued on other side**

Régie des rentes Québec

B-042-1A (11-07)

## How to apply

To apply for these benefits, you must fill out the necessary sections of this form. See the instructions below.

## Instructions

This booklet contains the forms needed for the 3 types of survivors' benefits. There are 4 detachable sections.

**PART 1: Information about the Deceased**
(This part **must be completed and sent to us**, regardless of the type of benefit you are applying for.)

**PART 2: Application for a Death Benefit**

**PART 3: Application for a Surviving Spouse's Pension**

**PART 4: Application for an Orphan's Pension**

1. Answer all the questions in **PART 1**.
2. Complete **PARTS 2, 3 or 4**, depending on the type of benefit for which you are applying.
3. Be sure to **sign** in the required spaces (in **each** form you have completed).
4. Send **PART 1** and **PARTS 2, 3 or 4** depending on the situation, as well as any required documents, to:

   Régie des rentes du Québec
   Case postale 5200
   Québec (Québec) G1K 7S9

**IMPORTANT:**
If the death occurred **in Québec**, there is no need to provide proof of death. However, we reserve the right to request proof of birth, marriage or death at any time.

## Access to documents held by public bodies and the protection of personal information

The information requested on this form is needed in order for the Régie to study your application. Failure to provide the information may result in delays in processing the application or in the application being rejected. Only authorized employees at the Régie will have access to the information. The information can be provided to other persons or agencies or verified with them only in the cases provided for by law. It could also be used for research, assessments, enquiries or surveys. Under the *Act respecting Access to documents held by public bodies and the Protection of personal information*, you may consult the information and have your personal information corrected.

## Time required to process the application

In our *Service Statement*, we are committed to replying to an application for a surviving spouse's pension within a maximum of 90 days. However, 3 times out of 4, you will not have to wait more than 35 days. The time required may be longer if you are a de facto spouse because we will contact you to obtain information proving your status.

## How to reach us

**By Internet**
www.rrq.gouv.qc.ca

**By telephone**
Québec region: 418 643-5185
Montréal region: 514 873-2433
Toll-free: 1 800 463-5185

**TTY**
Service for the hearing impaired
Toll-free: 1 800 603-3540

**You must provide the social insurance number of the deceased where requested to avoid delays in processing your application.**

B-042-1A (11-07)

0100003 LE

Régie des rentes Québec

## Application for Survivors' Benefits

### PART 1: Information about the Deceased

Answer **all the questions in this PART** and return it to us with PARTS 2, 3 or 4.

Please print

**Indicate the deceased's social insurance number**

**1.1 Information about the deceased's identity**

| Sex | Deceased's family name | Given name |
|---|---|---|
| ☐ F<br>☐ M | Family name at birth, if different | Given name at birth, if different |

| Date of birth (year, month, day) | Place of birth (city, province, country) |
|---|---|
| Date of death (year, month, day) | Place of death (city, province, country) |

| His or her mother's family name at birth | Mother's given name |
|---|---|
| His or her father's family name | Father's given name |

His or her permanent address at the time of the death (number, street, apt.)

| City | Province | Country | Postal code |
|---|---|---|---|

If the deceased was living outside Canada, indicate his or her last province of residence in Canada.

**1.2 Conjugal status**

Deceased's conjugal status **at the time of his or her death** (Check 1 box only.)

If the person was living in a de facto (common-law) relationship at the time of death and had never been married or in a civil union with another person, check "single" as the person's conjugal status.

- ☐ Single
- ☐ Widowed
- ☐ Married ........ Date of marriage (year, month, day)
- ☐ Legally separated ........ Date of separation
- ☐ Divorced ........ Date of divorce
- ☐ Civil union ........ Date of civil union
- ☐ Dissolved civil union ........ Date of dissolution

**1.3 Social security plans outside Canada**

Did the deceased person take part in the social security plan of a country other than Canada?

☐ No ☐ Yes, in the following country or countries: ____________

Foreign social security numbers: ____________

1

Régie des rentes du Québec B-042A (11-07)

Indicate the deceased's social insurance number

## 1.4 Information about children

The following situations could help give a person entitlement to a pension or increase the amount:

- if the deceased received family benefits for a child (Québec child assistance, Québec family allowance or the Canada Child Tax Benefit);
- if the deceased was entitled to family benefits, but did not receive any because the family income was too high.

**a)** Did the deceased have, or did he or she become responsible for, children born after 31 December 1958?

☐ Yes ☐ No. Go to PART 2 to apply for a death benefit,
PART 3 to apply for a surviving spouse's pension,
PART 4 to apply for an orphan's pension.

**b)** Did the deceased receive family benefits paid **in his or her name** for a child born after 31 December 1958 or, if he or she did not, was it because the family income was too high? (Benefits are usually paid to the mother.)

☐ Yes. Complete the following table. ☐ No. Go to PART 2 to apply for a death benefit,
PART 3 to apply for a surviving spouse's pension,
PART 4 to apply for an orphan's pension.

| | Information about children born after 31 December 1958 | | | |
|---|---|---|---|---|
| 1 | Family name at birth | Given name | | Date of birth (year, month, day) |
| | Place of birth (province, country) | Date of adoption or date child became a dependent (if applicable) (year, month) | | Date of death (if death occurred before age 7) (year, month) |
| | Child born outside Canada: Date of arrival in Canada (year, month) | Province of residence upon arrival in Canada | | |
| 2 | Family name at birth | Given name | | Date of birth (year, month, day) |
| | Place of birth (province, country) | Date of adoption or date child became a dependent (if applicable) (year, month) | | Date of death (if death occurred before age 7) (year, month) |
| | Child born outside Canada: Date of arrival in Canada (year, month) | Province of residence upon arrival in Canada | | |
| 3 | Family name at birth | Given name | | Date of birth (year, month, day) |
| | Place of birth (province, country) | Date of adoption or date child became a dependent (if applicable) (year, month) | | Date of death (if death occurred before age 7) (year, month) |
| | Child born outside Canada: Date of arrival in Canada (year, month) | Province of residence upon arrival in Canada | | |
| | **If you need more space, continue on a separate sheet.** | | | |

**c)** Between the birth and the 7th birthday of each child, were there any periods during which family benefits were **not paid in the deceased's name**? ☐ Yes ☐ No

**d)** Between each child's birth or arrival in Canada and that child's 7th birthday, did each of these children always **live with the deceased in Canada**? ☐ Yes ☐ No

Régie des rentes du Québec 2 B-042A (11-07)

Régie des rentes Québec

## Application for Survivors' Benefits

### PART 2: Application for a Death Benefit

**Be sure you have answered all the questions in PART 1 before continuing with your application.**

**Indicate the deceased's social insurance number** ▶ ☐ ☐ ☐

### 2.1 Application for a death benefit

The death benefit is payable:

- to the person or charitable organization that paid the funeral expenses. Payment is made on a **priority basis** if an application is filed with the Régie with proof of payment **within 60 days** of the death;

  ▶ If you choose **a)** or **e)** below: The cheque will be issued **in your name** (or the name of the charitable organization) for the amount of the funeral expenses paid (maximum 2 500 $).

or

- to the heirs or, if there are no heirs, to other persons.

  ▶ If you choose **b), c)** or **d)** below: The cheque will be made out to **"the Heirs of (name of the deceased)"** not before 60 days after the death.

Please indicate **in what capacity** you are applying for the death benefit. **(Check 1 box only.)**

a) ☐ **Person who paid the funeral expenses** ▶ Provide with this form (or **within 60 days of the death**) **proof of payment** of the funeral expenses **(photocopy of RECEIPTS or BILLS MARKED "PAID") made out in your name** in order to conserve your priority.

If the funeral expenses were less than the death benefit, the balance can be paid to the **heirs** or, if there are no heirs, to certain other persons. Provide the following information:

Are you an heir? ☐ Yes ☐ No

Did you legally renounce the estate? (by notarial deed or judicial declaration) ☐ Yes ☐ No

What was your relationship to the deceased? ______________________

Complete **Sections 2.2** and **2.4**.

b) ☐ **Heir**

Did you legally renounce the estate? (by notarial deed or judicial declaration) ☐ Yes ☐ No

What was your relationship to the deceased? ______________________

Complete **Sections 2.2** and **2.4**.

c) ☐ **Liquidator of the estate***

Complete **Sections 2.2** and **2.4**.

d) ☐ **Professional mandated to settle the estate**

Complete **Sections 2.3** and **2.4**.

e) ☐ **Charitable organization that paid the funeral expenses** ▶ Provide **proof of payment** of the funeral expenses **(photocopy of RECEIPTS or BILLS MARKED "PAID") made out in the name of the charitable organization**.

Complete **Sections 2.3** and **2.4**.

* Executor named in the will or if there is no will, the person named by the heirs.

3

Régie des rentes du Québec B-042A (11-07)

Indicate the deceased's social insurance number ▶

## 2.2 Information about the applicant

If you are also applying for a surviving spouse's pension (PART 3), you do not need to complete this section. **However, you must sign Section 2.4.**

| Sex ☐ F ☐ M | Family name | | Given name | |
|---|---|---|---|---|
| | **Social insurance number** | Date of birth (year month day) | Language of correspondence ☐ French ☐ English | |
| Your mother's family name at birth | | | Your mother's given name | |
| Your address (number, street, apt.) | | | | |
| City | Province | | Country | Postal code |
| Telephone Home (area code) | | Other (area code) | | Extension |

## 2.3 Information about the professional mandated to settle the estate, or about the charitable organization

Complete this section if you are filing the application in the capacity of professional mandated to do so or as the representative of the charitable organization.

| Sex ☐ F ☐ M | Family name of the professional or representative | | Given name | |
|---|---|---|---|---|
| | Profession (if applicable) | | | |
| Name of the charitable organization (if applicable) | | | Registration number of the charitable organization (if applicable) | |
| Address of the professional or the charitable organization (number, street, office) | | | | |
| City | Province | | Country | Postal code |
| Telephone (area code) | | Extension | Language of correspondence ☐ French ☐ English | |

## 2.4 Declaration and signature

I declare that all the information provided is true and correct.

**Signature** ____________________ Date (year month day)

**Important:** If the death occurred in Québec, no proof of death is required.

**To apply for a surviving spouse's pension, complete PART 3.**
**To apply for an orphan's pension, complete PART 4.**

Régie des rentes du Québec    4    B-042A (11-07)

Régie des rentes Québec

## Application for Survivors' Benefits

### PART 3: Application for a Surviving Spouse's Pension

**Be sure you have answered all the questions in PART 1 before continuing with your application.**

**Indicate the deceased's social insurance number**

**3.1 Information about the spouse of the deceased**

| Sex | Your family name | Your given name |
|---|---|---|
| ☐ F ☐ M | Your family name at birth, if different | Your given name at birth, if different |

| **Your social insurance number** | Your date of birth (year, month, day) | Language of correspondence ☐ French ☐ English |
|---|---|---|

Your place of birth (city, province, country)

| Your mother's family name at birth | Your mother's given name |
|---|---|
| Your father's family name | Your father's given name |
| Your permanent address **at the time of the death** | Your current address, if different (number, street, apt.) |
| City | City |
| Province / Country / Postal code | Province / Country / Postal code |

Telephone
Home (area code) Other (area code) Extension

**3.2 Relationship to the deceased**

**At the time of the death,** what was your relationship to the deceased? (Check 1 box only.)

☐ We had been **married** since ............ (year, month, day)

Place of marriage (city, province, country) ____

If you were not living together at the time of the death, but were still married, please indicate the reason.

____

If the marriage took place **outside Québec**, please provide proof of marriage issued by an officer of civil status.

☐ We had been **legally separated** since ............ (year, month, day)

☐ We had been **divorced** since ............

**If you had resumed living together, indicate since when.** (year, month, day)

☐ We had been **de facto spouses** since ............

☐ We had been in a **civil union** since ............

☐ Our **civil union had been dissolved** since ............

**If you had resumed living together, indicate since when.** (year, month, day)

5

Régie des rentes du Québec B-042A (11-07)

**Indicate the deceased's social insurance number**

**3.3 Other information**

**a)** Was a child born or is a child to be born of your union with the deceased? ☐ Yes ☐ No

**b)** Did you adopt a child together or did either of you adopt the other's child? ☐ Yes ☐ No

**c)** Are you disabled or do you consider yourself disabled? ☐ Yes ☐ No

**d) At the time of your spouse's death:**

Did you have any dependent disabled children? ☐ Yes ☐ No

Did you have any dependent children under 18? ☐ Yes ☐ No

**e) Since the death of your spouse:**

Have you become responsible for any disabled children? ☐ Yes ☐ No

Have you become responsible for any children under 18? ☐ Yes ☐ No

**f)** Are you receiving benefits (retirement pension, survivor's or disability benefits) under the Canada Pension Plan? **(Any pension other than the Old Age Security pension.)**

☐ No ☐ Yes, under the following social insurance number

**3.4 Application for direct deposit**

We suggest that you sign up for direct deposit if you would like your pension payments to be deposited in a financial institution in Canada. It's safe and easy.

If you are already receiving a pension from the Régie that is paid by direct deposit, your benefits will be paid into the same account. There is no need to provide any information about the account. Go directly to **Section 3.5**.

| Name of the bank or caisse | Branch number (transit number) | Number of the bank or caisse | Account number (folio) |
|---|---|---|---|
| Address (number, street) | | | |

The account provided must be in your name or that of the beneficiary if you are applying on his or her behalf. **Enclose a blank cheque with VOID written across it.** Write your name and your social insurance number on the back of the cheque.

**3.5 Declaration and signature of the deceased's spouse**

This section must be signed by the spouse or by a person authorized to act on his or her behalf, that is, a trust officer, a member of a professional order (lawyer, notary, accountant, etc.) or a person who has a mandate or power of attorney.

I declare that all the information given in this application is true and correct.

**Signature** ______________________ Date (year / month / day)

If this form was not completed by the spouse of the deceased, the person who completed it must provide the following information.

In what capacity have you signed (guardian, mandatary)? ______________________

| Sex | Family name | Given name | |
|---|---|---|---|
| ☐ F ☐ M | Address | | Postal code |

Telephone

Home (area code) Other (area code) Extension

**If you are an individual, you must also provide the following information:**

| **Your social insurance number** | Your date of birth (year / month / day) | Your mother's family name at birth |
|---|---|---|
| | | |

**To apply for an orphan's pension, complete PART 4.**

6

Régie des rentes du Québec B-042A (11-07)

Régie des rentes Québec

## Application for Survivors' Benefits

### PART 4: Application for an Orphan's Pension

**Be sure you have answered all the questions in PART 1 before continuing with your application.**
**Important:** Don't forget to indicate the **children's social insurance numbers,** if any.

**Indicate the deceased's social insurance number** ▶

**4.1 Information about children under age 18**

**a)** Indicate the names of the **children who were under 18** at the time of the death and for whom you are applying for an orphan's pension.

1

| Sex ☐ F ☐ M | Family name at birth | Given name | **Social insurance number** |
|---|---|---|---|
| | Date of birth (year, month, day) | Place of birth (city, province, country) | If the child was born outside Québec, provide proof of birth issued by a civil authority. |
| | Address **at the time of the death** | Current address, if different | |
| | Family name at birth of the child's mother | Mother's given name | |
| | Family name of the child's father | Father's given name | |

2

| Sex ☐ F ☐ M | Family name at birth | Given name | **Social insurance number** |
|---|---|---|---|
| | Date of birth (year, month, day) | Place of birth (city, province, country) | If the child was born outside Québec, provide proof of birth issued by a civil authority. |
| Provide this information if different from 1st child. | Address **at the time of the death** | Current address, if different | |
| | Family name at birth of the child's mother | Mother's given name | |
| | Family name of the child's father | Father's given name | |

3

| Sex ☐ F ☐ M | Family name at birth | Given name | **Social insurance number** |
|---|---|---|---|
| | Date of birth (year, month, day) | Place of birth (city, province, country) | If the child was born outside Québec, provide proof of birth issued by a civil authority. |
| Provide this information if different from 1st child. | Address **at the time of the death** | Current address, if different | |
| | Family name at birth of the child's mother | Mother's given name | |
| | Family name of the child's father | Father's given name | |

If you need more space, continue in Section 4.3.

**b)** Are any of the children named above already receiving an orphan's pension or a pension for a disabled person's child under the Québec Pension Plan or the Canada Pension Plan?

☐ No ☐ Yes, under the following social insurance number

7

Régie des rentes du Québec B-042A (11-07)

**Indicate the deceased's social insurance number** ▶

## 4.2 Information about the person supporting the children

Provide information on the identity of the person supporting the children. That person, to whom the orphan's pension will be paid, must notify the Régie if he or she stops supporting the children.

If you are the spouse of the deceased and you are also applying for a surviving spouse's pension (PART 3), you do not have to complete this section. Go directly to **Section 4.3**.

| Sex | Family name | Given name |
|---|---|---|
| ☐ F<br>☐ M | Family name at birth, if different | Given name at birth, if different |

| **Social insurance number** | Date of birth (year, month, day) | Language of correspondence ☐ French ☐ English |
|---|---|---|

| Mother's family name at birth | Mother's given name |
|---|---|

Address (number, street, apt.)

| City | Province | Country | Postal code |
|---|---|---|---|

Telephone
Home (area code) | Other (area code) | Extension

## 4.3 Other information

Use this space if needed. Indicate the question number concerned for any information provided here.

## 4.4 Declaration and signature

This section must be signed by the person to whom the orphan's pension will be paid or a person authorized to act on his or her behalf, that is, a trust officer, a member of a professional order (lawyer, notary, accountant, etc.), the liquidator of the estate or a person who has a mandate or power of attorney.

I declare that all the information provided on this application is true and complete.

**Signature** ______________________ Date (year, month, day)

If this form was not completed by the person to whom the orphan's pension will be paid, the person who completed it must provide the following information.

In what capacity have you signed (guardian, mandatary)? ______________________

| Sex | Family name | Given name |
|---|---|---|
| ☐ F<br>☐ M | Address | Postal code |

Telephone
Home (area code) | Other (area code) | Extension

**If you are an individual, you must also provide the following information:**

| **Your social insurance number** | Your date of birth (year, month, day) | Your mother's family name at birth |
|---|---|---|

Régie des rentes du Québec

B-042A (11-07)

# Sample Inventory — Assets of the Deceased

| RESIDENTIAL REAL ESTATE | Ownership and Transfer | Insurance | Market Value | Mortgage | Net Value |
|---|---|---|---|---|---|
| (1) Principal residence<br><br>Address:<br><br>Purchase price: | Joint tenancy:<br>Yes ____<br>No ____<br>Name of joint tenant:<br><br>Spousal trust under will:<br>Yes ____<br>No ____<br><br>Transfer to beneficiary under will:<br>Yes ____<br>No ____<br>Name of beneficiary: | Broker:<br><br>Coverage:<br><br>Premium payable: | | Balance outstanding:<br><br>Mortgagee:<br><br>Monthly payments:<br><br>Maturity date: | |
| (2) Cottage/ Chalet/ Additional home<br><br>Address:<br><br>Purchase price: | Joint tenancy:<br>Yes ____<br>No ____<br>Name of joint tenant:<br><br>Spousal trust under will:<br>Yes ____<br>No ____<br><br>Transfer tc beneficiary under will:<br>Yes ____<br>No ____<br>Name of beneficiary: | Broker:<br><br>Coverage:<br><br>Premium payable: | | Balance outstanding:<br><br>Mortgagee:<br><br>Monthly payments:<br><br>Maturity date: | |
| (3) Cottage/ Chalet/ Second home<br><br>Address:<br><br>Purchase price: | Joint tenancy:<br>Yes ____<br>No ____<br>Name of joint tenant:<br><br>Spousal trust under will:<br>Yes ____<br>No ____<br><br>Transfer to beneficiary under will:<br>Yes ____<br>No ____<br>Name of beneficiary: | Broker:<br><br>Coverage:<br><br>Premium payable: | | Balance outstanding:<br><br>Mortgagee:<br><br>Monthly payments:<br><br>Maturity date: | |

| COMMERCIAL REAL ESTATE | Tenants | Transfer | Insurance | Market Value | Mortgages | Net Value |
|---|---|---|---|---|---|---|
| (1) Commercial property<br><br>Address:<br><br>Purchase price or book value: | Tenant's name:<br><br>Tenant's address:<br><br>Tenant's phone no.: | Joint tenancy:<br>Yes ____<br>No ____ | Broker:<br><br>Coverage:<br><br>Premium payable: | | Balance outstanding:<br><br>Mortgagee:<br><br>Monthly payments:<br><br>Maturity date: | |
| (2) Commercial property<br><br>Address:<br><br>Purchase price or book value: | Tenant's name:<br><br>Tenant's address:<br><br>Tenant's phone no.: | Joint tenancy:<br>Yes ____<br>No ____ | | | Balance outstanding:<br><br>Mortgagee:<br><br>Monthly payments:<br><br>Maturity date: | |

| **CASH AND INVESTMENTS**<br>**Bank Accounts, Term and Saving Deposits, Guaranteed Investment Certificates** | Principal | Interest | Total |
|---|---|---|---|
| Type of account/investment:<br>Location:<br>Account number:<br>Contact phone number:<br>Registered plan: Yes/No. If yes, designated beneficiary: | | | |
| Type of account/investment:<br>Location:<br>Account number:<br>Contact phone number:<br>Registered plan: Yes/No. If yes, designated beneficiary: | | | |
| Type of account/investment:<br>Location:<br>Account number:<br>Contact phone number:<br>Registered plan: Yes/No. If yes, designated beneficiary: | | | |

| INSURANCE POLICY PAYABLE TO THE ESTATE | Face Value | Add Accumulated Dividends + Interest | Less Loans | Value |
|---|---|---|---|---|
| Name of insurance company:<br>Address of insurance company:<br>Agent name:<br>Phone no.: | | | | |
| Name of insurance company:<br>Address of insurance company:<br>Agent name:<br>Phone no.: | | | | |

| ANNUITIES, PENSION BENEFITS, SAVINGS PLANS | Issuer | Beneficiary | Principal | Interest | Value |
|---|---|---|---|---|---|
| Type of interest:<br>Description: | | | | | |
| Type of interest:<br>Description: | | | | | |
| Type of interest:<br>Description: | | | | | |
| Type of interest:<br>Description: | | | | | |

| SHARES | Number of Shares | Registered Owner | Issuer | Transfer Agent | Price per Share at Date of Death | Dividends Payable at Date of Death | Value |
|---|---|---|---|---|---|---|---|
| Certificate numbers: | | | | | | | |

| BONDS AND DEBENTURES | Issue Date | Issuer | Interest Rate | Face Value | Purchase Price and Date | Maturity Date | Value |
|---|---|---|---|---|---|---|---|
| Serial numbers: | | | | | | | |

| BUSINESS INTERESTS | Value |
|---|---|
| Give brief inventory of stock in trade and liabilities if deceased had interest in a sole proprietorship or a partnership. Include the location of relevant documents regarding the business and the names of key contacts (lawyer, accountant, etc.). | |

| FARMING INTERESTS | Value |
|---|---|
| Give description and value of all machinery, cattle and other farm animals, and produce as of date of death. | |

| PERSONAL PROPERTY | Value |
|---|---|
| List personal effects, household goods, and furniture, and give a description if the value appears to be significant. | |

| TOTAL VALUE OF ASSETS |
|---|

| ASSETS NOT PASSING THROUGH ESTATE | Value |
|---|---|
| Jointly held land | |
| Joint bank accounts | |
| Registered plans paid to a named beneficiary | |
| Insurance payable to a named beneficiary | |
| Other assets | |
| Total | |

## Sample Letter to Bank Concerning Accounts and/or Assets

[date]
[return address]

Attention: Accounts Manager
[financial institution's address]

Dear Sir or Madam:

Re: The Estate of ____________________

I am the personal representative [or liquidator in Quebec] of the Estate of ____________________ (the "deceased") who died on the _______ day of _______________, 20___. According to my records, the deceased dealt with your bank [or trust company/credit union, etc.] and I would ask that you provide me with the following information to complete my records:

1. Confirmation of account numbers;
2. The amount on deposit in the accounts as at the date of death;
3. The full names of all persons whose names were on the accounts and whether the accounts were joint accounts;
4. Full details of any term deposits, GICs, RRSPs, RRIFs, or other registered plans;
5. Details of all assets in which the deceased had an interest and which the bank held in safekeeping;
6. Whether the deceased had a safety deposit box at your branch; and
7. Whether the deceased had any loans, mortgages, guarantees or any other liabilities owning to your institution.

Enclosed, please find a notarial copy of the will [or, where there is no will, the grant of administration] and a copy of the death certificate for your records.

Please advise me of the information required in order that the deceased's assets held by you can be transferred to the Estate or the beneficiaries.

Thank you for your assistance in this matter and I can be reached at (area code) 123-4567.

Yours very truly,

Eddie Executor

## Sample Authorization To View Safety Deposit Box

[date]
[return address]

[financial institution's address]

Dear Sir or Madam:

Re: The Estate of ____________________ (the "Estate")

This letter is an authorization to allow [name of authorized person, e.g., lawyer, trust company representative, etc.] to view Safety Deposit Box No. __________

### AUTHORIZATION

This is an authorization to permit [name of authorized person] to attend on my behalf to list the contents of the aforementioned safety deposit box registered in the name of [the deceased's name]. Furthermore, [name of authorized person] is authorized to remove from the box documents or assets so required for the successful administration of the Estate and to ensure the protection of such assets. The signature of [name of authorized person] appears below.

DATED _______ day of
______________, 20_____.

Eddie Executor
Personal Representative of the Estate [or Estate Trustee of the Estate in Ontario]

[signature of authorized person]

________________________________
[name of authorized person]

Yours very truly,

Eddie Executor

## Sample Letter Regarding Life Insurance Policy

[date]
[return address]

[name of insurance company or institution]

Dear Sir or Madam:

Re: The Estate of ____________________ (the "Estate")

I am the personal representative [or liquidator in Quebec] of the Estate of ____________________ (the "deceased") who died on the _______ day of _______________, 20___. According to my records the deceased held a life insurance policy with your company. Please forward the following information to me:

1. The policy number;
2. The amount of the policy; and
3. The name of the beneficiary, if one has been designated.

In addition to this information, please notify me of the necessary documentation in order that the proceeds of the policy be paid out.

Enclosed please find a copy of the Death Certificate for your file.

Sincerely,

Eddie Executor

# Transfer or Redemption of Canada Savings Bonds from a Deceased Owner[1]

TESTATE - DIED WITH A WILL

| DIVISION OF ESTATE | LIMIT WITHOUT PROBATE | REQUIRED DOCUMENTS TO COMPLETE A TRANSFER/REDEMPTION NOTE: Any variation in the transaction request from what is set out in the Will, will require Probate |
|---|---|---|
| **Letters Probate**<br><br>Executor(s) will divide the estate between the beneficiaries in the Last Will and Testament<br><br>**Note: Bond series issued on or after November 1, 2008 (i.e., CSB S114 and higher, as well as CPB P064 and higher) will no longer be eligible to be transferred in the name of the estate.** | N/A | ✓Notarial or Court certified copy of Letters Probate (copy of the Last Will and Testament annexed).<br><br>✓Completed Transfer Form (2351) ETRF signed by the executor/s appointed in Letters Probate.<br><br>✓Signature of executor(s) must be guaranteed by a Canadian financial institution acceptable to the Bank of Canada or the form must have been signed in front of a notary public, who must also sign and seal the document . |
| **Specific Bequest of bonds** | Unlimited (Par value of the bonds) | ✓All documentation required for a non probated Will (e.g., Notarial copy of Will / Proof of Death) which is acceptable to the Bank and completed Transfer Form (2351) ETRF signed by all executors with signature guaranteed by a Canadian financial institution or the form must have been signed in front of a notary public, who must also sign and seal the document acceptable to the Bank of Canada. |
| **Spouse** is the sole beneficiary under the Will | $75,000 (Par value of the bonds) | ✓Notarial certified copy of the Will.<br><br>✓Proof of death acceptable to the Bank of Canada.<br><br>✓Completed Transfer Form (2351) ETRF signed by all executors named in the Will.<br><br>✓Signature of executor(s) must be guaranteed by a Canadian financial institution acceptable to the Bank of Canada or the form must have been signed in front of a notary public, who must also sign and seal the document.<br><br>✓In the case of Wills containing cash bequests, proof of payment of the bequest with a release signed by the recipient in front of a witness is necessary before accepting any transaction with respect to bonds. |

[1] Bank of Canada Business Rules. Applies to all provinces other than Quebec. These tables are available on the Canada Savings Bonds website at www.csb.gc.ca/wp-content/uploads/2009/04/bank-of-canada-business-rules.pdf.

| | | |
|---|---|---|
| **Children** are the sole beneficiary/ies under the Will (no surviving spouse) | $50,000 (Par value of the bonds) | ✓Notarial certified copy of the Will.<br>✓Proof of death acceptable to the Bank of Canada.<br>✓Proof of death of the spouse which is acceptable to the Bank of Canada.<br>✓Completed Transfer Form (2351) ETRF signed by all the executors and all the beneficiaries named in the Will.<br>✓Signature of executor(s) must be guaranteed by a Canadian financial institution acceptable to the Bank of Canada or the form must have been signed in front of a notary public, who must also sign and seal the document.<br>✓In the case of Wills containing cash bequests, proof of payment of the bequest with a release signed by the recipient in front of a witness is necessary before accepting any transaction with respect to bonds. |

| | | |
|---|---|---|
| **Spouse & Children** are the sole beneficiaries under the Will | $50,000 (Par value of the bonds) | ✓Notarial certified copy of the Will.<br>✓Proof of death acceptable to the Bank of Canada.<br>✓Completed Transfer Form (2351) ETRF signed by all the executors and all the beneficiaries named in the Will.<br>✓Signature of executor(s) must be guaranteed by a Canadian financial institution acceptable to the Bank of Canada or the form must have been signed in front of a notary public, who must also sign and seal the document.<br>✓In the case of wills containing cash bequests, proof of payment of the bequest with a release signed by the recipient in front of a witness is necessary before accepting any transaction with respect to bonds. |

| | | |
|---|---|---|
| **Children** are the sole beneficiaries under the Will (Spouse alive) | $50,000 (Par value of the bonds) | ✓Notarial certified copy of the Will.<br>✓Proof of death acceptable to the Bank of Canada.<br>✓Completed Transfer Form (2351) ETRF signed by all the executors and all the beneficiaries named in the Will.<br>✓Signature of executor(s) must be guaranteed by a Canadian financial institution acceptable to the Bank of Canada or the form must have been signed in front of a notary public, who must also sign and seal the document.<br>✓Release from surviving Spouse which must be witnessed.<br>✓In the case of Wills containing cash bequests, proof of payment of the bequest with a release signed by the recipient in front of a witness is necessary before accepting any transaction with respect to bonds. |

| | | |
|---|---|---|
| **Parents, siblings or other family members** are the sole beneficiaries under the Will (no spouse) (no children) | $20,000 (Par value of the bonds) | ✓ Notarial certified copy of the Will.<br><br>✓ Proof of death acceptable to the Bank of Canada.<br><br>✓ Proof of death of spouse (if applicable).<br><br>✓ Completed Transfer Form (2351) ETRF signed by all the executors and all the beneficiaries named in the Will.<br><br>✓ Signature of executor(s) must be guaranteed by a Canadian financial institution acceptable to the Bank of Canada or the form must have been signed in front of a notary public, who must also sign and seal the document.<br><br>✓ In the case of wills containing cash bequests, proof of payment of the bequest with a release signed by the recipient in front of a witness is necessary before accepting any transaction with respect to bonds. |
| **Common Law Spouse, same sex partner or friend** is the sole beneficiaries under the Will | $20,000 (Par value of the bonds) | ✓ Notarial certified copy of the Will.<br><br>✓ Proof of death acceptable to the Bank of Canada.<br><br>✓ Proof of death of spouse (if applicable).<br><br>✓ Completed Transfer Form (2351) ETRF signed by all the executors and all the beneficiaries named in the Will.<br><br>✓ Signature of executor(s) must be guaranteed by a Canadian financial institution acceptable to the Bank of Canada or the form must have been signed in front of a notary public, who must also sign and seal the document.<br><br>✓ In the case of wills containing cash bequests, proof of payment of the bequest with a release signed by the recipient in front of a witness is necessary before accepting any transaction with respect to bonds. |
| **Double Estates** (between spouses)<br><br>Bond owner is deceased<br><br>Bond owner's spouse is deceased<br><br>Children are the beneficiaries | $50,000 (Par value of the bonds) | ✓ Notarial certified copy of the Will for both bond owner and spouse.<br><br>✓ Proof of death of the bond owner and spouse acceptable to the Bank of Canada.<br><br>✓ Two completed Transfer Forms (2351) ETRF signed by the appropriate executors and beneficiaries named in the Wills of both deceased. One Transfer Form (2351) ETRF would transfer the bonds from the deceased bond owner to the estate of the spouse and the second would transfer the estate to the spouse's beneficiaries.<br><br>✓ Signature of executor must be guaranteed by a Canadian financial institution acceptable to the Bank of Canada or the form must have been signed in front of a notary public, who must also sign and seal the document.<br><br>✓ In the case of wills containing cash bequests, proof of payment of the bequest with a release signed by the recipient in front of a witness is necessary before accepting any transaction with respect to bonds. |

| | | |
|---|---|---|
| **Organization**<br>(e.g., charities, churches, etc. sole beneficiary under the Will) | Not accepted without probate | ✓Notarial certified copy of Letters Probate (copy of the Last Will and Testament annexed).<br><br>✓Completed Transfer Form (2351) ETRF signed by all the executors and all the beneficiaries named in the Will.<br><br>✓Signature of executor(s) must be guaranteed by a Canadian financial institution acceptable to the Bank of Canada or the form must have been signed in front of a notary public, who must also sign and seal the document |

| | | |
|---|---|---|
| **Trust in the Will**<br>(the residue must be kept invested) | Not accepted without probate | ✓Notarial certified copy of Letters Probate (copy of the Last Will and Testament annexed).<br><br>✓Completed Transfer Form (2351) ETRF signed by all the executors and all the beneficiaries named in the Will.<br><br>✓Signature of executor(s) must be guaranteed by a Canadian financial institution acceptable to the Bank of Canada or the form must have been signed in front of a notary public, who must also sign and seal the document. |

BONDS WITH SPECIAL REGISTRATIONS

| REGISTRATION | LIMIT WITHOUT LETTERS OF ADMINISTRATION | REQUIRED DOCUMENTS TO COMPLETE A TRANSFER/REDEMPTION |
|---|---|---|
| **Co-owners**<br>(two or more names without survivorship)<br>Estate of the deceased owner is entitled to the **deceased's** portion of the par value of the bond.<br><br>**Note: This registration only applies to series issued PRIOR to November 2008 (i.e., CSB series up to and including S113 and CPB series up to and including P063).** | Refer to estate limits of the deceased owner's share | ✓Letter of direction is required or the Transfer Form (2351) ETRF signed by the surviving co-owners before a witness authorizing the splitting of the bonds and the release of the deceased's share.<br><br>✓Refer to the appropriate transaction type for the estate documents required. |

| | | |
|---|---|---|
| **Sole proprietorship** (e.g., Mary Smith carrying on business as *Mary's Flower* Shop)<br><br>**Note: This registration only applies to series issued PRIOR to November 2008 (i.e., CSB series up to and including S113 and CPB series up to and including P063).** | Not accepted without probate | ✓ Refer to the transaction Letters Probate or Letters of Administration on page 1 for estate documents required.<br><br>✓ Please note that the bonds have to be redeemed. |

INTESTATE - DIES WITHOUT A WILL

| DIVISION OF ESTATE | LIMIT WITHOUT LETTERS OF ADMINISTRATION | REQUIRED DOCUMENTS TO COMPLETE A TRANSFER/REDEMPTION |
|---|---|---|
| **Letters of Administration**<br><br>**Note: Bond series issued on or after November 1, 2008 (i.e., CSB S114 and higher, as well as CPB P064 and higher) are not eligible to be transferred in the name of the estate.** | N/A | ✓ Notarial or court certified copy of Letters of Administration.<br><br>✓ Completed Transfer Form (2351) ETRF signed by the Administrator(s) named in the Letters of Administration.<br><br>✓ Signature of the Administrator must be guaranteed by a Canadian financial institution acceptable to the Bank of Canada or the form must have been signed in front of a notary public, who must also sign and seal the document. |
| **Spouse claiming bonds** (no children) | $75,000 (Par value of the bonds) | ✓ Proof of death acceptable to the Bank of Canada.<br><br>✓ Completed Transfer Form (2351) ETRF signed by spouse.<br><br>✓ Signature must be guaranteed by a Canadian financial institution acceptable to the Bank of Canada or the form must have been signed in front of a notary public, who must also sign and seal the document. |
| **Spouse and Children claiming bonds** | $50,000 (Par value of the bonds) | ✓ Proof of death acceptable to the Bank of Canada.<br><br>✓ Completed Transfer Form (2351) ETRF signed by spouse and all children of the deceased bond owner.<br><br>✓ Signature(s) must be guaranteed by a Canadian financial institution acceptable to the Bank of Canada or the form must have been signed in front of a notary public, who must also sign and seal the document. |

| | | |
|---|---|---|
| **Children claiming bonds** (no surviving spouse) | $50,000 (Par value of the bonds) | ✓ Proof of death of the bond owner and spouse which are acceptable to the Bank of Canada.<br>✓ Completed Transfer Form (2351) ETRF signed by all the children of the deceased bond owner.<br>✓ Signature(s) must be guaranteed by a Canadian financial institution acceptable to the Bank of Canada or the form must have been signed in front of a notary public, who must also sign and seal the document |

| | | |
|---|---|---|
| **Children claiming bonds** (Spouse alive) | $50,000 (Par value of the bonds) | ✓ Proof of death of the bond owner acceptable to the Bank of Canada.<br>✓ Completed Transfer Form (2351) ETRF signed by all the children of the deceased bond owner.<br>✓ Signature(s) must be guaranteed by a Canadian financial institution acceptable to the Bank of Canada or the form must have been signed in front of a notary public, who must also sign and seal the document.<br>✓ A release from the surviving spouse signed before a witness. |

| | | |
|---|---|---|
| **Parents or siblings if parents deceased**<br>(no spouse)<br>(no children) | $20,000<br>(Par value of the bonds) | ✓ Proof of death of the bond owner acceptable to the Bank of Canada.<br>✓ Completed Transfer Form (2351) ETRF signed by the parents or all siblings of the deceased bond owner.<br>✓ Signature(s) must be guaranteed by a Canadian financial institution acceptable to the Bank of Canada or the form must have been signed in front of a notary public, who must also sign and seal the document.<br>✓ If parents deceased, we require proof of death acceptable to the Bank of Canada. |

# Canada Savings Bonds — Estate Transfer Form and Guidelines (Form 2351)

IMPORTANT INFORMATION

✓ Form ETRF is used for all provinces except Quebec. For **Quebec Estates**, please complete the Quebec Estate Transfer Form (534) QETRF.

✓ The form must be completed in full in order to be processed. This includes the signatures of all authorized representatives as well as the estate beneficiaries/heirs, if applicable.

✓ **For the protection of the estate, incomplete forms, or forms with incorrect information, or incorrect documentation will be rejected and will result in the delay of your request.**

✓ Request for cheque payments payable to a law firm **"in trust"** will be rejected.

✓ If the transaction involves **physical certificate bonds,** the **unsigned physical certificates** in question must be sent along with the completed form.

✓ **Bond series issued on or after November 1, 2008 (i.e., CSB S114 and higher, as well as CPB P064 and higher) are not eligible to be transferred in the name of the estate.**

✓ For Estate value limits and documentation requirements refer to the Bank of Canada Business Rules available on our web site.

✓ For estates involving funds held in The Canada RSP or The Canada RIF, please contact us for further guidelines. Refer to the "For Inquiries" Section on page 4 of these guidelines for our contact information.

✓ If the surviving spouse wishes to transfer into the Canada RSP/RIF, it must be into an existing Canada RSP/RIF plan.

✓ When the bonds/plans are registered in two or more names with the words ***"and Survivor"*** (e.g., John Smith and Jane Smith and Survivor) and one or more of the registered co-owners die, the Estate Transfer Form ETRF is not required. The bonds/plans may be transferred to the survivor(s) when proof of death of the deceased is presented with a letter from the surviving co-owner(s) requesting the transfer or redemption of bonds/plans. The letter must include the address of the surviving co-owner(s) and social insurance number(s) required by income tax legislation.

✓ When bonds/plans are registered in two or more names **without rights of survivorship** and one or more of the registered owners die, no rights to a transfer of registration automatically accrue to the remaining owner(s). In order to transfer the bonds/plans, the Estate Transfer Form ETRF must be completed. Please note, this registration applies to certificate bonds series issued **prior** to November 2008 and all series purchased through the Payroll Savings Program.

✓ Any alterations made on the form must be initialed, by all authorized representatives, before the final declaration is signed.

✓ Any difference in name between bonds/plans and legal documents should be addressed by a letter of guarantee from a financial institution or a lawyer on their letterhead stating e.g., John Doe, John H Doe and John Harry Doe are one and the same person.

✓ Please note that Government of Canada Retail Debt Instruments are also referred to as bonds, plans and securities.

**DOCUMENTS REQUIRED TO TRANSFER OR REDEEM BONDS/PLANS (Government of Canada Retail Debt Instruments)**

Before proceeding further please:

✓ Refer to the Bank of Canada Rules (available on our web site) to determine the situation (Probate, Intestate, Testate) and the Estate value limits that applies to your request.

✓ Once the situation has been identified, please refer to that section of the guidelines below to determine how to proceed in having your request processed.

**Situation # 1 - Letters Probate or Letters of Administration**

| Required Document | Specific instructions |
|---|---|
| A Notarial/Court certified copy of either the Letters Probate with a copy of the Will annexed or the Letters of Administration (with a copy of the Will annexed if applicable).<br>**Note: Financial Institution certified copies are not acceptable.**<br><br>**and**<br><br>Form ETRF | On the ETRF form please complete Sections A, B, C and F.<br><br>The beneficiary's name, address and social insurance number (required by income tax legislation) must be noted in Section F.<br><br>The form must be dated and signed by the appointed estate representative(s). Their signature must be:<br>✓ Guaranteed by a Canadian Financial Institution acceptable to the Bank of Canada or by a member of the Medallion guarantee program.<br>**Note: The "endorsement guaranteed stamp" is not acceptable.**<br>**or**<br>✓ Witnessed by a Notary Public, properly identified with the Notary seal/stamp and signature present. |

**OR**

**Situation # 2 - Testate - Died with a Will**

| Required Document | Specific instructions |
|---|---|
| A Notarial certified copy of the Will and Codicils (if applicable) attached with the Notary's signature and seal/stamp of office.<br>**Note: Financial Institution certified copies are not acceptable.**<br><br>**and**<br><br>Proof of Death<br>(see page 3)<br><br>**and**<br><br>Form ETRF | On the ETRF form please complete Sections A, B, D and F.<br><br>The beneficiaries must sign in the consent area of Section D and have their signature witnessed.<br><br>The beneficiary's name, address and social insurance number (required by income tax legislation) must be noted in Section F.<br><br>The form must be dated and signed by the appointed estate representative(s). Their signature must be:<br>✓ Guaranteed by a Canadian Financial Institution acceptable to the Bank of Canada or by a member of the Medallion guarantee program.<br>**Note: The "endorsement guaranteed stamp" is not acceptable.**<br>**or**<br>✓ Witnessed by a Notary Public, properly identified with the Notary seal/stamp and signature present.<br>**Note:**<br><br>**Any survivorship clause in the Will must be respected (e.g., 30 day clause; therefore, the Estate Transfer Form (2351) ETRF can only be signed 30 days after the date of death).** |

**OR**

**Situation # 3 - Intestate - Died without a Will and no legal certificate was issued by the court for any other assets, (e.g., Letters of Administration)**

| Required Document | Specific instructions |
|---|---|
| Proof of Death (see below)<br><br>**and**<br><br>Form ETRF | On the ETRF form please complete Sections A, B, E and F.<br><br>All heirs must sign in the consent area of Section E and have their signature witnessed.<br><br>The heir's name, address and social insurance number (required by income tax legislation) must be noted in Section F.<br><br>The form must be dated and signed by the appointed estate representative(s). Their signature must be:<br>✓ Guaranteed by a Canadian Financial Institution acceptable to the Bank of Canada or by a member of the Medallion guarantee program.<br>**Note: The "endorsement guaranteed stamp" is not acceptable.**<br><br>**or**<br><br>✓ Witnessed by a Notary Public, properly identified with the Notary seal/stamp and signature present. |

**Proof of Death: One of the following is acceptable to the Bank of Canada.**

- ✓ An **ORIGINAL** Death Certificate issued by either a Provincial Registrar or a Notarial Certified copy with a Notary's signature and seal/stamp of office or certified by a Canadian Financial Institution;
- ✓ An **ORIGINAL** certificate of finding issued by a coroner properly identified or a Notarial certified copy with the Notary's signature and seal/stamp of office or certified by a Canadian Financial Institution;
- ✓ An **ORIGINAL** Death Certificate issued by a church under seal and minister of religion`s signature or a Notarial certified copy with the Notary's signature and seal/stamp of office or certified by a Canadian Financial Institution;
- ✓ An **ORIGINAL** Death Certificate from an undertaking establishment issued under corporate seal and **ORIGINAL** signature or a Notarial certified copy with the Notary's signature and seal/stamp of office or certified by a Canadian Financial Institution.

**FOR INQUIRIES**

Contact us, Monday to Friday from 8 a.m. to 8 p.m. ET.

Phone:
1 800 575-5151
1 888 646-2626 for Financial Institution
1 800 354-2222 for TTY (teletypewriter only)

Email:
csb@csb.gc.ca

Online:
www.csb.gc.ca

**HOW TO SUBMIT YOUR REQUEST**

Once fully completed, please mail the form along with the **unsigned physical certificate bond(s)** (if applicable) and the legal documents to:

Canada Savings Bonds
Transfer & Exchange
PO BOX 2770, STN D
Ottawa, ON, K1P 1J7

**SPECIFIC INSTRUCTIONS**

This form is used for all provinces except Quebec.
Please print clearly or type the required information into the form fields. Please be sure to complete all required Sections to avoid delays in processing your request. Sign page 3 and mail your request to the destination indicated on page 3.

**SECTION A - DETAILS REGARDING THE DECEASED AND THEIR REPRESENTATIVES**

Full name of the deceased *(list all variations seen within the legal documents. e.g. Death Certificate, Last Will and Testament, Codicil(s))*

Social Insurance Number | Date of death (yyyy/mm/dd) | Last address for the deceased

Civil Status
- ◯ Single
- ◯ Married
- ◯ Other, please specify (e.g., divorce, widow)

City | Prov | Postal code | Country

I / We

Insert full name of all authorized representatives for the deceased
*(e.g. spouse, legal estate representative(s), liquidator(s)/executor(s), court appointed administrator(s)/executor(s))*

of

Care of address (for estate purposes) | City | Prov | Postal code | Country

do solemnly declare as follows, I am / we are the ◯ Administrator/ Executor(s)
◯ Other, please specify (e.g., spouse) of the deceased named above

**SECTION B - BOND(S)/PLAN(S) DETAILS**

The following is a list of all Government of Canada securities (bonds/plans) which were registered to the deceased at the time of death.

*If space is insufficient, please complete and attach a separate sheet that includes the fields seen below. Please initial all attached sheets.*

| | Name(s) appearing on the bond(s) | | Registration Account # or Certificate Bond Serial #(s) | | $ par value |
|---|---|---|---|---|---|
| **Canada Savings Bonds / Canada Premium Bonds** | | **AND** | | **AND** | |
| | | **AND** | | **AND** | |

*- The Registration Account # is 10 digits and can be found on a statement or T5.*
*- The Bond Serial # is located on the top center of the certificate (e.g., CS101F1234567J).*

☐ I have attached the physical unsigned certificates to this request.

Total par value $

**AND/OR**

**Payroll Savings Program** — Name(s) appearing on the Plan **AND** Plan # (10 digits): 2 _ _ _ _ _ _ _ _ _

*- The 10 digit Plan # can be found on an annual statement or T5.*

**AND/OR**

**Canada RSP / Canada RIF** — Name appearing on the Plan; Plan # (up to 11 digits)

*- The **Canada RSP** plan number is located on the semi-annual statements*
*- The **Canada RIF** plan number is located on the quarterly statements*

## SECTION C - LETTERS PROBATE OR LETTERS OF ADMINISTRATION

☐ Select this box only if the following situation applies;

Letters Probate / Letters of Administration were obtained and I am / we are the estate's legal representative(s).
The original or a notarial certified copy of the Letters Probate with a copy of the Will attached or Letters of Administration (with a copy of the Will attached if applicable) issued by the court has been submitted with this request.

## SECTION D - TESTATE (DIED WITH A WILL)

☐ Select this box and complete the section below only if the following situation applies;

The deceased left a Last Will dated ____________ (yyyy/mm/dd) which was neither amended nor revoked and no application for Letters Probate for the estate has been made or is intended to be made in any jurisdiction.
A notarial certified copy of the deceased Will and Proof of Death that is acceptable to the Bank of Canada is attached.
The following are all the persons, besides myself / ourselves, who are entitled to a share of the securities according to the Last Will and have consented to the transfer / redemption of the securities by signing below:

| | | | |
|---|---|---|---|
| Name of the beneficiary | | Name of the beneficiary | |
| Relationship to deceased | Age (if minor) | Relationship to deceased | Age (if minor) |
| Signature of the beneficiary | WITNESS must sign here | Signature of the beneficiary | WITNESS must sign here |

*All signatures must be witnessed and the signatories must be of full age of maturity, qualified and duly authorized (submit tutorship or curatorship documents if necessary). If space is insufficient, please complete and attach a separate sheet that includes the fields seen above. Please initial all attached sheets.*

## SECTION E - INTESTATE (DIED WITHOUT A WILL)

☐ Select this box and complete the section below only if the following situation applies;

The deceased died intestate (without leaving a Last Will and Testament) and no application for Letters of Administration for the estate has been made or is intended to be made in any jurisdiction.
Attached is a Proof of Death that is acceptable to the Bank of Canada.
The following are all the persons, who are entitled to a distributed share of the securities under the laws respecting intestacy of the Province in which the deceased was domiciled at the time of death and have consented to the transfer / redemption of the securities by signing below:

| | | | |
|---|---|---|---|
| Name of the heir | | Name of the heir | |
| Relationship to deceased | Age (if minor) | Relationship to deceased | Age (if minor) |
| Signature of the heir | WITNESS must sign here | Signature of the heir | WITNESS must sign here |

*All signatures must be witnessed and the signatories must be of full age of maturity, qualified and duly authorized (submit tutorship or curatorship documents if necessary). If space is insufficient, please complete and attach a separate sheet that includes the fields seen above. Please initial all attached sheets.*

**SECTION F - FINAL DECLARATION**

In consideration of the transfer or redemption of the securities as requested, I / we undertake to indemnify and save harmless the Bank of Canada against any claim that should at any time arise as a result of such transfer or redemption.
I / we further undertake to administer and utilize the share of each beneficiary or heir only in accordance with the law.
By virtue of the foregoing it is requested that the securities be ☐ **Transferred** and/or ☐ **Redeemed** in favour of the following:

Enter the exact names that are to appear on the NEW bonds/plans or cheque payment (continue on next line if required)

☐ add ***"and Survivor"***

Preferred Language of Communication ◯ English ◯ French

Social Insurance Number (required by income tax legislation) | Date of birth (yyyy/mm/dd) | Series | $ par value

Care of (if applicable) | Address

City | Prov | Postal code | Country | Home phone (including area code) | Work phone (including area code)

*If more than one beneficiary/heir, please complete and attach a separate sheet that includes the fields seen above. Please initial all attachments.*

All debts of the estate have been or will be fully paid; I / we hereby undertake to be responsible for the same to the extent of the amount of the above mentioned securities.
I / we give all right, title and interest in the securities described above absolutely and the Bank of Canada is hereby authorized to make such entries in the books of registration as are required to give effect to such transfer/redemption.
I / we make this solemn declaration conscientiously believing it to be true and knowing that it is of the same force and effect as if made under oath and by virtue of the Canada Evidence Act.

Declared before me at ________ City on ________ Date (yyyy/mm/dd)

**FINANCIAL INSTITUTION**

*Place the Financial Institution Signature Guaranteed Stamp or Medallion Guaranteed Stamp in this area*

*Signature of all the authorized representative(s)* ***must be guaranteed*** *by either:*

*A Canadian Financial Institution acceptable to the Bank of Canada or by a member of the Medallion guarantee program.*

***OR***

*Witnessed by a Notary Public, properly identified with the Notary Stamp and Signature of the Notary present.*

**NOTARY PUBLIC**

*Place the notarial stamp or seal in this area*

Signature of a Notary Public properly identified above

***Note: The "endorsement guaranteed stamp" is NOT acceptable.***

Signature of legal estate representative | Signature of legal estate representative | Signature of legal estate representative

***Note: Any alterations should be initialed, by the estate representative(s) before the declaration is signed.***

Once fully completed, please mail the form, the legal documents and the **unsigned physical certificate bonds** (if applicable) to Canada Savings Bonds, Transfer and Exchange, PO BOX 2770, STN D, Ottawa, ON, K1P 1J7.

For inquiries, contact us by phone at 1 800 575-5151 or at 1 888 646-2626 for Financial Institution, Monday to Friday from 8 a.m. to 8 p.m. ET. We can also be contacted by TTY (teletypewriter only) at 1 800 354-2222.
Please visit us online at www.csb.gc.ca.

The personal information provided on this form is protected under the provisions of the **PRIVACY ACT** and will be used solely for the purpose for which it was collected.

# Canada Savings Bonds — Quebec Estate Transfer Form and Guidelines (Form 534)

Canada Savings Bonds
the way to save. guaranteed.

Print Form

Quebec Estate Transfer Form (534) and Guidelines

QETRF-07-11

GUIDELINES TO HELP YOU COMPLETE THE FORM

IMPORTANT INFORMATION

✓ Form QETRF is used for **Quebec Estates** only. For **all other provinces**, please refer to Estate Transfer Form (2351) ETRF.

✓ The form must be completed in full in order to be processed. This includes the signatures of all authorized representatives as well as the estate legatees, heirs, co-legatees and co-heirs if applicable.

✓ **For the protection of the estate, incomplete forms, or forms with incorrect information, or incorrect documentation will be rejected and will result in the delay of your request.**

✓ Requests for cheque payments payable to a law firm **"in trust"** will be rejected.

✓ If the transaction involves **physical certificate bonds,** the **unsigned physical certificates** in question must be sent along with the completed form.

✓ Where a deceased co-owner is a resident of Quebec, the words ***"and Survivor"*** will not be legally recognized. Therefore, the proceeds from bonds/plans registered to a deceased Quebec resident will be distributed according to the deceased's Will, regardless of whether the ***"and Survivor"*** designation appears on the registration.

✓ **Bond series issued on or after November 1, 2008 (i.e., CSB S114 and higher, as well as CPB P064 and higher) are not eligible to be transferred in the name of the estate.**

✓ Any alterations made on the form must be initialed by all authorized representatives before the final declaration is signed.

✓ Only the **ORIGINAL/AUTHENTIC** documents are acceptable. They will be returned by Registered Mail after completion of the transaction. **Photocopies or faxes will not be accepted.**

✓ Any difference in name between Government of Canada Retail Debt Instruments (bonds/plans) and legal documents should be addressed by a letter of guarantee from a financial institution or a lawyer or notary public on their letterhead stating e.g., John Doe, John H Doe and John Harry Doe are one and the same person.

✓ Please note that Government of Canada Retail Debt Instruments are also referred to as bonds, plans and securities.

✓ If the surviving spouse wishes to transfer into the Canada RSP/RIF, it must be into an existing Canada RSP/RIF plan.



Canadä

Canada Savings Bonds
the way to save. guaranteed.

Print Form

Quebec Estate Transfer Form (534) and Guidelines

QETRF-07-11

DOCUMENTS REQUIRED TO TRANSFER OR REDEEM BONDS/PLANS (Government of Canada Retail Debt Instruments)

**Situation # 1 - Died with a Notarial Will**

| Required Document | Specific Instructions |
|---|---|
| An **Authentic** copy of the Notarial Will signed and sealed by the notary who executed it and registered it or the notary's cessionary.<br>**Note: The authentic document will be returned by registered mail.**<br><br>**and**<br><br>Proof of Death<br>(see page 3)<br><br>**and**<br><br>Form QETRF | On the QETRF form complete Sections A, B, D and F.<br><br>All co-legatee/co-heir(s) must sign in the consent area of Section D and have their signature witnessed.<br><br>The legatee/heir's name, address and social insurance number (required by income tax legislation) must be noted in Section F.<br><br>The form must be dated and signed by the assigned estate representative(s) and must be witnessed by a Notary Public or a Commissioner for Oaths properly identified with stamp/seal and signature present.<br><br>**Notes:**<br><br>**When the value of the transaction is higher than $20,000 the form must be witnessed by a Notary.**<br><br>**If the Will contains a survivorship clause, then this must be respected (e.g., 30 day clause; therefore, the form can only be signed 30 days after the date of death.)** |

**OR**

**Situation # 2 - Letters Probate or Court Judgement**

| Required Document | Specific Instructions |
|---|---|
| The **ORIGINAL** registered court document or a court-certified true copy of the letters probate with the Will annexed.<br>**Note: The original document will be returned by registered mail.**<br><br>**and**<br><br>Form QETRF | On the QETRF form complete Sections A, B, D and F.<br><br>All co-legatee/co-heir(s) must sign in the consent area of Section D and have their signature witnessed.<br><br>The legatee/heir's name, address and social insurance number (required by income tax legislation) must be noted in Section F.<br><br>The form must be dated and signed by the assigned estate representative(s) and must be witnessed by a Notary Public or a Commissioner for Oaths properly identified with stamp/seal and signature present.<br><br>**Notes:**<br><br>**When the value of the transaction is higher than $20,000 the form must be witnessed by a Notary.**<br><br>**If the Will contains a survivorship clause, then this must be respected (e.g., 30 day clause; therefore, the form can only be signed 30 days after the date of death.)** |

Page 2 of 4 (guidelines)

Canada

Canada Savings Bonds
the way to save. guaranteed.

Print Form

Quebec Estate Transfer Form (534) and Guidelines

QETRF-07-11

**OR**

**Situation # 3 - Testate - Died with a marriage contract**

| Required Document | Specific Instructions |
|---|---|
| The **ORIGINAL** Marriage Contract containing a testamentary clause.<br>**Note: The original document will be returned by registered mail.**<br><br>**and**<br><br>Proof of Death (see page 3)<br><br>**and**<br><br>Form QETRF | On the QETRF form complete Sections A, B, C and F.<br><br>The legatee/heir's name, address and social insurance number (required by income tax legislation) must be noted in Section F.<br><br>The form must be dated and signed by the assigned estate representative(s) and must be witnessed by a Notary Public or a Commissioner for Oaths properly identified with stamp/seal and signature present.<br><br>**Note:**<br><br>**When the value of the transaction is higher than $20,000 the form must be witnessed by a Notary.** |

**OR**

**Situation # 4 - Intestate - Died without a Will or Marriage Contract**

| Required Document | Specific Instructions |
|---|---|
| Proof of Death (see page 3)<br><br>**and**<br><br>Form QETRF | On the QETRF form complete Sections A, B, E and F.<br><br>All co-legatee/co-heir(s) must sign in the consent area of Section E and have their signature witnessed.<br><br>The legatee/heir's name, address and social insurance number (required by income tax legislation) must be noted in Section F.<br><br>The form must be dated and signed by the assigned estate representative(s) and must be witnessed by a Notary Public or a Commissioner for Oaths properly identified with stamp/seal and signature present.<br><br>**Note:**<br><br>**When the value of the transaction is higher than $20,000 the form must be witnessed by a Notary.** |

**Proof of Death: One of the following is acceptable to the Bank of Canada.**

- ✓ An **ORIGINAL** Death Certificate issued by a Directeur de l'état civil or a Notarial Certified copy with either a Notary's signature and seal of office or certified by a Canadian Financial Institution;
- ✓ An **ORIGINAL** certificate of finding issued by a coroner properly identified or a Notarial certified copy with the Notary's signature and stamp/seal of office or certified by a Canadian Financial Institution;
- ✓ An **ORIGINAL** Death Certificate issued by a church under seal and minister of religion`s signature or a Notarial certified copy with the Notary's signature and stamp/seal of office or certified by a Canadian Financial Institution;
- ✓ An **ORIGINAL** Death Certificate from an undertaking establishment issued under corporate seal and **ORIGINAL** signature or a Notarial certified copy with the Notary's signature and seal of office or certified by a Canadian Financial Institution.

Page 3 of 4 (guidelines)

Canadä

Canada Savings Bonds
the way to save. guaranteed.

Print Form

Quebec Estate Transfer Form (534) and Guidelines

QETRF-07-11

FOR INQUIRIES

Contact us, Monday to Friday from 8 a.m. to 8 p.m. ET.

Phone:
1 800 575-5151
1 888 646-2626 for Financial Institution
1 800 354-2222 for TTY (teletypewriter only)

Online:
www.csb.gc.ca

HOW TO SUBMIT YOUR REQUEST

Once fully completed, please mail the form along with the **unsigned physical certificate bond(s)** (if applicable) and the legal documents to:

Canada Savings Bonds
Transfer & Exchange
PO BOX 2770, STN D
Ottawa, ON, K1P 1J7

Page 4 of 4 (guidelines)

Canada

Canada Savings Bonds
the way to save. guaranteed.

Print Form

Quebec Estate Transfer Form (534) and Guidelines

QETRF-07-11

Protected B (when completed)

**SPECIFIC INSTRUCTIONS**

This form is used for Quebec Estates only.
Please print clearly or type the required information into the form fields. Please be sure to complete all required Sections to avoid delays in processing your request. Sign page 3 and mail your request to the destination indicated on page 3.

**SECTION A - DETAILS REGARDING THE DECEASED AND THEIR REPRESENTATIVES**

Full name(s) of the deceased *(list all variations seen within the legal documents. e.g. death certificate, Last Will and Testament, Codicil(s) or Marriage Contract)*

Social Insurance Number | Date of death (yyyy/mm/dd) | Last address for the deceased

Civil Status
- ( ) Single
- ( ) Married
- ( ) Other, please specify (e.g., divorced, widow)

City | Prov | Postal Code | Country

I / We

Insert full name of all authorized representatives for the deceased
*(e.g. spouse, legal estate representative(s), liquidator(s)/executor(s), court appointed administrator(s)/executor(s))*

of

Care of Address (for estate purposes) | City | Prov | Postal Code | Country

do solemnly declare as follows, I am / we are the
- ( ) Liquidator(s)/ Executor(s)
- ( ) Other, please specify (e.g., spouse)

of the deceased named above.

**SECTION B - BOND(S)/PLAN(S) DETAILS**

The following is a list of all the Government of Canada securities (bonds/plans) which were registered to the deceased at the time of death.

*If space is insufficient, please complete and attach a separate sheet that includes the fields seen below. Please initial all attached sheets.*

| **Canada Savings Bonds / Canada Premium Bonds** | Name(s) appearing on the bond(s) | | Registration Account # or Certificate Bond Serial #(s) | | $ par value |
|---|---|---|---|---|---|
| | | **AND** | | **AND** | |
| | | **AND** | | **AND** | |

- *The Registration Account # is 10 digits and can be found on a statement or T5.*
- *The Bond Serial # is located on the top center of the certificate (e.g., CS101F1234567J).*

☐ I have attached the physical unsigned certificates to this request.

Total par value $

**AND/OR**

**Payroll Savings Program**

Name(s) appearing on the Plan | **AND** | Plan # (10 digits): 2

- *The Plan # can be found on an annual statement or T5.*

**AND/OR**

**Canada RSP / Canada RIF**

Name appearing on the Plan | **AND** | Plan # (up to 11 digits)

- *The **Canada RSP** plan number is located on the semi-annual statements.*
- *The **Canada RIF** plan number is located on the quarterly statements.*

Page 1 of 3 (form)

Canadä

Canada Savings Bonds
the way to save. guaranteed.

Print Form

Quebec Estate Transfer Form (534) and Guidelines

QETRF-07-11

Protected B (when completed)

## SECTION C - MARRIAGE CONTRACT

☐ Select this box and complete the section below only if the following situation applies;

The deceased left a Marriage Contract dated ______ (yyyy/mm/dd) which contains no unrevoked contractual disposition affecting the transaction.

The Marriage Contract and a Proof of Death (as per the guidelines) have been submitted with this request.

## SECTION D - TESTATE (DIED WITH A WILL OR LETTERS PROBATE)

☐ Select this box and complete the section below only if the following situation applies;

The deceased left a Notarial Will dated ______ (yyyy/mm/dd) which was neither amended nor revoked.

A Notarial Will and Proof of Death or Letters probate with the Will annexed (as per the guidelines) has been submitted with this request.

The deceased's legatees are as follows and hereby consent to the transfer or redemption of the securities as stated in Section F:

| Name of the legatee | | Name of the legatee | |
|---|---|---|---|
| Relationship to deceased | Age (if under 21) | Relationship to deceased | Age (if under 21) |
| Signature of the legatee | WITNESS must sign here | Signature of the legatee | WITNESS must sign here |

*If space is insufficient, please complete and attach a separate sheet that includes the fields seen above. Please initial all attached sheets.*

## SECTION E - INTESTATE (DIED WITHOUT A WILL)

☐ Select this box and complete the section below only if the following situation applies;

The deceased died intestate (without leaving a Notarial Will).
Attached is a Proof of Death that is acceptable to the Bank of Canada.
The sole heirs (heirs entitled to inherit) are as follows and hereby consent to the transfer or redemption of the securities as stated in Section F:

| Name of co-heir or co-legatee | Relationship to the deceased | Age (if under 21) | Signature of co-heir or co-legatee | WITNESS must sign here |
|---|---|---|---|---|
| | | | | |
| Name of co-heir or co-legatee | Relationship to the deceased | Age (if under 21) | Signature of co-heir or co-legatee | WITNESS must sign here |
| | | | | |
| Name of co-heir or co-legatee | Relationship to the deceased | Age (if under 21) | Signature of co-heir or co-legatee | WITNESS must sign here |

*All signatures must be witnessed and the signatories must be older than 21 years of age, qualified and duly authorized (submit tutorship or curatorship documents if necessary). If space is insufficient, please complete and attach a separate sheet that includes the fields seen above. Please initial all attached sheets.*

Page 2 of 3 (form)

Canadä

Canada Savings Bonds
the way to save. guaranteed.

Print Form

Quebec Estate Transfer Form (534) and Guidelines

QETRF-07-11

Protected B (when completed)

**SECTION F - FINAL DECLARATION**

In consideration of the transfer or redemption of the securities as requested, I / we undertake to indemnify and save harmless the Bank of Canada against any claim that should at any time arise as a result of such transfer or redemption.
I / we further undertake to administer and utilize the share of each legatee or heir only in accordance with the law.
By virtue of the foregoing it is requested that the securities be ( ) **Transferred** or ( ) **Redeemed** in favour of the following:

Enter the exact names that are to appear on the NEW bonds/plans or cheque payment (continue on next line if required)

[ ] add ***"and Survivor"***

Preferred Language of Communication ( ) English ( ) French

Social Insurance Number (required by income tax legislation) | Date of birth (yyyy/mm/dd) | Series | $ par value

Care of (if applicable) | Address

City | Prov | Postal code | Country | Home phone (including area code) | Work phone (including area code)

*If more than one legatee/heir, please complete and attach a separate sheet that includes the fields seen above. Please initial all attachments.*

All debts of the estate have been or will be fully paid; I / we hereby undertake to be responsible for the same to the extent of the amount of the above mentioned securities.
I / we give all right, title and interest in the securities described above absolutely and the Bank of Canada is hereby authorized to make such entries in the books of registration as are required to give effect to such transfer/redemption.
I / we make this solemn declaration conscientiously believing it to be true and knowing that it is of the same force and effects as if made under oath and by virtue of the Canada Evidence Act.

Declared before me at ____________ on ____________
City | Date (yyyy/mm/dd)

Signature of legal estate representative

Signature of legal estate representative

Signature of legal estate representative

*Signature of all the authorized representative(s)* ***must be witnessed*** *by a Notary Public or a commissioner for oaths, properly identified with the Notary stamp/seal and signature of the Notary present.*

*If the value is over $20,000 of securities, the form must be signed before a Notary Public. Any alterations should be initialed, by the estate representative(s) before the declaration is signed.*

NOTARY PUBLIC OR COMMISSIONER FOR OATHS

Place the stamp or seal in this area

Signature of a Notary Public or Commissioner for Oaths properly identified above

Once fully completed, please mail the form, the legal documents and the **unsigned physical certificate bonds** (if applicable) to Canada Savings Bonds, Transfer and Exchange, PO BOX 2770, STN D, Ottawa, ON K1P 1J7.

For inquiries, contact us at 1 800 575-5151 or at 1 888 646-2626 for Financial Institution, Monday to Friday from 8 a.m. to 8 p.m. ET. We can also be contacted by TTY (teletypewriter only) at 1 800-354-2222.

Please visit us online at www.csb.gc.ca.

The personal information provided on this form is protected under the provisions of the **PRIVACY ACT** and will be used solely for the purpose for which it was collected.

Page 3 of 3 (form)

Canada

## Sample Letter To Transfer Shares

Dear Sir or Madam:

Re: The Estate of ____________________ (the "Estate")

I am the personal representative [or liquidator in Quebec] of the Estate of ____________________ (the "deceased") who died on the _______ day of ______________, 20__.

I request that you transfer _______ (class) shares of ____________ (company) from the name of the deceased into the name of ________________________ (beneficiary's name) of the Estate.

Please find enclosed the following documents:

- Notarial copy of letters probate or letters of administration (certificate of appointment of estate trustee with/without a will in Ontario, or a true copy of the will or a declaration of heirship for intestate estate in Quebec, if required);
- Power of attorney;
- Declaration of transmission; and
- Original share certificate.

The new certificate should be forwarded to ____________________.

Sincerely,

Eddie Executor

## Sample Power of Attorney for Stocks

FOR VALUE RECEIVED the undersigned hereby sells, assigns and transfers unto

______________________________________________________

(Name of Transferee)

______________________________________________________

(Address)

______________________ shares of the ______________________

__________________________________________ Capital Stock of

______________________________________________________

standing in the name of the undersigned on the books of the said corporation represented by certificate(s) no.(s) __________________ and hereby irrevocably constitutes and appoints __________________ the attorney of the undersigned to transfer the said stock on the books of the said corporation with full power of substitution in the premises.

DATED ______ day of ____________, 20__.

In the presence of ________________________

NOTE: The signature to this assignment must correspond with the name as written upon the face of the certificate(s) in every particular without alteration or enlargement or any change whatever. The signature of the person executing this power must be guaranteed by a bank or trust company or a member that participates in one of the three medallion signature guarantee programs: STAMP (Securities Transfer Agents Medallion Program), SEMP (Stock Exchanges Medallion Program) or MSP (New York Stock Exchange Medallion Signature Program).

## Sample Power of Attorney for Bonds

FOR VALUE RECEIVED the undersigned hereby sells, assigns and transfers unto

________________________________________________________

(Name of Transferee)

________________________________________________________

(Address)

________________________________________________________

________________________________________________________

standing in the name of the undersigned on the books of the said corporation represented by certificate(s) no.(s) ______________ and hereby irrevocably constitutes and appoints __________________ the attorney of the undersigned to transfer the said bonds on the books of the said corporation with full power of substitution in the premises.

DATED _______ day of ______________, 20__.

In the presence of ______________________________

NOTE: The signature to this assignment must correspond with the name as written upon the face of the certificate(s) in every particular without alteration or enlargement or any change whatever. The signature of the person executing this power must be guaranteed by a bank or trust company or a member that participates in one of the three medallion signature guarantee programs: STAMP (Securities Transfer Agents Medallion Program), SEMP (Stock Exchanges Medallion Program) or MSP (New York Stock Exchange Medallion Signature Program).

## Sample Letter to Deceased's Employer

[date]
[return address]

Attention: Human Resources
[employer's address]

Dear Sir or Madam:

Re: The Estate of ____________________ (the "Estate")

I am the personal representative [or liquidator in Quebec] of the Estate of ____________________, (the "deceased") who died on the _______ day of _______________, 20__. The deceased was an employee of your organization and I would request that you inform me as to whether any benefits are owing as a result of the deceased's employment with your organization. Please provide me with the following information:

1. Death benefits owing;
2. Salaries or commissions owing;
3. Benefits available under a group pension plan;
4. Deferred profit sharing plan or retiring allowance; and
5. Any other benefit information relating to the deceased's employment.

Thank you for your assistance in this matter. If you require further information, please contact the undersigned at (area code) 123-4567.

Your very truly,

Eddie Executor

## Fact Sheet on Inherited Firearms[2]

If you inherit firearms, or if you are the executor of an estate with firearms, here is some information you need to know about the *Firearms Act*.

### If You Are the Heir

#### *Licence Requirements*

To be able to acquire a firearm by any means, including as an inheritance, you must be at least 18 years old and hold a valid Possession and Acquisition Licence (PAL). While a Possession-Only Licence allows you to keep firearms you have lawfully owned since December 1, 1998, it does not allow you to acquire more firearms, so if you have a POL, you will need to replace it with a PAL.

A PAL is only valid for the class or classes of firearms listed on it. The three classes of firearms are:

- non-restricted: most common rifles and shotguns;
- restricted: only allowed for approved purposes such as target shooting or as part of a collection; and
- prohibited: see below for information on grandfathering requirements.

To apply for a PAL or to upgrade your privileges for different classes of firearms, submit form CAFC 921. To be eligible for this licence, you must have met specific safety-training requirements.

#### *Grandfathering Requirements for Prohibited Firearms*

As a general rule, to be able to acquire a prohibited firearm, you need "grandfathering privileges" for that particular category of prohibited firearm. In other words, you must have continuously held a valid registration certificate for a firearm in that category since December 1, 1998. A registration certificate is valid only if you already have a valid licence authorizing you to possess that category of firearm.

**Exception:** You do not need grandfathering privileges to inherit a registered prohibited handgun that discharges .25 or .32 calibre ammunition or that has a barrel length of 105 mm or less if:

- the handgun was manufactured before 1946, **and**
- you are the spouse, brother, sister, child or grandchild of the registered owner; **and**
- the handgun is used for a permitted purpose such as target shooting or as part of a collection.

[2] This Fact Sheet is available on the Royal Canadian Mounted Police website at www.rcmp-grc.gc.ca/cfp-pcaf/fs-fd/will-testament-eng.htm.

### *Registering the Firearms*

The firearm will need to be registered to you as part of the transfer process that must take place when a firearm changes ownership. More information can be found in the section for executors.

You will receive a new registration certificate in the mail for each firearm transferred to you.

### *Fees*

The initial fee for a PAL is $60 for non-restricted firearms only, or $80 for any combination of non-restricted, restricted and prohibited firearms, except in the following cases:

- If you are renewing a PAL or changing your licence privileges, the fee is waived until **May 16, 2011**.
- You may not be required to pay a fee for a PAL if it would only be valid for non-restricted firearms and you need a firearm to hunt or trap in order to sustain yourself or your family.

There are no fees to register or transfer a firearm or to obtain an Authorization to Transport.

## If You Are the Executor

While the *Firearms Act* sets out how firearms may be transferred and who may have them, provincial estate laws determine the role of the executor.

Estate laws may vary from province to province. However, as a common principle of law, an executor of an estate generally has the same rights as the deceased had to possess firearms while the estate is being settled. Therefore, even if you are not personally licensed to possess firearms, you can generally possess a firearm left in an estate for a reasonable amount of time while the estate is being settled.

If a court has prohibited you from possessing firearms, you cannot take possession of firearms left in an estate, but you can still act as the executor in transferring the firearms to someone who can lawfully acquire them.

If the owner did not have a valid licence and registration certificate for the firearm, he or she was in illegal possession of the firearm, which puts you at risk of penalties for possessing the firearm unless you act quickly to comply with the law — for example, by transferring it to a properly licensed individual, deactivating the firearm or by turning it in to a police or firearms officer for disposal.

If you are not sure if the deceased had a licence or registration certificate, call 1 800 731-4000.

To be able to obtain information on a firearm that is registered to someone else, or to transfer the firearm to someone else, you need to be able to provide evidence that you are in a lawful position to do so.

To confirm that the registered owner is deceased, you will need to provide a copy of:

- the death certificate; or
- letters of probate; or
- a document from a police department or coroner on letterhead.

To provide proof that you are the executor, you are required to complete form RCMP 6016 "Declaration of Authority to Act on Behalf of an Estate".

### *Transferring Ownership of a Firearm*

When you transfer the firearm to the new owner, there is a specific process you must go through to ensure that the new owner is eligible to have the firearm, the Registrar is notified of the transfer and the firearm is registered to the new owner.

To initiate the transfer of a registered firearm, call 1 800 731-4000 and either complete the entire transfer process over the phone or request a paper application (form CAFC 681 for restricted and prohibited firearms or form CAFC 682 for non-restricted firearms). Both you and the new owner will need to be involved in the transfer process.

### *Firearm Verification*

A firearm must be verified by an approved verifier before it is transferred to a new owner unless:

- the firearm has already been verified; and
- the description of the firearm has not changed; and
- the Registrar is satisfied that the firearm does not need to be re-verified.

Restricted and prohibited firearms that have previously been registered in Canada are already deemed to be verified. They do not need to be verified again unless the Registrar requests another verification to confirm their description or classification. Some non-restricted firearms might not be verified yet. Call 1 800 731-4000 for help to verify a firearm.

### *Ineligible Heirs or Unwanted Firearms*

If there is no eligible heir, or if the heir does not want an inherited firearm, the estate may:

- sell or give the firearm to any individual, museum or business with a licence to acquire that particular type of firearms through the official transfer process; or
- export it to a country that allows it: call the Department of Foreign Affairs and International Trade at 1 800 267-8376 for information on requirements for an export permit; or
- have the firearm permanently deactivated so that it no longer meets the definition of a firearm, and therefore, is exempted from the requirements of the *Firearms Act*; or
- turn the firearm in to a police officer or firearms officer for disposal: Call first.

## Other Requirements

If the deceased owner had a valid firearms licence, please return it, along with a copy of their death certificate, to the following address:

Central Processing Site
PO Box 1200
Miramichi, New Brunswick E1N 5Z3

### *Transporting and Storing Firearms*

All firearms must be unloaded and transported or stored in a safe and secure manner to deter loss, theft and accidents, as set out in the *Storage, Display, Transportation and Handling of Firearms by Individuals Regulations.*

If you ship the firearms, you have two options:

- you may ship non-restricted firearms, restricted firearms and prohibited handguns to another location within Canada, using the most secure method offered by Canada Post that requires a signature upon delivery; or
- you may ship any class of firearm by licensed carrier to a location inside or outside Canada. This is the only option for shipping prohibited firearms other than prohibited handguns.

### *Information*

For more information, contact the CFP.

This fact sheet is intended to provide general information only. For legal references, please refer to the *Firearms Act* and its Regulations. Provincial, territorial and municipal laws, regulations and policies may also apply.

## Sample Advertisement for Creditors (Provinces Other Than Quebec)

Claims against the Estate of JIM DANDY, late of the City of Toronto, who died on March 8, 2011, must be filed with the undersigned personal representative on or before [date], after which date the estate will be distributed, having regard only to the claims of which the personal representative has had notice.

Dated at Toronto this ____ day of _________ 20___.

Trust Me Trust Company
Newton Ave
Oakville, Ontario
N51 2T3

## Sample Advertisement for Creditors (Quebec)

### Notice of Closure of Inventory

Notice is hereby given that [name of deceased] (the "deceased"), domiciled at _________ in his lifetime, died at _________ on _________ . An inventory of the deceased's property has been made in accordance with the law and can be consulted by interested parties at [place where the inventory can be consulted].

Given on this _____ day of _________ 20___.

[name of liquidator or successor or heir]

Attention of [name of trust officer]

## Sample Release of Executor/Liquidator

I, ______________________ of the City of ______________________
in the Municipality of ______________, [occupation]

DO HEREBY ACKNOWLEDGE that I have this day had and received of and from __________, of the City of ____________, in the Regional Municipality of ____________, executor [or liquidator in Quebec] of the last Will and Testament of ______________ late of the ______________ of in the Municipality of ____________, deceased, in full satisfaction and payment of such sum or sums of money, legacies and bequests as are given and bequeathed to me under the last Will and Testament aforesaid and all interest accrued thereon.

AND THEREFORE I, ____________ do release, quit claim and forever discharge the said ____________ and, as applicable, [his/her/its] estate, heirs, estate trustees, executors, administrators, other personal representatives, successors and assigns of and from any and all actions, claims, accounts and demands whatsoever which I now have or ever had against the said ____________ in respect of or in connection with the estate of the deceased.

In Witness Whereof I have hereunto set my hand and seal this _______ day of ______________, 20_____.

Signed, sealed and delivered
in the presence of:

[affix seal]
______________________
[beneficiary signature]

______________________

[witness signature]

______________________

[print witness name]

______________________

[full address of witness]

# Income Tax Forms and Guides

# What To Do Following a Death (Information Sheet RC4111)

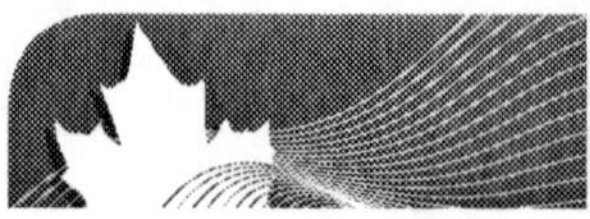

## Canada Revenue Agency
## What to do following a death

Coping with the death of a loved one is difficult. We at the Canada Revenue Agency (CRA) recognize that you are going through a very difficult time. With this in mind, we hope we can help you by answering some questions you may have.

This information sheet contains basic information that the family and legal representative should know to start settling the affairs of the deceased person. For more information, go to **www.cra.gc.ca/deceased** or see Guide T4011, *Preparing Returns for Deceased Persons*, and T4013, *T3 Trust Guide*.

### What should you do first?

You should provide us with the deceased's date of death as soon as possible. You can call us at **1-800-959-8281**, or complete the form on the back of this information sheet and send it to your tax services office or tax centre.

Arrangements must be made to stop payments and, if applicable, transfer them to a survivor, if **any** of the following situations apply:

- The deceased was receiving the goods and services tax/harmonized sales tax (GST/HST) credit.
- The deceased was receiving the working income tax benefit (WITB) advance payments.
- The deceased was receiving Canada Child Tax Benefit (CCTB) payments and/or Universal Child Care Benefit (UCCB) payments for a child.
- The deceased was a child for whom CCTB and/or UCCB and/or GST/HST credit payments are paid.

Service Canada should also be advised of the deceased's date of death. For more information, or to get the address of the Service Canada Centre nearest you, call **1-800-622-6232**.

#### Was the deceased paying tax by instalments?

If the deceased person was paying tax by instalments, **no** further instalment payments have to be made after his or her death. The only instalments that have to be paid are those that were due before the date of death, but not paid.

### What do you do with the GST/HST credit?

Generally, GST/HST credit payments are issued on the fifth day of the month in July, October, January, and April. If the deceased was receiving GST/HST credit payments, we may still send out a payment after the date of death because we are not aware of the death. If this happens, return the payment to us.

> **Note**
> We administer provincial programs that are related to the GST/HST credit. If the deceased was receiving payments under one of these programs, you do not have to take any further action. We will use the information provided for the GST/HST credit payments to adjust the applicable credit.

#### What if the deceased was single, separated, divorced, or widowed and received the GST/HST credit?

If the recipient died **before** the scheduled month in which we issue the credit, we cannot make any more payments in that person's name or to that person's estate.

If the recipient died **during or after** the scheduled month in which we issue the credit and the payment has not been cashed, return it to us so that we can send the payment to the person's estate.

If the deceased was getting a credit for a child, the child's new caregiver should contact us to request GST/HST credit payments for that child.

RC4111(E) Rev. 10

La version française de cette publication est intitulée *Agence du revenu du Canada – Quoi faire suivant un décès.*

Canada Revenue Agency Agence du revenu du Canada

### What if the deceased's GST/HST credit is for the deceased and his or her spouse or common-law partner?

If the deceased had a spouse or common-law partner, that person may be eligible to receive the GST/HST credit payments based on his or her net income alone. If the deceased's GST/HST credit included a claim for that spouse or common-law partner, he or she should:

- contact us at **1-800-959-1953**, and ask to receive the GST/HST credit payment for the remainder of the year for himself or herself and any children, if applicable; and
- file an *Income Tax and Benefit Return* for the applicable previous year if he or she has not already done so.

### What if the surviving spouse's or common-law partner's GST/HST credit includes a claim for the deceased?

If the surviving spouse's or common-law partner's GST/HST credit included an amount for the deceased, the payments will be recalculated based on his or her net income alone and will only include a claim for himself or herself and any children, if applicable.

### What if the deceased is an eligible child?

Entitlement to GST/HST credit payments for a deceased child stops the quarter after the child's date of death. You should notify us of the date of death so that we can update our records.

## What do you do with the Canada Child Tax Benefit (CCTB) and/or Universal Child Care Benefit (UCCB) payments?

### What if the deceased was receiving the CCTB and/or UCCB?

Contact us and let us know the date of death. If the deceased person was receiving CCTB and/or UCCB payments for a child, and the surviving spouse or common-law partner is the child's parent, we will usually transfer the CCTB and/or UCCB payments to that person.

If anyone else, other than the parent, is now primarily responsible for the child, that person will have to complete and submit Form RC66, *Canada Child Benefits Application*, to request benefit payments for the child.

Note
If the deceased was receiving payments under provincial or territorial child benefit and credit programs administered by the CRA, there is no need to apply separately to qualify. We will use the information from the application to determine the new caregiver's eligibility for these programs.

### What if the deceased's spouse or common-law partner receives the CCTB and/or UCCB?

If you are the surviving spouse or common-law partner and you receive CCTB and/or UCCB payments for a child, you can request that we recalculate the payments excluding the deceased person's net income. Provide the required information on the form on the back of this information sheet to make the request and send it to your tax services office or tax centre.

### What if the deceased is an eligible child?

Your entitlement to CCTB and UCCB payments stops the month after the child's date of death. You should notify us of the date of death so that we can update our records.

## Are you the legal representative?

You are the legal representative of a deceased person if:

- you are named as the executor in the will;
- you are appointed as the administrator of the estate by a court; or
- you are the liquidator for an estate in Quebec.

As the legal representative, your responsibilities under the *Income Tax Act* include:

- filing all required returns for the deceased;
- making sure all taxes owing are paid;
- letting the beneficiaries know which, if any, of the amounts they receive from the estate are taxable; and
- if necessary, obtaining a clearance certificate to certify that all amounts owing to the CRA are paid.

If you are the legal representative, you may need information from the deceased person's tax records. Before we can give you this information, we will need the following:

- a copy of the deceased's death certificate;
- the deceased's social insurance number; and
- a complete copy of the will or other legal document such as a grant of probate or letters of administration showing that you are the legal representative.

You should also give us your address so that we can reply directly to you. Send this information to your tax services office or tax centre.

**Note**
As the legal representative, you may wish to appoint an authorized representative to deal with the CRA for tax matters on your behalf. You may do so by completing Form T1013, *Authorizing or Cancelling a Representative*.

## What is the due date for the final tax return and any balance owing?

The deceased's final return and any balance owing are due on or before the following dates:

| Period when death occurred | Due date |
|---|---|
| January 1 to October 31 | April 30 of the following year |
| November 1 to December 31 | Six months after the date of death |

**Note**
The due date for filing the T1 return of a surviving spouse or common-law partner who was living with the deceased is the same as the due date for filing the deceased's final return indicated in the chart above. Any balance owing on the surviving spouse's or common-law partner's return still has to be paid on or before April 30 of the following year to avoid interest charges.

If the deceased or the deceased's spouse or common-law partner was carrying on a business during the year when the death occurred, the following filing due dates apply:

| Period when death occurred | Filing due date |
|---|---|
| January 1 to October 31 | June 15 of the following year, although any balance owing is still due on April 30 |
| November 1 to December 15 | June 15 of the following year, although any balance owing is due six months after the date of death |
| December 16 to December 31 | Six months after the date of death (including any balance owing) |

If you file the final return late and there is a balance owing, we will charge a late-filing penalty. If you do not pay the balance owing from the final return in full by the balance due date (whether April 30 of the following year or six months after death of the individual, as applicable), we will charge interest on the unpaid amount. The interest will start to accumulate from the day after the balance due date.

### Previous year return

If a person dies after December 31, but on or before the filing due date for his or her return (usually April 30), and that person had not yet filed that return, the due date for filing it, as well as for paying the balance owing, is six months after the date of death. The filing due dates for previous year returns that are already due but which the deceased had not yet filed, remain the same.

## How do you contact the CRA?

If you need help, call us at **1-800-959-8281**. To find more contact information go to **www.cra.gc.ca/contact**.

If you would like any of our publications, go to **www.cra.gc.ca/forms**, or call **1-800-959-2221**.

Canada Revenue Agency

Canada Revenue Agency | Agence du revenu du Canada

## Request for the Canada Revenue Agency to update records

**Complete the information below concerning the deceased.**

Name of deceased: ______________________________

Deceased's social insurance number: ______________________________

The deceased's date of birth: Year ________ Month ________ Day ________

The deceased's date of death: Year ________ Month ________ Day ________

Address: ______________________________

______________________________

**Complete the applicable information below concerning the surviving spouse or common-law partner**

☐ Please update the surviving spouse's or common-law partner's marital status and recalculate the CCTB and/or UCCB.

☐ Please update the surviving spouse's or common-law partner's marital status and recalculate the GST/HST credit.

☐ Please reassess the surviving spouse's or common-law partner's return to allow a claim for the GST/HST credit.

Name of surviving spouse or common-law partner: ______________________________

Surviving spouse's or common-law partner's social insurance number: ______________________________

Signature of surviving spouse or common-law partner: ________________ Date: ________________

Your name: ______________________ Your telephone number: ________________

Your address: ______________________________

Your relationship to the deceased*: ______________________________

*In addition to any personal relationship you may have had with the deceased, please specify whether you are the executor, administrator, or liquidator, or if you are acting in some other capacity.

*Privacy Act* Personal Information Bank number CRA PPU 040

## Preparing Returns for Deceased Persons 2010 (Guide T4011)

# Preparing Returns for Deceased Persons

# 2010

T4011(E) Rev. 10

Canada

## Before you start

### Is this guide for you?

Use this guide if you are the legal representative (see page 5) who has to file an *Income Tax and Benefit Return* for a deceased person. Use it together with the guide that came with the deceased person's return.

### Which return should you use?

You can use an *Income Tax and Benefit Return*. However, the deceased may have received a different return in the mail based on his or her situation last year. If the return covers the types of income you want to report and the deductions and credits you want to claim, you can use it instead of an *Income Tax and Benefit Return*. You cannot use a T1S-C, *Credit and Benefit Return*, to complete a return for a deceased person.

**Note**
If you cannot get a return for the year of death, use a blank one from a previous year. In the top right corner of page 1, write the year for which you are filing. We will assess the return based on the legislation in effect for the year of death.

## What's new for 2010?

**Rollover of registered retirement savings plan (RRSP) proceeds to a registered disability savings plan (RDSP)** – Under proposed changes, for deaths occurring after March 3, 2010, the existing RRSP rollover rules will be extended to allow a rollover of a deceased individual's RRSP proceeds to the RDSP of the deceased individual's financially dependent infirm child or grandchild. These proposed rules will also apply for amounts transferred to an RDSP from registered retirement income fund (RRIF) proceeds and certain lump-sum amounts paid from registered pension plans (RPP).

In addition, when the death of an RRSP annuitant occurs after 2007 and before 2011, special transitional rules will allow a contribution to be made to the RDSP of a financially dependent infirm child or grandchild of the annuitant that will provide a similar result to the proposed measures. It is important to note that in order to be eligible, the contribution to an RDSP can only be made **after June 30, 2011** and, when the death of the annuitant occurs after 2007 and before 2011, the contribution must be made **before January 1, 2012**.

For updated information on these proposed changes, go to **www.cra.gc.ca/rdsp**.

If you have a visual impairment, you can get our publications in braille, large print, or etext (CD or diskette), or MP3 by going to **www.cra.gc.ca/alternate** or by calling **1-800-959-2221**. You can also get your personalized correspondence in these formats by calling **1-800-959-8281**.

La version française de cette publication est intitulée *Déclarations de revenus de personnes décédées*

**www.cra.gc.ca**

## Table of contents

## Definitions

**Adjusted cost base (ACB)** – This is usually the cost of a property, plus any expenses to acquire it, such as commissions and legal fees.

The cost of a capital property is its actual or deemed cost, depending on the type of property and how you acquired it. It also includes capital expenditures, such as the cost of additions and improvements to the property. You cannot add current expenses, such as maintenance and repair costs, to the ACB of a property.

For more information on ACB, see Interpretation Bulletin IT-456, *Capital Property – Some Adjustments to Cost Base*, and its Special Release.

If the deceased filed Form T664 or T664 (Seniors), *Election to Report a Capital Gain on Property Owned at the End of February 22, 1994*, the ACB of the property may change. For more information, see Guide T4037, *Capital Gains*.

**Advantage** – See the definition of **Eligible amount of the gift** on this page.

**Annuitant** – Generally, an annuitant is the person for whom a retirement plan provides a retirement income. In certain circumstances, the surviving spouse or common-law partner may qualify as the annuitant when, because of the death, he or she becomes entitled to receive benefits out of the retirement plan.

**Annuity payment** – This is a fixed periodic payment that a person has the right to receive, either for life or for a specific number of years. These payments represent a partial recovery of financing and a return (interest) on the capital investment.

**Arm's length transaction** – This is a transaction between persons each of whom acts in his or her own self-interest. Related persons are not considered to deal with each other at arm's length. Related persons include individuals connected by a blood relationship, marriage or common-law partnership, or adoption (legal or in fact). Also, a corporation and a shareholder who controls the corporation are related.

Unrelated persons usually deal with each other at arm's length, although this might not be the case if, for example, one person is under the influence or control of the other.

For more information on arm's length, see Interpretation Bulletin IT-419, *Meaning of Arm's Length*.

**Capital cost allowance (CCA)** – In the year you buy a **depreciable property** (defined later on this page), such as a building, you cannot deduct the full cost. However, since this type of property wears out or becomes obsolete over time, you can deduct its capital cost over a period of several years. This deduction is called CCA. You cannot claim it for the fiscal period that ends on the date of death.

When we talk about CCA, a reference is often made to **class**. You usually group depreciable properties into classes. You have to base your CCA claim on the rate assigned to each class of property.

**Capital property** – This includes **depreciable property** and any property that, if sold, would result in a capital gain or a capital loss. You usually buy it for investment purposes or to earn income. Capital property does not include the trading assets of a business, such as inventory. Some common types of capital property include cottages, securities such as stocks, bonds, and units of a mutual fund trust, and land, buildings, and equipment used in a business or rental operation.

**Common-law partner** – This applies to a person who is **not your spouse**, with whom you are living in a conjugal relationship, and to whom at least **one** of the following situations applies. He or she:

a) has been living with you in a conjugal relationship for at least 12 continuous months;

b) is the parent of your child by birth or adoption; or

c) has custody and control of your child (or had custody and control immediately before the child turned 19 years of age) and your child is wholly dependent on that person for support.

An individual immediately becomes your common-law partner if you previously lived together in a conjugal relationship for at least 12 continuous months and you have resumed living together in such a relationship. **Under proposed changes**, this condition will no longer exist. The effect of this proposed change is that a person (other than a person described in b) or c) above) will be your common-law partner only after your current relationship with that person has lasted at least 12 continuous months. This proposed change will apply to 2001 and later years.

Reference to "12 continuous months" in this definition includes any period that you were separated for less than 90 days because of a breakdown in the relationship.

**Deemed disposition** – This expression is used when a person is considered to have disposed of a property, even though a sale did not take place.

**Deemed proceeds of disposition** – This is an expression used when a person is considered to have received an amount for the disposition of property, even though the person did not actually receive that amount.

**Depreciable property** – This is usually capital property used to earn income from a business or property. The capital cost can be written off as CCA over a number of years.

**Eligible amount of the gift** – Under proposed changes, this is generally the amount by which the **fair market value** (defined on page 5) of the gifted property exceeds the amount of the advantage, if any, received for the gift.

Under proposed changes, the **advantage** is generally the total value of all property, services, compensation, or other benefits to which you are entitled as partial consideration for, or in gratitude for, the gift. The advantage may be contingent or receivable in the future, and given either to you or a person not dealing at arm's length with you.

Under proposed changes, the advantage also includes any limited-recourse debt in respect of the gift at the time it was made. For example, there may be a limited-recourse debt if the property was acquired through a tax shelter that is a gifting arrangement. In this case, the eligible amount of the gift will be reported in **box 13** of Form T5003, *Statement of Tax Shelter Information*. For more information on gifting arrangements and tax shelters, see Guides T4068, *Guide for the T5013 Partnership Information Return* and T4068-1, *2010 supplement to the 2006 T4068*.

**Fair market value (FMV)** – This is usually the highest dollar value that you can get for your property in an open and unrestricted market between a willing buyer and a willing seller who are acting independently of each other.

**Locked-in** – In this guide, locked-in means that the beneficiary who is to receive the property has a right to absolute ownership of it. No future event or development can take this right away. In order for a property to be locked-in:

- for a spousal or common-law partner trust, it has to become locked-in before the surviving spouse or common-law partner dies; and
- for an individual, it has to become locked-in before the individual dies.

**Non-arm's length transaction** – This is a transaction between persons who were not dealing with each other at arm's length at the time of the transaction.

**Qualified donee** – A qualified donee generally includes:

- a registered Canadian charity;
- a registered Canadian amateur athletic association;
- a Canadian tax exempt housing corporation that only provides low-cost housing for seniors;
- a municipality in Canada or, under proposed changes, for gifts made after May 8, 2000, a municipal or public body performing a function of government in Canada;
- the United Nations (UN) or an agency of the UN;
- a prescribed university outside Canada;
- a charitable organization outside Canada to which the Government of Canada has made a donation in 2009 or 2010; and
- the Government of Canada, a province, or a territory.

**Spouse** – This is a person to whom you are legally married.

**Testamentary spousal or common-law partner trust** – This is a trust created by the deceased's will, or a court order in relation to the deceased's estate made under any law of a province or territory that provides for the relief or support of dependants. The surviving spouse or common-law partner is entitled to all the income of the trust that arises before he or she dies. No one else can receive or use the trust's income or capital before the surviving spouse's or common-law partner's death.

For more information, see Interpretation Bulletin IT-305, *Testamentary Spouse Trusts*.

**Testamentary debts** – These are debts or liabilities of all kinds that an individual incurred and did not pay before death. They also include amounts payable by the estate because of death.

**Undepreciated capital cost (UCC)** – Generally, UCC is equal to the total capital cost of all the properties of a class **minus** any capital cost allowance claimed in previous years. When property of the class is disposed of, you also have to subtract from the UCC one of the following two amounts, **whichever is less**:

- the proceeds of disposition of the property (either actual or deemed) **minus** the related outlays and expenses to sell it; or
- the capital cost of the property.

# Chapter 1 – General information

## Are you the legal representative?

If you are an executor, an administrator, or a liquidator, you are the legal representative of a deceased person.

**Executor** – This is someone a will names to act as the legal representative to handle a deceased's estate.

**Administrator** – There may not be a will, or the will may not name an executor. In this case, a court will appoint an administrator to handle the deceased's estate. An administrator is often the spouse, common-law partner, or the next of kin.

**Liquidator** – In Quebec, the liquidator is responsible for distributing assets of all estates. For estates with a will, the liquidator's role is similar to an executor's. For estates without a will, the liquidator acts as the administrator of the estate.

**Note**
As the legal representative, you may wish to appoint an authorized representative to deal with the CRA for tax matters on your behalf. You may do so by completing Form T1013, *Authorizing or Cancelling a Representative*.

## What are your responsibilities as the legal representative?

As the legal representative, you should provide us with the deceased's date of death as soon as possible. You can advise us by calling **1-800-959-8281**, by sending us a letter, or by completing and sending us a *Request for the Canada Revenue Agency to Update Records* form. This form is included with our Information Sheet RC4111, *What to Do Following a Death*. To get a copy of this publication, go to **www.cra.gc.ca/forms**, or call **1-800-959-2221**.

To keep our records up to date, also send us the following information:

- a copy of the death certificate; and
- a complete copy of the will or other legal document such as a grant of probate or letters of administration showing that you are the legal representative.

You must provide the deceased individual's social insurance number with any request you are making or with any information that you are submitting to us.

Include this information with the final return if you did not send it right after the deceased's death.

**Note**
Service Canada should also be advised of the deceased's date of death. For more information or to get the address of the Service Canada centre nearest you, call **1-800-622-6232**.

This guide deals only with your responsibilities under the *Income Tax Act* (the Act). Under the Act, as the legal representative, it is your responsibility to:

- file all required returns for the deceased;
- pay all taxes owing; and
- let the beneficiaries know which of the amounts they receive from the estate are taxable.

As the legal representative, you are responsible for filing a return for the deceased for the year of death. This return is called the **final return**. For more information, see Chapter 2, which begins on page 8.

You also have to file any returns for previous years that the deceased person did not file. If the person did not leave records about these returns, or if you cannot tell from existing records whether or not the returns were filed, contact us at **1-800-959-8281**. If you have to file a return for a year before the year of death, use a *T1 General Income Tax and Benefit Return* for that year. Previous year returns are available from our Web page at **www.cra.gc.ca/forms** or by calling **1-800-959-2221**.

You have to file a *T3 Trust Income Tax and Information Return*, for income the **estate** earned after the date of death. If the terms of a trust were established by the will or a court order in relation to the deceased individual's estate under provincial or territorial dependant relief or support law, you also have to file a *T3 Trust Income Tax and Information Return* for that trust. However, you may not have to file a T3 return (not to be confused with the final return, which always has to be filed) if the estate is distributed immediately after the person dies, or if the estate did not earn income before the distribution. In these cases, you should give each beneficiary a statement showing his or her share of the estate. See the T4013, *T3 Trust Guide*, for more information and, where a trust is created, to determine whether that return has to be filed. See Chart 2 on page 30 to find out what income to report on the T3 return.

## Do you need information from the deceased person's tax records?

You can contact us for information from the deceased's tax records. When you write for such information, include the words "The Estate of the Late" in front of the deceased person's name. Include your address so we can reply directly to you. Before we can give you information from the deceased's records, we need the following:

- a copy of the death certificate;
- the deceased's social insurance number; and
- a complete copy of the will or other legal document such as a grant of probate, trust agreement, or letters of administration showing that you are the legal representative.

If you make an appointment to see an agent at one of our tax services offices to get information from the tax records of the deceased, you also have to show us one piece of identification with your picture and signature on it, or two pieces with your signature on them.

## Goods and services tax/harmonized sales tax (GST/HST) credit received after the date of death

Generally, GST/HST credit payments are issued on the fifth day of the month in July, October, January, and April. If the deceased was receiving GST/HST credit payments, we may still send out a payment after the date of death because we are not aware of the death. If this happens, you should return the payment to the tax centre that serves your area.

**Note**
We administer provincial programs that are related to the GST/HST credit. If the deceased was receiving payments under such a program, you do not have to take any further action. We will use the information provided for the GST/HST credit payments to adjust the applicable credit.

### What if the deceased was single and received the GST/HST credit?

If a single person dies in a month before we send a quarterly GST/HST credit payment, no one else can receive the payment. We cannot make any more payments either in that person's name or to the estate.

If a single person dies during or after a month in which we issue the credit and the payment has not been cashed, return it to us so that we can send the payment to the person's estate.

If the deceased had children for whom he or she was receiving the GST/HST credit, the new caregiver should contact us at **1-800-959-1953**, as he or she may qualify to receive GST/HST credit payments for these children.

### What if the deceased's GST/HST credit is for the deceased and his or her spouse or common-law partner?

If the deceased had a spouse or common-law partner, that person may now be eligible to receive the GST/HST credit payments based on his or her net income alone. If the deceased's GST/HST credit included a claim for that spouse or common-law partner, he or she should:

- contact us at **1-800-959-1953** and ask to receive the GST/HST credit payment for the remainder of the year for himself or herself and any eligible children, if applicable; and
- file an *Income Tax and Benefit Return* for the applicable previous year if he or she has not already done so.

### What if the surviving spouse's or common-law partner's GST/HST credit included a claim for the deceased?

If the surviving spouse's or common-law partner's GST/HST credit included an amount for the deceased, the payments will be recalculated based on the surviving spouse's or common-law partner's net income and will only include a claim for himself or herself and any eligible children, if applicable.

### What if the deceased is an eligible child?

Entitlement to GST/HST credit payments for a deceased child stops the quarter after the child's date of death. You should notify us of the date of death so that we can update our records.

## Canada Child Tax Benefit (CCTB) and/or Universal Child Care Benefit (UCCB) credit received after the date of death

Contact us at **1-800-387-1193** and provide us with the date of death. If the deceased person was receiving CCTB and/or UCCB payments (which could include payments from related provincial or territorial child benefit and credit programs) for a child and the surviving spouse or common-law partner is the child's parent, we will usually transfer the CCTB and/or UCCB payments to that person. If anyone else, other than the parent, is now primarily responsible for the child, that person will have to complete and send us Form RC66, *Canada Child Benefits Application*, to ask for benefit payments for the child.

If the deceased is an eligible child, entitlement to CCTB and/or UCCB payments for the deceased child stops the month after the child's date of death. You should notify us of the date of death so that we can update our records.

## Clearance certificate

As the legal representative, you may want to get a clearance certificate before you distribute any property under your control. A clearance certificate certifies that all amounts for which the deceased is liable to us have been paid, or that we have accepted security for the payment. If you do not get a certificate, you can be liable for any amount the deceased owes. A certificate covers all tax years to the date of death. It is not a clearance for any amounts a trust owes. If there is a trust, a separate clearance certificate is needed for the trust.

To request a certificate, complete Form TX19, *Asking for a Clearance Certificate*, and send it to the Assistant Director, Audit, at your tax services office. Do **not** include Form TX19 with a return. Send it only **after** you have received the notices of assessment for all the returns filed, and paid or secured all amounts owing. You can find the mailing address of your tax services office at **www.cra.gc.ca/contact**.

If you need more information about clearance certificates, call **1-800-959-8281**. You can also see Information Circular IC82-6, *Clearance Certificate*.

## Getting started

This section covers the information you may need to prepare the return.

- Determine the deceased person's income from all sources. You can do this by:
  - checking previous year returns to get the names of employers and investment companies the deceased may have received income from in the past;
  - checking safety deposit boxes for additional sources of income and benefits;
  - contacting payers such as employers, banks, trust companies, stock brokers, and pension plan managers;
  - getting information slips from payers (for example, a T4, *Statement of Remuneration Paid*, from an employer, or a T5, *Statement of Investment Income*, from a bank or trust company); and
  - contacting the nearest Service Canada Centre at **1-800-622-6232**, if the deceased was receiving Canada Pension Plan benefits or was 65 years or older and in receipt of Old Age Security pension, and you do not have a T4A(P) slip or T4A(OAS) slip.

  Even if you cannot get the slips, you still have to report the income from all sources on either the final or the optional returns. We explain optional returns in Chapter 3, which begins on page 17. You can also claim any related deductions as outlined in Chart 1 on page 28. If a slip is not available, ask the payer to give you a note that shows the income and deductions. Attach this note to the return. If you cannot get a note from the payer, estimate the income and deduction amounts. For example, you can use pay stubs to estimate employment income and the amounts deducted for Canada Pension Plan or Quebec Pension Plan contributions, registered pension plan contributions, Employment Insurance premiums, union dues, and income tax. Attach a note to the return giving the amounts and the payer's name and address. If possible, also attach a photocopy of the pay stubs.

- Get the tax package for the province or territory where the deceased lived at the time of death. You will need a *T1 General Income Tax and Benefit Return* to report commission, partnership, rental, or self-employment income, and capital gains, or to claim deductions for attendant care expenses, security options deductions, and non-capital and capital losses of other years.
- Get any other guides, information circulars, interpretation bulletins, and forms that you may need. See page 31 for a list of forms and publications referred to in this guide.
- Prepare and file a final return and any optional returns. For information on how to prepare a final return, see Chapter 2, which begins on page 8. For information on optional returns, see Chapter 3, which begins on page 17.

- You may have to file a *T3 Trust Income Tax and Information Return*, in addition to a final return. For example, some of the amounts an employer pays are income for the estate. Estate amounts can appear on T4A slips, T4RSP slips, or in a letter from the issuing institution. See Chart 2 on page 30.
- When you have received the notice of assessment for all required returns, you can apply for a clearance certificate. See the "Clearance certificate" section on the previous page.

## Common questions and answers

Here are some common questions and answers you may want to look at before you read this guide.

Q. Can I deduct funeral expenses, probate fees, or fees to administer the estate?

A. No. These are personal expenses and cannot be deducted.

Q. Who reports a death benefit that an employer pays?

A. That depends on who received the death benefit. A death benefit is income of either the estate or the beneficiary who receives it. Up to $10,000 of the total of all death benefits paid (other than CPP or QPP death benefits) is not taxable. If the beneficiary received the death benefit, see line 130 in the *General Income Tax and Benefit Guide* or the guide that came with the beneficiary's return. If the estate received the death benefit, see the T4013, *T3 Trust Guide*.

Q. On what return do I report Canada Pension Plan (CPP) or Quebec Pension Plan (QPP) death benefits for the estate of the deceased?

A. A CPP or QPP death benefit can be reported either on the tax return of the recipient beneficiary of the deceased person's estate, or on a *T3 Trust Income Tax and Information Return*, for the estate of the deceased. If the estate then pays the death benefit to the beneficiary, a T3 slip will be issued in the beneficiary's name. The amount of the CPP or QPP death benefit is shown in box 18 of Form T4A(P), *Statement of Canada Pension Plan Benefits*. Do **not** report the amount on the deceased's return. Unlike a death benefit that an employer may pay to the estate or to a named beneficiary, this benefit is not eligible for the $10,000 death benefit exemption. You have to report all other CPP or QPP benefits on the deceased's return. For details, see line 114 on page 11.

Q. Who reports amounts an employer pays for vacation and unused sick leave?

A. Vacation pay is income of the deceased person and can be reported on a return for rights or things. See page 18 for more information. Payment for unused sick leave is considered a death benefit and is income of the estate or beneficiary who receives it. For details, see Interpretation Bulletin IT-508, *Death Benefits*.

Q The deceased had investments in a Tax-Free Savings Account (TFSA). Who reports any income earned in the TFSA?

A When the holder of a deposit or an annuity contract under a TFSA dies, the holder is considered to have received, immediately before death, an amount equal to the fair market value (FMV) of all the property held in the TFSA at the time of death. As a result, no income should be reported by the deceased on the final return or any optional returns. After the holder's death, the annuity contract is no longer considered a TFSA and all earnings after the holder's death are taxable to the beneficiaries in the year they receive this income. For more information, see Guide RC4466, *Tax-Free Savings Account (TFSA)*.

Q. If the deceased person was paying tax by instalments, do I have to continue making those instalment payments?

A. No. The only instalments we require are those that were due before the date of death but not paid.

Q. Why do I have to return the deceased person's GST/HST credit?

A. Since the payments are an advance on purchases for the current calendar year, you have to return GST/HST credit payments that were paid to the deceased after his or her death. If the deceased was single and the estate is entitled to the payment, another cheque will be issued to the estate. However, the cheque that was issued to the deceased person must be returned to us before we reissue the payment to the estate.

# Chapter 2 – Final return

This chapter explains how to complete and file the final return.

On the final return, report all of the deceased's income from January 1 of the year of death, up to and including the date of death. Report income earned **after** the date of death on a *T3 Trust Income Tax and Information Return*. To find out what income to report on the T3 return, see Chart 2 on page 30. For more information, see the T4013, *T3 Trust Guide*.

**Tax tip**
In addition to the final return, you can choose to file up to three optional returns for the year of death.

Information about the deceased's income sources will help you determine if you can file any of these optional returns. You do not report the same income on both the final and an optional return but you can claim certain credits and deductions on more than one return.

Although you do not have to file any of the optional returns, there may be a tax advantage if you file one or more of them in addition to the final return. You may be able to reduce or eliminate tax that you would otherwise have to pay for the deceased.

For more information, see "Chapter 3 – Optional returns" which begins on page 17, and Chart 1 on page 28.

## What date is the final return due?

Generally, the final return is due on or before the following dates:

| Period when death occurred | Due date for the return |
|---|---|
| January 1 to October 31 | April 30 of the following year |
| November 1 to December 31 | Six months after the date of death |

**Note**
The due date for filing the T1 return of a surviving spouse or common-law partner who was living with the deceased is the same as the due date for the deceased's final return indicated in the chart above. However, any balance owing on the surviving spouse's or common-law partner's return still has to be paid on or before April 30 of the next year to avoid interest charges.

If the deceased or the deceased's spouse or common-law partner was carrying on a business in 2010 (unless the expenditures of the business are mainly in connection with a tax shelter), the following due dates apply:

| Period when death occurred | Due date for the return |
|---|---|
| January 1 to December 15 | June 15 of the following year |
| December 16 to December 31 | Six months after the date of death |

**Tax tip**
**Previous year return** – A person may die after December 31, 2010, but on or before the filing due date for his or her 2010 return. If he or she has not filed that return, the due date for filing the return and paying any balance owing is **six months** after the date of death. For previous year returns that are already due but were not filed by the deceased, the due dates for filing those returns, as well as payment of any related taxes owing remain the same.

The deceased's will or a court order may set up a **testamentary spousal or common-law partner trust**. When testamentary debts of the deceased or the estate are being handled through the trust, the due date for the final return is extended to 18 months after the date of death. We define **testamentary spousal or common-law partner trust** and **testamentary debts** in the "Definitions" section, which begins on page 4. However, you have to pay any taxes owing on the final return by the due date shown in the section called "What is the due date for a balance owing?" on this page.

**Note**
If a person dies in 2011, the legal representative may choose to file the final return at any time after the date of death and the returns will generally be processed at that time as a service to the estate. In these cases, the returns will generally be processed using tax legislation applicable to the 2010 tax year. The legal representative can then request a reassessment of the return in the following year (2012) to apply any tax changes introduced for the 2011 tax year.

## What happens if you file the final return late?

If you file the final return late and there is a balance owing, we will charge a late-filing penalty. We will also charge you interest on both the balance owing and any penalty. The **penalty is 5%** of any balance owing, **plus 1%** of the balance owing for each full month that the return is late, to a maximum of 12 months. The late-filing penalty may be higher if we charged a late-filing penalty on a return for any of the three previous years.

**Tax tip**
Even if you cannot pay the full amount owing by the due date, you can avoid this penalty by filing the return on time.

In certain situations, we may cancel this penalty and interest if you file the return late because of circumstances beyond your control. If this happens, complete Form RC4288, *Request for Taxpayer Relief*, **or** include a letter with the return explaining why you filed the return late. For more information, go to **www.cra.gc.ca/fairness** or see Information Circular IC07-1, *Taxpayer Relief Provisions*.

## What is the due date for a balance owing?

The due date for a balance owing on a final return depends on the date of death.

| Period when death occurred | Due date for the amount owing |
|---|---|
| January 1 to October 31 | April 30 of the following year |
| November 1 to December 31 | Six months after the date of death |

If you do not pay the amount in full, we will charge compound daily interest on the unpaid amount from the day after the due date to the date you pay the amount owing.

In some cases, you can make an election to delay paying part of the amount due. For instance, you can delay paying part of the amount owing from rights or things (see page 18) and the deemed disposition of capital property (see page 24).

## How to complete the final return

In this section, we cover the most common lines on a deceased person's return. For more information on these and other lines on a return, see the guide that came with the deceased's return. If the types of income you want to report, or the deductions or credits you want to claim, are not on the return that you have, get a *T1 General Income Tax and Benefit Return*. You cannot use a T1S-C, *Credit and Benefit Return*, to complete a return for a deceased person.

### Identification

In this area of the return:

- Write "The Estate of the Late" before the name of the deceased.
- Give your address as the return address.
- Ensure the province or territory of residence on December 31 is the one where the deceased was living on the date of death.
- Tick the box that applies to the deceased's marital status at the time of death.
- Enter the date of death on the proper line.

If you use the personal label provided with the return, make sure the information on the label is correct. Attach the label to the return.

### Goods and services tax/harmonized sales tax (GST/HST) credit

Since there is no GST/HST credit based on the year of death, do not complete the GST/HST credit area when you file the final return.

### Foreign income

If the deceased earned foreign income or owned or held foreign property at any time in 2010, see the "Foreign income" section in the guide that came with the deceased's return.

### Total income

Report amounts that are paid regularly, even if the person did not receive them before he or she died. Some examples of these amounts are salary, interest, rent, royalties, and most annuities. These amounts usually accumulate in equal daily amounts for the time they are payable. For more information, see Interpretation Bulletin IT-210, *Income of Deceased Persons – Periodic Payments and Investment Tax Credit*.

There are two types of amounts that do **not** accumulate in equal daily amounts:

- certain amounts receivable by the deceased, but not payable to the deceased on or before the date of death; and
- amounts from some annuity contracts that we consider to have been disposed of on death.

For more information about amounts receivable on or before the date of death, see the section called "1. Return for rights or things" on page 18.

#### Amounts an employer pays to the deceased person's estate

There may be amounts that an employer will pay to a deceased employee's estate. For these amounts, an employer will usually complete a T4 or T4A slip.

Some of the amounts an employer pays will be part of the deceased's employment income for the year of death. Report these amounts on the final return. The amounts are employment income for the year of death even if they are received in a year after the year of death. Box 14 of the T4 slip should include the following amounts:

- salary or wages (including overtime) from the end of the last pay period to the date of death;
- salary or wages (including overtime) for a pay period finished before the date of death, but paid after death; and
- payment for vacation leave earned but not taken.

The employer may change any of these amounts later because of an agreement or promotion. If the document that allows the change was signed **before** the date of death, report these additional amounts on the final return. However, if the document was signed **after** the date of death, the additional amounts are not taxable (see Chart 3 on page 30).

Some of these amounts may be **rights or things**, and you may be able to report them on an optional return. For details, see the section called "1. Return for rights or things" on page 18. Some of the amounts an employer pays are income for the estate and should be reported on a *T3 Trust Income Tax and Information Return*. See Chart 2 on page 30.

#### Lines 101 to 104 – Employment income

Report all salary, wages, or commissions received from January 1 to the date of death. Also include amounts that accumulate from the start of the pay period in which the employee died to the date of death.

If the commissions are for a self-employed salesperson, see Guide T4002, *Business and Professional Income*, to determine how to report the commission income and claim expenses.

#### Line 113 – Old Age Security pension

Report the amounts from box 18 of the deceased's T4A(OAS) slip. A payment received after the date of death for the month in which the individual died may be reported on the final return or on a rights or things return.

**Do not report** on line 113 the amount in box 21 of the T4A(OAS) slip. Report this amount on "Line 146 – Net federal supplements." You may be able to claim a deduction for this amount on "Line 250 – Other payments deduction."

> **Note**
> If the deceased's net income before adjustments (line 234), **minus** the amounts reported on lines 117 and 125, **plus** the amount deducted on line 213 and/or any repayment of registered disability savings plans income (line 232), is more than $66,733, all or part of the OAS benefits may have to be repaid. For details, see line 235 in the *General Income Tax and Benefit Guide*, or the *Special Income Tax and Benefit Guide*.

**Line 114** – CPP or QPP benefits
Report the total Canada Pension Plan (CPP) or Quebec Pension Plan (QPP) benefits in box 20 of the deceased's T4A(P) slip, **minus** any amount in box 18. The amount in box 20 is the total of the amounts in boxes 14 to 18. A payment received after the date of death for the month in which the individual died may be reported on the final return or on a rights and things return.

**Do not report** a CPP or QPP death benefit shown in box 18 on the final return. This amount will be reported either by the recipient beneficiary of the deceased person's estate on his or her return, or on a *T3 Trust Income Tax and Information Return* for the estate. If the deceased received a lump-sum CPP or QPP benefit, or a CPP or QPP disability benefit, see line 114 in the *General Income Tax and Benefit Guide*, or the *Special Income Tax and Benefit Guide*.

A CPP or QPP death benefit will generally not be taxable where the recipient deals at arm's length with the estate (is not the beneficiary of the estate) and the benefit is received in the following circumstances:

- the amount is received by a taxpayer who paid the deceased's funeral expenses;
- the amount does not exceed the actual funeral expenses; and
- the deceased has no heirs and there is no other property in the estate.

**Line 115** – Other pensions or superannuation
Report any other pensions or superannuation the deceased received from January 1 to the date of death (box 016 on T4A slips and box 31 on T3 slips).

If the deceased received annuity or registered retirement income fund (RRIF) payments, including life income fund (LIF) payments, for the period from January 1 to the date of death, report that income on the final return. If the deceased was 65 or older, report the RRIF income on line 115. Also report the RRIF income on line 115 if the deceased was under 65 but received the RRIF payments because his or her spouse or common-law partner died. In all other cases, report the RRIF income on line 130 of the return. For more information, see the section called "Income from a registered retirement income fund (RRIF)" on page 13.

If there is a lump-sum amount shown in box 018 of the T4A slip or box 22 of the T3 slip, report it on line 130.

If the deceased person jointly elected with his or her spouse or common-law partner to split the pension, annuity, and RRIF (including LIF) payments that were reported on line 115 by the pensioner, the elected split-pension amount transferred from the pensioner to the pension transferee can be deducted on line 210. For more information, see "Line 210 – Deduction for elected split-pension amount" on page 14.

**Line 116** – Elected split-pension amount
To make this election, the deceased and his or her spouse or common-law partner must have jointly elected to split pension income by completing Form T1032, *Joint Election to Split Pension Income*. The elected split-pension amount from line E of Form T1032 must be entered on line 116 for the pension transferee.

Form T1032 must be filed by the filing due date for the 2010 return (see the section called "What date is the final return due?" on page 9). This form **must** be attached to **both** the deceased's paper return and his or her spouse's or common-law partner's paper return.

Both the deceased person and his or her spouse or common-law partner must sign Form T1032. If the form is being completed **after** the date of death, the surviving spouse or common-law partner **and** the executor of the deceased person's estate must sign the form. In some cases, the executor may be the spouse or common-law partner in which case this person must sign for the deceased person too.

**Line 119** – Employment Insurance benefits
Report any Employment Insurance (EI) benefits the deceased received from January 1 to the date of death (box 14 of the T4E slip). If the deceased's net income before adjustments (line 234), **minus** the amounts reported on lines 117 and 125, **plus** the amount deducted on line 213 and/or any repayment of registered disability savings plans income (line 232), is more than $54,000, part of these benefits may have to be repaid. For details, see line 235 in the *General Income Tax and Benefit Guide*, or the *Special Income Tax and Benefit Guide*. If the deceased repaid any EI benefits to Service Canada, he or she may be entitled to a deduction. For details, see line 232 in the *General Income Tax and Benefit Guide*.

**Lines 120 and 121** – Investment income
Report investment income received from January 1 to the date of death. This type of income includes dividends (line 120) and interest (line 121).

Also include the following:

- amounts earned from January 1 to the date of death that have not been paid;
- amounts earned from term deposits, guaranteed investment certificates (GICs), and other similar investments from the last time these amounts were paid to the date of death;
- bond interest earned from the last time it was paid to the date of death, if the deceased did not report it in a previous year; and
- compound bond interest that accumulated to the date of death, if the deceased did not report it in a previous year.

You can report some types of investment income as rights or things. For details, see the section called "1. Return for rights or things" on page 18. Report interest that accumulates after the date of death on a *T3 Trust Income Tax and Information Return*.

**Line 125** – Registered disability savings plan (RDSP) income

If the beneficiary of an RDSP dies, the RDSP must be closed no later than December 31 of the year following the year of the beneficiary's death. Any funds remaining in the RDSP, after any required repayment of government bonds and grants, will be paid to the estate. The RDSP must be closed and all amounts paid out of the plan by the end of the calendar year following the year in which the beneficiary dies. If a disability assistance payment (DAP) had been made and the beneficiary is deceased, the taxable portion of the DAP must be included in the income of the beneficiary's estate in the year the payment is made.

**Line 127** – Taxable capital gains

For information about this type of income, see Chapter 4, which begins on page 21.

**Line 129** – RRSP income

At the time of death, a person may have a registered retirement savings plan (RRSP). The RRSP may or may not have matured. Depending on the situation, the amount you include in the deceased's income can vary.

If the deceased person jointly elected with his or her spouse or common-law partner to split RRSP annuity payments that the pensioner received up until the date of death and reported on line 129, the elected split-pension amount can be deducted on line 210. For more information, see "Line 210 – Deduction for elected split-pension amount" on page 14.

**Payments from a matured RRSP** – A **matured** RRSP is one that is paying retirement income, usually in monthly payments. Report on line 129 the RRSP payments the deceased received from January 1 to the date of death.

If the surviving spouse or common-law partner is the beneficiary of the RRSP, as specified in the RRSP contract, he or she will begin receiving the remaining annuity payments from the plan. The surviving spouse or common-law partner has to report the remaining payments as income on his or her return.

If the surviving spouse or common-law partner is the beneficiary of the estate, that person and the legal representative can jointly elect, in writing, to treat the amounts the RRSP paid to the estate as being paid to the spouse or common-law partner. Attach a copy of the written election to the return of the surviving spouse or common-law partner. The election has to specify that this person is electing to become the annuitant of the RRSP.

If the amounts from the RRSP are paid to a beneficiary other than the deceased's spouse or common-law partner, see Guide T4040, *RRSPs and Other Registered Plans for Retirement*.

**Payments from an unmatured RRSP** – Generally, an **unmatured** RRSP is one that does not yet pay retirement income.

Generally, we consider a deceased annuitant to have received, immediately before death, an amount equal to the fair market value (FMV) of all the property of the unmatured plan at the time of death. The FMV of the property is shown in box 34 of the T4RSP slip issued to the deceased annuitant. You have to include this amount in the deceased's income for the year of death.

If a T4RSP slip showing the FMV of the plan at the time of death is issued in the deceased's name, you may be able to reduce the amount you include in the deceased's income. For details, see Information Sheet RC4177, *Death of an RRSP Annuitant*, and Guide T4040, *RRSPs and Other Registered Plans for Retirement*.

If **all** of the property held in the RRSP is to be paid to the surviving spouse or common-law partner, **and** that payment is directly transferred to his or her RRSP, RRIF, or to an issuer to buy the surviving spouse or common-law partner an eligible annuity (as specified in the RRSP contract) **before** the end of the year following the year of death, a T4RSP slip will not be issued in the deceased's name. In this case, the surviving spouse or common-law partner has to report the payment on his or her return and claim a deduction equal to the amount transferred.

Sometimes there can be an **increase** in the value of an RRSP between the date of death and the date of final distribution to the beneficiary or estate. This amount has to be included in the income of the beneficiary or the estate for the year it is received. A T4RSP slip will be issued for this amount. For more information, see Chart 4 - Amounts from a deceased annuitant's RRSP, in Chapter 3 of Guide T4040, *RRSPs and Other Registered Plans for Retirement*.

Sometimes, the FMV of the property of an unmatured RRSP can **decrease** between the date of death and the date of final distribution to the beneficiary or the estate. If the total of all distributions from the RRSP is less than the FMV of the property that was included in the deceased annuitant's income for the year of death, the deceased's legal representative can request that the difference between the FMV and the total of all distributions be deducted on the deceased's final return. Generally, for the deduction to be allowed, the final distribution must occur by the end of the year that follows the year of death. For further details, see Information Sheet RC4177, *Death of an RRSP Annuitant*.

If the amounts from the RRSP are paid to a beneficiary other than the deceased's spouse or common-law partner, see Guide T4040, *RRSPs and Other Registered Plans for Retirement*.

**Home Buyers' Plan (HBP)** – The deceased may have participated in the HBP. If so, the deceased would have made a withdrawal from his or her RRSP and may have been making repayments to the RRSP. In this case, include on line 129 the total of all amounts that remain to be repaid at the time of death. Any RRSP contributions that the deceased made in the year of his or her death can be designated as a repayment.

However, you do not have to report these amounts when the legal representative and the surviving spouse or common-law partner jointly elect to have the surviving spouse or common-law partner continue to make the repayments. For more information, see Guide RC4135, *Home Buyers' Plan (HBP).*

**Lifelong Learning Plan (LLP)** – The deceased may have participated in the LLP. If so, the deceased would have made a withdrawal from his or her RRSP and may have been making repayments to the RRSP. Treatment of these amounts is the same as with the Home Buyer's Plan, and a similar election is available. For more information, see Guide RC4112, *Lifelong Learning Plan (LLP).*

**Line 130** – Other income

Use this line to report taxable income not reported anywhere else on the return. Identify the type of income you are reporting in the space to the left of line 130. We discuss some of the types of income you report on this line below. For more information, see line 130 in the guide that came with the deceased's return.

**Death benefits (other than Canada or Quebec Pension Plan death benefits)** – A death benefit is an amount received after a person's death for that person's employment service. It is shown in box 106 of the T4A slip or box 26 of the T3 slip. A death benefit payable in respect of the deceased person is not reported on the final return for the deceased; rather, it is income of the estate or the beneficiary that receives it. Up to $10,000 of the total of all death benefits paid may not be taxable. For more information, see line 130 in the guide that came with the deceased's return or Interpretation Bulletin IT-508, *Death Benefits.*

**Income from a registered retirement income fund (RRIF)** – When a person dies, he or she may have a RRIF. Depending on the situation, the amount you include in the deceased's income can vary.

If the deceased received payments from a RRIF for the period from January 1 to the date of death, report that income on the final return. If the deceased was 65 or older, or if the deceased was under 65 and received the RRIF payments due to the death of his or her spouse or common-law partner, see "Line 115 – Other pensions or superannuation" on page 11. In all other cases, report the RRIF income on line 130.

If the annuitant made a written election in the RRIF contract or in the will to have the RRIF payments continue to be paid to his or her spouse or common-law partner after death, that person becomes the annuitant and will start to get the RRIF payments as the new annuitant.

If the annuitant did not elect in writing to have the RRIF payments continue to be paid to his or her spouse or common-law partner, that person can still become the annuitant of the RRIF after the annuitant's death. This is the case if the legal representative consents to the deceased's spouse or common-law partner becoming the annuitant, and the RRIF carrier agrees to continue the payments under the deceased annuitant's RRIF to the surviving spouse or common-law partner.

A T4RIF slip will not be issued in the deceased annuitant's name for the fair market value (FMV) of the property at the time of death if **all** of the following conditions exist:

- All of the property held by the RRIF is to be paid to the surviving spouse or common-law partner (as specified in the RRIF contract).
- The **entire** eligible amount of the designated benefit is directly transferred to the surviving spouse's or common-law partner's RRIF, RRSP, or to an issuer to buy an eligible annuity for the surviving spouse or common-law partner.
- All the RRIF property is distributed **before** the end of the year following the year of death.

In this case, the surviving spouse or common-law partner will receive a T4RIF slip, has to report the payment on his or her return, and is eligible to claim a deduction equal to the amount directly transferred.

For all other situations, we consider that the deceased received, immediately before death, an amount equal to the FMV of the plan at the time of death. The FMV of the property is shown in box 18 of the T4RIF slip issued in the deceased's name. Include this amount in the deceased's income for the year of death. However, you may be able to reduce the amount you include in income. For details, see Information Sheet RC4178, *Death of a RRIF Annuitant*, and Guide T4040, *RRSPs and Other Registered Plans for Retirement.*

Sometimes there can be an **increase** in the value of a RRIF between the date of death and the date of final distribution to the beneficiary or estate. Generally, this amount has to be included in the income of the beneficiary or the estate for the year it is received. A T4RIF slip will be issued for this amount. For more information, see Chart 5 – Amounts from a deceased annuitant's RRIF, in Chapter 3 of Guide T4040, *RRSPs and Other Registered Plans for Retirement.*

Sometimes, the FMV of the property of a RRIF can **decrease** between the date of death and the date of final distribution to the beneficiary or the estate. If the total of all distributions from the RRIF is less than the FMV of the property that was included in the deceased annuitant's income for the year of death, the deceased's legal representative can request that the difference between the FMV and the total of all distributions be deducted on the deceased's final return. Generally, for the deduction to be allowed, the final distribution must occur by the end of the year that follows the year of death. For further details, see Information Sheet RC4178, *Death of a RRIF Annuitant.*

**Lines 135 to 143** – Self-employment income

If the deceased had self-employment income, report the gross and net income or loss on the appropriate line. For more information, see lines 135 to 143 in the *General Income Tax and Benefit Guide.*

**Reserves in the year of death** – Sometimes, when a property is sold, some of the proceeds are not payable until after the year of sale. Similarly, a self-employed person may have amounts that he or she will receive in a later year for work done this year. An example is for work in progress.

Usually, a person can deduct from income the part of the proceeds that are not payable until a later year. This is called a reserve.

In most cases, you cannot deduct a reserve in the year of death. However, there may be a transfer to a spouse or common-law partner, or spousal or common-law partner trust, of the right to receive the proceeds of disposition or the income owing. When this happens, the legal representative and the beneficiary can choose to claim a reserve on the deceased's return. To do this, complete Form T2069, *Election in Respect of Amounts Not Deductible as Reserves for the Year of Death*, and attach a copy to the deceased's return.

This choice is available only if the deceased was a resident of Canada right before death. For a transfer to a spouse or common-law partner, that person also has to have been a resident of Canada right before the deceased's death. For a transfer to a spousal or common-law partner trust, the trust has to be resident in Canada right after the proceeds or income become locked-in for the trust. We define **locked-in** in the "Definitions" section, which begins on page 4.

The spouse or common-law partner, or spousal or common-law partner trust includes in income an amount equal to the reserve that is on Form T2069. This income has to be included on the return for the first tax year after death. You have to attach a copy of Form T2069 to that return.

**Lines 144 to 146** – Other types of income
Report the deceased's workers' compensation benefits, social assistance payments, and net federal supplements on the appropriate line. For details, see the guide that came with the deceased's return.

## Net income

**Line 208** – RRSP deduction
Use this line to deduct registered retirement savings plan (RRSP) contributions the deceased made before his or her death. These include contributions to both the deceased's RRSPs and the deceased's spouse or common-law partner's RRSPs, but do not include repayments under a Home Buyers' Plan or Lifelong Learning Plan described on pages 12 and 13.

After a person dies, no one can contribute to the deceased person's RRSPs. However, the deceased individual's legal representative can make contributions to the surviving spouse's or common-law partner's RRSPs in the year of death or during the first 60 days after the end of that year.

The amount you can deduct on the deceased's return for 2010 is usually based on the deceased's 2010 RRSP deduction limit. You can also deduct amounts for contributions the deceased made for certain income the deceased received and transferred to an RRSP.

For information, see Guide T4040, *RRSPs and Other Registered Plans for Retirement*. For information on other deductions the deceased may be entitled to (line 207 and lines 209 to 235), see the *General Income Tax and Benefit Guide*, or the guide that came with the deceased's return.

**Line 210** – Deduction for elected split-pension amount
If the deceased person jointly elected with his or her spouse or common-law partner to split pension income by completing Form T1032, *Joint Election to Split Pension Income*, the pensioner can deduct on this line, the elected split-pension amount from line E of this form.

Form T1032 must be filed by the filing due date for the 2010 return (see the section called "What date is the final return due?" on page 9). This form **must** be attached to both the deceased's paper return and his or her spouse's or common-law partner's paper return.

Both the deceased person and his or her spouse or common-law partner must sign the Form T1032. If the form is being completed **after** the date of death, the surviving spouse or common-law partner **and** the executor of the deceased person's estate must sign the form. In some cases, the executor may be the spouse or common-law partner in which case this person must sign for the deceased person too.

## Taxable income

**Line 253** – Net capital losses of other years
For information about these losses, see Chapter 5, which begins on page 25.

For information on other deductions the deceased may be entitled to (lines 244 to 252 and lines 254 to 256), see the *General Income Tax and Benefit Guide*, or the guide that came with the deceased's return.

## Federal non-refundable tax credits

**Personal amounts (lines 300 to 306)**
If the deceased was a resident of Canada from January 1 to the date of death, claim the full personal amounts.

If the deceased was a resident of Canada for **part** of the time from January 1 to the date of death, you may have to prorate the personal amounts. To do so, multiply the personal amount by the number of days the deceased lived in Canada and divide the result by the number of days in the year. The result is the amount you can claim on the deceased's return. If the deceased immigrated to Canada in the year of death, see Pamphlet T4055, *Newcomers to Canada*. If the deceased emigrated from Canada in the year of death, see Guide T4056, *Emigrants and Income Tax*.

The credits we refer to in this section are federal credits, which are claimed on Schedule 1, *Federal Tax*. If the deceased was a resident of a province or territory other than Quebec, use the appropriate form included in the forms book to calculate his or her provincial or territorial tax credits. For more information, see the provincial or territorial pages in the deceased's forms book.

**Line 300** – Basic personal amount
Claim the full basic personal amount for the year.

**Line 301** – Age amount
If the deceased was 65 or older, and his or her net income is less than $75,480, you can claim all or part of the age amount. The amount you can claim will depend on the deceased's net income for the year. For more information,

see line 301 in the guide that came with the deceased's return.

**Line 303** – Spouse or common-law partner amount
If the net income of the spouse or common-law partner is less than the base amount for the year (see line 303 in the guide that came with the deceased's return), you may be able to claim all or part of this amount. Use the net income of the spouse or common-law partner for the whole year, not just up to the deceased's date of death.

**Line 305** – Amount for an eligible dependant
If the deceased is entitled to claim this amount, use the dependant's net income for the whole year, not just up to the deceased's date of death. For more information, see line 305 in the guide that came with the deceased's return. Calculate the amount for line 305 on Schedule 1, and complete the appropriate part of Schedule 5, both of which are included in the forms book.

**Line 306** – Amount for infirm dependants age 18 or older
If the deceased is entitled to claim this amount, use the dependant's net income for the whole year, not just up to the deceased's date of death. For more information, see line 306 in the *General Income Tax and Benefit Guide*.

**Line 314** – Pension income amount
The deceased may have received eligible pension or annuity income before the date of death. If this is the case, you may be able to claim the pension income amount of up to $2,000. For more information, see line 314 in the guide that came with the deceased's return, and complete the chart for line 314 on the *Federal Worksheet* included in the forms book.

If the deceased and his or her spouse or common-law partner elected to split pension income, follow the instructions at Step 4 on Form T1032, *Joint Election to Split Pension Income*, to calculate the amount to enter on line 314.

**Line 315** – Caregiver amount
You may be able to claim this amount if the deceased cared for certain dependants. See line 315 in the *General Income Tax and Benefit Guide*, and complete the chart for line 315 on the *Federal Worksheet* included in the forms book.
For more information, see Guide RC4064, *Medical and Disability-Related Information*.

**Line 316** – Disability amount (for self)
You can claim a disability amount if the deceased met certain conditions. For more information about these conditions, see line 316 in the guide that came with the deceased's return.

**Tax Tip**
If the deceased or anyone else paid for certain eligible expenses, such as an attendant or for care in a nursing home or other establishment because of the deceased's impairment, it may be more beneficial to claim the amounts paid as medical expenses instead of the disability amount. In some circumstances, both amounts can be claimed.

For more information, see the section called "Attendant care or care in an establishment" in Guide RC4064, *Medical and Disability-Related Information*, and Interpretation Bulletin IT-519, *Medical Expense and Disability Tax Credits and Attendant Care Expense Deduction*.

**Line 318** – Disability amount transferred from a dependant
If the deceased had a dependant who is entitled to claim a disability amount, you may be able to claim all or a part of the dependant's disability amount. For more information, see line 318 in the *General Income Tax and Benefit Guide*, and complete the chart for line 318 on the *Federal Worksheet* included in the forms book.

**Line 319** – Interest paid on your student loans
You can claim an amount for most of the interest paid after 1997 on loans made to the deceased under the *Canada Student Loans Act*, the *Canada Student Financial Assistance Act*, or similar provincial or territorial government laws for post-secondary education. Enter the total amount shown on the receipts. Attach the receipts to the return. For more information, see the *General Income Tax and Benefit Guide* or Pamphlet P105, *Students and Income Tax*.

**Line 326** – Amounts transferred from your spouse or common-law partner
Sometimes there are amounts that a spouse or common-law partner does not need to reduce his or her federal income tax to zero. In these situations, you can transfer the remaining amounts to the deceased's final return.

Also, the deceased may have amounts that are not needed to reduce his or her federal tax to zero. If this is the case, you can transfer the remaining amounts to the return of the spouse or common-law partner. However, before you can do this, you have to reduce the federal tax to zero on the final return you file for the deceased.

For either situation, you can transfer the following amounts if the person transferring the credit meets the requirements for the credit:

- the age amount (line 301);
- the pension income amount (line 314);
- the disability amount (line 316);
- 2010 tuition, education, and textbook amounts (line 323); and
- the amount for children born in 1993 or later (line 367).

If you do transfer any of these amounts, complete Schedule 2, *Federal Amounts Transferred From Your Spouse or Common-law Partner*, and attach it to the final return for the deceased.

**Line 330** – Medical expenses for self, spouse or common-law partner, and your dependent children born in 1993 or later
You can claim medical expenses that are more than the **lower** of:

- $2,024; and

www.cra.gc.ca 15

- 3% of the deceased's total net income from line 236 of **all** returns for the year of death.

The expenses can be for any 24-month period that includes the date of death, as long as no one has claimed them on any other return.

Attach the receipts for medical expenses to the return.

> **Note**
> You may be able to claim a credit of up to $1,074 if you have an amount on line 215, "Disability supports deduction," or line 332, the allowable portion of medical expenses. Use the net income from the deceased's final return, and the spouse's or common-law partner's net income for the entire year, to calculate this credit. For details, see line 452, "Refundable medical expense supplement," in the *General Income Tax and Benefit Guide*, or in the *Special Income Tax and Benefit Guide.*

For more information on medical expenses, see line 330 in the *General Income Tax and Benefit Guide*, the *Special Income Tax and Benefit Guide*, or the T1S-A *Income Tax and Benefit Guide*.

**Line 349** – Donations and gifts

Use this line to claim charitable donations the deceased, or his or her spouse or common-law partner, made before the date of death. If you are using a *T1 General Income Tax and Benefit Return*, complete Schedule 9, *Donations and Gifts*. If you are using a T1 Special or T1S-A return, calculate the allowable amount on Schedule 1.

Support the claims for donations and gifts with official receipts that the registered charity or other qualified donee has issued, showing either the deceased's name, or the deceased's spouse's or common-law partner's name.

You can also claim charitable donations made through the will, as long as you support the donations. The type of support you have to provide depends on when the registered charity or other qualified donee will receive the gift:

- For gifts that will be received right away, provide an official receipt.
- For gifts that will be received later, provide a copy of each of the following:
  - the will;
  - a letter from the estate to the charitable organization that will receive the gift, advising of the gift and its value; and
  - a letter from the charitable organization acknowledging the gift and stating that it will accept the gift.

You may be able to claim a charitable donations tax credit for a donation of a direct distribution of proceeds to a qualified donee from an RRSP (including a group RRSP), RRIF, or life insurance policy (including a group life insurance policy) as a result of a beneficiary designation. The above does not apply if the qualified donee is the policy holder or an assignee of the deceased person's interest in the policy.

The deceased may have donated amounts in the five years before the year of death. As long as the deceased did not previously claim the amounts, you can claim them in the year of death. Where part of a donation has already been claimed, attach a note to the return giving the amounts and the year or years the donations were made. Also, attach any receipts that were not attached to previous returns, if applicable.

> **Note**
> Charitable donations cannot be carried forward from a T1 return to a T3 return.

The most you can claim is the **lower** of:

- the **eligible amount of the gift(s)** (defined in the "Definitions" section, which begins on page 4), donated in the year of death (including gifts by will), plus the unclaimed portion of the eligible amount of any gifts made in the five years before the year of death; and
- 100% of the deceased's net income (line 236) on the return.

Under proposed changes, for a gift of property made to a qualified donee, special rules may apply to limit the fair market value (FMV) of the property gifted, and thereby limit the eligible amount of the gift that can be used in computing the donation tax credit amount. When the rules apply, the FMV of the donated property will be deemed to be the **lesser** of the property's:

- FMV otherwise determined; and
- cost (or its adjusted cost base if it is capital property), at the time the gift was made. We define "**fair market value**" and "**adjusted cost base**" in the "Definitions" section, which begins on page 4.

The limitation on the eligible amount of a gift **will** apply where:

- the donated property was acquired under a gifting arrangement that is a tax shelter; or
- the property is being gifted otherwise than as a consequence of the taxpayer's death, and the property was acquired less than **3** years, or in some cases, less than **10** years, before making the gift.

The limitation on the eligible amount of a gift will **not** apply to gifts of:

- inventory;
- real property or an immovable property located in Canada;
- certified cultural property;
- ecologically sensitive land (including a covenant, an easement, or in the case of land in Quebec, a real servitude);
- a share, debt obligation, or right listed on a designated stock exchange;
- a share of the capital stock of a mutual fund corporation;
- a unit of a mutual fund trust;
- an interest in a related segregated fund trust;

- a prescribed debt obligation;
- shares of controlled corporations in certain circumstances; or
- property acquired by a corporation in certain circumstances where the property was acquired under a tax-deferred rollover.

There are also special anti-avoidance rules that may apply where a taxpayer has attempted to avoid the application of the limitation rules. For more information, see Pamphlet P113, *Gifts and Income Tax*.

If the property was acquired through a tax shelter that is a gifting arrangement, the eligible amount will be reported in box 13 of Form T5003, *Statement of Tax Shelter Information*.

On the return(s) for the year of death, you may not be able to claim all of the gifts the deceased made in the year of death. In that case, you can ask us to adjust the deceased's return for the preceding year to include the unused part of these gifts.

Sometimes, a capital property may be gifted. At the time the deceased gives the property, its FMV may be more than its adjusted cost base (ACB).

When the FMV is **more** than the ACB, you may designate an amount that is **less** than the FMV to be the proceeds of disposition. This may allow you to reduce the capital gain otherwise calculated. If you choose to designate an amount that is less than the FMV as the amount to be used as the proceeds of disposition, this will be the eligible amount of the donation. You can choose an amount that is **not greater than** the FMV and **not less** than the greater of:

- any **advantage** (defined in the "Definitions" section, which begins on page 4) in respect of the gift; and
- the ACB of the property (or, where the property was depreciable property, the lesser of its ACB and the undepreciated capital cost of the class of the property), at the time you made the donation.

Treat the amount you choose as the proceeds of disposition when you calculate any capital gain.

For more information about charitable donations and the special rules that may apply, see the guide that came with the deceased's return, and Pamphlet P113, *Gifts and Income Tax*.

**Line 363** – Canada employment amount

Employees are eligible to claim an employment amount.

Claim the **lesser** of:

- $1,051; and
- the total of the employment income reported on line 101 and line 104 of the deceased's return.

## Refund or Balance owing

You will find the details you need about tax and credits in the section called "Refund or Balance owing" in the guide that came with the deceased's return.

**Note**
We cannot accept direct deposit applications for individuals who died in the year, or the preceding year.

**Minimum tax**

Minimum tax limits the tax advantage a person can receive in a year from certain incentives. Minimum tax does not apply to a person for the year of death. However, the deceased may have paid this tax in one or more of the seven years before the year of death. If this is the case, you may be able to deduct part or all of the minimum tax the deceased paid in those years from the tax owing for the year of death. To do this, complete Part 8 of Form T691, *Alternative Minimum Tax*. Include Form T691 with the return.

**Line 453** – Working income tax benefit (WITB)

If the deceased died after June 30, he or she may qualify for the WITB. This benefit is for low-income individuals and families who have earned income from employment or business. For more information, see line 453 in the guide that came with the deceased's return.

**Provincial and territorial tax**

Use Form 428 included in the forms book to calculate the provincial or territorial tax for the province or territory where the deceased was living at the time of death.
To calculate the tax for the province of Quebec, you must use a Quebec provincial return.

## Signing the return

As the legal representative for the deceased, you have to sign the return in the area provided on the last page of the return. Sign your name and indicate your title (for example, executor or administrator).

# Chapter 3 – Optional returns

Optional returns are returns on which you report some of the income that you would otherwise report on the final return. By filing one or more optional returns, you may reduce or eliminate tax for the deceased. This is possible because you can claim certain amounts more than once, split them between returns, or claim them against specific kinds of income.

Chart 1 on page 28 summarizes the information in this chapter. You may also want to get Interpretation Bulletin IT-326, *Returns of Deceased Persons as "Another Person."*

You can choose to file up to three optional returns.
The optional returns are for income from:

- rights or things;
- a business as a partner or proprietor; or
- a testamentary trust.

**Note**
Do not confuse the optional return for income from a testamentary trust with the *T3 Trust Income Tax and Information Return*, described in the section called "What are your responsibilities as the legal representative?" on page 5. After someone dies, a will or a court order may create a trust, and the trustee, executor, or administrator may be required to file a T3 return. Also, an individual

may be required to file a T3 return to report income earned after the date of death or for CPP or QPP death benefits. For more information, see Chart 2 on page 30 and the T4013, *T3 Trust Guide*.

## Signing the optional return

You have to sign the optional return in the area provided on the last page of the return. Sign your name and indicate your title (for example, executor or administrator).

## What are the three optional returns?

### 1. Return for rights or things

Rights or things are amounts that had not been paid to the deceased at the time of his or her death and that, had the person not died, would have been included in his or her income when received. There are rights or things from employment and other sources.

You can file a return for rights or things to report the value of the rights or things at the time of death. However, if you file a return for rights or things, you have to report **all** rights or things on that return, except those transferred to beneficiaries. You **cannot** split rights or things between the final return and the return for rights or things.

If you **transfer** rights or things to a beneficiary, you have to do so within the time limit for filing a return for rights or things. The beneficiary must report the income from the transferred rights or things on his or her return.

#### Employment rights or things

Employment rights or things are salary, commissions, and vacation pay, as long as **both** of these conditions are met:

- The employer owed them to the deceased on the date of death.
- They are for a pay period that ended before the date of death.

#### Other rights or things

Other rights or things include the following:

- old age security (OAS) benefits that were due and payable before the date of death;
- uncashed matured bond coupons;
- bond interest earned to a payment date before death, but not paid and not reported in previous years;
- unpaid dividends declared before the date of death;
- supplies on hand, inventory, and accounts receivable if the deceased was a farmer or fisherman and used the cash method;
- livestock that is not part of the basic herd and harvested farm crops, if the deceased was using the cash method; and
- work in progress, if the deceased was a sole proprietor and a professional [an accountant, a dentist, a lawyer (in Quebec an advocate or notary), a medical doctor, a veterinarian, or a chiropractor] who had elected to exclude work in progress when calculating his or her total income.

For more information about rights or things, see Interpretation Bulletins IT-212, *Income of Deceased Persons – Rights or Things*, and its Special Release, IT-234, *Income of Deceased Persons – Farm Crops*, and IT-427, *Livestock of Farmers*.

Some items that are **not** rights or things include:

- elected split-pension amounts;
- amounts that accumulate periodically, such as interest from a bank account;
- bond interest accumulated between the last interest payment date before the person died and the date of death;
- registered retirement savings plan (RRSP) income;
- amounts withdrawn from the Net Income Stabilization Account (NISA) Fund 2;
- eligible capital property and capital property;
- Canadian or foreign resource properties;
- land in the deceased's business inventory; and
- income from an income-averaging annuity contract.

**How to file** – If you decide to file a return for rights or things, you will need to:

1. Get a *T1 General Income Tax and Benefit Return*.
2. Write "70(2)" in the top right corner of page 1 of the return.
3. Follow the instructions for completing a return in this guide and the *General Income Tax and Benefit Guide*.

You have to file this return by the **later** of:

- 90 days after we send the notice of assessment or notice of reassessment for the final return; and
- one year after the date of death.

However, the due date for any balance of tax owing on a rights or things return depends on the date of death. See the section called "What is the due date for a balance owing?" on page 9.

#### Election to delay payment of income tax

In some cases, you can delay paying part of the amount owing from rights or things. However, we still charge interest on any unpaid amount from the day after the due date to the date you pay the amount in full.

If you want to delay payment, you will have to give us security for the amount owing. You also have to complete Form T2075, *Election to Defer Payment of Income Tax, Under Subsection 159(5) of the Income Tax Act by a Deceased Taxpayer's Legal Representative or Trustee*. For more information, contact the Collections Division of your tax services office by calling **1-888-863-8657**.

#### How to cancel a return for rights or things

You may file a return for rights or things before the due date, but later want to cancel it. We will cancel the return if you send us a note asking us to do this. You have to send the note by the filing due date for the rights or things return.

### 2. Return for a partner or proprietor

A deceased person may have been a partner in, or the sole proprietor of, a business. The business may have a fiscal year that does not start or end on the same dates as the calendar year. If the person died after the end of the business's fiscal period but before the end of the calendar year in which the fiscal period ended, you can file an optional return for the deceased.

On this return, report the income for the time from the end of the fiscal period to the date of death. If you choose not to file this optional return, report all business income on the final return.

**Example**
A person who had a business died on May 28, 2010. The business has a March 31 fiscal year end. You have two choices when you report the person's 2010 income:

- One choice is to include the business income from April 1, 2009, to May 28, 2010, on the final return.
- The other choice is to file a return for a partner or proprietor in addition to the final return. On the final return, include business income from April 1, 2009, to March 31, 2010. On the return for a partner or proprietor, report the business income from April 1, 2010, to May 28, 2010.

**How to file** – If you decide to file a return for a partner or proprietor, you will need to:

1. Get a *T1 General Income Tax and Benefit Return.*
2. Write "150(4)" in the top right corner of page 1 of the return.
3. Follow the instructions for completing a return in this guide and the *General Income Tax and Benefit Guide.*

The due date for this optional return is the same as for the final return. The due date for a balance owing depends on the date of death. See the sections called "What date is the final return due?" and "What is the due date for a balance owing?" on page 9.

For more information, see Interpretation Bulletin IT-278, *Death of a Partner or of a Retired Partner.*

### 3. Return for income from a testamentary trust

You can file an optional return for a deceased person who received income from a testamentary trust. The trust may have a fiscal period (tax year) that does not start or end on the same dates as the calendar year. If the person died after the end of the fiscal period of the trust, but before the end of the calendar year in which the fiscal period ended, you can file an optional return for the deceased.

On this return, report the income for the time from the end of the fiscal period to the date of death. If you choose not to file this optional return, report all income from the trust on the final return.

**Example**
A husband gets income from a testamentary trust. The trust was formed as a result of his wife's death. The fiscal year of the trust is from April 1 to March 31. The husband died on June 11, 2010. You have two choices when you report the husband's income from the trust:

- One choice is to include the trust income from April 1, 2009, to June 11, 2010, on the final return.
- The other choice is to file a return for income from the trust in addition to the final return. On the final return, include the trust income from April 1, 2009, to March 31, 2010. On the optional return for income from the trust, report the trust income from April 1, 2010, to June 11, 2010.

**How to file** – If you decide to file a return for income from a testamentary trust, you will need to:

1. Get a *T1 General Income Tax and Benefit Return.*
2. Write "104(23)(d)" in the top right corner of page 1 of the return.
3. Follow the instructions for completing a return in this guide and the *General Income Tax and Benefit Guide.*

You have to file this optional return and pay any amount owing by the **later** of:

- April 30, 2011 (or June 15, 2011, if the deceased was a self-employed individual, although any balance owing is still due on April 30); and
- six months after the date of death.

## Amounts for optional returns

There are three groups of amounts you can claim on the optional returns. They are amounts you can:

- claim in full on each return;
- split between returns; and
- claim only against certain income.

### Amounts you can claim in full on each return

On each optional return and on the final return, you can claim:

- the basic personal amount (line 300);
- the age amount (line 301);
- the spouse or common-law partner amount (line 303);
- the amount for an eligible dependant (line 305);
- the amount for infirm dependants age 18 or older (line 306); and
- the caregiver amount (line 315).

### Amounts you can split between returns

There are certain amounts you cannot claim in full on the final return and optional returns. However, you can split these amounts between the returns.

When you split an amount, the **total** of the claims cannot be more than what would have been allowed if you were only filing the final return. Amounts you can split are:

- adoption expenses (line 313);
- disability amount for the deceased (line 316);
- disability amount transferred from a dependant (line 318);
- interest paid on certain student loans (line 319);
- tuition, education, and textbook amounts for the deceased (line 323);
- tuition, education, and textbook amounts you transfer from a child (line 324);
- charitable donations that are not more than the net income you report on that return (line 349);
- cultural, ecological, and Crown gifts (line 342 of Schedule 9);
- public transit passes amount (line 364);
- children's fitness amount (line 365);
- home buyers' amount (line 369); and
- medical expenses (line 330), which you can split any way you want between the final return and any optional returns. However, you have to reduce the total expenses by the lower of $2,024 or 3% of the **total** net income you report on all returns.

**Example**
In the year a woman died, her total medical expenses were $9,000. You decide to file a rights or things return in addition to the final return. The total of her net income on the two returns is $40,000. Of this, $30,000 is on the final return and $10,000 is on the rights or things return.

You decide to split the $9,000 of medical expenses and claim two-thirds on the final return and one-third on the rights or things return.

| | | |
|---|---|---|
| 2/3 of $9,000 | = | $6,000 (to claim on final return) |
| 1/3 of $9,000 | = | $3,000 (to claim on rights or things return) |

The medical expense reduction is the lower of $2,024 or 3% of the total net income. In this example, the reduction is $1,200 ($40,000 × 3%), which is lower than $2,024.

The medical expense reduction must also be split between the two returns in the same proportion as the medical expenses.

| | | |
|---|---|---|
| 2/3 of $1,200 | = | $800 |
| 1/3 of $1,200 | = | $400 |

| | | |
|---|---|---|
| Deductions for medical expenses on final return | | $6,000 |
| | – | 800 |
| | = | $5,200 |
| Deductions for medical expenses on rights or things return | | $3,000 |
| | – | 400 |
| | = | $2,600 |

The deductions for medical expenses are $5,200 on the final return and $2,600 on the rights or things return.

## Amounts you can claim only against certain income

There are some amounts you can only claim on those returns on which you report the related income. The amounts are:

- Canadian Forces personnel and police deduction (line 244);
- employee home relocation loan deduction (line 248);
- security options deductions (stock options and shares) (line 249);
- vow of perpetual poverty deduction (line 256);
- Canada Pension Plan (CPP) or Quebec Pension Plan (QPP) contributions (line 308 or line 310);
- Employment Insurance premiums (line 312);
- pension income amount (line 314);
- Canada employment amount (line 363); and
- social benefits repayment (line 422).

**Example**
A deceased person's total employment income in the year of death was $30,000, and the CPP amount was $800. Of the $30,000, $1,000 is a right or thing. Of the $800, $27 is the CPP contribution the person paid on the $1,000. You decide to file a return for rights or things.

On the final return, you report income of $29,000 and claim a CPP amount of $773. On the return for rights or things, you include income of $1,000 and claim a CPP amount of $27.

There are certain amounts you **cannot** normally claim on an optional return. They include:

- registered pension plan (RPP) deduction (line 207);
- registered retirement savings plan (RRSP) deduction (line 208);
- annual union, professional, or like dues (line 212);
- child care expenses (line 214);
- disability supports deduction (line 215);
- allowable business investment losses (line 217);
- moving expenses (line 219);
- support payments made (line 220);
- carrying charges and interest expenses (line 221);

- exploration and development expenses (line 224);
- losses from other years (lines 251 – 253);
- capital gains deduction (line 254);
- northern residents deduction (line 255); and
- amounts you transfer from a spouse or common-law partner (line 326).

You may be able to claim these amounts on the final return.

For more information on other credits, see Chart 1 on page 28.

## Chapter 4 – Deemed disposition of property

In this chapter, we discuss the tax treatment of capital property the deceased owned at the date of death. We deal with capital property in general, as well as the particular treatment of depreciable and farm and fishing property. We discuss only property acquired after December 31, 1971.

There are special rules for property that a deceased person owned before 1972. For details about these rules and for information about other property such as eligible capital property, resource property, or an inventory of land, contact us at **1-800-959-8281**.

We define some of the terms in this chapter in the "Definitions" section, which begins on page 4.

### General information

When a person dies, we consider that the person has disposed of all capital property right before death. We call this a deemed disposition.

Also, right before death, we consider that the person has received the deemed proceeds of disposition (throughout this chapter we will refer to this as **deemed proceeds**). Even though there was not an actual sale, there can be a capital gain or, except for depreciable property or personal-use property, a capital loss.

For depreciable property, in addition to a capital gain, there can also be a **recapture** of capital cost allowance. Also, for depreciable property, instead of a capital loss there may be a **terminal loss**. We explain these terms on this page.

#### What is a capital gain?

When the proceeds or deemed proceeds of disposition of a capital property are **more** than its adjusted cost base, the result is a capital gain. In most cases, one-half of the capital gain is the taxable capital gain.

Use Schedule 3, *Capital Gains (or Losses) in 2010*, to calculate the taxable capital gain to report on the final return.

#### What is a capital gains deduction?

This is a deduction you can claim for the deceased person against eligible taxable capital gains from the disposition or deemed disposition of certain capital property.

You may be able to claim the capital gains deduction on taxable capital gains the deceased had in 2010 from:

- dispositions or deemed dispositions of qualified farm property or, after May 1, 2006, qualified fishing property;
- dispositions or deemed dispositions of qualified small business corporation shares; and
- a reserve brought into income from either of the above.

The lifetime capital gains exemption has been increased from $500,000 to $750,000 for dispositions after March 18, 2007. Since the inclusion rate for capital gains and losses is 50%, the lifetime capital gains deduction limit has been increased from $250,000 (1/2 of $500,000) to $375,000 (1/2 of $750,000) for dispositions after March 18, 2007.

For more information, see Guide T4037, *Capital Gains*.

#### What is a capital loss?

When the proceeds or deemed proceeds of disposition of a capital property are **less** than its adjusted cost base, the result is a capital loss. One-half of the capital loss is the allowable capital loss. You cannot have a capital loss on the disposition of depreciable property or personal use property.

For more information on claiming a capital loss, see the section called "Net capital losses in the year of death" on page 25.

#### Recaptures and terminal losses

For depreciable property, when the proceeds or deemed proceeds of disposition are **more** than the undepreciated capital cost, you will usually have a recapture of capital cost allowance (see the definition of capital cost allowance in the "Definitions" section, which begins on page 4). Include the recapture in income on the deceased's final return.

For depreciable property, when the proceeds or deemed proceeds of disposition are **less** than the undepreciated capital cost, the result is a terminal loss. Deduct the terminal loss on the deceased's final return.

> **Note**
> A terminal loss is not allowed for depreciable property that was personal-use property of the deceased.

For more information about a recapture of capital cost allowance or a terminal loss, see Interpretation Bulletin IT-478, *Capital Cost Allowance – Recapture and Terminal Loss*.

### Capital property other than depreciable property

In this section, we explain how to determine the deemed proceeds for capital property, other than depreciable property. The rules for calculating the deemed proceeds for depreciable property are explained in the section called

"Depreciable property" on this page. If there is a transfer of farm or fishing property to a child, read the section called "Farm or fishing property transferred to a child" on the next page.

### **Deceased's deemed proceeds** – Transfer to spouse or common-law partner, or testamentary spousal or common-law partner trust

There may be a transfer of capital property (including farm property, or fishing property) from a deceased person who was a resident of Canada immediately before death to a spouse or common-law partner, or a testamentary spousal or common-law partner trust.

**For a transfer to a spouse or common-law partner**, the deemed proceeds are the same as the property's adjusted cost base right before death, if **both** of these **conditions** are met:

- The spouse or common-law partner was a resident of Canada right before the person's death.
- The property becomes locked-in for the spouse or common-law partner no later than 36 months after the date of death. If you need more time to meet this condition, you can make a written request to the director at your tax services office.

**For a transfer to a testamentary spousal or common-law partner trust**, the deemed proceeds are the same as the property's adjusted cost base right before death, if **both** of these **conditions** are met:

- The testamentary spousal or common-law partner trust is resident in Canada right after the property becomes locked-in for this trust.
- The property becomes locked-in for the testamentary spousal or common-law partner trust no later than 36 months after the date of death. If you need more time to meet this condition, you can make a written request to the director at your tax services office.

In most cases, the deceased will not have a capital gain or loss. This is because the transfer postpones any gain or loss to the date the beneficiary disposes of the property.

**Example**
A person's will transfers non-depreciable capital property to the spouse or common-law partner, and both of the conditions for transfer to a spouse or common-law partner are met. Right before death, the adjusted cost base of the property was $35,000. Therefore, the deemed proceeds are $35,000. You would not report any capital gain or loss on the deceased's final return.

**Tax tip**
You can choose not to have the deemed proceeds equal the adjusted cost base. If you make this choice, the deemed proceeds are equal to the property's fair market value right before death. You have to make this choice when you file the final return for the deceased.

You may want to do this to use a capital gains deduction (see page 21) or a net capital loss on the deceased's final return. It may be best to report a capital gain or loss on the final return instead of deferring it to the spouse or common-law partner, or spousal or common-law partner trust.

### **Deceased's deemed proceeds** – All other transfers

For all other transfers, the deemed proceeds are equal to the property's fair market value right before death.

## Depreciable property

In this section, we explain how to determine the deemed proceeds for depreciable property. If there is a transfer of farm or fishing property to a child, see the section "Farm or fishing property transferred to a child" on the next page.

### **Deceased's deemed proceeds** – Transfer to spouse or common-law partner, or testamentary spousal or common-law partner trust

There may be a transfer of depreciable property (including depreciable farm property or fishing property) to a spouse or common-law partner, or a testamentary spousal or common-law partner trust. For such transfers, you may be able to use a special amount for the deemed proceeds. When you use this special amount, the deceased will not have a capital gain, recapture of capital cost allowance, or a terminal loss. The transfer postpones any gain, recapture, or terminal loss to the date the beneficiary disposes of the property.

The conditions required to use this special amount are the same as those listed for a transfer of capital property to a spouse or common-law partner, or testamentary spousal or common-law partner trust.

The special amount (deemed proceeds) is the **lower** of:

- the capital cost of the property for the deceased; and
- the result of the following calculation:

$$\frac{\text{Capital cost of the property}}{\text{Capital cost of all the property in the same class that had not been disposed of previously}} \times \text{Undepreciated capital cost of all of the deceased's property in the same class}$$

**Example**
A woman had two trucks that were used in her business. The woman died in July 2010, and the will transferred one truck to her husband. Both of the conditions for transfer to a spouse or common-law partner are met.

You have the following details:

| | |
|---|---|
| Undepreciated capital cost of the two trucks right before death | $33,500 |
| Capital cost of transferred truck | $22,500 |
| Capital cost of the two trucks | $50,000 |

The deceased's deemed proceeds on the transferred truck are the lower of:

- $22,500; and
- $\frac{\$22{,}500}{\$50{,}000} \times \$33{,}500 = \$15{,}075.$

The deemed proceeds are $15,075.

When there is more than one property in the same class, you can choose the order in which the deceased is deemed to have disposed of the properties. When you calculate the special amount, adjust the undepreciated capital cost and the total capital cost of the properties in the class to exclude previous deemed dispositions.

**Note**
When determining the special amount, you will need to recalculate the capital cost of property in the class when:

- the property was acquired in a non-arm's length transaction (see the "Definitions" section, which begins on page 4);
- the property was previously used for something other than gaining or producing income; or
- the part of a property used for gaining or producing income changed.

For more information, contact us at **1-800-959-8281**.

**Tax tip**
You can choose not to use the special amount for the deemed proceeds. If you make this choice, the deemed proceeds are equal to the property's fair market value right before death. You have to make this choice when you file the final return for the deceased.

You may want to do this to claim a capital gains deduction (see page 21) on the final return. It may be best to report a capital gain, recapture, or terminal loss on the final return instead of deferring it to the spouse or common-law partner, or spousal or common-law partner trust.

### **Deceased's deemed proceeds** – All other transfers

For all other transfers, the deemed proceeds are equal to the property's fair market value right before death.

## Farm or fishing property transferred to a child

In this section, we explain how to determine the deemed proceeds when there is a transfer of farm or fishing property to a child. For this kind of transfer, you may be able to use a special amount for the deemed proceeds. When you use this special amount, the deceased will not have a capital gain, recapture of capital cost allowance, or a terminal loss. The transfer postpones any gain, recapture, or terminal loss to the date the beneficiary disposes of the property.

In this chapter, when we refer to the transfer of farm and fishing property, the terms **farm property, fishing property**, and **child** have the following meanings:

**Farm property** includes land and depreciable property of a prescribed class used for farming.

**Fishing property** includes land and depreciable property of a prescribed class used for fishing.

A **child** includes:

- the deceased's natural or adopted child;
- the child of the deceased's spouse or common-law partner;
- the deceased's grandchild or great-grandchild;
- a person who, while under the age of 19, was in the deceased's custody and control and was wholly dependent on the deceased for support; and
- the spouse or common-law partner of any of the above.

### Conditions

To use the special amount for the deemed proceeds, **all four** of the following conditions have to be met:

- The farm or fishing property is used principally in a farming or fishing business carried on in Canada.
- The child was a resident of Canada right before the deceased's death.
- The farm property becomes locked-in for the child no later than 36 months after the date of death. If you need more time to meet this condition, you can make a written request to the director at your tax services office.
- The deceased, the deceased's spouse or common-law partner, or any child of the deceased was using the farm property mainly for farming, on a regular and ongoing basis, before the deceased's death.

  The rollover provisions available for farm property also apply to land and depreciable property used principally in a woodlot farming business. They apply where the deceased, the deceased's spouse or common-law partner, or any of the deceased's children was engaged in the woodlot operation as required by a **prescribed forest management plan** in respect of the woodlot. These provisions apply to transfers of property that occur after December 10, 2001. For more information, see IT-373, *Woodlots*, or contact us at **1-800-959-8281**.

You may also be able to use a special amount for the deemed proceeds when a share of the capital stock of a family farm corporation or an interest in a family farm partnership is transferred to a child.

For details, see Interpretation Bulletin IT-349, *Intergenerational Transfers of Farm Property on Death.*

You may also be able to use a special amount for the deemed proceeds when a share of the capital stock of a family fishing corporation or an interest in a family fishing partnership is transferred to a child.

### **Deceased's deemed proceeds** – Transfer of farmland to a child

If all four conditions, listed on the previous page are met, you can choose to have the deemed proceeds equal the adjusted cost base of the land right before death. Therefore, the deceased will not have a capital gain or loss.

**Tax tip**
You can choose not to have the deemed proceeds equal the adjusted cost base. If you make this choice, you can transfer the land for any amount between its adjusted cost base and fair market value right before death. You have to make this choice when you file the final return for the deceased.

You may want to do this to claim the capital gains deduction (see page 21) or a net capital loss on the final return. It may be best to report a capital gain or loss on the final return instead of deferring it to a child.

### **Deceased's deemed proceeds** – Transfer of depreciable farm or fishing property to a child

If there is a transfer of depreciable farm property, or depreciable fishing property, you may be able to use a special amount for the deemed proceeds. To use this special amount, the four conditions listed on the previous page have to be met.

In most cases, when you use this special amount, the deceased will not have a capital gain, a recapture of capital cost allowance, or a terminal loss. This is because the transfer postpones any gain, recapture, or terminal loss to the date the beneficiary disposes of the property.

The special amount (deemed proceeds) is the **lower** of:

- the capital cost of the property for the deceased; and
- the result of the following calculation:

$$\frac{\text{Capital cost of the property}}{\text{Capital cost of the property in the same class that had not been disposed of previously}} \times \begin{array}{c}\text{Undepreciated capital cost of all}\\ \text{of the deceased's property in the}\\ \text{same class}\end{array}$$

**Example**
A man who owned three fishing boats died in August 2010. His will transferred one boat to his son. The four conditions for transfer of fishing property to a child are met. You have the following details:

| | |
|---|---|
| Undepreciated capital cost of the three boats right before death | $ 90,000 |
| Capital cost of transferred boat | $ 45,000 |
| Capital cost of all three boats | $100,000 |

The deceased's deemed proceeds on the transferred boat are the lower of:

- $ 45,000; and
- $\frac{\$45{,}000}{\$100{,}000} \times \$90{,}000 = \$40{,}500$.

The deemed proceeds are $40,500.

When there is more than one property in the same class, you can choose the order in which the deceased is deemed to have disposed of the properties. When you calculate the special amount, adjust the undepreciated capital cost and the total capital cost of the properties in the class to exclude previous deemed dispositions.

**Note**
When you determine the special amount, you will need to recalculate the capital cost of any property in the class when:

- the property was acquired in a non-arm's length transaction;
- the property was previously used for something other than gaining or producing income; or
- the part of a property used for gaining or producing income changed.

For more information, contact us at **1-800-959-8281**.

**Tax tip**
You can choose not to use the special amount for the deemed proceeds. If you make this choice, you can transfer the property for any amount between the special amount and its fair market value right before death. You have to make this choice when you file the final return for the deceased.

You may want to do this to claim the capital gains deduction (see page 21) on the final return. It may be best to report a capital gain, recapture, or terminal loss on the final return instead of deferring it to a child.

For more information, see Interpretation Bulletin IT-349, *Intergenerational Transfers of Farm Property on Death*, or contact us. You may also refer to Guide T4003, *Farming Income*, or Guide T4004, *Fishing Income*.

#### **Election to delay payment of income tax**

Generally, you have to pay any amount owing on a return when the return is due. In some cases, you can delay paying part of the income tax due. For instance, you can delay paying part of the amount owing from the deemed disposition of capital property. Remember that we charge interest on any unpaid amount, from the day after the due date to the date you pay the amount in full.

If you want to delay payment, you will have to give us security for the amount owing. You also have to complete Form T2075, *Election to Defer Payment of Income Tax, Under Subsection 159(5) of the Income Tax Act by a Deceased Taxpayer's Legal Representative or Trustee*. For more information, contact the Collections Division of your tax services office by calling **1-888-863-8657**.

## Chapter 5 – Net capital losses

In this chapter, we discuss how to apply a net capital loss that occurred in the year of death. We also explain how to apply net capital losses from earlier years to the final return and the return for the year before the year of death.

We define some of the terms in this chapter in the "Definitions" section, which begins on page 4.

### What is a net capital loss?

Generally, when allowable capital losses are more than taxable capital gains, the difference is a **net capital loss**. An allowable capital loss is 1/2 of a capital loss.

Generally, a taxable capital gain is 1/2 of a capital gain. The rate used to determine the taxable part of a capital gain and the allowable part of a capital loss is called an **inclusion rate**.

### Net capital losses in the year of death

To apply a net capital loss that happened in the year of death, you can use either Method A or Method B.

**Method A** – You can carry back a 2010 net capital loss to reduce any taxable capital gains in any of the three tax years before the year of death. If you are applying it against taxable capital gains realized in 2007, 2008, or 2009, you do not need to make any adjustment because the inclusion rate is the same in all three years. The loss you carry back cannot be more than the taxable capital gains in those years. To ask for a loss carryback, complete "Section III – Net capital loss for carryback" on Form T1A, *Request for Loss Carryback*, and send it to your tax centre. **Do not** file an amended return for the year to which you want to apply the loss.

After you carry back the loss, there may be an amount left. You may be able to use some of the remaining amount to reduce other income on the final return, the return for the year before the year of death, or both returns. However, before you do this, you have to calculate the amount you can use.

From the net capital loss you have left, subtract any capital gains deductions the deceased has claimed to date. Use any loss left to reduce other income for the year of death, the year before the year of death, or for both years.

If you claim any remaining net capital loss in the year of death, you should claim the amount at line 127 of the final return.

**Note**
Do not use a capital loss claimed against other income at line 127 in the calculation of net income for the purposes of calculating other amounts such as social benefit repayments, provincial or territorial tax credits, and those non-refundable tax credits requiring the use of net income.

**Method B** – You can choose not to carry back the net capital loss to reduce taxable capital gains from earlier years. You may prefer to reduce other income on the final return, the return for the year before the year of death, or both returns. However, before you do this, you have to calculate the amount you can use.

From the net capital loss, subtract any capital gains deductions the deceased has claimed to date. Use any loss remaining to reduce other income for the year of death, the year before the year of death, or for both years.

If you claim any remaining net capital loss in the year of death, you should claim it as a negative amount at line 127 of the final return.

**Example**
A man died on June 20, 2010. You have the following details about his tax matters:

| | |
|---|---|
| Net capital loss in 2010 | $11,000 |
| Taxable capital gains in 2008 | $ 4,000 |
| Taxable capital gains in 2007 | $ 2,000 |
| Total capital gains deductions claimed to date | $ 4,000 |

He did not claim any capital gains deductions for 2007 or 2008.

You can use Method A or Method B.

**Method A**
If you choose Method A, you can use the net capital losses to reduce his 2008 taxable capital gains to zero ($11,000 – $4,000). Then, you can use the remaining balance of $7,000 to reduce his 2007 taxable capital gain to zero ($7,000 – $2,000).

After you subtract his capital gains deductions ($5,000 – $4,000), you still have $1,000 left to reduce the man's other income for 2010 or 2009 or for both years.

**Method B**
If you choose to use this method, you will first deduct his capital gains deductions of $4,000 from his net capital loss in 2010 of $11,000. You can now use the remaining $7,000 to reduce the man's other income for 2010 or 2009, or for both years.

**Note**
If you claim any remaining net capital loss in the year before the year of death, you will need to complete Form T1-ADJ, T1 *Adjustment Request*, or send us a signed letter providing the details of your request. Send your Form T1-ADJ or letter **separately** from the deceased's final return. Applying a 2010 net capital loss to a previous year may reduce any capital gains deductions the deceased claimed in that year or a following year.

## Net capital losses before the year of death

The deceased may have had a net capital loss before the year of death but never applied it. If so, you can apply the loss against taxable capital gains on the final return. If the net capital loss arose after 1987 and before 2001, you will need to make an adjustment to the inclusion rate as explained below. If there is still an amount left, you may be able to use it to reduce other income on the final return, the return for the year before the year of death, or both returns. If you decide to claim this loss on the final return, report it at line 253.

> **Note**
> You cannot use the net capital losses of other years to create a negative taxable income for any year.

You have to apply net capital losses of earlier years before you apply net capital losses of later years. For example, if you have net capital losses in 1997 and 1999 and want to apply them against your taxable capital gains in 2010, you have to follow a certain order. First, apply your 1997 net capital loss against your taxable capital gain. Then apply your 1999 net capital loss against it.

The inclusion rate used to determine the taxable part of a capital gain and the allowable part of a capital loss has changed over the years. If the inclusion rate of 1/2 for 2010 is different from the inclusion rate in effect the year the loss occurred, you will need to adjust the loss before applying it to the taxable capital gain in 2010.

**To apply a previous year loss to 2010**, you will need to adjust the loss as follows:

- For a net capital loss from **1987 or earlier**, there is no adjustment required.
- For a net capital loss from **1988 or 1989**, multiply the loss by **3/4**.
- For a net capital loss from **1990 to 1999**, multiply the loss by **2/3**.
- For a net capital loss from **2000**, multiply the loss by **[1 ÷ (2 × IR)]**, where **IR** is the inclusion rate for 2000. This rate is from Line 16 of Part 4 of the deceased's Schedule 3 for 2000, or from the deceased's notice of assessment or latest notice of reassessment for 2000.
- For a net capital loss from **2001 or later**, there is no adjustment required.

When you make these calculations, you get the **adjusted net capital loss**.

Now you can reduce taxable capital gains in the year of death. To do this, use the **lower** of:

- the adjusted net capital loss; and
- the taxable capital gains in the year of death.

After you reduce the taxable capital gains, some of the loss may be left. You may be able to use this amount to reduce other income for the year of death, the year before the year of death, or for both years. However, before you do this, you may have to calculate the amount you can use.

If you had to adjust the loss before applying it to the 2010 taxable capital gain, you will now have to readjust the loss that remains as follows:

- For a net capital loss from **1987 or earlier**, there is no adjustment required.
- Multiply any adjusted net capital losses from **1988 or 1989** by **4/3**.
- Multiply any adjusted net capital losses from **1990 to 1999** by **3/2**.
- Multiply any adjusted net capital losses from **2000** by **2 × IR**, where **IR** is the inclusion rate for 2000.
- For a net capital loss from **2001 or later**, there is no adjustment required.

The result is your **readjusted balance** of net capital losses. From this balance, subtract all capital gains deductions claimed to date, including those on the final return. If there is an amount left, you can use it to reduce other income for the year of death, the year before the year of death, or for both years.

**Example**
A woman died in August of 2010. You have these details about her tax matters:

| | |
|---|---|
| Net capital loss in 1999, never applied | $18,000 |
| Taxable capital gain in 2010 | $ 6,000 |
| Capital gains deductions claimed to date | $ 4,000 |

You decide to use the 1999 loss to reduce the 2010 taxable capital gain and to use any amount left to reduce other income for 2010.

You have to adjust the 1999 net capital loss before you can apply it. Multiply it by **2/3** to get the adjusted net capital loss:

$18,000 × 2/3 = $12,000

To reduce the 2010 taxable capital gain, use the lower of:

- $12,000 (adjusted net capital loss); and
- $6,000 (2010 taxable capital gain).

After you use $6,000 of the loss to reduce the gain to zero, you still have $6,000 ($12,000 – $6,000) left. You can use this amount to reduce the deceased's other income for 2010.

To determine the amount to use, you have to readjust the $6,000. Because the loss occurred in 1999, multiply the amount left by **3/2** to get the readjusted balance:

$6,000 × 3/2 = $9,000

From the readjusted balance, subtract all capital gains deductions claimed to date:

$9,000 – $4,000 = $5,000

You can use $5,000 to reduce the deceased's other income for 2010. If you decide not to use the total of this balance in 2010, you can use the amount that is left to reduce other income for 2009.

**Note**
If you claim a capital gains deduction for the year of death or the year before the year of death, subtract it from the balance of net capital losses you have available to reduce other income in those years. For more details about capital gains and losses, as well as the capital gains deduction, see Guide T4037, *Capital Gains*.

## Disposition of estate property by the legal representative

As the legal representative, you may continue looking after the deceased's estate through a trust. If you dispose of capital property, the result may be a net capital loss. If you dispose of depreciable property, the result may be a terminal loss.

Usually, you would claim these losses on the trust's *T3 Trust Income Tax and Information Return*. However, in the trust's first tax year, you can choose to claim all or part of these losses on the deceased's final return. Any net capital loss realized after the date of death can only be applied to the year of death. For more information, see "164(6) election" in Chapter 3 of the T4013, *T3 Trust Guide*.

## Appendix

| Chart 1 – Returns for the year of death | | | | | |
|---|---|---|---|---|---|
| **Section of *General Income Tax and Benefit Return*** | **Line** | **Final return 70(1)** | **Return for rights or things 70(2)** | **Return for a partner or proprietor 150(4)** | **Return for income from a testamentary trust 104(23)(d)** |
| **Total income** | 101 to 146 | ▪ all income received before death<br>▪ all income from deemed dispositions<br>▪ all periodic payments (for example, rent, salary, and accrued interest) | ▪ salary, commissions, and vacation pay owed and paid after death (Note 1)<br>▪ retroactive salary adjustments owed and paid after death<br>▪ OAS, CPP/QPP paid after the date of death for the month of death<br>▪ CPP and EI arrears<br>▪ Universal Child Care Benefit (UCCB)<br>▪ accounts receivable, supplies, and inventory (Note 2)<br>▪ uncashed matured bond coupons<br>▪ bond interest earned but not received before death<br>▪ dividends declared before the date of death, but not received<br>▪ crops, livestock (Note 3)<br>▪ work in progress (Note 4) | ▪ income from the business from the end of the business' fiscal period to the date of death | ▪ income from the trust from the end of the trust's fiscal period to the date of death |
| **Deductions for calculating net income** | 207 to 232 | ▪ all deductions from lines 207 to 232 that are allowable | ▪ Universal Child Care Benefit (UCCB) repayment<br>▪ generally, none of the other deductions can be claimed | same as for return for rights or things 70(2) | same as for return for rights or things 70(2) |
| | 235 | ▪ social benefits repayments | Note 5 | not applicable | not applicable |
| **Deductions for calculating taxable income** | | | **Split deductions** (Note 6) | | |
| | 244 | ▪ Canadian Forces personnel and police deduction | Note 7 | not applicable | not applicable |
| | 248 | ▪ home relocation loans | Note 7 | not applicable | not applicable |
| | 249 | ▪ security options deductions | Note 7 | not applicable | not applicable |
| | 250 | ▪ other payments | not applicable | not applicable | not applicable |
| | 251-255 | ▪ losses or other deductions | no | no | no |
| | 256 | ▪ vow of perpetual poverty | yes | not applicable | not applicable |
| **Federal non-refundable tax credits** (Note 13) | 300-306, 367 | ▪ all personal amounts | yes – in full | yes – in full | yes – in full |
| | 315 | ▪ caregiver amount | yes – in full | yes – in full | yes – in full |
| | | | **Split amounts** (Note 6) | | |
| | 308 | ▪ CPP or QPP contributions | Note 7 | not applicable | not applicable |
| | 310 | ▪ CPP or QPP contributions on self-employed income | not applicable | yes | not applicable |
| | 312 | ▪ EI premiums | Note 7 | not applicable | not applicable |
| | 313 | ▪ adoption expenses | yes | yes | yes |

(continued on next page)

| Chart 1 – Returns for the year of death (continued) | | | | | |
|---|---|---|---|---|---|
| **Section of *T1 General Income Tax and Benefit Return*** | **Line** | **Final return 70(1)** | **Return for rights or things 70(2)** | **Return for a partner or proprietor 150(4)** | **Return for income from a testamentary trust 104(23)(d)** |
| **Federal Non-refundable tax credits** (Note 13) (continued) | **Split amounts** (Note 6) | | | | |
| | 314 | ▪ pension income amount | Note 8 | not applicable | Note 8 |
| | 316 | ▪ disability amount | yes | yes | yes |
| | 318 | ▪ disability amount transferred from a dependant | yes | yes | yes |
| | 319 | ▪ interest on student loans | yes | yes | yes |
| | 323-324 | ▪ tuition, education, and textbook | yes | yes | yes |
| | 326 | ▪ amounts transferred from spouse or common-law partner | no | no | no |
| | 330 | ▪ medical expenses | Note 9 | Note 9 | Note 9 |
| | 340 | ▪ charitable donations | Note 10 | Note 10 | Note 10 |
| | 342 | ▪ cultural and ecological gifts | yes | yes | yes |
| | 363 | ▪ Canada employment amount | yes | no | no |
| | 364 | ▪ public transit passes amount | yes | yes | yes |
| | 365 | ▪ children's fitness amount | yes | yes | yes |
| | 369 | ▪ Home buyers' amount | yes | yes | yes |
| **Refund or Balance owing** | 412 | ▪ investment tax credit | no | no | no |
| | 422 | ▪ social benefits repayment | Note 5 | not applicable | not applicable |
| | 425 | ▪ dividend tax credits | Note 11 | not applicable | Note 11 |
| | 427 | ▪ minimum tax carryover | no | no | no |
| | 452 | ▪ refundable medical expense supplement (Note 12) | no | no | no |
| | 453 | ▪ Working income tax benefit (WITB) | no | no | no |

**Notes**

1. Salary, commissions, and vacation pay are rights or things if **both** of these conditions are met:
   - the employer owed them to the deceased on the date of death; and
   - they are for a pay period that ended before the date of death.
2. Accounts receivable, supplies on hand, and inventory are rights or things if the deceased's business used the cash method.
3. This includes harvested farm crops and livestock that is not part of the basic herd. For more information, see Interpretation Bulletins IT-234, *Income of Deceased Persons – Farm Crops*, and IT-427, *Livestock of Farmers*.
4. **Work in progress** is a right or thing if the deceased was a sole proprietor and a professional [accountant, dentist, lawyer (in Quebec an advocate or notary), medical doctor, veterinarian, or chiropractor] who had elected to exclude work in progress when calculating his or her total income. For more information about rights or things, see Interpretation Bulletin IT-212, *Income of Deceased Persons – Rights or Things*, and its Special Release.
5. If OAS or EI benefits have been reported on this return, this amount can be claimed.
6. Claims split between returns cannot be more than the total that could be allowed if you were only filing the final return.
7. If related employment income has been reported on this return, this amount can be claimed.

(continued on next page)

www.cra.gc.ca 29

**Chart 1 – Returns for the year of death** (continued)

**Notes** (continued)

8. If pension or annuity income has been reported on line 115 or line 129 of this return, this amount can be claimed.
9. The medical expenses can be split between the returns. Allowable medical expenses have to be reduced by the lesser of $2,024 or 3% of the total net income reported on **all** the returns.
10. The amount that can be claimed is the **lesser** of the eligible amounts of charitable donations or 100% of the net income reported on this return. Also, the total charitable donations claimed on **all** the returns cannot be more than the eligible amount of charitable donations.
11. If dividend income has been reported on this return, this amount can be claimed.
12. Use the deceased's net income from the final return and the spouse's or common-law partner's net income for the entire year to calculate this credit.
13. If the deceased was a resident of a province or territory other than Quebec, he or she may now also be able to claim provincial or territorial tax credits. See the provincial or territorial pages in the deceased's forms book.

**Chart 2 – Income reported on the *T3 Trust Income Tax and Information Return***

Report the following amounts on line 19 of the *T3 Trust Income Tax and Information Return*, for the year in which you receive the income. If the income is received in a year after the year of death, report it on the T3 return for that later year.

| Type of income | Information slip |
|---|---|
| 1. Severance pay received because of death. Since this is a death benefit, up to $10,000 may be non-taxable. | T4A, Box 106 |
| 2. Future adjustments to severance pay regardless of when the collective agreement was signed. | T4A, Box 028 |
| 3. Refund of pension contributions payable because of death. | T4A, Box 018 |
| 4. Guaranteed minimum pension payment (this is not a death benefit). | T4A, Box 018 |
| 5. Deferred profit-sharing plan payment. | T4A, Box 018 |
| 6. Pension or superannuation periodic payments | T4A, Box 016 |
| 7. I.A.A.C. Annuity | T4A, Box 024 |
| 8. Income earned in a RRIF after annuitant dies | T4RIF, Box 22 |
| 9. Income earned in an RRSP after annuitant dies | T4RSP, Box 28 |
| 10. CPP or QPP death benefit, if not reported by the recipient. | T4A(P), Box 18 |

**Chart 3 – Non-taxable amounts**

Do not report the following amounts on a T1 final return for a deceased person or a T3 return for a trust:

1. Retroactive adjustments to the following employment income when a collective agreement or other authorizing instrument has been signed **after** the date of death:
   - salary or wages (including overtime) from the end of the last pay period to the date of death;
   - salary or wages (including overtime) for a pay period finished before the date of death, but paid after death; and
   - payment for vacation leave earned but not taken.
2. Group term insurance such as the federal government's supplementary death benefit.

## References

The following publications are available at **www.cra.gc.ca** or by calling **1-800-959-2221**.

### Forms

RC4288 *Request for Taxpayer Relief*
T1A *Request for Loss Carryback*
T1013 *Authorizing or Cancelling a Representative*
T1090 *Death of a RRIF Annuitant – Designated Benefit*
T1136 *Old Age Security Return of Income*
T2019 *Death of an RRSP Annuitant – Refund of Premiums*
T2075 *Election to Defer Payment of Income Tax, Under Subsection 159(5) of the Income Tax Act by a Deceased Taxpayer's Legal Representative or Trustee*
TX19 *Asking for a Clearance Certificate*

### Guides

P113 *Gifts and Income Tax*
RC4060 *Farming Income and the AgriStability and AgriInvest Programs Guide*
RC4064 *Medical and Disability-Related Information*
RC4112 *Lifelong Learning Plan (LLP)*
RC4135 *Home Buyers' Plan (HBP)*
RC4288 *Request for Taxpayer Relief*
RC4408 *Farming Income and the AgriStability and AgriInvest Programs Harmonized Guide*
RC4466 *Tax-Free Savings Account (TFSA)*
T4002 *Business and Professional Income*
T4003 *Farming Income*
T4013 *T3 Trust Guide*
T4037 *Capital Gains*
T4040 *RRSPs and Other Registered Plans for Retirement*
T4055 *Newcomers to Canada*
T4056 *Emigrants and Income Tax*

### Information circulars

IC82-6 *Clearance Certificate*
IC07-1 *Taxpayer Relief Provisions*

### Interpretation bulletins

IT-210 *Income of Deceased Persons – Periodic Payments and Investment Tax Credit*
IT-212 *Income of Deceased Persons – Rights or Things*, and its Special Release
IT-234 *Income of Deceased Persons – Farm Crops*
IT-244 *Gifts by Individuals of Life Insurance Policies as Charitable Donations*
IT-278 *Death of a Partner or of a Retired Partner*
IT-305 *Testamentary Spouse Trusts*
IT-326 *Returns of Deceased Persons as "Another Person"*
IT-349 *Intergenerational Transfers of Farm Property on Death*
IT-419 *Meaning of Arm's Length*
IT-427 *Livestock of Farmers*
IT-456 *Capital Property – Some Adjustments to Cost Base*, and its Special Release
IT-478 *Capital Cost Allowance – Recapture and Terminal Loss*
IT-508 *Death Benefits*
IT-519 *Medical Expense and Disability Tax Credits and Attendant Care Expense Deduction*

### Information sheets

RC4111 *What to Do Following a Death*
RC4177 *Death of an RRSP Annuitant*
RC4178 *Death of a RRIF Annuitant*

## For more information

### What if you need help?

If you need help after reading this publication, go to **www.cra.gc.ca/deceased** or call **1-800-959-8281**.

If we cannot resolve your enquiry by telephone, you can meet with an agent in person at a tax services office. Call us at the number listed above to make an appointment with an agent.

### Forms and publications

To get any forms or publications, go to **www.cra.gc.ca/forms** or call **1-800-959-2221**.

### TIPS (Tax Information Phone Service)

For personal and general tax information by telephone, use our automated service, TIPS, by calling **1-800-267-6999**.

### Teletypewriter (TTY) users

TTY users can call **1-800-665-0354** for bilingual assistance during regular business hours.

### Our service complaint process

#### Step 1 – Talk to us

If you are not satisfied with the **service** you have received from us, you have the right to make a formal complaint. Before you make a complaint, we recommend that you try to resolve the matter with the CRA employee you have been dealing with (or call the phone number you have been given).

If you still disagree with the way your concerns are being addressed, ask to discuss the matter with the employee's supervisor.

#### Step 2 – Contact CRA – Service Complaints

This program is available to individual and business taxpayers and benefit recipients who have dealings with us. It is meant to provide you with an extra level of review if you are not satisfied with the results from the **first step** of our complaint process. In general, service-related complaints refer to the quality and timeliness of the work we performed.

If you choose to bring your complaint to the attention of CRA – Service Complaints, complete Form RC193, *Service Related Complaint*, which you can get by going to **www.cra.gc.ca/complaints** or by calling **1-800-959-2221**.

#### Step 3 – Contact the office of the Taxpayers' Ombudsman

If, **after following steps 1 and 2**, you are still not satisfied with the way the CRA has handled your complaint, you can file a complaint with the Taxpayers' Ombudsman.

For more information on the Taxpayers' Ombudsman and on how to file a complaint, visit their Web site at **www.taxpayersrights.gc.ca**.

### Your opinion counts!

If you have any comments or suggestions that could help us improve our publications, we would like to hear from you. Please send your comments to:

**Taxpayer Services Directorate**
**Canada Revenue Agency**
**750 Heron Road**
**Ottawa ON K1A 0L5**

## Index

# Taxpayer Relief Provisions (Information Circular IC07-1)

Canada Revenue Agency    Agence du revenu du Canada

**INCOME TAX**
**INFORMATION CIRCULAR**

NO.: **IC07-1**    DATE: May 31, 2007

SUBJECT: **Taxpayer Relief Provisions**

**This version is only available electronically.**

## Contents



Canada

## Application

¶ 1. This information circular consolidates and cancels information circulars IC 92-1, *Guidelines for Accepting Late, Amended or Revoked Elections, IC 92-2, Guidelines for the Cancellation and Waiver of Interest and Penalties, and IC 92-3, Guidelines for Refunds Beyond the Normal Three Year Period*, all dated March 18, 1992.

¶ 2. In this information circular, the term **taxpayer** includes an individual, an employer or a payer, a corporation, a partnership, a trust, an estate, and an organization, all of which can request relief from the Minister of National Revenue (Minister) to mitigate the strict application of certain provisions as a result of not satisfying various rules and obligations required under the *Income Tax Act.*

¶ 3. Unless otherwise specified, all legislative references in this information circular refer to the *Income Tax Act* (Act).

¶ 4. In this information circular, the terms **fairness provisions** and **fairness legislation** commonly used on the Canada Revenue Agency (CRA) Web site and in CRA publications have been replaced with the term **taxpayer relief provisions**.

## Introduction

¶ 5. This information circular provides information on the discretionary authority the Minister has under the Act to grant taxpayers relief in accordance with the legislative provisions described in ¶ 9. It also explains how a taxpayer makes a request for relief, including the proper information and documentation needed to support such a request, and outlines the administrative guidelines the CRA will follow in making a discretionary decision whether to grant or deny relief based on a taxpayer's situation.

¶ 6. These are only guidelines. They are not intended to be exhaustive, and are not meant to restrict the spirit or intent of the legislation.

¶ 7. This information circular is divided into five parts:

| | |
|---|---|
| Part I | Legislation |
| Part II | Guidelines for the Cancellation or Waiver of Penalties and Interest |
| Part III | Guidelines for Accepting Late, Amended, or Revoked Elections |
| Part IV | Guidelines for Refunds or Reduction in Amounts Payable Beyond the Normal Three-Year Period |
| Part V | Rules and Procedures When Relief Is Granted or Denied |

## *Part I*

### Legislation

¶ 8. The legislation gives the CRA the ability to administer the income tax system fairly and reasonably by helping taxpayers to resolve issues that arise through no fault of their own, and to allow for a common-sense approach in dealing with taxpayers who, because of personal misfortune or circumstances beyond their control, could not comply with a statutory requirement for income tax purposes.

#### *Taxpayer Relief Provisions*

¶ 9. A taxpayer can ask for relief in accordance with the provisions of the Act listed in this paragraph. After consideration of the relevant facts and circumstances, a delegated official of the CRA (see ¶ 17) will decide whether it is appropriate to:

(a) waive or cancel penalties and interest under subsection 220(3.1);

(b) extend the filing-due date for making certain elections or grant permission to amend or revoke certain elections under subsection 220(3.2);

(c) authorize a refund to an individual (other than a trust) or a testamentary trust under paragraph 164(1.5)(a), even though an income tax return is filed outside the normal three-year period; or

(d) authorize a reassessment or redetermination for an individual (other than a trust) or a testamentary trust beyond the three-year normal reassessment period under subsection 152(4.2), where the adjustment would result in a refund or a reduction in an amount payable.

¶ 10. While paragraph 164(1.5)(a) and subsection 152(4.2) apply only to individuals (other than a trust) and testamentary trusts, subsections 220(3.1) and (3.2) apply to all taxpayers.

¶ 11. The Minister does not have to grant relief under the taxpayer relief provisions. Each request will be reviewed and decided on its own merit. If relief is denied or partly granted, the CRA will provide the taxpayer with an explanation of the reasons and factors for the decision.

#### *Limitation Period on Exercising Ministerial Discretion and Deadline to Apply for Relief*

¶ 12. For requests or income tax returns filed on or after January 1, 2005, the Minister may grant relief for any tax year (or fiscal period in the case of a partnership) that ended within 10 years before the calendar year in which the taxpayer's request or income tax return is filed.

¶ 13. Due to this limitation, a taxpayer has 10 years from the end of the calendar year in which the tax year or fiscal period at issue ended to make a request to the CRA for relief. This limitation applies to each of the legislative provisions described in ¶ 9.

¶ 14. The 10-year limitation period rolls forward every January 1. For requests or income tax returns that are filed in the current calendar year, the Minister has no authority to:

- waive or cancel penalties and interest;
- accept a late, amended, or revoked income tax election; or
- issue a refund or adjustment beyond the normal three-year period;

where the request is for a tax year or fiscal period of the taxpayer that ended more than 10 years before the calendar year in which the request was made.

#### *Examples*

- An initial request or income tax return filed during the 2007 calendar year must deal with an issue related to a taxpayer's 1997 and later tax years (or fiscal periods) to be eligible for relief.
- An initial request or income tax return filed on or after January 1, 2008, related to a taxpayer's 1997 and previous tax years (or fiscal periods) is not eligible for relief, since those tax years (or fiscal periods) are beyond the 10-year period. Only requests or returns filed for the 1998 and later tax years (or fiscal periods) are eligible for relief as of this date.
- The Minister has no authority to grant relief for the 1998 tax year (or fiscal period) unless the taxpayer has filed an initial request or income tax return for that year before January 1, 2009.

¶ 15. If an assessment or reassessment for a tax year is issued by the CRA in a later year, or if an objection or appeal filed by a taxpayer may take considerable time to resolve, the taxpayer should send in their request for any potential relief before the 10-year time limit for that tax year expires.

¶ 16. Unless an initial request or income tax return was filed before the 10-year limitation rule coming into effect on January 1, 2005, requests filed for the 1985 to 1994 tax years will not be accepted and refunds beyond the normal three-year period will not be issued. For any active requests made before January 1, 2005, the taxpayer relief provisions in ¶ 9 and the redress process described in ¶ 103 and ¶ 105 continue to apply for the taxpayer's 1985 to 1994 tax years.

### *Who Is Authorized to Make the Decision?*

¶ 17. Subsection 220(2.01) authorizes the Minister to delegate his/her powers and duties conferred in various provisions of the Act to designated officials within the CRA. The officials delegated to exercise the Minister's discretionary authority under the taxpayer relief provisions described in ¶ 9 are authorized through administrative delegation instruments. These instruments are available at **http://www.cra-arc.gc.ca/tax/technical/delegationofpowers/menu-e.html**.

¶ 18. These officials are authorized to conduct a review of a taxpayer's request for relief and to make a decision whether to grant, partly grant, or deny, the request. It is a general administrative practice of the CRA for another CRA official, or a committee of CRA officials, to prepare a decision report for the delegated official's consideration, including a recommendation on whether or not granting relief is justified. The final decision and notification of the decision to the taxpayer rests with the delegated official.

## *Part II*

## Guidelines for the Cancellation or Waiver of Penalties and Interest

¶ 19. The information in Part II of this information circular deals with the Minister's discretion to allow relief from the application of the penalty and interest provisions of the Act. The Minister may also provide relief from interest amounts, and in some cases penalty amounts, if he or she is satisfied that a taxpayer has an inability to pay or suffers from financial hardship related to a debt owed to the CRA.

### *General*

¶ 20. Subsection 220(3.1) gives the Minister the discretionary authority to waive or cancel all or part of any penalty and interest otherwise payable by a taxpayer under the Act. The request must be made within the 10-year time limit described in ¶ 13.

¶ 21. The ability of the CRA to waive or cancel penalties and interest is not to be used by taxpayers as a way to arbitrarily reduce or settle their tax debt.

¶ 22. A **waiver** refers to penalties and interest otherwise payable by a taxpayer for which relief is granted by the CRA before these amounts are assessed or charged to the taxpayer. A **cancellation** refers to penalties and interest amounts that were assessed or charged to the taxpayer for which relief is granted by the CRA.

### *Circumstances Where Relief From Penalty and Interest May Be Warranted*

¶ 23. The Minister may grant relief from the application of penalty and interest where the following types of situations exist and justify a taxpayer's inability to satisfy a tax obligation or requirement at issue:

(a) extraordinary circumstances

(b) actions of the CRA

(c) inability to pay or financial hardship

¶ 24. The Minister may also grant relief if a taxpayer's circumstances do not fall within the situations stated in ¶ 23.

#### Extraordinary Circumstances

¶ 25. Penalties and interest may be waived or cancelled in whole or in part where they result from circumstances beyond a taxpayer's control. Extraordinary circumstances that may have prevented a taxpayer from making a payment when due, filing a return on time, or otherwise complying with an obligation under the Act include, but are not limited to, the following examples:

(a) natural or man-made disasters such as, flood or fire;

(b) civil disturbances or disruptions in services, such as a postal strike;

(c) a serious illness or accident; or

(d) serious emotional or mental distress, such as death in the immediate family.

**Actions of the CRA**

¶ 26. Penalties and interest may also be waived or cancelled if the penalty and interest arose primarily because of actions of the CRA, such as:

(a) processing delays that result in the taxpayer not being informed, within a reasonable time, that an amount was owing;

(b) errors in material available to the public, which led taxpayers to file returns or make payments based on incorrect information;

(c) incorrect information provided to a taxpayer, such as in the case where the CRA wrongly advises a taxpayer that no instalment payments will be required for the current year;

(d) errors in processing;

(e) delays in providing information, such as when a taxpayer could not make the appropriate instalment or arrears payments because the necessary information was not available; or

(f) undue delays in resolving an objection or an appeal, or in completing an audit.

**Inability to Pay or Financial Hardship**

¶ 27. It may be appropriate, in circumstances where there is a confirmed inability to pay all amounts owing, to consider waiving or cancelling interest in whole or in part to enable taxpayers to pay their account. For example:

(a) when collection had been suspended due to an inability to pay and substantial interest has accumulated or will accumulate;

(b) when a taxpayer's demonstrated ability to pay requires an extended payment arrangement, consideration may be given to waiving all or part of the interest for the period from when payments start until the amounts owing are paid, as long as the agreed payments are made on time and compliance with the Act is maintained; or

(c) when payment of the accumulated interest would cause a prolonged inability to provide basic necessities (financial hardship) such as food, medical help, transportation, or shelter, consideration may be given to cancelling all or part of the total accumulated interest.

¶ 28. Consideration would not generally be given to cancelling a penalty based on an inability to pay or financial hardship unless an extraordinary circumstance, as described in ¶ 25 has prevented compliance. However, there may be exceptional situations that may give rise to cancelling penalties, in whole or in part. For example, when a business is experiencing extreme financial difficulty, and enforcement of such penalties would jeopardize the continuity of its operations, the jobs of the employees, and the welfare of the community as a whole, consideration may be given to providing relief of the penalties.

### *Making a Request*

¶ 29. Taxpayers or their authorized representatives can make their requests in writing and send them to the tax centre where they file their returns or to the tax services office serving their area. Alternatively, Form RC4288, *Request for Taxpayer Relief*, can be used to make a request. A copy of this form is available from the CRA Web site at **http://www.cra-arc.gc.ca/formspubs/menu-e.html** or by telephone at 1-800-959-2221.

¶ 30. Taxpayer requests on the basis of inability to pay or financial hardship should be sent to the taxpayer's tax services office.

¶ 31. For addresses and telephone numbers of CRA offices, see the listings in the government section of telephone books and on the "Contact us" page of the CRA Web site at **www.cra-arc.gc.ca**.

¶ 32. Taxpayers should include all the circumstances (as listed in ¶ 23) that they intend to rely on in their initial request. It is important that taxpayers provide the CRA with a complete and accurate description of their circumstances to explain why their situation should merit relief. To support a request, taxpayers should provide all relevant information including the following, where applicable:

(a) the name, address, telephone number, social insurance number, account number, partnership number, trust account number, and business number or any other identification tax number assigned by the CRA to the taxpayer;

(b) the tax year(s) or fiscal period(s) involved;

(c) the facts and reasons supporting that the interest or penalties were either mainly caused by factors beyond the taxpayer's control, or were as a result of actions of the CRA;

(d) an explanation of how the circumstances affected the taxpayer's ability in meeting their tax obligation;

(e) the facts and reasons supporting the taxpayer's inability to pay the interest or penalties levied, or to be levied;

(f) any relevant documentation such as death certificates, doctor's statements, or insurance statements to support the facts and reasons;

(g) in cases involving financial hardship (inability to pay), a meaningful payment arrangement which covers at least the tax and the penalty part, if applicable, and full financial disclosure including a statement of income and expenses, as well as a statement of assets and liabilities;

(h) supporting details of incorrect information given by the CRA in the form of written answers, published information, or other objective evidence;

(i) where incorrect information given by the CRA is of a oral nature, the taxpayer should give all possible details they have documented, such as date, time, name of the CRA official spoken to, and details of the conversation; and

(j) a complete history of events including what measures were taken (e.g., payments and payment arrangements) and when they were taken to resolve the non-compliance.

### *Factors Used in Arriving at the Decision*

¶ 33. Where circumstances beyond a taxpayer's control, actions of the CRA, or inability to pay or financial hardship has prevented the taxpayer from complying with the Act, the following factors will be considered when determining whether or not the CRA will cancel or waive penalties and interest:

(a) whether or not the taxpayer has a history of compliance with tax obligations;

(b) whether or not the taxpayer has knowingly allowed a balance to exist on which arrears interest has accrued;

(c) whether or not the taxpayer has exercised a reasonable amount of care and has not been negligent or careless in conducting their affairs under the self-assessment system; and

(d) whether or not the taxpayer has acted quickly to remedy any delay or omission.

### *Special Consideration Due to Extraordinary Events*

¶ 34. When an extraordinary event (e.g., natural disaster) has prevented a large number of taxpayers from meeting their tax obligations, the Minister may issue a news release to announce that special consideration will be given to providing relief, such as a waiver or cancellation of penalty and interest charges on late tax remittances or late filing of a return. In such cases, taxpayers need to make a request to get relief. CRA news releases on extraordinary events that qualify for relief can be found at **http://www.cra-arc.gc.ca/newsroom/releases/menu-e.html**.

### *Third-Party Actions*

¶ 35. Taxpayers are generally considered to be responsible for errors made by third parties acting on their behalf for income tax matters. A third party who receives a fee and gives incorrect advice, or makes arithmetic or accounting errors, is usually regarded as being responsible to their client for any penalty and interest charges that the client has because of the party's action. However, there may be exceptional situations, where it may be appropriate to provide relief to taxpayers because of third-party errors or delays.

¶ 36. It may be appropriate to consider granting relief from penalties and interest, in whole or in part, where an extraordinary circumstance beyond the control of a taxpayer's representative or actions of the CRA (as described in ¶ 25 and ¶ 26) have prevented the taxpayer from complying with an obligation or requirement under the Act.

### *Gross Negligence Penalties*

¶ 37. Relief from a gross negligence penalty assessed under the Act can be considered under subsection 220(3.1). However, since the levy of these penalties indicates a degree of negligence and absence of care and diligence on the part of the taxpayer in the conduct of their tax affairs, the cancellation of a gross negligence penalty may be appropriate only in exceptional circumstances.

¶ 38. Given the nature of a gross negligence penalty, it is more appropriate for a taxpayer to dispute the assessment of such a penalty by filing a notice of objection. For more information on a taxpayer's right of objection, see Pamphlet P148, *Resolving Your Dispute: Objection and Appeal Rights Under the Income Tax Act* on the CRA Web site.

### *Accrual of Arrears Interest*

¶ 39. Arrears interest that has accumulated on an outstanding balance during a calendar year that is within the 10 preceding calendar years, but relates to a liability that arose for a tax year or fiscal period beyond the 10-year limit (described in ¶ 12), is not eligible for relief. For example, a request made in the 2007 calendar year for relief from arrears interest that accumulated over the 1997 to 2007 calendar years in regard to a tax amount owed for the 1996 tax year cannot be given consideration.

### *Administrative Charge on Dishonoured Payments*

¶ 40. An administrative charge payable under the *Financial Administration Act* for a dishonoured payment made to the CRA before April 1, 2007 cannot be cancelled under subsection 220(3.1). However, this charge may be waived or reduced under the *Financial Administration Act* and *Interest and Administrative Charges Regulations* where circumstances beyond the taxpayer's control, including an error made by the financial institution resulted in the payment being dishonoured. Taxpayers or their authorized representatives can make their requests in writing and send them to the tax centre where they file their returns or to the tax services office serving their area.

### *Employment Insurance Premiums and Canada Pension Plan Contributions*

¶ 41. The 10-year limit in ¶ 12 and the guidelines in this part also apply to penalties and interest provided for in the *Employment Insurance Act* and *Canada Pension Plan* regarding the collection and payment of premiums and contributions required to be made.

### *Voluntary Disclosures Program*

¶ 42. The Voluntary Disclosures Program is a CRA initiative that gives taxpayers the opportunity to come forward and to correct inaccurate or incomplete information, or to disclose previously unreported information, without penalties or fear of prosecution. Taxpayers who are considered to have made a valid voluntary disclosure will have to pay the taxes owing and arrears interest, and the CRA will waive the penalties that would otherwise be imposed under the Act. Under this program, and on a case-by-case basis, the CRA may provide some relief on the amount of arrears interest outstanding, after it is determined that the taxpayer made a valid voluntary disclosure. For more details, see Information Circular 00-1R, *Voluntary Disclosures Program*.

¶ 43. Arrears interest payable on a valid voluntary disclosure may be cancelled or waived under subsection 220(3.1). For more details, see Part II in this information circular called "Guidelines for the Cancellation or Waiver of Penalties and Interest."

### *Goods and Services Tax/Harmonized Sales Tax*

¶ 44. Section 281.1 of the *Excise Tax Act* (ETA) gives the Minister the discretion to waive or cancel penalties and interest payable under section 280 of the ETA, and effective April 1, 2007, the failure-to-file penalty payable under section 280.1. For more details on requesting relief from penalties and interest regarding the goods and services tax/harmonized sales tax (GST/HST), see GST Memorandum G500-3-2-1, *Cancellation or Waiver of Penalties and Interest*.

# *Part III*

## Guidelines for Accepting Late, Amended, or Revoked Elections

¶ 45. The Act and *Income Tax Regulations* contain many elections that give taxpayers the opportunity to decide on an alternative tax treatment in conducting their financial affairs for income tax purposes. Most elections do not have tax rules that permit a taxpayer to file an election once the prescribed time for making that election expires or that give the taxpayer the ability to modify or cancel an original election filed on time. The information in Part III of this information circular deals with the Minister's discretion to allow a taxpayer the benefit of certain elections even though they missed the due date, and to permit a taxpayer to modify or cancel certain elections already filed.

### *General*

¶ 46. Subsection 220(3.2) gives the Minister the discretionary authority to extend the statutory time for filing certain elections or to permit certain elections to be amended or revoked. The request must be made within the 10-year time limit described in ¶ 13.

### *Prescribed Elections*

¶ 47. A request by a taxpayer to have a late or amended election accepted or to revoke an election is limited to the elective provisions of the Act and Regulations listed in section 600 of the Regulations. For the list of prescribed elections, see Appendix A at the end of this information circular.

¶ 48. A late, amended, or revoked election must be correct in law based on the relevant legislation in place for the applicable tax year to which the election applies.

¶ 49. When accepted by the CRA, a late or amended election will be considered to have been made at the time it was required to be made. For amended and revoked elections, the earlier election will be cancelled. To give effect to acceptance of a late, amended, or revoked election, the CRA will reassess the affected returns for the tax years in question even if the years are beyond the taxpayer's normal reassessment period (i.e., statute-barred years).

¶ 50. Any assessments or reassessments resulting from the CRA's acceptance of the request is subject to the general provisions concerning arrears interest charged on the balance owing.

### *Penalty for Late, Amended, or Revoked Elections*

¶ 51. A taxpayer is liable to a penalty if the CRA accepts a late, amended, or revoked election. The penalty, calculated under subsection 220(3.5), is whichever amount is less:

(a) $8,000; or

(b) $100 for each complete month from the election's original due date to the date the application was made in a form satisfactory to the CRA.

¶ 52. The date on which the request (application) was made in a satisfactory form to the CRA is when the CRA has been provided with complete and accurate information for the election under review. To minimize the amount of penalty, the taxpayer should satisfy the application procedures described in ¶s 58 through 63.

¶ 53. It is CRA policy not to accept late, amended, or revoked elections, or to process the necessary adjustments to give an election effect, unless the amount of the penalty described in ¶ 51 is paid. Taxpayers should remit the penalty amount with their request. The CRA will determine and assess any unpaid balance of the penalty, which the taxpayer must pay at once. Interest will be charged on the unpaid balance of the penalty from the date of the *Notice of Assessment* to the date of payment.

¶ 54. The penalty described in ¶ 51 is subject to the provisions of subsection 220(3.1). For details on the cancellation or waiver of this penalty, see Part II in this information circular called "Guidelines for the Cancellation or Waiver of Penalties and Interest."

### Deemed Prescribed Elections

¶ 55. The rules and guidelines under this part also apply to the following designations and allocations that are considered prescribed elections, under subsection 220(3.21):

(a) Paragraph 80(2)(i) of the Act allows a taxpayer to designate the order in which commercial debt obligations settled at the same time are to be applied for the purpose of the debt forgiveness rules.

(b) Subsections 80(5) to 80(11) allow a taxpayer who has designated a forgiven amount to apply any remaining part of the forgiven amount in certain circumstances.

(c) Subsection 80.03(7) allows a taxpayer to designate a capital gain that would otherwise arise under subsection 80.03(2) as a forgiven amount for the purpose of the debt forgiveness rules.

(d) Subsection 132.11(6) allows a mutual fund trust, as well as any electing trust with a December 15 year-end, to choose an amount designated by it for a tax year to be added in computing its income for the year.

### Acceptance of a Late, Amended, or Revoked Election

¶ 56. A request may be accepted in the following situations:

(a) There have been tax consequences not intended by the taxpayer, and there is evidence that the taxpayer took reasonable steps to comply with the law. This could include, for example, the situation where the taxpayer obtained a bona fide valuation for a property, but after the CRA's review the valuation was found to be not correct.

(b) The request arises from circumstances that were beyond the taxpayer's control. Such extraordinary circumstances could include natural or man-made disasters such as flood or fire; civil disturbances or disruptions in services, such as a postal strike; a serious illness or accident; or serious emotional or mental distress, such as death in the immediate family.

(c) It is evident that the taxpayer acted on incorrect information given by the CRA. This could include incorrect written replies to queries and errors in CRA publications.

(d) The request results from what is a mechanical error. This could include using the net book value amount when obviously the taxpayer intended to use the undepreciated capital cost or using an incorrect cost.

(e) The later accounting of the transactions by all parties is as if the election had been made, or had been made in a particular manner.

(f) The taxpayer can demonstrate that they were not aware of the election provision, even though they took a reasonable amount of care to comply with the law, and took remedial action as quickly as possible.

### Denial of a Late, Amended, or Revoked Election

¶ 57. A request will not be accepted in the following instances:

(a) It is reasonable to conclude that the taxpayer made the request for retroactive tax planning purposes. This could include taking advantage of changes to the law enacted after the due date of the election.

(b) Adequate records do not exist.

(c) It is reasonable to conclude that the taxpayer had to make the request because he or she was negligent or careless in complying with the law.

### Making a Request

¶ 58. Taxpayers or their authorized representatives can make their requests in writing and send them to the tax centre where they file their returns or to the tax services office serving their area. Alternatively, Form RC4288, *Request for Taxpayer Relief*, can be used to make a request. A copy of this form is available from the CRA Web site at **http://www.cra-arc.gc.ca/formspubs/menu-e.html** or by telephone at 1-800-959-2221. To find the addresses and telephone numbers of CRA offices, see ¶ 31.

¶ 59. To support a request, taxpayers should provide all relevant information including the following, where applicable:

(a) the name, address, telephone number, social insurance number, partnership number, trust account number, and business number or any other identification tax number assigned by the CRA to the taxpayer;

(b) the tax year(s) or fiscal period(s) involved;

(c) the dates and details of the transactions;

(d) the date and details of the original election, including an explanation of why the taxpayer is asking to have an election amended or revoked; and

(e) details of a late election, and an explanation of why it is late.

¶ 60. For a request to accept a late or amended election, the election needs to be made in the appropriate manner required by the specific provisions of the Act concerning that election (e.g., filing the election in prescribed form or in a prescribed manner).

¶ 61. The request should briefly describe the income tax implications of the acceptance or refusal of the request for all the parties involved.

¶ 62. If accepting the request involves changes to continuing tax account balances, taxpayers should submit appropriate revised schedules reflecting these changes. This could include, for example, capital cost allowance schedules, reserve account schedules, and Canadian exploration or development expense account schedules.

¶ 63. When the request involves more than one taxpayer, an agreement, signed by all parties, to the changes requested should be included with the request.

## *Part IV*

## Guidelines for Refunds or Reduction in Amounts Payable Beyond the Normal Three-Year Period

¶ 64. The Act sets a three-year limitation period from the end of the tax year of an individual (other than a trust) and testamentary trust to file an income tax return to claim a tax refund and a three-year limitation period from the date of the original *Notice of Assessment* to ask for an adjustment to an assessment issued for a previous tax year. The information in Part IV of this information circular deals with the Minister's discretion to relieve an individual (other than a trust) and a testamentary trust from the limitation period and, in certain circumstances, to accept late requests to give the individual or testamentary trust a refund or reduction in tax.

### *General*

¶ 65. The relief provided under paragraph 164(1.5)(a) and subsection 152(4.2) applies only to individuals (other than trusts) and testamentary trusts.

### *Refund Entitlement*

¶ 66. Subsection 164(1) restricts the CRA from refunding an overpayment of tax unless:

(a) an income tax return was filed within three years from the end of the tax year; or

(b) the CRA received a request for a refund within three years from the date of the original *Notice of Assessment* and the related income tax return was filed within three years from the end of the tax year. This is referred to as the normal reassessment period.

### *Discretion to Allow a Statute-Barred Refund*

¶ 67. However, paragraph 164(1.5)(a) gives the Minister the discretionary authority to refund to an individual or a testamentary trust all or any part of an overpayment of tax for a tax year even if the tax return was filed later than three years from the end of the tax year. The request must be made within the 10-year time limit described in ¶ 13.

### *Reassessment or Redetermination*

¶ 68. Subsection 152(4) generally restricts the CRA from reassessing a return of income for a tax year that is beyond three years from the date of the original *Notice of Assessment* or of an original notification that no tax was payable for the year. When the normal three-year reassessment period for a tax year ends, the return is considered statute-barred.

### *Discretion to Refund or Reduce Tax Payable for a Statute-Barred Return*

¶ 69. However, subsection 152(4.2) gives the Minister the discretionary authority to make a reassessment or a redetermination beyond the normal reassessment period for a statute-barred tax year, when requested by an individual or a testamentary trust in order to determine a refund or to reduce tax payable. The request must be made within the 10-year time limit described in ¶ 13.

¶ 70. An individual or testamentary trust, as the case may be, can ask the CRA to redetermine certain amounts that are considered either as payments on account of tax or overpayment of tax under the Act. Paragraph 152(4.2)(b) refers to the following amounts for which a redetermination could be issued:

(a) refundable Quebec abatement for income earned in Quebec by an individual resident of Quebec under subsection 120(2);

(b) refundable First Nations abatement for individuals who are subject to income tax legislation of certain First Nations under subsection 120(2.2);

(c) goods and services tax/harmonized sales tax (GST/HST) credit available to eligible individuals under subsection 122.5(3);

(d) refundable medical expense supplement available to eligible individuals under subsection 122.51(2);

(e) refundable investment tax credit available to taxpayers under subsection 127.1(1);

(f) the tax credit that a beneficiary of a mining reclamation trust can claim under subsection 127.41(3);

(g) the tax credit that certain beneficiaries can claim under subsection 210.2(3) for the Part XII.2 tax paid by a trust;

(h) the tax credit a Canadian partnership flows through to its partners for the Part XII.2 tax paid by a trust under subsection 210.2(4); and

(i) Canada Child Tax Benefit (CCTB) payments available to eligible individuals for qualified dependants under subsection 122.61(1).

### *Acceptance of a Refund or Adjustment Request*

¶ 71. The CRA may issue a refund or reduce the amount owed if it is satisfied that such a refund or reduction would have been made if the return or request had been filed or made on time, and provided that the necessary assessment is correct in law and has not been already allowed.

¶ 72. Individuals and testamentary trusts can make a request if they were not aware of, or missed, claiming a deduction or a non-refundable tax credit that was available for the year, such as child care expenses or the amount for an eligible dependant. Individuals can also ask for refunds or reductions of amounts owing for refundable tax credits such as provincial tax credits that have not been claimed. In addition, payroll deductions may have resulted in an overpayment of taxes for which a refund can be requested.

¶ 73. The purpose for requesting an adjustment under subsection 152(4.2) is not to dispute or disagree on the correctness or validity of a previous assessment. The ability of the CRA to allow an adjustment to amounts for a statute-barred tax year should not be used as a means to have issues reconsidered, such as an audit reassessment, where the individual or testamentary trust chose not to challenge the issues through the normal objection/appeals processes or where the issues were already dealt with under the objection/appeal. For more information on a taxpayer's right of objection, see Pamphlet P148, *Resolving Your Dispute: Objection and Appeal Rights Under the Income Tax Act*, on the CRA Web site.

¶ 74. The CRA will generally not accept a request for an adjustment to a statute-barred tax year of an individual where the adjustment would result in the increase of taxes, interest, or penalties to the returns of other individuals that are statute-barred and cannot be reassessed by the CRA.

### *Making a Request*

¶ 75. Individuals and testamentary trusts, or their authorized representatives, can apply for a refund from a statute-barred tax year by filing the income tax return(s) together with documentation or explanations to support their claim(s). If the returns were previously filed, they can make a written request.

¶ 76. To ask for a refund or a reduction of amounts owing under subsection 152(4.2), individuals and testamentary trusts can make their requests in writing and include the following information:

(a) the name, address, telephone number, social insurance number, and trust account number or any other identification tax number assigned by the CRA to the taxpayer;

(b) the tax year(s) involved;

(c) all relevant documents to support any claims being made; and

(d) an explanation for the adjustment they are requesting.

¶ 77. Individuals and testamentary trusts, or their authorized representatives, can send returns, written requests, and supporting documentation to the tax centre where they file their returns or to the tax services office serving their area. Alternatively, Form RC4288, *Request for Taxpayer Relief*, can be used to make a request. A copy of this form is available from the CRA Web site at **http://www.cra-arc.gc.ca/formspubs/menu-e.html** or by telephone at 1-800-959-2221. To find the addresses and telephone numbers of CRA offices, see ¶ 31.

¶ 78. To support a return or a request for an adjustment, individuals and testamentary trusts should provide the following information, if relevant:

(a) official receipts or certified true copies of receipts (e.g., tuition, registered retirement savings plan, or charitable donation receipts);

(b) copies of information slips (e.g., T3, T4, T5);

(c) details or calculations of expenses or deductions being claimed; and

(d) proof of payment, such as cancelled cheques for rental payments or a letter from a landlord.

¶ 79. If T4 information slips are relevant but are not available, individuals should provide a letter from their present or former employer(s), which states their income and deductions for the year. Otherwise, they should provide the full name and address of the present or former employer(s), as well as copies of pay stubs or cancelled cheques.

¶ 80. If other types of information slips are not available, an individual and testamentary trust should provide the name and address of the slip issuer and the amount on the slip.

¶ 81. If it is impossible to get the proper documentation, individuals and testamentary trusts should submit full details and a written explanation for consideration.

¶ 82. The CRA will try to reconstruct and validate the claim or claims by referring to CRA records.

¶ 83. If the CRA cannot validate a claim after referring to its records, a refund will not be issued.

### *Provincial Benefits or Credits*

¶ 84. If there are time limitations to claim certain provincial benefits or credits (which are administered by the CRA for provinces) stipulated in a provincial act, subsection 152(4.2) and paragraph 164(1.5)(a) do not override provincial limitations, unless provincial law allows for it.

### *Permissive Deductions*

¶ 85. The CRA will not process requests for adjustments if the requested decrease in tax is the result of an increased claim for capital cost allowance or other allowable deductions, where the taxpayer originally claimed less than the maximum amount allowed. For more information, see Information Circular 84-1, *Revision of Capital Cost Allowance Claims and Other Permissive Deductions*.

### *Employment Insurance Premiums and Canada Pension Plan Contributions*

¶ 86. The relief described in ¶ 67 and ¶ 69 does not affect refunds for overpayments of Employment Insurance premiums and Canada Pension Plan contributions. The time limit for refunds remains at three and four years under the *Employment Insurance Act* and *Canada Pension Plan* respectively.

### *Requests Based on a Court Decision or Other Resolution*

¶ 87. CRA policy does not allow for the reassessment of a statute-barred return if the request is made as a result of a court decision (for more information, see Information Circular 75-7R3, *Reassessment of a Return of Income*). Requests made to reassess a statute-barred return based only on the successful appeal by another taxpayer will not be granted under subsection 152(4.2).

¶ 88. Similarly, knowledge of another taxpayer's negotiated settlement to resolve an objection, or another taxpayer's consent to judgment on an appeal, will not be extended to permit a reassessment of a taxpayer's statute-barred return under subsection 152(4.2), if the taxpayer has chosen not to protect his or her right of objection or appeal.

## *Part V*

## Rules and Procedures When Relief is Granted or Denied

¶ 89. Part V of this information circular deals with rules and procedures for interest paid on overpayments, issuing refunds, and the right of objection to an assessment or reassessment issued as a result of a decision made by the CRA to grant relief to a taxpayer. Part V also explains the recourse taxpayers have to ask for a second administrative review from the CRA or to have the Minister's decision reviewed by the Federal Court, when taxpayers do not agree with the Minister's decision for denying relief or partly granting relief.

### *Reductions in Refunds*

¶ 90. Paragraph 164(1.5)(b) gives the Minister the discretion to refund an overpayment of tax that results from a reassessment or redetermination relating to:

(a) an adjustment made beyond the normal reassessment period under subsection 152(4.2);

(b) the cancellation of penalties and interest under subsection 220(3.1); or

(c) the application of subsection 220(3.4) for the accepting of a late, amended, or revoked election under subsection 220(3.2).

¶ 91. Under certain circumstances, the CRA may reduce the amount of a refund to which an individual or testamentary trust might otherwise be entitled. For example, this may happen when a requested adjustment for a year beyond the normal reassessment period results in a refund for that particular year, but the adjustment would result in an increase of taxes, interest, or penalties for another year that is statute-barred. Under these circumstances, the CRA will usually grant a refund only if it is more than the taxes, interest, and penalties that would otherwise have been paid if the other year had not been statute-barred.

¶ 92. Similarly, if a redetermination of Canada Child Tax Benefit (CCTB) or goods and services tax/harmonized sales tax (GST/HST) credit requested by an individual results in a refund for the particular year, but would necessitate a redetermination to repay CCTB or GST/HST overpayments received for another year(s) which is statute-barred, the refund may be reduced accordingly.

### *Refund Interest*

¶ 93. For requests received after June 30, 2003, subsection 164(3.2) provides for the payment of interest on a refund arising from a reassessment or redetermination that:

- cancels all or part of any penalty and interest previously paid; or
- reduces the amount of tax previously paid as a result of accepting an adjustment or a late, amended, or revoked election.

¶ 94. Compound daily interest at the prescribed rates will start to accumulate on the 31st day after a written request to waive or cancel penalty and interest, accept a late, amended, or revoked election, or to allow an adjustment beyond the normal three-year limit was received in a manner satisfactory to the CRA.

¶ 95. The date on which the request was received in a manner satisfactory to the CRA is the date when the CRA has been given complete and accurate information about the request under review. In certain circumstances, refund interest may begin later than the day stated in ¶ 94. For example, refund interest may begin on a later date if there was not enough documentation given to support the taxpayer's claim for an adjustment, or a new request is made for penalty and interest relief, which relies on different grounds than the previous request that was denied by the CRA. Taxpayers should satisfy the procedures described in this information circular in the section called "Making a Request."

¶ 96. Under subsection 164(3) and for the filing of a tax return for a tax year of an individual or testamentary trust that ended after June 30, 2003, refund interest on an overpayment will start to accumulate on the 31st day after the date the return was filed. For tax years that ended on or before June 30, 2003, refund interest will start on the 46th day after the date the return was filed.

¶ 97. There is no interest paid on a refund or part of a refund for GST/HST or CCTB payments made to an individual.

### *Application of Refund to Other Debts*

¶ 98. Under subsection 164(2), the amount of any refund (except for CCTB payments) may be applied against any amount the taxpayer owes or is about to owe.

### *Refund Withheld Until Outstanding Returns Are Filed*

¶ 99. Effective April 1, 2007, under subsection 164(2.01), a refund will not be paid to a taxpayer, applied to other debts, or used to set off amounts under the Act until such time as all outstanding returns that are required to be filed by the taxpayer under the *Income Tax Act*, the *Air Travellers Security Charge Act*, the *Excise Act, 2001*, and the *Excise Tax Act* have been filed with the CRA.

### Right of Objection

¶ 100. If the Minister has waived or cancelled in whole or in part any penalties and interest under subsection 220(3.1) or has issued a *Notice of Reassessment* beyond the normal reassessment period under subsection 152(4.2), a taxpayer is prohibited under subsection 165(1.2) from filing an objection to dispute the assessment or reassessment.

¶ 101. If the Minister has accepted a late, amended, or revoked election under subsection 220(3.2), a taxpayer can file an objection under subsection 165(1.1) to dispute the assessment or reassessment made under subsection 220(3.4). However, objections are limited to matters that give rise to the assessment.

¶ 102. The normal objection procedures under subsection 165(1) apply to an individual (other than a trust) or testamentary trust for an original *Notice of Assessment* made to allow a refund from filing an income tax return beyond the normal three-year period. For more information on a taxpayer's right of objection, see Pamphlet P148, *Resolving Your Dispute: Objection and Appeal Rights Under the Income Tax Act*.

### Redress – Second Administrative Review

¶ 103. If a request was denied or partly granted, there is no right of objection for a taxpayer to dispute a decision under the taxpayer relief provisions. However, if the taxpayer believes that the Minister's discretion has not been properly exercised, the taxpayer can write to ask that the director of the tax services office or the tax centre reconsider the original decision and review the situation again. During the second review, the taxpayer will have the opportunity to make more representations for the CRA's consideration. To find the addresses of CRA offices, see ¶ 31.

¶ 104. CRA officials not involved in the first administrative review and decision would carry out the second administrative review. They would prepare a decision report for the director or another delegated official for his or her consideration, including a recommendation on whether or not granting relief is justified. The final decision and notification of the decision to the taxpayer rests with the director or another delegated official, such as an assistant director.

### Redress – Judicial Review

¶ 105. If a taxpayer believes that the Minister's discretion was not properly exercised, the taxpayer can apply for judicial review of that decision to the Federal Court under section 18.1 of the *Federal Courts Act*, within 30 days of the date the decision was first received by the taxpayer.

¶ 106. To ask for judicial review, the taxpayer must send a completed Form 301, *Notice of Application*, with the appropriate filing fee to the registrar of the Federal Court. For more information on how to file an application for judicial review or other general enquiries, contact the Courts Administration Service or see their Web site at **http://www.cas-satj.gc.ca**.

¶ 107. If it is determined that the Minister's discretion was not properly exercised, the Federal Court cannot substitute its decision for a decision of the CRA but can only refer the decision back to the CRA to be reconsidered by another delegated official.

¶ 108. As a general rule, taxpayers should ask for a second administrative review (described in ¶ 103) from the CRA before filing an application for judicial review with the Federal Court.

### Requests Made While an Objection or Appeal Is in Progress

¶ 109. A request to cancel penalty and interest on the grounds of extraordinary circumstances or actions of the CRA for an assessment under objection or appeal may be reviewed and an informal decision may be communicated to the taxpayer. However, a final decision about the taxpayer's request for relief will be held until the objection or appeal is resolved or until all rights of appeal have expired.

¶ 110. A taxpayer's request to cancel penalty and interest on the grounds of inability to pay or financial hardship under subsection 220(3.1), for an adjustment under subsection 152(4.2), or to accept a late, amended, or revoked election under subsection 220(3.2) that relates to an assessment that is under objection or appeal will generally be held in abeyance until the outcome of the objection or appeal process or until all rights of appeal have expired.

### Comments

¶ 111. If you have any comments about this information circular, please write to:

Taxpayer Relief and Service Complaints Directorate
Canada Revenue Agency
Ottawa ON K1A 0L5

## *Appendix A – List of prescribed elections*

Section 600 of the *Income Tax Regulations* lists the provisions of the *Income Tax Act* and *Income Tax Regulations* under which a taxpayer or a partnership can apply under subsection 220(3.2) of the Act to make a late or amended election, or to revoke an election.

The list of eligible elections reflects the amendments to section 600 that were registered in the *Canada Gazette*, Part II, on August 29, 2006, as SOR/2006-200.

Below is a list of the prescribed provisions, and a brief description of related elections:

### Deferral on non-Canadian controlled private corporation employee options

Subsection 7(8) of the Act allows an employee to defer the taxing of an employment benefit realized from a qualifying acquisition of a particular security under an agreement with the employer (or a person not dealing at arm's length with the employer) until the year in which the employee disposes of the security, becomes a non-resident of Canada or dies, whichever occurs first, if the employee elects in accordance with subsection 7(10) to have subsection 7(8) apply.

### Deemed outlay or expense

Paragraph 12(2.2)(b) of the Act allows a taxpayer to elect to reduce the amount of an outlay or expense (other than an outlay or expense which relates to the cost of the property) incurred in the year, the immediately following year or any preceding year, by all or part of any related government assistance received in the year which would otherwise be included in income by virtue of paragraph 12(1)(x).

### Interest income accrual rules

Former subsection 12.2(4) of the Act allowed an individual or a trust with individuals as beneficiaries to elect to report accrued interest income annually for certain life insurance policies and annuity contracts last acquired before December 20, 1980, rather than tri-annually under former subsection 12.2(3). Subsection 12.2(4) was repealed, after the introduction of mandatory annual reporting of accrued income on life insurance policies last acquired or materially altered after 1989.

### Available-for-use rules on long-term projects

Subsection 13(29) of the Act allows a taxpayer to elect to include an amount, within limits, as undepreciated capital cost for long-term project depreciable property under the available-for-use provisions of subsections 13(26) to 13(28), before the completion of the project.

### Amounts paid for undertaking future obligations

Subsection 20(24) of the Act allows a taxpayer to deduct from income certain payments made to obtain another person's agreement to undertake certain future obligations for which an amount was included in the taxpayer's income under paragraph 12(1)(a), if the taxpayer and the recipient jointly elect under subsection 20(25).

### Cost of borrowed money

The elections contained in section 21 of the Act allow a taxpayer to elect to capitalize, instead of deducting as a current expense, the cost of borrowed money used to acquire depreciable property (subsections 21(1) and 21(3)) or used for exploring, developing, or acquiring a resource property (subsections 21(2) and 21(4)).

### Exchanges of property

Subsections 13(4), 14(6), 44(1), and (6) of the Act allow a taxpayer to elect to defer an income inclusion or the recognition of a capital gain when a replacement property is acquired for a property that was stolen, expropriated, or destroyed, or for a former business property that was sold.

### Adjustments to cost base

Subsections 13(7.4) and 53(2.1) of the Act allow a taxpayer to elect to reduce the capital cost of depreciable property and the adjusted cost base of non-depreciable capital property, respectively, by the amount of any related inducement, refund, reimbursement, contribution, allowance, or other assistance that would otherwise be included in income under paragraph 12(1)(x).

### Election where change of use

Subsection 45(2) of the Act allows a taxpayer to elect to designate a property as his principal residence although there has been a change in use to an income producing property.

Subsection 45(3) of the Act allows a taxpayer to elect to defer a capital gain on the change of use of a property from an income producing property to a principal residence.

### Debts established to be bad debts and shares of bankrupt corporation

Subsection 50(1) of the Act applies to debts established to have become bad debts in a tax year and to certain shares, and allows a taxpayer to elect to have a deemed disposition at the end of the year and a reacquisition immediately thereafter at a cost of nil.

### Successor rules for resource properties

Paragraphs 66.7(7)(c), (d), and (e), and (8)(c), (d), and (e) of the Act allow a predecessor corporation and a successor corporation to elect to transfer the unused pools of resource expenses from the predecessor to the successor corporation.

### Transfers or distributions to a taxpayer's spouse, common-law partner, or spousal/partner trust on the death of the taxpayer

Subsection 70(6.2) of the Act allows a taxpayer's legal representative to elect to have the rollover rules under subsections 70(6) and 70(6.1) not to apply, thus causing the deemed disposition of assets at fair market value under subsection 70(5) and the deemed payment of amounts in NISA Fund No.2 under subsection 70(5.4).

### Transfer of farm property, or family farm corporations and partnerships to a child

Subsection 70(9) of the Act allows a taxpayer's legal representative to elect an amount, within limits, as proceeds of disposition for farm property that is transferred to a child on the taxpayer's death.

Subsection 70(9.1) of the Act allows a spousal or common-law partner trust to elect an amount, within limits, as proceeds of disposition for farm property that is transferred from the trust to a child on the spouse or common-law partner's death.

Subsection 70(9.2) of the Act allows a taxpayer's legal representative to elect an amount, within limits, as proceeds of disposition for a share in a family farm corporation, or an interest in a family farm partnership that is transferred to a child on the taxpayer's death.

Subsection 70(9.3) of the Act allows a spousal or common-law partner trust to elect an amount, within limits, as proceeds of disposition for a share in a family farm corporation, or an interest in a family farm partnership that is transferred from the trust to a child on the spouse or common-law partner's death.

### Election by legal representative and transferee re reserves

Subsection 72(2) of the Act lets a legal representative of a deceased taxpayer elect to claim a deduction for certain reserves, as long as the amount so deducted is then included in the income of the taxpayer's spouse or common-law partner or a spousal or common-law partner trust.

### Inter vivos transfer of property

Subsection 73(1) of the Act allows a taxpayer to elect to have the rollover provisions for an inter vivos transfer of assets to a spouse or common-law partner or certain trusts not to apply, thus causing the assets to be considered to be transferred at fair market value for tax purposes.

### Deemed settlement on winding-up

Paragraph 80.01(4)(c) of the Act allows a parent corporation to elect to reduce the amount to which subsection 80(1) (debt forgiveness rules) might otherwise apply in cases where a debt owed between a parent corporation and its subsidiary is settled on the winding up of the subsidiary for less than both the principal amount and the cost amount of the debt.

### Expropriation assets acquired as compensation for, or as consideration for sale of, foreign property taken by or sold to a foreign issuer

Subsection 80.1(1) of the Act applies to a Canadian resident taxpayer who has acquired expropriation assets issued or guaranteed by a foreign government as compensation for the expropriated or forced sale of shares of a foreign affiliate, or foreign property used to carry on business in a foreign country. The election establishes the deemed cost of the expropriation assets and the deemed proceeds of disposition of the property that was expropriated or sold.

### Dividends received by taxpayer's spouse or common-law partner

Subsection 82(3) of the Act allows a taxpayer to elect to have a taxable dividend from a taxable Canadian corporation received by the taxpayer's spouse or common-law partner included in the taxpayer's income where such an inclusion increases the taxpayer's spouse or common-law partner credit under paragraph 118(1)(a).

### Capital dividend

Subsection 83(2) of the Act allows a private corporation to elect to have the full amount of a dividend that is payable by it to be treated as a capital dividend, which effectively allows those dividends to be paid on a tax-free basis.

### Eligible distributions of foreign spin-off shares

Paragraph 86.1(2)(f) of the Act allows a taxpayer to elect to defer the tax on eligible distributions of foreign spin-off shares.

### Election to defer the 21-year deemed disposition date

Subsection 104(5.3) of the Act allowed certain family trusts to elect to defer the 21-year deemed disposition date. This provision was ended with the result that the deferred disposition date is no later than January 1, 1999.

07-1

## Preferred beneficiary election

Subsection 104(14) of the Act allows a trust and its preferred beneficiaries to elect to have the income of the trust included in the income of the preferred beneficiaries, instead of being taxed in the trust.

## No rollover on election by trust

Subsection 107(2.001) of the Act allows a personal trust or prescribed trust resident in Canada at the time of the distribution to elect not to have the rollover in subsection 107(2) applied to a distribution of certain property to a beneficiary to satisfy the beneficiary's capital interest in the trust.

## Deemed disposition on emigration

Paragraph 128.1(4)(d) of the Act allows an individual (other than a trust) to elect to treat certain properties that would otherwise be exempt from the deemed disposition that occurs when the individual ceases to be resident in Canada as having been disposed of.

## Departure tax adjustment for a returning former resident

Paragraphs 128.1(6)(a) and 128.1(6)(c) of the Act apply to an individual (other than a trust) who ceases to be resident in Canada after October 1, 1996, and later returns to reside in Canada. The effect of the election is to unwind the deemed disposition under subsection 128.1(4) for certain properties still held on the individual's return to Canada.

## Departure tax adjustment for a returning trust beneficiary

Paragraphs 128.1(7)(d) and 128.1(7)(g) of the Act apply to an individual trust beneficiary (other than a trust) who ceases to be resident in Canada after October 1, 1996, receives a distribution of property from the trust while a non-resident, and later returns to reside in Canada while still owning the property. These rules allow the beneficiary and the trust to jointly elect, on the beneficiary's return to Canada, to unwind the deemed disposition under subsection 107(2.1), which was triggered when the trust distributed the property to the non-resident beneficiary.

## Post-emigration loss on disposition

Paragraph 128.1(8)(c) of the Act applies to an individual (other than a trust) who disposes of taxable Canadian property, after having ceased to be resident in Canada after October 1, 1996, for proceeds that are less than the deemed proceeds that arose on the deemed disposition on emigration under paragraph 128.1(4)(b) of the Act. The individual can elect to reduce the deemed proceeds of disposition that arose when the individual emigrated.

## Allocation of income by communal organizations

Subsection 143(2) of the Act allows a communal organization to elect to have its taxable income, earned by the deemed trust under subsection 143(1), allocated to members of the organization.

## Home Buyers' Plan

Subsection 146.01(7) of the Act allows a deceased taxpayer's legal representative and the surviving spouse or common-law partner to elect not to have the full outstanding balance of the Home Buyers' Plan included on the deceased taxpayer's final return. The practical effect of the election is to put the surviving spouse or common-law partner in the same position as the deceased taxpayer with respect to the balance outstanding.

## Disposition of property by legal representative of deceased taxpayer

Subsection 164(6) of the Act allows a deceased taxpayer's legal representative to elect to treat certain capital losses or terminal losses of the taxpayer's estate for its first tax year as capital losses or terminal losses of the deceased taxpayer for the year of death.

## Realization of deceased employees' options

Subsection 164(6.1) of the Act allows a deceased taxpayer's legal representative to elect to treat the amount of the loss realized on the exercise, disposition, or expiration of rights to acquire certain securities within the first tax year of the taxpayer's estate as a loss of the deceased taxpayer for the year of death.

## Excess capital dividend

Subsection 184(3) of the Act allows a corporation to elect to have the amount of the elected capital dividend in excess of the balance in the corporation's capital dividend account treated as a separate, taxable dividend, thereby avoiding the tax otherwise payable under Part III.

## Date of acquisition of control

Subsection 256(9) of the Act allows a corporation to elect not to have the acquisition of control deemed to occur at the start of the day on which the acquisition took place. If the corporation makes an election, the particular time of day that the acquisition of control took place will be recognized.

## Elections to include properties in Class 1

Subsection 1103(1) of the Regulations allows a taxpayer to elect, for capital cost allowance purposes, to include in Class 1 all properties included in Classes 2 to 10 and Classes 11 and 12.

## Elections to include properties in Class 2, 4, or 17

Subsection 1103(2) of the Regulations allows a taxpayer to elect, for capital cost allowance purposes, to include in Class 2, 4, or 17, a property acquired before May 26, 1976, that would otherwise be included in another class when the chief depreciable properties of the taxpayer are included in Class 2, 4, or 17.

## Elections to make certain transfers

Subsection 1103(2d) of the Regulations allows a taxpayer to elect to defer a capital cost allowance recapture by transferring the property disposed of to a new class of which the taxpayer has property, when the property disposed of would have been a property of the new class if it had been acquired when the property of the new class was acquired.

## Earnings of a foreign affiliate

Subsection 5907(2.1) of the Regulations allows that, in calculating the active business earnings of a foreign affiliate, a corporation can make an election for the cost of a foreign resource property or the cost of a capital property.

# Principal Residence (Interpretation Bulletin IT-120R6)

NO.: **IT-120R6** DATE: July 17, 2003

SUBJECT: INCOME TAX ACT
**Principal Residence**

REFERENCE: The definition of "principal residence" in section 54, and paragraphs 40(2)(*b*) and 40(2)(*c*) (also sections 54.1 and 110.6; subsections 13(7), 40(4), 40(6), 40(7), 40(7.1), 45(1), 45(2), 45(3), 45(4), 107(2), 107(2.01), 107(4), 110.6(19) and 220(3.2); paragraph 104(4)(*a*); and subparagraph 40(2)(*g*)(iii) of the *Income Tax Act*; and Part XXIII of the *Income Tax Regulations*)

At the Canada Customs and Revenue Agency (CCRA), we issue income tax interpretation bulletins (ITs) in order to provide technical interpretations and positions regarding certain provisions contained in income tax law. Due to their technical nature, ITs are used primarily by our staff, tax specialists, and other individuals who have an interest in tax matters. For those readers who prefer a less technical explanation of the law, we offer other publications, such as tax guides and pamphlets.

While the comments in a particular paragraph in an IT may relate to provisions of the law in force at the time they were made, such comments are not a substitute for the law. The reader should, therefore, consider such comments in light of the relevant provisions of the law in force for the particular taxation year being considered, taking into account the effect of any relevant amendments to those provisions or relevant court decisions occurring after the date on which the comments were made.

Subject to the above, an interpretation or position contained in an IT generally applies as of the date on which it was published, unless otherwise specified. If there is a subsequent change in that interpretation or position and the change is beneficial to taxpayers, it is usually effective for future assessments and reassessments. If, on the other hand, the change is not favourable to taxpayers, it will normally be effective for the current and subsequent taxation years or for transactions entered into after the date on which the change is published.

Most of our publications are available on our Web site at: **www.ccra.gc.ca**

***If you have any comments regarding matters discussed in an IT, please send them to:***

***Manager, Technical Publications and Projects Section***
***Income Tax Rulings Directorate***
***Policy and Legislation Branch***
***Canada Customs and Revenue Agency***
***Ottawa ON K1A 0L5***

***or by email at the following address:*** **bulletins@ccra.gc.ca**

## *Contents*

## *Application*

This bulletin replaces and cancels Interpretation Bulletin IT-120R5, dated November 30, 1999 and applies for the 2001 and subsequent taxation years. Unless otherwise stated, all statutory references throughout the bulletin are to the *Income Tax Act.*

## *Summary*

This bulletin discusses the principal residence exemption, which can eliminate or reduce (for income tax purposes) a capital gain on the disposition of a taxpayer's principal residence.

In order for a property to qualify for designation as the taxpayer's principal residence, he or she must own the property. Joint ownership with another person qualifies for this purpose.

The housing unit representing the taxpayer's principal residence generally must be inhabited by the taxpayer or by his or her spouse or common-law partner, former spouse or common-law partner, or child.

A taxpayer can designate only one property as his or her principal residence for a particular taxation year. Furthermore, for a taxation year that is after the 1981 year, only one property per family unit can be designated as a principal residence.

If the land on which the housing unit is situated is not in excess of one-half hectare, it usually qualifies as part of the taxpayer's principal residence. Land in excess of one-half hectare may also qualify, but only to the extent that it is established to be necessary for the use and enjoyment of the housing unit as a residence.

If the taxpayer's principal residence is located on his or her farm, the taxpayer has a choice of two methods for determining what portion of any gain on a disposition of the farm can be eliminated by the principal residence exemption.

A complete or partial change in the use of a property from a principal residence to income-producing, or vice-versa, results in a deemed disposition of the property by the taxpayer at fair market value. The taxpayer may be able to elect that the deemed disposition on a complete change in use does not apply. A property covered by such an election may qualify as the taxpayer's principal residence for up to four years, or possibly longer in the case of a work relocation.

It is also possible for a personal trust to claim the principal residence exemption on the disposition of a property. Modifications to the normal principal residence exemption rules exist for this purpose.

The above topics are discussed more fully below, as well as other topics relating to the principal residence exemption.

The appendices to the bulletin contain illustrations of some of the rules discussed in the bulletin.

## *Discussion and Interpretation*

### Introduction

**¶ 1.** Various topics concerning the principal residence exemption are discussed in this bulletin, as indicated in the "*Contents*" section at the beginning of the bulletin. It should be noted that some of these topics are not relevant for all taxpayers. For example, a resident of Canada who owns only one housing unit which is situated in Canada on land of one-half hectare or less and which has been used since its acquisition strictly as his or her residence, will usually find that ¶s 14 to 44 have no particular relevance.

**¶ 2.** If a property qualifies as a taxpayer's principal residence, he or she can use the principal residence exemption to reduce or eliminate any capital gain otherwise occurring, for income tax purposes, on the disposition (or deemed disposition) of the property. The term "principal residence" is defined in section 54 of the *Income Tax Act.* The principal residence exemption is claimed under paragraph 40(2)(*b*) of the Act, or under paragraph 40(2)(*c*) where land used in a farming business carried on by the taxpayer includes his or her principal residence.

Unless otherwise stated, any reference in this bulletin to a "taxation year" or "year" means a particular taxation year for which the principal residence exemption is being claimed.

Various references are made throughout this bulletin to a taxpayer's spouse or common-law partner and child. For the 1993 to 2000 taxation years, former subsection 252(4) of the Act extended the meaning of the term "spouse" to include a common-law spouse of the opposite sex. Effective in 2001, the extended meaning of spouse in subsection 252(4) has been replaced with the term "common-law partner" in subsection 248(1) which can now also include a person of the same sex. A transitional rule for the 1998, 1999 and 2000 taxation years allowed same-sex couples to elect to be treated as common-law partners under the Act for those years. For more information about the meaning of the terms "spouse" and "common-law partner", see the current version of the *General Income Tax and Benefit Guide*. For purposes of applying the rules in subsections 70(6) and 73(1) as discussed in ¶ 38, see also the extended meaning of "spouse" and "former spouse" in subsection 252(3), as it reads for the particular taxation year being considered. Subsection 252(1), as it reads for the particular taxation year being considered, extends the meaning of "child" for purposes of applying all the rules in the Act, including the principal residence exemption rules, for that year.

It is also possible for a personal trust to claim the principal residence exemption on the disposition of a property. This is discussed in ¶s 35 and 38.

## Types of Property That Can Qualify as a Principal Residence

**¶ 3.** The following are the types of property that can qualify as a "principal residence":

- a housing unit, which includes:
  - a house,
  - an apartment or unit in a duplex, apartment building or condominium,
  - a cottage,
  - a mobile home,
  - a trailer, or
  - a houseboat;
- a leasehold interest in a housing unit; or
- a share of the capital stock of a co-operative housing corporation, if such share is acquired for the sole purpose of obtaining the right to inhabit a housing unit owned by that corporation. The term "co-operative housing corporation" means an association, incorporated subject to the terms and conditions of the legislation governing such incorporation, and formed and operated for the purpose of providing its members with the right to inhabit, by reason of ownership of shares therein, a housing unit owned by the corporation.

Land on which a housing unit is situated can qualify as part of a principal residence, subject to certain restrictions (see ¶s 14 to 23).

## Ownership is Required

**¶ 4.** For a property to be a taxpayer's principal residence for a particular year, he or she must own the property in the year. The meaning of "ownership of property" for this purpose is discussed in the current version of IT-437, *Ownership of Property (Principal Residence)*. The taxpayer's ownership of the property qualifies for purposes of the section 54 definition of "principal residence" whether such ownership is "jointly with another person or otherwise". These latter words include sole ownership or a form of co-ownership such as joint tenancy or tenancy-in-common.

## The "Ordinarily Inhabited" Rule

**¶ 5.** Another requirement is that the housing unit must be "ordinarily inhabited" in the year by the taxpayer or by his or her spouse or common-law partner, former spouse or common-law partner, or child.

The question of whether a housing unit is ordinarily inhabited in the year by a person must be resolved on the basis of the facts in each particular case. Even if a person inhabits a housing unit only for a short period of time in the year, this is sufficient for the housing unit to be considered "ordinarily inhabited in the year" by that person. For example, even if a person disposes of his or her residence early in the year or acquires it late in the year, the housing unit can be considered to be ordinarily inhabited in the year by that person by virtue of his or her living in it in the year before such sale or after such acquisition, as the case may be. Or, for example, a seasonal residence can be considered to be ordinarily inhabited in the year by a person who occupies it only during his or her vacation, provided that the main reason for owning the property is not to gain or produce income. With regard to the latter stipulation, a person receiving only incidental rental income from a seasonal residence is not considered to own the property mainly for the purpose of gaining or producing income.

If the housing unit is not ordinarily inhabited in the year by any of the above-mentioned persons, it is still possible for the property (as described in ¶ 3) to be considered to be the taxpayer's "principal residence" for the year, by means of an election under subsection 45(2) or (3). For a discussion of these provisions, see ¶s 25 to 29.

## Designation of a Property as a Principal Residence

**¶ 6.** For a property to be a taxpayer's principal residence for a particular year, he or she must designate it as such for the year and no other property may have been so designated by the taxpayer for the year. Furthermore, no other property may have been designated as the principal residence of any member of the taxpayer's family unit for the year. For purposes of the latter rule, which applies if the taxpayer is designating a property as his or her principal residence for 1982 or a subsequent year, the taxpayer's family unit for the year includes, in addition to the taxpayer, the following persons (if any):

- the taxpayer's spouse or common-law partner throughout the year, unless the spouse or common-law partner was throughout the year living apart from, and was separated under a judicial separation or written separation agreement from, the taxpayer;
- the taxpayer's children, except those who were married, in a common-law partnership or 18 years of age or older during the year; and
- where the taxpayer was not married, in a common-law partnership or 18 years of age or older during the year,
  - the taxpayer's mother and father, and
  - the taxpayer's brothers and sisters who were not married, in a common-law partnerhip or 18 years of age or older during the year.

As discussed in ¶ 2, for the 1993 to 2000 taxation years, a spouse included a common-law partner of the opposite sex. Accordingly, these individuals will be considered a family unit for the purposes of the principal residence exemption for the 1993 and subsequent taxation years (see Example 2 in Appendix A). In the case of same-sex common-law partners, they will be considered a family unit for the 2001 and subsequent taxation years. However, if a same-sex couple filed a joint election to be treated as common-law partners for the 1998, 1999 and/or 2000 taxation years, then they will be considered a family unit for those years.

**¶ 7.** According to section 2301 of the *Income Tax Regulations*, a taxpayer's designation of a property as a principal residence for one or more taxation years is to be made in his or her income tax return for the taxation year in which he or she has disposed of the property or granted an option to another person to acquire the property. The designation form used for this purpose is Form T2091(IND), *Designation of a Property as a Principal Residence by an Individual (Other Than a Personal Trust)*. However, in accordance with our practice, Form T2091(IND) need not be completed and filed with the taxpayer's income tax return unless

(a) a taxable capital gain on the disposition of the property remains after using the principal residence exemption formula (as shown in ¶ 8), or

(b) form T664 or T664(Seniors), *Election to Report a Capital Gain on Property Owned at the End of February 22, 1994* was filed with respect to the property by the taxpayer, or his or her spouse or common-law partner; and the property was the taxpayer's principal residence for 1994, or it was designated in the year as the principal residence for any taxation year.

Note that if a taxpayer using the principal residence exemption formula (as shown in ¶ 8) to eliminate a gain on the disposition of a property is not, because of the above-mentioned practice, required to complete and file Form T2091(IND), he or she is still considered to have designated the property as his or her principal residence (i.e., to have claimed the principal residence exemption for that property) for the years in question as far as the limitations discussed earlier in this paragraph are concerned.

## Calculating the Gain on the Disposition of a Principal Residence – The Principal Residence Exemption

**¶ 8.** Under the principal residence exemption provision contained in paragraph 40(2)(*b*) of the Act, a taxpayer's gain from the disposition (or deemed disposition) of any property that was his or her principal residence at any time after his or her "acquisition date" (see definition below) with respect to the property, is equal to his or her "gain otherwise determined" (see explanation below) less two amounts, which are described later in this paragraph.

The taxpayer's "acquisition date" with respect to the property is the later of the following two dates:

- December 31, 1971, and
- the date on which the taxpayer last acquired or reacquired the property or is deemed to have last acquired or reacquired it. (Note that, by virtue of subsection 40(7.1), if a subsection 110.6(19) capital gains election was made in respect of the property, the deemed reacquisition of the property under that election is not considered to be a reacquisition for purposes of determining the "acquisition date" used in paragraph 40(2)(*b*).)

The taxpayer's "gain otherwise determined" means the amount that the gain (if any) from the taxpayer's disposition (or deemed disposition) of the property would be—before the two reductions described later in this paragraph—if the capital gains election provision in subsection 110.6(19) and the related provision in subsection 110.6(21) were not taken into account. Thus, if a subsection 110.6(19) capital gains election has been made in respect of the property, the taxpayer's gain otherwise determined is calculated without reference to the deemed disposition and reacquisition of the property under that election. That is, the gain otherwise determined is calculated without taking into account the increase to the adjusted cost base of the property under subsection 110.6(19) or the decrease to that adjusted cost base under subsection 110.6(21).

The first amount by which the taxpayer's gain otherwise determined is reduced under paragraph 40(2)(*b*) is calculated by using the following formula:

$$A \times \frac{B}{C}$$

The variables in the above formula are as follows:

A is the taxpayer's gain otherwise determined, as described above.

B is 1 + the number of taxation years ending after the acquisition date for which the property was the taxpayer's principal residence and during which he or she was resident in Canada. (Note that both these conditions must be satisfied for a particular year in order for that year to qualify for inclusion in the numerator B.)

C is the number of taxation years ending after the acquisition date during which the taxpayer owned the property (whether jointly with another person or otherwise—see ¶ 4).

For a discussion of the meaning of "resident in Canada", see the current version of IT-221, *Determination of an Individual's Residence Status*. The word "during" in reference to a taxation year means "at any time in" rather than "throughout the whole of" the taxation year.

The second amount by which the taxpayer's gain otherwise determined is reduced is shown in paragraph 40(2)(*b*) as variable "D" and it is referred to in this bulletin as the "capital gains election reduction amount". It occurs only if

- the taxpayer's acquisition date with respect to the property (as described above) is before February 23, 1994, and
- the taxpayer, or his or her spouse, or common-law partner (see ¶ 7(b)), made a subsection 110.6(19) capital gains election for the property or for an interest in the property—if such an election was made, Form T664 or T664(Seniors), *Election to Report a Capital Gain on Property Owned at the End of February 22, 1994*, would have been filed.

The inclusion of the 110.6(19) election amount of a spouse or common-law partner of the taxpayer, when calculating the capital gains election reduction amount for the taxpayer, ensures that any elected gain reported by the spouse or common-law partner in 1994 with respect to a property that was subsequently transferred to the taxpayer through a spousal or common-law partner roll-over provision after February 1994, is properly reflected in the ultimate disposition of the property by the taxpayer. In other words, in situations where a spouse or common-law partner has transferred property to the taxpayer subsequent to 1994 and pursuant to the roll-over provisions of subsection 73(1) or 70(6), the calculation of the capital gains reduction amount of the taxpayer at the time the property is sold, must include any 1994 elected gain reported by the spouse or common-law partner with respect to the transferred property. Qualifying transfers of property under these subsections are discussed later in ¶ 38.

The capital gains election reduction amount essentially represents the total amount of the gains that resulted from the taxpayer's and his or her spouse or common-law partner's capital gains elections for the property, after taking into account any reduction in calculating those gains by virtue of the property having been designated as the principal residence of the taxpayer or his or her spouse or common-law partner for any taxation year up to and including the taxation year that included February 22, 1994. The capital gains election reduction amount cannot, however, be more than such gains—after taking into account any reduction thereto by virtue of the property having been the principal residence of the taxpayer or his or her spouse or common law partner for any taxation year up to and including the taxation year that included February 22, 1994—that would have resulted from such capital gains elections if the fair market value of the property as at the end of February 22, 1994 had been used as the designated proceeds for the property.

The taxpayer calculates his or her capital gains election reduction amount on Form T2091(IND)-WS, *Principal Residence Worksheet*, which the taxpayer files with his or her T2091(IND) designation form (see ¶ 7).

The remaining discussions in this bulletin regarding paragraph 40(2)(*b*) are concerned with the first reduction to the gain otherwise determined, i.e., the reduction provided for by means of the above-mentioned formula, A × B/C. Unless stated to the contrary, it is assumed for purposes of those discussions that the taxpayer did not make a capital gains election and thus that there is no second reduction to the gain otherwise determined, i.e., no capital gains election reduction amount.

## Ownership of a Property by Both Spouses or Common-Law Partners

**¶ 9.** Where there is a gain on the disposition of a property owned both by a taxpayer and his or her spouse or common-law partner in one of the forms of ownership described in ¶ 4, both spouses or common-law partners will generally have a gain on the disposition. It should be kept in mind that if one of the spouses or common-law partners designates the property as his or her principal residence for any taxation year after the 1981 year, the other spouse or common-law partner will be able to designate only that same property as his or her principal residence for that year if the rule described in ¶ 6 prevents him or her from so designating any other property for that year.

## More Than One Residence in a Taxation Year

**¶ 10.** While only one property may be designated as a taxpayer's principal residence for a particular taxation year (see ¶ 6), the principal residence exemption rules recognize that the taxpayer can have two residences in the same year, i.e., where one residence is sold and another acquired in the same year. The effect of the "one plus" in variable B (the numerator of the fraction) in the formula in ¶ 8 is to treat both properties as a principal residence in such a year, even though only one of them may be designated as such for that year.

## Construction of a Housing Unit on Vacant Land

**¶ 11.** If a taxpayer acquires land in one taxation year and constructs a housing unit on it in a subsequent year, the property may not be designated as the taxpayer's principal residence for the years that are prior to the year in which the taxpayer, his or her spouse or common-law partner, former spouse or common-law partner, or child commences to ordinarily inhabit the housing unit. Such prior years (when the taxpayer owned only the vacant land or the land with a housing unit under construction) would not be included in the numerator "B" in the formula in ¶ 8 (or in the years included in the statement in ¶ 22(b)). However, all years, commencing with the year in which the taxpayer acquired the vacant land, would be included in the denominator "C". Therefore, it is possible that when the property is later disposed of, only part of the gain otherwise determined will be eliminated by the principal residence exemption.

***Example***

In 1992, Mr. A acquired vacant land for $25,000. In 1995, he constructed a housing unit on the land, costing $75,000, and started to ordinarily inhabit the housing unit. In 2001, he disposed of the property for $150,000. Mr. A's gain otherwise determined on the disposition of the property is equal to his $150,000 proceeds minus his $100,000 adjusted cost base = $50,000 (assume there were no costs of disposition). Mr. A can designate the property as his principal residence for the years 1995 to 2001 inclusive, but not for the years 1992 to 1994 inclusive because no one lived in a housing unit on the property during those years. The principal residence exemption formula in ¶ 8 cannot, therefore, eliminate his entire $50,000 gain otherwise determined, but rather can eliminate only $40,000 of that gain:

$$A \times \frac{B}{C} = \$50{,}000 \times \frac{1 + 7\ (1995\ \text{to}\ 2001)}{10\ (1992\ \text{to}\ 2001)} = \$40{,}000$$

## Property Owned on December 31, 1981

¶ **12.** A property may not be designated as a taxpayer's principal residence for any taxation year after the 1981 year if another property has been designated for that year as the principal residence of another member of his or her family unit (for further particulars on this rule, see ¶ 6). If the taxpayer disposes of a property he or she has owned (whether jointly with another person or otherwise) continuously since before 1982 and the property cannot be designated as the taxpayer's principal residence for one or more years after the 1981 year because of the above-mentioned rule, a transitional provision in subsection 40(6) puts a cap on the amount of the taxpayer's gain (if any) on the disposition. Appendix A at the end of this bulletin provides examples which illustrate how the rule in subsection 40(6) works.

## Loss on the Disposition of a Residence

¶ **13.** A property which is used primarily as a residence (i.e., for the personal use and enjoyment of those living in it)—or an option to acquire a property which would, if acquired, be so used—is "personal-use property". Therefore, a loss on the disposition of such a property or option is deemed to be nil by virtue of subparagraph 40(2)(*g*)(iii).

## Land Contributing to the Use and Enjoyment of the Housing Unit as a Residence

¶ **14.** By virtue of paragraph (*e*) of the section 54 definition of "principal residence", a taxpayer's principal residence for a taxation year shall be deemed to include, except where the property consists of a share of the capital stock of a co-operative housing corporation, the land upon which the housing unit stands and any portion of the adjoining land that can reasonably be regarded as contributing to the use and enjoyment of the housing unit as a residence. Evidence is not usually required to establish that one-half hectare of land or less, including the area on which the housing unit stands, contributes to the use and enjoyment of the housing unit as a residence. However, where a portion of that land is used to earn income from business or property, such portion will not usually be considered to contribute to such use and enjoyment. Where the taxpayer claims a portion of the expenses related to the land (such as property taxes or mortgage interest) in computing income, the allocation of such expenses for this purpose is normally an indication of the extent to which he or she considers the land to be used to earn income.

## Land in Excess of One-Half Hectare

¶ **15.** Where the total area of the land upon which a housing unit is situated exceeds one-half hectare, the excess land is deemed by paragraph (*e*) of the section 54 definition of "principal residence" not to have contributed to the use and enjoyment of the housing unit as a residence and thus will not qualify as part of a principal residence, except to the extent that the taxpayer establishes that it was necessary for such use and enjoyment. The excess land must clearly be necessary for the housing unit to properly fulfill its function as a residence and not simply be desirable. Generally, the use of land in excess of one-half hectare in connection with a particular recreation or lifestyle (such as for keeping pets or for country living) does not mean that the excess land is necessary for the use and enjoyment of the housing unit as a residence.

Land in excess of one-half hectare may be considered necessary where the size or character of a housing unit together with its location on the lot make such excess land essential to its use and enjoyment as a residence, or where the location of a housing unit requires such excess land in order to provide its occupants with access to and from public roads. Other factors may be relevant in determining whether land in excess of one-half hectare is necessary for the use and enjoyment of the housing unit as a residence, such as, for example, a minimum lot size or a severance or subdivision restriction (see ¶ 16). In all cases, however, it is a question of fact as to how much, if any, of the excess land is necessary for the use and enjoyment of the housing unit as a residence.

¶ **16.** In order to acquire a property for use as a residence, a taxpayer may be required by a law or regulation of a municipality or province with respect to residential lots to acquire more than one-half hectare of the property. Such a law or regulation could, for example,

(a) require a minimum lot size for a residential lot in a particular area, or

(b) impose a severance or subdivision restriction with respect to residential lots in a particular area.

To the extent that a taxpayer, in order to acquire a property as a residence, is required because of such a law or regulation to acquire land that exceeds one-half hectare, the land that must be so acquired is generally considered to be necessary for the use and enjoyment of the housing unit as a residence throughout the period that the property is continuously owned by the taxpayer after the acquisition date. However, it should be noted that the mere existence of such a municipal law or regulation on the date the taxpayer acquired the property does not immediately qualify the excess land for purposes of the principal residence exemption. For example, if the taxpayer could have made an application for severance of the excess land and it is likely that such a request would have been approved, the taxpayer would generally not be considered to have been required to acquire the excess land.

Furthermore, regardless of the above, where any portion of the land in excess of one-half hectare is not used for residential purposes but rather for income-producing purposes, such portion is usually not considered to be necessary for the use and enjoyment of the housing unit as a residence.

## Disposition of Bare Land in Excess of One-Half Hectare

**¶ 17.** If the housing unit is situated on land in excess of one-half hectare and part or all of that excess land is severed from the property and sold, the land sold is generally considered not to be part of the principal residence unless the housing unit can no longer be used as a residence due to the land sale. If the housing unit can still be so used, such a sale indicates that the land sold was not necessary for the use and enjoyment of the housing unit as a residence.

Circumstances or events beyond the taxpayer's control may cause a portion of the land to cease to be necessary for the use and enjoyment of the housing unit as a residence (e.g., a minimum lot size requirement or severance or subdivision restriction in effect at the date of acquisition is subsequently relaxed). If the taxpayer then subdivides the excess land, it will be considered to have been "necessary" until the time of its subdivision. After subdivision, each newly created lot is a separate property and only the property on which the housing unit is located may continue to be designated as the taxpayer's principal residence. Furthermore, it is possible for the vacant land which previously formed part of the principal residence to be considered to have been converted to inventory at the time of the subdivision (see the rules on partial changes of use in ¶ 30).

## Disposition of Part of a Principal Residence

**¶ 18.** Where only a portion of a property qualifying as a taxpayer's principal residence is disposed of (e.g. the granting of an easement or the expropriation of land), the property may be designated as the taxpayer's principal residence in order to use the principal residence exemption for the portion of the property disposed of. It is important to note that such a designation is made on the entire property (including the housing unit) that qualifies as the principal residence, and not just on the portion of the property disposed of. Accordingly, when the remainder of the property is subsequently disposed of, it too will be recognized as the taxpayer's principal residence for the taxation years for which the above-mentioned designation was made. No other property may be designated as a principal residence for any of those years by the taxpayer (or, for any of those years that are after the 1981 taxation year, by the taxpayer or any of the other members of his or her family unit) as discussed in ¶ 6.

## Disposition of a Property Where Only Part of It Qualifies as a Principal Residence

**¶ 19.** In some cases, only a portion of a property that is disposed of for a gain will qualify as a principal residence (see ¶s 14 to 16). If such qualifying portion of the property is designated as the taxpayer's principal residence, it will be necessary to calculate the gain on such portion separately from the gain on the remaining portion of the property which does not qualify as the taxpayer's principal residence. This is because the gain otherwise determined on the portion of the property designated as the principal residence may be reduced or eliminated by the principal residence exemption, whereas the gain on the remaining portion of the property results in a taxable capital gain. The allocation of the proceeds of disposition and adjusted cost base of the total property between the two portions does not necessarily have to be on the basis of area—consideration should be given to any factors which could have an effect on the relative value of either of the two portions.

***Example***

Mr. A's house is on a property with a total land area of three-quarters of a hectare. He sells the property at fair market value and realizes an actual gain on the disposition. The house and one-half hectare of land qualify as his principal residence for all the years he has owned it. The extra one-quarter hectare does not qualify as part of his principal residence for these reasons:

- There has never been any law or regulation requiring the extra one-quarter hectare to be part of the property as a residence (see ¶ 16)—it has always been severable from the one-half hectare on which the house is situated.
- There has never been, as elaborated on below, any other valid reason for considering the extra one-quarter hectare to be necessary for the use and enjoyment of the house as a residence (see ¶ 15).

If the extra one-quarter hectare were severed, it would still be accessible from the road by which the principal residence's one-half hectare is accessed. However, it would be difficult to sell the extra one-quarter hectare on its own because it forms part of a shallow gully through which a small brook flows. In fact, the only feasible use for the extra one-quarter hectare is to enhance the enjoyment of Mr. A's residence or, if severed, the residence of his next door neighbour, i.e., by providing the owner with the enjoyment of such additional land with its natural beauty. Nevertheless, the extra one-quarter hectare is not necessary for the use and enjoyment of Mr. A's house as a residence. Note that in these circumstances, the portion of Mr. A's gain that is considered to pertain to the extra one-quarter hectare may not simply be one-third of the gain pertaining to the entire three-quarters of a hectare of land he sold, but would probably be a lower amount (a determination of the actual amount in such a case could require a real estate appraisal).

The comments in this paragraph do not apply if the property includes land used in a farming business (see instead ¶s 20 to 23).

## Principal Residence on Land Used in a Farming Business

¶ **20.** If a taxpayer disposes of land used in a farming business which he or she carried on at any time and such land includes property that was at any time his or her principal residence, paragraph 40(2)(*c*) of the Act provides that any gain on the disposition of the land may be calculated using either of the two methods discussed below. It should be noted that the reference to "land" in paragraph 40(2)(*c*) includes the buildings thereon.

¶ **21.** *First Method*: The taxpayer may regard the property as being divided into two portions: the principal residence portion and the remaining portion, part or all of which was used in the farming business. The proceeds of disposition and adjusted cost base of the total property must be allocated on a reasonable basis between the two portions in order to determine the gain for each portion. The gain otherwise determined for the principal residence portion may be reduced or eliminated by the principal residence exemption provided for in paragraph 40(2)(*b*) of the Act, as described in ¶ 8 (including, if applicable, the capital gains election reduction amount, i.e., variable "D" in paragraph 40(2)(*b*)); the gain on the remainder of the property results in a taxable capital gain (see, however, ¶ 24). For purposes of determining what portion of the proceeds of disposition of the land may reasonably be allocated to the principal residence, it is our usual practice to accept the greater of the following two amounts:

(a) the fair market value, as of the date of disposition of the land, of one-half hectare of land estimated on the basis of comparable sales of similar farm properties in the same area (the fair market value of more than one-half hectare could be used to the extent that such excess land was necessary for the use and enjoyment of the housing unit as a residence – see ¶s 15 and 16); and

(b) the fair market value, as of the date of disposition of the land, of a typical residential lot in the same area.

Whichever basis is chosen, (a) or (b), for allocating a portion of the proceeds of disposition of the land to the principal residence, the same basis should be used to allocate a portion of the adjusted cost base of the land to the principal residence. For purposes of making this allocation of the land's adjusted cost base, the fair market value of the land referred to in (a) or (b), as the case may be, would be as of the taxpayer's acquisition date for the land rather than as of the date of its disposition.

Appendix B at the end of this bulletin provides an example which illustrates the use of the first method allowed under paragraph 40(2)(*c*).

¶ **22.** *Second Method*: The taxpayer may elect under subparagraph 40(2)(*c*)(ii) to compute the gain on the disposition of the total property (including the property that was the principal residence) without making the allocations described above or using the principal residence exemption provided for in paragraph 40(2)(*b*) of the Act as described in ¶ 8. With regard to this election under subparagraph 40(2)(*c*)(ii) of the Act, section 2300 of the *Income Tax Regulations* requires that a letter signed by the taxpayer be attached to the income tax return filed for the taxation year in which the disposition of the property took place. The letter should contain the following information:

(a) a statement that the taxpayer is electing under subparagraph 40(2)(*c*)(ii) of the Act;

(b) a statement of the number of taxation years ending after the acquisition date for which the property was the taxpayer's principal residence and during which he or she was resident in Canada (for the meanings of "resident in Canada" and "during", see ¶ 8); and

(c) a description of the property sufficient to identify it with the property designated as the taxpayer's principal residence.

Under the subparagraph 40(2)(*c*)(ii) election, the gain on the disposition of the total property is equal to the gain otherwise determined less the total of $1,000 plus $1,000 for each taxation year in (b) above. Two points should be noted for purposes of calculating the gain under subparagraph 40(2)(*c*)(ii):

- The "acquisition date" mentioned in (b) is the later of
  - December 31, 1971; and
  - the date on which the taxpayer last acquired or reacquired the property or is deemed to have last acquired or reacquired it. If the taxpayer made a subsection 110.6(19) capital gains election in respect of the property, the deemed reacquisition of the property immediately after the end of February 22, 1994 under that election is considered to be a reacquisition for purposes of determining the "acquisition date" when calculating the gain otherwise determined. The reason for this is that, although subsection 40(7.1) prevents a subsection 110.6(19) deemed reacquisition from being considered a reacquisition for purposes of determining the "acquisition date" used in paragraph 40(2)(*b*) (as indicated in ¶ 8), neither subsection 40(7.1) nor any other provision prevents a subsection 110.6(19) deemed reacquisition from being considered a reacquisition for purposes of determining the "acquisition date" used in subparagraph 40(2)(*c*)(ii).
- If the "acquisition date" is in fact the date of the deemed reacquisition under a subsection 110.6(19) capital gains election, i.e., immediately after the end of February 22, 1994, the gain otherwise determined is calculated by taking into account the taxpayer's cost of the property under that deemed reacquisition rather than his or her actual cost at some earlier date. (Variable "A" in paragraph 40(2)(*b*), as discussed in ¶ 8, does not apply for the purposes of subparagraph 40(2)(*c*)(ii).)

Appendix B at the end of this bulletin provides an example which illustrates the use of the second method allowed under paragraph 40(2)(*c*).

¶ **23.** When the second method is used, the exemption of $1,000 per year, which is to allow for the fact that a portion of the total property pertains to the principal residence rather than the farm, is not reduced where part of the residence itself is used to earn income (e.g., there could be an office in the house which is used in connection with a business). However, any gain or recapture of capital cost allowance pertaining to the portion of the residence (i.e., building) so used to earn income (either or both of which can occur, for example, where the use of such portion of the residence is changed back from income-producing to non-income-producing – see ¶s 30 and 34) cannot be reduced by the $1,000 per year exemption.

¶ **24.** Where an individual has a taxable capital gain from the disposition of a farm property, a section 110.6 capital gains deduction (which is a deduction in calculating taxable income) may be possible on the basis that the property is qualified farm property. For further particulars on this topic, see either the *Farming Income* tax guide or the *Farming Income and NISA* tax guide.

## Complete Change in Use of a Property From Principal Residence to Income-Producing

¶ **25.** If a taxpayer has completely converted his or her principal residence to an income-producing use, he or she is deemed by paragraph 45(1)(*a*) to have disposed of the property (both land and building) at fair market value (FMV) and reacquired it immediately thereafter at the same amount. Any gain otherwise determined on this deemed disposition may be eliminated or reduced by the principal residence exemption. The taxpayer may instead, however, defer recognition of any gain to a later year by electing under subsection 45(2) to be deemed not to have made the change in use of the property. This election is made by means of a letter to that effect signed by the taxpayer and filed with the income tax return for the year in which the change in use occurred. If the taxpayer rescinds the election in a subsequent taxation year, he or she is deemed to have disposed of and reacquired the property at FMV on the first day of that subsequent year (with the above-mentioned tax consequences). If capital cost allowance (CCA) is claimed on the property, the election is considered to be rescinded on the first day of the year in which that claim is made.

Subsection 220(3.2) of the Act, in conjunction with section 600 of the *Income Tax Regulations*, provides the authority for the Canada Customs and Revenue Agency (the CCRA) to accept a late-filed subsection 45(2) election. Such a late-filed election may be accepted under certain circumstances, one of which is that no CCA has been claimed on the property since the change in use has occurred and during the period in which the election is to remain in force. For further particulars on the acceptance of late-filed elections, see the current version of Information Circular 92-1, *Guidelines for Accepting Late, Amended or Revoked Elections*.

¶ **26.** A property can qualify as a taxpayer's principal residence for up to four taxation years during which a subsection 45(2) election remains in force, even if the housing unit is not ordinarily inhabited during those years by the taxpayer or by his or her spouse or common-law partner, former spouse or common-law partner, or child (see ¶ 5). However, the taxpayer must be resident, or deemed to be resident, in Canada during those years for the full benefit of the principal residence exemption to apply (see the numerator "B" in the formula in ¶ 8 or the years included in the statement in ¶ 22(b), as the case may be). It should also be noted that the rule described in ¶ 6 prevents the designation of more than one property as a principal residence for any particular year by the taxpayer (or, for any particular year after the 1981 taxation year, by the taxpayer or any other member of his or her family unit). Thus, for example, a taxpayer's designation for the same year of one property by virtue of a subsection 45(2) election being in force, and another property by virtue of the fact that he or she ordinarily inhabited that other property, would not be permitted.

***Example***

Mr. A and his family lived in a house for a number of years until September 30, 1993. From October 1, 1993 until March 31, 1998 they lived elsewhere and Mr. A rented the house to a third party. On April 1, 1998, they moved back into the house and lived in it until it was sold in 2001. When he filed his 2001 income tax return, Mr. A designated the house as his principal residence for the 1994 to 1997 taxation years inclusive (i.e., the maximum four years) by virtue of a subsection 45(2) election (which he had already filed with his 1993 income tax return) having been in force for those years. (He was able to make this designation because no other property had been designated as a principal residence by him or a member of his family unit for those years.) He designated the house as his principal residence for all the other years in which he owned it by virtue of his having ordinarily inhabited it during those years, including the 1993 and 1998 years. Having been resident in Canada at all times, Mr. A's gain otherwise determined on the disposition of the house in 2001 was, therefore, completely eliminated by the principal residence exemption.

Any income in respect of a property (e.g., the rental income in the above example), net of applicable expenses, must be reported for tax purposes. However, for taxation years covered by a subsection 45(2) election, CCA should not be claimed on the property (see ¶ 25).

¶ **27.** Section 54.1 removes the above-mentioned four-year limitation for taxation years covered by a subsection 45(2) election if all of the following conditions are met:

(a) the taxpayer does not ordinarily inhabit the housing unit during the period covered by the election because the taxpayer's or his or her spouse's or common-law partner's place of employment has been relocated;

(b) the employer is not related to the taxpayer or his or her spouse or common-law partner;

(c) the housing unit is at least 40 kilometers farther from such new place of employment than is the taxpayer's subsequent place or places of residence; and

(d) either

- the taxpayer resumes ordinary habitation of the housing unit during the term of employment by that same employer or before the end of the taxation year immediately following the taxation year in which such employment terminates; or
- the taxpayer dies during the term of such employment.

With regard to condition (d), two corporations that are members of the same corporate group, or are otherwise related, are not considered to be the same employer.

## Complete Change in Use of a Property From Income-Producing to Principal Residence

**¶ 28.** If a taxpayer has completely changed the use of a property (for which an election under subsection 45(2) is not in force) from income-producing to a principal residence, he or she is deemed by paragraph 45(1)(*a*) to have disposed of the property (both land and building), and immediately thereafter reacquired it, at FMV. This deemed disposition can result in a taxable capital gain. The taxpayer may instead defer recognition of the gain to a later year by electing under subsection 45(3) that the above-mentioned deemed disposition and reacquisition under paragraph 45(1)(*a*) does not apply. This election is made by means of a letter to that effect signed by the taxpayer and filed with the income tax return for the year in which the property is ultimately disposed of (or earlier if a formal "demand" for the election is issued by the CCRA). Also, subsection 220(3.2) of the Act, in conjunction with section 600 of the *Income Tax Regulations*, provides the authority for the CCRA to accept a late-filed subsection 45(3) election. Such a late-filed election may be accepted under certain circumstances. For further particulars on the acceptance of late-filed elections, see the current version of Information Circular 92-1, *Guidelines for Accepting Late, Amended or Revoked Elections.*

Even if a subsection 45(3) election is filed in order to defer recognition of a gain from the change in use of a property from income-producing to principal residence, the net income from the property for the period before the change in use must still be reported. However, for purposes of reporting such net income, it should be noted that an election under subsection 45(3) is not possible if, for any taxation year ending after 1984 and on or before the change in use of the property from income-producing to a principal residence, CCA has been allowed in respect of the property to

- the taxpayer;
- the taxpayer's spouse or common-law partner; or
- a trust under which the taxpayer or his or her spouse or common-law partner is a beneficiary.

CCA so allowed would cause subsection 45(4) to nullify the subsection 45(3) election.

**¶ 29.** Similar to the treatment for a subsection 45(2) election (see ¶ 26), a property can qualify as a taxpayer's principal residence for up to four taxation years prior to a change in use covered by a subsection 45(3) election, in lieu of fulfilling the "ordinarily inhabited" rule (discussed in ¶ 5) for these years. As in the case of a subsection 45(2) election, residence or deemed residence in Canada during these years is necessary for the full benefit of the principal residence exemption to apply. Furthermore, the rule described in ¶ 6 prevents the designation of more than one property as a principal residence for any particular year by the taxpayer (or, for any particular year after the 1981 taxation year, by the taxpayer or any other member of his or her family unit).

***Example***

Mr. X bought a house in 1993 and rented it to a third party until mid-1999. Mr. X and his family then lived in the house until it was sold in 2001. Mr. X has been resident in Canada at all times. When he filed his 2001 income tax return, Mr. X designated the house as his principal residence for the 1999 to 2001 taxation years inclusive, by virtue of his having ordinarily inhabited it during those years. He also designated the house as his principal residence for the 1995 to 1998 years inclusive (i.e., the maximum 4 years) by virtue of a subsection 45(3) election, which he filed with his 2001 income tax return (he was able to make this designation because (i) no other property had been designated by him or a member of his family unit for those years, and (ii) he did not claim any CCA when reporting the net income from the property before the change in use). However, his gain otherwise determined on the disposition of the house in 2001 could not be fully eliminated by the principal residence exemption formula in ¶ 8 because he could not designate the house as his principal residence for the 1993 and 1994 years.

## Partial Changes in Use

**¶ 30.** If a taxpayer has partially converted a principal residence to an income-producing use, paragraph 45(1)(*c*) provides for a deemed disposition of the portion of the property so converted (such portion is usually calculated on the basis of the area involved) for proceeds equal to its proportionate share of the property's FMV. Paragraph 45(1)(*c*) also provides for a deemed reacquisition immediately thereafter of the same portion of the property at a cost equal to the very same amount. Any gain otherwise determined on the deemed disposition is usually eliminated or reduced by the principal residence exemption. If the portion of the property so changed is later converted back to use as part of the principal residence, there is a second deemed disposition (and reacquisition) thereof at FMV. A taxable capital gain attributable to the period of use of such portion of the property for income-producing purposes can arise from such a second deemed disposition or from an actual sale of the whole property subsequent to the original partial change in use. An election under subsection 45(2) or (3) cannot be made where there is a partial change in use of a property as described above.

**¶ 31.** The above-mentioned deemed disposition rule applies where the partial change in use of the property is substantial and of a more permanent nature, i.e., where there is a structural change. Examples where this occurs are the conversion of the front half of a house into a store, the conversion of a portion of a house into a self-contained domestic establishment for earning rental income (a duplex, triplex, etc.), and alterations to a house to accommodate separate business premises. In these and similar cases, the taxpayer reports the income and may claim the expenses pertaining to the altered portion of the property (i.e., a reasonable portion of the expenses relating to the whole property) as well as CCA on such altered portion of the property.

**¶ 32.** It is our practice not to apply the deemed disposition rule, but rather to consider that the entire property retains its nature as a principal residence, where all of the following conditions are met:

(a) the income-producing use is ancillary to the main use of the property as a residence,

(b) there is no structural change to the property, and

(c) no CCA is claimed on the property.

These conditions can be met, for example, where a taxpayer carries on a business of caring for children in his or her home, rents one or more rooms in the home, or has an office or other work space in the home which is used in connection with his or her business or employment. In these and similar cases, the taxpayer reports the income and may claim the expenses (other than CCA) pertaining to the portion of the property used for income-producing purposes. Certain conditions and restrictions are placed on the deductibility of expenses relating to an office or other work space in an individual's home—see the current version of IT-514, *Work Space in Home Expenses* (if the income is income from a business) or the current version of IT-352, *Employee's Expenses, Including Work Space in Home Expenses*. In the event that the taxpayer commences to claim CCA on the portion of the property used for producing income, the deemed disposition rule is applied as of the time at which the income-producing use commenced.

## Change in Use Rules Regarding CCA, Deemed Capital Cost, and Recapture

**¶ 33.** If a taxpayer has completely or partially changed the use of property from principal residence to income-producing, subsection 13(7) provides for a deemed acquisition of the property or portion of the property so changed that is depreciable property. For purposes of claiming CCA, the deemed capital cost of such depreciable property is its FMV as of the date of the change in use unless that FMV is greater than its cost to the taxpayer. In that case, the deemed capital cost of such depreciable property is equal to its cost to the taxpayer plus an amount which represents the taxable portion of the accrued gain on the property (before any reduction to that gain by means of the principal residence exemption) to the extent that a section 110.6 capital gains deduction has not been claimed in respect of that amount (this latter rule has no particular significance for dispositions of residence properties occurring after February 22, 1994, because of the elimination of the $100,000 lifetime capital gains exemption for dispositions after that date).

***Example***

Mr. A completely converted his house to a rental property in January 2001, at which time its cost to him and its FMV were $60,000 and $100,000 respectively (both amounts pertain only to the housing unit and not the land). The change in use resulted in a deemed disposition of the property at FMV (see ¶s 25 and 26—assume that Mr. A did not make a subsection 45(2) election in respect of the property because he wanted to use the principal residence exemption for his cottage for the years after 2001). Mr. A was able to use the principal residence exemption formula in ¶ 8 to bring his gain on the January 2001 deemed disposition of the house to nil. Mr. A's deemed capital cost for the house (i.e., for CCA purposes) at the time of its change in use to a rental property was $80,000. This amount was calculated by taking the $60,000 cost and adding $20,000, the latter amount being one-half of the excess of the $100,000 FMV over the $60,000 cost. (Note that the $20,000 potentially taxable portion of the gain was included in Mr. A's deemed capital cost for CCA purposes even though he eliminated the gain by means of the principal residence exemption.)

In the case of a complete change in use of a property from principal residence to income-producing, a subsection 45(2) election will cause subsection 13(7), as described above, not to apply. However, if the election is rescinded in a subsequent taxation year (e.g., by claiming CCA on the property—see ¶ 25), a subsection 13(7) deemed acquisition of depreciable property will occur on the first day of that subsequent year.

Because a subsection 45(2) election is not available where there is only a partial change in use of a property from principal residence to income-producing, subsection 13(7) applies in such a situation in the manner described above (except where conditions (a) to (c) in ¶ 32 have been met, including the condition not to claim CCA on the portion of the property used to earn income).

**¶ 34.** If a taxpayer completely or partially changes the use of a property from income-producing to principal residence, there is a deemed disposition at FMV, by virtue of subsection 13(7), of the portion of the property so changed that is depreciable property. This can result in a recapture of CCA previously claimed on the property. A subsection 45(3) election cannot be used to defer such a recapture (e.g., a recapture of CCA claimed for a taxation year ending before 1985—see the comments regarding CCA in ¶ 28).

## Personal Trusts

**¶ 35.** It is possible for a "personal trust" (this term is defined in subsection 248(1) of the Act) to claim the principal residence exemption to reduce or eliminate a gain that the trust would otherwise have on the disposition of a property. For this purpose, the normal principal residence exemption rules generally apply, subject to the following modifications:

(a) When a personal trust designates a property as its principal residence for one or more taxation years, the trustee of the trust should complete and file Form T1079, *Designation of a Property as a Principal Residence by a Personal Trust.* For purposes of calculating a capital gains election reduction amount (see ¶ 8) for the trust, the trustee should complete Form T1079–WS, *Principal Residence Worksheet*, and file it with the T1079 designation form.

(b) For each taxation year for which the trust is designating the property as its principal residence, the trust must specify in the above-mentioned designation each individual who, in the calendar year ending in that taxation year,
   - was beneficially interested in the trust, and
   - ordinarily inhabited the housing unit or who had a spouse or common-law partner, former spouse or common-law partner, or child who ordinarily inhabited the housing unit (a subsection 45(2) or (3) election can be used, however, in essentially the same manner as, and subject to the limitations discussed in, ¶s 26 and 29, to remove the requirement that the "ordinarily inhabited" rule be fulfilled for the year by one of these persons).

   Any individual specified by the trust to be an individual as described above is referred to as a "specified beneficiary" of the trust for the year.

(c) For each taxation year for which the trust is designating the property as its principal residence, there must not have been any corporation (other than a registered charity) or partnership that was beneficially interested in the trust at any time in the year.

(d) For each taxation year for which the trust is designating the property as its principal residence (including years before 1982), no other property may have been designated as a principal residence, for the calendar year ending in the year, by any specified beneficiary of the trust for the year, or by any person who throughout the calendar year ending in the year was a member of such a beneficiary's family unit. For this purpose, a specified beneficiary's "family unit" includes, in addition to the specified beneficiary, the following persons (if any):
   - the specified beneficiary's spouse or common-law partner throughout the calendar year ending in the year, unless the spouse or common-law partner was throughout that calendar year living apart, and was separated pursuant to a judicial separation or written separation agreement, from the specified beneficiary;
   - the specified beneficiary's children, except those who were married, in a common-law partnership or 18 years of age or older during the calendar year ending in the year; and
   - where the specified beneficiary was not married, in a common-law partnership or 18 years of age or older during the calendar year ending in the year,
     - the specified beneficiary's mother and father, and
     - the specified beneficiary's brothers and sisters who were not married, in a common-law partnership or 18 years of age or older during that calendar year.

Furthermore, if a personal trust designates a property as its principal residence for a particular taxation year, the property is deemed to be property designated, for the calendar year ending in the year, as the principal residence of each specified beneficiary of the trust. This deeming rule can be applied, in conjunction with the other principal residence exemption rules, to various situations not explicitly described in those rules.

***Example***

Personal Trust A owned a house in its taxation year ended December 31, 2001. The house was ordinarily inhabited in 2001 by Mr. X, a specified beneficiary of Personal Trust A (and also by his spouse, Mrs. X). The trust has designated the house as its principal residence for its taxation year ended December 31, 2001. The house is therefore deemed to have been designated as Mr. X's principal residence for 2001.

Personal Trust B owned a cottage (see ¶ 3) in its taxation year ended December 31, 2001. The cottage was ordinarily inhabited (see ¶ 5) in 2001 by Mrs. X, a specified beneficiary of Personal Trust B (and also by Mr. X). As discussed in ¶ 6, a taxpayer and his or her spouse or common-law partner cannot designate different properties for the same year. Therefore, since the house has already been deemed to have been designated as Mr. X's principal residence for 2001, Personal Trust B cannot designate the cottage as its principal residence for 2001 because that would have resulted in the cottage being deemed to have also been designated as Mrs. X's principal residence for 2001.

**¶ 36.** Where a beneficiary has acquired a property from a personal trust in satisfaction of all or any part of the beneficiary's capital interest in the trust and

- the rollover provision in subsection 107(2) applied (see discussion in ¶ 37 for an exception to this rollover provision) and

- subsection 107(4) did not apply,

subsection 40(7) provides a deeming rule when the beneficiary disposes of the property. For purposes of claiming the principal residence exemption, the beneficiary is deemed by subsection 40(7) to have owned the property since the trust last acquired it.

The following example illustrates the effect of this deemed ownership provision in subsection 40(7) (in conjunction with subsection 107(2)).

***Example***

A personal trust acquired a residential property on October 1, 1997 for $75,000. On January 10, 1999, the property was distributed to Mr. X in satisfaction of his capital interest in the trust. Subsection 107(4) did not apply with respect to this distribution, and the rollover provision in subsection 107(2) prevented the gain on the property accrued to January 10, 1999 from being taxed in the hands of the trust. Instead, the potential for taxing that gain was transferred to Mr. X because subsection 107(2) deemed him to have acquired the property at a cost equal to $75,000, i.e., the cost amount of the property to the trust. Mr. X lived in the residence from October 15, 1997 until he disposed of the property on December 1, 2001 for $125,000, incurring no costs in connection with the disposition. Mr. X's gain otherwise determined on the disposition of the property was equal to his $125,000 proceeds minus his $75,000 adjusted cost base = $50,000. Subsection 40(7) deemed him to have owned the property from October 1, 1997 rather than from January 10, 1999. Since Mr. X ordinarily inhabited the residence in all of the years from 1997 to 2001 inclusive (i.e., all of the years in which he either owned the property or was deemed to have owned it), he was able to designate the property as his principal residence for all those years. Thus, he was able to use the principal residence exemption formula in ¶ 8 to fully eliminate his $50,000 gain otherwise determined. However, if neither Mr. X nor his current or former spouse or common-law partner, or child had ordinarily inhabited the residence (see the rule discussed in ¶ 5) until it was distributed by the trust to Mr. X on January 10, 1999, he would have been able to designate the property as his principal residence only for 1999 to 2001. In other words, he would have been able to use the formula in ¶ 8 to eliminate only the following portion of his $50,000 gain otherwise determined:

$$A \times \frac{B}{C} = \$50{,}000 \times \frac{1 + 3\ (1999\text{ to }2001)}{5\ (1997\text{ to }2001)} = \$40{,}000$$

**¶ 37.** In order to prevent the rollover rule in subsection 107(2) from applying with respect to a trust's distribution, to a beneficiary, of a property that qualifies for designation as the trust's principal residence before the distribution, a personal trust can use an election under subsection 107(2.01) of the Act. Under this election, the trust would instead be deemed, just before the distribution of the property to the beneficiary, to have disposed of and then to have reacquired the property at fair market value. This could be done, for example, in order for the trust to use the principal residence exemption to eliminate or reduce any gain on the property accrued to that point in time (see ¶ 35), ideal in circumstances where the recipient beneficiary is not the specified beneficiary and has owned another home during the period in which the trust owned the home being distributed. The cost of the property to the beneficiary would be that same fair market value, and the beneficiary would not be deemed by subsection 40(7) (see ¶ 36) to have owned the property during the period of time in which it was owned by the trust prior to the distribution.

## Transfer of a Principal Residence

**¶ 38.** Subsection 40(4) can apply if a property of a taxpayer (hereinafter referred to as the "transferor")

- has been transferred *inter vivos* to:
  - the transferor's spouse or common-law partner,
  - the transferor's former spouse or common–law partner,
  - a spousal or common-law partner trust,
  - a joint spousal or common-law partner trust or
  - an alter ego trust

and the subsection 73(1) rollover rule has applied; or

- has been transferred or distributed, as a consequence of the transferor's death, to his or her spouse or common-law partner or to a spousal or common-law partner trust, and the subsection 70(6) rollover rule has applied.

If the spouse or common-law partner, former spouse or common-law partner, spousal or common-law partner trust, joint spousal or common-law partner trust, or alter ego trust (hereinafter referred to as the "transferee") subsequently disposes of the property, subsection 40(4) can apply with respect to a principal residence exemption, claimed by the transferee, for the property. For purposes of the transferee's claiming the principal residence exemption under either paragraph 40(2)(*b*) (see the formula in ¶ 8) or paragraph 40(2)(*c*) (see ¶s 20 to 23), the following rules apply under subsection 40(4):

(a) The transferee is deemed to have owned the property throughout the period that the transferor owned it.

(b) The property is deemed to have been the transferee's principal residence

- in a case where the subsection 73(1) rollover rule applied—for any taxation year for which it was the transferor's principal residence; and
- in a case where the subsection 70(6) rollover rule applied—for any taxation year for which it would have been the transferor's principal residence if he or she had so designated it.

(c) If the transferee is a trust, it is deemed to have been resident in Canada during each of the taxation years during which the transferor was resident in Canada.

Any year included in the period described in (a) is included by the transferee in variable C (the denominator of the fraction) in the formula in ¶ 8. Any year described in (b) is included by the transferee in variable B (the numerator of the fraction) in the formula in ¶ 8 or in the years included in the statement in ¶ 22(b), as the case may be, assuming that the transferee meets the residence requirement mentioned therein, as the case may be, for that year. (If the transferee is a trust, see (c) above with regard to this residence requirement.)

### *Example 1*

Mr. X was the sole owner of a house in Canada, which he had acquired in 1985. In 1990, Mr. X got married and his spouse, Mrs. X, moved into the house with him. In 1995, Mr. X died and the house was transferred to a spousal trust for Mrs. X. The trust was a trust as described in subsection 70(6). The trust's taxation year-end was December 31. If Mr. X had not died (and if he had sold his house in 1995), he could have designated it as his principal residence for any of the years 1985 to 1995 inclusive.

Under the rollover rule in subsection 70(6), Mr. X was deemed to have disposed of the house immediately before his death for proceeds equal to his cost of the house. Thus, Mr. X had no gain or loss on the deemed disposition of the house. The spousal trust for Mrs. X was deemed under subsection 70(6) to have acquired the house, at the time of Mr. X's death, at a cost equal to Mr. X's deemed proceeds, i.e., at Mr. X's cost of the house.

In 2001, Mrs. X died and the trust sold the house at fair market value. Since this amount was greater than the trust's deemed cost of the house, the trust had a "gain otherwise determined" from the disposition, which the trust (i.e., its trustee) wishes to eliminate by using the principal residence exemption.

Subsection 40(4) deems the trust to have owned the house in all the years in which Mr. X owned it, i.e., 1985 to 1995 inclusive, in accordance with the rule described in (a) above. (The house was, of course, owned by the trust in 1995 in any event.) This means that the years that the trust must include in variable C (the denominator of the fraction) in the principal residence exemption formula in ¶ 8 are 1985 to 2001 inclusive.

Since the trust is a personal trust resident in Canada and also since Mrs. X lived in the house and qualified as a specified beneficiary of the trust for the years 1995 to 2001 inclusive (see ¶ 35), the trust can designate the house as its principal residence for those years. The trust cannot designate the house as its principal residence for the years 1985 to 1994 inclusive; however, such a designation by the trust is not necessary—the house is already deemed by subsection 40(4) to have been the trust's principal residence for those years, in accordance with the rule described in (b) above, because Mr. X could have designated the house as his principal residence for those years. Also, in accordance with the rule described in (c) above, the trust is deemed to have been resident in Canada for the years 1985 to 1994 because Mr. X was resident in Canada during those years. Therefore, the trust is able to include all of the years from 1985 to 2001 inclusive in variable B (the numerator of the fraction) in the formula in ¶ 8. In other words, the trust is able to use the principal residence exemption formula in ¶ 8 to completely eliminate the gain otherwise determined on its disposition of the house in 2001.

### *Example 2*

Assume all the same facts as in Example 1, except the following: Mr. X could not have designated the house as his principal residence for the years 1985 to 1988 inclusive because he had already designated his cottage (see ¶s 3 and 5) as his principal residence for those years (see the designation rules discussed in ¶ 6). Under these circumstances, the house that was transferred to the spousal trust for Mrs. X cannot be deemed to have been the principal residence of the trust for the years 1985 to 1988 inclusive. Therefore, the trust can only partially eliminate the gain otherwise determined on its disposition of the house in 2001 by means of the principal residence exemption formula in ¶ 8.

In the case of an *inter vivos* transfer of property under subsection 73(1) of the Act, the following should be noted for purposes of any subsequent disposition of the property by the transferee:

- A designation of the property as the principal residence of the transferor—for one or more years prior to the transfer—may be needed in order for the property to be deemed to have been the principal residence of the transferee for those years by means of subsection 40(4) (see (b) above). Note that the transferor will not be able to designate the property as a principal residence for any particular year if another property is designated as a principal residence for that year by the transferor (or, if the year is after the 1981 taxation year, by the transferor or any of the other members of the transferor's family unit)—see ¶ 6. If the transferor is able to, and does in fact, designate the property as his or her principal residence for one or more years prior to the transfer, this does not necessarily mean that the transferor must actually file the designation form with the return for the year of the transfer (although the transferor may do so)—for further comments on the necessity to file a designation form, see ¶ 7. The transferor should, in any event, complete the designation form and, if it is not filed by the transferor, **it should be retained by the transferee**. Subsequently, if the transferee disposes of the property (or grants an option to another person to acquire the property) and wishes to use the principal residence exemption, the transferee would need to file the designation forms—i.e., the transferee's designation form for any years for which the transferee is designating the property as a principal residence and the transferor's designation form for any years for which his or her designation of the property causes the property to be deemed to have been the principal residence of the transferee

- if the transferee is the transferor's spouse or common-law partner—only when the situation described in ¶ 7(a) or (b) exists in connection with the transferee's disposition of the property; or
- if the transferee is a personal trust—in every case (see ¶ 35(a)).

- Any taxable capital gain of the transferee (excluding an alter ego trust) from the disposition of the property or substituted property (which might occur, for example, because the transferee was not able to completely eliminate the gain otherwise determined by means of the principal residence exemption) could be deemed to be the taxable capital gain of the transferor by virtue of the attribution rules in section 74.2 of the Act. For a discussion of these rules, see the current version of IT-511, *Interspousal and Certain Other Transfers and Loans of Property*.

## Partnership Property

**¶ 39.** Although a housing unit, a leasehold interest therein, or a share of the capital stock of a co-operative housing corporation (see ¶ 3) can be a partnership asset, a partnership is not a taxpayer and it cannot use the principal residence exemption on the disposition of any such property. However, a member of the partnership could use the principal residence exemption to reduce or eliminate the portion of any gain on the disposition of the property which is allocated to that partner pursuant to the partnership agreement, provided that the other requirements of the section 54 definition of "principal residence" are met (e.g., if the partner resides in the partnership's housing unit, this would satisfy the "ordinarily inhabited" requirement discussed in ¶ 5).

## A Principal Residence Outside Canada

**¶ 40.** A property that is located outside Canada can, depending on the facts of the case, qualify as a taxpayer's principal residence (see the requirements discussed in ¶s 2 to 6). A taxpayer that is resident in Canada and owns such a qualifying property outside Canada during a particular taxation year can designate the property as a principal residence for that year in order to use the principal residence exemption (see ¶ 8 for the meanings of "resident in Canada" and "during"). Should a non-resident of Canada who owns a property outside Canada become a resident of Canada at any particular time, the provisions of the Act normally apply to deem that person to acquire the property at that time at fair market value, thereby ensuring that any unrealized gain on the property accruing to that time will not be taxable in Canada. Thereafter, the comments in the first two sentences of this paragraph may apply.

## Non-Resident Owner of a Principal Residence in Canada

**¶ 41.** It may be possible for a property in Canada that is owned in a particular taxation year by a non-resident of Canada to qualify as the non-resident's principal residence (i.e., satisfy all the requirements of the section 54 definition of "principal residence" for the non-resident) for that year. The non-resident's spouse could be the one, for example, who satisfies the "ordinarily inhabited" rule—see ¶ 5 (or, alternatively, a subsection 45(2) or (3) election could make the designation of the property as the non-resident's principal residence possible—see ¶s 26 and 29). However, the use of the principal residence exemption by a taxpayer is limited by reference to the number of taxation years ending after the acquisition date during which the taxpayer was resident in Canada—see ¶s 8 and 22 (as indicated in ¶ 8, "during" a year means at any time in the year). Thus, even if a property in Canada owned by a non-resident qualifies as the non-resident's principal residence, the above-mentioned "residence in Canada" requirement typically prevents the non-resident from using the principal residence exemption to eliminate a gain on the disposition of the property.

**¶ 42.** In spite of the limitation mentioned in ¶ 41 in connection with the principal residence exemption, an election under subsection 45(2) or (3) could allow a non-resident owning a property in Canada to defer a taxable capital gain which would otherwise result from a deemed disposition of a property on a change in its use (see ¶s 25 and 28).

**¶ 43.** Where a non-resident owner of a property in Canada has rented out the property in a particular taxation year and has filed a subsection 45(2) or (3) election in respect of the property, see ¶s 25 and 28 regarding the restrictions on claiming CCA. These restrictions apply where the non-resident elects to report the rental income under section 216. (That election is discussed in the current version of IT-393, *Election re Tax on Rents and Timber Royalties – Non-Residents*.)

## Section 116 Certificate for a Disposition of a Principal Residence in Canada by a Non-Resident Owner

**¶ 44.** Where a non-resident wishes to obtain a certificate under section 116 of the Act for a property in Canada which the non-resident proposes to dispose of or has disposed of within the last 10 days, a prepayment on account of tax must be made or security acceptable to the CCRA must be given before the certificate will be issued. Form T2062, *Request by a Non-Resident of Canada for a Certificate of Compliance Related to the Disposition of Taxable Canadian Property*, or a similar notification, must be filed in connection with a request for a section 116 certificate. Further particulars regarding the above are contained in the current version of Information Circular 72-17, *Procedures Concerning the Disposition of Taxable Canadian Property by Non-Residents of Canada – Section 116*. Where part or all of any gain otherwise determined on the disposition of the property by the non-resident is or will be eliminated by the principal residence exemption, the amount of prepayment on account of tax to be made or security to be given may be reduced accordingly. An application for such a reduction should be made by means of a letter signed by the taxpayer and attached to the completed Form T2062 or similar notification. Such letter should contain a calculation of the portion of the gain otherwise determined that is or will be so eliminated by the principal residence exemption.

## Appendix A – Illustration of the Rule in Subsection 40(6)

If a taxpayer disposes (or is deemed to dispose) of a property which the taxpayer has owned (whether jointly with another person or otherwise) continuously since before 1982, the rule in subsection 40(6) (see ¶ 12) provides that the gain calculated under the usual method, using the principal residence exemption formula in ¶ 8, cannot be greater than the maximum total net gain determined under an alternative method. Under the alternative method, there is a hypothetical disposition on December 31, 1981 and reacquisition on January 1, 1982 of the property at fair market value (FMV). The maximum total net gain determined under the alternative method is then calculated as follows:

**pre-1982 gain + post-1981 gain – post-1981 loss = maximum total net gain**

where

- the **pre-1982 gain** is the gain (if any), as reduced by the principal residence exemption formula in ¶ 8, that would result from the hypothetical disposition at FMV on December 31, 1981,
- the **post-1981 gain** is the gain (if any), as reduced by the principal residence exemption formula in ¶ 8 without the "1 +" in the numerator "B" in that formula, that would result from the hypothetical acquisition at FMV on January 1, 1982 and the subsequent actual (or deemed) disposition, and
- the **post-1981 loss** is the amount of any loss that has accrued from December 31, 1981 to the date of the subsequent actual (or deemed) disposition, i.e., the excess (if any) of the FMV on December 31, 1981 over the proceeds (or deemed proceeds) from the subsequent actual (or deemed) disposition.

The examples which follow illustrate the rule in subsection 40(6). It has been assumed in these examples that, on each actual disposition, no costs were incurred in connection with that disposition.

### *Example 1*

Mrs. X acquired a house in 1975 for $50,000. She and her husband lived in it until February 1996, when she sold it for $115,000, resulting in an actual gain of $65,000 ($115,000 – $50,000). Ever since the sale of the house in 1996, Mr. and Mrs. X have been living in rented premises. In filing her 1996 income tax return, Mrs. X designated the house as her principal residence for 1975 to 1995 inclusive, and thus her gain otherwise determined was completely eliminated by the principal residence exemption formula in ¶ 8:

| | | |
|---|---|---|
| Gain otherwise determined ($115,000 – $50,000) | | $ 65,000 |
| Reduce by principal residence exemption: | | |
| $A \times \frac{B}{C} = \$65,000 \times \frac{1 + 21 \text{ (1975 to 1995)}}{22 \text{ (1975 to 1996)}}$ | | 65,000 |
| Gain | | $ NIL |

Mr. X acquired a lot in 1975 for $7,000 and built a cottage on it in 1979 for $13,000. Mr. and Mrs. X used the cottage as a seasonal residence from 1979 to 2001 inclusive. In the fall of 2001 Mr. X sold the cottage for $65,000, resulting in an actual gain of $45,000 ($65,000 – ($7,000 + $13,000)). In filing his 2001 income tax return, Mr. X designated the cottage property as his principal residence for 1979 to 1981 inclusive, as well as for 1996 to 2001 inclusive. He could not designate the property as his principal residence for 1975 to 1978 inclusive because it was only a vacant lot and thus no one "ordinarily inhabited" it in those years (see ¶ 11); nor could he designate the property as his principal residence for 1982 to 1995 inclusive because of his wife's designation of the house as her principal residence for those years (see ¶ 6). As a result, not all of his $45,000 gain otherwise determined was eliminated by the principal residence exemption formula in ¶ 8. However, because the property had been owned by Mr. X continuously since before 1982, subsection 40(6) applied for purposes of computing his gain. The fair market value of the cottage on December 31, 1981 was $30,000.

In addition to the above facts, assume also that Mr. X did not make a subsection 110.6(19) capital gains election with respect to the cottage (see the discussion of this election in ¶ 8) because he had already used up his $100,000 lifetime capital gains exemption before 1994. Therefore, he had no capital gains election reduction amount (as described in ¶ 8) with respect to the cottage.

The calculations under subsection 40(6) in connection with Mr. X's 2001 gain on the cottage were as follows:

USUAL METHOD FOR CALCULATING GAIN:

| | |
|---|---|
| Gain otherwise determined ($65,000 – $20,000) | $ 45,000 |
| Reduce by principal residence exemption: | |
| $A \times \frac{B}{C} = \$45,000 \times \frac{1 + 9 \text{ (1979 to 1981 and 1996 to 2001)}}{27 \text{ (1975 to 2001)}}$ | 16,667 |
| Gain | $ 28,333 |

ALTERNATIVE METHOD – CALCULATION OF MAXIMUM TOTAL NET GAIN:

| | |
|---|---|
| Pre-1982 gain: | |
| Gain otherwise determined ($30,000 – $20,000) | $ 10,000 |
| Reduce by principal residence exemption: | |
| $A \times \frac{B}{C} = \$10,000 \times \frac{1 + 3 \text{ (1979 to 1981)}}{7 \text{ (1975 to 1981)}}$ | 5,714 |
| Gain | $ 4,286 |
| Post-1981 gain: | |
| Gain otherwise determined ($65,000 – $30,000) | $ 35,000 |
| Reduce by principal residence exemption: | |
| $A \times \frac{B}{C} = \$35,000 \times \frac{6 \text{ (1996 to 2001)}}{20 \text{ (1982 to 2001)}}$ | 10,500 |
| Gain | $ 24,500 |
| Post-1981 loss: | |
| N/A | $ NIL |

Pre-1982 gain + post-1981 gain – post-1981 loss
= $4,286 + $24,500 – $Nil
= $28,786.

RESULT: Mr. X's gain remained at the $28,333 calculated under the usual method since that amount did not exceed the maximum total net gain of $28,786 calculated under the alternative method.

***Example 2***

Assume the same facts in Example 1 except that the couple are in a common-law relationship rather than a married couple.

In filing his 2001 income tax return, Mr. X designated the cottage property as his principal residence for 1979 to 1992 inclusive, as well as for 1996 to 2001 inclusive. He could not designate the property as his principal residence for 1975 to 1978 inclusive because it was only a vacant lot and thus no one "ordinarily inhabited" it in those years (see ¶ 11); nor could he designate the property as his principal residence for 1993 to 1995 inclusive because of his common-law partner's designation of the house as her principal residence for those years (see ¶ 6). As a result, not all of his $45,000 gain otherwise determined was eliminated by the principal residence exemption formula in ¶ 8.

The calculations under subsection 40(6) in connection with Mr. X's 2001 gain on the cottage were as follows:

USUAL METHOD FOR CALCULATING GAIN:

| | |
|---|---|
| Gain otherwise determined ($65,000 – $20,000) | $ 45,000 |
| Reduce by principal residence exemption: | |
| $A \times \frac{B}{C} = \$45,000 \times \frac{1 + 20 \text{ (1979 to 1992 and 1996 to 2001)}}{27 \text{ (1975 to 2001)}}$ | 35,000 |
| Gain | $ 10,000 |

ALTERNATIVE METHOD – CALCULATION OF MAXIMUM TOTAL NET GAIN:

| | |
|---|---|
| Pre-1982 gain: | |
| Gain otherwise determined ($30,000 – $20,000) | $ 10,000 |
| Reduce by principal residence exemption: | |
| $A \times \frac{B}{C} = \$10,000 \times \frac{1 + 3 \text{ (1979 to 1981)}}{7 \text{ (1975 to 1981)}}$ | 5,714 |
| Gain | $ 4,286 |

| | |
|---|---|
| Post-1981 gain: | |
| Gain otherwise determined ($65,000 – $30,000) | $ 35,000 |
| Reduce by principal residence exemption: | |
| $A \times \frac{B}{C} = \$35,000 \times \frac{17 \text{ (1982 to 1992 and 1996 to 2001)}}{20 \text{ (1982 to 2001)}}$ | 29,750 |
| Gain | $ 5,250 |
| Post-1981 loss: | |
| N/A | $ NIL |

Pre-1982 gain + post-1981 gain – post-1981 loss
= $4,286 + $5,250 – $Nil
= $9,536.

RESULT: Although Mr. X's gain calculated under the usual method was $10,000, such gain could not exceed the maximum total net gain of $9,536 calculated under the alternative method. Therefore, the gain was reduced to $9,536.

## Appendix B – Illustration of Calculation of Gain on Disposition of a Farm Property

Assume that a taxpayer resident in Canada sold a 50 hectare farm. The taxpayer owned the farm and occupied the house on it from July 30, 1993 to June 15, 2001. The house and one-half hectare of the land have been designated as the taxpayer's principal residence for the 1993 to 2001 taxation years inclusive. The taxpayer's calculations of the gain on the disposition of the farm property, using the two methods permitted by paragraph 40(2)(*c*) of the Act, are as follows:

FIRST METHOD (see ¶ 21)

| | Principal Residence | Farm | Total Property |
|---|---|---|---|
| Proceeds of disposition | | | |
| Land | $ 10,000* | $ 90,000 | $ 100,000 |
| House | 50,000 | — | 50,000 |
| Barn | — | 35,000 | 35,000 |
| Silo | — | 15,000 | 15,000 |
| | $ 60,000 | $ 140,000 | $ 200,000 |
| Adjusted cost base | | | |
| Land | $ 2,000* | $ 58,000 | $ 60,000 |
| House | 20,000 | — | 20,000 |
| Barn | — | 11,000 | 11,000 |
| Silo | — | 4,000 | 4,000 |
| | $ 22,000 | $ 73,000 | $ 95,000 |
| Gain otherwise determined | $ 38,000 | $ 67,000 | $ 105,000 |
| Less: Principal residence exemption | 38,000 | — | 38,000 |
| Gain | $ NIL | $ 67,000 | $ 67,000 |

* Since the principal residence portion of the land is 1/100 of the total land (i.e., one-half hectare divided by 50 hectares), one way (as described in ¶ 21(a)) of assigning values to the principal residence portion of the land would be to simply use $1,000 (i.e., 1/100 of $100,000) for the proceeds for such portion of the land and $600 (i.e., 1/100 of $60,000) for the adjusted cost base of such portion. Assume, however, that a typical residential lot in the area, although less than one-half hectare in this example, had a fair market value of $10,000 as of the date of sale and $2,000 as of the date of acquisition. As indicated in ¶ 21(b), we would accept the taxpayer's use of the latter amounts, which in this case would result in a greater portion of the gain otherwise determined being eliminated by the principal residence exemption.

SECOND METHOD (see ¶ 22)

| | |
|---|---|
| Proceeds of disposition for total farm property | $ 200,000 |
| Adjusted cost base for total farm property | 95,000 |
| Gain otherwise determined | $ 105,000 |
| Less: Principal residence exemption using subparagraph 40(2)(c)(ii) election: $1,000 + (9 × $1,000) | 10,000 |
| Gain | $ 95,000 |

RESULT: In this example, the first method results in a lower gain to the taxpayer.

IT-120R6

## *Explanation of Changes*

### Introduction

The purpose of the *Explanation of Changes* is to give the reasons for the revisions to an interpretation bulletin. It outlines revisions that we have made as a result of changes to the law, as well as changes reflecting new or revised CCRA interpretations.

### Reasons for the Revision

This bulletin is being revised to reflect legislative changes enacted under S.C. 2000, c.12 (formerly Bill C-23) and S.C. 2001, c.17 (formerly Bill C-22). The comments in the bulletin are not affected by any proposed legislation released before June 9, 2003.

### Legislative and Other Changes

The bulletin has been revised to reflect the repeal of subsection 252(4) and the addition of the term "common-law partner" to the Act. Specific discussions on this topic have been added to ¶s 2 and 6 of the bulletin.

The discussion in former ¶ 12 on spousal trusts and subsection 107(4) has been removed since paragraph 104(4)(a) now also refers to joint spousal or common-law partner trusts and alter ego trusts. A discussion on these types of trusts and the application of subsection 107(4) to these trusts is outside of the scope of this bulletin. The remainder of former ¶ 12 has been moved to ¶ 36.

We have added a comment in ¶ 15 regarding recreational or lifestyle uses for land in excess of one-half hectare.

¶ 17 has been expanded to clarify the CCRA's interpretation. The previous version contemplated that a taxpayer would subdivide and immediately sell the newly created lots. Comments have been added to also address the situation where a taxpayer subdivides his or her property but then holds the lots for a period of time.

¶ 38 (formerly ¶ 36) now addresses the rules in subsection 40(4) as they relate to alter ego trusts and joint spousal and common-law partner trusts by virtue of their addition to the list of qualifying transfers set out in new subsection 73(1.01) of the *Income Tax Act*. Specific references to spousal trusts have been removed from ¶ 38 as the rules now apply to the aforementioned trusts as well.

The various examples in the bulletin and its appendices have been updated to reflect more current years and current law.

Throughout the bulletin, we have made other changes for clarification or readability purposes, and we have deleted items which were redundant or which no longer have any relevance.

# Election To Defer Payment of Income Tax (Form T2075)

Canada Revenue Agency / Agence du revenu du Canada

**ELECTION TO DEFER PAYMENT OF INCOME TAX, UNDER SUBSECTION 159(5) OF THE INCOME TAX ACT BY A DECEASED TAXPAYER'S LEGAL REPRESENTATIVE OR TRUSTEE**

- For use by a deceased taxpayer's legal representative or trustee when electing to pay income tax in up to ten equal consecutive annual instalments. The first instalment is required to be paid on or before the day on which payment of that tax was otherwise payable if no election had been made.
- This election is to be filed at the Tax Services Office in the area in which the taxpayer resided prior to death on or before the day on which payment for the first of the equal consecutive annual instalments is required to be made.
- Security acceptable to the Minister must be provided with respect to the tax, the payment of which is being deferred. Contact the Collections Section at the Tax Services Office in the area in which the taxpayer resided prior to death to complete security arrangements.

| NAME OF DECEASED IN FULL (Print) | DATE OF DEATH Year Month Day |
|---|---|
| LAST ADDRESS | SOCIAL INSURANCE NUMBER |
| NAME(S) AND ADDRESS(ES) OF LEGAL REPRESENTATIVE(S) (Print) | |

Amount of increase in taxable income by virtue of subsections 70(2), 70(5), 70(5.2) or 70(9.4) of the Income Tax Act $ ______

Amount of tax subject to deferment $ ______

Payment to be made in instalments as follows:

| Payment | (A) Instalments to be paid or 1/10th of Tax Deferred | (B) Interest on Instalment | (C) (A) + (B) Total Payment | Due Not Later Than (Date) |
|---|---|---|---|---|
| 1 | | | | |
| 2 | | | | |
| 3 | | | | |
| 4 | | | | |
| 5 | | | | |
| 6 | | | | |
| 7 | | | | |
| 8 | | | | |
| 9 | | | | |
| 10 | | | | |

At the time of payment of any amount, payment of which is deferred by this election, the taxpayer shall pay to the Receiver General interest, compounded daily, on the amount at the prescribed rate in effect at the time the election is made.The interest is computed from the day on or before which the amount would, but for the election, have been required to be paid to the day of

Note: Payment of the first instalment as required, on or before the date that the tax would, but for the election, have been required to be paid, attracts no interest on the amount of that instalment.

**ELECTION**

I/We, in the capacity of ______
(Legal Representative(s) or Trustee(s))

HEREBY ELECT to have the provisions of subsection 159(5) of the Income Tax Act applied in accordance with the terms set forth above.

| Signature | Date |
|---|---|
| Signature | Date |
| Signature | Date |

T2075 (00/10) Form authorized by the Minister of National Revenue (Français au verso)

Printed in Canada

Canada

# Death of an RRSP Annuitant (Information Sheet RC4177)

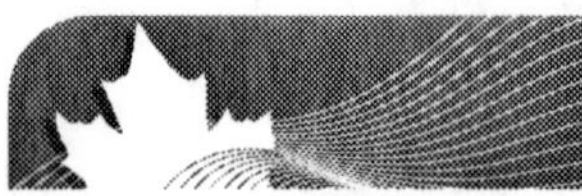

## Death of an RRSP Annuitant

Generally, an annuitant is the person for whom a retirement plan provides retirement income. This information sheet contains general information about the taxation of amounts held in a registered retirement savings plan (RRSP) at the time the annuitant died and the taxation of amounts paid out of an RRSP because the annuitant died. It explains how these amounts are generally reported, and the options that are available to the deceased annuitant's legal representative (liquidator) and the qualified beneficiaries to reduce or defer the tax liability resulting from the annuitant's death.

**Under proposed changes,** as of July 1, 2011, for deaths occurring after March 3, 2010, the existing registered retirement savings plan (RRSP) rollover rules will be extended to allow a rollover of a deceased individual's RRSP proceeds to the RDSP of the deceased individual's financially dependent infirm child or grandchild. Similar rules will also apply in respect of registered retirement income fund (RRIF) proceeds and certain lump-sum amounts paid from registered pension plans (RPP). In addition, where the death of an RRSP annuitant occurs after 2007 and before 2011, special transitional rules will allow a contribution to be made to the RDSP of a financially dependent infirm child or grandchild of the annuitant that will provide a similar result to the proposed measures. It is important to note that in order to be eligible, the contribution to an RDSP can only be made **after June 30, 2011** and, where the death of the annuitant occurs after 2007 and before 2011, the contribution must be made before 2012, i.e. individuals will have six months in which to make the contribution to an RDSP

For updated information on these proposed changes, go to **www.cra.gc.ca/rdsp**.

## Slips issued by the RRSP issuer

The chart below shows how the RRSP issuer generally prepares the slips used to report the amounts paid from a deceased annuitant's RRSP.

**Chart 1 – How the RRSP issuer prepares the slips used to report the amounts paid from a deceased annuitant's RRSP**

| **Period** | Day the annuitant died* | **From** the day after the day the annuitant died **to** December 31 of the year after the year of death | From January 1 of the year after the period described in the previous column to the date the RRSP property is distributed |
|---|---|---|---|
| **Amount** | Fair market value (FMV) of the RRSP | Income earned in the RRSP during this period | Income earned in the RRSP during this period |
| **How the RRSP issuer generally reports the amount** | We consider that the annuitant received this amount at the time of death, so the amount is reported in box 34 of a T4RSP slip issued in the name of the annuitant for the year of death. This slip also shows any other amounts the annuitant received in the year. | **Unmatured RRSP:**<br>■ If the annuitant's spouse or common-law partner is named as a beneficiary in the RRSP contract, income paid to that beneficiary is reported in box 18 of a T4RSP slip issued in his or her name, for the year of payment.<br>■ For all other beneficiaries named in the RRSP contract or the annuitant's estate (if no beneficiary is named), income paid is reported in box 28 of a T4RSP slip issued to each beneficiary or the estate, for the year of payment.<br>**Matured RRSP:**<br>■ Income is paid to the beneficiaries named in the RRSP contract or the annuitant's estate (if no beneficiary is named) and reported in box 28 of a T4RSP slip issued to each beneficiary or the estate, for the year of payment. | **Depositary RRSP** – Income is paid to the beneficiaries named in the RRSP contract or the annuitant's estate (if no beneficiary is named) and reported in box 13 of a T5 slip issued to each beneficiary or the estate, for the year in which the income is credited or added to the deposit.<br>**Trusteed RRSP** – Income is paid to the beneficiaries named in the RRSP contract or the annuitant's estate (if no beneficiary is named) and reported in boxes 28 and 40 of a T4RSP slip issued to each beneficiary or the estate, for the year of payment.**<br>**Insured RRSP** – Income is paid to the beneficiaries named in the RRSP contract or the annuitant's estate (if no beneficiary is named) and reported in the same way as described in the previous column. |

The shaded areas represent amounts that qualify as a **refund of premiums** if received by a **qualified beneficiary** (see the definitions on the next page). If you do not know the type of RRSP the annuitant has, or need a breakdown of the amount reported in box 28, contact the plan issuer.

* An exception to the reporting requirement is provided where the spouse or common-law partner is the sole beneficiary of the RRSP. Go to "Exception – Spouse or common-law partner is the sole beneficiary of the RRSP" on the next page for details.

** Only the part of the income earned in this period that is not taxable to the RRSP trust is reported to the beneficiary. A beneficiary will not have to pay tax on any part of the amount he or she receives, to the extent that the funds can reasonably be regarded as having been included in the RRSP trust's income.

RC4177 (E) Rev. 10

La version française de cette publication est intitulée *Décès du rentier d'un RERR*.

Canada Revenue Agency Agence du revenu du Canada

## Unmatured RRSP

An unmatured RRSP is an RRSP that has not yet started to pay a retirement income. Chart 1 on page 1 shows how the RRSP issuer usually prepares the slips that report the amounts paid out of a deceased annuitant's unmatured RRSP.

### General rule – deceased annuitant

When the annuitant of an unmatured RRSP dies, we consider that the annuitant received, immediately before death, an amount equal to the FMV of all the property held in the RRSP at the time of death. This amount and all other amounts the annuitant received from the RRSP during the year have to be reported on the annuitant's tax return for the year of death.

A beneficiary will not have to pay tax on any payment made out of the RRSP if it can reasonably be regarded as having been included in the annuitant's income.

**Exception – Spouse or common-law partner is the sole beneficiary of the RRSP** – We **do not** consider the deceased annuitant to have received an amount from the RRSP at the time of death if the annuitant had a spouse or common-law partner when he or she died and **both** the following conditions are met:

- the spouse or common-law partner is named in the RRSP contract as the **sole** beneficiary of the RRSP; and
- **by** December 31 of the year following the year of death, all the RRSP property is directly transferred to an RRSP or a RRIF under which the spouse or common-law partner is the annuitant, or to an issuer to buy an eligible annuity for the spouse or common-law partner.

If **both** these conditions are met, only the spouse or common-law partner will receive a T4RSP slip. The transferred amount will be shown in box 18 of the slip. This amount has to be reported on line 129 of the spouse's or common-law partner's tax return for the year the transfer was made. The spouse or common-law partner will receive an official receipt for the amount that was transferred. To find out how to claim a deduction for the transfer, see "Qualified beneficiaries – transfers," on page 4.

### General rule – beneficiaries of the RRSP

Amounts paid from the RRSP that represent the income earned in the RRSP after the date the annuitant died have to be reported by the beneficiaries named in the RRSP contract or by the annuitant's estate (if no beneficiary is named). These payments have to be included in the income of the beneficiaries or the estate for the year they are received.

### Optional reporting for an unmatured RRSP

Read this section if the exception described under the above heading "Exception – Spouse or common-law partner is the sole beneficiary of the RRSP," in the section does not apply.

If a **qualified beneficiary** (see below) **receives** an amount from a deceased annuitant's **unmatured** RRSP that qualifies as a **refund of premiums** (see below), the annuitant's legal representative can claim a reduction to the amount we consider that the annuitant received at the time of death. The reduction, which is determined by completing Chart 2 on page 5, allows for a redistribution of the annuitant's income to the qualified beneficiary who actually received it. This redistribution of income allows the deceased annuitant and the qualified beneficiary to pay the least amount of tax the law allows. If none of the payments out of the RRSP are made to a qualified beneficiary or designated as a refund of premiums, the amount we consider that the annuitant received at the time of death cannot be reduced.

**Qualified beneficiary** – A **qualified beneficiary** is the deceased annuitant's spouse or common-law partner, or a financially dependent child or grandchild. A child or grandchild of a deceased annuitant is generally considered financially dependent on that annuitant at the time of death if, before that person's death, the child or grandchild ordinarily resided with and was dependent on the annuitant and they meet one of the following conditions:

- the child or grandchild's net income for the previous year (shown on line 236 of their return) was less than the basic personal amount (line 300 from Schedule 1) for that previous year; or
- the child or grandchild is infirm and their net income for the previous year was equal to or less than the basic personal amount **plus** the disability amount (line 316 from Schedule 1) for that previous year.

If, before the annuitant's death, the child or grandchild is away from home because they were attending school, we still consider them to have resided with the annuitant.

If the child or grandchild's net income was **more than the amounts described above**, we will **not** consider them to be financially dependent on the annuitant at the time of death, unless they can establish the contrary. In such a case, the child or grandchild or the legal representative should submit a request in writing to the child or grandchild's tax services office outlining the reasons why we should consider them to be financially dependent on the annuitant at the time of death.

**Refund of premiums** – A **refund of premiums** is any of the amounts shown in the shaded areas of Chart 1 on the first page if paid to a qualified beneficiary. If these amounts are paid to the annuitant's estate, they will qualify as a refund of premiums if **both** the following conditions are met:

- there is a qualified beneficiary who is a beneficiary of the annuitant's estate; and
- the annuitant's legal representative and the qualified beneficiary jointly file Form T2019, *Death of an RRSP Annuitant – Refund of Premiums*, to designate all or part of the amounts paid to the estate as a refund of premiums received by the qualified beneficiary.

Sometimes there can be an **increase** in the value of an unmatured RRSP between the date of death and the date of the final distribution to the beneficiary or estate. Generally, this amount has to be included in the income of the beneficiary or the estate for the year it is received. A T4RSP slip may be issued for this amount. For more information, see Chart 6 – Amounts from a deceased annuitant's RRSP, in Chapter 4 of Guide T4040, *RRSP and Other Registered Plans for Retirement*.

If there is a **decrease** in the value of an unmatured RRSP **between** the date of death and the date of the final distribution after 2008, the deceased's legal representative can request the amount of the decrease be deducted on the deceased's final return through a reassessment. However, if the final distribution is made in the year of death, the deduction will be claimed when filing the final return. The deduction is claimed on line 232 of the T1, *General Income Tax and Benefit Return*.

The amount of that deduction is the total of:

- the part of the FMV of the RRSP at the time of death included in the deceased annuitant's income as a result of the annuitant's death;
- all amounts received after the annuitant's death that have been included in the recipient's income as a benefit from the RRSP, other than the "tax-paid amounts"; and
- all "tax-paid amounts" (see box 40 of T4RSP slip);

  **MINUS**

- the total of all amounts distributed from the RRSP after the death of the annuitant.

Generally, the deduction will not be available if the RRSP held a non-qualified investment after the annuitant dies or if the final distribution is made after the end of the year that follows the year in which the annuitant died. However, this rule may be waived to allow the deduction to deceased annuitants on a case-by-case basis.

If an unmatured RRSP experiences a post-death decline in value, and the exceptional reporting described starting above does not apply, the financial institution that holds the RRSP will issue Form RC249, *Post-Death Decline in the Value of an Unmatured RRSP or a RRIF – Final Distribution made in 20___*.

This form will be issued to the executor of the deceased annuitant's estate for the year in which the final distribution is made.

## Matured RRSP

A matured RRSP is an RRSP that is paying a retirement income. Chart 1 on the first page shows how the RRSP issuer usually prepares the slips that report the amounts paid out of a deceased annuitant's matured RRSP.

### General rule – deceased annuitant

When the annuitant of a matured RRSP dies, we consider that the annuitant received, immediately before death, an amount equal to the FMV of all remaining annuity payments under the RRSP at the time of death. This amount, and any other amount the annuitant received in the year from the RRSP, has to be reported on the deceased annuitant's return for the year of death.

A beneficiary will not have to pay tax on any payment made out of the RRSP, if it can reasonably be regarded as having been included in the annuitant's income.

**Exception – Spouse or common-law partner is the sole beneficiary of the RRSP** – We do **not** consider the annuitant to have received an amount from the RRSP at the time of death if, in the RRSP contract, the deceased annuitant named his or her spouse or common-law partner as the sole beneficiary of the RRSP. In this situation, the RRSP continues and the spouse or common-law partner becomes the successor annuitant under the plan. All annuity payments made after the date the annuitant died become payable to that successor annuitant. The successor annuitant will receive a T4RSP slip for the year of death and for future years. The slip will show the annuity payments he or she received in box 16. The successor annuitant has to report the annuity payments on line 129 of his or her tax return for the year they are received.

If, in the RRSP contract, the annuitant named his or her **spouse** or **common-law partner** and **someone else** as beneficiaries of the RRSP, the spouse or common-law partner becomes the successor annuitant of the part of the remaining annuity payments that represents his or her share of the RRSP. In this situation, the FMV of the annuity payments that are not receivable by the spouse or common-law partner has to be included in the income of the deceased annuitant for the year of death.

When no beneficiary is named in the RRSP contract, the deceased annuitant's estate becomes entitled to receive the RRSP property. If the deceased's will states that the spouse or common-law partner is entitled to the amounts paid under the RRSP, or that the spouse or common-law partner is the sole beneficiary of the estate, the spouse or common-law partner can elect in writing, jointly with the legal representative, to be the successor annuitant under the plan. Common-law partners who are of the same sex can make this election if the annuitant died after 1997.

If this election is made, we consider the spouse or common-law partner to have received the annuity payments, and he or she will have to include the annuity payment in income for the year the legal representative received them. To make this election, the legal representative and the spouse or common-law partner need only to write a letter explaining their intention. A copy of the letter must be provided to the payer of the annuity and another copy attached to the spouse's or common-law partner's return.

### General rule – beneficiaries of the RRSP

Amounts paid from the RRSP, which represent income earned in the RRSP after the date the annuitant died, have to be reported by the beneficiaries named in the RRSP contract or by the annuitant's estate (if no beneficiary is named). These payments have to be included in the income of the beneficiaries or the estate for the year they are received.

## Optional reporting for a matured RRSP

If a **qualified beneficiary** (see below) receives an amount that qualifies as a **refund of premiums** (see below) from a deceased annuitant's matured RRSP, the annuitant's legal representative can claim a reduction to the amount we consider that the annuitant received at the time of death. The reduction, which is determined by completing Chart 2 on page 5, allows for a redistribution of the annuitant's income to the qualified beneficiary who actually received it. The redistribution of income allows the deceased annuitant and

the qualified beneficiary to pay the least amount of tax the law allows.

If none of the payments out of the RRSP are made to a qualified beneficiary or designated as a refund of premiums, the amount we consider that the annuitant received at the time of death cannot be reduced.

**Qualified beneficiary** – A **qualified beneficiary** is the annuitant's financially dependent child or grandchild.

**Refund of premiums** – A **refund of premiums** is any of the amounts shown in the shaded areas of Chart 1 on the first page if paid to a qualified beneficiary. If these amounts are paid to the annuitant's estate, they will qualify as a refund of premiums if **both** the following conditions are met:

- there is a qualified beneficiary who is a beneficiary of the annuitant's estate; and
- the annuitant's legal representative and the qualified beneficiary jointly file Form T2019, *Death of an RRSP Annuitant – Refund of Premiums*, to designate all or part of the amounts paid to the estate as a refund of premiums received by the qualified beneficiary.

## Qualified beneficiaries – transfers

When a qualified beneficiary includes a refund of premiums in income, he or she can defer paying tax on the amount by transferring it to an RRSP or RRIF, or to an issuer to buy an eligible annuity. See the definitions for **qualified beneficiary** and **refund of premiums** in the previous section.

The following chart shows the transfers that different qualified beneficiaries can choose.

| Refund of premiums paid to: | Can be transferred to: | | |
|---|---|---|---|
| | RRSP* | RRIF | Annuity |
| ■ the annuitant's spouse or common-law partner | ✔ | ✔ | ✔ |
| ■ the annuitant's financially dependent child or grandchild who: | | | |
| – was dependent because of a physical or mental impairment | ✔ | ✔ | ✔ |
| – was dependent but **not** because of a physical or mental impairment | | | ✔** |

* The qualified beneficiary must be 71 years of age or younger at the end of the year the transfer is made.

** The annuity can provide for payments based on a period of not more than 18 years minus the child's or grandchild's age at the time the annuity was purchased. The payments from the annuity have to begin no later than one year after the purchase.

The transfer or purchase has to be completed in the year the refund of premiums is received or within 60 days after the end of the year. If the qualified beneficiary is 71 years of age in the year the refund of premiums is received, the transfer to an RRSP must be completed by December 31 of that year.

The carrier or issuer who receives the transferred funds will issue an official receipt to the qualified beneficiary. The beneficiary can use the receipt to claim a deduction on his or her tax return for the year the refund of premiums was received. The following chart shows where on the tax return the beneficiary should claim the deduction.

| Refund of premiums transferred to: | Claim deduction on: | |
|---|---|---|
| | line 208 | line 232 |
| an RRSP | ✔ | |
| a RRIF | | ✔ |
| an annuity | | ✔ |

**Example**

Martin died in June 2008. When he died the fair market value (FMV) of his unmatured trusteed RRSP was $185,000. The FMV of the RRSP on December 31, 2009, was $215,000. On June 30, 2010, the day the RRSP property was distributed, the FMV of the RRSP was $225,000. The RRSP contract named Martin's spouse, Elaine, as the sole beneficiary. Elaine, who is also the legal representative of Martin's estate, received the following slips:

- a T4RSP slip for 2010 issued in her name, showing $30,000 in box 18, and $10,000 in boxes 28 and 40; and
- a T4RSP slip for 2008 in Martin's name, showing $185,000 in box 34. Although Elaine is the sole beneficiary, the slip was issued to Martin because the second condition in the exception described in the section called "General rule – deceased annuitant," on page 2, is not met.

Elaine wants to know if it would be beneficial to request a reduction to the amount we consider that Martin received from his RRSP when he died. She completes Chart 2 on the next page and determines that she can claim a reduction of $185,000. She reviews Martin's tax situation and her own, and decides to claim a $100,000 reduction. This reduces the amount reported on line 129 of Martin's 2008 return to $85,000 ($185,000 – $100,000), and increases the amount reported on line 129 of her 2010 return to $140,000 ($100,000 + $30,000 + $10,000).

Because the FMV of the RRSP at the time of death was included in Martin's income for 2008, Elaine has to write a letter to request an adjustment to that year's return. To minimize her 2010 taxes, she transfers $130,000 to her RRIF. This is the difference between the amount she included in income ($140,000) and the amount shown in boxes 28 and 40 of her T4RSP slip ($10,000). Elaine claims a $130,000 deduction on line 232 of her 2010 return.

**Chart 2 – How to calculate the reduction to the amount we consider that the deceased annuitant received at death**

Complete a separate calculation for each RRSP belonging to the deceased annuitant.

| | | | Example from the previous page | |
|---|---|---|---|---|
| 1. Enter the amount shown in box 34 of the T4RSP slip issued to the annuitant for the year of death. | $ | 1 | $ 185,000 | 1 |
| 2. Enter the FMV of the RRSP on the later of the following dates (you may need to contact the deceased annuitant's RRSP issuer to determine these amounts):<br>■ December 31 of the year after the year the annuitant died; or<br>■ the end of the day the last time a designated benefit was paid out of the RRSP. | $ | 2 | $ 0 | 2 |
| 3. Enter the total of all amounts paid out of the RRSP after the annuitant died. | + $ | 3 | + $ 225,000 | 3 |
| 4. **Add** lines 2 and 3. | = $ | 4 | = $ 225,000 | 4 |
| 5. Enter the amount from either line 1 or line 4, **whichever is less**. | – $ | 5 | – $ 185,000 | 5 |
| 6. Line 4 **minus** line 5. | = $ | 6 | = $ 40,000 | 6 |
| 7. Enter the total of the following amounts:<br>■ amount designated as a refund of premiums on each Form T2019 filed for the RRSP;<br>■ the part of the amounts shown in box 40 of all T4RSP slips and box 13 of all T5 slips issued in the name of the estate that the qualified beneficiaries are entitled to receive from the estate;<br>■ amounts shown in boxes 18 and 28 of all T4RSP slips and box 13 of all T5 slips issued to qualified beneficiaries;<br>■ the part of the amount shown in box 40 of all T4RSP slips that were issued to the qualified beneficiaries that is not required to be included in income (contact the deceased annuitant's RRSP issuer to determine these amounts); and<br>■ the part of the amount shown in box 34 of the T4RSP slip that was issued to the deceased annuitant for the year of death and that the qualified beneficiaries are entitled to receive. | $ | 7 | $ 225,000 | 7 |
| 8. Enter the result of the following calculation:<br>1 – ( $ ______ (amount from line 6) / $ ______ (amount from line 4) ) | × | 8 | × 0.822222* | 8 |
| 9. Maximum reduction to the amount we consider that the deceased annuitant received at the time of death (line 7 **multiplied** by line 8). The reduction can be any amount, from zero to the amount on this line. | = $ | 9 | = $ 185,000 | 9 |

If the reduction is claimed in the year the annuitant died, the legal representative has to attach a letter to the annuitant's return for that year to explain how the amount reported on line 129 was calculated. If the reduction is claimed after the year of death, the legal representative has to write us a letter requesting an adjustment to the annuitant's return for the year of death.

* Calculation of line 8

1 – ( $ 40,000 / $ 225,000 )

www.cra.gc.ca 5

## For more information

### What if you need help?

If you need help after reading this guide, visit **www.cra.gc.ca** or call **1-800-959-8281**.

### Forms and publications

To get any forms or publications, go to **www.cra.gc.ca/forms** or call **1-800-959-2221**.

### My Account

My Account is a secure, convenient, and time-saving way to access and manage your tax and benefit information online, seven days a week! Discover all that My Account can do for you. Take the tour at **www.cra.gc.ca/myaccount** or see Pamphlet RC4059, *My Account for individuals*.

### TIPS (Tax Information Phone Service)

For personal and general tax information by telephone, use our automated service, TIPS, by calling **1-800-267-6999**.

### Teletypewriter (TTY) users

TTY users can call **1-800-665-0354** for bilingual assistance during regular business hours.

### Our service complaint process

If you are not satisfied with the **service** you have received, contact the CRA employee you have been dealing with (or call the phone number you have been given). If you still disagree with the way your concerns are being addressed, ask to discuss the matter with the employee's supervisor.

If the matter is still not resolved, you have the right to file a service complaint by completing Form RC193, *Service-Related Complaint*. If you are still not satisfied with the way the CRA has handled your complaint, you can contact the Taxpayers' Ombudsman.

For more information, go to **www.cra.gc.ca/complaints** or see Booklet RC4420, *Information on CRA – Service Complaints*.

### Related forms and publications

**Forms**

| | |
|---|---|
| 5005-R | T1 *General Income Tax and Benefit Return* |
| RC193 | *Service-Related Complaint* |
| RC249 | *Post-Death Decline in the Value of an Unmatured RRSP or a RRIF – Final Distribution made in 20___* |
| T2019 | *Death of an RRSP Annuitant – Refund of Premiums* |

**Publications**

| | |
|---|---|
| 5000-G | *General Income Tax and Benefit Guide* |
| RC4059 | *My Account for individuals* |
| RC4420 | *Information on CRA – Service Complaints.* |
| T4040 | *RRSP and Other Registered Plans for Retirement* |

## Your opinion counts

If you have any comments or suggestions that could help us improve our publications, we would like to hear from you. Please send your comments to:

**Taxpayer Services Directorate**
**Canada Revenue Agency**
**750 Heron Road**
**Ottawa ON K1A 0L5**

## Home Buyers' Plan (Guide RC4135)

# Home Buyers' Plan (HBP)

Includes Form T1036

RC4135(E) Rev.10

Canada

## Before you start

### Is this guide for you?

Use this guide if you want information about the rules that apply to the Home Buyers' Plan (HBP).

Chapter 1 explains the Home Buyers' Plan and the conditions of participation.

Chapter 2 provides information concerning the repayment of withdrawals made under the HBP and different situations for these withdrawals.

Chapter 3 describes other rules to be considered.

**Definitions** – In the definitions section on page 4, we have included definitions of some of the terms used in this guide. You may want to read through the glossary before you start.

If you have a visual impairment, you can get our publications in braille, large print, or etext (CD or diskette), or MP3 by going to **www.cra.gc.ca/alternate**, or by calling **1-800-959-2221**. You can also get your personalized correspondence in these formats by calling **1-800-959-8281**.

La version française de cette publication est intitulée *Régime d'accession à la propriété (RAP)*.

## Table of contents

## Definitions

This section provides a general description of the technical terms that we use in this guide.

**Arm's length** – at arm's length is a concept describing a relationship in which the parties are acting independently of each other. The opposite, **not at arm's length**, includes individuals:

- related to each other by blood, marriage, adoption, or common-law partnerships; or
- acting in concert without separate interests, such as those with close business ties.

An individual is not at arm's length with a corporation they control.

**Common-law partner** – This applies to a person who is **not your spouse** (see the definition of spouse on the next page), with whom you are living in a conjugal relationship, and to whom at least **one** of the following situations applies. He or she:

a) has been living with you in such a relationship for at least 12 continuous months;

b) is the parent of your child by birth or adoption; or

c) has custody and control of your child (or had custody and control immediately before the child turned 19 years of age) and your child is wholly dependent on that person for support.

In addition, an individual immediately becomes your common-law partner if you previously lived together in a conjugal relationship for at least 12 continuous months and you have resumed living together in such a relationship.

**Under proposed changes**, this condition will no longer exist. The effect of this proposed change is that a person (other than a person described in b) or c) above) will be your common-law partner only after your current relationship with that person has lasted at least 12 continuous months. This proposed change will apply to 2001 and later years.

Reference to "12 continuous months" in this definition includes any period that you were separated for less than 90 days because of a breakdown in the relationship.

**Person with a disability** – You are considered a person with a disability if you are entitled to the disability amount. For purposes of the HBP, a person with a disability includes you or a person related to you by blood, marriage, common-law partnership or adoption. A related person with a disability does not have to reside with you in the same home.

We consider a person to be entitled to the disability amount if one of the following situations applies:

- the person was entitled to the disability amount on line 316 of his or her return for the year before the HBP withdrawal, and still meets the eligibility requirements for the disability amount when the HBP withdrawal is made; or
- the person was not entitled to the disability amount for any year before the HBP withdrawal, but a Form T2201, *Disability Tax Credit Certificate*, certified by a medical doctor or appropriate medical practitioner (that is, an optometrist, audiologist, psychologist, physiotherapist, occupational therapist or speech language pathologist), is filed for the person for the year of the HBP withdrawal. If Form T2201 is not approved, your withdrawals will not be considered eligible withdrawals under the HBP, and will have to be included in your income for the year you receive them.

If all other eligibility requirements are met, we consider a person to be entitled to the disability amount even if costs for an attendant or for care in a nursing home were claimed as a medical expense by or on behalf of that person.

**Eligible withdrawal** – This is an amount you withdraw from your RRSP after you have met the HBP conditions that apply to your situation.

**HBP balance** – When you withdraw funds from your RRSPs under the HBP, you create an HBP balance. Your HBP balance at any time is the total of all eligible withdrawals you made from your RRSPs **minus** the total of all amounts you designated as an HBP repayment and amounts included in your income (because they were not repaid to your RRSPs) in previous years.

**Participant** – You are considered an HBP participant if:

- you make an eligible withdrawal from your RRSP to buy or build a qualifying home for yourself;
- You make an eligible withdrawal from your RRSP under the HBP to buy or build a qualifying home for a related person with a disability or to help such a person buy or build a qualifying home; or
- you are the spouse or common-law partner of a deceased HBP participant and you have elected to continue making the repayments of the deceased participant.

**Participation period** – Your HBP participation period starts on January 1 of the year you receive an eligible withdrawal from your RRSP and ends in the year your HBP balance is zero.

**Qualifying home** – A qualifying home is a housing unit located in Canada. This includes existing homes and those being constructed. Single-family homes, semi-detached homes, townhouses, mobile homes, condominium units, and apartments in duplexes, triplexes, fourplexes, or apartment buildings all qualify. A share in a co-operative housing corporation that entitles you to possess, and gives you an equity interest in a housing unit located in Canada, also qualifies. However, a share that only provides you with a right to tenancy in the housing unit does not qualify.

**RRSP deduction limit** – This refers to the maximum amount you can deduct for a year for contributions you made to your own RRSP, or to your spouse's or common-law partner's RRSP.

**Spouse** – You have a spouse when you are legally married.

## Chapter 1 – Participating in the HBP

### What is the HBP?

The HBP is a program that allows you to withdraw funds from your RRSPs to buy or build a qualifying home. You can withdraw up to $25,000 in a calendar year.

The home can be for you, or it can be for a related person with a disability. If the home is acquired by a person with a disability or for a related person with a disability, one of the following should apply:

- it is more accessible to that person than his or her current home; or
- it is better suited to that person's needs.

As an HBP participant, you can acquire the home for the related person with a disability, or you can provide the withdrawn funds to the related person with a disability to acquire the home.

You do not have to include eligible withdrawals in your income, and your RRSP issuer will not withhold tax on these amounts. You can withdraw a single amount or make a series of withdrawals throughout the same calendar year, provided the total of your withdrawals is not more than $25,000. If you buy the qualifying home with your spouse or common-law partner, or with other individuals, each of you can withdraw up to $25,000. However, under existing requirements, you or your spouse or common-law partner may not own the qualifying home for more than 30 days before the final withdrawal is made in 2010.

**Note**
Your RRSP contributions must remain in the RRSP for at least 90 days before you can withdraw them under the HBP, or they may not be deductible for any year. For more information, refer to the shaded area on page 9.

Generally, you have to repay all withdrawals to your RRSPs within a period of no more than 15 years. You will have to repay an amount to your RRSPs each year until your HBP balance is zero. If you do not repay the amount due for a year, it will have to be included in your income for that year.

**Note**
Situations may arise where the repayments may have to be made in less than 15 years. These situations are explained starting on page 11.

### Can a withdrawal be made from any RRSP?

You (the participant) can only withdraw funds from an RRSP under which you are the annuitant. In the case of spousal or common-law partner RRSPs, the annuitant is the person who will receive benefits from the plan. For more information about spousal or common-law partner RRSPs, see Guide T4040, *RRSPs and Other Registered Plans for Retirement*.

Some RRSPs, such as locked-in or group RRSPs, do not allow you to withdraw funds from them. Your RRSP issuer can give you more information about the types of RRSPs that you have and whether or not withdrawals can be made from these plans to participate in the HBP.

**Note**
If you or your spouse or common-law partner withdraws an amount from an RRSP to which you or your spouse or common-law partner had made contributions during the **89-day period just before** the withdrawal, you may **not be able to deduct** part or all of these contributions for any year. For more information, see "How to make an HBP withdrawal," on page 9.

### What are the conditions for participating in the HBP?

A number of conditions have to be met in order to participate in the HBP. While some conditions have to be met **before** you can withdraw funds from your RRSPs, others apply **when** or **after** you receive the funds.

Generally, if you participate in the HBP, you have to meet all the HBP conditions yourself. However, depending on your situation, some conditions may apply to another person. For example, if you withdraw funds from your RRSPs to buy or build a qualifying home for a related person with a disability, or to help a related person with a disability buy or build a qualifying home, some conditions have to be met by that person.

Regardless of the situation, you are responsible for making sure that all applicable HBP conditions are met. If, at any time during your participation period, a condition is not met, your withdrawal will not be considered an eligible withdrawal and it will have to be included in your income for the year it is received.

The following chart lists all the HBP conditions, and who has to meet them in different situations. **We explain each condition in greater detail following the chart.**

**Conditions for participating in the HBP**

**Situation 1** – You buy or build a qualifying home for yourself.

**Situation 2** – You, a person with a disability, buy or build a qualifying home for yourself.

**Situation 3** – You buy or build a qualifying home for a related person with a disability.

**Situation 4** – You help a related person with a disability buy or build a qualifying home.

| **Situation** | 1 | 2 | 3 | | 4 | |
|---|---|---|---|---|---|---|
| **Person responsible for meeting the HBP conditions** | You | You | You | Related person with a disability | You | Related person with a disability |
| Conditions you have to meet **before** applying to withdraw funds under the HBP | | | | | | |
| You have to enter into a written agreement to buy or build a qualifying home. | ✔ | ✔ | ✔ | N/A | N/A | ✔ |
| You have to intend to occupy the qualifying home as your principal place of residence no later than one year after buying or building it. | ✔ | ✔ | * | N/A | * | N/A |
| You have to be considered a first-time home buyer. | ✔ | N/A | N/A | N/A | N/A | N/A |
| Your HBP balance on January 1 of the year of the withdrawal has to be zero. | ✔ | ✔ | ✔ | N/A | ✔ | N/A |
| Conditions you have to meet **when** a withdrawal is made | | | | | | |
| Neither you nor your spouse or common-law partner can own the qualifying home more than 30 days before a withdrawal is made. | ✔ | ✔ | ✔ | N/A | N/A | ✔ |
| You have to be a resident of Canada. | ✔ | ✔ | ✔ | N/A | ✔ | N/A |
| You have to complete Form T1036 for each eligible withdrawal. | ✔ | ✔ | ✔ | N/A | ✔ | N/A |
| You have to receive all withdrawals in the same calendar year. | ✔ | ✔ | ✔ | N/A | ✔ | N/A |
| You cannot withdraw more than $25,000. | ✔ | ✔ | ✔ | N/A | ✔ | N/A |
| Condition you have to meet **after** all your withdrawals have been made | | | | | | |
| You have to buy or build the qualifying home before October 1 of the year after the year of the withdrawal. | ✔ | ✔ | ✔ | N/A | N/A | ✔ |

* You must intend that the related person with a disability occupy the qualifying home as his or her principal place of residence.

## You have to enter into a written agreement to buy or build a qualifying home

To withdraw funds from your RRSPs under the HBP, when you are buying or building a qualifying home for yourself or a related person with a disability, you must first have entered into a written agreement to buy or build a qualifying home. Obtaining a pre-approved mortgage does not satisfy this condition.

**Note**
If you are withdrawing funds from your RRSPs to help a related person with a disability who is buying or building a qualifying home, it is the related person with a disability who must have entered into such an agreement.

## You have to intend to occupy the qualifying home as your principal place of residence

When you withdraw funds from your RRSPs under the HBP, you have to intend to occupy the qualifying home as your principal place of residence no later than one year after buying or building it. Once you occupy the home, there is no minimum period of time in which you have to live there.

In some cases, you may not occupy the qualifying home by the end of the 12-month period after you bought or built it. If this happens, you are still considered to have satisfied this condition if, at the time you withdrew funds under the HBP, you did in fact, intend to occupy the home as your principal place of residence no later than one year after buying or building it.

**Note**
If you are withdrawing funds from your RRSPs to buy or build a qualifying home for a related person with a disability or to help a related person with a disability buy or build a qualifying home, you must intend that the related person with a disability will meet this condition.

## You have to be considered a first-time home buyer

Generally, before you can withdraw funds from your RRSPs to buy or build a qualifying home, you have to meet the first-time home buyer's condition. If you are a person with a disability, or you are acquiring a home for a related person with a disability or helping such a person acquire a home, you may not have to meet this condition. Refer to the section called "Exception to the first-time home buyer's condition ," on page 7.

You are not considered a first-time home buyer if, at any time during the period beginning January 1 of the fourth year before the year of the withdrawal and ending 31 days before the withdrawal, you or your spouse or common-law partner owned a home that you occupied as your principal place of residence.

If, at the time of the withdrawal you have a spouse or common-law partner, it is possible that only one of you will be considered a first-time home buyer (see the example below).

To determine if you are considered a first-time home buyer in 2010, complete the following questionnaire.

**Are you considered a first-time home buyer in 2010?**

**Question 1** – Did you, at any time during the period beginning January 1 of the fourth year before the year of the withdrawal (2006) and ending 31 days before the withdrawal, own a home that you occupied as your principal place of residence?

Yes ☐ You **are not** considered a first-time home buyer.

No ☐ Go to question 2.

**Question 2** – Do you have a spouse or common-law partner?

Yes ☐ Go to question 3.

No ☐ You **are** considered a first-time home buyer.

**Question 3** – Did your spouse or common-law partner have an owner-occupied home, at any time during the period beginning January 1 of the fourth year before the year of the withdrawal (2006) and ending 31 days before the withdrawal, that you occupied with that individual while you were living together as spouses or common-law partners?

Yes ☐ You **are not** considered a first-time home buyer.

No ☐ You **are** considered a first-time home buyer.

If you could not participate in the HBP in a particular year because you did not meet this condition, see the section entitled "If I could not participate in the HBP in a particular year, can I participate in a later year?" on page 14.

**Example**
In 2007, Paul sold the home he had occupied as his principal place of residence for five years. He then moved into a rented apartment. In 2007, he met Jane and she moved in with him. Jane had been renting her own apartment, and had never owned a home.

Jane and Paul were married in August 2010. They wanted to withdraw funds from their RRSPs to participate in the HBP in September 2010. Since Paul owned and occupied his home during the period beginning January 1 of the fourth year before the year he wants to make the withdrawal, he is not considered a first-time home buyer, so he cannot participate in the HBP in 2010.

However, Jane is considered a first-time home buyer, since she never owned a home, and she did not live with Paul during the period in which he owned and occupied his home as his principal place of residence. She can participate in the HBP in 2010, providing all the other requirements are met.

If Jane does not participate in the HBP in either 2010 or 2011, Paul can participate in the HBP in 2012 as he will not have owned a home that he occupied as his principal place of residence since January 1, 2008. If they want to participate together in the HBP, they both have to wait until 2012 at which time they can withdraw funds under the HBP to buy or build a qualifying home.

**Exception to the first-time home buyer's condition** – You do not have to meet this condition to participate in the HBP if any of the following situations apply to you at the time you make a withdrawal from your RRSPs under HBP:

- you are a person with a disability and you withdraw funds under the HBP to acquire a home that is more accessible, or better suited to your needs;
- you withdraw funds under the HBP to acquire a home for a person with a disability related to you by blood, marriage, common-law partnership or adoption, and the home is more accessible or better suited to the needs of that person; or
- you withdraw funds under the HBP and give those funds to a person with a disability related to you by blood, marriage, common-law partnership or adoption, to acquire a home that is more accessible, or better suited to the needs of that person.

## Your repayable HBP balance on January 1 of the year of the withdrawal has to be zero

If you have previously participated in the HBP, you may be able to do so again if:

- your HBP balance is zero on January 1 of the year during which you plan on making another HBP withdrawal; and
- you meet **all** the other HBP conditions that apply to your situation.

Your HBP balance is zero when the total of your designated HBP repayments and the amounts included in your income (because they were not repaid to your RRSPs) in previous years **equals** the total eligible withdrawals you received.

> **Note**
> The RRSP contributions you make in the first 60 days of a year, and designate as HBP repayments for the previous year reduce your HBP balance for purposes of determining whether your balance is zero on January 1 of the current year. For more information about designating HBP repayments, see "Chapter 2 – Repaying your withdrawals," on page 10 .

## Neither you nor your spouse or common-law partner can own the qualifying home more than 30 days before the withdrawal

You cannot withdraw an amount from your RRSP under the HBP if you or your spouse or common-law partner owned the home described on Form T1036, *Home Buyers' Plan (HBP) – Request to Withdraw Funds from an RRSP*, more than 30 days before the date of your withdrawal.

**Example**
Kate buys a qualifying home with a closing date (acquisition date) of November 1, 2010. She must make her final withdrawal under the HBP no later than 30 days after the closing date. Therefore, Kate has until December 1, 2010, to make her last withdrawal under the HBP. If she makes a withdrawal after December 1, 2010, it will not be considered an eligible withdrawal and will have to be included in her income for the year it is received.

**Note**
If you are withdrawing funds from your RRSPs to help a related person with a disability to buy or build a qualifying home, the person with a disability and his or her spouse or common-law partner (if applicable) must meet this condition.

### You have to be a resident of Canada

You have to be a resident of Canada when you receive funds from your RRSPs under the HBP and up to the time a qualifying home is bought or built. For more information about residency status, contact us at **1-800-267-5177** (from anywhere in Canada and the U.S.) and **613-952-3741** (call collect from outside Canada and the U.S.).

If you become a non-resident after you receive your funds but before a qualifying home is bought or built, you may cancel your participation in the HBP. For more information, see the section entitled "Cancelling your participation," on page 13.

If you become a non-resident after a qualifying home is bought or built, your withdrawal will be considered to be eligible. However, special rules will apply to the repayment of your HBP balance. For more information, see the section called "You become a non-resident," on page 12.

### You have to complete Form T1036 for each eligible withdrawal

To make an eligible withdrawal under the HBP, you have to use Form T1036, *Home Buyers' Plan (HBP) – Request to Withdraw Funds from an RRSP.*

You have to complete this form for each withdrawal you make. A copy is included at the end of this guide, or you can print a copy from our Web site at **www.cra.gc.ca/forms** or order a copy by calling **1-800-959-2221**. For more information about completing this form, see the section entitled "How to make an HBP withdrawal," on page 9.

### You have to receive all withdrawals in the same calendar year

To participate in the HBP, you have to receive all the withdrawals from your RRSPs in the same calendar year. However, if you receive a withdrawal in one year and another **in January** of the following year, we consider the January withdrawal to have been received in the year the first withdrawal was made.

**Note**
If the January withdrawal is received before you acquire your qualifying home, or no later than 30 days after you acquire it, and all the other relevant conditions described in the chart on page 6 are met, it is an eligible withdrawal. For this purpose, your HBP balance on January 1 is not a relevant condition and does not have to be zero.

**Example**
On October 15, 2009, Chloe withdrew $7,500 from her RRSP under the HBP. Before the withdrawal, Chloe had entered into a written agreement to buy a qualifying home. In January 2010, she withdrew an additional $1,500 to pay expenses she had not anticipated. Chloe acquired the qualifying home in March 2010. The January withdrawal is an eligible HBP withdrawal because Chloe received it before she acquired her qualifying home. She does not have to include it in her income for 2010.

### You cannot withdraw more than $25,000

You can make more than one withdrawal, as long as the total of your withdrawals is not more than $25,000. If you buy the qualifying home with your spouse or common-law partner, or with other individuals, each of you can withdraw up to $25,000.

**Note**
If the total of your RRSP withdrawals under the HBP is more than $25,000, you will have to include the excess amount in your income for the year you received it. In addition, your RRSP issuer will have to withhold tax on the excess amount at the time of the withdrawal.

### You have to buy or build the qualifying home before October 1 of the year after the year of the withdrawal

Generally, if you participate in the HBP in a particular year, you have to buy or build the qualifying home before October 1 of the year following the year of the withdrawal.

We consider you to have bought or built a qualifying home if you bought or built it alone or with one or more individuals. If you are building a qualifying home, we consider you to have built the home on the date it becomes habitable.

**Note**
If you are withdrawing funds from your RRSPs under the HBP to help a related person with a disability to buy or build a qualifying home, the person with a disability must meet this condition.

If you do not buy or build the qualifying home before October 1 of the year after the year of the withdrawal, you can:

- cancel your participation in the HBP (for more information, see the section called "Cancelling your participation," on page 13); or
- buy or build a different home, called a replacement property, before October 1 of the year following the year of the withdrawal.

A replacement property has to meet the same conditions as a qualifying home. You do not have to complete another Form T1036 to advise us that you are buying or building a replacement property. Just send a letter to:

Pension Workflow Section,
Ottawa Technology Centre,
875 Heron Road,
Ottawa ON K1A 1A2.

Give your name, address, and social insurance number, as well as the address (and phone number, if possible) of the replacement property. Also, you have to state in the letter that you intend to occupy the replacement property as your principal place of residence no later than one year after you buy or build it.

**Note**
If you have already withdrawn from your RRSPs the $25,000 maximum allowed under the HBP, you cannot make any more withdrawals to buy or build the replacement property.

**Extensions for buying or building a qualifying home or replacement property** – If you do not buy or build the qualifying home you indicated on Form T1036 (or a replacement property) before October 1 of the year following the year of the withdrawal, we still consider you to have met the deadline if **either** of the following situations applies to you:

- You had a written agreement, in effect on October 1 of the year following the year of the withdrawal, to buy a qualifying home or replacement property, and you buy the property before October 1 of the second year following the year of the withdrawal. In addition, you have to be a Canadian resident up to the time of purchase (see Example 1 below).
- You had paid an amount after the date of the first withdrawal and before October 1 of the following year to the contractors or suppliers (with whom you deal at arm's length) for materials for the home being built, or towards its construction, that was at least equal to the total of all withdrawals under the HBP (see Example 2 in the opposite column).

**Example 1**
On February 10, 2008, Steven, a Canadian resident, entered into an agreement to buy a duplex, the ground floor of which he intends to occupy as his principal place of residence. Because of an existing lease, the possession date is May 4, 2010. On February 20, 2008, Steven withdrew $15,000 from his RRSPs under the HBP. On May 4, 2010, he takes possession of the duplex and moves in.

Since Steven withdrew his funds in 2008, he had to buy the home before October 1, 2009. Although Steven took possession of the home after this deadline, we consider him to have bought the home by the deadline because he had an agreement in effect on October 1, 2009, he bought the home before October 1, 2010, and he was a Canadian resident when he bought it.

**Example 2**
In January 2009, Clara withdrew $10,000 from her RRSPs under the HBP. Earlier in the same month, she had finalized a contract to have her home built. She paid $7,000 when construction started in April 2009, and $6,000 more in August 2010, for a total of $13,000. Clara dealt at arm's length with the contractor.

Construction of the home is not completed until December 15, 2010, because the building materials arrived late.

Since Clara withdrew her funds in 2009, she has to have the home built before October 1, 2010.

Although construction of the home is not completed until December 15, 2010, we consider Clara's home to have been built by the deadline because the $13,000 she paid towards its construction before this deadline is more than the total amount of her withdrawals ($10,000), and because she dealt at arm's length with the contractor.

## How to make an HBP withdrawal

To make an eligible withdrawal under the HBP, you have to use Form T1036, *Home Buyers' Plan (HBP) – Request to Withdraw Funds from an RRSP*.

You have to complete Form T1036 for each withdrawal you make. A copy is included at the end of this guide.

After completing Area 1 of Form T1036, give it to your RRSP issuer who will fully complete Area 2. Your RRSP issuer will not withhold tax from the funds you withdraw if you meet the applicable HBP conditions. Your RRSP issuer will send you a T4RSP slip, *Statement of RRSP Income*, showing the amount you withdrew under the HBP in box 27. You have to attach this slip to your income tax return.

**Your RRSP deduction may be affected by HBP participation**

If you participate in the HBP, certain rules limit your RRSP deduction for contributions you made to your **RRSP during the 89-day period** just before your withdrawal under the HBP. Under these rules, you may not be able to deduct all or part of the contributions made during this period for any year.

You cannot deduct the amount by which the total of your contributions to an RRSP, during the 89-day period just before your withdrawal from that RRSP, is more than the fair market value of that RRSP after the withdrawal.

The same rules apply if you contributed to your spouse's or common-law partner's RRSP during the 89-day period just before that individual made the withdrawal from the same RRSP under the HBP.

In other words, for contributions to be fully deductible that are made to an RRSP in the 89-day period just before an HBP withdrawal from that RRSP, the value of that RRSP after the withdrawal must be at least equal to those contributions.

You and your spouse or common-law partner can use the chart on page 17 to determine the part of the contributions you or your spouse or common-law partner made to an RRSP that is not deductible for any year.

### You have to file an income tax return

Starting in the year you make your first HBP withdrawal, you have to complete and send us a return every year until you have repaid all of your HBP withdrawals or included them in your income. You have to send us a return even if you do not owe any tax. Attach the T4RSP slips that your RRSP issuer sends you for your HBP withdrawals.

Complete Schedule 7, *RRSP Unused Contributions, Transfers, and HBP or LLP Activities* (included in your General Income Tax and Benefit Package), and attach it to your return to show your total HBP withdrawals and repayments in the year. Do not report these amounts on line 129 of your return. This will help both you and us to keep track of them.

## Chapter 2 – Repaying your withdrawals

Over a period of no more than 15 years, you have to repay to your RRSPs the amounts you withdrew under the HBP. Generally, for each year of your repayment period, you have to repay 1/15 of the total amount you withdrew, until the full amount is repaid to your RRSPs. Your repayment period starts the second year following the year you made your withdrawals.

You will receive a *Home Buyers' Plan (HBP) Statement of Account*, each year with your notice of assessment or notice of reassessment. This statement will show the total HBP withdrawals, the amounts you have repaid to date, your HBP balance, and the amount you have to contribute to your RRSP and designate as a repayment for the following year.

**Note**
Even if you declare bankruptcy, you still have to make the annual repayment to your RRSPs for each year remaining in your HBP participation period, until all amounts withdrawn under the HBP are repaid. If you do not make the repayment for a year, it will have to be included in your income for that year.

### How to make your repayment

To make a repayment under the HBP, you have to make contributions to your RRSPs in the year the repayment is due or in the first 60 days of the following year. You can contribute the repayments to any of your RRSPs. Once your contribution is made, you can designate all or part of the contribution as a repayment under the HBP.

To designate your repayment, complete lines 245 and 246 of Schedule 7, *RRSP Unused Contributions, Transfers, and HBP or LLP Activities*, and file it with your tax return. You have to do this even if you would not otherwise have to file a return for the year.

**Contributions you cannot designate** – **Not all** contributions you make to your RRSPs in the repayment year or in the first 60 days of the following year can be designated as a repayment under the HBP. You **cannot** designate contributions that:

- you make to your **spouse's or common-law partner's RRSPs** (or that he or she makes to your RRSPs);
- are amounts you transfer directly to your RRSPs from a registered pension plan, deferred profit sharing plan, registered retirement income fund, the Saskatchewan Pension Plan, or another RRSP;
- are amounts you deducted as a re-contribution of an excess qualifying withdrawal that you designated to have a past service pension adjustment approved;
- are amounts that you designate as a repayment under the Lifelong Learning Plan (LLP) for the year;
- are amounts you contribute in the first 60 days of the repayment year, that you:
  - deducted on your return for the previous year, or
  - designated as a repayment for the previous year under the HBP or the LLP; or
- are amounts you receive in the year (such as retiring allowances) that you transfer to your RRSPs and deduct or will deduct on your return for that year.

**Note**
If your RRSP deduction limit for the repayment year is zero, you can still contribute to your RRSPs and designate the amount you contributed as a repayment under the HBP. We do not consider an amount you designate as a repayment under the HBP to be an RRSP contribution. Therefore, you cannot claim a deduction for this amount on your return

**Example**
In 2008, Robert withdrew $6,000 from his RRSPs to participate in the HBP. Robert's repayment for 2010 is $400 ($6,000 ÷ 15).

In 2010, Robert contributes $8,200 to his RRSPs. Robert could deduct the full amount as an RRSP contribution on line 208 of his 2010 return because his notice of assessment for 2009, shows that he has an RRSP deduction limit of $11,000 for 2010. However, he knows an HBP repayment is required.

Therefore, Robert files Schedule 7 with his 2010 return and records his $8,200 RRSP contribution on line 245. He designates $400 of this amount as an HBP repayment on line 246 of Schedule 7. Robert deducts the remaining $7,800 as an RRSP contribution on line 208 of his 2010 return.

## What happens if I choose to begin my repayments earlier?

In such case, your repayment period will remain the same. Any repayments made before you are required to start your repayments will reduce the amount you have to repay for the first year. If your early repayments are **more** than this required amount for the first year, the difference will reduce your HBP balance and your remaining repayment amounts over the entire repayment period.

## What happens if I repay more than the amount I have to repay for the year?

If your designated HBP repayment is more than the amount you are required to repay for the year, the HBP balance for later years will be reduced. You will still have to make the required payment for the following year.

The annual *Home Buyers' Plan (HBP) Statement of Account,* that we send you with your notice of assessment or notice of reassessment takes into account any additional payments you made, and will give you the minimum amount you have to repay for the next year. If you want to calculate the minimum amount you have to repay for the next year, divide your HBP balance by the number of years remaining in your repayment period.

**Example**
In 2004, Suzanne withdrew $16,500 from her RRSPs to participate in the HBP. Her minimum annual repayment starting in 2006 was $1,100 ($16,500 ÷ 15). Suzanne made the repayment for 2006, 2007 and 2008. In 2009, Suzanne receives an inheritance and decided to contribute $8,000 to her RRSPs and designate that amount as a repayment under the HBP for 2009. She calculates the amount she has to repay for the year 2010, using the chart below.

**Calculating the annual amount Suzanne has to repay**

| Year | Column A<br>HBP balance (column A **minus** column C for the previous year) | Column B<br>Amount Suzanne has to repay for the year | Column C<br>Amount Suzanne repays and designates as a repayment for the year |
|---|---|---|---|
| 2006 | $16,500 | $1,100<br>(16,500 ÷ 15) | $1,100 |
| 2007 | $15,400 | $1,100<br>(15,400 ÷ 14) | $1,100 |
| 2008 | $14,300 | $1,100<br>(14,300 ÷ 13) | $1,100 |
| 2009 | $13,200 | $1,100<br>(13,200 ÷ 12) | $8,000 |
| 2010 | $5,200 | $472.73<br>(5,200 ÷ 11) | $472.73 |

## What happens if I repay less than the amount I have to repay for the year?

If your designated HBP repayment is less than the amount you are required to repay for the year, you have to include the difference as RRSP income on line 129 of your return. You cannot include more than the required repayment for the year **minus** the amount you repay and designate as an HBP repayment. You cannot include in income an amount that is more than the result of this calculation.

## What happens if I do not repay the amount I have to repay for the year?

If you do not repay the amount you have to repay for the year, you have to include it as income on line 129 of your return. The amount you include on line 129 is the minimum amount you have to repay as shown on your *Home Buyers' Plan (HBP) Statement of Account.* Your HBP balance will be reduced accordingly.

## Special repayment situations

Special repayment rules apply if an HBP participant:

- dies;
- becomes a non-resident; or
- reaches the age of 71.

### The HBP participant dies

**General rule** – If an HBP participant dies, the legal representative has to include the participant's HBP balance in the participant's income for the year of death.

The amount to be included in a deceased participant's income for the year of death is equal to the participant's HBP balance before death less any RRSP contributions (made before the participant died) designated as an HBP repayment for the year of death.

**Example**
John dies in 2010. At the time of death, his HBP balance was $7,000. He had made a $1,000 RRSP contribution before he died, which he intended to designate as an HBP repayment for 2010. John's legal representative has to include $6,000 ($7,000 – $1,000) as RRSP income on line 129 of John's final return for 2010.

**HBP election** – If, at the time of death, the participant had a spouse or common-law partner who is a resident of Canada, that individual can jointly elect with the deceased participant's legal representative, to make the repayments under the HBP and to not have the income inclusion rule apply for the deceased participant. The participant's HBP balance at the time of death less any RRSP contributions designated as an HBP repayment for the year of death is treated as if the surviving spouse or common-law partner withdrew it, and it has to be repaid to that individual's RRSPs.

**Note**
Prior to the year of death or in the year of death but before the participant dies, the surviving spouse or common-law partner may have also become a participant by, withdrawing an amount under the HBP (up to $25,000) from his or her RRSPs. There are no adverse tax consequences to the surviving spouse or common-law partner if, as a result of electing to treat the deceased participant's HBP balance as his or her own, the new HBP balance exceeds $25,000.

If at the time of death the participant's surviving spouse or common-law partner is also a participant and the election described above is made, the surviving spouse's or common-law partner's revised HBP balance has to be repaid over the remaining number of years in his or her repayment period.

However, if the surviving spouse or common-law partner was not a participant, the deceased participant's HBP balance has to be repaid over the same number of years remaining in the participation period of the deceased.

To make a joint election, the surviving spouse or common-law partner and the deceased participant's legal representative should attach a signed letter to the final return of the deceased. The letter should state that an election is being made to have the surviving spouse or common-law partner continue making repayments under the HBP, and to not have the income inclusion rule apply for the deceased.

Generally, if the surviving spouse or common-law partner was not participating in the HBP but elects to continue making the repayments of the deceased individual, the surviving spouse or common-law partner would be considered a participant and cannot make any withdrawals under the HBP until the HBP balance is completely repaid and all the other applicable HBP conditions are met.

**Note**
If the deceased had not made an HBP repayment for the year of death, and the election is made, the annual repayment for that year for the deceased would not be required.

**Example 1**
Ron died June 10, 2010. At the time of death, Ron was a participant in the HBP but his common-law partner, Joanne, was not. At the time of death, Ron has an HBP balance of $5,000. Unless Joanne elects to make Ron's HBP repayments, the $5,000 HBP balance will have to be included in income on Ron's final return for 2010.

Joanne, who is the legal representative of the estate, decides to repay Ron's HBP balance. She attaches a letter to Ron's 2010 final return stating that she elects to repay Ron's HBP balance and to not have the income inclusion rules apply for Ron. Joanne will continue making the repayments to her RRSPs according to Ron's repayment period.

As a result of making the election, Joanne is now considered a participant. She cannot make an HBP withdrawal from her RRSPs until the HBP balance has been completely repaid, and all the other applicable conditions are met.

**Example 2**
Susan and David are married. In 2004, they each withdrew $20,000 from their respective RRSPs to participate in the HBP. The repayment period for both Susan and David is from 2006 to 2020.

On December 7, 2010, Susan dies. At that point, she still had $12,000 of her total withdrawal left to repay. She had not made her repayment for 2010.

David, who is the legal representative of the estate, attaches a letter to Susan's final return stating that he elects to repay her $12,000 HBP balance to his RRSPs. As a result of making the election, the unpaid balance of $12,000 does not have to be included in Susan's income for 2010 and a repayment for Susan for the year of death does not have to be made.

David had made his repayment for 2010. His balance to be repaid is $10,000. Susan's unpaid balance of $12,000 is added to David's $10,000. He will now have an HBP balance of $22,000. Therefore, his annual repayment for the next 10 years (2011 to 2020, inclusive), will be $2,200, calculated as follows: ($10,000 + $12,000) ÷ 10 years.

## You become a non-resident

You may cease to be a resident of Canada after a qualifying home is bought or built. If this is the case, you have to repay the balance of the funds you withdrew from your RRSPs under the HBP before the date you file your return for the year, or no later than 60 days after you cease to be a Canadian resident, whichever date is earlier. If you do not make the repayment by this deadline, you have to include the amount that you have not repaid in your income for the year that you became a non-resident. The amount is included in income for the period you were resident in Canada.

**Example**
In 2006, Jeannie withdrew $10,000 from her RRSPs under the HBP to buy a qualifying home. On November 10, 2010, she leaves Canada to live in France. At that time, her unpaid HBP balance is $4,000.

Jeannie has 60 days after becoming a non-resident, that is, until January 9, 2011, to repay the balance. She contributes $2,500 to her RRSPs on December 2, 2010, and $1,000 to her RRSPs on January 7, 2011, for a total contribution of $3,500. Jeannie completes and files Schedule 7 with her 2010 return to designate this contribution as a repayment under the HBP. Because she has not repaid the full amount, Jeannie has to include $500 in her 2010 income, calculated as $4,000 – ($2,500 + $1,000).

### Your options in the year you reach the age of 71

After the end of the year you reach the age of 71, you will not be able to contribute to your RRSPs to repay your withdrawals made under the HBP. This is because you cannot contribute to your RRSP after the end of the year in which you turn 71.

In the year you reach the age of 71, you can choose to contribute to your RRSPs to repay all or part of your HBP balance. If you do not repay your entire HBP balance, you will have to include in your income, for each year remaining in your repayment period, the amount that would be your required annual repayment.

**Example**
In 2002, Mary withdrew $18,000 from her RRSPs to participate in the HBP. Her repayment period began in 2004. In 2010, Mary reaches the age of 71.

Mary's HBP balance is $10,800 at the beginning of 2010. For 2010, Mary can choose to make an HBP repayment, or to include $1,200 in her income. Mary decides to contribute $5,000 to her RRSPs and designates that amount as a 2010 repayment under the HBP. This leaves her with an unpaid balance of $5,800 at the end of 2010. Mary will have to include $725 ($5,800 ÷ 8 = $725) in income for each year from 2011 to 2018.

If Mary did not repay any part of the $10,800, she would have to include $1,200 in income each year from 2011 to 2018. If Mary repaid the entire $10,800 by the end of December 2010, she would not have to include any of this amount in her income, since her balance would be zero.

## Chapter 3 – Other rules you should know

### What happens if I do not meet all the HBP conditions?

If you do not meet all the HBP conditions, your RRSP withdrawals will not be considered eligible and they will have to be included in income for the year you received them. If we have already assessed your return for that year, we will reassess it to include the withdrawals.

### Cancelling your participation

You can cancel your participation in the HBP if you have met all the applicable HBP conditions, but **one** of the following applies:

- you did not buy or build a qualifying home or replacement property; or
- you became a non-resident before buying or building a qualifying home or a replacement property.

You can also cancel your participation, if you withdrew funds under the HBP to help a related person with a disability acquire a home, and:

- that person does not buy or build a qualifying home or replacement property; or
- you become a non-resident before that person buys or builds a qualifying home or a replacement property.

If either of these situations applies to you, complete the cancellation form on page 15 of this guide.

> **Note**
> If you make a withdrawal from your RRSP after having met all applicable HBP conditions, you **cannot** cancel your participation.

If you repay to your RRSPs the full amount you withdrew under the HBP, you will not be taxed on your withdrawal. Any portion of your withdrawal that is not repaid will have to be included in your income for the year you received the funds.

You can make your cancellation payments to any of your RRSPs or to a new RRSP, with any issuer.

**Due date for making cancellation payments** – If you cancel your participation because a qualifying home or replacement property was not bought or built, your cancellation payments are due by December 31 of the year after the year you received the funds.

If you cancel your participation because you became a non-resident before a qualifying home or replacement property was bought or built, your due date will depend on when you became a non-resident. If you were a non-resident at the time you filed a return for the year you received the funds, your cancellation payments are due by the earlier of the following two dates:

- December 31 of the year after the year you received the funds; or
- the day you filed a return for the year you received the funds.

In all other situations, your cancellation payments are due by December 31 of the year after the year you received the funds.

**How to cancel your participation** – To cancel your participation, you have to complete the *Home Buyers' Plan (HBP) – Cancellation* form, provided on page 15. Send us the completed form and all official RRSP contribution receipt(s) that your RRSP issuer gave you, by the cancellation payment due date that applies to you.

**Example**
Jason and his spouse Karen each completed Form T1036, *Home Buyers' Plan (HBP) Request to Withdraw Funds from an RRSP*, on April 10, 2009, to withdraw amounts from their RRSPs under the HBP. Jason withdrew $12,000 from his RRSPs and Karen withdrew $14,000 from her RRSPs. They had entered into a written agreement on March 20, 2009, to buy a qualifying home on September 12, 2009.

In August 2009, Jason and Karen decided not to buy the home and to cancel their participation in the HBP. Jason repaid $12,000 to one of his RRSPs by December 31, 2010. He completes the cancellation form and sends it to us with all copies of his official RRSP receipts so we can cancel his HBP participation.

Karen chose to repay to her RRSP only $8,000 of the $14,000 withdrawal she made under the HBP. She repaid this amount by December 31, 2010. She also completes the cancellation form and sends it to us with all copies of her official RRSP receipts so we can cancel that part of her HBP participation. Karen has to report $6,000 as income on her 2009 return, because she did not repay these funds to her RRSP.

## If I could not participate in the HBP in a particular year, can I participate in a later year?

If you could not participate in the HBP in a particular year, because you did not meet the first-time home buyer's condition or because your HBP balance was not zero on January 1 of the year you wanted your participation period to start, you may be able to participate in a later year.

**First-time home buyer** – If, during the period beginning January 1 of the fourth year before the year of the withdrawal and ending 31 days before the withdrawal, neither you nor your spouse or common-law partner owned a home that you occupied as your principal place of residence, you may be able to participate in the HBP. For example, if in 2005 you sold the home you previously lived in, you may be able to participate in 2010. Or if you sold the home in 2006, you may be able to participate in 2011.

**HBP balance** – If you have previously participated in the HBP, you can do so again if your HBP balance on January 1 of the year in which you want your new participation to begin is zero, and you meet the first-time home buyer's condition as well as all the other HBP conditions that apply to your situation.

For example, if you withdrew funds from your RRSPs under the HBP in 1999, your repayment period is from 2001 to 2015. If you repay the funds you withdrew over the full 15-year repayment period, you may be able to participate in the HBP again in 2016. If you completed repaying the funds in 2010, you may be able to participate in the HBP again in 2011.

**Note**
If you repay the remainder of your HBP balance owing by designating an RRSP contribution made in the first 60 days of the following year, we consider your HBP balance to be zero on January 1 of the year in which the contribution was made.

## Can I use funds withdrawn under the HBP for other purposes?

As long as you buy or build a qualifying home, and you meet all the applicable conditions to participate in the HBP, you can use the funds you withdrew under the HBP for any purpose.

## Can I participate in the Lifelong Learning Plan (LLP) at the same time?

You can participate in the HBP even if you have withdrawn funds from your RRSPs under the LLP that you have not yet fully repaid. For more information about the LLP, see Guide RC4112, *Lifelong Learning Plan (LLP)*.

**HOME BUYERS' PLAN (HBP) – CANCELLATION**

Complete this form to advise us if either of the following situations occurs (please check the box that applies to you):

☐ A qualifying home or replacement property was not bought or built.

☐ I ceased to be a resident of Canada before a qualifying home or replacement property was bought or built.

If you repay your HBP withdrawals to your RRSPs, the amount will not have to be included in your income. If you do not repay all of the amounts withdrawn, the unpaid amounts will have to be included in your income for the year you received the funds. You can make your cancellation payments to any of your RRSPs or to a new RRSP, with any issuer. For information on making cancellation payments, see "Cancelling your participation" on page 13.

| Last name | First name and initials | | | Social insurance number |
|---|---|---|---|---|
| Address | | | | Amount of cancellation payment (Please attach all official receipts.) |
| City | Province or Territory | Postal code | Telephone number | $ |

Participant's signature ____________________ Date ____________

Send this form and the official receipts for your RRSP contribution (if applicable) to:

Pension Workflow Section
Ottawa Technology Centre
875 Heron Road
Ottawa ON K1A 1A2

## For more information

### What if you need help?

If you need help after reading this guide, visit **www.cra.gc.ca** or call **1-800-959-8281**.

### Forms and publications

To get any forms and publications, go to **www.cra.gc.ca/forms**, or call **1-800-959-2221**.

### My Account

My Account is a secure, convenient, and time-saving way to access and manage your tax and benefit information online, seven days a week! Discover all that My Account can do for you. Take the tour at **www.cra.gc.ca/myaccount** or see Pamphlet RC4059, *My Account for individuals*.

### TIPS (Tax Information Phone Service)

For personal and general tax information by telephone, use our automated service, TIPS, by calling **1-800-267-6999**.

### Teletypewriter (TTY) users

TTY users can call **1-800-665-0354** for bilingual assistance during regular business hours.

### Our service complaint process

#### Step 1 – Talk to us

If you are not satisfied with the **service** you have received from us, you have the right to make a formal complaint. Before you make a complaint, we recommend that you try to resolve the matter with the CRA employee you have been dealing with (or call the phone number you have been given).

If you still disagree with the way your concerns are being addressed, ask to discuss the matter with the employee's supervisor.

#### Step 2 – Contact CRA – Service Complaints

This program is available to individual and business taxpayers and benefit recipients who have dealings with us. It is meant to provide you with an extra level of review if you are not satisfied with the results from the **first step** of our complaint process. In general, service-related complaints refer to the quality and timeliness of the work we performed.

If you choose to bring your complaint to the attention of CRA – Service Complaints, complete Form RC193, *Service-Related Complaint*, which you can get by going to **www.cra.gc.ca/complaints** or by calling **1-800-959-2221**.

#### Step 3 – Contact the office of the Taxpayers' Ombudsman

If, **after following steps 1 and 2**, you are still not satisfied with the way the CRA has handled your complaint, you can file a complaint with the Taxpayers' Ombudsman.

For more information on the Taxpayers' Ombudsman and on how to file a complaint, visit their Web site at **www.taxpayersrights.gc.ca**.

### Related forms and publications

#### Forms

T1036 *Home Buyers' Plan (HBP) – Request to Withdraw Funds from an RRSP*

#### Guides

RC4112 *Lifelong Learning Plan (LLP)*

### Your opinion counts

If you have any comments or suggestions that could help us improve our publications, we would like to hear from you. Please send your comments to:

**Taxpayer Services Directorate**
**Canada Revenue Agency**
**750 Heron Road**
**Ottawa ON K1A 0L5**

**Calculating the part of the contributions you or your spouse or common-law partner made to an RRSP that is not deductible for any year**

Use a separate chart for each withdrawal made under the HBP.

**Area 1 – Complete this area if you are the only one who contributed to your RRSP during the 89-day period just before you withdrew an amount from that RRSP.**

| | | | |
|---|---|---|---|
| 1. | RRSP account number ______ 1 | | |
| 2. | Amounts you contributed to the above RRSP during the 89-day period just before your withdrawal under the HBP from that RRSP. * | $ ______ | 2 |
| 3. | Fair market value of the property held in the above RRSP just after your withdrawal. | – ______ | 3 |
| 4. | Line 2 **minus** line 3 (if negative, enter "0"). This is the amount of your contribution to the RRSP indicated on line 1 that you cannot deduct for any year. | = $ ______ | 4 |

**Area 2 – Complete this area if you contributed to your spouse's or common-law partner's RRSP during the 89-day period just before your spouse or common-law partner withdrew an amount from that RRSP.**

| | | | |
|---|---|---|---|
| 5. | RRSP account number ______ 5 | | |
| 6. | Amounts you and your spouse or common-law partner contributed to the above RRSP during the 89-day period just before your spouse's or common-law partner's withdrawal under the HBP from that RRSP. ** | $ ______ | 6 |
| 7. | Fair market value of the property held in the above RRSP just after your spouse's or common-law partner's withdrawal. | – ______ | 7 |
| 8. | Line 6 **minus** line 7 (if negative, enter "0"). This is the amount of the contributions to the RRSP indicated on line 5 that is not deductible for any year. *** | = $ ______ | 8 |

* **Do not include**:

- any amounts for which you did not receive an official RRSP receipt;
- contributions representing lump-sum amounts (for example, retiring allowances) that you transferred to this RRSP. However, you have to include lump-sum amounts that represent contributions you made to another RRSP during the 89-day period just before your withdrawal, and that were transferred to the RRSP identified on line 1;
- the excess amount that you withdrew from your RRSPs in connection with the certification of a provisional past service pension adjustment that you re-contributed to this RRSP in the 89-day period just before your withdrawal, and for which you claim or will claim a deduction; or
- an amount you contributed to this RRSP that was refunded to you as an unused amount (you may have completed Form T3012A, *Tax Deduction Waiver on the Refund of Your Unused RRSP Contributions*).

** **Do not include**:

- any amounts for which you or your spouse or common-law partner did not receive an official RRSP receipt;
- contributions your spouse or common-law partner made for amounts that he or she transferred to this RRSP. However, you have to include amounts that your spouse or common-law partner contributed to another RRSP during the 89-day period just before your spouse's or common-law partner's withdrawal, and that he or she transferred to the RRSP identified on line 5;
- the excess amount that your spouse or common-law partner withdrew from his or her RRSPs in connection with the certification of a provisional past service pension adjustment that your spouse or common-law partner recontributed to this RRSP in the 89-day period just before his or her withdrawal, and for which your spouse or common-law partner claims or will claim a deduction; or
- an amount you or your spouse or common-law partner contributed to this RRSP that was refunded to you or your spouse or common-law partner as an unused amount (you or your spouse or common-law partner may have completed Form T3012A, *Tax Deduction Waiver on the Refund of Your Unused RRSP Contributions*).

*** If both you and your spouse or common-law partner contributed to the above RRSP during the 89-day period just before your spouse's or common-law partner's withdrawal under the HBP, the earliest contributions made during this period are the non-deductible contributions.

www.cra.gc.ca 17

Canada Revenue Agency / Agence du revenu du Canada

## HOME BUYERS' PLAN (HBP) REQUEST TO WITHDRAW FUNDS FROM AN RRSP

Use this form to make a withdrawal from your registered retirement savings plan (RRSP) under the Home Buyers' Plan (HBP). Answer the questions in Part A of Area 1 to determine if you are eligible to make a withdrawal from your RRSP under the HBP. Although some conditions may apply to another person in certain situations, you (the participant) are responsible for making sure that all the conditions are met. For more details about the HBP, see Guide RC4135, *Home Buyers' Plan (HBP)*. **Generally, you must receive all your HBP withdrawals in the same calendar year. The maximum you can withdraw is $25,000.** Complete Area 1 and give the form to your financial institution.

### Area 1 – To be completed by the participant

**Part A – Complete the following questionnaire to determine if you can make a withdrawal from your RRSP under the HBP.**

1. Are you a resident of Canada?
   Yes ☐ Go to question 2. No ☐ You cannot make an HBP withdrawal.

2. Has the person who is buying or building a qualifying home entered into a written agreement to do so?
   Yes ☐ Go to question 3(a). No ☐ You cannot make an HBP withdrawal.

3a). Have you ever, before this year, withdrawn funds from your RRSP under the HBP to buy or build a qualifying home?
   Yes ☐ Go to question 3(b). No ☐ Go to question 4(a).

3b). Are you making this request in January as part of the participation you began last year?
   Yes ☐ Go to question 4(a). No ☐ Go to question 3(c).

3c). Was your repayable balance from your previous HBP participation zero on January 1 of this year?
   Yes ☐ Go to question 4(a). No ☐ You cannot make an HBP withdrawal.

4a). Are you a person with a disability?
   Yes ☐ Go to question 5. No ☐ Go to question 4(b).

4b). Are you withdrawing funds from your RRSP to buy or build a qualifying home for a related person with a disability or to help such a person buy or build a qualifying home?
   Yes ☐ Go to question 5. No ☐ Go to question 4(c).

4c). Are you considered a first-time home buyer?
   Yes ☐ Go to question 5. No ☐ You cannot make an HBP withdrawal.

5. Does the person who is buying or building the qualifying home intend to occupy it as his or her principal place of residence no later than one year after buying or building it? If you are acquiring the home for a related person with a disability or helping a related person with a disability acquire the home, you must intend that the related person with a disability occupy the home as his or her principal place of residence.
   Yes ☐ Go to question 6. No ☐ You cannot make an HBP withdrawal.

6. Has the person who is buying or building the qualifying home or his or her spouse or common-law partner owned the home more than 30 days before receiving this withdrawal?
   Yes ☐ You cannot make an HBP withdrawal. No ☐ You are eligible (complete Part B).

**Part B – Complete this part to make a withdrawal from your RRSP under the HBP.**

| First name and initials | Last name | | | Social insurance number (SIN) |
|---|---|---|---|---|
| Address of **qualifying home being bought or built** (include number, street, rural route, or lot and concession number) | | | | If you are a person with a disability, check this box. ☐ |
| City | Province or Territory | Postal code | Telephone number | |

If you answered "Yes" to question 4(b) above, provide the following information about that person:

Person's name ______ Relationship to you ______ SIN of person with the disability

**Part C – Certification**

Amount of requested withdrawal $ ______

Date withdrawal required ▶ Year Month Day

I certify that the information given in Area 1 of this form is correct.

Date ▶ Year Month Day

______
Participant's signature

Account number of the RRSP from which the withdrawal is made

### Area 2 – To be completed by the RRSP issuer (Do not send this form to the CRA. Keep it for your records.)

| Issuer's name | Telephone number | Amount paid (maximum $25,000) $ |
|---|---|---|
| Issuer's address | | Date withdrawal paid ▶ Year Month Day |

Privacy Act, Personal Information Bank Number CRA PPU 005

T1036 (10)

Canada

## Lifelong Learning Plan (Guide RC4112)

 Canada Revenue Agency Agence du revenu du Canada

# Lifelong Learning Plan (LLP)

Includes Form RC96

RC4112(E) Rev. 10

Canada

## Before you start

### Is this guide for you?

Use this guide if you want information about participating in the Lifelong Learning Plan (LLP).

The LLP allows you to withdraw amounts from your registered retirement savings plans (RRSPs) to finance training or education for you, your spouse or your common-law partner. You do not have to include the withdrawn amounts in your income, and the RRSP issuer will not withhold tax on these amounts.

You have to repay these withdrawals to your RRSPs over a period of no more than 10 years. Any amount that you do not repay when due will be included in your income for the year it was due.

The definitions section on page 4 gives general definitions of the terms we use. Chapter 1 gives information on how the LLP works. Chapter 2 explains how to repay withdrawals under the LLP.

If you have a visual impairment, you can get our publications in braille, large print, etext (CD or diskette), or on MP3 by going to **www.cra.gc.ca/alternate** or by calling **1-800-959-2221**. You can also get your personalized correspondence in these formats by calling **1-800-959-8281**.

La version française de cette publication est intitulée *Régime d'encouragement à l'éducation permanente (REEP).*

**www.cra.gc.ca**

## Table of contents

## Definitions

These definitions provide a general description of the technical terms that we use in this guide.

**Common-law partner** – this applies to a person who is **not your spouse** (see definition on next page), with whom you are living in a conjugal relationship, and to whom at least **one** of the following situations applies. He or she:

a) has been living with you in such a relationship for at least 12 continuous months;

b) is the parent of your child by birth or adoption; or

c) has custody and control of your child (or had custody and control immediately before the child turned 19 years of age) and your child is wholly dependent on that person for support.

In addition, an individual immediately becomes your common-law partner if you previously lived together in a conjugal relationship for at least 12 continuous months and you have resumed living together in such a relationship.

**Under proposed changes,** this condition will no longer exist. The effect of this proposed change is that a person (other than the person described in b) or c) above), will be your common-law partner only after your current relationship with that person has lasted at least 12 continuous months. This proposed change will apply to 2001 and later years.

Reference to "12 continuous months" in this definition includes any period that you were separated for less than 90 days because of a breakdown in the relationship.

**Designated educational institution** – this is a university, college, or other educational institution that qualifies for purposes of the education amount on line 323 of your return.

**LLP balance** – your LLP balance is the total of the amounts you have withdrawn from your RRSPs that meet the LLP rules, **minus** the amounts you have repaid to your RRSPs or have included in your income.

**LLP student** – this is the individual whose education you are financing under the LLP. It can be you, your spouse, or your common-law partner, but not your child or the child of your spouse or common-law partner. You have to participate in the LLP for the same LLP student each year until the year after you have reduced your LLP balance to zero.

**LLP withdrawal** – this is an amount that you withdraw from your RRSPs under the LLP rules.

**Qualifying educational program** – this is an educational program that requires a student to spend 10 hours or more per week on courses or work in the program, and that lasts three or more consecutive months. The educational program must be offered at a designated educational institution. Where an educational institution, other than one certified by Human Resources and Skills Development Canada offers the educational program, the educational program must be at a post-secondary school level.

**Repayment year** – this is a year in which you are required to make a repayment under the LLP. You have to make the repayment no later than 60 days after the end of that year.

**RRSP contribution** – this is the amount you pay, in cash or in kind, when you contribute to an RRSP.

**RRSP deduction** – this is the amount you indicate on line 208 of your return.

**RRSP deduction limit** – this is the maximum amount you can deduct for a year for contributions you made to your own, or to your spouse's or common-law partner's RRSPs.

**RRSP owner** (also called annuitant) – this is the individual named in the RRSP contract as the one who will receive the RRSP money at maturity.

**Spouse** – you have a spouse when you are legally married.

# Chapter 1 – Participating in the LLP

The Lifelong Learning Plan allows you to withdraw up to $10,000 in a calendar year from your registered retirement savings plans (RRSPs) to finance full-time training or education for you, your spouse or common-law partner. You cannot participate in the LLP to finance your children's training or education, or the training or education of your spouse's or common-law partner's children. As long as you meet the LLP conditions **every year,** you can withdraw amounts from your RRSPs until January of the fourth year after the year you make your first LLP withdrawal. You cannot withdraw more than $20,000 in total.

You do not have to include the withdrawn amounts in your income, and the RRSP issuer will not withhold tax on these amounts. You have to repay these withdrawals to your RRSPs over a period of no more than 10 years. Any amount that you do not repay when it is due will be included in your income for the year it was due. This chapter explains the conditions that you and the LLP student have to meet to participate in the LLP, and how to make an LLP withdrawal. The following chart summarizes the LLP withdrawal process.

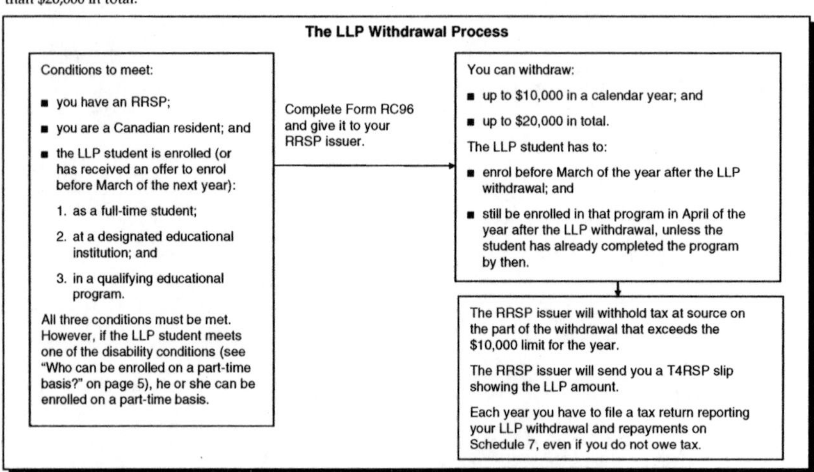

The LLP Withdrawal Process
Conditions to meet:
■ you have an RRSP;
■ you are a Canadian resident; and
■ the LLP student is enrolled (or has received an offer to enrol before March of the next year):
1. as a full-time student;
2. at a designated educational institution; and
3. in a qualifying educational program.
All three conditions must be met. However, if the LLP student meets one of the disability conditions (see "Who can be enrolled on a part-time basis?" on page 5), he or she can be enrolled on a part-time basis.
Complete Form RC96 and give it to your RRSP issuer.
You can withdraw:
■ up to $10,000 in a calendar year; and
■ up to $20,000 in total.
The LLP student has to:
■ enrol before March of the year after the LLP withdrawal; and
■ still be enrolled in that program in April of the year after the LLP withdrawal, unless the student has already completed the program by then.
The RRSP issuer will withhold tax at source on the part of the withdrawal that exceeds the $10,000 limit for the year.
The RRSP issuer will send you a T4RSP slip showing the LLP amount.
Each year you have to file a tax return reporting your LLP withdrawal and repayments on Schedule 7, even if you do not owe tax.


## Who can participate in the LLP?

If you are an RRSP owner, you can usually participate in the LLP to withdraw funds from your RRSPs for your own, your spouse's or your common-law partner's education.

Certain types of RRSPs, such as locked-in RRSPs, do not allow you to withdraw funds from them. Your RRSP issuer can give you more information about the types of RRSPs that you have.

You cannot participate in the LLP after the end of the year you reach the age of 71.

For more information, see "Options when you turn 71 " on page 13.

You have to be a resident of Canada when you receive funds from your RRSPs under the LLP. If you are not sure whether you are considered a resident or non-resident of Canada, or if you need more information about residency status, go to **www.cra.gc.ca**, or call us at **1-800-959-8281**.

If you become a non-resident after you make an LLP withdrawal, see "If you become a non-resident," on page 12.

## What conditions does the LLP student have to meet?

The LLP student can be you, your spouse or your common-law partner. You cannot name your child or the child of your spouse or common-law partner as an LLP student.

The LLP student must enrol on a **full-time basis** in a **qualifying educational program at a designated educational institution.**

If the LLP student meets the disability conditions, the student can enrol on a part-time basis (see "Who can be enrolled on a part-time basis?" on this page). If you are not sure whether the LLP student is enrolling on a full-time basis, check with the educational institution.

The educational institution determines when the student is considered to be enrolled in a program, and when the student is no longer enrolled. Usually, the student is considered to be enrolled when part or all of his or her fees are paid.

If the LLP student is not already enrolled in a program, the student must have received a written offer to enrol before March of the year after you withdraw funds from your RRSPs. A conditional written offer is acceptable.

You cannot participate in the LLP if the student has already completed the program and is no longer enrolled.

### What is a qualifying educational program?

A **qualifying educational program** is an educational program offered at a designated educational institution. Where an educational institution, other than one certified by Human Resources and Skills Development Canada, offers the educational program, the program must be at a post-secondary school level. The program has to:

- last three consecutive months or more; and
- require a student to spend 10 hours or more per week on courses or work in the program. Courses or work includes lectures, practical training, and laboratory work, as well as research time spent on a post-graduate thesis. It **does not** include study time.

### What is a designated educational institution?

A **designated educational institution** is a university, college, or other educational institution that qualifies for the education amount on line 323 of your return. Contact us at **1-800-959-8281** if you are not sure whether a particular institution qualifies as a designated educational institution.

### Who is a full-time student?

The educational institution determines who is a full-time or part-time student. The requirement that the student enrol as a full-time student is separate from the qualifying educational program requirement. The qualifying educational program requirement can be met by a person taking courses by correspondence or by a person enrolled in a distance education program. Even if the student is enrolled in a program that requires spending 10 hours or more per week on courses or work in the program, the institution may consider the student to be enrolled on a part-time basis. If this is the case, you cannot participate in the LLP. The following section explains the only exception to this rule.

### Who can be enrolled on a part-time basis?

An LLP student who meets one of the disability conditions can be enrolled on a part-time basis. The program in which the student is enrolled must still be a qualifying educational program that usually requires a student to spend 10 hours or more per week on courses or work in the program. However, a student who meets the disability conditions can spend less than 10 hours per week on courses or work in the program.

We consider the LLP student to meet the disability conditions if **one** of the following situations applies:

- the student cannot reasonably be expected to be enrolled as a full-time student because of a mental or physical impairment, and a medical doctor, an optometrist, a speech-language pathologist, an audiologist, an occupational therapist, a physiotherapist, or a psychologist has certified this on Form T2202, *Education and Textbook Amount Certificate*; or
- the student is entitled to the disability amount on line 316 of the student's tax return for the year of the LLP withdrawal.

**Note**
If the student was allowed the disability amount on his or her return for the previous year and still meets the eligibility requirements for the disability amount, the student will meet the disability condition for the LLP. The student will also meet this condition if someone else claimed the disability amount for the student in the previous year and the student still meets the eligibility requirements for the disability amount. If you have questions about the disability amount, contact us at **1-800-959-8281**.

### What if the LLP student does not enrol in the program?

If the LLP student is not already enrolled when you make the withdrawal, the student has to enrol in a qualifying educational program before March of the year after the LLP withdrawal.

If the LLP student does not enrol in the program in time, you have to cancel your LLP withdrawals. For more information, see "How to cancel your LLP withdrawal," on page 8.

## How much can you withdraw?

Under the LLP, you can withdraw up to $10,000 in a calendar year from your RRSPs. This is your **annual LLP limit**. The amount you withdraw is not limited to the amount of tuition or other education expenses. Your spouse or common-law partner can also withdraw up to $10,000 from RRSPs under the LLP in the same year you do. For more information, see "Can my spouse or common-law partner and I participate in the LLP at the same time?" on page 8.

You can keep withdrawing amounts from your RRSPs until January of the fourth year after the year you made your first LLP withdrawal, as long as the LLP student continues to meet the conditions explained on page 5 under "What conditions does the LLP student have to meet?"

**Example 1**
Eugene makes his first LLP withdrawal in 2010 for himself as the LLP student. He continues to meet the LLP student conditions every year. He has to make his last withdrawal before February 2014.

You cannot withdraw more than $20,000 each time you participate in the LLP. This is your **total LLP limit**. You can participate in the LLP again, starting the year after you bring your LLP balance to zero.

If you withdraw more than the annual LLP limit of $10,000, the excess will be included in your income for the year of the withdrawal. The excess does not reduce your total LLP limit of $20,000.

If you withdraw more than the total LLP limit of $20,000, the excess will be included in your income for the year you exceed the total LLP limit.

## How do you make the withdrawal?

To make an LLP withdrawal, use Form RC96, *Lifelong Learning Plan (LLP) – Request to Withdraw Funds From an RRSP*. You have to complete Form RC96 for each withdrawal that you make. You can use the form at the end of this guide. To get more copies of the form, go to our Web site at **www.cra.gc.ca/forms**, or call **1-800-959-2221**.

Complete Part 1 of Form RC96. You can name yourself, your spouse or your common-law partner as the LLP student in Part 1. After you complete this part, give the form to your RRSP issuer, who will complete Part 2. Your RRSP issuer will not withhold tax from the funds you withdraw if you meet the LLP conditions. Your RRSP issuer will send you a T4RSP slip, showing the amount you withdrew under the LLP. Attach this slip to your tax return.

### Filing a tax return

Starting in the year you make your first LLP withdrawal, you have to complete and send us a return every year until you have repaid all of your LLP withdrawals or included them in your income. You have to send us a return even if you do not owe any tax. Attach the T4RSP slips that your RRSP issuer sends you for your LLP withdrawals.

Complete Schedule 7, *RRSP Unused Contributions, Transfers, and HBP or LLP Activities* (included in your income tax package), and attach it to your return to show your total LLP withdrawals and repayments in the year. This will help both you and CRA to keep track of them.

When you file your return for the first year you are participating in the LLP, you can use Schedule 7 to change the LLP student that you named on Form RC96. If you named your spouse or common-law partner as the LLP student, you can change it to yourself. If you named yourself as the LLP student, you can change it to your spouse or common-law partner. You **cannot** change the LLP student you have named **after you file** your return for that first year.

## How does your withdrawal affect your RRSP deduction?

You can continue to make contributions to RRSPs and deduct them from your income on your return after you have made an LLP withdrawal. However, you may not be able to deduct contributions you made **before** the withdrawal. The following explains the restrictions that apply.

If you do not have an RRSP, you cannot set one up and then make an LLP withdrawal immediately. The contribution has to be in the RRSP for 90 days before you can deduct it from your income on your tax return.

If you already have an RRSP and you contribute to it in the 89-day period before you make an LLP withdrawal, you may not be able to deduct the contribution from your income on your return at any time even if you repay this amount to your RRSP under the LLP. If the value of the RRSP right after the LLP withdrawal is **more than** or the **same as** the amount of the RRSP contribution, you can deduct the entire contribution. If the value of the RRSP right after the LLP withdrawal is **less than** the amount of the RRSP contribution, you cannot deduct some or all of the contribution. To find out how much you **cannot** deduct, use the following formula for each RRSP from which you make an LLP withdrawal:

Total contributions you made to the RRSP in the 89-day period before the LLP withdrawal
**Minus:**
Value of the RRSP immediately after you made the LLP withdrawal
**Equals:**
The part of the contributions you **cannot** deduct at any time

**Example 2**
Stephen has an RRSP with a value of $6,500. He contributes $8,000 to the RRSP on February 10, 2010. He then makes an LLP withdrawal of $10,000 on March 1, 2010. The value of the RRSP after the withdrawal is $4,500.

| | |
|---|---|
| **February 10, 2010** | |
| Value of RRSP before contribution | $ 6,500 |
| February 10, 2010, contribution | + $ 8,000 |
| Value after the contribution | = $ 14,500 |
| **March 1, 2010** | |
| LLP withdrawal | – $ 10,000 |
| Value after withdrawal | = $ 4,500 |
| Stephen determines the part of his contribution that is not deductible as follows: | |
| Contribution in the 89 days before the LLP withdrawal | $ 8,000 |
| **Minus:** the value after the withdrawal | – $ 4,500 |
| **Result** | = $ 3,500 |

Stephen **cannot** deduct $3,500 of the contribution he made on February 10, 2010, for any year.

You can use the Appendix on page 14 to determine the part of the RRSP contributions you or your spouse or common-law partner made that is not deductible for any year.

## What happens if the LLP student leaves the educational program?

For you to be able to repay the LLP withdrawals over a 10-year period, the LLP student usually has to either:

- complete the program; or

- continue to be enrolled in the educational program at the end of March of the year after the LLP withdrawal.

If the LLP student leaves the program before April of the year after the withdrawal, you can still make your repayments over a 10-year period **if less than 75%** of the student's tuition is refundable by the educational institution.

If the LLP student leaves the program before April of the year after the withdrawal, and **75% or more** of the LLP student's tuition is refundable, you have to cancel the LLP withdrawal. For more information, see "How to cancel your LLP withdrawal?" on this page. If you do not cancel it, the amount you withdrew will be included in your income for the year you withdrew it.

We check the LLP student's education amount on line 323 of the student's return for the year you make the withdrawal and for the following year. If we cannot determine from the education amount that the LLP student has continued in the program, we will contact you to find out if you still meet the conditions to make the repayments over a 10-year period.

**Example 3**
In September 2010, George withdraws $1,000 from his RRSPs under the LLP. Earlier in the same month, he enrolled in a four-month college program and paid $750 in tuition fees. George completes the program in January 2011. Therefore, he can repay his LLP amounts over a 10-year period.

**Note**
Special rules apply if the LLP student dies.
For more information, see "If the person who made the LLP withdrawal dies," on page 11.

## How to cancel your LLP withdrawal?

You can cancel your LLP withdrawal by paying it back to your RRSPs if **any** of the following situations applies:

- the LLP student was not enrolled in the qualifying educational program when you made the withdrawal and did not enrol in time;
- the LLP student left the program before April of the year after the withdrawal and 75% or more of the student's tuition was refundable; or
- you became a non-resident of Canada **before** the end of the year in which you made an LLP withdrawal.

You cannot make your cancellation payment if the withdrawal did not meet the LLP rules **when you made the withdrawal**. One or more of the situations listed above must apply for you to cancel your withdrawal.

You can make the payment to any of your RRSPs with any issuer, or you can open a new RRSP. You cannot make a cancellation payment to your spouse's or common-law partner's RRSPs.

When you make the cancellation payment to your RRSP, your RRSP issuer will give you a receipt. Complete the cancellation form at the end of this guide and send it, along with the receipt, to the address on the form.

Any amount that you do not repay will be included in your income for the year you withdrew it. If we have already assessed your return for that year, we will reassess it to include the unpaid amount. Interest will be charged and penalties assessed, if applicable.

### Due date for cancellation payment

If you are a resident of Canada when you file your tax return for the year in which you made the withdrawal, the due date for the cancellation payment is December 31 of the year after the year you made the withdrawal.

If you are a non-resident of Canada when you file your tax return for the year in which you made the withdrawal, the due date for the cancellation payment is the **earlier of**:

- before the time you file your return for the year in which you made the withdrawal; or
- December 31 of the year after the year of the withdrawal.

**Example 4**
On May 3, 2010, Patrick applies to three Canadian universities as a full-time student. On July 12, 2010, Patrick receives a written offer to enrol in a program at one of the universities. On July 13, 2010, he makes an LLP withdrawal of $10,000. Since Patrick withdrew the funds in 2010, he has to enrol in the program before March 1, 2011. If he does not, Patrick will have to cancel the LLP withdrawal by paying back the $10,000 to his RRSP by December 31, 2011. We will include any amount he does not repay in his income for 2010.

## Questions you may have

### How often can I participate in the LLP?

There is no limit on the number of times you can participate in the LLP over your lifetime. Starting in the year after you bring your LLP balance to zero, you can participate in the LLP again and withdraw up to $20,000 over a new qualifying period.

### Can my spouse or common-law partner and I participate in the LLP at the same time?

Yes. You can do any of the following:

- you can participate in the LLP for yourself while your spouse or common-law partner participates in the LLP for him or herself;
- you can both participate in the LLP for either of you; or
- you can participate in the LLP for each other.

Each of you can withdraw up to the annual LLP limit of $10,000 in a year and up to the total LLP limit of $20,000 over the period you are participating in the LLP.

### Can I make LLP withdrawals from more than one RRSP?

You can make LLP withdrawals for you, your spouse or common-law partner from more than one RRSP if you are the RRSP owner of each one. Your total LLP withdrawals in a year from all of your RRSPs cannot be more than the annual LLP limit of $10,000. In addition, your total LLP withdrawals over the period that you are participating in the LLP cannot be more than the total LLP limit of $20,000.

### Can I make LLP withdrawals for other purposes?

As long as you meet all of the LLP conditions when you make the withdrawal, you can use the funds you withdrew for any purpose. For example, you could use other savings to pay for your tuition and books and use your LLP withdrawal to pay for living expenses.

### Can I participate in the LLP and in the Home Buyers' Plan at the same time?

You can participate in the LLP even if you have withdrawn amounts from your RRSPs under the Home Buyers' Plan that you have not yet fully repaid. For more information about the Home Buyers' Plan, see Guide RC4135, *Home Buyers' Plan (HBP)*.

### What if the LLP student does not qualify for the education amount?

It is possible to participate in the LLP even if the LLP student does not qualify for the education amount on line 323 of his or her return. The LLP student **may not be able to** claim the education amount because he or she is receiving a reimbursement, benefit, grant, or allowance for the educational program. If it is only for one of these reasons that the LLP student cannot claim the education amount, you can still participate in the LLP. However, we may ask you for documentation to show that you qualify to participate in the LLP.

## Chapter 2 – Repaying your withdrawals

You have to make repayments to your RRSPs over a period of no more than 10 years. Usually, each year you have to repay 1/10 of the total amount you withdrew until the full amount is repaid. You do not have to pay any interest on the amounts you withdrew.

### When and how much to repay

You will receive an LLP Statement of Account each year on your notice of assessment or notice of reassessment. This statement will show the total LLP withdrawals, the amount you have repaid to date, your LLP balance, and the amount you have to repay the following year.

To determine when you have to start repaying your LLP withdrawals, use the chart on page 10. In some situations, the latest year you can start repaying your LLP withdrawals is the fifth year after your first LLP withdrawal. However, in most cases, you have to start repaying your withdrawals before that year.

We determine when your repayment period starts by checking on line 323 of the LLP student's return to see if the student was entitled to the education amount as a full-time student for at least three months. If the LLP student does not meet this education amount condition two years in a row, your repayment period usually starts in the second of those two years. If the LLP student continues to meet this condition every year, your repayment period starts in the fifth year after your first LLP withdrawal.

In some cases, the LLP student is not entitled to the education amount for three months in any year. This can happen if the program is a short one and the student starts it near the end of a year. In that case, your first repayment year is the second year after the year of your LLP withdrawal. If the student is not entitled to the education amount for three months in any year because the student left the program, see "What happens if the LLP student leaves the educational program?" on page 7.

**Example 5**
Sarah makes LLP withdrawals from 2007 to 2010. She continues her education from 2007 to 2012, and is entitled to claim the education amount as a full-time student for at least three months on her return every year. Sarah's repayment period is from 2012 to 2021, since 2012 is the fifth year after the year of her first LLP withdrawal.

The due date for her first repayment is March 1, 2013, which is 60 days after the end of 2012, her first repayment year.

**Example 6**
Joseph makes an LLP withdrawal in 2009 for a qualifying educational program he is enrolled in during 2009. He is entitled to the education amount as a full-time student for five months of 2009. Joseph completes the educational program in 2010, and he is entitled to the education amount as a full-time student for five months on his return for 2010. He is not entitled to the education amount for 2011 or 2012. Joseph's repayment period begins in 2012.

**Note**
Even if you become bankrupt, you still have to repay all your LLP withdrawals to your RRSPs. If you do not, you have to include the required amounts in your income each year as they become due.

| When to start repaying your LLP withdrawals | |
|---|---|
| Use this chart to determine when you have to start repaying your LLP withdrawals. This chart does not cover cancelling your withdrawal. For that situation, see "How to cancel your LLP withdrawal," on page 8. | |
| **Step 1**<br>**Is this the year of your first LLP withdrawal?**<br>If **no**, go to Step 2. | If **yes**, you do not have to start repaying your LLP withdrawal this year. |
| **Step 2**<br>**Is this the fifth year after your first LLP withdrawal?**<br>(If you made your first LLP withdrawal in 2007, then 2012 would be the fifth year after your first LLP withdrawal.)<br>If **no**, go to Step 3. | If **yes**, you have to start repaying your LLP withdrawals this year. |
| **Step 3**<br>**Will the LLP student be entitled to the education amount as a full-time student on line 323 of his or her return for at least three months this year?**<br>If **no**, go to Step 4. | If **yes**, you do not have to start repaying your LLP withdrawals this year. |
| **Step 4**<br>**Was the LLP student entitled to the education amount as a full-time student for at least three months on his or her return for last year?**<br>If **no**, you have to start repaying your LLP withdrawals this year. | If **yes**, you do not have to start repaying your LLP withdrawals this year. |

## How to make your repayments

To make your repayments, you have to contribute to your RRSPs in the repayment year or in the first 60 days of the following year. You can make the repayments to any of your RRSPs with any issuer, or you can open a new RRSP.

You **cannot** designate a contribution you made to your spouse's or common-law partner's RRSPs (or a contribution your spouse or common-law partner made to your RRSPs) as a repayment under the LLP. You have to designate your repayment for the year by completing Schedule 7, *RRSP Unused Contributions, Transfers, and HBP or LLP Activities* (included in your income tax package), and filing it with your tax return for the repayment year.

You have to make your repayments to your RRSPs even if your RRSP deduction limit is zero or a negative amount. We do not consider an amount you designate as a repayment under the LLP to be an RRSP contribution. Therefore, you cannot claim a deduction for this amount on your return.

**Example 7**
Betty has an LLP balance of $7,500. Her repayment period is from 2010 to 2019. For her first repayment year, she needs to repay $750, which is 1/10 of the amount she withdrew. Betty contributes $6,000 to her RRSPs in 2010.
To designate $750 as her 2010 repayment, she has to file Schedule 7 with her 2010 return. Betty can deduct the remaining $5,250 she contributed if the RRSP deduction limit shown on her notice of assessment for 2009 is at least $5,250.

## Contributions you cannot designate

You may have made contributions to your RRSPs from January 1 of the repayment year up to the 60th day of the following year that **cannot** be designated as repayments under the LLP.

You **cannot** designate amounts that:

- you contributed to your spouse's or common-law partner's RRSPs (or that your spouse or common-law partner contributed to your RRSPs);
- you transferred directly to your RRSPs from a registered pension plan, deferred profit sharing plan, registered retirement income fund, the Saskatchewan Pension Plan, or another RRSP;
- you deducted as a recontribution of an excess qualifying withdrawal that you designated to have a past service pension adjustment approved;
- you contributed in the first 60 days of the repayment year, that you deducted on your return for the previous year, or that you designated as a repayment for the previous year under the Home Buyers' Plan or LLP; or
- you received in the repayment year, such as retiring allowances, that you transferred to your RRSPs and deducted or will deduct on your return for that year.

### What if you want to repay earlier?

Any payments you make before the first repayment year reduce your first required repayment. For example, assume your first repayment year is 2011 and $1,000 is your required repayment. If you make an early repayment of $600 in 2010, your required repayment for 2011 is $400.

### What if you repay less than the amount required?

If you designate an amount that is **less** than the amount you have to repay, you have to include the difference in your income on line 129 of your return. The amount you include in your income is equal to the amount you have to repay **minus** the amount you designate as a repayment for the year. The amount you include in your income cannot be more than the result of this calculation.

Your LLP balance is reduced by the amount you repay **plus** the amount you include in income. If you want to calculate the amount you have to repay for the next year, divide your LLP balance by the number of years remaining in your repayment period.

**Example 8**
Josée makes a $10,000 LLP withdrawal in 2008 for a four-month qualifying educational program that finishes in 2008. For 2010, Josée's repayment is $1,000 ($10,000 ÷ 10). Josée contributes $700 to her RRSPs in 2010, and she files Schedule 7 with her return to designate the $700 as a repayment under the LLP. Josée has to include $300 in her income on line 129 of her 2010 return. She determined this as follows:

| | |
|---|---|
| Amount she has to repay for 2010 | $ 1,000 |
| **Minus:** Amount she designates as a repayment on Schedule 7 | – $ 700 |
| Amount she includes as income on line 129 | = $ 300 |

She cannot claim a deduction for the $700 contributed to her RRSPs because she designated those contributions as a repayment under the LLP. In 2011, she will have to repay $1,000 ($9,000 ÷ 9).

### What if you repay more than the amount required?

If you repay and designate more than you have to repay for a year, the amount you have to repay in each of the following years will be less. The LLP Statement of Account on your notice of assessment or notice of reassessment takes into account any additional payments you make and tells you how much you have to repay for the next year. If you want to calculate the amount you have to repay for the next year, divide your LLP balance by the number of years left in your repayment period.

**Example 9**
Alexander's repayment period is from 2006 to 2015. His LLP balance is $8,500. Alexander's repayment for 2006 was $850 ($8,500 ÷ 10). He made the repayment for 2006, 2007, and 2008. In 2009, he received an inheritance and decided to contribute $4,000 to his RRSPs and designate that amount as a repayment under the LLP for 2009. He calculates the amount he has to repay for 2010 using the following chart:

**Calculating the annual amount Alexander has to repay**

| Year | LLP balance at the beginning of the year | Amount Alexander has to repay for the year | Amount Alexander designates as a repayment for the year | LLP balance for the following year |
|---|---|---|---|---|
| 2006 | $8,500 | $850 ($8,500 ÷ 10) | $850 | $7,650 |
| 2007 | $7,650 | $850 ($7,650 ÷ 9) | $850 | $6,800 |
| 2008 | $6,800 | $850 ($6,800 ÷ 8) | $850 | $5,950 |
| 2009 | $5,950 | $850 ($5,950 ÷ 7) | $4,000 | $1,950 |
| 2010 | $1,950 | $325 ($1,950 ÷ 6) | $325 | $1,625 |

## Situations where the repayments have to be made in less than 10 years

Additional repayment rules apply if you:

- die;
- become a non-resident; or
- are over the age of 71.

### If the person who made the LLP withdrawal dies

Usually, if the person who made the LLP withdrawal dies, the legal representative (liquidator) has to include the LLP balance in the deceased person's income for the year of death.

If the deceased person contributed to an RRSP in the year of death, the legal representative (liquidator) can designate the contributions as a repayment under the LLP using Schedule 7, *RRSP Unused Contributions, Transfers, and HBP or LLP Activities*. This reduces the LLP balance that the legal representative (liquidator) has to include in the deceased person's income.

**Note**
An LLP student who dies may not have been the person who made the LLP withdrawal. If this is the case, the person who made the withdrawal makes the required LLP repayments over the usual 10-year period.

**LLP election on death**

If, at the time the person who made the LLP withdrawal dies, he or she has a spouse or common-law partner who is a resident of Canada, that individual can elect jointly with the deceased person's legal representative (liquidator) to make the repayments and to not include the LLP balance in the deceased person's income. If the surviving spouse or common-law partner is also the legal representative (liquidator), he or she makes the election.

To make this election, the surviving spouse or common-law partner and the deceased person's legal representative (liquidator) sign a letter and attach it to the deceased person's tax return for the year of death. The letter should state that an election is being made to have the surviving spouse or common-law partner make the repayments under the LLP, and to not have the income inclusion rule apply for the deceased person. The deceased person's LLP balance then becomes the survivor's LLP balance. The surviving spouse or common-law partner makes the repayments to his or her own RRSPs.

> **Note**
> If an election is made and the deceased person had not made a repayment for the year of death, no repayment will be required for that year for the deceased.

**If the surviving spouse or common-law partner has no LLP balance of his or her own,** he or she is considered to be the student under the new plan. The surviving spouse will have to make repayments to his or her RRSP over the normal 10-year repayment period. For more information on when the repayment period will begin see "When and how much to repay," on page 9 and the chart on page 10.

**Example 10**

Isabelle died in 2010. At the time of death, she had an LLP balance of $7,200. Her repayment period is from 2009 to 2018. Her husband Bruno is her legal representative (liquidator). If Bruno does not make the election, he will have to include $7,200 as income on line 129 of Isabelle's final return for 2010.

If Bruno elects to make the repayments when he prepares Isabelle's return for 2010, he does not include her LLP balance in her income. Instead, he writes a letter explaining that he is electing to make his late wife's LLP repayments. He signs the letter and attaches it to her return. Bruno will become an LLP participant in 2010 due to the spousal transfer of $7,200.

If Bruno is not a full-time student in either 2011 or 2012, his 10-year repayment period will begin in 2012. He may choose to make repayments in 2010 or 2011, in which case they will be applied to the balance to reduce or eliminate the required repayment in 2012 and subsequent years. For more information see "What if you want to repay earlier?" on page 10.

If Bruno is a full-time student and wants to withdraw funds under the LLP from his own RRSP, his total LLP limit is now $20,000 **minus** the LLP balance transferred from Isabelle. In addition, his annual LLP limit for 2010 is $10,000 **minus** the LLP balance transferred from Isabelle. His required repayments on his LLP balance (spousal transfer amount plus any subsequent personal LLP withdrawals) will begin in the second year after ceasing to be a full-time student or the fifth year after the spousal transfer, whichever is earliest.

**If the surviving spouse or common-law partner already had an LLP balance of his or her own** at the time the person dies, the deceased person's LLP balance is added to the survivor's LLP balance. This may cause the survivor's LLP balance to be more than the $10,000 annual limit or the $20,000 total limit. If this occurs, we will not include the excess in the income of either the survivor or the deceased person. The surviving spouse or common-law partner has to repay the new balance over his or her own repayment period.

**Example 11**

Irene died on June 10, 2010. At the time of death, she had an LLP balance of $7,000 to be repaid. Irene's common-law partner Paul is the estate's legal representative (liquidator). He decides to make Irene's LLP repayments. He has his own LLP balance of $14,000, and his repayment period is from 2010 to 2019. Paul will add Irene's LLP balance of $7,000 to his own LLP balance of $14,000. However, Paul is only required to make a repayment of $1,400 in 2010 based on his own LLP balance of $14,000 at the beginning of the year. If he pays only the required amount, in 2011, his minimum LLP repayment will be $2,177 ($19,600 ÷ 9).

## If you become a non-resident

If you become a non-resident of Canada **after the year you make an LLP withdrawal**, your LLP balance becomes payable for the year that you become a non-resident. The due date for the repayment is the **earlier of**:

- the date you file your return for the year you became a non-resident; or
- 60 days after you stop being a Canadian resident.

You have to designate your repayment for the year by completing Schedule 7 and filing it with your tax return for the year that you become a non-resident. If you do not repay your LLP balance by the due date, you have to include the unpaid amount in your income for the year that you became a non-resident. The amount is included in income for the period you were a resident of Canada.

If you become a non-resident **before the end of the year in which you make an LLP withdrawal**, you have to cancel your LLP withdrawals by paying them back to your RRSPs.

If you are a non-resident of Canada when you file your tax return for the year in which you made the LLP withdrawal, the due date for the cancellation payment is whichever is **earlier**:

- before the time you file your return for the year in which you made the withdrawal; or
- December 31 of the year after the year of the withdrawal.

If you are a resident of Canada when you file your tax return for the year in which you made the LLP withdrawal, the due date for the cancellation payment is December 31 of the year after the year you made the withdrawal.

When you make the cancellation payment to your RRSPs, your RRSP issuer will give you a receipt. Complete the cancellation form at the end of this guide and send it, along with the receipt, to the address shown on the form.

If you do not make the cancellation payment by the due date, we will include the LLP withdrawal in your income for the year you made it. You may be charged interest, if applicable.

## Options when you turn 71

After the end of the year you reach the age of 71, you are no longer able to make contributions to your RRSP and therefore are not able to repay your LLP balance.
In the year you reach the age of 71, you can choose to repay all or part of your unpaid balance. After that, you will have to include your annual repayment in your income, on line 129 of your return, each year as it becomes due.

**Example 12**
In 2003, at the age of 64, Henry makes an LLP withdrawal of $9,000. His repayment period began in 2008.
The required annual repayment is $900.

In 2010, he reaches the age of 71. Henry's LLP balance at the beginning of 2010 is $7,200 and he can choose to make an LLP repayment, or to include $900 in his income.

In 2010, Henry decides to contribute $3,000 to his RRSPs and to designate that amount as a repayment under the LLP. This leaves him with an unpaid balance of $4,200 at the end of 2010. Henry will have to include $600 ($4,200 ÷ 7) in income for each year from 2011 to 2017.

If he did not repay any part of the $7,200, he would have to include $900 in income each year from 2010 to 2017.
If he repaid the entire $7,200, he would not have to include any part of this amount in his income.

## Appendix – Effect of LLP on RRSP deductions

**Calculating the part of RRSP contributions that is not deductible for any year**

Use a separate chart for each LLP withdrawal.

**Area 1 – Complete this area if you are the only one who contributed to your RRSP during the 89-day period just before you made an LLP withdrawal from that RRSP.**

| | | | |
|---|---|---|---|
| 1. | RRSP account number | ______ | 1 |
| 2. | Amounts you contributed to the above RRSP during the 89-day period just before you made an LLP withdrawal from that RRSP* | $ ______ | 2 |
| 3. | Fair market value of the above RRSP right after you made an LLP withdrawal | – ______ | 3 |
| 4. | Line 2 **minus** line 3 (if negative, enter "0"). This is the amount of your contributions to the RRSP shown on line 1 that you cannot deduct for any year. | = $ ______ | 4 |

**Area 2 – Complete this area if you contributed to your spouse's or common-law partner's RRSP during the 89-day period just before your spouse or common-law partner made an LLP withdrawal from that RRSP.**

| | | | |
|---|---|---|---|
| 5. | RRSP account number | ______ | 5 |
| 6. | Amounts you and your spouse or common-law partner contributed to the above RRSP during the 89-day period just before your spouse or common-law partner made an LLP withdrawal from that RRSP** | $ ______ | 6 |
| 7. | Fair market value of the above RRSP right after your spouse or common-law partner made an LLP withdrawal | – ______ | 7 |
| 8. | Line 6 **minus** line 7 (if negative, enter "0"). This is the amount of the contributions to the RRSP shown on line 5 that is not deductible for any year.*** | = $ ______ | 8 |

* **Do not include:**

- any amounts for which you did not receive an official RRSP receipt;
- contributions representing lump-sum amounts (for example, retiring allowances) that you transferred to this RRSP (you have to include amounts you contributed to another RRSP during the 89-day period just before your withdrawal that were transferred to the RRSP identified on line 1);
- the excess amount that you withdrew from your RRSPs in connection with the certification of a provisional past service pension adjustment, which you recontributed to this RRSP for the year and for which you claim or will claim a deduction;
- an amount you contributed to this RRSP that was refunded to you as an undeducted amount (you may have completed Form T3012A, *Tax Deduction Waiver on the Refund of Your Unused RRSP Contributions Made in* __ ); or
- amounts you contributed as a repayment or cancellation payment under the Home Buyers' Plan.

** **Do not include:**

- any amounts for which you or your spouse or common-law partner did not receive an official RRSP receipt;
- contributions your spouse or common-law partner made for amounts that he or she transferred to this RRSP (you have to include amounts that your spouse or common-law partner contributed to another RRSP during the 89-day period just before the withdrawal that he or she transferred to the RRSP identified on line 5);
- the excess amount that your spouse or common-law partner withdrew from his or her RRSPs in connection with the certification of a provisional past service pension adjustment, which he or she recontributed to this RRSP for the year and for which he or she claims or will claim a deduction;
- an amount you or your spouse or common-law partner contributed to this RRSP that was refunded to the designated person as an undeducted amount (the designated person may have completed Form T3012A, *Tax Deduction Waiver on the Refund of Your Unused RRSP Contributions Made in* __ ); or
- amounts you or your spouse or common-law partner contributed as a repayment or cancellation payment under the Home Buyers' Plan.

*** If both you and your spouse or common-law partner made contributions to the above RRSP during the 89-day period just before your spouse or common-law partner made an LLP withdrawal, the earliest contributions made during this period are non-deductible.

Canada Revenue Agency Agence du revenu du Canada

## LIFELONG LEARNING PLAN (LLP) REQUEST TO WITHDRAW FUNDS FROM AN RRSP

- Use this form to make a withdrawal from your RRSP under the LLP. Complete Part 1, and give the form to your RRSP issuer.
- For more information about the LLP and who qualifies to use it, see Guide RC4112, *Lifelong Learning Plan (LLP)*.

### Part 1 – Complete this part to make an LLP withdrawal from your RRSP

| Name | | Social insurance number |
|---|---|---|
| Address | | |
| City | Province or territory | Postal code |

**Who is the LLP student? (check one)** You ☐ Your spouse or common-law partner ☐

| If you checked "Your spouse or common-law partner", enter his or her name and social insurance number. | Social insurance number |
|---|---|

1. Has the LLP student enrolled in a qualifying educational program at a designated educational institution, or received a written offer to enrol before March of next year in such a program? For information about **qualifying educational programs** and **designated educational institutions**, see Guide RC4112, *Lifelong Learning Plan (LLP)*.
   Yes ☐ *Go to question 2.* No ☐ *You cannot make an LLP withdrawal.* **Do not complete the rest of this form.**

2. Is the student enrolling as a full-time student or a part-time student?
   Full-time ☐ *Go to question 4.* Part-time ☐ *Go to question 3.*

3. Does the student meet one of the disability conditions explained in Guide RC4112, *Lifelong Learning Plan (LLP)*?
   Yes ☐ *Go to question 4.* No ☐ *You cannot make an LLP withdrawal.* **Do not complete the rest of this form.**

4. How much do you want to withdraw? $________ A

5. Is this your first LLP withdrawal this year?
   Yes ☐ *Go to question 6.* No ☐ How much have you already withdrawn under the LLP this year? $________ B

   If the total of lines A and B is **more** than $10,000, your RRSP issuer will withhold tax on the part of your withdrawal that exceeds the $10,000 limit. You have to include the part that exceeds the $10,000 limit in your income on your return.

6. How much have you withdrawn under the LLP in previous years of your current participation? **Do not** include amounts that you repaid to your RRSPs after participating in the LLP in the past **or** the amounts you included in your previous year's T1 return because you exceeded the $10,000 limit. If the total of lines A, B, and C is **more** than $20,000, your RRSP issuer will withhold tax on the part of your withdrawal that exceeds the $20,000 limit.
   You have to include the part that exceeds the $20,000 limit in your income on your return. $________ C

7. What is the account number of the RRSP from which you want to make the LLP withdrawal? ________

I certify that the information given in Part 1 of this form is correct and complete.

____________ Signature of participant ________ Date

### Part 2 – To be completed by the RRSP issuer

- **Do not** send us a copy of this form. However, keep one for your records.
- Withhold tax if the total of lines A and B above exceeds $10,000, or if the total of lines A, B, and C above exceeds $20,000, withhold tax only on the excess.
- Report the amount withdrawn in box 25 of a T4RSP slip issued in the name of the RRSP annuitant for the year of the withdrawal.
- For more information on how to report LLP withdrawals, see Guide T4079, *T4RSP and T4RIF Guide*.

| RRSP issuer's name | | | |
|---|---|---|---|
| Address | City | Province or territory | Postal code |
| Phone number | Amount withdrawn | Date of withdrawal YYYY MM DD | |

RC96E (09) Privacy Act Personal Information Bank Number CRA PPU 005
(Ce formulaire existe en français) Canada

**LIFELONG LEARNING PLAN (LLP)**
**CANCELLING A WITHDRAWAL MADE IN ______**
**(year)**

Complete this form to tell us that you are cancelling an LLP withdrawal. Complete the title by writing the year you made the withdrawal on the blank line.

You can only cancel a withdrawal if you met the LLP rules when you made the withdrawal. The reasons listed below are the only acceptable ones for cancelling an LLP withdrawal. Please tick ( ) the box beside the reason that applies to you.

☐ The student was not enrolled in the qualifying educational program when you made the withdrawal and did not enrol in time.

☐ The student left the program before April of the year after the withdrawal, and 75% or more of the tuition was refundable.

☐ You became a non-resident of Canada before the end of the year in which you made the withdrawal.

You can cancel a withdrawal by repaying the amount you withdrew from your RRSP. You can make your cancellation payment to any of your RRSPs, or open a new RRSP. If you do not repay all the funds you withdrew, you have to include the unpaid amounts in your income for the year they were withdrawn.

**Information about the RRSP owner (this is the individual who made the RRSP withdrawal)**

| Last name | First name and initials | Social insurance number |
|---|---|---|
| Address | | |

| City | Province or territory | Postal code | Telephone number |
|---|---|---|---|
| | | | |

| Amount you withdrew | Amount of cancellation payment | Date of cancellation payment |
|---|---|---|
| $ | $ | Year / Month / Day |

______________________________
RRSP owner's signature

Send this form and your official RRSP contribution receipt to: Pension and RRSP Processing Group
Ottawa Technology Centre
875 Heron Road
Ottawa ON K1A 1A2

## For more information

### Contact us

In this publication, we use plain language to explain the most common tax situations. If you need more information after reading the guide, visit our LLP Web site at **www.cra.gc.ca** or contact us at **1-800-959-8281**.

### Teletypewriter (TTY) users

TTY users can call **1-800-665-0354** for bilingual assistance during regular business hours.

### My Account

My Account is a secure, convenient, and time-saving way to access and manage your tax and benefit information online, seven days a week! If you are not registered with My Account but need information right away, use **Quick Access** to get fast, easy and secure access to some of your information now. For more information, go to **www.cra.gc.ca/myaccount** or see Pamphlet RC4059, *My Account for individuals*.

### Forms and publications

To get any forms and publications, go to **www.cra.gc.ca/forms**, or call **1-800-959-2221**.

#### Forms

| | |
|---|---|
| Schedule 7 | *RRSP Unused Contributions, Transfers, and HBP or LLP Activities* |
| RC96 | *Lifelong Learning Plan (LLP) Request to Withdraw Funds from an RRSP* |
| T2202 | *Education and Textbook Amount Certificate* |

#### Publications

| | |
|---|---|
| RC4135 | *Home Buyers' Plan (HBP)* |
| RC4059 | *My Account for Individuals* |

### Your opinion counts

If you have any comments or suggestions that could help us improve our publications, we would like to hear from you. Please send your comments to:

**Taxpayer Services Directorate**
**Canada Revenue Agency**
**750 Heron Road**
**Ottawa ON K1A 0L5**

# Death of a RRIF Annuitant (Information Sheet RC4178)

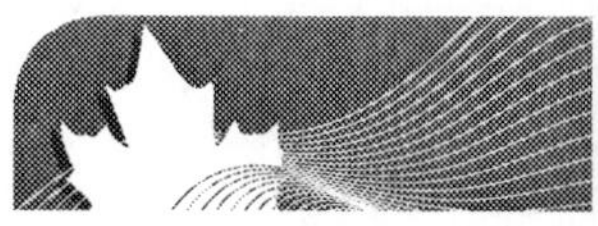

## Death of a RRIF Annuitant

A RRIF annuitant is the owner of a RRIF. This information sheet explains the taxation of registered retirement income fund (RRIF) amounts when the annuitant dies. It explains how they are reported, and the options that are available to reduce or defer the tax liability resulting from the annuitant's death.

**Under proposed changes**, as of July 1, 2011, for deaths occurring after March 3, 2010, the existing registered retirement savings plan (RRSP) rollover rules will be extended to allow a rollover of a deceased individual's RRSP proceeds to the RDSP of the deceased individual's financially dependent infirm child or grandchild. These proposed rules will also apply for amounts transferred to an RDSP from registered retirement income fund (RRIF) proceeds and certain lump-sum amounts paid from registered pension plans (RPP).

In addition, where the death of an RRSP annuitant occurs after 2007 and before 2011, special transitional rules will allow a contribution to be made to the RDSP of a financially dependent infirm child or grandchild of the annuitant that will provide a similar result to the proposed measures. It is important to note that in order to be eligible, the contribution to an RDSP can only be made **after June 30, 2011** and, where the death of the annuitant occurs after 2007 and before 2011, the contribution must be made before 2012, i.e. individuals will have six months in which to make the contribution to an RDSP.

For updated information on these proposed changes, go to **www.cra.gc.ca/rdsp**.

## Slips issued by the RRIF issuer

The chart below shows how the RRIF carrier generally prepares the slips that report the amounts paid out or considered to have been received from a deceased annuitant's RRIF.

**Chart 1 – How the RRIF carrier generally prepares the slips that report the amounts paid out of a deceased annuitant's RRIF**

| | | | |
|---|---|---|---|
| **Period** | Day the annuitant died* | **From** the day after the day the annuitant died **to** December 31 of the year after the year of death | **From** January 1 of the year after the period described in the previous column **to** the date the RRIF property is distributed |
| **Amount** | Fair market value (FMV) of the RRIF | Income earned in the RRIF during this period | Income earned in the RRIF during this period |
| **How the RRIF carrier generally reports the amount** | We consider that the annuitant received this amount at the time of death, so the amount is reported in box 18 of a T4RIF slip issued in the same of the annuitant for the year of death. This slip also shows any other amounts the annuitant received in the year. | ■ If the annuitant's spouse or common-law partner is named as a beneficiary in the RRIF contract, income paid to that beneficiary is reported in box 16 of a T4RIF slip issued in his or her name, for the year of payment.<br>■ For all other beneficiaries named in the RRIF contract or the annuitant's estate (if no beneficiary is named), income paid is reported in box 22 of a T4RIF slip for the year of payment. | **Depositary RRIF** – Income is paid to the beneficiaries named in the RRIF contract or the annuitant's estate (if no beneficiary is named) and reported in box 13 of a T5 slip issued to each beneficiary or the estate, for the year in which the income is credited or added to the deposit.<br>**Trusteed RRIF** – Income is paid to the beneficiaries named in the RRIF contract or the annuitant's estate (if no beneficiary is named) and reported in boxes 22 and 36 of a T4RIF slip issued to each beneficiary or the estate, for the year of payment.**<br>**Insured RRIF** – Income is paid to the beneficiaries named in the RRIF contract or the annuitant's estate (if no beneficiary is named) and reported in the same way as described in the previous column. |

The shaded areas represent amounts that qualify as a **designated benefit** if received by a **qualified beneficiary** (see the definitions on the next page). If you do not know the type of RRIF the annuitant has, or need a breakdown of the amount reported in box 22, contact the fund carrier.

* Two exceptions to the reporting requirement are provided where the spouse or common-law partner is the successor annuitant or the sole beneficiary of the RRIF. See the next page for details.

** Only the part of the income earned in this period that is not taxable to the RRIF trust is reported to the beneficiary. A beneficiary will not have to pay tax on any part of the amount he or she receives, to the extent that it can reasonably be regarded as having been included in the RRIF trust's income.

RC4178 (E) Rev. 10

La version française de cette publication est intitulée *Décès du rentier d'un FERR*.

Canada Revenue Agency Agence du revenu du Canada

Canada

## General rule – deceased annuitant

When the annuitant of a RRIF dies, we consider that the annuitant received, immediately before death, an amount equal to the FMV of all the property held in the RRIF at the time of death. This amount and all other amounts the annuitant received from the RRIF during the year have to be reported on the annuitant's return for the year of death.

A beneficiary will not have to pay tax on any payment made out of the RRIF if it can reasonably be regarded as having been included in the deceased annuitant's income.

**Exception 1 – Spouse or common-law partner as successor annuitant** – We **do not** consider the deceased annuitant to have received an amount at the time of death if the RRIF contract or the annuitant's will names his or her spouse or common-law partner as the successor annuitant of the RRIF. In this situation, the RRIF continues and the spouse or common-law partner becomes the successor annuitant. All payments made out of the RRIF after the date the annuitant died become payable to that successor annuitant. The successor annuitant will receive a T4RIF slip for the year of death (if applicable) and for future years showing the payments he or she received. The successor annuitant has to report the payments on his or her tax return for the year they are received.

If the spouse or common-law partner is not named as the successor annuitant, he or she can still be considered as a successor annuitant if the deceased annuitant's legal representative consents to the designation and the RRIF carrier agrees. For common-law partners of the same sex, this only applies if the annuitant died after 1997.

**Exception 2 – Spouse or common-law partner is the sole beneficiary of the RRIF** – We **do not** consider the deceased annuitant to have received an amount from the RRIF at the time of death if the annuitant had a spouse or common-law partner when he or she died and **both** the following conditions are met:

- the spouse or common-law partner is named in the RRIF contract as the **sole** beneficiary of the RRIF; and
- by December 31 of the year following the year of death, the entire eligible part of the RRIF property is directly transferred to an RRSP or RRIF under which the spouse or common-law partner is the annuitant, or to an issuer to buy an eligible annuity for the spouse or common-law partner.

If **both** these conditions are met, only the spouse or common-law partner will receive a T4RIF slip. The total amount that was paid out of the RRIF will be shown in box 16 of the slip, and the part that was transferred will be shown in box 24 of the slip. The amount shown in box 16 has to be reported on line 115 of the spouse's or common-law partner's tax return for the year the transfer was made. The spouse or common-law partner will receive an official receipt for the amount that was transferred. To find out how to claim a deduction for the transfer, see "Qualified beneficiaries – transfers" on the next page.

## General rule – beneficiaries of the RRIF

Amounts paid from the RRIF, which represent income earned in the RRIF after the date the annuitant died, have to be reported by the beneficiaries named in the RRIF contract or the annuitant's estate (if no beneficiary is named). These payments have to be included in the income of the beneficiaries or the estate for the year they are received. Chart 1 on the first page shows how RRIF carriers usually prepare the slips that report the amounts paid out of a deceased annuitant's RRIF.

## Optional reporting

Read this section if neither of the exceptions described above applies.

If a **qualified beneficiary** (see below) **receives** an amount from a deceased annuitant's RRIF that qualifies as a **designated benefit** (see below), the annuitant's legal representative can claim a reduction to the amount we consider that the annuitant received at the time of death.

The reduction, which is determined by completing Chart 2 on page 4, allows for a redistribution of the annuitant's income to the qualified beneficiary who actually received it. This redistribution of income allows the deceased annuitant and the qualified beneficiary to pay the least amount of tax the law allows.

If none of the payments out of the RRIF are made to a qualified beneficiary or designated as a designated benefit, the amount we consider that the annuitant received at the time of death cannot be reduced.

**Qualified beneficiary** – A **qualified beneficiary** is the deceased annuitant's spouse or common-law partner, or a financially dependent child or grandchild. A child or grandchild of a deceased annuitant is generally considered financially dependent on that annuitant at the time of death if, before that person's death, the child or grandchild ordinarily resided with and dependent on the annuitant and they meet one of the following conditions:

- the child or grandchild's net income for the previous year (shown on line 236 of their return) was less than the basic personal amount (line 300 from Schedule 1) for that previous year; or
- the child or grandchild is infirm and their net income for the previous year was equal to or less than the basic personal amount **plus** the disability amount (line 316 from Schedule 1) for that previous year.

If, before the annuitant's death, the child or grandchild is away from home because they were attending school, we still consider them to have resided with the annuitant.

If the child or grandchild's net income was **more** than **the amounts described above**, we will **not** consider them to be financially dependent on the annuitant at the time of death, unless they can establish the contrary. In such a case, the child or grandchild or the legal representative should submit a request in writing to the child or grandchild's tax services office outlining the reasons why we should consider them to be financially dependent on the annuitant at the time of death.

**Designated benefit** – A **designated benefit** out of a RRIF is any of the amounts shown in the shaded areas of Chart 1 on first page if paid to a qualified beneficiary. If these amounts are paid to the annuitant's estate, they will qualify as a designated benefit if **both** the following conditions are met:

- there is a qualified beneficiary who is a beneficiary of the annuitant's estate; and
- the annuitant's legal representative and the qualified beneficiary jointly file Form T1090, *Death of a RRIF Annuitant – Designated Benefit*, to designate all or part of the amounts paid to the estate as a designated benefit received by the qualified beneficiary.

Sometimes there can be an **increase** in the value of a RRIF between the date of death and the date of the final distribution to the beneficiary or estate. Generally, this amount has to be included in the income of the beneficiary or the estate for the year it is received. A T4RIF slip may be issued for this amount. For more information, see Chart 7 – Amounts from a deceased annuitant's RRIF, in Chapter 4 of Guide T4040, *RRSPs and Other Registered Plans for Retirement*.

If there is a **decrease** in the value of a RRIF **between** the date of death and the date of the final distribution after 2008 to the beneficiary or the estate, the deceased's legal representative can request the amount of the decrease be carried back and deducted on the deceased's final return through a reassessment. However, if the final distribution is made in the year of death, the deduction will be claimed when filing the final return. The deduction is claimed on line 232 of the *T1 General Income Tax and Benefit Return*.

The amount of that deduction is the total of:

- the part of the FMV of the RRIF at the time of death included in the deceased annuitant's income as a result of the annuitant's death;
- all amounts received after the annuitant's death that have been included in the recipient's income as a taxable payment from the RRIF other than "tax-paid amounts"; and
- all "tax-paid amount" (see box 36 of T4RIF slip);

**MINUS**

- the total of all amounts distributed from the RRIF after the death of the annuitant.

Generally, the deduction will not be available if the RRIF held a non-qualified investment after the annuitant dies or if the final distribution is made after the end of the year that follows the year in which the annuitant died. However, this rule may be waived to allow the deduction to deceased annuitants on a case-by-case basis.

If a RRIF experiences a post-death decline in value, and the exceptional reporting described starting at exception 1 does not apply, the financial institution that holds the RRIF will issue Form RC249, *Post-Death Decline in the Value of an Unmatured RRSP or a RRIF – Final Distribution Made in 20___*.

This form will be issued to the executor of the deceased annuitant's estate for the year in which the final distribution is made.

## Qualified beneficiaries – transfers

When a qualified beneficiary includes a designated benefit in income, he or she can defer paying tax on the eligible part of it by transferring it to an RRSP or RRIF, or to an issuer to buy an eligible annuity. See the definitions of **qualified beneficiary** and **designated benefit** in the previous section. To determine the **eligible part of a designated benefit**, which is the amount that can be transferred, complete Chart 3 on page 5.

The following chart shows the transfers that different qualified beneficiaries can choose.

| Designated benefit paid to: | Can be transferred to: | | |
|---|---|---|---|
| | RRSP* | RRIF | Annuity |
| ■ the annuitant's spouse or common-law partner | ✔ | ✔ | ✔ |
| ■ the annuitant's financially dependent child or grandchild who: | | | |
| – was dependent because of a physical or mental impairment | ✔ | ✔ | ✔ |
| – was dependent but **not** because of a physical or mental impairment | | | ✔** |

* The qualified beneficiary must be 71 years of age or younger at the end of the year the transfer is made.

** The annuity can provide for payments based on a period of not more than 18 years minus the child's or grandchild's age at the time the annuity was purchased. The payments from the annuity have to begin no later than one year after the purchase.

The transfer or purchase has to be completed in the year the designated benefit is received or within 60 days after the end of the year. If the qualified beneficiary is 71 years of age in the year the designated benefit is received, the transfer to an RRSP must be completed by December 31 of that year.

The carrier or issuer who receives the transferred funds will issue an official receipt to the qualified beneficiary. The beneficiary can use the receipt to claim a deduction on his or her tax return for the year the designated benefit was received.

The following chart shows where on the tax return the beneficiary should claim the deduction.

| Designated benefit transferred to: | Claim deduction on: | |
|---|---|---|
| | line 208 | line 232 |
| an RRSP | ✔ | |
| a RRIF | | ✔ |
| an annuity | | ✔ |

**Example**
Sarah died in December 2008 at the age of 67.

- The FMV of her trusteed RRIF at the time of death was $150,000.
- The FMV of the RRIF on December 31, 2009, was $160,000.
- The distribution of the RRIF property was delayed until 2010.

The RRIF contract named Sarah's husband, Dan, as the sole beneficiary of the RRIF. On June 30, 2010, he received $165,000 from the RRIF carrier.

Dan, who is also the legal representative of Sarah's estate, received the following slips from the RRIF carrier:

- a 2010 T4RIF slip issued in his name, showing $10,000 in box 16 and $5,000 in boxes 22 and 36.
- a 2008 T4RIF slip issued in Sarah's name, showing $150,000 in box 18. Although Dan is the sole beneficiary of the RRIF, the slip was issued to Sarah because both conditions listed in Exception 2 and under the section called "General rule – deceased annuitant", on page 2, were not met.

Had Sarah not died, the minimum payment under the RRIF for 2010 would have been $6,000. Dan decides that it would be beneficial to request a reduction to the amount Sarah is considered to have received from her RRIF. This would allow him to shift some of her income onto his return.

After completing Chart 2, Dan decides to claim a $130,000 reduction. This reduces the amount reported on line 115 of Sarah's 2008 return to $20,000 ($150,000 – $130,000). Because the FMV of the RRIF at the time of death was included in Sarah's income for 2008, Dan has to write a letter to request an adjustment to that year's return. Dan is required to report $145,000 ($130,000 + $10,000 + $5,000) on line 115 of his 2010 return.

To minimize his 2010 taxes, he decides to transfer the eligible part of his designated benefit to his RRIF. The amount that qualifies as a designated benefit is $140,000 ($145,000 – $5,000). Dan completes Chart 3 on the last page, and determines that he can transfer $134,000 to his RRIF. He claims a $134,000 deduction on line 232 of his 2010 return.

| **Chart 2 – How to calculate the reduction to the amount we consider that the deceased annuitant received at death**<br>Complete a separate calculation for each RRIF belonging to the deceased annuitant. | | | **Example from the previous page** |
|---|---|---|---|
| 1. Enter the amount shown in box 18 of the T4RIF slip issued to the annuitant for the year of death. | $ | 1 | $ 150,000 1 |
| 2. Enter the FMV of the RRIF on the later of the following dates (you may need to contact the deceased annuitant's RRIF carrier to determine these amounts):<br>■ December 31 of the year after the year the annuitant died; or<br>■ the end of the day the last time a designated benefit was paid out of the RRIF. | $ | 2 | $ 0 2 |
| 3. Enter the total of all amounts paid out of the RRIF after the annuitant died. | + $ | 3 | + $ 165,000 3 |
| 4. **Add** lines 2 and 3. | = $ | 4 | = $ 165,000 4 |
| 5. Enter the amount from either line 1 or line 4, **whichever is less**. | – $ | 5 | – $ 150,000 5 |
| 6. Line 4 **minus** line 5. | = $ | 6 | = $ 15,000 6 |
| 7. Enter the total of the following amounts:<br>■ amount designated as a designated benefit on each Form T1090 filed for the RRIF;<br>■ the part of the amounts shown in box 36 of all T4RIF slips and box 13 of all T5 slips issued in the name of the estate that the qualified beneficiaries are entitled to receive from the estate;<br>■ amounts shown in boxes 16 and 22 of all T4RIF slips and box 13 of all T5 slips issued to qualified beneficiaries;<br>■ the part of the amount shown in box 36 of all T4RIF slips that were issued to the qualified beneficiaries that is not required to be included in income (contact the deceased annuitant's RRIF carrier to determine these amounts); and<br>■ the part of the amount shown in box 18 of the T4RIF slip that was issued to the deceased annuitant for the year of death and that the qualified beneficiaries are entitled to receive. | $ | 7 | $ 165,000 7 |
| 8. Enter the result of the following calculation:<br>1 – ( $ (amount from line 6) / $ (amount from line 4) ) | × | 8 | × 0.909091* 8 |
| 9. Maximum reduction to the amount we consider that the deceased annuitant received at the time of death (line 7 **multiplied** by line 8). The reduction can be any amount, from zero to the amount on this line. | = $ | 9 | = $ 150,000 9 |
| If the reduction is claimed in the year the annuitant died, the legal representative has to attach a letter to the annuitant's return for that year to explain how the amount included in income was calculated.<br>If the reduction is claimed after the year of death, the legal representative has to write us a letter requesting an adjustment to the annuitant's return for the year of death. | | | * Calculation of line 8<br>1 – ( $ 15,000 / $ 165,000 ) |

**Chart 3 – How to calculate the eligible part of a designated benefit**

Complete a separate calculation for each RRIF of the deceased annuitant, for each year in which a designated benefit is paid and transferred, and for each beneficiary who receives a designated benefit. You may have to contact the deceased annuitant's RRIF carrier to determine certain amounts.

| | | Line | Example from the previous page | |
|---|---|---|---|---|
| 1. Enter the total of all amounts included in the income of **all** qualified beneficiaries for the year as a designated benefit from this RRIF. | $ | 1 | $ 140,000 | 1 |
| 2. Enter the minimum amount that is required to be paid from this RRIF for the year. | $ | 2 | $ 6,000 | 2 |
| 3. Enter the amount from line 2, or the total of the amounts the deceased annuitant received from this RRIF during the year and included in income, **whichever is less.** | – $ | 3 | – $ 0 | 3 |
| 4. Line 2 **minus** line 3. | = $ | 4 | = $ 6,000 | 4 |
| 5. Enter the part of all designated benefits from this RRIF that is included in the beneficiary's income for the year. | $ | 5 | $ 140,000 | 5 |
| 6. Enter the result of the following calculation: $1 - \left(\frac{\$\_\_\_\_ \text{ (amount from line 4)}}{\$ \text{ (amount from line 1)}}\right)$ | × | 6 | × 0.957143* | 6 |
| 7. Eligible part of the designated benefit that can be transferred (line 5 **multiplied** by line 6) | = $ | 7 | = $ 134,000 | 7 |

* Calculation of line 6

$$1 - \left(\frac{\$\ 6{,}000}{\$\ 140{,}000}\right)$$

## For more information

### What if you need help?

If you need help after reading this guide, visit **www.cra.gc.ca** or call **1-800-959-8281**.

### Forms and publications

To get any forms or publications, go to **www.cra.gc.ca/forms** or call **1-800-959-2221**.

### My Account

My Account is a secure, convenient, and time-saving way to access and manage your tax and benefit information online, seven days a week! Discover all that My Account can do for you. Take the tour at **www.cra.gc.ca/myaccount** or see Pamphlet RC4059, *My Account for individuals*.

### TIPS (Tax Information Phone Service)

For personal and general tax information by telephone, use our automated service, TIPS, by calling **1-800-267-6999**.

### Teletypewriter (TTY) users

TTY users can call **1-800-665-0354** for bilingual assistance during regular business hours.

### Our service complaint process

If you are not satisfied with the **service** you have received, contact the CRA employee you have been dealing with (or call the phone number you have been given). If you still disagree with the way your concerns are being addressed, ask to discuss the matter with the employee's supervisor.

If the matter is still not resolved, you have the right to file a service complaint by completing Form RC193, *Service-Related Complaint*. If you are still not satisfied with the way the CRA has handled your complaint, you can contact the Taxpayers' Ombudsman.

For more information, go to **www.cra.gc.ca/complaints** or see Booklet RC4420, *Information on CRA – Service Complaints*.

### Related forms and publications

**Forms**

| | |
|---|---|
| 5005-R | T1 *General Income Tax and Benefit Return* |
| RC193 | *Service-Related Complaint* |
| RC249 | *Post-Death Decline in the Value of an Unmatured RRSP or a RRIF – Final Distribution made in 20___* |
| T1090 | *Death of a RRIF Annuitant – Designated Benefit for Year 20__* |

**Publications**

| | |
|---|---|
| 5000-G | *General Income Tax and Benefit Guide* |
| RC4059 | *My Account for individuals* |
| RC4420 | *Information on CRA – Service Complaints.* |
| T4040 | *RRSP and Other Registered Plans for Retirement* |

## Your opinion counts

If you have any comments or suggestions that could help us improve our publications, we would like to hear from you. Please send your comments to:

**Taxpayer Services Directorate**
**Canada Revenue Agency**
**750 Heron Road**
**Ottawa ON K1A 0L5**

Canada Revenue Agency

# Designation of an Exempt Contribution Tax-Free Savings Account (Form RC240)

Canada Revenue Agency | Agence du revenu du Canada

**DESIGNATION OF AN EXEMPT CONTRIBUTION TAX-FREE SAVINGS ACCOUNT (TFSA)**

**General information**

Complete this form if you are the recipient of a **survivor payment** and you wish to contribute all or a portion of it to your own TFSA, designating the contribution as an **exempt contribution**. This form will help you determine the maximum amount that may be designated as an **exempt contribution**. Many of the terms used on this form are explained below.

Generally, if the deceased holder had an **excess TFSA amount** at the time of death, if payments are being received by more than one **survivor**, or if the **survivor payment** and/or the contribution is made after the **rollover period**, **no** amount of the **survivor payment** may be designated as an **exempt contribution**. For more information on the **excess TFSA amount**, or how to determine whether one exists in the deceased's TFSA, go to **www.cra.gc.ca/tfsa** or call **1-800-959-8281**. Call us to find out whether a designation can still be made if an **excess TFSA amount** does exist, if a payment was made to more than one **survivor**, or if the **survivor payment** and/or the contribution is made after the **rollover period**.

In addition, to complete this form you have to obtain from the executor of the estate, or possibly from the TFSA issuer, the fair market value (FMV), at the time of the **holder**'s death, of the TFSA from which the **survivor payment** was received. If the deceased holder had more than one TFSA, a separate form will be required in order to designate each TFSA contribution as an **exempt contribution**.

Once you have completed Part 3 and, if required, Part 4, to determine the **maximum** amount that you can contribute and designate as an **exempt contribution**, fill in the amount you wish to designate in Part 5.

**Note**: It is not necessary to complete this form if you have become the **successor holder** of the TFSA of your deceased spouse or common-law partner.

Submit this completed form to the Canada Revenue Agency within **30 days** of making the contribution listed in Part 5. Send the form to: **TFSA Processing Unit, PO Box 9768 STN T, Ottawa ON K1G 3X9.**

**Part 1 – Survivor TFSA holder information (print)**

| Last name | First name and initial(s) | Social Insurance Number |
|---|---|---|
| Address | | |
| City | Province or Territory | Postal code |

**Part 2 – Deceased TFSA holder information (print)**

| Last name | First name and initial(s) | | | Social Insurance Number |
|---|---|---|---|---|
| Address | | TFSA contract or account number | | Name of TFSA Issuer |
| City | Province or Territory | Postal code | Date of holder's death (Year, Month, Day) | FMV of TFSA at time of death $ |

**Part 3 – Calculation of the amount that may be designated as an exempt contribution**

Date the survivor payment was received. ____________ (YYYY/MM/DD) Amount of the survivor payment received. $ ____________

| | | |
|---|---|---|
| Total survivor payments received to date from the TFSA entered in Part 2 | $ | 1 |
| Total of any previous designations related to the payments on line 1 | $ – | 2 |
| Line 1 **minus** line 2. | $ = | **A** |
| Fair market value (FMV) of the deceased holder's TFSA at the time of death from Part 2 | $ | 3 |
| Total of any previous designations related to the payments on line 1 | $ – | 4 |
| Line 3 **minus** line 4. | $ = | **B** |
| Enter the **lesser** amount from lines A or B. | $ | **C** |

If the deceased holder did not have an **excess TFSA amount**, you were the only person to receive **survivor payments** from the TFSA and the contribution is made within the **rollover period**, continue to Part 5.

**However, if the deceased holder had an excess TFSA amount and you received the authorization from us to designate an amount, continue to Part 4.**

RC240 E (11) (Vous pouvez obtenir ce formulaire en français à **www.arc.gc.ca** ou au **1-800-959-3376**.) Canada

**Part 4 – Complete this part according to CRA instructions when the TFSA of the deceased holder includes an excess TFSA amount**

Fair market value of **all** deceased holder's TFSAs at date of death that ceased to be a TFSA.......... $ ____________ 5

Excess TFSA amount included in line 5.................................... $ ____________ 6

Total of **all** previous designations related to **any** of the deceased holder's TFSAs.......................................................... $ + ____________ 7

Line 6 **plus** line 7. $ = ____________ 8 ▶ $ – ____________ 8

Line 5 **minus** line 8. $ = ____________ D

**Part 5 – Designation of exempt contribution and certification**

If Part 4 **does not apply**, enter the amount from line C in Part 3.
In this situation, this is the maximum amount eligible to be designated as an exempt contribution. $ ____________

If Part 4 **does apply**, enter the **lesser** of line C in Part 3 and line D in Part 4.
In this situation, this is the maximum amount eligible to be designated as an exempt contribution. $ ____________

**I designate the following amounts as an exempt contribution to a TFSA of which I am the holder.**

| Date the exempt contribution was made | Amount of exempt contribution | Survivor TFSA contract number |
|---|---|---|
| ____________ | $ ____________ | ____________ |
| ____________ | $ ____________ | ____________ |
| ____________ | $ ____________ | ____________ |

**I certify that the information given on this form is, to the best of my knowledge, correct and complete.**

| Survivor Signature | Date | Telephone number |
|---|---|---|
| ____________ | ____________ | ____________ |

**Definitions**

An **excess TFSA amount** is the total of all contributions made by the **holder** to all their TFSAs at a particular time in the calendar year, excluding a **qualifying transfer** or an exempt contribution; **minus**:

- the unused TFSA contribution room at the end of the preceding calendar year;
- the total of all withdrawals made under the holder's TFSA in the preceding calendar year, other than a **qualifying transfer**;
- for a resident of Canada at any time in the year, the TFSA dollar limit for the calendar year; for any other case, nil; and
- the total of all withdrawals made in the calendar year under all TFSAs of the **holder**, other than a **qualifying transfer** or withdrawals that are more than the excess TFSA amount determined at that time.

For distributions (withdrawals) occuring after October 16, 2009, a distribution from a TFSA that is a **specified distribution** cannot reduce or eliminate an individual's excess TFSA amount.

An **exempt contribution** is a contribution made during the **rollover period** and designated as exempt by the **survivor** in prescribed form in connection with a payment received from the deceased holder's TFSA.

A TFSA **holder** is the individual who entered into the TFSA and, after their death, the individual's surviving spouse or common-law partner and, **under proposed legislation**, subsequent survivors, if designated as the **successor holder** of the TFSA. A **successor holder** designation is effective only if it is permitted under applicable provincial and territorial law and only if the survivor acquired all of the deceased holder's rights under the TFSA including the right to revoke any previous beneficiary designation.

A **qualifying transfer** is a direct transfer between a **holder**'s TFSAs, or a direct transfer between a **holder**'s TFSA and the TFSA of their current or former spouse or common-law partner if the transfer relates to payments under a decree, order or judgment of a court, or under a written agreement, relating to a division of property in settlement of rights arising from the breakdown of their relationship and they are living separate and apart at the time of the transfer.

The **rollover period** is the period that begins when the holder of the TFSA dies and ends at the end of the calendar year that follows the year of death.

A **specified distribution** is a distribution from a TFSA that is reasonably attributable to certain TFSA amounts that are subject to tax.

A **survivor** is an individual who is, immediately before the TFSA **holder**'s death, a spouse or common-law partner of the **holder**.

A **survivor payment** refers to a payment received by a **survivor** during the **rollover period**, as a consequence of the **holder**'s death, directly or indirectly out of or under an arrangement that ceased, because of the holder's death, to be a TFSA.

If you need more information regarding distributions or payments, go to **www.cra.gc.ca/tfsa**, or see RC4466, *Tax-Free Savings Account (TFSA), Guide for Individuals.*

*Privacy Act*, Personal Information Bank Number Tax-Free Savings Account PPU 054

## Tax-Free Savings Account Guide for Individuals (Guide RC4466)

# Tax-Free Savings Account (TFSA), Guide for Individuals

RC4466(E) Rev. 11

Canada

## Before you start

### Is this guide for you?

This guide is intended for individuals who have opened or who are considering opening a Tax-Free Savings Account (TFSA). It provides general background on what this new investment opportunity is, who is eligible to open one, contribution limits, possible tax situations, non-resident implications, transfers on marriage or relationship breakdown, extensive coverage on what happens when a TFSA **holder** dies, and various other topics. For additional information on the TFSA, go to **www.cra.gc.ca/tfsa**.

This guide does not deal with every tax situation. It is not intended to cover all possible situations or to replace professional financial, tax or estate planning services. As with making any other important investment decisions, you should speak with your financial advisor or a representative at your financial institution to ensure you are aware of any conditions, limitations, or administrative fees which may be applicable.

### Definitions

We have included definitions of some of the terms used in this guide in the "Definitions" section starting on page 4. You may want to read this before you start.

If you have a visual impairment, you can get our publications in braille, large print, etext (CD or diskette), or MP3 by going to **www.cra.gc.ca/alternate** or by calling **1-800-959-2221**. You can also get your personalized correspondence in these formats by calling **1-800-959-8281**.

## What's new?

### Advantage

Effective October 17, 2009, an "advantage" also includes any earnings and gains reasonably attributable to deliberate over-contributions, prohibited investments, asset transfer (swap) transactions and specified non-qualified investments.

### Specified distribution

For distributions (withdrawals) occurring after October 17, 2009, a distribution from a TFSA that is a specified distribution cannot reduce or eliminate an individual's excess TFSA amount nor increase the unused TFSA contribution room in the following year.

### Holder

**Under proposed changes**, a subsequent survivor to the holder may be considered a TFSA holder if designated as the successor holder of the TFSA.

La version française de cette publication est intitulée *Guide du Compte d'épargne libre d'impôt (CELI) pour les particuliers*.

www.cra.gc.ca

## Table of Contents

## Definitions

**Advantage** – an advantage is any benefit, loan or debt that depends on the existence of the TFSA other than: TFSA distributions, administrative or investment services in connection with a TFSA, loans on arm's length terms, and payments or allocations to the TFSA by the issuer, including bonus interest and other reasonable payments to the TFSA by the issuer.

An advantage also includes any benefit that is an increase in the fair market value (FMV) of the TFSA that can reasonably be considered attributable, directly or indirectly, to one of the following elements:

- a transaction or event (or a series of transactions or events) that would not have occurred in an open market between arm's length parties acting prudently, knowledgeably and willingly and one of the main purpose of which is to enable the holder (or another person or partnership) to benefit from the tax-exempt status of the TFSA; or
- a payment received in substitution for either:
  - a payment for services rendered by the holder or a person not at arm's length with the holder; or
  - a payment of a return on investment or proceeds of disposition in respect of property held outside of the TFSA by the holder or a person not at arm's length with the holder.

**Note**
If the advantage is extended by the issuer of the TFSA, or by a person with whom the issuer is not dealing at arm's length, the issuer, and not the holder of the TFSA, is liable to pay the tax in respect of the advantage.

For transactions occurring after October 16, 2009, an advantage also includes:

- any benefit that is an increase in the FMV of the TFSA that can reasonably be considered attributable, directly or indirectly; to
  - a swap transaction; or
  - specified non-qualified investment income that has not been distributed from the TFSA within 90 days of the holder of the TFSA receiving a notice from us requiring them to remove the amount from the TFSA; and
- any benefit that is income (including a capital gain) that is reasonably attributable, directly or indirectly, to a deliberate over-contribution to the TFSA or a prohibited investment in respect of any TFSA of the holder.

A **swap transaction** means a transfer of property (other than a contribution or distribution) occurring between the TFSA and the holder of the TFSA or a person not dealing at arm's length with the holder.

**Specified non-qualified investment income** means income (including a capital gain) that is reasonably attributable, directly or indirectly, to an amount that is taxable for any TFSA of the holder (for example, subsequent generation income earned on non-qualified investment income or on income from a business carried on by a TFSA.)

**Arm's length** – at arm's length is a concept describing a relationship in which the parties are acting independently of each other. The opposite, **not at arm's length**, includes individuals:

- related to each other by blood, marriage, adoption, and common-law relationships; or
- acting in concert without separate interests, such as those with close business ties.

An individual is not at arm's length with their TFSA.

**Common-law partner** – a person who is not the holder's **spouse**, with whom the holder is living in a conjugal relationship, and to whom at least one of the following situations applies. He or she:

a) has been living with the holder in such a relationship for at least 12 continuous months;

b) is the parent of the holder's child by birth or adoption; or

c) has custody and control of the holder's child (or had custody and control immediately before the child turned 19 years of age) and the child is wholly dependent on that person for support.

In addition, an individual immediately becomes the holder's common law partner if they previously lived together in a conjugal relationship for at least 12 continuous months and they have resumed living together in such a relationship. **Under proposed changes,** this condition will no longer exist. The effect of this proposed change is that a person (other than a person described in b) or c) above) will be a common law partner only after the current relationship with that person has lasted at least 12 continuous months. This proposed change will apply to 2001 and later years.

Reference to "12 continuous months" in this definition includes any period that they were separated for less than 90 days because of a breakdown in the relationship.

**Deliberate over-contribution** – a contribution made under a TFSA by an individual that results in, or increases, an excess TFSA amount, unless it is reasonable to conclude that the individual neither knew nor ought to have known that the contribution could result in liability for a tax or similar consequences. Income that is reasonably attributable, directly or indirectly, to a deliberate over-contribution constitutes an advantage subject to the special tax on advantages.

**Excess TFSA amount** – the total of all contributions made by the holder to all their TFSAs at a particular time in the calendar year, **excluding** a qualifying transfer or an exempt contribution,

MINUS:

- the unused TFSA contribution room at the end of the preceding calendar year;
- the total of all withdrawals made under the holder's TFSA in the preceding calendar year, other than a qualifying transfer;

- for a resident of Canada at any time in the year, the TFSA dollar limit for the calendar year; for any other case, nil; and
- the total of all withdrawals made in the calendar year under all TFSAs of the holder, other than a qualifying transfer or withdrawals that are more than the excess TFSA amount determined at that time.

For distributions (withdrawals) occurring after October 17, 2009, a distribution from a TFSA that is a specified distribution cannot reduce or eliminate an individual's excess TFSA amount.

**Exempt contribution** – a contribution made during the rollover period and designated as exempt by the survivor in prescribed form in connection with a payment received from the deceased holder's TFSA.

**Exempt period** – period that begins when the holder dies and that ends at the end of the first calendar year that begins after the holder's death, or when the trust ceases to exist, if earlier.

**Fair market value (FMV)** – this is usually the highest dollar value you can get for property in an open and unrestricted market between a willing buyer and a willing seller who are acting independently of each other. For information on the valuation of securities of closely-held corporations, see Information Circular IC89-3, *Policy Statement on Business Equity Valuations*.

**Holder** – the individual who entered into the TFSA and, after their death, the individual's surviving spouse or common-law partner and, **under proposed changes**, subsequent survivors, if designated as the successor holder of the TFSA. A **successor holder** designation is effective only if it is permitted under applicable provincial and territorial law and only if the survivor acquired all of the deceased holder's rights under the TFSA including the right to revoke any previous beneficiary designation.

**Issuer** – a trust company, a licensed annuities provider, a person who is, or is eligible to become, a member of the Canadian Payments Association or a credit union with which an individual has a qualifying arrangement.

**Non-qualified investment** – any property that is not a qualified investment for the trust. See the definition of "Qualified Investment" on this page.

**Prohibited investment** – this is an investment to which the TFSA holder is closely connected. It includes:

- a debt of the holder;
- a debt or equity investment in an entity in which the holder has a significant interest (generally a 10% or greater interest); and
- a debt or equity investment in an entity with which the holder, or an entity described in the previous bullet, does not deal at arm's length.

A prohibited investment does not include a mortgage loan that is insured by the Canada Mortgage and Housing Corporation (CMHC) or by an approved private insurer.

**Qualified donee** – the *Income Tax Act* permits qualified donees to issue official tax receipts for donations they receive from individuals or corporations. Some examples of qualified donees are registered charities, Canadian municipalities, registered Canadian amateur athletic associations, the United Nations or one of their agencies, or a university outside Canada that accepts Canadian students.

**Qualified investment** – common types of qualified investments include: money, guaranteed investment certificates (GICs), government and corporate bonds, mutual funds, and securities listed on a designated stock exchange. The types of investments that qualify for TFSAs are generally similar to those that qualify for registered retirement savings plans (RRSPs).

**Qualifying arrangement** – an arrangement that is entered into after 2008 between an issuer and an individual (other than a trust) who is at least 18 years of age, that is:

- an arrangement in trust with an issuer that is authorized in Canada to offer to the public its services as a trustee;
- an annuity contract with an issuer that is a licensed annuities provider; or
- a deposit with an issuer that is a person who is a member, or is eligible to be a member, of the Canadian Payments Association, or a credit union that is a shareholder or member of a "central" for the purposes of the *Canadian Payments Act*.

**Qualifying transfer** – a direct transfer between a holder's TFSAs, or a direct transfer between a holder's TFSA and the TFSA of their current or former spouse or common-law partner if the transfer relates to payments under a decree, order or judgment of a court, or under a written agreement relating to a division of property in settlement of rights arising from the breakdown of their relationship and they are living separate and apart at the time of the transfer.

**Qualifying portion of a withdrawal** – that portion of a withdrawal from a TFSA (excluding a qualifying transfer or a specified distribution), made in the year, which was required to reduce or eliminate a previously determined excess amount.

**Rollover period** – the period that begins when the holder dies and ends at the end of the calendar year that follows the year of death.

**Self-directed TFSA** – a vehicle which allows you to build and manage your own investment portfolio by buying and selling a variety of different types of investments.

**Specified distribution** – a distribution from a TFSA to the extent that it is, or is reasonably attributable to, an amount that is:

- an advantage;
- specified non-qualified investment income;
- income that is taxable in a TFSA trust; or
- income earned on excess contributions or non-resident contributions.

A specified distribution does not create or increase unused TFSA contribution room in the following year, nor does it reduce or eliminate an excess TFSA amount.

**Spouse** – an individual has a spouse when he or she is legally married.

**Successor holder** – see "Holder" on the previous page.

**Survivor** – a survivor is an individual who is, immediately before the TFSA holder's death, a spouse or common-law partner of the holder.

**Survivor payment** – a payment received by a survivor during the rollover period, as a consequence of the holder's death, directly or indirectly out of or under an arrangement that ceased, because of the holder's death, to be a TFSA.

**Unused TFSA contribution room** – the amount, either positive or negative, at the end of a particular calendar year after 2008, determined by the holder's unused TFSA contribution room at the end of the year preceding the particular year,

PLUS:

- the total amount of all withdrawals made under the holder's TFSA in the preceding calendar year, excluding a qualifying transfer or a specified distribution;
- the TFSA dollar limit for the particular year if, at some point in that year, the individual is at least 18 years old and a resident of Canada. In all other cases, the amount is nil.

MINUS:

- the total of all TFSA contributions made by the holder in the particular year excluding a qualifying transfer or an exempt contribution.

# Chapter 1 – What is a TFSA

A Tax-Free Savings Account (TFSA) is a new way to set money aside tax-free throughout your lifetime.

Contributions to a TFSA are not deductible for income tax purposes. The initial amount contributed as well as the income earned in the account (for example, investment income and capital gains) is tax-free, even when it is withdrawn.

Administrative or other fees in relation to a TFSA and any interest on money borrowed in order to contribute to a TFSA are not tax-deductible.

Management fees related to a TFSA trust paid by the holder do not constitute a contribution to the TFSA. The payment of investment counsel, transfer, or other fees by a TFSA trust will not result in a distribution (withdrawal) from the TFSA trust.

## Types of TFSAs

There are three different types of TFSAs that can be offered: a deposit, an annuity contract and an arrangement in trust.

Banks, insurance companies, credit unions, and trust companies can all issue TFSAs.

For more information about a certain type of TFSA, contact a TFSA issuer.

## Who is eligible to open a TFSA?

Any individual (other than a trust) who is 18 years of age or older and who has a valid Canadian social insurance number (SIN) is eligible to open a TFSA.

You cannot open a TFSA or contribute to one until you turn 18. However, when you turn 18, you will be able to contribute up to the full TFSA dollar limit for that year.

**Example**
Julie turns 18 years old on May 13, 2011. She will not be able to open and contribute to a TFSA until that date, however, as of May 13, 2011, she can open and contribute to a TFSA the full 2011 dollar limit of $5,000.

**Note**
In certain provinces and territories, the legal age at which an individual can enter into a contract (which would include opening a TFSA) is 19. In 2009 or later, in such jurisdictions, an 18-year-old who would be otherwise eligible, would accumulate $5,000 contribution room for that year and carry it over to the following year.

The account holder is the only person who can contribute to their TFSA. You can give your spouse or common-law partner money to contribute to their own TFSA without either that amount or any earnings on the amount being attributed back to you. The total of all contributions your spouse or common-law partner makes to their TFSA must not be more than their TFSA contribution room. For more information on TFSA contribution room, see "Chapter 2 – TFSA contribution room" on the next page.

## How to open a TFSA

To open a TFSA, you must contact your financial institution, credit union, or insurance company (issuer).

In order to become a TFSA holder, you will need to provide the issuer with your valid social insurance number (SIN) and date of birth so that the issuer can register your qualifying arrangement as a TFSA.

If you fail to provide this information or provide incorrect information to your issuer, this may cause the registration of your TFSA to be denied. If your TFSA is not registered, any income that is earned will have to be reported on your income tax return.

If the information that you provided to your issuer does not agree with CRA's records, your issuer may ask to see supporting documentation. If the information provided to your issuer is correct, you should contact us at **1-800-959-8281**.

You can set up a self-directed TFSA if you prefer to build and manage your own investment portfolio by buying and selling a variety of different types of investments. If you are considering this type of arrangement, you may want to consult with your financial institution.

## Chapter 2 – TFSA contribution room

Since January 1, 2009, Canadian residents who are 18 years of age or older with a valid social insurance number (SIN) are eligible to contribute up to $5,000 annually to a TFSA.

The $5,000 TFSA dollar limit is indexed based on the inflation rate. The indexed amount will be rounded to the nearest $500. For example, assuming that the inflation rate is 2% for 2010 and 2011, the TFSA dollar limit would be $5,000 for 2010 and 2011.

The TFSA contribution room is made up of:

- your TFSA dollar limit ($5,000 per year plus indexation, if applicable);
- any unused TFSA contribution room from the previous year; and
- any withdrawals made from the TFSA in the previous year, excluding qualifying transfers or specified distributions.

TFSA contribution room accumulates every year, if at any time in the calendar year you are 18 years of age or older and a resident of Canada. **You do not have to set up a TFSA or file a tax return to earn contribution room.**

If, for example, an individual who is 18 years or older in 2009 is not obligated to file a tax return until 2016, they would be considered to have accumulated TFSA contribution room for each year starting in 2009.

An individual will not accumulate TFSA contribution room for any year during which the individual is a non-resident of Canada throughout the entire year.

The TFSA dollar limit is not prorated in the year an individual:

- turns 18 years old;
- dies; or
- becomes a resident or a non-resident of Canada.

Investment income earned by, and/or changes in the value of TFSA investments will not affect your TFSA contribution room for the current or future years.

**Example**
John was eager to open his TFSA. He contributed the full $5,000 on January 2, 2009. On the advice of his broker, he had opened a self-directed TFSA and invested in stocks that overperformed the market. By the end of 2009, the value in John's TFSA had increased to $6,800. John was worried that for 2010, he would only be able to contribute $3,200 (the TFSA dollar limit of $5,000 for 2010 less the $1,800 increase in value in his TFSA through 2009). Neither the earnings generated in the account nor the increase in its value will reduce the TFSA contribution room in the following year, so John can contribute up to another $5,000 in 2010 to his TFSA.

**Note**
You can have more than one TFSA at any given time, as long as the total amount contributed to all your TFSAs during a year is not more than your available TFSA contribution room for that year.

## Determining your contribution room

The Canada Revenue Agency (CRA) will determine the TFSA contribution room for each eligible individual based on information provided by you and the TFSA issuers. Your TFSA contribution room will be shown on your income tax notice of assessment or a notice of reassessment.

However, if at the time we issue your notice of assessment or your notice of reassessment we have not received or finished processing the information from your TFSA issuer(s), the amount indicated may not reflect the correct amount. You should verify the amount indicated on your notice of assessment or your notice of reassessment to make sure it corresponds to your records. Contact us if you notice any discrepancies.

If you are not required to file an income tax return for the year, and decide not to do so, you will not receive a notice of assessment showing your TFSA contribution room. In that case, you should keep track of your available TFSA contribution room to ensure that your contributions do not exceed your limit.

**Example**
In March 2009, Jack contributed $5,000 to his TFSA. He did not make any other contributions and he did not withdraw any funds in 2009. His unused TFSA contribution room at the end of 2009 was zero.

His TFSA contribution room at the beginning of 2010 was $5,000 (his 2010 TFSA dollar limit).

On June 15, 2010, Jack made a contribution of $500. On October 26, 2010, he withdrew $4,000.

His unused TFSA contribution room at the end of 2010 was $4,500 ($5,000 – $500).

Jack makes the following calculation to determine his TFSA contribution room at the beginning of 2011:

**TFSA contribution room at the beginning of 2011**

| | | |
|---|---|---|
| TFSA contribution room at the beginning of 2010 | | $5,000 |
| Minus: Contributions made in 2010 | – | $500 |
| **Unused TFSA contribution room at the end of 2010** | | $4,500 |
| Plus: Total withdrawal made in 2010 | + | $4,000 |
| Plus: 2011 TFSA dollar limit | + | $5,000 |
| **TFSA contribution room at the beginning of 2011** | | **$13,500** |

After you file a tax return, in addition to advising you of your unused TFSA contribution room on your notice of assessment, the CRA may also send a *TFSA Room Statement*, later in the year, if the calculated amount of your unused TFSA contribution room has changed from the previously stated amount. A *TFSA Transaction Summary* of your contribution and withdrawal details as received from your TFSA issuer(s) will be available on request.

If you disagree with any of the information on your *TFSA Room Statement*, or *TFSA Transaction Summary*, such as dates or amounts of contributions or withdrawals which your TFSA issuer has provided to the CRA, you should contact your TFSA issuer. If any information initially provided by the issuer regarding your account is incorrect, the issuer must send us an amended information return so that we can update our records.

**Note**
You can get TFSA contribution room information from My Account at **www.cra.gc.ca/myaccount**, or from our TIPS telephone service at **1-800-267-6999**.

## Types of investments allowed

Generally, the types of investments that will be permitted in a TFSA are the same as those permitted in a registered retirement savings plan (RRSP). This includes cash, mutual funds, securities listed on a designated stock exchange, guaranteed investment certificates (GICs), bonds, and certain shares of small business corporations.

You can contribute foreign funds to a TFSA. However, your issuer will convert the funds to Canadian dollars, using the date of the transaction, when reporting this information to the CRA. The total amount of your contribution, in Canadian dollars, **cannot exceed** your unused TFSA contribution room.

If a dividend income from a foreign country is paid to a TFSA, the dividend income could be subject to foreign withholding tax.

You can also make "in kind" contributions (for example, securities you hold in a non-registered account) to your TFSA, as long as the property is a qualified investment. You will be considered to have disposed of the property at its fair market value (FMV) at the time of the contribution. If the FMV is more than the cost of the property, you will have to report the capital gain on your income tax return. However, if the cost of the property is more than its FMV, you cannot claim the resulting capital loss. The amount of the contribution to your TFSA will be equal to the FMV of the property.

If you want to transfer an investment from your RRSP to your TFSA, you will be considered to have withdrawn the investment from the RRSP at its FMV, and that amount will be reported as an RRSP withdrawal, and included in your income in that year. Tax will be withheld on the withdrawal, which can be claimed on your tax return. If the transfer into your TFSA takes place immediately, the same value will be used as the amount of the contribution to the TFSA. If the contribution to the TFSA is deferred, the amount of the contribution will be the FMV of the investment at the time of that contribution.

However, you cannot exchange securities for cash, or other securities of equal value, between your accounts, either between two registered accounts or between a registered and a non-registered account (swap).

## Withdrawals

Depending on the type of investment held in your TFSA, you can generally withdraw any amount from the TFSAs at any time and for any reason, with no tax consequences. For information on withdrawing amounts from your TFSA, contact your TFSA issuer.

Withdrawals, excluding qualifying transfers and specified distributions, made from your TFSA in the year will be added back to your TFSA contribution room at the beginning of the following year.

**Note**
You cannot contribute more than your TFSA contribution room in a given year, even if you make withdrawals from the account during the year. Withdrawals from the account in the year will be added to your contribution room in the following year. If you over-contribute in the year, you will be subject to a tax equal to 1% of the highest excess TFSA amount in the month, for each month you are in an excess contribution position.

**Example 1**
In 2009, Sarah contributed $5,000 to her TFSA. In 2010, she makes another $5,000 contribution to her TFSA. Later that year, she withdraws $3,000 for a trip. Unfortunately, her plans change and she cannot go. Since Sarah already contributed the maximum to her TFSA earlier in the year, she has no TFSA contribution room left. If she wishes to re-contribute part or all of the $3,000, she will have to wait until the beginning of 2011 to do so. If she re-contributes before 2011, she will have an excess amount in her TFSA and will be charged a monthly tax of 1% on the highest excess TFSA amount for each month that an excess exists in the account. The $3,000 will be added to her TFSA contribution room at the beginning of 2011.

**Example 2**
In 2009, Carl is allowed to contribute $5,000. He contributes $2,000 for that year.

| | | |
|---|---|---|
| 2009 TFSA dollar limit............................ | | $5,000 |
| 2009 contributions................................ | – | $2,000 |
| Unused TFSA contribution room available for future years......................... | | $3,000 |

In 2010, Carl does not contribute to his TFSA, but he makes a $1,000 withdrawal from his account (this withdrawal will be add only on his TFSA contribution room for 2011).

| | | |
|---|---|---|
| 2009 unused TFSA contribution room........ | | $3,000 |
| 2010 TFSA dollar limit............................ | + | $5,000 |
| 2010 unused TFSA contribution room available for future years......................... | | $8,000 |

Carl's TFSA contribution room for 2011

| | | |
|---|---|---|
| 2010 unused TFSA contribution room......... | | $8,000 |
| 2010 withdrawal........................................ | + | $1,000 |
| 2011 TFSA dollar limit................................ | + | $5,000 |
| TFSA contribution room at the beginning of 2011.................................. | | **$14,000** |

## Chapter 3 – Non-residents of Canada

You may be considered a non-resident for tax purposes if you:

- normally, customarily, or routinely live in another country and are not considered a resident of Canada;
- live outside Canada throughout the tax year;
- stay in Canada for less than 183 days in the tax year; or
- do not have residential ties in Canada.

Even if you do not live in Canada, you may have residential ties in Canada that are sufficient for you to be considered a factual or deemed resident of Canada. These ties may include a home or personal property situated in Canada and a spouse, common-law partner or dependants residing in Canada. Other ties that may be relevant include social ties in Canada, a Canadian driver's licence, Canadian bank accounts or credit cards, and provincial or territorial health insurance coverage. For more information, see Interpretation Bulletin IT-221R, *Determination of an Individual's Residence Status*.

If you become a non-resident of Canada, or are considered to be a non-resident for income tax purposes, you will be allowed to keep your TFSA and you will not be taxed **in Canada** on any earnings in the account or on withdrawals from it.

No TFSA contribution room will accrue for any year throughout which you are a non-resident of Canada.

Any withdrawals made during the period that you were a non-resident will be added back to your unused TFSA contribution room in the following year, but will only be available if you re-establish your Canadian residency status for tax purposes.

You can contribute to a TFSA up to the date that you become a non-resident of Canada. The TFSA dollar limit (for example $5,000 in 2010) is not pro-rated in the year of emigration or immigration.

If you make a contribution, except for a qualifying transfer or an exempt contribution, while you are a non-resident, you will be subject to a 1% per-month tax for each month the contribution stays in the account. You may also be subject to other taxes. For more information, see "Tax payable on non-resident contributions" on page 15.

## Chapter 4 – Impact on your income-tested benefits

You can withdraw money from the TFSA at any time, for any reason, with no tax consequences, and without affecting your eligibility for federal income-tested benefits and credits.

Your Old Age Security (OAS) benefits, Guaranteed Income Supplement (GIS) or Employment Insurance (EI) benefits will not be reduced as a result of the income earned in, or the amount withdrawn from, your TFSA.

The income earned in the account or amounts withdrawn from a TFSA will also not affect your eligibility for federal credits, such as the Canada Child Tax Benefit (CCTB), the working income tax benefit (WITB), the goods and services tax/harmonized sales tax credit, or the age amount.

**Example**
Denis is retired and, in addition to his pension, he receives OAS and Canada Pension Plan (CPP) benefits. He earns $500 a year in interest income from his TFSA savings. Neither this income nor any TFSA withdrawals will affect any federal income-tested benefits or credits he receives. If this $500 was earned in a regular savings account, it would have to be included as income on his tax return and, in addition to additional tax payable, could result in a social benefit repayment.

| Denis' income | Funds in a TFSA | Funds outside a TFSA |
|---|---|---|
| Total pension income | $48,250 | $48,250 |
| Total CPP benefits | $12,017 | $12,017 |
| Total OAS benefits | $5,933 | $5,933 |
| Interest income to be reported on the tax return | $0 | $500 |
| Total income | $66,200 | $66,700 |
| Fictitious base amount for social benefits repayments | $66,250 | $66,250 |
| Amount over base amount | $0 | $450 |
| Multiplied by 15% | × 15% | × 15% |
| Amount to be included on the tax return as a social benefit repayment | **$0** | **$67.50** |

## Chapter 5 – Qualifying transfers

### Between TFSAs of the same individual

If you have more than one TFSA, you can transfer funds between them without affecting your TFSA contribution room, as long as you arrange for the transfer to be done **directly** between the TFSAs. This would be considered as a qualifying transfer, and would have **no** tax consequences. If the transfer is not done directly, that is, if you withdraw the funds from one TFSA and subsequently contribute that amount to another TFSA, the subsequent contribution will be considered a separate contribution that will reduce, and may even exceed, your TFSA contribution room for the year, and as a result you may be subject to the tax on excess contributions. For more information, see "Chapter 7 – Tax payable" on page 13.

### Upon marriage or common-law partnership breakdown

When there is a breakdown in a marriage or common-law partnership, an amount can be transferred directly from one individual's TFSA to the other's TFSA without affecting either individual's contribution room. To do this, you must meet the following conditions:

- you and your current or former spouse or common-law partner are living separate and apart at the time of the transfer; and
- you are entitled to receive the amount under a decree, order or judgment of a court, or under a written separation agreement to settle rights arising out of your relationship on or after the breakdown of your relationship.

The transfer must be made **directly** between the TFSAs.

When these conditions are met, the transfer is a qualifying transfer and will not reduce the recipient's eligible TFSA contribution room. Since this transfer is not considered a withdrawal, the transferred amount will not be added back to the transferor's contribution room at the beginning of the following year.

Also, the transfer will not eliminate any excess TFSA amount, **if applicable**, in the payer's TFSA.

> **Note**
> If, instead of choosing to have the amount directly transferred, an individual chooses to receive the settlement amount before deciding to contribute part or all of it to their own TFSA, then any such contribution would be characterized as a regular contribution that would reduce their balance of unused TFSA contribution room.

## Chapter 6 – Death of the TFSA holder

After the holder of a TFSA dies, possible tax implications may vary somewhat depending on one or more of the following factors, as applicable:

- the type of TFSA;
- the type of beneficiary(ies);
- whether any income was earned after the date of death; and
- how long, after the date of death, amounts are distributed to beneficiaries.

Depending on which combination of the above factors applies, the following can be affected:

- whether or not the deceased's TFSA continues to exist or is considered to have ceased;
- how income earned after the date of death may be reported and taxed;
- whether a beneficiary can transfer amounts received to their own TFSA, within certain limits, and whether such a transfer would affect their unused TFSA contribution room.

### Types of beneficiaries

There are different types of beneficiaries for TFSA purposes:

- a survivor who has been designated as a successor holder; and
- designated beneficiaries, for example, a survivor who has not been named as a successor holder, former spouses or common-law partners, children, and qualified donees.

Determining the type of beneficiary is an important initial step and can be affected by:

- designations which may have been made in the deceased holder's TFSA contract;
- the provisions of the deceased holder's will, if there is one; and
- provincial or territorial succession legislation.

> **Note**
> If you wish to amend a prior beneficiary or successor holder designation, contact your TFSA issuer to determine the possibility of doing so according to the provisions of your plan.

### Successor holder

In provinces or territories that recognize TFSA beneficiary designation, the survivor can be designated as a successor holder in the TFSA contract or in the will.

A survivor can be named in the deceased holder's will as a successor holder to a TFSA, if the provisions of the will state that the successor holder acquires all of the holder's rights including the unconditional right to revoke any beneficiary designation, or similar direction imposed by the deceased holder under the arrangement or relating to property held in connection with the arrangement.

If named as the successor holder, the survivor will become the new holder of the TFSA immediately upon the death of the original holder.

This is the case for all three types of TFSA: deposit, annuity contract, and trust arrangement.

The deceased holder is not considered to have received an amount from the TFSA at the time of death if the holder named his or her survivor as the successor holder of the TFSA. In this situation, the TFSA continues to exist and the successor holder assumes ownership of the TFSA contract and all of its contents. However, where the TFSA contract is a trust arrangement, the trust continues to be the legal owner of the property held in the TFSA.

The TFSA continues to exist and both its value at the date of the original holder's death and any income earned after that date continue to be sheltered from tax under the new successor holder.

Except in cases where an excess TFSA amount existed in the deceased holder's TFSA at the time of their death, the successor holder's unused TFSA contribution room is unaffected by their having assumed ownership of the deceased holder's account.

The issuer will notify the CRA of this change in ownership.

The successor holder, after taking over ownership of the deceased holder's TFSA, can make tax-free withdrawals from that account. The successor holder can also make new contributions to that account, subject to their own unused TFSA contribution room.

If the successor holder already had their own TFSA, then they would be considered as the holder of two separate accounts. If they wish, they can **directly transfer** part or all of the value from one to the other (for example, to consolidate accounts). This would be considered as a qualifying transfer and would not affect available TFSA contribution room.

In certain cases, a survivor, designated as the successor holder of a TFSA, may not have a valid Canadian social insurance number (SIN), which is one of the eligibility requirements for opening a TFSA. If the survivor is a Canadian resident, they should apply to Service Canada to obtain a valid Canadian SIN.

If the survivor is a non-resident, they should request an individual tax number from the CRA by completing Form T1261, *Application for a Canada Revenue Agency Individual Tax Number (ITN) for Non-Residents*.

**Example**
Joan is living with her husband, George, in a province that recognizes TFSA beneficiary designation. Joan is the holder of a TFSA and designated George as the successor holder. Joan dies on February 15, 2010. The value of her TFSA on that date is $10,000. There is no excess TFSA amount in her account. Her estate is finally settled on September 1, 2010. By that time, an additional amount of $200 of income has been earned. As George meets all the conditions to be considered the successor holder, he becomes the successor holder of Joan's TFSA as of the date of her death.

The fair market value (FMV) of $10,000 as of the date of death is not taxable to George. Similarly, the $200 of income earned after the date of death (and any subsequent income earned) is also not taxable to George. No T4A slip would be issued and completion of Form RC240, *Designation of an Exempt Contribution Tax-Free Savings Account (TFSA)*, would not be necessary in this situation.

This is because Joan was a resident, at the time of her death, in a province that recognizes TFSA beneficiary designations.

### Excess TFSA amount at the time of death

If, at the time of death, there was an excess TFSA amount in the deceased holder's TFSA, a tax of 1% per month is applicable to the deceased holder on the highest excess TFSA amount for each month in which the excess existed, up to and including the month of death. The executor of the estate (liquidator) must file an RC243, *Tax-Free Savings Account (TFSA) Return*, and Form RC243-SCH-A, *Schedule A – Excess TFSA Amounts*, for that period.

Also, the successor holder is **deemed** to have made, at the beginning of the month following the date of death, a contribution to their TFSA equal to the amount by which the excess TFSA amount is more than the total FMV, at the date of the holder's death, of all property under any arrangements that ceased to be a TFSA because of the holder's death. If that contribution creates an excess TFSA amount in the successor holder's TFSA, they will be subject to a tax of 1% per month on the highest amount for each month they are in an excess contribution position.

**Example 1**
Bob and Betty were a married couple. Each had TFSA contribution room of $5,000 for 2009. They each opened their own TFSA on January 10, 2009. Bob initially contributed $4,000 to his TFSA and Betty contributed $1,000 to hers. On June 12, 2009, Bob contributed an additional $3,000 to his TFSA, bringing his total contributions for 2009 to $7,000.

As Bob only had contribution room of $5,000 for 2009, he had an excess TFSA amount of $2,000. Bob passed away on September 18, 2009, and the value of his TFSA on that date was $7,000. Bob had designated Betty as the successor holder of his TFSA in the event of his death. As Betty meets all the conditions to be considered a successor holder, she becomes the holder of the TFSA as of September 18, 2009.

Since an excess TFSA amount existed in Bob's TFSA at the time of his death, Betty is deemed to have made, as of October 1, 2009, a $2,000 contribution to her TFSA (which is the excess amount in Bob's TFSA). As Betty had only previously contributed $1,000 to her own TFSA, she still had unused TFSA contribution room for 2009 of $4,000. As such, the $2,000 deemed contribution does not create an excess TFSA amount in her account. Therefore, there are no tax consequences to Betty based on this deemed contribution. Her unused contribution room for the rest of 2009 is $2,000. However, the executor of Bob's estate must file an RC243, *Tax-Free Savings Account (TFSA) Return*, and Form RC243-SCH-A, *Schedule A – Excess TFSA Amounts*, for the period from June up to and including September 2009.

**Example 2**
From the scenario above, if Betty had initially contributed $4,500 to her own TFSA on January 10, 2009, instead of the $1,000 previously noted, the $2,000 deemed contribution on October 1, 2009, would have resulted in total contributions to her TFSA in 2009 of $6,500.

As Betty's TFSA contribution room for 2009 was $5,000, as a result of the deemed contribution, she would be considered to have an excess TFSA amount of $1,500 ($6,500 – $5,000). In such a situation, Betty would be subject to a tax of 1% per month on this excess TFSA amount for as long as this excess TFSA amount would stay in her account.

## Designated beneficiaries

Designated beneficiaries may include a survivor who has not been named as a successor holder, former spouses or common-law partners, children and qualified donees.

A designated beneficiary will not have to pay tax on payments made out of the TFSA the total of which does not exceed the FMV of all the property held in the TFSA at the time of the holder's death.

Beneficiaries (other than a survivor) can contribute any of the amounts they receive to their own TFSA as long as they have available unused TFSA contribution room.

A survivor who is a beneficiary has the option to contribute and designate all or a portion of a survivor payment as an exempt contribution to their own TFSA, without affecting their own unused TFSA contribution room, as long as they meet certain conditions and limits. For more information, see "Designation of an exempt contribution by a survivor" on the next page.

As noted earlier, if, at the time of death, there was an excess TFSA amount in the deceased holder's TFSA, a tax of 1% per month is applicable on the highest excess amount for each month in which the excess existed, up to and including the month of death. The executor of the estate (liquidator) must file an RC243, *Tax-Free Savings Account (TFSA) Return*, and Form RC243-SCH-A, *Schedule A – Excess TFSA Amounts*.

When no successor holder or beneficiary is designated in the TFSA contract or will, the TFSA property is directed to the deceased holder's estate and distributed in accordance with the terms of the will.

### General rules – deposit or annuity contract

If there is no successor holder, when the holder of a deposit or an annuity contract under a TFSA dies, the TFSA ceases to exist and the holder is considered to have disposed of the contract or the deposit immediately before the time that the TFSA ceased to be a TFSA for an amount equal to the FMV of all the property held in the TFSA at the time of death.

After the holder's death, the deposit or annuity contract is considered to be a separate contract and is no longer considered as a TFSA. All earnings that accrue after the holder's death will be taxable to the beneficiary.

The normal rules would apply for the reporting of income or gains accrued after the date of death, depending on the specific characteristics of the deposit or annuity contract. For example, interest earned would be reported on a T5 slip, *Statement of investment income*.

### General rules – arrangement in trust

If there is no successor holder, a TFSA that is an arrangement in trust is deemed to continue and it remains a non-taxable trust until the end of the exempt period.

All income earned during the exempt period and paid to the beneficiaries, will be included in their income, while earnings that accrued before death would remain exempt. In other words, any amount up to the FMV of the deceased holder's TFSA as of the date of death can be paid to beneficiaries, without them having to report any amount as income. Any amount paid to beneficiaries, that represents an increase in the FMV after the date of death is taxable to the beneficiaries and would have to be reported by them as income. Such payments will appear in box 028, "Other income," and with a footnote explanation code 134 "Tax-Free Savings Account (TFSA) taxable amount," in the "Other information" section of a T4A slip, *Statement of Pension, Retirement, Annuity, and Other Income*.

The trust has the exempt period within which to distribute both the taxable and non-taxable amounts. The trustee will designate the part of each payment that represents non-taxable FMV at the date of death with the rest being taxable.

Payments of amounts earned above the FMV made by the trust to a non-resident beneficiary, including a non-resident survivor, from a deceased holder's TFSA during the exempt period would be reported on an NR4 slip, *Statement of Amounts Paid or Credited to Non-residents of Canada*, and would be subject to non-resident withholding tax.

If the trust continues to exist beyond the end of the exempt period (for example, not all amounts from the deceased's TFSA have been paid to beneficiaries), it will be taxable from that point forward. It becomes a taxable inter vivos trust with a taxation year beginning January 1 of the following calendar year. The trust will be treated as having disposed of, and having immediately reacquired, its property for its FMV at that time. For as long as it would continue to exist, the trust would itself be taxable on any undistributed income (including, for its first taxation year, any undistributed income or gains during the exempt period) and required to annually file a T3RET, *T3 Trust Income Tax and Information Return*. The trust will also be required to prepare T3 slips, *Statement of Trust Income Allocations and Designations*, in that year or subsequent years for any distributions of taxable amounts to beneficiaries.

**Example**
Martin's mother passed away on January 9, 2010. The value of her TFSA on that date was $11,000. There was no excess TFSA amount in her account. In her TFSA contract, she had named Martin as the sole beneficiary. Her estate was settled on June 7, 2010. By that time, $200 in additional income had been earned and the full amount of $11,200 was paid to Martin.

The value of Martin's late mother's TFSA as of the date of her death—$11,000, is not taxable. The income earned after the date of her death—$200, is taxable to Martin. He will receive a T4A slip showing this amount in box 028, "Other income," and with a footnote explanation code 134 "Tax-Free Savings Account (TFSA) taxable amount," in the "Other information" section. Martin can contribute any of the amounts he receives to his own TFSA as long as he has available unused TFSA contribution room.

### Designation of an exempt contribution by a survivor

A survivor is an individual who is, immediately before the TFSA holder's death, a spouse or common-law partner of the holder.

If designated as a beneficiary, the survivor has the option to contribute and designate all or a portion of a survivor payment as an exempt contribution to their own TFSA, without affecting their own unused TFSA contribution room, subject to certain conditions and limits.

Beneficiaries (other than the survivor) in receipt of a payment from the deceased holder's TFSA are not able to contribute and designate any amount as an exempt contribution.

For the survivor to designate an exempt contribution, the amount must be received and contributed to their TFSA during the rollover period. Also, the survivor must designate their survivor payments as an exempt contribution on Form RC240, *Designation of an Exempt Contribution Tax-Free Savings Account (TFSA)*, and submit the designation within 30 days after the day the contribution is made.

The total exempt contributions designated during the rollover period cannot exceed the FMV of the deceased holder's TFSA at the time of death.

Generally, if the TFSA of the deceased holder includes an excess TFSA amount at the time of death, if payments are being received by more than one survivor, or if the survivor payment and/or the contribution is made after the rollover period, no amount of the survivor payment may be designated as an exempt contribution. If any of these circumstances are present, contact us to find out whether a designation can still be made.

**Example**
Emma died on February 2, 2010. She was living with her common-law partner, Fred, in Ontario. The value of her trusteed TFSA on that date was $9,000. There was no excess TFSA amount in her account. In her TFSA contract, she had not filled out the part about a successor holder, but she named Fred as the beneficiary. Her estate was settled on August 14, 2010. By that time, an additional amount of $150 of income had been earned and the full amount of $9,150 was paid to Fred.

The value of Emma's TFSA as of the date of her death—$9,000, is not taxable. The additional income earned after the date of death—$150, is taxable to Fred. His T4A slip will show this amount in box 028 as "Other income," and with a footnote explanation code 134 "Tax-Free Savings Account (TFSA) taxable amount," in the "Other information" section.

The amount paid to Fred, as the surviving common-law partner, is considered a survivor payment. Since the survivor payment was made during the rollover period, it is possible for Fred to rollover up to $9,000 (the value of the TFSA as of the date of death) to his own TFSA, as an exempt contribution.

An exempt contribution does not affect Fred's unused TFSA contribution room. For the contribution of a survivor payment to be considered an exempt contribution during the rollover period, Fred must designate it as such on Form RC240, *Designation of an Exempt Contribution Tax-Free Savings Account (TFSA)*, within 30 days after the contribution is made.

### Donation to a qualified donee

If a qualified donee was named as a beneficiary of the deceased holder's TFSA, the transfer of funds to the qualified donee must generally occur within the 36-month period following the holder's death. If necessary, once the donation has been completed, it is possible to ask to have the deceased's tax return for the year of death adjusted in order to claim the charitable donation tax credit.

## Chapter 7 – Tax payable

Generally, interest, dividends or capital gains earned in respect of investments in a TFSA are not subject to tax—either while held in the account or when withdrawn.

There are, however, certain circumstances under which one or more taxes may be payable with respect to a TFSA. The following sections will provide information and examples of when and how these taxes are payable, and by whom.

## Tax payable on excess TFSA amount

You have an excess TFSA amount at any time in a year if the total of all TFSA contributions you made in the year up to that time (other than a qualifying transfer or an exempt contribution) exceeds the total of your TFSA contribution room at the beginning of the year plus any qualifying portion of a withdrawal made in the year up to that time. The qualifying portion of the withdrawal is the lesser of the amount of the withdrawal or the previously determined excess TFSA amount. Any portion of a withdrawal which does not reduce or eliminate a previously determined excess TFSA amount is not a qualifying portion of the withdrawal and cannot be used to reduce or eliminate any future excess TFSA amount that may be created.

If, at any time in a month, you have an excess TFSA amount, you are liable to a tax of 1% on your highest excess TFSA amount in that month.

> **Note**
> If an excess TFSA amount exists in the account as of the date of death of a TFSA holder and there is a successor holder, see "Excess TFSA amount at the time of death" on page 11.

The tax of 1% per month will continue to apply for each month that the excess amount remains in the TFSA. It will continue to apply, on a pro-rata basis, until the earlier of:

- when the entire excess amount is withdrawn; or
- for eligible individuals, when the entire excess amount is absorbed by additions to your unused TFSA contribution room in the following and later years.

> For distributions (withdrawals) occurring after October 17, 2009, a distribution from a TFSA that is a specified distribution cannot reduce or eliminate an individual's excess TFSA amount.

This tax is similar to the tax of 1% per month on excess RRSP contributions except that in the case of a TFSA, there is no $2,000 "grace" amount. The tax of 1% on an excess TFSA amount is applicable from the first $1 of excess contributions.

This tax of 1% per month is applicable on the highest excess TFSA amount in your account for each month in which an excess exists. Since it is based on the highest excess TFSA amount, this means that the 1% tax would be applicable for a particular month even if an excess amount was contributed and later withdrawn during the same month.

For any year in which tax is payable by the holder of a TFSA on an excess TFSA amount in their account, it is necessary to complete and file an RC243, *Tax-Free Savings Account (TFSA) Return*, and Form RC243-SCH-A, *Schedule A – Excess TFSA Amounts*.

For information on the filing deadline for this return, see "TFSA Return and payment of tax" on page 18.

> Effective October 17, 2009, any earnings or increase in value reasonably attributable to "deliberate excess contributions" will be considered an **advantage** and treated accordingly. For more information, see "Tax payable on an advantage" on page 18.

**Example 1**
Theresa is a 31-year-old Canadian resident. She opened a TFSA on February 6, 2009, and contributed $3,000 at that time. Later in the year she received a windfall of $4,100. She forgot that her contribution limit for 2009 was $5,000 and she decided to contribute the entire $4,100 to her TFSA on October 29.

After making this contribution, Theresa had an excess TFSA amount of $2,100 in her account. This is because her total contributions as of October 29 were $7,100 ($3,000 + $4,100) and this total exceeded her available contribution room of $5,000.

Assuming Theresa makes no further TFSA contributions and no withdrawals during the remainder of 2009, she would be subject to a tax of $63 on her excess TFSA amount. This amount is calculated as 1% per month for each of October to December × the highest excess amount in each month. In other words, $2,100 × 1% × 3 months = $63.

If, after making her $4,100 contribution on October 29, Theresa had realized her mistake and withdrawn $2,100 on October 31, she would still be subject to the tax of 1% on the excess TFSA amount of $2,100 but only for the month of October. As such, her tax payable would be $21 ($2,100 × 1% × 1 month).

**Example 2**
Jamal is a 43-year-old Canadian resident. He opened his TFSA in 2009 and made the following transactions during that year:

- contribution on January 6 $4,000
- contribution on March 10 $500
- contribution on June 3 $2,700
- withdrawal on October 2 $800

Jamal's contribution room for that year was $5,000. The first contribution which created the excess TFSA amount was the $2,700 contribution on June 3. As of that date, his total contributions in 2009 were $7,200 ($4,000 + $500 + $2,700). This means that as of June 3, he had an excess amount in his TFSA of $2,200 ($7,200 of total contributions minus $5,000 of contribution room).

Jamal will be subject to a tax on his excess contributions. This tax is equal to 1% of the highest excess TFSA amount in each month and is applicable until Jamal either withdraws the entire excess amount or until he becomes entitled to enough unused TFSA contribution room to absorb the excess.

In this example, Jamal's tax would be $138 for 2009, calculated as follows:

- Highest excess TFSA amount per month for January to May = 0. No penalty tax applicable for those months.
- Highest excess TFSA amount per month for June to October = $2,200. Tax = 1% per month on the highest excess amount = $2,200 × 1% × 5 months, which is $110.

Note that although $800 was withdrawn in October, the tax is calculated based on the highest excess TFSA amount in each month. The highest excess TFSA amount in October was still $2,200.

For the months of November and December, Jamal still has an excess TFSA amount, but because of the withdrawal he made, his remaining excess TFSA amount for those last two months was $1,400 (the prior excess amount of $2,200 less the withdrawal of $800).

This means that for November and December, Jamal's tax is $1,400 × 1% × 2 months, which is $28. Therefore, in total for 2009, his tax is $138 ($110 for June to October + $28 for November to December).

**Example 3**
Luisa is a 60-year-old Canadian resident. On June 18, 2009, she received a $12,000 bonus from work. She decided to open a TFSA and she contributed the entire amount on June 25, 2009.

Assuming the TFSA dollar limit remains at $5,000 for 2009 to 2011, and also assuming Luisa makes no further contributions or withdrawals, she would be subject to a tax on an excess TFSA amount in both 2009 and 2010. The amount of tax payable for each of the respective years would be calculated as follows:

**2009**
After having made her $12,000 contribution on June 25, Luisa had an excess TFSA amount of $7,000 ($12,000 less her TFSA dollar limit of $5,000). The highest excess TFSA amount which existed in her account was therefore $7,000 for every month from June to December. This means she would be subject to a tax payable of $490 ($7,000 × 1% × 7 months).

**2010**
Luisa's unused TFSA contribution room at the end of 2009 was negative (–) $7,000. On January 1, 2010, she became entitled to her 2010 TFSA dollar limit of $5,000. Although this helped to reduce the excess TFSA amount from $7,000 to $2,000, it did not completely absorb it. Luisa will continue to have an excess TFSA amount of $2,000 in her account through all of 2010. As such, she would be subject to a tax of $240 ($2,000 × 1% × 12 months).

**2011**
Luisa's unused TFSA contribution room at the end of 2010 was negative (–) $2,000. As of January 1, 2011, she will be entitled to a new TFSA dollar limit of $5,000. This will fully eliminate or absorb the excess TFSA amount in her account. Luisa would have available contribution room of $3,000 and, as long as she does not contribute more than this amount to her TFSA through the remainder of 2011, she will not be subject to any tax on an excess TFSA amount for 2011.

**Example 4**
Gilles, a 36-year-old Canadian resident, opened his TFSA on February 6, 2009, and contributed $5,000 on that date. On March 3, 2010, he contributed an additional $7,000. Since Gilles' unused TFSA contribution room as of the beginning of 2010 was only $5,000 (the TFSA dollar limit for that year), his contribution of $7,000 on March 3 resulted, as of that date, in an excess TFSA amount of $2,000.

On May 17, 2010, Gilles withdrew $3,200 from his TFSA. The qualifying portion of this withdrawal is $2,000, since this is the maximum amount which eliminated the previously determined excess TFSA amount in his account.

No part of the $1,200 portion of his withdrawal (the full amount of $3,200 less the qualifying portion of $2,000) could be used in the year to reduce any subsequent excess TFSA amount. In other words, if Gilles was to make a new contribution of $1,000 on July 6, 2010, this would result in an excess TFSA amount, as of that date, of $1,000, even though Gilles previously withdrew $1,200 more than his excess TFSA amount on May 17, 2010.

**Example 5**
From the previous example, had Gilles withdrawn $900 on May 17 (instead of withdrawing $3,200), the qualifying portion of the withdrawal would have been the full $900, since the entire amount would have reduced (but not totally eliminated) his previously determined excess TFSA amount of $2,000.

In this case, an excess TFSA amount of $1,100 would remain in his account as of the date of the May 17 withdrawal (the previously determined excess TFSA amount of $2,000 minus the $900 qualifying portion of the withdrawal). If, in this scenario, Gilles were to have made a new contribution of $1,000 on July 6, 2010, this would result in an excess TFSA amount, as of that date, of $2,100 ($1,100 + $1,000).

## Tax payable on non-resident contributions

If, at any time during the year, your TFSA contains contributions (other than a qualifying transfer or an exempt contribution) you have made while a non-resident of Canada, you will be liable to a tax of 1% per month on these contributions.

This tax, calculated on the full amount of the contribution, will apply for each month that any portion of the amount contributed while a non-resident remains in the TFSA and will continue to apply until the earlier of:

- when these contributions are withdrawn in full from the account and designated as a withdrawal of non-resident contributions; or
- when you become a resident of Canada.

An individual is not subject to the tax of 1% on non-resident contributions for the month in which the full amount of the contribution is withdrawn or, if applicable, the month in which Canadian residency is resumed.

**Note**
Unlike in the case of excess TFSA contributions where a partial withdrawal can reduce the tax payable, a partial withdrawal of a contribution made while a non-resident does not proportionately reduce the tax otherwise payable. It is necessary for the full amount of a non-resident contribution to be withdrawn in order for the full tax to no longer apply.

For any year in which tax is payable by the holder of a TFSA on contributions made while a non-resident, it is necessary to complete and file an RC243, *Tax-Free Savings Account (TFSA) Return*, and Form RC243-SCH-B, *Schedule B – Non-Resident Contributions to a Tax-Free Savings Account (TFSA)*.

**Note**
In addition to the tax of 1% per month on the contributions made while a non-resident, you may also be subject to a separate tax of 1% per month if any of the same contributions create an excess amount in your TFSA. To determine whether you have excess TFSA amounts, you will need to complete Form RC243-SCH-A, *Schedule A – Excess TFSA Amounts*.

For information on the filing deadline for this form, see "TFSA Return and payment of tax" on page 18.

**Example 1**
Hassan is 25 years old and opened a TFSA in 2009 when he was a resident of Canada. His total contributions in 2009 were $1,000 and he made no withdrawals. Hassan became a non-resident of Canada on February 17, 2010. He contributed $3,000 to his TFSA on August 8, 2010. He re-established his Canadian residency for tax purposes on December 8, 2010.

Hassan's unused TFSA contribution room at the end of 2009 was $4,000 (the $5,000 limit for that year less the $1,000 he contributed). Hassan also accumulated an additional $5,000 TFSA dollar limit for 2010. This is the case because this amount is not pro-rated in the year an individual becomes a non-resident and he was considered a Canadian resident for part of 2010. This means that as of January 1, 2010, Hassan has a total TFSA contribution room of $9,000 (the $4,000 carried over from the end of 2009 + the annual limit of $5,000 for 2010).

Even though he has unused TFSA contribution room, a tax is applicable if any contributions are made while he is a non-resident. Since the $3,000 he contributed was while he was a non-resident, he would be subject to a tax of 1% of this amount for each month from August to November. He is not subject to tax for the month of December as he re-established Canadian residency in that month. Accordingly, Hassan would be subject to $120 in tax based on his non-resident contribution ($3,000 × 1% × 4 months).

**Example 2**
Gemma opened a TFSA on March 2, 2009, when she was 41 years old and a Canadian resident. She contributed $4,000 on that date. On September 7, 2009, she became a non-resident. On July 12, 2010, she contributed an additional $2,500 to her TFSA. By the end of 2010, Gemma is still a non-resident of Canada and she has not made any withdrawals from her account.

For 2010, Gemma will be subject to tax on the contribution she made while she was a non-resident and she will also be subject to tax on the excess TFSA amount in her account.

Gemma's unused TFSA contribution room at the end of 2009 was $1,000 (the TFSA dollar limit of $5,000 less her contribution of $4,000). Gemma is not entitled to the TFSA dollar limit of $5,000 for 2010 since she was a non-resident throughout that entire year. Gemma's $2,500 contribution on July 12, 2010, results in an excess TFSA amount in her account at that time of $1,500. This is the amount by which her contribution exceeded her available room.

Gemma's tax on non-resident contributions for 2010 would be $150 since the full amount of her $2,500 contribution was made while she was a non-resident and this amount remained in her account through the end of the year. Since the tax is equal to 1% per month of the amount of non-resident contributions, the tax on her non-resident contributions would be $150 ($2,500 × 1% × the 6 months including July to December 2010).

In addition, since part of Gemma's contribution while a non-resident also created an excess TFSA amount ($1,500, as described above) in her account, she is also subject to the tax of 1% per month on this amount for July to December 2010. Her tax on excess TFSA amounts would therefore be $90 ($1,500 × 1% × 6 months).

For 2010, Gemma would therefore be subject to a total tax of $240 on her TFSA, made up of $150 in tax on her non-resident contribution plus $90 in tax on her excess TFSA amount.

Gemma will not accumulate any room in 2011 unless she re-establishes Canadian residency in that year. She will have to withdraw the entire $2,500 contributed while she was a non-resident in order to avoid any additional tax of 1% per month on the non-resident contributions as well as on the $1,500 excess TFSA amount.

## Tax payable on non-qualified investments

If, in a calendar year, a trust governed by a TFSA acquires property that is a non-qualified investment or if previously acquired property becomes non-qualified, there are consequences in terms of reporting requirements and tax payable on the part of the TFSA trust as well as the holder of the TFSA.

**Note**
For the purposes of TFSA taxes, if a trust governed by a TFSA holds property at any time that is, for the trust, both a prohibited investment and a non-qualified investment, the property is not considered to be, at that time a non-qualified investment, but remains a prohibited investment.

### Reporting requirements and tax payable by the TFSA holder

A **one-time tax** is payable by the holder of a TFSA when a non-qualified investment is acquired or when a previously acquired qualified investment becomes non-qualified.

The tax is equal to 50% of the fair market value (FMV) of the property at the time it was acquired or it became non-qualified.

An individual subject to this tax is required to complete and file an RC243, *Tax-Free Savings Account (TFSA) Return*.

For information on the filing deadline for this return, see "TFSA Return and payment of tax" on page 18.

## Refund of taxes paid

The TFSA holder may be entitled to a refund of the one-time 50% of the FMV tax paid on non-qualified investments or prohibited investments held in the account before the end of the calendar year following the calendar year in which the liability for the tax arose or such later time as is permitted by the Minister, if either:

- the TFSA trust disposes of the non-qualified or prohibited investment; or
- the property ceases to be a non-qualified or prohibited investment.

However, no refund will be issued if it is reasonable to expect that the holder knew, or should have known, at the time the property was obtained by the TFSA trust, that the property was, or would become, a non-qualified investment or a prohibited investment.

To claim a refund, send a letter explaining why you are requesting a refund along with the documents detailing the information relating to the acquisition and disposition of the non-qualified or prohibited property. The documents must contain the name and description of the property, the number of shares or units, the date the property was acquired or became non-qualified or prohibited property and the date of the disposition or the date that the property became qualified or ceased to be prohibited. Send your letter to:

**TFSA Processing Unit**
**Post Office Box 9768 Station T**
**Ottawa ON K1G 3X9**

If the non-qualified investment becomes a qualified investment while it is held by a trust governed by a TFSA, the trust is considered to have disposed of and immediately re-acquired the property at its FMV.

### Reporting requirements by the trust governed by a TFSA

The TFSA issuer is required, by no later than the end of February in the year following the year in which the non-qualified property was acquired or previously acquired property became non-qualified, to provide relevant information to the CRA and the holder of the TFSA. Such information would include, where applicable, description(s) of the property(ies), date(s) of acquisition or disposition, and the FMV at the relevant time(s). This information is necessary for the TFSA holder in order to enable them to determine the amount of any tax payable or of any possible refund of tax previously paid.

## Tax payable on prohibited investments

If, in a calendar year, a trust governed by a TFSA acquires property that is a prohibited investment or if previously acquired property becomes prohibited, there are consequences in terms of reporting requirements and tax payable on the part of the TFSA holder.

**Note**
For the purposes of TFSA taxes, if a trust governed by a TFSA holds property at any time that is, for the trust, both a prohibited investment and a non-qualified investment, the property is not considered to be, at that time, a non-qualified investment, but remains a prohibited investment.

### Reporting requirements and tax payable by the TFSA holder

Where a trust that is governed by a TFSA holds a prohibited investment during the calendar year, the holder of the TFSA is liable to pay two amounts of tax.

A **one-time tax** is payable by the holder of a TFSA when a prohibited investment is acquired or when a previously-acquired property becomes a prohibited investment.

If the prohibited investment ceases to be a prohibited investment while it is held by the trust, the trust is considered to have disposed of and immediately reacquired the property at its FMV.

The tax is equal to 50% of the FMV of the property at the time it was acquired or it became prohibited.

An **additional tax** is payable by the holder of a TFSA that holds a prohibited investment. This additional tax is equal to 150% of the amount of tax that would be payable by the TFSA trust for the taxation year that ends in the calendar year, if the trust had no income or losses other than from the prohibited investments that it held in the year and no capital gains or capital losses other than from the disposition of its prohibited investments.

An individual subject to these taxes is required to complete and file an RC243, *Tax-Free Savings Account (TFSA) Return*.

Since October 16, 2009, for transactions after that date, the additional tax on income or gain on prohibited investments as noted in the preceding paragraph is no longer applicable. Instead, the earnings or increase in value reasonably attributable to a prohibited investment meets the definition of advantage and is subject to tax under the advantage rules. For more information, see "Tax payable on an advantage" on the next page.

For information on the filing deadline for this return, see "TFSA Return and payment of tax" on the next page.

## Refund of taxes paid

The TFSA holder may be entitled to a refund of the one-time 50% of FMV tax paid on non-qualified investments or prohibited investments held in the account before the end of the calendar year following the calendar year in which the liability for the tax arose or such later time as is permitted by the Minister, if either:

- the TFSA trust disposes of the non-qualified or prohibited investment; or
- the property ceases to be a non-qualified or prohibited investment.

However, no refund will be issued if it is reasonable to expect that the holder knew, or should have known, at the time the property was obtained by the TFSA trust, that the property was, or would become, a non-qualified investment or a prohibited investment.

To claim a refund, send a letter explaining why you are requesting a refund along with the documents detailing the information relating to the acquisition and disposition of the non-qualified or prohibited property. The documents must contain the name and description of the property, the number of shares or units, the date the property was acquired or became non-qualified or prohibited property and the date of the disposition or the date that the property became qualified or ceased to be prohibited. Send your letter to:

**TFSA Processing Unit**
**Post Office Box 9768 Station T**
**Ottawa ON K1G 3X9**

## Tax payable on an advantage

If the holder of a TFSA or a person not dealing at arm's length with the holder was provided with an advantage in relation to their TFSA during the year, a tax is payable which is:

- in the case of a benefit, the FMV of the benefit; and
- in the case of a loan or a debt, the amount of the loan or debt.

For a more complete definition of an advantage, see the "Definitions" section starting on page 4.

The tax payable on an advantage extended in relation to a TFSA may be applicable to the holder of the TFSA or the TFSA issuer, depending on the specifics of each situation.

If the advantage is considered to be extended by the TFSA issuer, or by a person not dealing at arm's length with the issuer, the issuer is liable to pay the tax, rather than the holder.

An individual subject to this tax is required to complete and file an RC243, *Tax-Free Savings Account (TFSA) Return*.

Effective October 17, 2009, an "advantage" also includes any earnings and gains reasonably attributable to deliberate over-contributions, prohibited investments, asset transfer (swap) transactions and specified non-qualified investments.

## TFSA Return and payment of tax

Normally, in most TFSA situations, there is no tax payable, and therefore, no tax return is required; however, where one or more of the TFSA taxes are applicable a tax return is required to be completed and filed.

For each year where a TFSA holder is subject to one or more taxes, they must complete and file an RC243, *Tax-Free Savings Account (TFSA) Return*, by June 30 of the year following the calendar year in which the tax arose, along with a remittance of any tax owing.

In advance of the due date, the CRA may use information provided by the TFSA issuers in order to calculate the tax payable on your behalf and send you a proposed RC243-P, *Proposed Tax-Free Savings Account (TFSA) Return*, setting out the transactions that gave rise to tax payable. You would then be asked to review, sign and return a copy of that return, along with payment, by the due date. Additional instructions will be provided with the return in the event that you disagree with our calculations. Your return will be assessed based on the existing information and any new information or documentation which has been provided, by you and your TFSA issuer(s), and a TFSA notice of assessment will be issued. If no TFSA return is received, the CRA will assess the return based on the information available and issue a TFSA notice of assessment.

A late filing penalty, as well as interest, may be charged if the return was received after **June 30**, and the tax owing was not paid on time.

## What should you do if you disagree with your assessment?

If you disagree with the assessment or reassessment of your return, contact us for more information. If you still disagree, you can make a formal objection by sending a completed Form T400A, *Objection – Income Tax Act*, or a signed letter to the Chief of Appeals at your tax services office or tax centre **within 90 days** of the date of the notice of assessment or notice of reassessment.

For more information, see Pamphlet P148 – *Resolving your Dispute: Objections and Appeal Rights under the Income Tax Act*.

## For more information

### What if you need help?

If you need help after reading this guide, go to **www.cra.gc.ca/tfsa** or call **1-800-959-8281**.

### Forms and publications

To get any forms or publications, go to **www.cra.gc.ca/forms** or call **1-800-959-2221**.

### My Account

My Account is a secure, convenient, and time-saving way to access and manage your tax and benefit information online, seven days a week! If you are not registered with My Account but need information right away, use Quick Access to get fast, easy, and secure access to some of your information now. For more information, go to **www.cra.gc.ca/myaccount** or see Pamphlet RC4059, *My Account for individuals*.

### TIPS (Tax Information Phone Service)

For personal and general tax information by telephone, use our automated service, TIPS, by calling **1-800-267-6999**.

### Teletypewriter (TTY) users

TTY users can call **1-800-665-0354** for bilingual assistance during regular business hours.

### Related forms and publications

#### Forms

RC240 *Designation of an Exempt Contribution Tax-Free Savings Account (TFSA)*

RC243 *Tax-Free Savings Account (TFSA) Return*

RC243-SCH-A *Schedule A – Excess TFSA Amounts*

RC243-SCH-B *Schedule B – Non-Resident Contributions to a Tax-Free Savings Account (TFSA)*

T400A *Objection – Income Tax Act*

#### Interpretation Bulletins

IT-110R *Gifts and Official Donation Receipts*

IT-221R *Determination of an Individual's Residence Status*

IT-320R *Qualified Investments – Trusts Governed by Registered Retirement Savings Plans, Registered Education Savings Plans and Registered Retirement Income Funds*

IT-419R *Meaning of Arm's Length*

#### Pamphlets

P148 *Resolving your Dispute: Objections and Appeal Rights under the Income Tax Act*

RC4059 *My Account for Individuals*

### Our service complaint process

If you are not satisfied with the **service** you have received, contact the CRA employee you have been dealing with (or call the phone number you have been given). If you still disagree with the way your concerns are being addressed, ask to discuss the matter with the employee's supervisor.

If the matter is still not resolved, you have the right to file a service complaint by completing Form RC193, *Service-Related Complaint*. If you are still not satisfied with the way the CRA has handled your complaint, you can contact the Taxpayers' Ombudsman.

For more information, go to **www.cra.gc.ca/complaints** or see Booklet RC4420, *Information on CRA – Service Complaints*.

### Your opinion counts

If you have any comments or suggestions that could help us improve our publications, we would like to hear from you. Please send your comments to:

**Taxpayer Services Directorate**
**Canada Revenue Agency**
**750 Heron Road**
**Ottawa ON K1A 0L5**

# Asking for a Clearance Certificate (Form TX19)

Canada Revenue Agency   Agence du revenu du Canada

## ASKING FOR A CLEARANCE CERTIFICATE

**DO NOT USE THIS AREA**

Use this form if you are the legal representative for an estate, business, or property and you are asking for a clearance certificate before distributing the assets of the estate, business, or trust. A legal representative includes an executor, administrator, liquidator, trustee, or like person other than a trustee in bankruptcy.

Send this form to the Assistant Director, Audit, at your tax services office. Do **not** attach this form to the return. You can find the address of your tax services office on our Web site at **www.cra.gc.ca/contact**.

Do **not** send us this form until:

- you have filed all the required tax returns and have received the related notices of assessment; and
- we have received or secured all income taxes (including the provincial or territorial taxes we administer), Canada Pension Plan contributions, Employment Insurance premiums, and any related interest and penalties.

Attach to this form the documents listed below to help us issue the certificate without delay:

- a copy of the will, including any codicils, renunciations, disclaimers, and all probate documents. If the taxpayer died intestate, also attach a copy of the document appointing an administrator (for example, the Letters of Administraton or Letters of Verification issued by a probate court);
- a copy of the trust document for inter vivos trusts;
- a statement showing the list of assets and distribution plan, including a description of each asset, adjusted cost base, and the fair market value at the date of death and at the date of distribution, if not at the same time. Also include the names, addresses, and social insurance numbers or account numbers of the recipients and his or her relationship to the deceased. If a statement of properties has been prepared for a probate court, we will usually accept a copy, and a list of any properties that the deceased owned before death and that passed directly to beneficiaries;
- any other documents that are necessary to prove that you are the legal representative; and
- a letter of authorization that you have signed if you want us to communicate with any other person or firm, or you want the clearance certificate sent to any address other than your own.

For more information, refer to the Information Circular 82-6, *Clearance Certificate* or call **1-800-959-8281**.

**Identification area**

| | |
|---|---|
| Name of deceased, corporation, or trust, whichever applies | |
| Address | |
| Social insurance number, Business Number, or trust number, whichever applies | Date of death **or** date of wind-up, whichever applies |
| Legal representative's name (if there is more than one, please provide the details on a separate sheet) | |
| Legal representative's address (we will send the clearance certificate to this address) | |
| Legal representative's capacity (for example, executor, administrator, liquidator, or trustee) | Telephone number |

**Period covered**

I am asking for a clearance certificate for the period ending ____________________

**Tax returns filed**

Have you filed any tax returns for the year of death? ☐ Yes ☐ No

If *yes*, indicate what type of tax return(s) you filed. For more information, get guides T4011, *Preparing Returns for Deceased Persons*, T4012, *T2 Corporation Income Tax Guide*, and/or T4013, *T3 Trust Guide*.

| | | |
|---|---|---|
| ☐ T1 final return | ☐ T1 return for rights or things | ☐ T2 Corporation Income Tax Return |
| ☐ T1 return for income from a testamentary trust | ☐ T1 return for partner or proprietor | ☐ T3 Trust Income Tax and Information Return |

**Certification and undertaking**

I am asking for a clearance certificate from the Minister of National Revenue. The certificate will certify that all taxes (including provincial or territorial taxes administered by the Canada Revenue Agency), Canada Pension Plan contributions, Employment Insurance premiums, and any related interest and penalties for which the deceased, corporation, or trust named above is liable (or can reasonably be expected to become liable) have been paid or that the Minister has accepted security for the amounts. The certificate will apply to the tax year in which the distribution is made and any previous year for which I am liable (or can reasonably be expected to become liable) as the legal representative of the deceased, corporation, or trust identified. I will complete the distribution of all of the property as soon as possible after I receive the clearance certificate.

| Date | Capacity (for example, executor, administrator, liquidator, or trustee) | Signature |
|---|---|---|
| Date | Capacity (for example, executor, administrator, liquidator, or trustee) | Signature |

*Privacy Act*, Personal Information Bank numbers CRA PPU 005 and CRA PPU 015

TX19 (10)   (Français au verso)   Canada

# Clearance Certificate (Information Circular IC82-6R8)

Canada Revenue Agency / Agence du revenu du Canada

INCOME TAX INFORMATION CIRCULAR

NO.: **IC82-6R8** DATE: December 10, 2010

SUBJECT: **Clearance Certificate**

*This circular cancels and replaces Information Circular IC82-6R7 dated November 23, 2009.*

1. This circular explains the need for a clearance certificate issued under the *Income Tax Act*. To ask for a clearance certificate, complete Form TX19, *Asking for a Clearance Certificate*. Also, give us the documents we ask for on Form TX19. This will help us to issue the certificate without delay.

## Why you need a clearance certificate

2. Subsection 159(2) of the *Income Tax Act* (the Act), requires a legal representative, which we define in paragraph 3, to obtain a clearance certificate before distributing property that he or she controls in their capacity as the legal representative. As a legal representative, if you distribute the property without a certificate, you are liable for any unpaid amounts (see paragraphs 4 and 5). You do not need a clearance certificate before each distribution, as long as you keep enough property to pay any liability to us.

3. A legal representative is a person who administers, winds up, controls, or otherwise deals with a property, business, or estate of another person who may be an individual, a trust, or a corporation. The legal representative for the purposes of subsection 159(2) must be an assignee, liquidator, curator, receiver of any kind, trustee, heir, administrator, executor, committee, or any other like person other than a trustee in bankruptcy. The reference to any other like person includes any person acting as a liquidator, whether or not the person was formally appointed. For instance, in a voluntary dissolution, there may be no formally appointed liquidator and the responsibility may be assumed by an auditor, director, officer, or other person. The facts of each particular case will determine whether a person is a legal representative.

4. A clearance certificate certifies that all amounts for which the taxpayer is, or can reasonably be expected to become, liable under the Act at or before the time of distribution have been paid, or that the Minister of National Revenue has accepted security for payment. The certificate applies to amounts for which you are or may become liable for payment as the legal representative. These amounts include all income taxes (including provincial and territorial taxes that we administer), along with any interest and penalties. The certificate also covers the payment of any outstanding Canada Pension Plan contributions and Employment Insurance premiums, including any associated interest and penalties.

5. If you do not get a clearance certificate before you distribute property, you are liable for unpaid amounts, whether assessed before or after the actual distribution of property. You will be personally liable for the taxpayer's debt, up to the value of the property you distributed. Under proposed legislation, for assessments completed after December 20, 2002, you will also be responsible for any and all interest that is charged as a result of these assessments.

6. When you give up control and transfer a property to the person entitled to receive it, we consider you to have distributed the property on that date. The date on which a person acquires the right to receive a property does not determine the distribution date.

## How to ask for a clearance certificate

7. To ask for a clearance certificate, you have to complete Form TX19, *Asking for a Clearance Certificate*. Send it to the Assistant Director, Audit, at your tax services office. Usually, that office will process the certificate. However, under some conditions, another tax services office may process your certificate. This may happen, for example, if the deceased's properties are located in an area served by a tax services office other than yours.

8. To avoid delays, make sure Form TX19 is as complete as possible, and include the attachments. Identify the person(s) asking for the certificate by providing the name, address, telephone number, and title (for example, executor, trustee, liquidator, administrator). For a deceased person, Form TX19 has to include the full name, last address, social insurance number, and date of death. For a trust, include the name of the trust, the name and address of the trustee(s), the trust account number, and the wind-up date. In the case of a corporation, give the full corporate name, the Business Number, and the wind-up date.

9. If you have not sent us the following documents, attach them to Form TX19:

(a) a copy of the will, including any codicils, renunciations, or disclaimers, and all probate documents. If the individual died intestate, also attach a copy of the document appointing an administrator (for example, the Letters of Administration or Letters of Verification issued by a probate court);

(b) a copy of the trust document for inter vivos trusts;

Cette publication existe aussi en français.

Canada

(c) a statement showing the list of assets and distribution plan, including a description of each asset, adjusted cost base and the fair market value at the date of death or at the date of distribution if not the same. Also include the names, addresses, and social insurane numbers or account numbers of the recipients and his or her relationship to the deceased. If a statement of properties has been prepared for a probate court, we will usually accept a copy, and a list of any properties (such as real estate held in joint ownership, RRSPs with named beneficiaries, etc.) that the deceased owned before death and that passed directly to beneficiaries;

(d) any other documents that are necessary to prove that you are the legal representative; and

(e) a letter of authorization that you have signed if you want us to communicate with any other person or firm, or you want the clearance certificate sent to any other address other than your own.

10. When you receive the clearance certificate, you have to complete, as soon as possible, the actual transfer or distribution of any property over which you have control.

## Issuing a clearance certificate

11. All clearance certificates will be issued on Form TX21, *Clearance Certificate*. We will issue a clearance certificate only when:

(a) you have filed and we have assessed the required tax return(s); and

(b) we have received or secured all amounts for which the taxpayer is liable. These amounts include income tax (including the provincial and territorial tax that we administer), Canada Pension Plan contributions, Employment Insurance premiums, interest, and penalties.

For an estate or trust, where the provisions of subsections 106(3), 107(4), or 107(5) apply to a distribution, and where any tax payable by the estate or trust can be determined only after the fair market value of the property to be distributed has been determined on the date of distribution, we will issue a clearance certificate as long as you do **all** of the following:

(a) you establish a scheme of distribution by a date chosen by you, which is prior to the date of your request for a clearance certificate (see paragraph 12);

(b) you calculate the tax payable as if the distribution had occurred on the chosen date;

(c) you file a final tax return for the tax year ending on the chosen date and pay any taxes, interest, and penalties that are chargeable against or payable out of the estate or trust property; and

(d) you submit your request in writing, and include a statement that you will complete the actual transfer of all the property of the estate or trust as soon as possible after you receive the clearance certificate.

We may not issue a clearance certificate if you have not filed a tax return or paid an amount for which the estate or trust is liable, or if there is an indication that the actual distribution will not take place as soon as possible after we issue the clearance certificate.

Once we issue the certificate, we consider the chosen date to be the actual date of distribution for tax purposes and regard the estate or trust representative as holding the properties for the beneficiaries since that date.

Do not file Form TX19, *Asking for a Clearance Certificate,* until you receive the assessment notice(s). However, there may be exceptions for an estate or trust (see paragraph 12).

12. There may be times when you cannot determine the date of distribution because it may depend on completing the final assessment and issuing the clearance certificate. Since the final assessment has to include the period up to and including the date of distribution of property, it may seem we cannot issue the final assessment or the clearance certificate. For example, this situation could arise when the properties of an operating corporation continue to generate income until they are distributed. In such circumstances, you should contact the Assistant Director, Audit, at the tax services office where you file Form TX19 to make alternative arrangements.

13. A clearance certificate covers only the properties you controlled from the date you received control to the date you asked for the clearance certificate. After you receive a clearance certificate, you may discover another property that affects the amounts of income or capital gains you reported on the taxpayer's tax return(s). If so, you will have to get another clearance certificate before you distribute the newly identified property. In this circumstance, you should contact the Assistant Director, Audit, at the tax services office where you file Form TX19.

## Individuals

14. For an individual, you should ask for a clearance certificate only for properties you will distribute in your capacity as a legal representative.

## Estates or trusts

15. There may be situations when an estate or a trust will continue to exist to pay or allocate its income to the beneficiaries until a certain situation occurs (for example, a beneficiary reaches the age of majority). In such cases, we do not consider the payment or allocation of trust income to a beneficiary as a distribution of property. As a result, you do not need to ask for a clearance certificate.

## Corporations

16. Under subsection 87(2) (amalgamation), you can transfer a corporation's assets and liabilities on a rollover basis to another corporation. If all conditions of the rollover are satisfied, the amalgamation should not create any additional tax liability. In this case, you do not need a clearance certificate. If you are not sure that the rollover is complete, you should apply for a clearance certificate. For any other type of corporate dissolution, you should get a clearance certificate before you distribute the corporate property.

## *Excise Tax Act* (goods and services tax/harmonized sales tax)

17. Section 270, Part IX of the *Excise Tax Act* (goods and services tax/harmonized sales tax) includes similar provisions requiring you, as a **receiver** or **representative**, to get a clearance certificate by completing Form GST352, *Application for Clearance Certificate*, before you distribute any property or money you control. For more information on clearance certificates related to the goods and services tax/harmonized sales tax, contact your tax services office.

# United States Estate (and Generation-Skipping Transfer) Tax Return (Form 706-NA)

Form **706-NA**

(Rev. July 2011)

Department of the Treasury
Internal Revenue Service

**United States Estate (and Generation-Skipping Transfer) Tax Return**

**Estate of nonresident not a citizen of the United States**

**To be filed for decedents dying after December 31, 2009.**

**▶ See instructions.**

OMB No. 1545-0531

Attach supplemental documents and translations. Show amounts in U.S. dollars.

**Part I Decedent, Executor, and Attorney**

| | | | |
|---|---|---|---|
| 1a Decedent's first (given) name and middle initial | b Decedent's last (family) name | | 2 U.S. taxpayer ID number (if any) |
| 3 Place of death | 4 Domicile at time of death | 5 Citizenship (nationality) | 6 Date of death |
| 7a Date of birth | b Place of birth | 8 Business or occupation | |

| | | |
|---|---|---|
| **In United States** | 9a Name of executor | 10a Name of attorney for estate |
| | b Address | b Address |
| **Outside United States** | 11a Name of executor | 12a Name of attorney for estate |
| | b Address | b Address |

**Part II Tax Computation**

| | | | |
|---|---|---|---|
| 1 | Taxable estate from Schedule B, line 9 | 1 | |
| 2 | Total taxable gifts of tangible or intangible property located in the U.S., transferred (directly or indirectly) by the decedent after December 31, 1976, and not included in the gross estate (see section 2511) | 2 | |
| 3 | Total. Add lines 1 and 2 | 3 | |
| 4 | Tentative tax on the amount on line 3 (see instructions) | 4 | |
| 5 | Tentative tax on the amount on line 2 (see instructions) | 5 | |
| 6 | Gross estate tax. Subtract line 5 from line 4 | 6 | |
| 7 | Unified credit. Enter smaller of line 6 amount or maximum allowed (see instructions) | 7 | |
| 8 | Balance. Subtract line 7 from line 6 | 8 | |
| 9 | Other credits (see instructions) — 9 | | |
| 10 | Credit for tax on prior transfers. Attach Schedule Q, Form 706 — 10 | | |
| 11 | Total. Add lines 9 and 10 | 11 | |
| 12 | Net estate tax. Subtract line 11 from line 8 | 12 | |
| 13 | Total generation-skipping transfer tax. Attach Schedule R, Form 706 | 13 | |
| 14 | **Total transfer taxes.** Add lines 12 and 13 | 14 | |
| 15 | Earlier payments. See instructions and attach explanation | 15 | |
| 16 | Balance due. Subtract line 15 from line 14 (see instructions) | 16 | |

Under penalties of perjury, I declare that I have examined this return, including accompanying schedules and statements, and to the best of my knowledge and belief, it is true, correct, and complete. I understand that a complete return requires listing all property constituting the part of the decedent's gross estate (as defined by the statute) situated in the United States. I (executor) understand that if any other person files a Form 8939 or Form 706 (or Form 706-NA) with respect to this decedent or estate, that my name and address will be shared with such person, and I (executor) also hereby request the IRS share with me the name and address of any other person who files a Form 8939 or Form 706 (or Form 706-NA) with respect to this decedent or estate. Declaration of preparer other than the executor is based on all information of which preparer has any knowledge.

**Sign Here**

▶ Signature of executor ▶ Date

▶ Signature of executor ▶ Date

| **Paid Preparer Use Only** | | | | |
|---|---|---|---|---|
| Print/Type preparer's name | Preparer's signature | Date | Check ☐ if self-employed | PTIN |
| Firm's name ▶ | | | Firm's EIN ▶ | |
| Firm's address ▶ | | | Phone no. | |

**For Privacy Act and Paperwork Reduction Act Notice, see the separate instructions.** Cat. No. 10145K Form **706-NA** (Rev. 7-2011)

Form 706-NA (Rev. 7-2011) Page 2

**Part III General Information**

| | | Yes | No |
|---|---|---|---|
| 1a | Did the decedent die testate? | | |
| b | Were letters testamentary or of administration granted for the estate? | | |
| | *If granted to persons other than those filing the return, include names and addresses on page 1.* | | |
| 2 | Did the decedent, at the time of death, own any: | | |
| a | Real property located in the United States? | | |
| b | U.S. corporate stock? | | |
| c | Debt obligations of (1) a U.S. person, or (2) the United States, a state or any political subdivision, or the District of Columbia? | | |
| d | Other property located in the United States? | | |
| 3 | Was the decedent engaged in business in the United States at the date of death? | | |
| 4 | At the date of death, did the decedent have access, personally or through an agent, to a safe deposit box located in the United States? | | |
| 5 | At the date of death, did the decedent own any property located in the United States as a joint tenant with right of survivorship; as a tenant by the entirety; or, with surviving spouse, as community property? | | |
| | *If "Yes," attach Schedule E, Form 706.* | | |
| 6a | Had the decedent ever been a citizen or resident of the United States (see instructions)? | | |
| b | If "Yes," did the decedent lose U.S. citizenship or residency within 10 years of death? (see instructions) | | |

| | | Yes | No |
|---|---|---|---|
| 7 | Did the decedent make any transfer (of property that was located in the United States at either the time of the transfer or the time of death) described in sections 2035, 2036, 2037, or 2038 (see the instructions for Form 706, Schedule G)? | | |
| | *If "Yes," attach Schedule G, Form 706.* | | |
| 8 | At the date of death, were there any trusts in existence that were created by the decedent and that included property located in the United States either when the trust was created or when the decedent died? | | |
| | *If "Yes," attach Schedule G, Form 706.* | | |
| 9 | At the date of death, did the decedent: | | |
| a | Have a general power of appointment over any property located in the United States? | | |
| b | Or, at any time, exercise or release the power? | | |
| | *If "Yes" to either a or b, attach Schedule H, Form 706.* | | |
| 10a | Have federal gift tax returns ever been filed? | | |
| b | Periods covered ▶ | | |
| c | IRS offices where filed ▶ | | |
| 11 | Does the gross estate in the United States include any interests in property transferred to a "skip person" as defined in the instructions to Schedule R of Form 706? | | |
| | *If "Yes," attach Schedules R and/or R-1, Form 706.* | | |

**Schedule A. Gross Estate in the United States** (see instructions)

| | Yes | No |
|---|---|---|
| Do you elect to value the decedent's gross estate at a date or dates after the decedent's death (as authorized by section 2032)? ▶ | | |

*To make the election, you must check this box "Yes." If you check "Yes," complete **all** columns. If you check "No," complete columns (a), (b), and (e); you may leave columns (c) and (d) blank or you may use them to expand your column (b) description.*

| (a) Item no. | (b) Description of property and securities For securities, give CUSIP number | (c) Alternate valuation date | (d) Alternate value in U.S. dollars | (e) Value at date of death in U.S. dollars |
|---|---|---|---|---|
| 1 | | | | |
| | *(If you need more space, attach additional sheets of same size.)* | | | |
| Total | | | | |

**Schedule B. Taxable Estate**

**Caution. You must document lines 2 and 4 for the deduction on line 5 to be allowed.**

| | | | |
|---|---|---|---|
| 1 | Gross estate in the United States (Schedule A total) | 1 | |
| 2 | Gross estate outside the United States (see instructions) | 2 | |
| 3 | Entire gross estate wherever located. Add amounts on lines 1 and 2 | 3 | |
| 4 | Amount of funeral expenses, administration expenses, decedent's debts, mortgages and liens, and losses during administration. Attach itemized schedule. (see instructions) | 4 | |
| 5 | Deduction for expenses, claims, etc. Divide line 1 by line 3 and multiply the result by line 4 | 5 | |
| 6 | Charitable deduction (attach Schedule O, Form 706) and marital deduction (attach Schedule M, Form 706, and computation) | 6 | |
| 7 | State death tax deduction (see instructions) | 7 | |
| 8 | Total deductions. Add lines 5, 6, and 7 | 8 | |
| 9 | Taxable estate. Subtract line 8 from line 1. Enter here and on line 1 of Part II | 9 | |

Form **706-NA** (Rev. 7-2011)

# Instructions for Form 706-NA

# Instructions for Form 706-NA

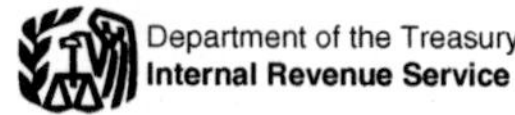

(Rev. August 2011)

**United States Estate (and Generation-Skipping Transfer) Tax Return**
**Estate of nonresident not a citizen of the United States**
**(To be used with the July 2011 revision of Form 706-NA for decedents dying after December 31, 2010.)**

Section references are to the Internal Revenue Code unless otherwise noted.

## What's New

- The provision for estates of nonresident aliens allowing for an exemption of a portion of the decedent's stock in a regulated investment company from U.S. estate tax was extended by the Tax Relief, Unemployment Insurance Reauthorization and Job Creation Act of 2010 (Act) at section 726(a). The provision will apply to estates of nonresident alien decedents dying on or before December 31, 2011.
- The Act also included several other provisions affecting the Form 706-NA. They are:

1. The maximum estate tax rate is 35% (Act section 302(a)(2)).
2. The applicable rate for generation-skipping transfers is 35% (Act section 302(c)).
3. Prior gifts must be calculated at the rate in effect at the decedent's date of death (Act section 302(d)(1)).

- Executors must provide documentation of their status.
- These instructions are for use with the July 2011 revision of Form 706-NA.

## General Instructions

### Purpose of Form

Form 706-NA is used to compute estate and generation-skipping transfer (GST) tax liability for nonresident alien decedents. The estate tax is imposed on the transfer of the decedent's taxable estate rather than on the receipt of any part of it.

*For information about transfer certificates for U.S. assets, write to the following address.*

Internal Revenue Service
Cincinnati, OH 45999
Stop 824G

**Note.** In order to complete this return, you must obtain Form 706, United States Estate (and Generation-Skipping Transfer) Tax Return, and its instructions. You must attach schedules from Form 706 if you intend to claim a marital deduction, a charitable deduction, a qualified conservation easement exclusion, or a credit for tax on prior transfers, or if you answer "Yes" to question 5, 7, 8, 9a, 9b, or 11 in Part III, *General Information.* You will need the instructions to Form 706 to explain how to value stocks and bonds. Make sure that you use the version of Form 706 that corresponds to the date of the decedent's death.

## Definitions

The following definitions apply in these instructions.

**United States.** The United States means the 50 states and the District of Columbia.

**Nonresident alien decedent.** A nonresident alien decedent is a decedent who is neither domiciled in nor a citizen of the United States at the time of death. For purposes of this form, a citizen of a U.S. possession is not a U.S. citizen.

**Long-term United States resident.** A long-term U.S. resident is an alien who has been a lawful permanent resident of the U.S. (green card holder) in at least 8 of the last 15 tax years ending with the tax year in which U.S. residency is terminated.

**Executor.** An executor is the personal representative, executor, executrix, administrator, or administratrix of the deceased person's estate. If no executor is appointed, qualified, and acting in the United States, every person in actual or constructive possession of any of the decedent's property must file a return. If more than one person must file, it is preferable that they join in filing one complete return. Otherwise, each must file as complete a return as possible, including a full description of the property and each person's name who holds an interest in it.

Executors must provide documentation proving their status. Documentation will vary but may include a certified copy of the will or a court order designating the executor(s). A statement by the executor(s) attesting to their status is insufficient.

**U.S. expatriate.** Generally, a U.S. expatriate is one who, within 10 years before the date of death, lost U.S. citizenship or (in certain cases) ended long-term U.S. residency with the principal purpose of avoiding U.S. taxes. See the instructions for *Question 6a* and *Question 6b*, below. Also, see effective dates below for more information.

***Note.*** U.S. citizens and long-term residents who relinquished their U.S. citizenship or ceased to be lawful permanent residents (green card holders) on or after June 17, 2008, are not considered U.S. expatriates for purposes of this form. U.S. citizens and residents who receive bequests from such individuals, however, may be subject to tax under section 2801.

***After June 3, 2004, but before June 17, 2008.*** A citizen or long-term resident who lost U.S. citizenship or residency after June 3, 2004, but before June 17, 2008, is subject to the alternative tax regime of section 877 when the individual:

1. Had an average annual net income tax liability for the 5 tax years ending before the date of expatriation greater than:
   - $124,000 if expatriated in 2004
   - $127,000 if expatriated in 2005
   - $131,000 if expatriated in 2006
   - $136,000 if expatriated in 2007
   - $139,000 if expatriated in 2008;
2. Had a net worth of $2,000,000 or more on the date of expatriation; or
3. Fails to certify compliance with all federal tax obligations for the 5 preceding taxable years, unless he or she is a minor or a dual citizen without substantial contact with the United States. See sections 877(c)(2)(B) and (c)(3), for more information.

Sep 16, 2011

Cat. No. 63118N

***On or after February 6, 1995, but before June 3, 2004.*** Under prior law, citizens or certain long-term residents (as defined in section 877(e)) who lost U.S. citizenship or residency on or after February 6, 1995, but before June 3, 2004, are presumed to have the principal purpose of avoiding U.S. taxes if the decedent's average annual net income tax liability or net worth exceeds certain limits. However, the executor has an opportunity to prove otherwise. See sections 877(a)(1), (a)(2), and (c), before its amendment by P.L. 108-357, for more information.

## Who Must File

The executor must file Form 706-NA if the date of death value of the gross estate located in the United States exceeds the filing limit of $60,000. The total value of the gross estate may be reduced by the sum of:

- The gift tax specific exemption (section 2521) allowed for gifts made between September 9, 1976, and December 31, 1976, inclusive, and
- The amount of adjusted taxable gifts made after December 31, 1976.

## When To File

File Form 706-NA within 9 months after the date of death unless an extension of time to file was granted.

If you are unable to file Form 706-NA by the due date, use Form 4768, Application for Extension of Time To File a Return and/or Pay U.S. Estate (and Generation-Skipping Transfer) Taxes, to apply for an automatic 6-month extension of time to file. Check the "Form 706-NA" box in Part II of Form 4768.

## Where To File

File Form 706-NA at the following address.

Department of the Treasury
Internal Revenue Service Center
Cincinnati, OH 45999

## Penalties

The law provides for penalties for both late filing of returns and late payment of tax unless there is reasonable cause for the delay. There are also penalties for willful attempts to evade or defeat payment of tax.

The law also provides for penalties for valuation understatements that cause an underpayment of tax. See sections 6662(g) and (h) for more details.

**Reasonable cause determinations.** If you receive a notice about penalties after you file Form 706-NA, send an explanation and we will determine if you meet reasonable cause criteria. Do not attach an explanation when you file Form 706-NA. Explanations attached to the return at the time of filing will not be considered.

**Return preparer.** The Small Business and Work Opportunity Tax Act of 2007 (2007 Act) extended the application of return preparer penalties to preparers of estate tax returns. Under section 6694, as amended by the 2007 Act, estate tax return preparers who prepare any return or claim for refund that reflects an understatement of tax liability due to willful or reckless conduct are subject to a penalty of $5,000 or 50% of the income derived (or income to be derived), whichever is greater, for the preparation of each such return. See section 6694, T.D. 9436 (2009-3 I.R.B. 268, available at *http://www.irs.gov/pub/irs-irbs/irb09-03.pdf*), and Ann. 2009-15, 2009-11 I.R.B. 687 (available at *http://www.irs.gov/pub/irs-irbs/irb09-11.pdf*) for more information.

## Death Tax Treaties

Death tax treaties are in effect with the following countries.

| | |
|---|---|
| Australia | Ireland |
| Austria | Italy |
| Canada* | Japan |
| Denmark | Netherlands |
| Finland | Norway |
| France | South Africa |
| Germany | Switzerland |
| Greece | United Kingdom |

*Article XXIX B of the United States—Canada Income Tax Treaty

If you are reporting any items on this return based on the provisions of a death tax treaty or protocol, attach a statement to this return indicating that the return position is treaty-based. See Regulations section 301.6114-1 for details.

# Specific Instructions

## Attachments

If the decedent died testate, attach a certified copy of the will to Form 706-NA. If you are unable to obtain a certified copy, attach a copy of the will and explain why it could not be certified.

You must also attach a copy of the decedent's death certificate.

For closely held or inactive corporate stock, attach the balance sheets, particularly the one nearest the valuation date, and statements of the net earnings or operating results and dividends paid for each of the 5 preceding years. Attach any other documents, such as appraisals, needed for explanation. Also attach copies of all available U.S. gift tax returns the decedent filed. Other documents may be required as explained in these instructions.

Attach an English translation to all documents in other languages.

## How To Complete Form 706-NA

First, enter the decedent's name and the other information called for in Part I. For item 2, enter the decedent's social security number (SSN) or individual taxpayer identification number (ITIN), whichever is applicable. Then answer all of the questions in Part III.

The estate tax is imposed on the decedent's gross estate in the United States, reduced by allowable deductions. Compute the gross estate in the United States on Schedule A. Reduce the Schedule A total by the allowable deductions to derive the taxable estate on Schedule B, and figure the tax due using Part II–Tax Computation.

### Part III. General Information

**Question 6a.** If you answer "Yes," please attach a statement listing:

- The citizenship of the decedent's parents,
- Whether the decedent became a U.S. citizen through a naturalization proceeding in the United States, and
- When the decedent lost U.S. citizenship or residency.

**Question 6b.** If you answered "Yes," and the decedent lost his or her U.S. citizenship or long-term residence within 10 years of death and prior to June 17, 2008, but maintain that avoiding U.S. taxes was not a principal purpose for the decedent's loss of citizenship or residency, attach documents to sustain your position. See *Definitions*, above.

**Question 9.** A *general power of appointment* is any power of appointment exercisable in favor of the decedent, the decedent's estate, the decedent's creditors, or the creditors of the decedent's estate, and includes the right of a beneficiary to appropriate or consume the principal of a trust. For a complete definition, see section 2041(b).

### Schedule A

Before you complete Schedule A, you must determine what assets are included in the decedent's entire gross estate, wherever located. However, list on Schedule A only those assets located in the United States. Enter the total value of assets located outside the United States on line 2 of Schedule B.

**Entire gross estate.** The entire gross estate is figured the same way for a nonresident alien decedent as for a U.S. citizen or resident. It consists of all property the decedent beneficially owned, wherever located, and includes the following property interests:

- Generally, the full value of property the decedent owned at the time of death as a joint tenant with right of survivorship (but if the surviving spouse is a U.S. citizen, then only half the value of property held by the decedent and surviving spouse either as joint tenants with right of survivorship or as tenants by the entirety). For exceptions, see the instructions for Form 706, Schedule E;
- Property the decedent and a surviving spouse owned as community property to the extent of the decedent's interest in the property under applicable state, possession, or foreign law;
- A surviving spouse's dower or curtesy interest and all substitute interests created by statute;
- Proceeds of insurance on the decedent's life, generally including proceeds receivable by beneficiaries other than the estate;
- Several kinds of transfers the decedent made before death;
- Property in which the decedent either held a general power of appointment at the time of death, or used or released this power in certain ways before death; and
- Certain annuities to surviving beneficiaries.

For additional information concerning joint tenancies, tenancies by the entirety, annuities, life insurance, transfers during life, and powers of appointment, see the Instructions for Form 706.

Enter on Schedule A all of the assets that meet both the following tests.

- They are included in the *entire gross estate* and
- They are located in the United States.

**Determining where assets are located.** Unless a treaty provides otherwise (see *Death Tax Treaties*, above), use the following rules to determine whether assets are located in the United States.

***Real estate and tangible personal property.*** Real estate and tangible personal property are located in the United States if they are physically located there.

**Note.** An exception is made for works of art that are owned by a nonresident alien and are located within the United States, if on the date of death the works of art are:

- Imported solely for public exhibition,
- On loan to a non-profit public gallery or museum, and
- On exhibition or en route to or from exhibition.

***Stock.*** Generally, no matter where stock certificates are physically located, stock of corporations organized in or under U.S. law is property located in the United States, and all other corporate stock is property located outside the United States.

***Stock in a Regulated Investment Company (RIC).*** For a nonresident alien decedent who died after 2004, a portion of stock in a RIC is treated as property located outside the United States in the proportion of the RIC's qualifying assets in relation to the total assets owned by the RIC at the end of the quarter immediately preceding the decedent's death.

Qualifying assets are assets that, if owned directly by the decedent, would have been:

- Bank deposits and amounts described in section 871(i)(3),
- Portfolio debt obligations,
- Certain original issue discount obligations,
- Debt obligations of a U.S. corporation that are treated as giving rise to foreign source income, and
- Other property not within the United States.

See section 2105(d) for details.

***Insurance proceeds.*** Proceeds of insurance policies on the decedent's life are property located outside the United States.

***Debt obligations within U.S.*** Debt obligations are generally property located in the United States if they are debts of a U.S. citizen or resident, a domestic partnership or corporation, a domestic estate or trust, the United States, a state or state's political subdivision, or the District of Columbia.

***Debt obligations outside U.S.*** The following debt obligations are generally treated as located outside the United States:

- Debt obligations (whether registered or unregistered) issued after July 18, 1984, if the interest on them would be eligible for tax exemption under section 871(h)(1) had such interest been received by the decedent at the time of his death. However, if the debt earns contingent interest, some or all of it may be considered property in the United States (section 2105(b)(3)).
- A debt obligation of a domestic corporation if the interest from it (had it been received at the time of death) would have been treated as income from outside the United States because the corporation derived less than 20% of its gross income from sources in the United States during its 3 tax years before the decedent's death (section 861(a)(1)(A)).
- Certain short-term original issue discount debt obligations.

See section 2105(b)(4) for details.

***Deposits.*** The following deposits are treated as located outside the United States if they are not effectively connected with conducting a trade or business within the United States:

- A deposit with a U.S. bank or a U.S. banking branch of a foreign corporation,
- A deposit or withdrawable account with a savings and loan association chartered and supervised under federal or state law,
- An amount held by a U.S. insurance company under an agreement to pay interest, and
- A deposit in a foreign branch of a U.S. bank.

If an asset is included in the total gross estate because the decedent owned it at the time of death, apply the above location rules as of the date of the decedent's death. However, if an asset is included in the decedent's total gross estate under one of the transfer provisions (sections 2035, 2036, 2037, and 2038), it is treated as located in the United States if it fulfills these rules either at the time of the transfer or at the time of death.

For example, if an item of tangible personal property was physically located in the United States on the date of a section 2038 transfer but had been moved outside the United States at the time of the decedent's death, the item would be considered still located in the United States and should be listed on Schedule A.

Describe the property on Schedule A in enough detail to enable the IRS to identify it. To determine the fair market value of stocks and bonds, use the rules in the Instructions for Form 706, Schedule B—Stocks and Bonds.

***Stocks.*** In descriptions of stock, include:

- The corporation's name;
- The number of shares;
- Whether common or preferred (if preferred, what issue);
- The par value (when needed for identification);
- Nine-digit CUSIP number (defined below); and
- The quotation at which reported.

Give the main exchange for listed stock. For unlisted stock, give the post office address of the main business office of the corporation, the state in which incorporated, and the incorporation date.

***Bonds.*** In bond descriptions, include:

- The quantity and denomination,
- Obligor's name,
- Maturity date,
- Interest rate,
- Each date when interest is payable,
- Nine-digit CUSIP number, and
- Series number (if more than one issue).

-3-

Give the exchange where the bond is listed. If it is unlisted, give the corporation's main business office.

The CUSIP (Committee on Uniform Security Identification Procedure) number is a nine-digit number that is assigned to all stocks and bonds traded on major exchanges and many unlisted securities. Usually the CUSIP number is printed on the face of the stock certificate. If you do not have a stock certificate, the CUSIP may be found on the broker's or custodian's statement or by contacting the company's transfer agent.

If you are required to file Schedule E, G, or H from Form 706, you need not enter the assets reported on those schedules on Schedule A of this Form 706-NA. Instead, attach the schedules to Form 706-NA, in column (b) enter "Total from Schedule _ _ _ _ _, Form 706," and enter the total values from the attached schedules in either column (d) or (e).

If the decedent was a U.S. expatriate, the decedent is treated as owning a prorated share of the U.S. property held by a foreign corporation in which he or she directly owned at least 10% of the voting stock and, with related interests, controlled over 50% of it (section 2107(b)).

**Property valuation date.** Generally, property must be valued as of the date of death. Columns (c) and (d) do not apply in this case, and you may use the space to expand descriptions from column (b).

However, you may elect to use the alternate valuation date. To make this election, check the "Yes" box at the beginning of Schedule A. If you do so, the election applies to all property, and you will need to complete each column in Schedule A. Under this election, any property distributed, sold, exchanged, or otherwise disposed of within 6 months after the decedent's death is valued as of the date of the disposition. Any property not disposed of during that period is valued as of the date 6 months after the decedent's death.

You may not elect alternate valuation unless the election will decrease both the value of the gross estate and the net estate tax due after application of all allowable credits.

## Qualified Conservation Easement Exclusion

Under section 2031(c), you may elect to exclude a portion of the value of land that is subject to a qualified conservation easement. You make the election by attaching Schedule U of Form 706 with all the required information. To elect the exclusion, you must include on Schedule A:

1. The decedent's interest in the land that is subject to the exclusion and
2. Exclude the applicable value of the land (amount from line 20, Schedule U) that is subject to the easement on Schedule A.

You must make the election on a timely filed Form 706-NA, including extensions. For more information, see the Instructions for Form 706.

## Canadian Small Estate Relief

If you are claiming a small estate exemption (worldwide estate of a Canadian resident decedent not more than $1.2 million) from tax on U.S. securities or certain other U.S. *situs* property under the 1995 Protocol to the Canadian income tax treaty, do not list the exempt assets on Schedule A.

Instead, list those assets and their values in a statement attached to the return specifying that you are relying on the treaty. To determine initially whether the small estate exemption applies, however, you must include the exempt assets in the value of the entire gross estate, wherever located, on lines 2 and 3 of Schedule B.

## United Kingdom-United States Treaty

If the decedent was a British national, the estate may figure its worldwide estate tax as if the decedent had been domiciled in the United States just before his or her death. If the amount is lower than the estate tax figured on a nonresident alien basis, the lower amount may be shown as the tax due on the Form 706-NA. Attach to the estate's Form 706-NA a statement showing the alternate computation and claiming the benefit of the treaty provision. See Paragraph 5 or Article 8 of the Treaty.

## Schedule B. Taxable Estate

*For the line 5 deduction to be allowed, you must complete lines 1 through 4 and document the amounts you include on lines 2 and 4.*

To document the line 2 amount, attach a certified copy of the foreign death tax return or, if none was filed, a certified copy of the estate inventory and the schedule of debts and charges that were filed with the foreign probate court or as part of the estate's administration proceedings. Supplement these documents with attachments if they do not set forth the entire gross estate outside the United States. If more proof is needed, you will be notified.

To document the line 4 amount, attach an itemized schedule. For each expense or claim, specify the nature and amount and give the creditor's name. Describe other deductions fully and identify any particular property to which they relate.

**Line 2.** The amount on line 2 is the total value of the assets included in the entire gross estate that were located outside the United States. If you claim deductions on line 5 of Schedule B, you must also document the amount you enter on line 2. See the first paragraph under Schedule B, above.

If you elected the alternate valuation date for property listed on Schedule A, use it also for the assets reported on line 2. Otherwise, value the amounts as of the date of death.

**Line 4.** You may deduct the following items whether or not they were incurred or paid in the United States:
- Funeral expenses;
- Administration expenses;
- Claims against the estate;
- Unpaid mortgages and liens; and
- Uncompensated losses that were incurred during settlement of the estate and that arose from theft or from casualties, such as fires, storms, or shipwrecks.

You may deduct only that part of a debt or mortgage that was contracted in good faith and for full value in money or money's worth. You may deduct mortgages only if you included the full value of the mortgaged property in the total gross estate on line 3. Do not deduct tax on income received after death or property taxes accrued after death. See *Line 7*, below, for details on deducting death taxes.

On line 4, show the total of these deductible items. In general, the total is limited to the amount on line 3.

**Line 6.** Use line 6 to enter the following deductions.

***Charitable deduction.*** Unless a treaty allows otherwise, you may take a charitable deduction only if the transfer was to a domestic entity or for use in the United States as described in the Instructions for Form 706.

Attach Schedule O of Form 706. If you claim the deduction under a treaty, specify the applicable treaty and attach a computation of the deduction.

***Marital deduction.*** Unless a treaty allows otherwise, you may only take a marital deduction if the surviving spouse is a U.S. citizen or if the property passes to a qualified domestic trust (QDOT) described in section 2056A and an election is made on Schedule M of Form 706.

Attach Schedule M of Form 706, and a statement showing your computation of the marital deduction.

-4-

See section 2518 for the rules governing disclaimers of interests in property.

**Line 7.** You may take a deduction on line 7 for death taxes (estate, inheritance, legacy, or succession taxes) you paid to any state or the District of Columbia on property listed in Schedule A. To calculate the deduction for state death taxes, use the formula below. Enter the result on line 7.

$$\frac{\text{Total value of assets in the gross estate subject to state death taxes}}{\text{Gross estate located in the U.S. (line 1 of Schedule B)}} \times \text{Total state death taxes paid}$$

Generally, you must claim this deduction within 4 years of filing the return. However, see section 2058(b) for exceptions and periods of limitations.

For the deduction to be allowed, you must file a certificate signed by the appropriate official of the taxing state. The certificate should show:

- The total tax charged,
- Any discount allowed,
- Any penalties and interest imposed,
- The tax actually paid, and
- Each payment date.

If possible, attach the certificate to this return; otherwise, please file it as soon as possible.

If you later recover any of the state tax for which you claim this deduction, you must notify the IRS at the following address within 30 days of receiving any refund of state taxes.

Department of the Treasury
Internal Revenue Service Center
Cincinnati, OH 45999

## Part II. Tax Computation

**Line 4 and Line 5.** To determine the tentative tax on the amount on line 2 (to be entered on line 4) and the tentative tax on the amount on line 3 (to be entered on line 5), use *Table A—Unified Rate Schedule* in the version of the Instructions for Form 706 that corresponds to the decedent's date of death.

**Line 7.** Enter the unified credit. The unified credit is allowed for the smaller of the line 6 amount or the maximum unified credit. In general, the maximum unified credit is $13,000.

For a citizen of a U.S. possession (see section 2209), the maximum unified credit is the greater of:

- $13,000 or
- The product of $46,800 times a fraction.

The numerator of the fraction is the part of the gross estate located in the United States (line 1 of Schedule B), and the denominator is the entire gross estate wherever located (line 3 of Schedule B).

If the unified credit is affected by a treaty, see section 2102(b)(3)(A).

**Note.** At the time this form went to print, treaties with Australia, Canada, Finland, France, Germany, Greece, Italy, Japan, Norway, and Switzerland contained provisions to which section 2102(b)(3)(A) applies.

*Any amount previously allowed as a unified credit against the gift tax will reduce, dollar for dollar, the unified credit allowed the estate (section 2102(b)(3)(B)).*

**Line 9.** Use line 9 to enter the following credits.

***Credit for federal gift taxes.*** See sections 2102 and 2012. Attach computation of credit.

***Canadian marital credit.*** In addition to the unified credit, a nonrefundable marital credit may be allowed if the executor elects this treaty benefit and waives the benefit of any estate tax marital deduction allowable under U.S. law. The credit amount is generally limited to the lesser of:

- The unified credit allowed to the estate (before reduction for any gift tax unified credit) or
- The amount of estate tax that would otherwise be imposed by the United States on the transfer of qualifying property to the surviving spouse.

See the 1995 Canadian income tax treaty protocol for details on computing the credit. Also, attach a computation of the credit and on the dotted line to the left of the line 9 entry, write "Canadian marital credit."

**Line 13.** If you answered "Yes" to Question 11 of Part III, you must complete and attach Schedules R and/ or R-1 from Form 706.

For the purposes of Form 706-NA, the GST tax is imposed only on transfers of interests in property that are part of the gross estate in the United States. Therefore, when completing Schedules R and/or R-1, you should enter only transfers of interests in property that you listed on Schedule A of Form 706-NA. Otherwise, complete Schedules R and/ or R-1 according to their instructions and enter the total GST tax from Schedule R on line 13.

For details, see Regulations section 26.2663-2.

**Line 15.** Attach an explanation if earlier payments were made to the IRS.

**Line 16.** Pay the balance due within 9 months after the decedent's death unless an extension of time to pay was granted. Make the check or money order payable to the "United States Treasury" for the face value in U.S. dollars.

## Signature(s)

CAUTION *If there is more than one executor, all listed executors are responsible for the return. However, it is sufficient for only one of the co-executors to sign the return.*

Form 706-NA must be signed. The executor must verify and sign the declaration on page 1 under penalties of perjury. The executor may use Form 2848, Power of Attorney and Declaration of Representative, to authorize another person to act for him or her before the IRS. See the instructions for Form 2848 and Circular 230, section 10.7(c)(1)(vii), for information on representing a person or entity located outside the United States.

Generally, anyone who is paid to prepare the return must sign the return in the space provided and fill in the "Paid Preparer Use Only" area. See section 7701(a)(36)(B) for exceptions.

In addition to signing and completing the required information, the paid preparer must give a copy of the completed return to the executor.

**Note.** A paid preparer may sign original or amended returns by rubber stamp, mechanical device, or computer software program.

-5-

**Privacy Act and Paperwork Reduction Act Notice.** We ask for the information on this form to carry out the Internal Revenue laws of the United States. You are required to give us the information. We need it to ensure that you are complying with these laws and to allow us to figure and collect the right amount of tax. Subtitle B and section 6109, and the regulations, require you to provide this information.

You are not required to provide the information requested on a form that is subject to the Paperwork Reduction Act unless the form displays a valid OMB control number. Books or records relating to a form or its instructions must be retained as long as their contents may become material in the administration of any Internal Revenue law. Generally, tax returns and return information are confidential as required by section 6103. However, section 6103 allows or requires the Internal Revenue Service to disclose information from this form in certain circumstances. For example, we may disclose information to the Department of Justice for civil or criminal litigation, and to cities, states, the District of Columbia, and U.S. commonwealths or possessions for use in administering their tax laws. We may also disclose this information to other countries under a tax treaty, to federal and state agencies to enforce federal nontax criminal laws, or to federal law enforcement and intelligence agencies to combat terrorism. Failure to provide this information, or providing false information, may subject you to penalties.

The time needed to complete and file this form will vary depending on individual circumstances. The estimated average time is:

| Recordkeeping | Learning about the law or the form | Preparing the form | Copying, assembling, and sending the form to the IRS |
|---|---|---|---|
| 1 hr., 25 min. | 52 min. | 1 hr., 36 min. | 34 min. |

If you have comments concerning the accuracy of these time estimates or suggestions for making this form simpler, we would be happy to hear from you. You can write to the Internal Revenue Service, Tax Products Coordinating Committee, SE:W:CAR:MP:T:M:S, 1111 Constitution Ave. NW, IR-6526, Washington, DC 20224. Do not send the tax form to this address. Instead, see *Where To File*.

# Websites and Organizational Tools

## Websites

### Income Taxation

Canada Revenue Agency ⇨ www.cra-arc.gc.ca
United States Internal Revenue Service ⇨ www.irs.gov

### Provincial and Territorial Governments

Alberta ⇨ http://alberta.ca
British Columbia ⇨ www.gov.bc.ca
Manitoba ⇨ www.gov.mb.ca
New Brunswick ⇨ www.gnb.ca
Newfoundland and Labrador ⇨ www.gov.nl.ca
Northwest Territories ⇨ www.gov.nt.ca
Nova Scotia ⇨ www.gov.ns.ca
Nunavut ⇨ www.gov.nu.ca
Ontario ⇨ www.ontario.ca
Prince Edward Island ⇨ www.gov.pe.ca
Quebec ⇨ www.gouv.qc.ca
Saskatchewan ⇨ www.gov.sk.ca
Yukon ⇨ www.gov.yk.ca

### Federal Government

Canadian Government ⇨ www.canada.gc.ca
Service Canada ⇨ www.servicecanada.gc.ca
Canada Savings Bonds ⇨ www.csb.gc.ca

### Workers' Compensation Boards

Alberta ⇨ www.wcb.ab.ca
British Columbia ⇨ www.worksafebc.com
Manitoba ⇨ www.wcb.mb.ca
New Brunswick ⇨ www.worksafenb.ca
Newfoundland and Labrador ⇨ www.whscc.nf.ca
Northwest Territories and Nunavut ⇨ www.wcb.nt.ca
Nova Scotia ⇨ www.wcb.ns.ca
Ontario ⇨ www.wsib.on.ca
Prince Edward Island ⇨ www.wcb.pe.ca
Quebec ⇨ www.csst.qc.ca
Saskatchewan ⇨ www.wcbsask.com
Yukon ⇨ www.wcb.yk.ca

### Funeral Information

Last Post Fund
⇨ www.lastpostfund.ca
Veterans Affairs Canada: Funeral, Burial and Gravemarking Assistance
⇨ www.veterans.gc.ca/eng/bereavement/gravevac

### Death Certificates

Alberta
⇨ www.servicealberta.ca/770.cfm
British Columbia
⇨ www.vs.gov.bc.ca/death
Manitoba
⇨ http://vitalstats.gov.mb.ca/pdf/application_death_certificate.pdf
New Brunswick
⇨ www.snb.ca/e/1000/1000-01/e/certificates-e.asp#
Newfoundland and Labrador
⇨ www.gs.gov.nl.ca/birth/death_certificate
Northwest Territories
⇨ www.hlthss.gov.nt.ca/english/services/vital_statistics/death_certificate
Nova Scotia
⇨ www.gov.ns.ca/snsmr/access/vitalstats/death-certificate.asp
Nunavut
⇨ www.gov.nu.ca/en/death.aspx
Ontario
⇨ www.ontario.ca/en/life_events/death/STEL02_119205.html
Prince Edward Island
⇨ www.gov.pe.ca/health/index.php3?number=1020360&lang=E
Quebec
⇨ www.etatcivil.gouv.qc.ca/en/death.html
Saskatchewan
⇨ www.isc.ca/VitalStats/Deaths
Yukon
⇨ www.hss.gov.yk.ca/death.php

### Legal Resources

CCH Canadian Limited (legal publisher)
⇨ www.cch.ca
CanLII (provides free access to legislative materials)
⇨ www.canlii.org

## Contacts

### LEGAL COUNSEL

Name: ______________________________

Phone Number: ______________________________

Fax Number: ______________________________

Address: ______________________________

Email Address: ______________________________

### ACCOUNTANT

Name: ______________________________

Phone Number: ______________________________

Fax Number: ______________________________

Address: ______________________________

Email Address: ______________________________

### FUNERAL DIRECTOR

Name: ______________________________

Phone Number: ______________________________

Fax Number: ______________________________

Address: ______________________________

Email Address: ______________________________

### BANKS AND OTHER FINANCIAL INSTITUTIONS

Name: ______________________________

Phone Number: ______________________________

Fax Number: ______________________________

Address: ______________________________

Email Address: ______________________________

Name: ______________________________

Phone Number: ______________________________

Fax Number: ______________________________

Address: ______________________________

Email Address: ______________________________

## INSURANCE COMPANY

Name: ______________________________

Phone Number: ______________________________

Fax Number: ______________________________

Address: ______________________________

Email Address: ______________________________

## BENEFICIARIES

Name: ______________________________

Phone Number: ______________________________

Fax Number: ______________________________

Address: ______________________________

Email Address: ______________________________

Name: ______________________________

Phone Number: ______________________________

Fax Number: ______________________________

Address: ______________________________

Email Address: ______________________________

Name: ______________________________

Phone Number: ______________________________

Fax Number: ______________________________

Address: ______________________________

Email Address: ______________________________

Name: ______________________________

Phone Number: ______________________________

Fax Number: ______________________________

Address: ______________________________

Email Address: ______________________________

## OTHER CONTACTS

### A-B-C

Name: ____________________________
Phone Number: ____________________________
Fax Number: ____________________________
Address: ____________________________
Email Address: ____________________________

Name: ____________________________
Phone Number: ____________________________
Fax Number: ____________________________
Address: ____________________________
Email Address: ____________________________

Name: ____________________________
Phone Number: ____________________________
Fax Number: ____________________________
Address: ____________________________
Email Address: ____________________________

### D-E-F

Name: ____________________________
Phone Number: ____________________________
Fax Number: ____________________________
Address: ____________________________
Email Address: ____________________________

Name: ____________________________
Phone Number: ____________________________
Fax Number: ____________________________
Address: ____________________________
Email Address: ____________________________

## G-H-I

Name: __________________________________

Phone Number: __________________________________

Fax Number: __________________________________

Address: __________________________________

Email Address: __________________________________

Name: __________________________________

Phone Number: __________________________________

Fax Number: __________________________________

Address: __________________________________

Email Address: __________________________________

## J-K-L

Name: __________________________________

Phone Number: __________________________________

Fax Number: __________________________________

Address: __________________________________

Email Address: __________________________________

Name: __________________________________

Phone Number: __________________________________

Fax Number: __________________________________

Address: __________________________________

Email Address: __________________________________

Name: __________________________________

Phone Number: __________________________________

Fax Number: __________________________________

Address: __________________________________

Email Address: __________________________________

## M-N-O

Name: ____________________
Phone Number: ____________________
Fax Number: ____________________
Address: ____________________
Email Address: ____________________

Name: ____________________
Phone Number: ____________________
Fax Number: ____________________
Address: ____________________
Email Address: ____________________

Name: ____________________
Phone Number: ____________________
Fax Number: ____________________
Address: ____________________
Email Address: ____________________

## P-Q-R

Name: ____________________
Phone Number: ____________________
Fax Number: ____________________
Address: ____________________
Email Address: ____________________

Name: ____________________
Phone Number: ____________________
Fax Number: ____________________
Address: ____________________
Email Address: ____________________

## S-T-U

Name: ____________________
Phone Number: ____________________
Fax Number: ____________________
Address: ____________________
Email Address: ____________________

Name: ____________________
Phone Number: ____________________
Fax Number: ____________________
Address: ____________________
Email Address: ____________________

## V-W-X

Name: ____________________
Phone Number: ____________________
Fax Number: ____________________
Address: ____________________
Email Address: ____________________

Name: ____________________
Phone Number: ____________________
Fax Number: ____________________
Address: ____________________
Email Address: ____________________

## Y-Z

Name: ____________________
Phone Number: ____________________
Fax Number: ____________________
Address: ____________________
Email Address: ____________________

Name: ____________________
Phone Number: ____________________
Fax Number: ____________________
Address: ____________________
Email Address: ____________________

## Sample Time Sheets

<table>
<tr><td rowspan="2">Matter:<br>☐ Assets<br>☐ Debts<br>☐ Income Tax<br>☐ Application for Letters Probate/Administration<br>☐ Miscellaneous</td><td rowspan="2">Person or Organization Contacted:<br><br>Telephone:<br>Fax:<br>Email:</td><td>Time Spent:</td></tr>
<tr><td>Date:</td></tr>
<tr><td colspan="3">Explanation of Work Performed:</td></tr>
<tr><td colspan="3"></td></tr>
<tr><td colspan="3"></td></tr>
<tr><td colspan="3"></td></tr>
<tr><td colspan="3"></td></tr>
<tr><td colspan="3"></td></tr>
<tr><td colspan="3"></td></tr>
<tr><td colspan="3"></td></tr>
</table>

<table>
<tr><td rowspan="2">Matter:<br>☐ Assets<br>☐ Debts<br>☐ Income Tax<br>☐ Application for Letters Probate/Administration<br>☐ Miscellaneous</td><td rowspan="2">Person or Organization Contacted:<br><br>Telephone:<br>Fax:<br>Email:</td><td>Time Spent:</td></tr>
<tr><td>Date:</td></tr>
<tr><td colspan="3">Explanation of Work Performed:</td></tr>
<tr><td colspan="3"></td></tr>
<tr><td colspan="3"></td></tr>
<tr><td colspan="3"></td></tr>
<tr><td colspan="3"></td></tr>
<tr><td colspan="3"></td></tr>
<tr><td colspan="3"></td></tr>
<tr><td colspan="3"></td></tr>
</table>

## Notes

# Glossary

**Abatement:** If, after all debts and liabilities have been paid, the estate does not have sufficient assets to satisfy all the gifts in full, some or all of the gifts will have to be reduced. The gift has abated.

**Ademption:** If a specific gift under the will is not in the deceased's possession at the time of death or cannot be located, the gift cannot be made. The gift has adeemed.

**Adjusted Cost Base:** This is usually the cost of a property plus any expenses incurred to buy it, such as commissions and legal fees.

**Administrator/Administratrix:** In all provinces except Ontario and Quebec, an administrator/administratrix is a person appointed by the court to administer the estate when: (1) the deceased dies without a will (intestate); (2) the will does not name a personal representative; or (3) the only personal representative in the will (a) is deceased, (b) has become incapable, (c) has renounced the appointment, or (d) is unable or refuses to act. The role is called an "estate trustee without a will" in Ontario and a "liquidator" in Quebec.

**Ascendant:** A person to whom one is related in the ascending line (e.g., father and mother).

**Beneficiary:** A person entitled to receive a benefit under a trust or a will. Beneficiary may also refer to a person who is named as the recipient of insurance proceeds or an RRSP, RRIF, LIF, pension, or annuity. The estate of a deceased may also be a beneficiary.

**Bequest:** A gift of personal property under the will (see also "legacy", "personal property", and "devise").

**Capital Gain/Capital Loss:** The profit earned or loss suffered on the sale of an asset **or** the profit/loss deemed to be realized on the death of an individual, as if the asset had been sold immediately prior to death. The CRA deems that the proceeds of disposition are equal to the property's fair market value at the time of the deemed disposition.

**Class:** Individuals who belong to a group identified in a will by the testator; for example, "my nieces and nephews".

**Codicil:** A written document that makes a change or an addition to the will. It is executed by the testator in accordance with the same formalities as a will.

**Collaterals:** Blood relatives who are neither ascendants nor descendants; for example, brothers, sisters, and cousins of the deceased. In Quebec, the brothers and sisters of the deceased and their descendants in the first degree are called privileged collaterals.

**Compensation:** Money to be paid to the executor/administrator for his or her work in the administration of an estate.

**Custodian:** A person appointed by a will to have custody of the testator's minor children. In Quebec, this person is called a tutor.

***Cy-près*:** A rule that relates to charitable gifts. It applies where a testator's charitable intent is either impossible or too impracticable to be carried out. If the testator has expressed a general charitable intent, the court may use the *cy-près* doctrine to allow the gift to be used to achieve an object as close as possible to that specified by the testator.

**Dependant:** A dependant includes certain family members who are financially dependent upon the deceased, such as the spouse or child of the deceased.

**Descendant:** A person to whom one is related in the descending line (e.g., children, grandchildren, great-grandchildren).

**Devise:** In common law, a devise is a gift of land or realty under the will.

**Devolution of Executorship:** When an executor of an estate dies, his or her executor becomes executor of that estate, in addition to the estate of the deceased executor. For example, X is the executor of the estate of Y. X dies during the administration of Y's estate. Z is the executor of X's estate and therefore becomes the executor of Y's estate as well. (Not applicable in Quebec.)

***Donatio mortis causa*.** A gift of property made in contemplation of death.

**Escheat:** When a person dies intestate without heirs, the estate vests in the provincial government.

**Estate Trustee:** A person appointed in the will to administer the estate of the testator or testatrix (i.e., an executor), or, where there is no will, a person who applies for and is granted a certificate of appointment of estate trustee (see also "executor", "administrator", and "liquidator").

**Executor/Executrix:** A person appointed in a will to administer the estate of the testator or testatrix. In Quebec, this person is called the liquidator.

**Gift-over:** A provision that specifies that a gift is to be given to another beneficiary, if the original beneficiary predeceases the testator or dies before becoming entitled to the gift.

**Guardian:** A person or trust company appointed to care for the property of a minor or an incompetent person. Guardian may also refer to a person appointed in a will to have custody of a child. In Quebec, this person is called a "tutor" if appointed to care for the property of a minor, or a "tutor, curator, or mandatary" if appointed to care for the property of an incompetent person.

**Holograph Will:** A will written completely in the testator's writing, signed by the testator and without the necessity of witnesses.

**Intestate:** The act of dying without a valid will; for example, "John died intestate". It also refers to a person who dies without a valid will; for example, "the intestate owned a cottage in Prince Edward Island".

**Issue:** The descendants of an individual, i.e., an individual's children, grandchildren, great-grandchildren, etc.

**Joint Tenancy:** Co-ownership with right of survivorship (right of survivorship does not apply in Quebec).

**Legacy:** The disposition of personal property by will (see also "bequest"). There are four categories of legacy:

- **Demonstrative Legacy:** A bequest of a certain sum of money with a direction that it shall be paid out of a particular fund.
- **General Legacy:** A bequest of a sum of money or an annuity, payable out of the general assets of the testator.
- **Specific Legacy:** A gift of a specific thing distinguished from all other things (e.g., the collectible porcelain figurine identified as "Marsha").
- **Residuary Legacy:** A bequest of all the testator's personal estate that was not dealt with in the testator's will.

In Quebec, there are three types of legacy:

- **Legacy by particular title:** A gift of a particular thing, specified and distinguished from all other things.
- **Legacy by general title:** A bequest of (a) the ownership of an aliquot share of the succession; (b) a dismemberment of the right of ownership of the whole or of an aliquot share of the succession; or (c) the ownership or a dismemberment of the right of ownership of the whole or of an aliquot share of all the immovable or movable property of the deceased.
- **Universal legacy:** A bequest of the entirety of a person's property.

**Letters of Administration/Certificate of Appointment of an Estate Trustee Without a Will:** A grant from the court to the administrator (known as "estate trustee without a will" in Ontario) to administer the estate of an individual who died intestate.

**Letters Probate/Certificate of Appointment of Estate Trustee with a Will:** Letters probate (known as "certificate of appointment of estate trustee with a will" in Ontario) provide evidence to third parties that the will has been proved and registered in court and that the executor is authorized to deal with the estate. (Not applicable to notarial wills in Quebec.)

**Life Estate:** A benefit that allows a person to use certain property during his or her lifetime or the lifetime of another. Life estate may also refer to an arrangement whereby the beneficiary is entitled to income from property for his or her life. Upon the death of the beneficiary, the property will go to the person or persons who hold the remainder interest (see "remainderman"). In Quebec, a "usufruct" or "substitution" is similar.

**Liquidator:** A person appointed to administer the estate of the deceased in Quebec.

**Next of Kin:** The nearest blood relatives of a person.

**Passing of Accounts:** The submission of the estate accounts by the executors and administrators for scrutiny by the court. Not applicable in Quebec.

***Per Capita*:** The method of dividing an estate where an equal share is given to each of a number of persons, all of whom stand in equal degree to the deceased. A division *per capita* means by a number of individuals equally, or share and share alike. Under a *per capita* distribution, if a beneficiary predeceases, his or her share is divided among the surviving beneficiaries. The children or descendants of the deceased beneficiary get nothing. A *per capita* distribution is the antithesis of a *per stirpes* distribution.

**Personal Property:** All property with the exception of real property (also known as "personalty").

**Personal Representative:** The executor or administrator of a deceased's estate (see also "estate trustee" and "liquidator").

***Per Stirpes*:** *Per stirpes* denotes a method of dividing an estate, where a class or group of distributees take the share to which their deceased ancestor would have been entitled. They take by their right of representing such ancestor, one share for each line of descendants. For example, if a member of a group among which the assets are being divided is not alive at the time of distribution but all of her children are alive, the share of assets that the deceased member would have received is divided equally among her children.

**Probate:** Probate is the procedure by which a will is accepted as valid (in Ontario, the procedure is referred to as an application for a "certificate of appointment of estate trustee").

**Real Property:** Real property means land and buildings. It is also known as "real estate" and "realty".

**Remainderman/Remainderer:** The person entitled to the remainder of the estate after the death of the life tenant.

**Residuary estate:** The portion of the estate that has not otherwise been particularly bequeathed or devised.

**Residue:** The surplus of a testator's estate remaining after all debts, legacies, and devises have been looked after.

**Survivorship:** Survivorship is where a person becomes entitled to property by reason of his or her having survived another person who had an interest in the property. Not applicable in Quebec.

**Tenancy in Common:** Co-ownership that does not include a right of survivorship.

**Testamentary Capacity:** Testamentary capacity refers to the testator's ability to make a valid will. The testator/testatrix must:

- understand what he or she is doing;
- comprehend and remember the nature and extent of his or her property;

- be aware of which persons might expect to benefit by his or her will; and
- understand the claims of those persons he or she is excluding from his or her will, and what he or she is giving to each beneficiary.

**Testate:** The act of dying with a will.

**Testator:** The name given to a man who makes a will.

**Testatrix:** The name given to a woman who makes a will.

**Will:** A declaration in writing that provides for the distribution and/or administration of one's property after one's death, and which does not take effect until death.

# Topical Index